EIGHTEENTH-CENTURY EUROPE

◆

The Longman History of European Women

Women in Medieval Europe, 1200–1500
Jennifer Ward

Women in Early Modern Europe, 1500–1700
Cissie Fairchilds

Women in Eighteenth-Century Europe
Margaret R. Hunt

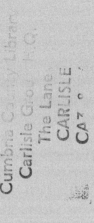

WOMEN IN EIGHTEENTH-CENTURY EUROPE

◆

MARGARET R. HUNT

Longman
is an imprint of

Harlow, England • London • New York • Boston • San Francisco • Toronto • Sydney • Singapore • Hong Kong
Tokyo • Seoul • Taipei • New Delhi • Cape Town • Madrid • Mexico City • Amsterdam • Munich • Paris • Milan

PEARSON EDUCATION LIMITED

Edinburgh Gate
Harlow CM20 2JE
United Kingdom
Tel: +44 (0)1279 623623
Fax: +44 (0)1279 431059
Website: www.pearsoned.co.uk

First edition published in Great Britain in 2010

ISBN: 978-0-582-30865-7

British Library Cataloguing in Publication Data
A CIP catalogue record for this book can be obtained from the British Library

Library of Congress Cataloging in Publication Data
Hunt, Margaret R., 1953–
    Women in eighteenth-century Europe / Margaret R. Hunt. — 1st ed.
        p. cm. — (The Longman history of European women)
    Includes bibliographical references and index.
    ISBN 978-0-582-30865-7 (pbk.)
    1. Women—Europe—History—18th century.   2. Women—Europe—Social
conditions—18th century.   3. Sex role—Europe—History—18th century.
4. Europe—History—18th century.   5. Europe—Social conditions—18th century.
I. Title.
HQ1587.H86 2009
305.4094′09033—dc22

                                                    2009020860

10   9   8   7   6   5   4   3   2   1
13   12   11   10   09

Set in 11.5/14pt Garamond by 35
Printed and bound in Malaysia (CTP-VVP)

The Publisher's policy is to use paper manufactured from sustainable forests.

CONTENTS

———— ◆ ————

LIST OF PLATES

◆

ACKNOWLEDGEMENTS

This book was an adventure, and like most good adventures it involved unfamiliar places, unexpected collaborations and new friendships. But it also taught me to appreciate what I already had, and, in truth, the project would not have been completed without the combined generosity both of old friends and new. My colleague Peter Czap supplied early and crucial assistance on early modern Russia; my Five College colleagues Jutta Sperling and Lois Dubin helped me with (respectively) Portuguese and Italian marriage and property laws, and early modern rabbinical law; Henry Horwitz and Amy Erickson taught me much of what I know about English equity law; Jennifer Heuer, Margaret Darrow and Darline Levy helped me with French revolutionary and Napoleonic law. Maria Ågren allowed me to read her forthcoming book on gender and early modern Swedish law in manuscript and Karin Jansson passed on to me her book on rape in early modern Sweden. Jan Lindegren, Barbara Donagan and Nick Rogers opened my eyes to new ways of thinking about early modern war, and Elektra Petropoulos advised me on Ottoman Greece and the history of Greeks in Turkey. Amy Froide dispensed advice on the history of single women; Lynn Botelho on old people in the early modern period; Jill Shefrin on literature for children; and Rachel Weil on gender, politics and royalty. Tim Hitchcock, Tim Wales, Jessica Warner, Robert Shoemaker and Jennine Hurl-Eamon all helped me with questions relating to poverty and the law in the early modern period; Faramerz Dabhoiwala, Janice Irvine, Susan Lanser, Jeffrey Merrick and, before his untimely death, Alan Bray, advised me on the history of love and sexuality; and Cathy Crawford, Laura Gowing, Vilma Hunt, Lisa Cody and Patricia Crawford advised me on the history of the body, medicine, epidemiology, midwifery and breast-feeding. My colleagues Ute Brandes and Anston Bosman helped me make sense of, respectively, early German women writers, and theatre and commerce in the early modern period. My colleagues Nasser Hussain and Sean Redding and my former colleague Durba Ghosh helped with colonial law; Mary Beth Norton helped on colonial American race and gender politics and much else; my colleagues Celso Castro Alves and Rick Lopez provided citations and primary source material on Latin American slavery; and Jennifer Morgan, Susan Amussen and my colleagues Hilary

Moss and Kevin Sweeney advised me on comparative slave systems and notions of race. Judith Bennett, Beverly Lemire, Danielle van den Heuvel, Anne McCants, Maxine Berg, Laurence Fontaine, Daniel Rabuzzi and Barbara Todd passed on sources and advice on women, trade, credit networks, investment, manufacturing and charity in Britain, France, the Netherlands and the Baltic region. Siep Stuurman gave me citations on early eighteenth-century feminists. Gail Hornstein perused sources in the Cambridge University Library on my behalf. Linda Semple and Rhona Hotchkiss advised me on Scottish history and took me on historical excursions. Marni Sandweiss provided advice on photographs and set me a good writerly example. Ann King put me up in Oxford and reminded me of the necessity of cultivating one's own garden. Lisa Baskin generously allowed me to use her remarkable library and drew my attention to numerous sources and lines of inquiry I would never have hit upon otherwise. Amrita Basu, Cathy Crawford, Jan Lambertz, Michele Barale and Rose Olver offered help and friendship in times of need. The membership of the Berkshire Conference of Women Historians was a source of philosophical insight, moral support and good times.

I was a relative newcomer to Ottoman, Balkan, Middle Eastern, Islamic and Turkish Studies when I embarked upon this project and it was only because of the enormous generosity of scholars in those interlinked fields that this book has taken its present form. One of these was my dear departed colleague, John Petropoulos, who first introduced me to Ottoman history. I miss him still. My colleague, Monica Ringer, my former colleague, Jamal Elias, and my Five College colleagues, Mary Wilson, Lorna Peterson and Walter Denny, were generous with citations and expertise; my former colleagues, Nadia El Cheikh, Anissa Helie and Nadia Guessous, helped with theoretical issues; and Mary Anne Fay, Fatma Gök, Nikki Keddie, Tijana Krstic, Elif Şafak, Irvin Schick, Selim Sirri Kuru and Madeline Zilfi all shared their knowledge and, in some cases, their unpublished writings with me. If this book succeeds in conveying to readers even a small part of the remarkable work that has been done in recent years in early modern Ottoman women's history, it will be largely due to them.

Bella Barmak and Jamie Rounds provided research assistance at a critical early phase of the project. Anya Zilberstein was brilliant, both as research assistant and travel companion. Many people allowed themselves to be enlisted for other kinds of help, especially of a linguistic sort. My colleagues Ron Rosbottom and Manuela Picq helped correct my French, Anne McCants my Dutch, and Angelica Cesario my Portuguese. Maria Ågren supplied some

Swedish translations; Jan Lindegren drew my attention to Swedish and Danish sources and translated several on my behalf; Tijana Krstic drew my attention to several Serbo-Croatian sources, and translated one of them; Stephanie Reitter and my colleague David Schneider helped with Hungarian; Tadeusz Pudlik helped with Polish; Amanda Collins and my colleague Paola Zamperini helped with Italian; my former colleague, Cynthia Damon, helped with Latin; my colleague Fred Cheyette helped with Catalan; Dagmar Powitz and Catherine Epstein helped with German; Anya Zilberstein did several Russian translations; and Cathy Ciepiela helped with both Russian and Bulgarian. Irvin Schick did a beautiful translation of an Ottoman poem, and my Five College colleague, Walter Denny, provided advice on Ottoman images. Bogdan State, research assistant extra-ordinaire, provided help with databases, map-making, indexing, programming and translations from German, Italian, Spanish, Swedish and Romanian. He made the whole project more manageable and a lot more fun.

Many people have commented on parts of the manuscript, including my colleagues Jamal Elias, Monica Ringer, Kim Brandt, Amrita Basu, Uday Mehta, Martha Saxton, Sean Redding, Catherine Ciepiela and Susan Niditch. In addition, Beverly Lemire, Judith Walkowitz, Martha Howell, Madeline Zilfi, Janice Irvine, Patricia Crawford, Pam Sharpe, Joan Cocks and Carolyn Sachs all read chapters or parts of chapters. I have been saved from many errors of fact and infelicities of interpretation through these generous efforts, and where errors remain it is likely because I failed to follow my readers' sage advice.

Money changes almost everything, and my Amherst College colleagues, particularly Dean Greg Call and (earlier) Dean Lisa Raskin, were generous with research funds. Several other institutions and individuals supplied funds, or a temporary research base, or both. Thanks to a grant from the National Endowment for the Humanities I was able to spend four months at the Huntington Library, and I am grateful to the Library staff, particularly Robert Ritchie and Susie Krasnoo, for their hospitality. The other Huntington fellows that year, especially Judith Bennett, Konstantin Dierks, Barbara Donagan, Cynthia Herrup, Roger Knight, Andrew Lewis, Maria Lepowsky, Jaya Mehta, Mary Beth Norton, Jenny Price, Dana Rabin, and Nicholas Rogers, greatly improved my life with their excellent conversation, political sanity in insane times, and generosity with citations and bird-watching advice. During that same period Margaret Jacob and Lynn Hunt opened up their home and shared their friends in a way that was truly beyond the call. The Penn State University Women's Studies Department offered me a free office and peace and quiet for one whole summer, and I especially thank Carolyn Sachs for arranging that and Paula Greaser for being such good company. A Folger Shakespeare Library Fellowship allowed me to work there for four months, where my fellow researchers, Carole Levin, Paul Hammer, Tim Harris, Kimberly Hossain, Bernhard Klein and Denise Walen, made the time pass all too quickly. Finally, the American Philosophical Society gave me a much needed sabbatical grant to live and work for a lengthy period in London.

This book was researched and written in the British Library; the Bodleian Library in Oxford; the Biblioteca Nacional de España in Madrid; the Institute of Historical Research, London; the Vatican Library; the Library of Contemporary History in Rome; the library of the University of Amsterdam; the Uppsala University Library; The Folger Shakespeare Library, the Library of Congress, the Penn State University Library; the Széchény National Library, Budapest; the Women's Library and Information Center (Kadin Eserleri Kütüphanesi ve Bilgi Merkezi), Istanbul; the Boğaziçi University Library, Istanbul; the Huntington Library in San Marino, California; the library of the University of California, Los Angeles; the library of the University of Massachusetts Amherst; and the Amherst College Library. I thank the staffs of all of these institutions, but my deepest gratitude goes to my friends at the Amherst College Library, especially Margaret Groesbeck, Michael Kasper, Daria D'Arienzo, John Lancaster and Juliet Demeter. I also want to acknowledge the countless positive interventions made by the Amherst College Department of Information Technology, especially Debra K. McCulloch, on my behalf. Finally, and from the bottom of my heart, I thank the members of the Amherst College History Department, especially Rhea Cabin, and the members of the Women's and Gender Studies Department, especially Amy Ford, for their friendship and support. One could not wish for better colleagues.

Barbara Balliet, Cheryl Clarke, Rhonda Cobham-Sander, Mitzi Goheen, Anne Knowlton and the Hunt-Marro-Rounds-Lebret-Gonzalez-Fullman 'tribe' enriched my life during the writing of this book with their generosity of spirit, love, and intellectual and political companionship. This book is dedicated to my mother, Vilma R. Hunt, whose boundless curiosity and love of adventure have been an inspiration to many, and not least to me.

PUBLISHER'S ACKNOWLEDGEMENTS

———— ◆ ————

We are grateful to the following for permission to reproduce copyright material:

Extract on pages 232–3 from *Seyder Tkhines: the Forgotten Book of Common Prayer for Jewish Women*, The Jewish Publication Society (Devra Kay (ed. and trans.) 2004) © 2004 by Devra Kay, published by the Jewish Publication Society, with permission of the copyright holder.

Plate 1 courtesy of Amherst College Library and Collections; plate 2 courtesy of the Museum of Fine Arts, Budapest; plate 3 courtesy of the Schlesinger Library, Radcliffe Institute for Advanced Study, Harvard; plate 4 courtesy of the Princes Czartoryski Foundation; plate 5 courtesy of the John Johnson Collection, Bodleian Library; plate 6 courtesy of the council of the National Army Museum, London; plate 7 courtesy of the German Archaeological Institute, Istanbul; plate 9 © the State Hermitage Museum, St. Petersburg; plate 10 courtesy of the Library of Congress; plate 11 © RMN/ Droits reserves.

In some instances we have been unable to trace the owners of copyright material, and we would appreciate any information that would enable us to do so.

INTRODUCTION

◆

The eighteenth century was heavy with contradiction, and some of its after-effects are with us still. Its intellectuals helped invent modern conceptions of freedom and equality, but only a tiny minority thought to extend 'freedom' or 'equality' to women, slaves or non-elite men. Some of the most powerful women ever to sit on a European throne reigned in the eighteenth century, while at the same time moralists and philosophers were busy developing influential new arguments for why women should eschew politics. The later eighteenth century birthed one of the most ambitious and internationalist revolutionary movements ever seen, and yet ended in a toxic morass of political reaction that, in many regions, set back political reform – including reforms that would have benefited women – for generations. And those are only a few of the complexities with which the historian of the period must grapple. To write a history of women in that bewildering time is no small task, and anyone who embarks upon it finds herself owing a large debt to earlier historians. Articles, books and edited collections by Maxine Berg, Natalie Zemon Davis, Arlette Farge, Suraiya Faroqhi, Olwen Hufton, Lynn Hunt, Natalia Pushkareva, Merry Wiesner, Heide Wunder, Madeline Zilfi and others have brought extraordinary evidentiary precision and interpretive power to the study of late seventeenth- and eighteenth-century women and work, the law, politics, popular violence, religion, and revolutionary fervour.[1] They have also expanded our understanding of 'Europe' and 'European culture', by emphasizing the shifting and permeable boundaries between Europe and adjoining regions, especially Africa and the Middle East, and by excavating the multidirectional cultural influences that formed the era. The questions historians of European women ask today about women in the early modern period, the ethical problems we are preoccupied with, our conception of the relationship between the history of women and the larger surround, all spring from the seeds these scholars sowed.

The reasons for telling this story anew and in my own way are three-fold. First, general studies focusing only on women in the eighteenth century are few and it is, I believe, a century that deserves to be treated on its own. Second, a great deal of work has appeared since the last attempt to draw together a general study of women in early modern Europe, with particularly rich offerings in countries or regions (Russia, Scandinavia, the Iberian Peninsula) which, despite the best efforts of historians, sometimes featured relatively little in earlier generalist accounts. And third, there is today a pressing need more fully to acknowledge the importance of Europe's historical connections to the Middle East, and particularly to that hybrid European/Middle Eastern entity, the Ottoman Empire. It is not that we lack a literature on the Ottoman Empire, or, more importantly for this project, on Ottoman women. Ottoman women's history has fully emerged as an area of research in the last twenty or so years, yielding information on family life, property-ownership patterns, work, the arts, charitable activity, slavery, minority status, the law-courts, religious conversion and much else. The problem, rather, has been a fairly comprehensive lack of attention on the part of many self-described 'European' historians to the Ottomans except at those moments when they posed a military threat to people or places with which they identify. The failed Ottoman siege of Vienna in 1683 has generated and continues to generate a large literature; yet many historians are ignorant of even the most basic facts about Ottoman social and political life.

What explains this reluctance? Partly it springs from the way the Ottoman Empire confounds simple definition of 'Europe' and 'Europeanness'. In the early modern period it was a behemoth of a state that straddled most of the European Balkans and for long periods extended well into Hungary (and, more fleetingly, Austria) as well as present-day Ukraine, the Crimea and the Caucasus. It had its main capital city in Istanbul (formerly Byzantine Constantinople), on what is still sometimes thought of as the 'European' side of the Bosphorus. Its heartland was the mainly Turkic-speaking, predominantly Muslim Anatolian peninsula, roughly coterminous with modern Turkey, and it encircled the Mediterranean all the way around to Egypt and beyond. But the more compelling reason for not treating the Ottoman Empire as part of Europe was and is religion. The Ottoman Empire was, in fact, a multi-confessional state, that supported large Eastern Orthodox, Coptic Christian and Armenian Christian, as well as Jewish populations. But its official religion – Islam – belied and still belies a very deeply held belief, even among many secularists, in Europe's essentially Christian character. For European women's historians a further impediment to imagining the Ottomans as even partially European has been some extremely enduring myths, dating from the early modern period, which assumed a close relationship between Islam and an (alleged) especially pernicious form of women's oppression. Their corollary was the self-serving belief that European Christian women were existentially 'free' while 'Oriental' and Muslim women were imprisoned body and soul behind veils, religion, polygamy and harem walls. Ottoman women and Muslim women more generally thus became foils for a belief in European and Christian superiority and exceptionalism that came to be shared even by people critical of aspects of European culture. All of this has made it difficult to view the Ottomans as anything other than a profoundly alien people – never European even though the Empire and its successor states have been part of Europe for over half a millennium.

Europe is a more notional entity than some other continents. Not only does it share a four-thousand-kilometre land border with Asia, one crisscrossed by innumerable trade, travel and migration routes, but it is closely linked culturally, politically and economically to the Middle East and Africa via the Mediterranean Sea, the Black Sea, the Bosphorus and the Strait of Gibraltar. This proximity has affected food ways, languages, faith systems, population movements, war, technology transfer, and much else. This book understands 'Europe' to be the land stretching from Ireland to the Ural Mountains in Russia, and from the Scandinavian countries (including far-off Iceland) down to the four main Mediterranean peninsulas, Iberia, Italy, the Balkans, and Anatolia, not excluding the Mediterranean Islands. In fact the story moves past even those boundaries, as it must if it hopes to follow the dynamic rhythms of eighteenth-century life. Though this is a book about Europe I have not hesitated, on occasion, to talk about the Massachusetts Bay Colony, or Haiti, or Mexico, or even the Philippines. Somewhat closer to home I have paid some attention to Aleppo and Damascus, two major Ottoman colonial cities in what is now Syria.

The push to expand 'European women's history' beyond western and central Europe, as a number of historians are now trying to do,[2] is not merely a compensatory device. The historical narrative begins to change when one takes into account a more diverse array of people and regions. Expanding our purview also has the effect of casting doubt upon the assumption that northwestern Europe has always and in every way been the most 'progressive' region where women are concerned. The realm of politics illustrates this well. Eastern Europe, on the whole, had more top-level political participation by women than almost any western nations in the eighteenth century. Russia, the most striking case, was ruled for sixty-seven of the years between 1700 and 1800 by four different women, including one, Catherine II ('the Great'), considered by many at the time, and since, to be one of the most capable rulers of her time. Next door, in Poland, noblewomen repeatedly intervened in the debates in the *Sejm* (the noble assembly), engaged in numerous political intrigues, acted as foreign diplomats, were already setting up political salons in the 1730s (well before women's salons turned overtly political in most other countries), participated openly in electioneering, and played leading roles in several revolts. In the eighteenth century, elite women in eastern Europe wielded immense power, very directly, and for an extended period. This sort of thing, for a variety of reasons, was much rarer in western Europe.

Protestant Europe was, with only a few exceptions, also slow to innovate in the area of women's property rights. The first Married Women's Property Law in Christian Europe was promulgated in 1753 in Orthodox Russia, a century or more before such laws were passed in Protestant Europe, while the country in western Europe with the most advantageous property laws for women (along with other legal benefits) was probably Catholic Portugal, and Iberia more generally. Women's property rights were also very strong in the Ottoman Empire, particularly among Muslims, because the *sharia* courts offered strong support for married women's rights to their own property, even against depredations by their husbands or male kin, and had done so since the very beginning of Islam. The contrast between Muslim law and Christian and Jewish law on this point was so pronounced that by the early modern period we find both Christian and Jewish women deliberately resorting to Muslim courts in hopes of getting a more favourable hearing. The various mid- to late nineteenth-century Scandinavian, British and American Married Women's Property Acts were often put forward at the time as proof of the superiority of the West's treatment of women. But such claims were based upon an abysmal and, at times, wilful ignorance of the legal position of women elsewhere. The reforms end up looking rather belated, or at least far less remarkable, when we match them up against the situation in large parts of southern and eastern Europe and the Middle East.

If we cast our nets more broadly we will also get a more realistic view of those features of eighteenth-century western European culture that almost certainly *were* advantageous to women. Western Europe boasted a considerably more developed popular print culture than was true elsewhere, relatively high – and rising – literacy rates, and a fairly strong commitment to girls' and women's education, though the latter was far truer of the cities than the rural areas. Female literacy rates were especially high in Protestant regions and higher still in Protestant cities, but some Catholic areas were drawing even by the later eighteenth century, in good part because of the energetic educational efforts of Catholic women's religious organizations. (Incidentally, women's organizations – which were far scarcer in Protestant than in Catholic parts of western and central Europe – serve to remind us that 'the West' was in no sense a homogeneous region with respect to women.)

The 'Big European' view also yields some trends that appear to have affected the entire region and even beyond, though with much local variation. One of these was an accelerating resort to the law-courts by women. Hundreds of thousands of European, Middle Eastern and colonial women of every status, from peasants and slaves to duchesses, went to court in the early modern period, pursuing cases relating to inheritance, marital abuse, dowries, conjugal support, divorce, widows' rights, slave emancipation, forced marriage, rape, sexual abuse by priests, business contracts, debt, and commercial and guild monopolies. The enormous volume of early modern women's litigation and the rich records it has left, has turned legal history into one of the most expansive areas of women's history scholarship, and literally revolutionized our understanding of pre-modern women, particularly women below the level of the elite.[3] This new scholarship turns up frequently in this book.

Women's extensive use of the courts across many regions and locales has at least partially resolved the problem – a longstanding one in women's history – of whether or not pre-modern women possessed historical agency. The past quarter of a century of research by historians of Christian Europe as well as Ottoman historians (and, for that matter, historians of other parts of the globe) has made it clear that the women we write about were thinking, acting people who, where they had the opportunity, often sought to improve their lot as well as to exert an influence on the world around them. They did not always get that opportunity, of course. Class, age, race, condition of servitude and other factors often severely constrained their opportunities for action, and many had little or no choice over key life decisions modern people assume will be ours to make. Nevertheless, most early modernists (including this author) now assume that where early modern women could they were perfectly capable of exercising agency.

It must, however, be acknowledged that at that point consensus breaks down. In fact, the term 'women's agency' raises a number of vexed theoretical and methodological questions, and it has done so especially urgently in recent years.[4] There are several dimensions to this problem. The first, especially if we are talking about the fairly distant past, is a problem of sources. The woman who foments a food riot or takes her abusive husband or master to court is far more likely to leave a mark on the written record, and hence be noticed by historians, than the woman who starves in silence or decides that there is nothing she can do about the beatings, and who may even think she deserves them. Because the writing of history is based primarily upon record survival this bias toward quite possibly unrepresentative actions may be unavoidable (it is certainly evident in this book). But there are many actions in between the two notional and perhaps unrealistic extremes of 'heroic resistance' and 'pure inaction' that must sometimes have been efficacious in their own way. (Did the abused person pray for her tormentor to die, for example? Or try to bewitch him or her? Or, give in to the abuser's sexual demands in hopes of gaining a stronger position later on?) One aim of this book is to explore that bumpy and morally ambiguous middle ground, one that is, arguably, particularly complex for women.

Another potential problem with the concept of female agency is the tendency on the part of the researcher to emphasize forms of agency to which she or he feels personally sympathetic – notably explicit acts of resistance to male or state power – while largely dismissing other kinds. This vision of agency has recently been challenged by the anthropologist Saba Mahmood in *Politics of Piety: The Islamic Revival and the Feminist Subject* (2005), a study of the women's mosque movement in contemporary Egypt.[5] For Mahmood there is no question that this extremely vibrant movement constitutes an expression of female agency. However, she insists that a movement focused on piety, bodily discipline and the attainment of paradise simply cannot be shoved in under the rubric of resistance to patriarchal forms. It demands to be understood on its own terms, something gender studies researchers, with their typically secular and individualist bias, and their tendency to search for resistance to the patriarchal status quo, often fail to do. Mahmood's critique has considerable relevance for the study of eighteenth-century women, not least because, while there is much evidence that women grew more publicly active in this period – publishing more, founding and joining more organizations, starting more charitable institutions, and travelling more than women in earlier centuries – a large proportion of their active concern revolved around religion. Women across Europe and beyond became deeply involved in new or relatively new movements of religious renewal in the eighteenth and early nineteenth centuries: the Sufi revival that swept across the Muslim world, powerful movements in Catholic countries related to the veneration of the Virgin Mary, pietistic and heterodox movements in Protestant ones, women's conventual and dissident movements in Orthodox lands, and kabbalistic and pietist movements among Jewish women. It is true that many of these movements did, in practice, expand women's sphere of action, and gender egalitarian themes do crop up fairly often within them – as they also do in the Egyptian women's mosque movement. Jewish and Christian women's interest in de-emphasizing the sin of Eve (Chapter 7 of this book) is a case in point. But in virtually all of these movements the activists' stated aim (and, almost certainly, their main aim) was religious and, at least in part, other-worldly. 'Feminism' (or at least some variant of gender-egalitarian rhetoric or practice) was an occasional tactic; saving their own and others' souls was the goal.

The third problem with the concept of female agency derives from another of the traditional preoccupations of feminists and political activists almost everywhere – the search for evidence of mutual solidarity on the part of the downtrodden of history. There is no question that solidarity between women can sometimes be found in the early modern period. But if we confine our view of female agency to actions that seem positive on twentieth- or twenty-first-century terms while leaving aside the less savoury things early modern women got up to, we risk consigning a large part of our subjects' lives to oblivion. The fact is that a good deal of eighteenth-century women's agency was exercised at other people's expense – people who were just a bit more (and sometimes a good deal more) vulnerable and easy to exploit, due to age, race, religion, social status, condition of servitude, foreignness or some other factor. Most of the time, of course, this meant exploiting other women or girls. Some of it – informing on a fellow-servant for gain, for instance – might have been recognized at the time as morally problematic, at least by other servants. But plenty of other activities were thoroughly legitimate, even virtuous by the standards of the time, though they seem deeply tainted today. Eighteenth-century women often exercised their entrepreneurial agency by investing in the slave trade, while mistresses did everything in their power to undermine the position of those slaves or servants they thought were competing with them sexually or reproductively.[6] Women who wrote books or who participated in politics generally could do so only because they had servants, serfs or slaves to do most of the other work, which was hardly conducive to thinking expansively about the common lot of womankind. And when solidarity did exist it was often directed at aims that seem reprehensible to us today. A number of eighteenth-century all-women charities were explicitly devoted to the coercive conversion of other people's children to the dominant religion. And some of the more spectacular examples of early modern 'women's solidarity' consisted of violent collective attacks by women on minority groups, most commonly, though not exclusively, Jews.

The approach to agency and female subjectivity adopted in this book is eclectic and composed of careful, if subjective, judgement, a dose of scepticism and strenuous attempts at analytical humility. I do not assume, even if it looks that way on the surface, that women always subsumed their interests beneath those of their family or kin-group – even though that is what they were incessantly told to do. And I am not averse to calling upon recent, feminist modifications of social choice theory, such as the notion of situated agency, for help in trying to untangle the details. In recent years such approaches have opened up a wide field of inquiry into the often unequal ways resources are and were distributed in families, and the conflicts, negotiations and bargains about money, food, sex, work and power that keep the system going.[7] But I also try to remain attuned to the possibility that eighteenth-century people approached power and possibility, self and risk, in ways quite different from modern people. Some acts seemed justifiable, even virtuous, to them and to the people around them precisely because they were selfless and done on others' behalf, often for other-worldly reasons. We are entitled to be a bit cynical about some of this – as eighteenth-century people were themselves. Then, as now, some very self-serving behaviour could be concealed under the mantle of preserving one's children's future estate, working for one's own or someone else's spiritual well-being, protecting the family name, or being charitable. But by the same token we cannot simply assume an ability either to recognize or to understand eighteenth-century women's deepest desires and aims. The theoretical problems posed by the concept of women's agency will certainly not be definitively decided as a result of this book, but I do have some hopes that fleshing out these problems with reference to real women, facing dilemmas both similar to and very different from our own, will cause modern readers to think about them in some new and more complex ways.

BOOK STRUCTURE

Chapter 1 (Hierarchy and Difference)

One of the fundamental differences between the eighteenth century and today concerns the ways dominance and subordination 'looked' and functioned in society. Women were, on the whole, subordinate to men, but there were other kinds of subordination that crosscut and complicated the picture. Moreover, where subordination today (e.g. racial or gender discrimination in relation to work) tends to be indirect or relatively concealed, in the eighteenth century hierarchy was completely overt, and the 'performance' of it, by both superiors and inferiors, was a central concern for those charged with maintaining the social order. This chapter looks at a variety of different kinds of subordination in the eighteenth century, including some that readers may be less familiar with, such as the rampant exploitation of orphan girls and the inferior position of younger, in-marrying women in complex families. It also examines some of the functional uses of subordination, particularly in relation to controlling mobility and the distribution of work, in a society in which almost everything had to be done by the sweat of someone's brow. Finally it looks at some of the ways people tried to lighten the load, and either make sense of or resist the more dehumanizing aspects of subordination.

Chapter 2 (Families)

When it came to the formation of families, eighteenth-century women had a good deal less freedom to follow their inclinations than we do today. This chapter looks first at the very different regimes of choice and lack of choice over fundamental aspects of daily life that obtained in early modern Europe, and the implications this had for women. It then moves on to the theory and practice of marriage in both Christian Europe and the Ottoman Empire, including discussions of marital relations, of monogamy and polygamy, of different married women's property regimes, and of the rise of marital litigation. It also takes up the dissolution of marriage and examines various alternatives to marriage including the rising trend of women refusing to marry.

Chapter 3 (Sexuality and Reproduction)

During the eighteenth century many Europeans began having second thoughts about the extremely repressive policies that had been put in place during the Protestant and Catholic Reformations with respect to extramarital sexuality. Here we trace what those policies were and the larger assumptions they reveal about women, sexuality and God. We also look at the most important European institutional response to unwed motherhood and infanticide, the foundling home. Children were a source of tremendous ambivalence for eighteenth-century people. They were very likely to die (about half did so before their tenth birthday), many of them were unwanted, and rates of child-murder were much higher than they are today (abandonment was even higher); at the same time children were often greatly loved, and they were central to ongoing family survival strategies, as well as to the welfare of their parents in old age. Here we explore women's role as both willing and unwilling bearers of children, and as the people charged with the often impossible task of keeping those children alive. The last part of the chapter looks at adultery, rape and same-sex love.

Chapter 4 (Food and Consumption)

Food was probably the single area in which early modern women had the most informal power. They had primary responsibility for obtaining fuel and water and they supplied a lot of most families' food supplies through foraging and gardening, both traditional areas of female expertise. Many things changed in the eighteenth century, however, with respect to women and food. Foraging grew more difficult because of growing population pressures, environmental degradation (especially deforestation) and enclosure of common lands. But gardening grew more important, partly due to the spread of new-world garden crops, notably potatoes and maize. Though women had crucial roles in the provision of food, they also *were* food, by virtue of the fact that most children had to be breast-fed if they were to survive. We look here at some of the broader cultural implications of this, particularly in terms of ideas about female self-denial and sacrifice. The chapter also delves into women's experience of famines and their role in food riots, discusses the problem of living standards during the agricultural revolution, and looks at women in relation to cookbooks and new luxury imports like tea, coffee and sugar.

Chapter 5 (Work and Money)

Almost all women worked in the early modern period, and increasingly, especially in the cities, and in central and western Europe, most worked for pay. This chapter examines the wide range of ways women made a living, from selling fruit or milk in the street, to working as domestic servants, from running businesses inherited from their husbands, to building up empires in millinery or textile production, from investing in equities or real estate to surviving through begging and prostitution. In the eighteenth century, capitalist relations spread definitively through virtually all of Europe (in some places this had happened considerably earlier), and England, after about 1760, also saw the beginnings of industrialization. This chapter shows how these changes affected women's subsistence and money-making activities, both for better and for worse, and it takes up several long-running debates about women's work, women and capitalism, and women and industrialization.

Chapter 6 (Pathways of the Spirit)

In the early modern period belief in God, and often other supernatural forces and entities as well, was both widespread and normative. This offered women tremendous scope, even as it also supplied important ideological justifications for female subordination. The chapter starts with an examination of women's healing practices, which were often both eclectic and syncretic. The second part of the chapter looks at the five largest faith-systems of Europe: Catholicism, Eastern Orthodoxy, the Protestant denominations, Islam and Judaism, and describes women's efforts, within many faiths, to encourage greater female participation in worship, emphasize female religious figures from the past, de-emphasize the original sin of Eve, and, in the case of a few radical individuals and groups, introduce quite feminine, androgynous and non-anthropomorphic reinterpretations of the divine. The chapter concludes with a discussion of the rise of religious toleration and Enlightenment secularism and their impact on women.

Chapter 7 (Cultures of Women)

It is a severe challenge to try to recreate women's popular art and culture in the eighteenth century. This chapter discusses gendered restrictions in activities like music and storytelling, and analyses such diverse forms as singing, folktales, laments and jokes as vehicles for expressing both individual and collective concerns. The second section analyses a variety of eighteenth-century literary genres that were strongly associated with women, including letters and didactic literature, autobiography, poetry, novels and children's literature, particularly looking for the ways women used such forms to comment on women's role and status. The third section takes up performance arts, including the ambiguous role of actresses, and musicianship, particularly women composers. The fourth and final section discusses professional women artists and the problem of the division between the 'fine' and the 'decorative' arts.

Chapter 8 (Civil Society and the State)

Though it is often imagined that women had little or no 'public' role in the eighteenth century, the reality is far more complex. Opportunities for women to act publicly expanded markedly in this period, due to, among other factors, the expansion of state power, the growth of commercial media, the rise of new forms of sociability, and women's own efforts to push the boundaries of what was publicly acceptable. The first part of the chapter examines some of the justifications women used for taking public action, as well as some of the many new secular and faith-based societies and institutions, both single-sex and mixed-sex, to which women were drawn in the eighteenth century. The middle section looks at plebeian, middling and elite women petitioning, confronting, celebrating, rebelling against, making deals with, fighting in uniform for, and attempting to influence the early modern state, particularly its military institutions. It also examines women's entry into both individual and institutional charity work, particularly on issues relating to children and health. The third section deals with aristocratic women and political power, and with the challenges and opportunities presented by female rule in the eighteenth century.

Chapter 9 (Age of Revolutions)

In the 1770s, 1780s and 1790s the American Revolution, and soon after it a succession of other revolts and revolutions, severely destabilized the entrenched power of monarchy, aristocracy and church. Women participated in many of these revolutions and revolutionary movements, insisting on their right to fight and sometimes die for patriotic ideals, and, especially in the case of the French Revolution, launching a serious bid to make the revolution more gender egalitarian. Jacobin women activists took up both traditional women's concerns, like education and marriage law, and new ones, such as the 'right' to form women's battalions and the demand for the vote. Efforts to dampen down female militancy began well before the revolution ended, though; here we examine what happened to women activists as the French Revolution turned more radical and violent in 1793, as well as the effects upon women's political aspirations of the Thermidorian Reaction in France and conservative movements outside France. The last section examines the Revolution as an inspiration to women and other subordinated groups in places as far-flung as Hungary and Saint-Domingue-Haiti, and as near as Denmark and Italy, as well as its tendency, over the long run, to tamp down egalitarian feminist impulses, while encouraging a variety of other kinds of political and organizational activity for women. The chapter concludes with the massive conservative reaction that the Revolutions inadvertently set in motion, one in which the status of women was a central concern.

Chapter 1

◆

HIERARCHY AND DIFFERENCE

To early modern people, domination and subordination were the very warp and woof of reality. Efforts to subvert the old order, or even to rethink its hierarchical assumptions, tended to be viewed, particularly by those at the top, as assaults upon God's plan. The eighteenth-century 'Age of Enlightenment' is, of course, associated with a series of systematic attempts to do just that. But throughout the century, and still more urgently in the face of the revolutionary movements that brought it to a close, conservative sentiments continued to issue from the mouths of most preachers, inform childrearing, define labour relations, and permeate the laws. There were, to be sure, always doubts as to whether or not God had personally ordained abuse and exploitation by status superiors (many thought not), but hierarchy and inequality remained the default mode. A central feature of this system was the assumed superiority of most men over virtually all women. And yet, even this apparently simple proposition was anything but straightforward when arrayed next to the many other status categories that helped define early modern life. In this chapter we try to untangle some of these categories and think about how they affected the lives of flesh and blood women.

DEFINING AND ENFORCING SUBORDINATION

Varieties of women's subordination

In the normal course of events a woman would leave the authority of her parents, or, if she was a servant, her master, and come under the authority of her husband (or, in compound or complex families, her father and mother-in-law[1]), often for the rest of her life. That life was supposed to be, and often was, a fairly narrow one. As a woman she was presumptively unfit for most prestige-bearing and potentially powerful roles and opportunities, including the parish clergy, higher education, the military, many skilled crafts, village and town governance, and official state policy making – unless she happened to be an aristocrat or a queen. The amount of wealth and status a woman could accumulate was similarly quite constrained and often dependent upon her connections to men. Women were far more likely to accrue status by virtue of their husband or male relatives coming into an inheritance or advancing in their craft, profession or status-group, than by their own talents or connections.

One of the central markers of status for women was the ability to delegate heavy or time-consuming tasks away to other women or girls. Bearing children conferred status at least in part because of the labour and, often, wages children could contribute. In areas where domestic service was common, even a not-very-prosperous woman might preside over a meagrely paid maidservant, perhaps a young, half-starved, local orphan, or someone whose family could not afford to keep her. In areas where serfdom or slavery flourished, the ownership of other people was a major source of prestige for the better-off. In regions characterized by large, complex or multigenerational households a woman's status rose considerably when she had daughters-in-law to supervise (before she acquired daughters-in-law she had, obviously, to have borne sons).[2] Money was also important. A minority of women could and did exchange subordination to a husband for financial independence later in life, especially in legal regimes that favoured, or at least were not incompatible with, wealth accumulation by women. But both the ability to control other women's or children's labour and financial independence were very contingent where women were concerned. Prosperity could count for little if a wife lacked the support and loyalty of her husband, or if he routinely beat her, publicly shamed her, or took and spent monies earmarked for her widowhood and old age. Everywhere demographic bad luck (the early death of a spouse or failure to bear children) affected women's economic and social status more than it did men's; moreover, they were very vulnerable to having their property and inheritance rights trampled upon by relatives. Consequently, the proportion of women who actually achieved a comfortable and honoured old age, while not negligible, was probably never large. It was extremely easy for women to fall through the tattered safety net of family obligation and love, and because of the many constraints and limitations upon them the landing was often rock-hard.[3]

The everyday disadvantages of femaleness were greatly complicated by other factors. Stigma was an open and unapologetic feature of early modern life, and it had many faces. There were literally stigmatized people, those with birth defects (for instance a hare-lip or a withered arm), obvious skin-diseases, or acquired disabilities, such as polio or a face ruined by smallpox. Many other kinds of stigma were essentially social. In much of Christian Europe people of illegitimate birth were barred from many employment opportunities, including guild membership, municipal citizenship and the priesthood; often it was difficult, and sometimes it was impossible for them to inherit from either parent. Bastards of either sex were, on the whole, undesirable marriage partners, and in some places, especially late in our period, they were disproportionately likely to be abandoned or starved in infancy.[4] Certain occupations also bore the mark of stigma, which is to say that they were considered sufficiently dirty, polluting or uncivilized to render their practitioners (and their kin) unfit for borough citizenship, guild membership, or marriage to honourable people, and sometimes access to the sacraments of the Catholic Church. Women who married men in these groups were, in many places, unwelcome at other women's gatherings or otherwise shunned. Depending on the place, stigmatized occupations could include: executioners, skinners, tanners, shepherds, charcoal-burners, traveling musicians, actors and actresses, professional women mourners, grave-diggers and prostitutes.[5] Ethnic and religious minorities endured many gradations of stigma. This diverse and variable group included Jews, the Roma (Gypsies), Africans, the Scandinavian Saami, various Russian 'tribal' groupings, Protestants in some Catholic countries; Catholics in some Protestant countries, Muslims in Russia, Shi'ites in the Ottoman Empire, and many others. In the early modern period the numbers of the potentially or actually stigmatized expanded considerably with Europe's incursions into the Americas, Asia, Africa and the Pacific, and especially with the exponential growth of the transatlantic slave trade.

Norms and practices relating to stigmatized groups varied greatly. A disability could be somewhat offset by a supportive and loving family, and some disabilities evoked more pity than others. Bastardy could be partially balanced out by a high-born father, by wealth, and, probably most important of all, by having a father who loved and acknowledged all his offspring. Among Muslims, children born to concubines inherited equally with a man's legitimate children if he recognized them as his own; some illegitimates in Iberia and its colonies also inherited on an equal basis with their legitimate half-siblings.[6] Single mothers were not everywhere bereft of support: charities sometimes helped them; and in some places they seem to have been supported by their families and assimilated back into the marriage or the labour market with little fuss (see Chapter 3). Jews were treated far better in some cities or realms (Amsterdam, Ottoman cities like Salonika/Thessaloniki and Smyrna/Izmir, and in many parts of Poland) than in others. Toleration allowed a respite, albeit sometimes only temporary, from the siege mentality and crippling economic burdens that persecution usually brought with it. This inevitably affected women for the better. In early modern Poland, on the whole a place of opportunity for Jews despite some shocking outbreaks of mass violence, Jewish women sometimes supervised charitable collections in their communities, and a few were very active in estate management, sometimes forging close working relationships with Christian noblewomen.[7]

Slavery and serfdom

In the English and Dutch colonies and former colonies, slavery was tantamount to social death.[8] Slaves had no right to property. African abductees had their family ties systematically destroyed, and the new families they tried to form could be broken up on an owner's whim. Though in many places it was, technically, against the law, in practice male slave-owners had virtually unlimited sexual access to their slaves. The children of free men and slave women were considered illegitimate, did not usually automatically inherit from their white fathers, and remained slaves unless special steps were taken by their owner to manumit them. Manumission was relatively rare, and increasingly illegal, so for most people slavery was a life-long status that they passed on to their children and their children's children. Slaves could not, for the most part, sue in court, much less sue their masters. In addition slavery was so strongly linked to race that even free people of African descent inherited a variety of legal and cultural disabilities, as well as the possibility that they or their children might be kidnapped and re-enslaved. This is the model of slavery that most northwestern Europeans are most familiar with: it is what prevailed in the British and Dutch West Indies and in the North American colonies (later the United States), and there is general agreement that it was one of the most extreme forms of slavery in recorded history.[9]

Slavery looked quite different in the Ottoman Empire, while Spain, Portugal (and arguably France) and their colonies lay between the extremes. One would not want to exaggerate the contrasts. To take the Ottomans first, it is quite clear that their form of slavery was saturated with coercion. It is true that some slaves sold themselves (or were sold by their families) into slavery – because, as we will see, enslavement tended to be a temporary state and was quite often a route to upward mobility. But many others, particularly those of African or Balkan origin, were dragged by force from their homelands and their families. The forced march of central African and Sudanese captives north across the Sahara desert to slavery among the Ottomans was every bit as brutal and dangerous as the Middle Passage of slaves to the New World. In some other respects, however, slavery in the Ottoman mode was a hybrid form, located somewhere between slavery, indentured servitude, and fictive kinship. In the Ottoman Empire slaves were generally freed after five or seven years, and if they were not they could petition the courts to free them. They could also arrange to have themselves sold to a new owner if their first owner mistreated them, and they had a right, enshrined in the Qur'an, to purchase their freedom. Strong social pressure, sometimes buttressed by the law, was brought to bear on masters who refused to let their slaves go.[10] Masters were supposed to feed and clothe their slaves with the same food and clothes they themselves wore and ate, and to consider them their brothers, and freeing a slave was not only to be done in expiation for a variety of crimes or missteps, but was mandated (as several *hadiths*[11] report) if a master struck or otherwise mistreated his slave. The position of slave women is especially indicative of the hybrid character of Ottoman slavery. A woman did not have the right to refuse sexual relations with her master and many women were specifically bought for sexual purposes. On the other hand, a slave who bore children to her master could not be sold and was automatically freed on his death if she had not been previously. In addition, her children were free and inherited equally with the master's other children *if he acknowledged them*, though this was entirely up to him, and it would have been greatly in the interests of his other wives for him not to do so.[12] Ottoman slaves tended to have marriages arranged for them, either before or after manumission, by their owners or former owners (which was probably usually considered a benefit), and often subsequently became valued members of their master's or mistress's clientage network. This not infrequently led to extraordinary upward mobility: many of the most powerful people in the Ottoman Empire in the early modern period were slaves or former slaves, and the Sultan himself was invariably the son of a slave. Women could also move up through slavery, and often did, especially if they were attractive and musically talented or had administrative or accounting skills; moreover, the Qur'an strongly encourages men to marry their slaves, and even to choose pious slave-women as wives over less-pious free ones, and forbids an owner to prostitute his or her slaves 'if she [the slave] desires chastity'.[13] As one authority, Y. Hakan Erdem, has remarked, '[t]he Ottoman slave system was an open one in which slaves were continually integrated into society as full members . . .'[14] On the other hand, it is also clear that black slaves (who became significantly more common in the eighteenth and nineteenth centuries than they had been) were much less likely to experience this sort of upward mobility than white or Ethiopian slaves were, and they tended to be consigned to menial household tasks (African women could sometimes improve their lot by becoming wet nurses, a very important position in elite households, not least because it conferred a form of kinship between the wet nurse's own children and the children she nursed).[15] The treatment of slaves prescribed in the Qur'an and *hadiths* was clearly an ideal. It did demonstrably affect the conditions under which slaves lived: many slaves *did* become fictive kin and marry up into the families or networks of their owners; it is likely that it emboldened slaves to try to better their lot, and it certainly translated into very high manumission rates. Still, there is no question that Ottoman slavery, especially to the extent that it was located in the private household (as female slavery, at least, almost always was) could be abusive and exploitative in ways that were quite comparable to what we see in other closed family systems. And many slaves (perhaps especially menial slaves, who were also likely to be Africans), achieved manumission only to find themselves, essentially, abandoned to their fate.

Similar paradoxes and inconsistencies characterized slave conditions in the various Iberian and French colonies. Slaves' living and working conditions, especially in the West Indian and Brazilian plantation economies, were often horrific. Slaves *did* have a right to petition the court for manumission if they were ill-treated, and they could also purchase their own freedom, but one wonders how well either of these worked on remote plantations (throughout the early modern world legal rights tended to be more available to people in or near urban areas). Be that as it may, slave manumission does seem to have been a good deal more common in the Iberian colonies than in the Northern European colonies. Unlike in the Ottoman system, slave-women in the Iberian colonies did, in theory, have the right to refuse to have sexual relations with their master (and, as we will see, it was sometimes enforceable in court). Moreover, in both Portuguese and Spanish colonies, and to some extent in French ones, this was buttressed by strong, if inconsistent, pressure from the Catholic Church and the courts on owners to marry slave-women with whom they cohabited (assuming the men were not already married, that is) or at least to provide child-support. One result was a significantly higher rate of interracial marriage than one sees in the Northern European colonies (where cross-racial marriage was more likely to be illegal), with some children of slaves even ending up as heirs to a share of the estate of their mother's former owner.[16]

Conversely, even with their somewhat more liberal views on intermarriage, there is also much evidence of race prejudice in Spain, Portugal, France and their colonies. One symptom of this was that municipalities were perpetually trying to forbid slaves, and often free blacks or mulattos too, from gambling, dancing, playing loud music, or wearing clothes or personal adornments that seemed to compete with those of white and/or free people. There were also a variety of laws (which all historians agree grew more onerous over the course of the eighteenth and early nineteenth centuries) excluding blacks and mixed-race people from public office or from attending university, limiting their ability to bear arms, and generally seeking to deny them the benefits and the opportunities afforded to free whites. Predictably, in a world where white men routinely preyed sexually upon non-white women, considerable discursive and legislative effort was expended to define black and mixed-race women as essentially dishonourable (because they were allegedly naturally disposed to 'sexual ardours')[17] while white women were supposedly both honourable and chaste. This doctrine was convenient for white men because it left women of colour more vulnerable to both verbal and physical sexual attack. It was convenient for white women because it suggested that the paternity of 'entirely white' children was far more certain than that of mixed-race children. In short, it struck a pre-emptive blow against the efforts of slave-women concubines to get the white fathers of their children to recognize them as their own, and undermined the ability of the offspring of irregular unions to compete, either morally or legally, with legitimate children for shares in the master's estate. Interestingly, even places (chiefly Catholic countries and their colonies) that did give rights to slave-women to, say, sue for child-support, that encouraged men to marry their slave-concubines, that automatically enfranchised the children of free men, or that gave inheritance rights to illegitimate children, had back-tracked by the second half of the eighteenth century, and grew even more illiberal in the nineteenth. There are many reasons for this, but it is hard to avoid the suspicion that at least some of the impetus came from the growing cultural influence of white women, who had the least to gain from such arrangements. Certainly by the early nineteenth century, even in Catholic colonies, both law and custom proceeded as if all or almost all black and mixed-race people were illegitimate or at least of doubtful paternity, and therefore presumptively dishonourable.[18]

The famous 'second serfdom', largely established in the sixteenth and seventeenth centuries, and at its apex in the eighteenth, affected a good proportion of the rural and parts of the urban labour force of east central and eastern Europe, including various German states, Lithuania, Livonia (now

Latvia and Estonia), Poland, Hungary, Bohemia, Silesia, Romania and Russia. It also had a western European outpost in Denmark. Like slavery, serfdom systematically undermined the cultural, economic and political power of those at the receiving end, though it differed from most slavery in the sense that, since serfs were supposed to be 'tied to the land', they also generally stayed connected to their kin-group. Serfdom was essentially a way to capture a large agricultural labour force and then monopolize it. It involved a phalanx of efforts aimed at stopping people from leaving the estate where they were born, extracting their labour with relatively minimal return, and gradually depriving them of traditional avenues of redress. Over time, landowners – most of them members of the nobility – gained more and more rights over their serfs, including, in some countries, the right actually to buy and sell them away from their natal villages. In many areas it became difficult or illegal for serfs to use any courts other than the one presided over by their owner. Owners could typically interfere with their serfs' right to marry (or not marry), force them to pay a variety of special taxes, monopolize their labour, require that they use only the master's mill or other service (for a steep fee of course), inflict beatings and other punishments on them, sexually exploit them, and even, in practice, kill them with relative impunity. Everywhere there was a great deal of diversity in terms of the conditions and degree of unfreedom, though, even within a given state, region or estate. So, for example, on most estates, as in New World slave plantations, there was a distinction between domestic serfs and field-hands, with different advantages and disadvantages accruing to each, and often significant social divisions as well (since domestic serfs were often women this particularly affected them). In all serf families and villages the subordination of serfs to their owner, the state, and the estate manager both competed and colluded with other hierarchies based upon gender, marital status, and age. Thus, in most Russian serf villages, local governance was in the hands of councils of old men, and both women and younger men could suffer at their hands.[19]

Both serfdom and slavery came under attack in the early modern period. This happened earliest in some Catholic countries, some of it, as we now know, spearheaded by former slaves themselves, particularly members of Portuguese, Spanish, Angolan, Kongolese and Brazilian black confraternities.[20] In 1773, Portugal, which supported some important and under-recognized early abolitionists, became the first European country to outright abolish slavery, but the provisions applied only in Portugal and its Indian colonies, not in Brazil or the African colonies.[21] Most other European powers (and colonies and former colonies) abolished the trade in slaves and, usually somewhat later, the *institution* of slavery, sometime between about 1800 and the last quarter of the nineteenth century. Among the last to abolish slavery were the Netherlands (1863), the United States (1865), Puerto Rico (1873), Cuba (1886), Brazil (1888) and the Ottoman Empire (for most intents and purposes in the 1890s). Most countries also abolished serfdom in the late eighteenth or early nineteenth century; the main holdout was Russia, which retained the institution until 1861 and abolished it only slowly over the ensuing decades. These events are mostly beyond the scope of the present study, but their protracted nature speaks volumes about how deep-rooted these most extreme forms of subordination actually were.

Violence

In the Europe of today legitimate resort to violence is almost entirely confined to the state. Society operates on the assumption that most people will choose to go to work each day, cooperate with (how different from obey!) their superiors, pay their taxes, and refrain from stealing from, assaulting or killing each other, without the constant threat of a beating or worse. For that matter, the arm of the state is far less heavy (or at least heavy in a different way) than it used to be. An obvious example is that, unlike in the eighteenth century, hardly anyone any longer believes that arraying the rotting corpses or body parts of malefactors around major cities, rebellious villages, or colonies with large subject populations, or burning people at the stake, is essential to convince others of the wages of defying authority.[22] One of the central characteristics differentiating early modern hierarchies from modern ones is that the former were founded on swift and virtually universal resort to the threat or reality of physical violence. In the resource-poor and highly stratified eighteenth-century world, positive rewards for work well done were few and meagre, especially among lower-status groups. In their place negative incentives (pain, fear, and food deprivation most notably) loomed large in almost everyone's conception of how essential tasks got accomplished. A farmer beating or threatening to beat his cow or dog, an overseer his serfs, a husband his wife, a military officer his men, a schoolmaster his pupils, or a mother or mistress her children, servants, slaves or daughters-in-law, were all pursuing the standard method of 'getting things done' – *not* the only one by any means, but one of the main ones. Private violence was buttressed by very widespread use of judicial violence that usually featured the purposeful inflicting of pain. Judicial flogging and branding were ubiquitous across most countries' criminal justice systems, inflicted for crimes or sins as diverse as bearing an illegitimate child, engaging in prostitution, vagrancy, begging, petty theft, rudeness to social superiors, and wearing clothes or ornaments not befitting one's station in life. Torture was also rather widely utilized in criminal investigations, at least for more serious crimes, though it was in increasing disrepute among jurists (the eighteenth-century assault on the use of torture to elicit confessions is an important feature of the Enlightenment; though it is revealing that punitive torture – flogging and the like – lasted much longer). At the same time there were very strong taboos against inferiors of any kind hitting back. We hear about this most often in relation to wives striking their husbands or slaves their masters, but it suffused the whole system, including the criminal law. Almost everywhere hurting or killing a superior was treated as one of the most heinous of crimes and savagely punished (burning at the stake, impalement, being buried alive, being hung up in chains until dead, being flogged to death, and having one's severed head stuck on a pike for public view were all practised in the eighteenth century, and in the case of slaves well into the nineteenth), though there is some evidence that, over the course of the eighteenth century, a number of countries began to punish husband-murder more like other kinds of manslaughter and homicide.[23] Islamic law had a somewhat more refined system, but it was not any more democratic, since it assigned a different 'bloodprice' to people of different status (bloodprice was the amount of compensation that had to be paid by a killer or his/her kin to the family of the victim). Thus, a slave had a lower bloodprice than a free person, a *dhimmi* (a non-Muslim subject of the Empire) a lower bloodprice than a Muslim; a woman a lower bloodprice than a man. Moreover there was a tendency to assume that execution would only follow if a person with a lower bloodprice killed someone with a higher one.[24]

Children, the poor, women, servants, orphans, slaves, animals and other lower-status beings were the ones most likely to be on the receiving end of violent acts, and also the ones *least* likely to leave any record of their feelings about it. But even where punishment was immoderate by contemporary standards there were probably fewer effective avenues of recourse than there are today. Other people quite often tried to intervene, and were sometimes successful; moreover, as we will see, the authorities were sometimes prepared to step in when the violence was life-threatening, inappropriately public (as when a man abused his wife in front of half the parish), or incommensurate with the victim's social status. But in the final analysis, precisely because high status was so bound up with the right to disciplinary violence, status superiors had relatively few checks, beyond their own conscience, on their ability to dispense punishment to their inferiors if, when and in the way they saw fit.

This atmosphere of relative, if not total, impunity encouraged a good many quite ordinary people to look to violence as a solution to most managerial problems and quite a few more personal ones. The horrific forms of abuse detailed in divorce court proceedings of the time, in inquests into the untimely deaths of servants and apprentices at the hands of masters or mistresses, in folk-tales about cruel masters and murderous stepmothers, and in narratives of maltreatment at the hands of both male and female slave- or serf-owners, were not the norm – they came to people's attention because of a death or a maiming or because they were intrinsically exciting stories (a fascination with murder and atrocity was as typical of those times as it is of our own). However, petty tyrants who lorded it over their wives, children, servants, serfs or slaves, using threats and liberal (but not maiming or life-threatening) doses of violence and mental cruelty, were all-too-common. And so was the unthinking callousness and insensitivity of more average people – both male and female – whose daily plans simply did not factor in their subordinates' well-being or humanity.

Not all relations of domination were the same. Physical punishment may have been, by our standards, common, but it was also extremely degrading. There was a strong presumption in early modern society that adults of noble status (and most particularly *men* of noble status) should not be subjected to it, and indeed, contemporary notions of honour and dishonour tracked closely with whether one was in a position to inflict pain or order it to be inflicted (honourable) or on the receiving end of it (deeply dishonourable, especially when done in public). Judiciaries often gave the guilty the choice *either* to receive a public whipping *or* to pay a fine, a practice which meant that the rich (or at least the adult rich) seldom suffered corporal punishment. In the *sharia* courts it seems often to have been assumed that a public reprimand from the *kadi* (judge) would be just as effective for the rich as a flogging was for the poor.[25] This sort of double standard was sometimes made explicit with respect to slaves. It was common in eighteenth- and nineteenth-century Brazil for laws to specify two types of punishments, based on whether the culprit was free or a slave. A free person paid a fine or served a jail sentence; slaves were punished with pain. Thus, according to the law code of one Brazilian town: 'The individual who publicly washed himself at any place in the river in front of town or in its vicinity, in such a manner that he offends public morality, because he is seen by those passing by, a fine of ten milréis paid at the jail; *if a slave, the offender will be punished with fifty lashes.*'[26] Some famous and widely publicized exceptions notwithstanding, almost everywhere the rich, and particularly the nobility, were also much less likely to be executed for any crime.

The question of who could legitimately discipline whom was especially complicated for women, and it was a problem precisely because of the anxious way that status categories cross-cut one another. There was considerable discomfort with women administering physical punishment to male inferiors, apart, perhaps, from very young boys. Male servants and journeymen who would submit to a thrashing from a master simply would not work for a mistress who tried the same thing. Even when dealing with non-free subordinates, such as male serfs or slaves, many women probably delegated punishment to others, because that way it would seem more 'legitimate', and hence, in the punitive calculus of the time, have a more salutary effect. The perceived 'problem' of the inappropriateness of women disciplining men helped bolster the belief that women householders could not control their male servants, contributed to the difficulty widows had of carrying on their husbands' trades or farms, and helped justify men seizing managerial control of widows' estates. On the other hand some women clearly did wield considerable authority over inferiors, including male inferiors. So we should not underestimate the ability of the system to adapt itself to figures of authority of either sex.

The identification of marriage with husband-on-wife violence was virtually axiomatic, which is quite different from saying that everyone approved of it (they did not). Possibly marriage really *was* the locus, proportionally speaking, of more violence than other relationships. Anna Clark argues that, in eighteenth- and nineteenth-century Britain, wife-beating was reinforced by prevailing patterns of all-male sociability. These often involved a good deal of alcohol consumption, which encouraged men to defend with violence their right to spend household resources on socializing with their friends rather than feeding their families. In addition, men often deepened their ties to other men by celebrating their ability to dominate their wives and other women sexually and with their fists.[27] This formulation, if true, is unlikely to have been unique to Britain. However, the stereotypically close cultural association, almost everywhere, between marriage and violence could also derive from the fact that many more people married than had servants or slaves, or even than owned domestic animals; because the marriage relation, and especially marriages in trouble, were considered particularly exciting and humorous topics of discussion (as they still are in many cultures); or because getting one's wife to submit was an unusually challenging task and hence required more cultural ammunition.

The stigmatized were particularly vulnerable to violence, and they generally had little recourse against it. People routinely set their dogs on itinerant beggars and other strangers or forcibly ejected them from villages and towns.

Old beggar women and the Roma also sometimes encountered local vigilante actions aimed at countering their alleged propensity for malevolent magic. Crowds of boys, and sometimes even of adults, threw stones at, heckled or played cruel tricks on people with physical disabilities when they ventured into view. And the ritualized humiliation and killing of Jews at the hands of states, municipalities and pumped-up crowds is an extremely well-documented feature of the medieval and early modern periods.[28]

Controlling mobility, attire and social contacts

At a rough guess, at any one time in the eighteenth century, somewhere around four-fifths of European women and up to one-half of men (and a much higher percentage in some places), were not allowed to leave where they were without getting someone else's permission first. Controls on mobility had a variety of aims. One was to 'capture' and keep a labour force in a context where the rewards accruing to work were few or very unevenly distributed, or labour was scarce. Slaves, serfs, 'life-cycle' servants during the duration of their contract, apprentices, soldiers and sailors, minor male children *and* adult married men who were not heads of household were usually forbidden to desert their owners, masters, commanding officers or parents. In Russia even the nobility (deemed essential for military service) had to get the tsar or tsarina's permission to leave the country.[29]

Another reason for controls on mobility was lingering fears about certain groups' alleged designs upon other people's well-being. Jews had long been thought to be in league with the devil, and to be full of plans for destroying or harming Christian communities and individual Christians, both through magic and more secular means. Many Christians believed that toleration of Jews displeased God and helped bring on collective punishments (the plague was especially linked to Jews), and that punishing or killing them would bring divine blessings. If anything, the early modern period saw an increase in this kind of thinking. The first Jewish ghetto was established in Venice in 1516: it was a confined area, locked at night, so as to keep Jews from carrying out their nefarious anti-Christian plans under cover of darkness. Thereafter ghettos spread across Italy and central and eastern Europe (they were less common in western Europe because Jews had been expelled *en masse* from most western European countries during the Medieval and Renaissance periods). The consequences could be deadly. When the bubonic plague came to Prague in 1713 the Jews were essentially locked up in the ghetto to die.[30]

Almost everywhere, women were more encircled by unfreedom and constraint than men, the result of a felt need to monopolize and control their productive, reproductive, and emotional labour, to exclude them from occupations or activities men preferred to monopolize, and to neutralize or channel their magical sexual power so that it would not cause social disorder. There were also far more rules for women than for men concerning with whom they could converse or keep company, what kind of work they could do, and where and with whom they could live. Everywhere men were permitted to lock up their wives (and daughters) in their own houses, and where madhouses existed they could also confine them there. Tens of thousands of early modern women, mostly daughters of the elite, entered locked convents, some only until they married, some for their entire lives. Much, though not all, of the latter was voluntary: convents had much to recommend them to upper-class women (see Chapter 6). But the fact remains that once one had taken permanent vows one was generally a prisoner for life. Convents were also a favoured dumping ground for unwanted upper-class wives and sexually uncontrollable noblewomen, and both could be consigned to them without a trial.[31] In Orthodox Russia a man could put away his wife in a convent simply by claiming she was an adulteress, and then go on to marry another. To be fair, though, there were efforts in the eighteenth century to curtail this practice, just as, in England, relatives began seeking writs of *habeas corpus* to stop men using private madhouses to confine their wives.[32]

There were numerous laws and customs prescribing what clothes, and especially what head-gear, women should wear. Today many people associate rules about veiling and headscarves with the Muslim world, but in the eighteenth century they were common among Christians as well, in line with 1 Corinthians 11:4–13 which appears not only to prescribe head-coverings for any woman who prays or goes to church, but explicitly to associate it with female subordination, which Islamic veiling traditions do not typically do. Many Christian women wore a head-covering all the time, and certainly when they went outside; those who did not would have been barred from church and likely harassed on the street. It was a sin for Jewish women to appear before any man other than their husband without a head covering (as it still is for many Orthodox Jews). Russians believed that it was dangerous for a married woman's hair to be seen in public, while some Baltic peoples cut women's hair off when they married.[33] For Jews, Muslims *and* Christians *not* wearing a head-covering was often interpreted to mean that the person was a prostitute or adulteress, or at least sexually available, and tearing off a woman's head-covering, or refusing to let her wear one when she wanted to, was a way to say that she was a whore (not surprisingly, 'tearing off a woman's head-clothes' was a common form of domestic abuse or defamation – actionable in some places – it also often turns up in neighbourhood vigilante actions against women deemed to be unchaste). Veils were, of course, required for Catholic nuns, and a veil that actually obscured the face was also a mark of elite status throughout most of Europe. Spanish noblewomen wore them well into the eighteenth century, and so did Venetian women, both elites and non-elites. Across Europe almost any woman who could afford them also wore them to travel.[34]

It was generally easier to limit the mobility of women than of men because girls and women on their own knew they were very vulnerable both to attacks on their reputations and to actual sexual assault. There is much evidence that unaccompanied girls and women on the move were thought, by definition, to be sexually available to all comers, especially if they were lower class or marked as racially 'other'.[35] Women also tended to be discouraged from establishing contacts with people outside their immediate family circle or village, which meant that they had fewer places to go if they needed to flee. It has been estimated that between 1719 and 1727 200,000 Russian serfs fled their owners for the Urals, the lower Volga, Siberia or Poland; in some cases entire villages departed. But unless they fled in large groups (as some clearly did), women serfs, whether seeking to escape their husbands and in-laws or the local estate overseer, sometimes found it difficult to flee much farther than their own parents' home, whence they could easily be extracted. Both free and enserfed or enslaved women were also tied to particular households by the difficulty and expense of getting other work, especially if they lacked anyone to vouch for them. In many areas, and particularly in the countryside, maidservants received only room and board and no cash compensation for their work (an arrangement that was far rarer for men) so they had no savings to call upon if they decided to leave; nor could their natal families, if they had any, necessarily afford, legally or financially, to offer them sanctuary. Mothers of children were often unwilling to leave behind children they knew they could not support on their own, which both kept them in abusive marriages and was one of the reasons why slave women with children were less likely to try to escape than either men or unencumbered women. It seems that, for women, the social stigma, the illegality and the pragmatic difficulties of flight were all unusually strong.[36]

Women's mobility in the Ottoman Empire

Most early modern commentators thought that the Ottoman Empire placed greater constraints upon women's mobility than other regions did, though some other places (notably Venice) came close.[37] It is not easy to gauge how true this is, especially since travellers tended to generalize from the experience of elite women; and virtually everywhere in Europe and the Middle East elite women encountered more restraints upon their movements than the generality of women (or at least different kinds of restraints). In the early modern Ottoman Empire, honourable women could never be seen doing their own work (drawing water, doing what were clearly errands, and probably most shopping, were the jobs of servants or slaves) and they only went out in public accompanied by a retinue. But French noblewomen did not draw their own water or stir abroad without retinues either. Travellers' observations raise more questions than they answer. For example, was avoidance of visible, out-in-public work more widely practised among Ottoman city-dwellers than it was in large parts of Christian Europe, perhaps because of the absence of a distinct Ottoman aristocracy? Or was it the case that travellers overlooked or ignored the activities of lower-class women? And what of the majority of Ottoman women, who had neither servants nor slaves, routinely shared their crowded homes with other families, and did their own chores, including shopping, begging, drawing water, etc.? Did they lack honour, or did they simply assert it in some other way?[38]

Two things did differentiate Ottoman elite (and to some extent other) women from most travellers' country-women. First, they had very few social interactions with men who were not close relatives. In most cases (the exception, as we will see, being the special case of the sultan's harem) these women were not shut in anywhere near as definitively as, say, Counter-reformation Catholic nuns were enclosed in their convents. Since most Ottoman women went out a good deal (see below), but virtually always socialized in single-sex groupings, many scholars prefer to characterize their lives using terms like 'spatial autonomy' (that is, from men) or 'segregation' rather than 'seclusion' or 'confinement'.[39] Second, the famous souks or bazaars of most Ottoman cities were apparently more male than many marketplaces in Christian Europe, a product of the concerns about mixed-sex interaction, of an especially entrenched system of guild monopolies of trade, manufacture, street-selling, and even many urban service-professions (e.g. water-carrying), and of an increased programme of surveillance of women that, for reasons that are yet to be explained, seems to have set in from the later sixteenth century on.[40]

There were a number of women shop owners (this was a popular area of investment for Ottoman women), but the impression we get is that it was rarer for women to operate a shop than to collect rents on it (though not unheard of). On the other hand there were plenty of travelling saleswomen, many of them Jewish (goods often went to where women buyers were rather than the reverse), at least some women street-sellers, and special segregated or semi-segregated women's street markets in Istanbul and several other Ottoman towns (see Chapter 5).

Ottoman women did shop. Popular tales and pictures from the period depict women bargaining with male shopkeepers, and there were periodic efforts to stop women from congregating in certain kinds of shops, though the fact that this sort of legislation was so often repeated suggests that it did not work very well.[41] Most women went to the public bathhouses frequently, and a lot of buying and selling, real-estate deals, slave-trading and marriage-brokerage went on in this all-woman space as well as in women's homes.[42] Picnics and promenades were also common features of eighteenth-century women's lives, even elite women, as contemporary pictures demonstrate (Plate 1), and in the late seventeenth century Jewish women from Smyrna (now Izmir), on the Aegean Sea, and probably other Ottoman cities, apparently frequented coffee-houses on the Sabbath and Jewish holidays.[43] There was much visiting by all religious groups to medical practitioners of both sexes, and to shrines. One eighteenth-century traveller named Alexander Russell remarked, tongue in cheek, of one Ottoman town: 'were a stranger to judge from the number [of women] he daily meets in the streets, he would hardly think himself in a country, where the women generally are supposed to be prisoners for life'.[44] Not only were most women not 'prisoners for life' but they frequently owned the home or part of a home in which they lived, and some went to court against both neighbours and their own relatives in order to control 'their space'.[45]

Only one eighteenth-century Western woman socialized fairly extensively with elite Ottoman women and then subsequently wrote about it (unfortunately she had little to say about non-elite women). Lady Mary Wortley Montagu (1689–1762) was the wife of the British Ambassador and lived in Istanbul from 1717 to 1718. She also appears to have spoken at least a smattering of Ottoman Turkish. Like Russell, Montagu was sceptical of the claim, made by so many western Europeans, that Turkish women lived in 'miserable confinement'; in her view they were '(perhaps) freer than any Ladys in the universe' and 'have more Liberty than we English have'.[46] Montagu clearly exaggerated for effect, she was more backhanded in her praise than at first meets the eye, and her basis for comparison was limited. (The universe? How could she know?) Nevertheless, her words need to be taken seriously, if not literally. The Ottomans clearly practised modes of limiting women's options – particularly elite women's options – that differed in some respects from those many western Europeans were accustomed to, though the larger purposes are very recognizable and in no sense unique. What is far less clear is that this made Ottoman women – whether elite or non-elite – existentially more 'oppressed' than elsewhere, given the benefits of 'spatial autonomy', Ottoman married women's extensive property rights, and fairly extensive access to the law courts (see below and Chapter 2).

The only institution in the Ottoman Empire as comprehensively confining as the Catholic convent system was the Imperial Harem, the inner family sanctum of the sultan's palace. It involved far fewer women than did Catholic convents, however. In the eighteenth century the Imperial Harem enclosed between 450 and 1,000 women of whom, on average, fewer than a dozen were actually concubines or potential concubines of the sultan, with the rest being attendants, women civil servants, and pensioners from previous sultans' reigns.[47] The Imperial Harem was a central part of the mystique of the house of Osman (from which the empire took its name), and linked to a conception of sovereignty that preferred that neither males nor females of the royal household appear very much in public. It fascinated both the Ottomans themselves and foreigners, but it was not representative. Other elite households did not practise this sort of extreme seclusion for either women or men (as Mary Wortley Montagu quickly realized), and it was distant indeed from the crowded spaces in which ordinary urban women lived, worked and socialized.

The women of the Imperial Harem had even less in common with women who lived in rural areas (the majority of the population in the Ottoman Empire as in Christian Europe). Most rural women were out and about throughout the day, doing laundry in streams, carrying water, collecting fuel, foraging, tending animals, gardening, attending fairs, and participating in religious activities such as shrine-visiting. These girls' and women's lives were certainly confined, and like rural women in many parts of Europe and the Middle East they were often under fairly heavy surveillance, largely by other women, but they did not live secluded in their homes.

Justifications

Human hierarchies almost always come along with complex justifications on the part of those who benefit from them. These justifications are often pragmatic: in the early modern period temporary service in other people's homes supplied – it was thought – better discipline and better training for otherwise potentially unruly youths than their over-indulgent parents were likely to be able to offer. It also gave householders the opportunity to fine-tune their labour force instead of depending on their own children, who might not be old enough or skilled enough to do the requisite work. Life-cycle subordination, such as temporary domestic service during a person's teens, often relied heavily on common-sense rationales that could have broad appeal, including to subordinates themselves.

However, subordination in early modern Europe also needed more powerful justifications, perhaps because the day-to-day reality of it so often, and so transparently, favoured the interests of elites, household heads, adults, etc., at everyone else's expense. There was, for example, the belief that aristocrats were braver and more intelligent than other groups, and hence more fit to lead. Sometimes, as happened in Poland, this gave rise to curious proto-'scientific' claims, such as the 'Sarmatian myth', that held that *szlachta* (nobles) were of a different and superior race to peasants. In keeping with this, savage penalties could be exacted upon peasant men who had sexual relations with *szlachta* women (it is important to note that many Polish nobles were not any better off economically than peasants, so this is not as unlikely as it sounds). The men risked castration and death, and the sexual relations between them were actually denominated as 'sodomy', and alleged to give rise to natural disasters. Moreover, the bastard children of mixed liaisons were stigmatized and barred from testifying in court, inheriting property, or holding membership in a guild.[48] This is a fairly extreme case, and one assumes it was inconsistently enforced, but it strikingly parallels evolving taboos in New World slave societies against interracial sex and marriage between white women and non-white men, as well as these societies' growing reluctance to legitimize the unions or the offspring of white men and black, mixed-race or slave-women.[49] At a more quotidian level, there were tireless efforts, throughout Europe and her colonies, to associate subordinates with intellectual inferiority, dirtiness, bad manners, cowardice, promiscuity and other undesirable traits, as well as to argue that they 'needed' the oversight of their betters in order to work at peak efficiency.[50] Very few status superiors thought that inferiors living independently and working for themselves for decent wages could possibly be making their best effort; the contrary view would be one of the eighteenth-century Scottish political economist Adam Smith's great contributions to European managerial theory as well as to the progress of humanity.[51] Theories about racial and religious minorities tended to be especially lurid and hypersexualized (see Voices from the Past 1.1).

VOICES FROM THE PAST 1.1

Gender, race and sexual dishonour

Most racialist thought focuses a good deal of attention on the alleged promiscuity, shamelessness, and seductive wiles of the women of the 'Other' group (usually minority men are also assumed to have sexual designs on the dominant group's women). Rumours about women served to undermine their honour as well as that of the men in the group under attack — the latter since they supposedly colluded in the debauchery. These theories helped to justify the whole group's inferior, servile or enslaved status (the Edward Long quote is actually part of an extended defence of slavery). In addition they offered a pre-emptive rationale for sexual depredations upon minority women by men of the dominant group.

On Romany Women

Their dances are the most disgusting that can be conceived, always ending with fulsome grimaces, or the most lascivious attitudes and gestures, uncovering those parts, which the rudest and most uncultivated people carefully conceal; nor is this indecency confined to the married women only, but is rather more practised by young girls, travelling with their fathers, who are also musicians, and for a trifling acknowledgement, exhibit their dexterity to any body who is pleased with these unseemly dances.

Nothing can exceed the unrestrained depravity of manners, existing among these people, I allude particularly to the other sex [i.e. women]. Unchecked by any idea of shame, they give way to every desire. The mother endeavors, by the most scandalous arts, to train her daughter for an offering to sensuality, and [she] is scarce grown up, before she becomes the seducer of others.

Source: Heinrich Moritz Gottlieb Grellman, *Dissertation on the Gipsies* (London: P. Elmsley, T. Cadell and J. Sewell, 1787), 34, 67.

On Jewish Women

For the love of God, may I be preserved from all contact with these damned souls!

Among these people [Jews] every women belongs to [that is, is sexually available to] all men; girls and boys belong to each and everyone [that is, the paternity of children cannot be determined].

Source: Fazil-Bey, *Le Livre des Femmes (Zenan-Nameh)*, trans. J.A. Decourdemanche, Bibliothèque Orientale Elzévirienne 25 (Paris: E. Leroux, 1879), 94 (the *Zenan-Nameh* dates from around 1793).

On Black and Mulatto Women

The girls arrive very early at the age of puberty; and, from the time of their being about twenty-five, they decline very fast, till at length they grow horribly ugly. They are lascivious; yet, considering their want of instruction, their behaviour in public is remarkably decent; and they affect a modesty which they do not feel . . .

. . . The major part, nay, almost the whole number [of mulatto women], with very few exceptions, have been *filles de joye* [prostitutes] before they became wives.

They are all married (*in their way*) to a husband, or wife, *pro tempore*, or have other family connexions, in almost every parish throughout the island; so that one of them, perhaps, has six or more husbands, or wives, in several different places . . .

They laugh at the idea of marriage, which ties two persons together indissolubly. Their notions of love are, that it is free and transitory.

Source: Edward Long, *The History of Jamaica* (London: T. Lowndes 1774), II, 335–6, 414–15.

Organized religion played a major role in justifying European hierarchies. Scriptural passages, parables or teachings that related to social order and precedence were quite well known to ordinary lay-people, and often appealed to by status superiors. 'The rich man in his castle/The poor man at his gate/God made them, high or lowly/And ordered their estate' runs one well-known Anglican hymn from the period, and it was matched by similar sentiments in every faith. Gender hierarchy was especially well defended by such bulwarks. Most Christians, Jews and Muslims knew little about the theological arcana of their respective faiths, but they knew that Eve was created out of Adam's body (as both the book of Genesis and the Qur'an report) and hence was subordinate to him. Of course, order of precedence in Creation was only one, and arguably not even the most compelling, rationale for male supremacy. Far more important was the fact that the Genesis story, sacred to both Jews and Christians and revered by Muslims, blamed Original Sin, in the first instance, on a woman, and punished her and all future women by putting a confirmation of male supremacy – as well as a reproductive curse – in the very mouth of God: 'I will greatly increase your pangs in childbearing; in pain you shall bring forth children, yet your desire will be for your husband and he shall rule over you' (Genesis 3:16). The Qur'an's version of the story of the temptation of Adam and Eve is more egalitarian and less punitive, but it is made perfectly clear elsewhere that women are subordinate to men – and educated Muslims as well as popular glosses on the Expulsion from the Garden were thoroughly conversant with the more misogynist Genesis account. All three traditions were deeply anxious about female sexuality which they saw as dangerous for men and likely to tempt them away from heaven, just as Eve had used her wiles to tempt Adam to bite into the forbidden fruit. And all three associated menstruation and childbirth with ritual uncleanness, dangerous magic and disruptions in the natural world.

Many other hierarchies also received the stamp of divine approval. As we have seen, in the book of Genesis (and this is followed in the Qur'an) God gave humans supremacy over the animals very early in the process of Creation, and it is made very clear that this includes confining, as well as killing them as sacrifice and for food. All three traditions condone slavery (though the Qur'an is considerably more concerned about the good treatment and freeing of slaves than are the other holy books), and Jewish, Christian and Muslim theologians all contributed versions of the so-called 'curse of Ham', a garbled gloss on Genesis 9:1–27 often used across Europe, the Middle East and the colonies, to justify the enslavement of people with dark skin.[52] There is clear scriptural warrant in the Old Testament for fathers dominating their daughters (and sons), arranging their marriages, directing their movements, and even killing them for insubordination, while, as we have seen, the New Testament urges women to veil as a mark of their subjection. There are also, in all these traditions, strong defences of subjects obeying duly constituted authority, servants obeying their masters, lay-people obeying the religious authorities, and people paying taxes and tithes.

In lands where most people are illiterate, appeals to scripture will only go so far. We need also to look at other kinds of sources, most notably the vast body of folk-tales, proverbs, songs, and the like, generally transmitted orally, that explained and justified the poor treatment and general exclusion of stigmatized groups. According to oral tradition, Jews were believed to be extortionate *and* to be engaged in satanic cultic practices that involved the murder of Christian children, in addition to having supposedly arranged the murder of Jesus. Gypsies were thought to be natural thieves and cannibals and to steal children (ironically, in the eighteenth century there were several state campaigns that involved stealing Roma children from their parents, so that, as one Austro-Hungarian scheme put it, 'at a distance from their parents or relations, they [the Roma] might be more usefully educated, and become accustomed to work'). The Gypsies were also supposed to have played a role in the death of Jesus: a Romanian tradition had it that a gypsy had forged the nails with which Jesus was hung on the cross.[53] Witchcraft accusations often focused on crimes such as consorting with the devil, having unnatural relations with animals, and killing, and even eating, children (the association, in popular myth, of stigmatized groups with murderous attacks on the dominant group's children is a recurrent theme in European history).[54] The physically deformed were believed in some places to have been evil people, crippled when they were cast out of heaven and fell to earth, and there was a very widespread belief that, if a pregnant woman beheld a maimed or malformed person, her infant would also be born deformed.[55] Folk-tales represented old maids as grotesquely ugly, and so frustrated that they would avidly seek sexual inter-course with wild animals, and even with the devil himself.[56]

As all this suggests, stigmatized groups were the source of a tremendous amount of cultural anxiety, even open suspicion in early modern Europe. In good part this was because envy (which the stigmatized, and subordinates in general, were supposed to be consumed by) could translate so readily into dangerous magic. Beliefs about the Evil Eye demonstrate this well. The Evil Eye was associated with a range of ills including the deaths of young children and domestic animals, bad relations between husbands and wives, miscarriages, barrenness, impotence and sickness. Young men, new brides and grooms, and young children, especially sons (in short, lucky, entitled people with everything to live for), were thought to be especially vulnerable. The Evil Eye was an especially ominous form of magic because its possessor, unlike, say, a witch, was not necessarily even conscious of the fact that she or he was blighting the lives of others. Any manifestly unlucky or shunned person might be dangerously envious and capable of projecting unluckiness through looking – which helps explains why beggars, elderly women, or any women past childbearing age, people with physical defects, spinsters, women who failed to have children, gypsies, poor foreigners, Jews, etc., were viewed with such suspicion and disproportionately accused of trying to harm their neighbours. The term in parts of Germany for 'evil eye' was 'Judenblick', which translates as 'Jewish glance'.[57]

Belief in ordinary people's capacity for malevolent magic was not simply a form of victim blaming (though it certainly was that). In the day to day it may well have encouraged people to help neighbours in distress, to respond positively to people asking for alms, and the like – because they feared being the object of that person's anger or envy. However, while fear can be an incentive it can turn swiftly from grudging conciliation to a desire to hurt. Europeans were probably as likely to throw stones at or taunt, say, a person with an obvious disability, as they were to give him or her alms (ritual humiliation or the inflicting of pain on the hated or feared person or animal is a traditional means of neutralizing or warding off evil magic). Belief in the evil eye, like witchcraft beliefs, especially divided women. A number of historians have suggested that, because they had more to lose than men from forces that were beyond their control, women may have been more likely than men to accuse others of supernatural crimes. Moreover, they often targeted other women, both close women neighbours and women in their own households, precisely the people most likely to be envious of a woman's fleeting good fortune.[58]

Many of the claims made about stigmatized groups centred on the fact that they did not always fall in easily with the plans of their betters. Jews were 'a stiff-necked race' because they refused to adopt Christianity, even though they 'knew' Jesus to be the true Messiah – or so some Christians convinced themselves. Slaves and serfs were 'naturally thievish' because they attempted to compensate themselves by dipping into their masters' food or goods. Inferiors in general were 'lazy' because they did not work as hard as their masters believed they should. An even more insidious set of claims revolved around pain. A Scottish traveller named Janet Schaw had this to say in 1775 of the field slaves she saw being flogged on a West Indian plantation:

> When one comes to be better acquainted with the nature of the Negroes, the horror of it [flogging] must wear off. It is the suffering of the human mind that constitutes the greatest misery of punishment, but with them [slaves] it is merely corporeal. As to the brutes [slaves again] it inflicts no wound on their mind, whose Natures seem made to bear it, and whose sufferings are not attended with shame or pain beyond the present moment.[59]

In other words, nature intended these people for subordination, and, like cattle, they forget the pain almost as soon as the overseer puts by his whip. Moreover, according to Schaw, they can be made to work no other way. It was common to argue that, because low-status people had no inner life, inflicting pain on them led to no lasting psychic damage. And indeed, Schaw's stated views were fully in line with the practice of punishing serfs, slaves, and the desperately poor, but not (or far less often) the nobility, slave owners or respectable householders, with pain for breaking the law (see above). But the inner life argument rings hollow. Scoring the imperative to obey onto an inferior's flesh, senses and memory, over and over at the slightest pretext, and sometimes on no pretext at all, was surely intended to mould the inner man or woman, to give inferiors a consciousness that was visceral, reflexive and deep about their place in the hierarchy of being. And much of the time, at least at the phenomenological level, this strategy must have worked. By modern standards this was a regime (or series of regimes) characterized by an extraordinary amount of free-floating fear – fear of painful punishment on the part of inferiors; fear that their inferiors were plotting overt or covert revenge on the part of superiors. How did eighteenth-century women try to contain this fear and turn this often unpropitious situation to their advantage? Was it ever possible to succeed when they tried? That is the question to which we now turn.

LIVING IN SUBORDINATION

Higher powers

It has always been a prerogative of the weak and oppressed to appeal to God and the saints for relief. In societies where most people believe in God this can have real force. 'Have mercy in the name of God' really could both stay the hand of an abuser and encourage intervention from others who would rather be on the side of good religion than a bad husband, father, master or mistress. Islam has a particularly rich body of teachings, in the Qur'an, the *hadiths* and various jurisprudential traditions, that encourage slave-owners to free their slaves, to feed and clothe them with the same food and clothing they (the owners) enjoy, and to allow them to buy their freedom. Several *hadiths* suggest that those who beat their slaves will go to hell unless they immediately emancipate them, and this was often interpreted to mean that a slave who was beaten or abused automatically became free. Traditions like these helped make the act of individual manumission far commoner in the Ottoman Empire than in any of the Christian European colonies, though, as Madeline Zilfi has remarked, there were material incentives to masters as well, most notably that ex-slaves formed a cheap pool of domestic labour.[60] Verbal appeals to (say) the Virgin Mary were just as well established in Catholic and Orthodox contexts, and must, at least some of the time, have been efficacious in moderating abuse, if less often in gaining people their freedom (though it has to be said, at least for the Iberian colonies, that the Catholic Church was often more solicitous of the rights of slaves than the secular authorities or individual slave-owners).

Higher powers of an earthly, rather than celestial, kind also had a role to play. Inferiors often sought the aid of relatives. It was commonplace, all over Europe and the Middle East, for kin-folk to intervene to take abusive masters to court, to assist daughters, sisters or more distant kin in obtaining formal and informal separations and divorces, and to give them a place to stay. Of course one had to have cooperative – and living – kin for this to work. One of the signal markers of unluckiness in the early modern period was not having any relatives upon whom to call for help; which is one reason why orphans were so pitied and so often taken advantage of. It is also one of the main reasons why slaves, often captives from distant lands and hence bereft of family, were so singularly disadvantaged. Many of the most efficacious strategies probably originated in households. A husband might be willing to intervene to stop the abuse or exploitation of his wife by his mother, sisters, or sisters-in-law, and it would certainly be in his interests to stop the sexual abuse of his young bride by her father-in-law – a common nexus of abuse in extended families.[61] The negotiations both in and out of the household must have been incredibly complex. People in crisis are often willing to turn to any source of help; thus frantic women called upon – and not infrequently received the help of – higher-ups such as estate overseers, village elders, serf-owners, local nobles, members of the clergy, local convents or monasteries, justices of the peace, their own or their husband's employers, and even local military garrisons.

In a highly stratified society this kind of paternalism is the other side of violent coercion, a necessary leaven that keeps open lines of communication between the governors and the governed, addresses the worst (or at least the most public) abuses of power, offers feelings of satisfaction and a sense of spiritual well-being to the dispenser of benefits, and encourages grateful subservience in those with little power. Women were well placed to appeal to their superiors' paternalistic instincts because they were forced to learn the theatre of subservience at an earlier age and more thoroughly than men. It is impossible to know how many women *internalized* subservience, but it does seem that women were especially well schooled at simultaneously conveying their worshipful respect for authority and making melodramatic appeals for help. They were the ideal supplicants in a culture that demanded that those who receive help loudly and continually confirm and dramatize their notional support for the status quo.[62]

The law-courts

The law is not necessarily the natural ally of those of lower status. In the early modern period numerous laws were precisely designed to draw attention to and confirm status and difference, such as rules that required slaves, servants or religious minorities not to dress above their station, and not to carry arms or ride a horse. Almost all law courts implicitly or explicitly valued higher status people's word more than others. And, as we have seen, lower-status people who assaulted or killed higher status people were almost always much more savagely punished than when the positioning was reversed. And yet, despite all this, resort to the law by quite humble people, and specifically by women, became much more common in the early modern period, to the extent of becoming a genuine resource for coping with abuses of power. This began quite early in the lands around the Mediterranean. Litigation by plebeian women had become a standard part of court business in parts of Ottoman Europe and the Middle East at least by the late fifteenth century, and there was also a much older tradition of women appealing to the law in Islamic regimes that went back to the time of the Prophet.[63] Litigation by urban women, often quite humble in status, also became fairly commonplace in Italy, Portugal, and Spain in the late medieval period. Starting perhaps a century later (in most cases between the early seventeenth and early eighteenth centuries) plebeian women also began resorting to the courts in appreciable numbers in urbanized parts of France, the Netherlands, England, the Hapsburg Empire, Scandinavia, and Russia, among other places.

No courts in any nation were much interested in undermining social hierarchy. However, legal intervention was important in the larger scheme of things because it represented a very public response to extreme abuse or exploitation, and because, when such cases did come to court, judges rather often ruled in favour of the abused person or persons (part of the reason for this, then as now, was that cases that got as far as the courtroom were likely to be especially egregious). Standing up for individual status inferiors – including women – also represented an excellent opportunity for emerging national states and their personnel, from court clerks to appellate judges, and ultimately monarchs or sultans, to identify themselves with disinterested justice, almost everywhere an esteemed ideal.

It is impossible at this point to come up with an aggregate figure for how many women actually used the courts, but it was clearly a lot. In just one Ottoman court from the early seventeenth century, the *kadi* (*sharia*) court of Kayseri in central Anatolia, 10,593 cases were heard in the two and a half decades between 1603 and 1627, and just over seventeen per cent, or 1,827, involved one or more women. In this court, as in many other *sharia* courts, women were especially prominent in cases involving land and property transfers: forty per cent of real property cases involved one or more women.[64] Many of the cases involved women buying property from or selling it to their husbands, and it was not uncommon for women to sue their husbands over property matters, as well as to turn to the courts to moderate their husband's violence and to obtain divorces. If the Kayseri figures are representative, and research in at least a dozen other Ottoman cities suggests they were, tens of thousands of Ottoman women were bringing suit by the early seventeenth century. Few Christian European courts had such a high percentage of women litigating this early, at least not on property or marital issues (though they were quite active in defence of their sexual reputations in defamation cases),[65] but their numbers were increasing. By the eighteenth century cases involving women plaintiffs comprised up to twenty per cent of the business in some civil courts in England, France, Spain, Portugal, the Netherlands, and parts of the Italian peninsula and the German-speaking territories, and they covered a considerably wider range of issues than earlier ones had done. In England, in the two courts of Chancery and Exchequer alone, around sixty thousand women brought suit, generally over property or inheritance, in the eighteenth century. Women sued individually (widows and spinsters were especially active), jointly (often, but not always, with their husbands) and in larger groupings, complaining against fathers, stepfathers and stepmothers, guardians, brothers, and, yes, husbands, on issues like inheritance, marriage settlements, and conjugal support, as well as a wide range of other personal and business concerns.[66] All over Europe and the Middle East, many more women turned to the law-courts much earlier than historians used to think. This phenomenon constitutes a major challenge to an older historiography that took it for granted that plebeian women had no public agency before the advent of suffrage and 'modernity'.

One might think that only independent householders and free people would be in a position to sue, but in fact, servants and slaves were surprisingly active in the early modern courts. There are many cases of women servants and (in the Ottoman Empire) slaves suing for their wages or legacies,[67] and slave-women (at least in the Iberian colonies) complaining about abusive masters or suing for the right to buy their freedom. In societies accustomed to viewing human beings as saleable commodities there is always a risk that people who are not 'supposed' be enslaved will be carried off and sold by kidnappers. Accordingly a number of cases have turned up in the Ottoman records of free women who had been abducted and sold coming to court to sue for their freedom. In two typical cases, a women called Fatma Hatun, of Greek origin, proved she was of free origin and was manumitted in 1710, while at the other end of the century in 1793 another woman, also called Fatma, proved in court that she 'was of free Muslim lineage and daughter of Ibrahim and Ayse of Batum province on Black Sea Coast'. Similar cases can be found in the New World involving free black or indigenous women who had been abducted and illegally enslaved.[68] There are also cases from Portugal, France and England where slaves sought to be freed from their masters on the basis of edicts, precedents and rumors that put time limits on how long a slave could remain in the mother country, or that suggested that slaves automatically became free on setting foot on Portuguese, French or English soil. In France between 1750 and 1790 some 153 French slaves were freed as a result of their bringing law-suits, a number of them women, though there were also persistent efforts to police freed blacks and send them back to the colonies, sometimes only to be resold.[69]

Women also used the courts to try to equalize their disadvantages in the realm of marriage and sexuality. Women routinely sued men for breach of promise (promising to marry them and then reneging).[70] And mistresses went to court to force heirs to honour bonds from their former paramours. The Englishwoman Katherine Rooke was one such litigant. Rooke had lived with and had an illegitimate child by one Jeremiah Cray. When Cray married someone else he promised Rooke an annuity or flat payment of a significant sum of money. Unfortunately he then died and his heirs refused to honour the contract. But the court sided with Rooke, having heard from her counsel that she had 'been prevailed upon' to surrender her virtue in expectation of financial support.[71] Women also sued both women and unrelated men for assault and defamation. In some English courts by the first third of the eighteenth century women comprised the majority of complainants in assault cases.[72] All over Europe and the Middle East, women went to court to prosecute or try to get recompense for sexual harassment and rape.

Because the law was beginning to count in more and more women's lives, transfers of territory from one legal jurisdiction to another could have major consequences, and, as we will see, so could a change in religion. The Ottoman conquest of Cyprus in 1571 was rather swiftly followed by a significant influx of *Christian* women into the newly established *sharia* courts, seeking to settle matters involving divorce, conjugal non-support, domestic violence and property disputes, and this despite the fact that Christians had their own separate courts, generally run by Orthodox priests. Almost certainly this was due to the fact that the Muslim courts accorded more property and dowry rights to married women than the Christian courts did. The problem of Cypriot Christian, and later Jewish women, who preferred the Muslim courts was still worrying the Orthodox clergy and the rabbinate in the eighteenth century.[73] The negative side of property transfer for women's legal rights – in this case the rights of slave women – can be seen with the transfer of most of Florida from Spanish to permanent United States suzerainty after 1821. As we have seen, Spanish (and Portuguese) colonial laws and cultures were somewhat more tolerant toward interracial marriage and mixed-race offspring than were Anglo-derived laws and cultures, and gave more rights to slave concubines and their children. Children of slaves often inherited from their fathers, and manumission was common (since slaves had some property rights under Spanish law they often accumulated enough money to buy their own freedom). After 1821, both free blacks and slaves encountered a far less hospitable climate. The repressive legal regime of the American southern slave states was extended to Florida, and a wide range of constraints were placed on free blacks, including a requirement that they post a bond for their good behaviour, and the extension to them of sumptuary and other laws previously applicable only to slaves. Interracial marriage was prohibited (1832), and the children of mixed liaisons were decisively divested of inheritance rights. Slaves were no longer permitted to sue in court, manumission was forbidden, and neither male nor female slaves were any longer permitted to own property.[74] For Florida's black and mulatto population an increasingly draconian racial caste system replaced an oppressive, but still relatively flexible, set of social arrangements. And slavery, already bad enough as it was, was systematically turned into something that really *did* approximate social death.

In the early modern period a number of European regimes adopted the principle that a woman of a minority religion who converted to the dominant religion could have her marriage tacitly or officially annulled (at least so long as her husband did not also convert). In 1830 the wife of an Ionian Greek merchant arrived in Tunis on a ship from Syria, ostensibly to be reunited with her husband. But when the husband went to claim her he found to his horror that she had converted to Islam and gone to work for someone in the bey's (governor's) palace. The British consulate, under whose protection the merchant was, tried to intercede so that the man could 'regain possession of her'. But when the envoy got to the palace, 'the woman declared it was of her own free will she turned a Musulwoman [Muslim] and that she would know no other religion, and from her husband having deserted and ill-treated her, she would remain where she was [in Tunis] and would not return either to him or to her parents back [in Greece]'.[75] She was taking advantage of a law that annulled the marriage of any *dhimmi* woman who converted to Islam (*dhimmi* was the general term for Jews and Christians – non-Muslims – who lived in settled Ottoman lands). In another spectacular case, from 1796, a Venetian noblewoman and wife of a diplomat in the Dardanelles, poisoned her husband and fled with her daughter to a *kadi* (judge's) house (these were common places of refuge) where both of them promptly converted to Islam. Similar arrangements obtained in a number of Christian countries, at least if the convert was coming from a non-Christian or, technically, an 'un-baptized' background (e.g. Jewish, Muslim, pagan, though conceivably other groups, such as Anabaptists and Russian Orthodox Old Believers).[76]

Conversion was also often a way for some slaves either to gain their freedom or obtain a better place, since few regimes were happy about allowing a slave, particularly a woman slave, of the dominant religion to be under the control of someone of a minority religion, lest they be put under irresistible pressure to apostasize. 'Saving' recently converted female slaves from non-Islamic owners became an important project for some elite Ottoman men in the second half of the seventeenth century, and there is no question that women used this for their own devices, both to escape owners they did not like and to obtain more prestigious Muslim owners who would either marry them or arrange a more social elevated marriage than they would otherwise have had available to them. Between wives converting to Islam to escape bad marriages (most of them less dramatic than the two detailed above) and slaves converting to Islam to improve their social standing and marriage prospects, hundreds of women took this step in the second half of the seventeenth century and an as-yet-uncounted number in the eighteenth.[77]

Conversion had benefits in some Christian countries as well. Slave-women and men from North Carolina and Georgia in the North American Colonies (soon to be the new United States) often fled south to Spanish territory in the eighteenth century to take advantage of the religious sanctuary laws which permitted escaped slaves from Protestant countries who indicated an interest in converting to Catholicism to claim their freedom.[78] In Italy we find Balkan slaves seeking to escape abusive owners by throwing themselves on the mercy of special Catholic 'conversion' hostels (*catecumeni*), and simply refusing to leave. In 1693 a group of seventeen originally Muslim women from Bosnia, presumably captured by Venetian slave-traders, insisted to the Venetian *catecumeni*'s director that they would rather die than 'be subjected to their masters' cruelty'.[79] As these examples suggest, Europe, the Middle East and the various colonies were more regionally and globally linked in the eighteenth century than ever before. War, national rivalries, racial and religious prejudice, and the enormous expansion of the transatlantic slave trade, brought tragedy for many. But the proximity of diverse faiths and legal systems also opened up unexpected opportunities both for women and for men to escape or renegotiate oppressive relationships of all kinds.

Female solidarity

Women's feelings of solidarity with other women cannot be presumed; still, groups of women (and mixed groups as well) routinely intervened to try to stop other women being abused by their husbands and masters or mistresses. When a Londoner named Elizabeth Spinkes lay bleeding on the ground, having jumped out of the window to escape her abusive husband, 'some of the women of the neighborhood . . . came to her assistance'; however, they were forced to retreat when John, a physician, and therefore of relatively high status, loudly threatened to arrest their husbands for debt.[80] Julie Hardwick, in an important study of domestic violence in early modern France, finds many interventions of this type. She has also identified some 'high-status neighbourhood women' who became what she calls 'community specialists' in domestic viole   They took an interest in abused women in their neighborhoods, visit   .em, and sometimes took them into their own homes to recover. One noblewoman sent along her sedan-chair to bring the injured woman away, no doubt having ordered her bearers – presumably fairly brawny fellows – to face down the woman's husband. Such women were also prepared to try to mobilize their influence to get doctors or other higher-status men to bring pressure on lower-status abusive husbands. This comports well with what we know of the kinds of paternalistic charitable activities engaged in by high-status women (see Chapter 8). Hardwick and others have also noted that women servants sometimes intervened to try to protect their mistresses, even getting into physical fights with the husbands.[81] Servants also routinely testified on their mistresses' behalf in court cases, though they also sometimes turned against them. In the Spinkes case her servant, Marie Nuby, testified in court that her mistress deserved to be beaten because she was licentious, verbally abusive, prone to drunkenness, and had tried to bewitch her husband with the help of a Whitechapel fortune teller who specialized in 'plague[ing]' difficult husbands.[82] On the plus side, it was common for both French and Polish battered women to take refuge in convents, and indeed, it is likely that this was the case across Catholic Europe. There are also several known cases in which slave-women seeking to escape abusive masters received material aid from Catholic convents, and one Senegalese woman, with the slave-name Catherine Morgan, received help and support from a network of free black women in Nantes.[83]

There are also numerous cases of women coming together to stage protests of one sort or another. As we saw earlier, Balkan slaves in Italy are known to have staged dramatic protests in the *catecumeni* homes. Women often joined together to petition the authorities (particularly legislative and military bodies or monarchs) over grievances, a topic we will take up in detail in Chapter 8. There are also cases of women clubbing together to sue in court. More than seventy-five women were involved in a sequence of suits around 1700 designed to pressure the British East India Company to pay them their male relatives' pay after the men all drowned in a shipwreck.[84] About the same time a dozen young Dutch girls joined together to successfully prosecute the director of a Rotterdam poorhouse for rape (see Chapter 3). There were numerous lawsuits, throughout Europe and probably elsewhere, brought by small groups of servant women against employers or their heirs for non-payment of wages or bequests. The heavy involvement of women experts, such as midwives, as witnesses in infanticide cases could make the difference between conviction and acquittal, and few rape trials went forward without the support of older or higher-status women (though the conviction rate was still low). On a more visceral level, there are instances of groups of neighbourhood women physically attacking men accused of raping little girls.[85]

Moral dilemmas of womanhood

Flight, revolts, demonstrations and other fairly morally clear-cut public sphere activities of that kind are the ones historians have traditionally focused on when they think about agency and resistance on the part of lower-status people. Though eighteenth-century women did participate in all of these to some degree (see Chapters 4, 8 and 9), they were much less likely to do so than men, even when (it would seem) the provocations were very great. Does this mean that 'resistance' was primarily a male enterprise and that women simply passively submitted to their lot? Well clearly not, but then what were women doing? And is it really useful to think about it using terms like resistance? This problem has been especially perceptively analysed by historians of New World slavery, though their discussions have implications for thinking about women in less constrained circumstances as well. In a recent collection of essays on women and (mostly) New World slavery, Gwyn Campbell, Suzanne Miers and Joseph C. Miller address with great clarity the dichotomy between the position of some slave-women and most slave-men, arguing that the peculiar division of agricultural, sexual, emotional and reproductive labour characteristic of New World slavery tended to endow slave-women both with a different set of vulnerabilities and a different set of strategic possibilities than most men. African male slaves in the New World were, for the most part, subjected to hard manual labour, under the lash, on sugar, rice and tobacco plantations, with few opportunities to do or be anything else. For a significant proportion of men the hyper-exploitation, surveillance and systematic regime of terror that was plantation production for the global capitalist marketplace *did*, in effect, reduce their choices to fleeing, revolting or submitting. While some female slaves worked as field hands they also presented their owners with a broader set of exploitive possibilities. As Campbell, Miers and Miller explain:

> Unlike men, female slaves were also valued for their reproductive capacities, for their nurturing ability as uniquely female wet-nurses and maternally experienced nannies, for their more arbitrarily gendered domestic house skills, and for sexual service that only they – as physically women – could provide for white males ... This greater variety of often intimate positions available to women slaves in turn presented them with a potentially wider range of strategies than the violent few at the disposal of enslaved males. Sex [by which I take them to mean both gender and sexuality] is a powerful tool, emotionally as well as physically.[86]

As a great many historians have shown, slave-women deployed these 'tools' in diverse ways. They tried to win more freedoms for themselves by making themselves loved, or at least needed, by the white babies and children they nurtured, by the white women whose lives they made easier, and by the white men with whom they sometimes had sex or formed relationships, both willingly and under coercion. They used that slightly larger ambit to engage in trade and other economic activities, to pursue religious and associational interests – often with other black women and men – and to negotiate for or purchase their own and others' freedom. Sometimes they married their masters and became slave-owners themselves. Sometimes they tried to resist parts of the system – the coerced sex, the forced break-up of families, the tendency of white men to abandon their responsibilities to their mixed-race children – through the courts and by any other means at their disposal. And for all that they paid a terrible price that hit at some of the most fundamental aspects of early modern women's identity, both in Europe and in Africa. They had their sexual honour stolen from them, their ability to form stable emotional relationships with men of any race was significantly impaired and, to a large extent, they lost control of the ability to raise their own children, do right by them, and, in turn, be cared for by them in old age.[87]

There can be no doubt that New World slave-women's experiences were different from those of most European women, and, arguably, worse than those of many serfs. Few European women suffered abduction, death, violence, loss of kin and country, and loss of honour in the comprehensive way that African abductees did. Still, in a great many respects, slave-women were situated at the extreme end of a continuum rather than radically distinct from other women – especially poor women or those who belonged to a racial or religious minority, but not only them. Slave-women were radically incapable of controlling their sexuality. But, for reasons that will become clear in later chapters, few early modern women 'controlled their sexuality' or had a 'right to their own body' in any way that would be recognizable to us today. Slave-women's mobility was severely constrained, and they had to negotiate hard for the little they had. They were also denounced as licentious for participating in the market even though the capital they accumulated from petty trade often helped to finance their own and others' emancipation.[88] (In fact many eighteenth-century women were involved in petty commodities trading – these were the proverbial market-women whose diverse activities we will deal with at various points in this study. The work was frequently crucial to their own and their families' survival, and their sexual honour was routinely impugned because of it.) Slave-women's ability to form permanent family ties was unusually contingent. As people who were also property, slaves were often used as collateral for loans, even as one would use a house, or a field or a horse. They were not just at the mercy of slave-owners' goodwill but of the weather (bad harvests), the economy (downturns in the price of sugar), fecklessness (some young heir's gambling problem), or an owner's death. You just never knew. Few other Europeans (or colonials) had to live with that degree of insecurity. On the other hand, non-slave women – especially poor women – also had to struggle to keep their families together, in the face of challenges that were far greater than what most of us face today – little or no effective birth-control, shockingly high infant mortality rates, poverty, unfeeling families, desertion, abusive husbands, the military draft, and numerous other problems.

Slave-women inhabited the outer limits of 'agency'. They had control over very little in their lives, so they tried to be strategic with the few assets they had. If a chance presented itself they often took it. Some asserted themselves in ways that seem incredible today. Going to court, where the odds were stacked against them, and the potential for retaliation great, was a gamble. But many did it, even though they may have lost as often as they won.[89] And yet, they were no less fallible than the next person, and if they could collude with the system for some temporary or longer-term gain, or exchange the role of exploited for exploiter, some of them were fully prepared to walk that road. People in situations of sustained and extreme stress are not always heroic, resistance often seems futile, and they frequently end up permanently damaged in body and spirit. Unfortunately, it is likely that that was also true of these women. They were, in short, ordinary people, with all kinds of personalities, temperaments, strengths, weaknesses, and capacities, trying to improvise lives for themselves in the face of an extraordinarily exploitative regime. Most early modern European women *did* have more strategic opportunities than New World slaves did, though not always very many more (and it is telling that, as with slave-women, sexuality and nurture were both a locus of extreme exploitation and a source of opportunity). But slave-women's diverse approaches to life, survival and control, or its absence, have much to teach us both about what was possible and about what a complicated moral terrain 'agency' occupied in the early modern period.

LOOKING TOWARD THE FUTURE

Many of the old ways of marking hierarchy and enforcing stigma were on the wane by the end of the eighteenth century. Sumptuary laws were in decline, at least in Europe itself if not in the colonies or former colonies. Curtseying and bowing replaced kneeling before one's social superiors. A good number of people stopped believing in Original Sin or started to think of it in much more abstract terms (see Chapter 6). Official use of the death penalty (though not of vigilante violence) to control people's religious beliefs, largely disappeared by the end of the eighteenth century. The more far-fetched tales about Jews (notably accusations of ritual murder of Christian children) and other groups, like the Roma, began to seem less credible, though they were sometimes replaced by more secular attacks, focusing on these groups' alleged unassimilability, tribalism, criminality or greed (ritual murder accusations would actually be revived, to considerable effect, in eastern Europe in the nineteenth and early twentieth centuries, and also turned up in the nineteenth-century Ottoman Empire).

Progress came slowly and with many setbacks. Even as both male dominance and slavery were coming under attack, new, allegedly more 'scientific', justifications for racial and gender inequality came into being and flourished. Paternalism died faster than elite's demands for deference and a return on their investments, and in many places (including large parts of Ireland and Scotland, France, Italy, the Balkans and Russia) servile tenures were replaced by crippling indebtedness to the local nobility, rich landowners, land developers, or military officials who cared little about their dependants' welfare. Slavery in the United States, the West Indies and South America would in most cases be replaced by share-cropper economies, a sort of buy-out scheme for former slave-owners that kept millions of ex-slaves and some poor whites immiserated for generations after slavery had gone. The eighteenth century is the last century in which most Europeans still lived within an old-style, deferential world. By the end of it the wheels were in motion that would utterly transform that universe, though these changes would take a very long time in some places, and every region changed in a different way. Women had been powerfully enmeshed within early modern hierarchies, most often toward the bottom, yet sometimes able to dominate others within a household setting, and very occasionally in a position to accrue real political or economic power (see Chapter 8). Much of the process of transforming eighteenth-century subordination into the complexly graded societies of today, freer in some important senses, but also still capable of spectacular instances of ethnic and religious violence, is a later story than the one we are telling here. This chapter has been an effort to describe some of that perhaps too frequently idealized pre-nineteenth-century world.

Chapter 2

◆

FAMILIES

'Both marriage and the shroud are brought by heaven' runs a traditional Spanish proverb.[1] Today it seems perverse to speak in the same breath of marriage (to most of us a matter of individual choice) and death (very seldom anyone's choice). Even in the eighteenth century choice played a more prominent role in marriage than it did in death. But this perplexing phrase also points to some real differences in the way marriages were embarked upon in the early modern period as compared to today. Most modern marriage systems are orientated, at base, around the assumption that young people can and should be able to choose their own mates and their own future. By contrast, marriage in most pre-modern societies was more likely to be seen as a family matter, a group investment in the future whose success or failure affected everyone in the family or lineage. Property-owning or noble families enhanced their prestige, enriched themselves, and established or ratified new patronage, business and political linkages if one of their children or other dependants made a 'good' marriage; conversely they stood to lose honour, money, and connections with a 'bad' one, or one that came unstuck. Even relatively poor and propertyless families, and slaves or former slaves, could benefit to some degree from a marriage that, say, brought them into a new or more lavish clientage network.

Ironically, their family's pursuit of honour and connections often meant that aristocratic girls did not marry at all. In most of Christian Europe honour required that better-off families supply their marrying daughters with a dowry, but many such families were strapped for cash, and were reluctant to split the family patrimony by endowing daughters. As a result many elite women found themselves pressured to remain unmarried or, in Catholic countries, to enter a convent. In the Milanese aristocracy in the first half of the eighteenth century thirty-four per cent of the women did not marry (most went into convents). Men, especially younger sons, were also affected. In a sample of seven families from the Catalonian petty nobility, tracked across several generations, less than a quarter of younger sons married, while a remarkable 42.6 per cent went into the church (the rest of the non-marriers did not take holy orders but remained lifelong bachelors). It is, of course, possible that early modern Catalonia supported an especially pious and sexually diffident cohort of minor noblemen who just happened to be younger sons – but unlikely. These figures reflect family strategies, not these youths' own choices. The story was much the same in Protestant countries, which had neither convents nor monasteries. Among the British upper aristocracy in the eighteenth century, twenty-four per cent of, or almost one in four, women, most of them Protestants, never married. And between twenty-nine and thirty-two per cent of Genevan upper-middle-class women in the eighteenth century (again, Protestants) were still unmarried at the age of fifty.[2]

A different set of obstacles stood in the way of poor women. Part of the reason some regions had low marriage rates was because local officials put barriers in the way of poor men and women marrying. In eighteenth-century England it was common to require poor couples who wanted to marry to post a money bond that they would not later seek parish relief. If they refused to comply they could be banished from the town. In Württemberg, Germany, poor women (most of them migrant textile workers) were forbidden to marry until 1871. They were also subjected to very intrusive forms of moral oversight, and they risked banishment if they acquired a 'bad reputation' in the eyes of employers or the authorities. In much of western and central Europe, servants and apprentices, both male and female, lost their positions if they were found to have married.

Women were also affected by disadvantageous sex-ratios. Many regions lacked enough marriageable men to meet the demand, generally due to men going into the military (see below) or migrating away in search of a job, or to a significant influx of young women coming to work as servants or in manufacture. These regions virtually always saw reduced numbers of women marrying. In late eighteenth-century Galicia, on the coast of Northern Spain, where many more men than women migrated away to find work, around fourteen per cent of women never married, while in some locales the figure was almost forty per cent. In eighteenth-century Amsterdam, partly as a result of the shocking death-rate of Dutch East India Company sailors (a phenomenon known to Dutch historical demographers as 'the Indian leak') and partly due to the fact that men going to the colonies were generally not allowed to marry, there were, in many neighbourhoods, at least four women for every three men.[3] This may have opened up some job opportunities for women; however, the fact that the poorest districts in the city tended to be those with the highest proportion of women suggests a drearier picture. With fewer men, with their higher wages, to marry, many of the women in these communities had no way to pull themselves out of abject poverty.[4] In Colyton in East Devon, England, a town with a substantial lace-making and wool-spinning industry in the late seventeenth and early eighteenth centuries, the flow of labour went the opposite way, and women flocked in. These women, too, had a lower rate of marriage than normal, especially if they were poor; during the early modern period almost thirteen per cent of poor women in Colyton were still unmarried at the age of forty-five.[5]

The rise of large, professional militaries from the seventeenth century on (part of what many historians call 'the Military Revolution of the seventeenth century'), and the attendant leap in rates of conscription, also affected the marriage prospects of poor women. Most women did not dress up as men so as to replace their brothers in the army, as a number of ballads suggest. But many women were called upon to give up their dowries or inheritance in order to buy replacements or exemptions for male kin vulnerable to conscription, or to 'bump up' brothers' inheritance so as to put them over the property limit beyond which mandatory conscription ceased to apply (early modern wars were made more palatable to local elites by taking their sons last; but the growing demand for soldiers in some regions tended to raise property thresholds). In the German state of Hesse-Kassel there was a perceptible drop in the size of dowries in the eighteenth century: women's family share was, in effect, being redistributed toward the military state.[6] A different kind of female sacrifice obtained in the central Balkans. An area that had been fought over for centuries, and the main dividing line between the Ottomans and the Austrians, large swathes of land along the military border on both sides were specially organized for defensive purposes, with low taxes for 'fighting farmers'. The officially favoured family form both on the Austro-Hungarian and Ottoman sides of the border was the *zadruga*, the classic multiple family of the Balkans, preferred because the large size of each family offered economies of scale, and allowed a good proportion of the men to fight, supposedly without disrupting agricultural production. It disrupted other things, though. A recent study of maternal mortality in eighteenth-century Croatia shows that a woman was more at risk of dying in or shortly after childbirth if her husband had been mobilized into the military, probably because she was likely to be starved and exploited by her in-laws.[7]

The new military state was, at least initially, often overtly hostile both to the formation of families and the maintenance of those already formed. In the German states, France and elsewhere, particularly in the first half of the eighteenth century, there were strict quotas on the number of soldiers who could marry, they had to get permission from their commanding officer (which was often refused), and those who married without a licence could be severely punished. In a number of the German territories soldiers who married without permission were made repeatedly to run the gauntlet; their wives were put in the workhouse for a minimum of a year. Married officers could find themselves demoted or cashiered. The bans on marriage meant that even soldiers who got women pregnant were often not permitted to marry them, or did not have it within their means to pay the large sums of money it could take to get their commanding officer's permission (demanding bribes in return for marriage licences soon became a standard method for officers to supplement their pay). Predictably, a high percentage of women executed for infanticide in the German lands in the late seventeenth and early eighteenth centuries had been impregnated by soldiers (see Chapter 3).[8] More surprising, perhaps, is the number of soldiers who, in spite of the impediments, tried their best to form permanent relationships, albeit without the benefit of official marriage. Still, this meant that their children were illegitimate, at a time when illegitimacy often carried civil disabilities. Irregular relationships were always frowned upon and sometimes treated as criminal, especially in Protestant lands. The woman was easily abandoned (though she also had an easier time leaving a bad relationship). Women in these relationships were vulnerable to being accused of prostitution. And they were ineligible for military benefits, such as widows' pensions.

An especially callous policy obtained in Russia. There, early age at marriage meant most men were already married when they were conscripted. Russian soldiers were drafted essentially for life, and furloughs were rare. Every effort seems to have been made to thwart men's ability to maintain connections to their wives and children. Consequently, the 'soldatkas' (women married to soldiers) evolved into the most desperate subgroup in almost any Russian village. Tied by marriage to a man they were unlikely ever to see again and unable to travel (most of these women were serfs), the soldatkas were routinely cast out by their in-laws, and often ended up prostitutes. Over time, as the army grew they became a clearly identifiable outcast subculture, shunned by the respectable, and constantly under suspicion for sexual irregularities, infanticide and theft.[9]

Decisions about marriage were not always the prerogative of one's own family – assuming one had one. Lords, masters of servants and slave or serf owners routinely sought to influence or control the marriage choices of their dependants or human property. Peasants and tenant farmers were often required to obtain the permission of their landlords to marry, and sometimes to pay a 'fine' or premium for doing so. At the same time they could come under severe pressure if they did *not* marry, or tried to marry the 'wrong' person. New World slave-owners often interfered with slaves' right to marry, refusing it entirely at times, or trying to control their slaves' marriage choices. Slaves, for their part, often tried to marry free persons, or at least to marry 'off the plantation', partly as a way to dilute their total dependence on their master.[10] In Russia landlords both owned their serfs and collected taxes from them, so they were anxious to encourage the formation of new households. Some landlords levied fines on the fathers of girls who had not married by a certain age (sometimes as young as fifteen), and fines might also extend to widows who failed to remarry. Conversely, in Kurland (part of present-day Latvia) serfs were not allowed to marry outside the duchy's borders, and serf women could not marry free Germans, because it would automatically make them and their children free.[11] Limits on whom one could marry were probably especially common near national borders, as was the case with Kurland, and in multi-confessional regions: virtually everywhere marriage was forbidden or regulated across religious lines (of course, love being the unpredictable thing it is, such liaisons did happen).

Plenty of young people resisted the direction of their elders and betters, and married whomever they wanted; however, the impression one gets is that most young people were unresentful about someone else choosing their marriage partner. Many of them no doubt believed that the superior contacts and prestige of a parent, or even an owner or former owner, would be likely to produce a better match than they would be able to negotiate on their own. This was especially true in relatively high nuptiality areas, like much of eastern and southeastern Europe. For so many people up and down the social scale to marry, especially in societies or social groups where unrelated women and men rarely socialized, there had to be a considerable amount of patronage and organizational help from status superiors. Thus, in the Ottoman Empire marriage-arranging, where the higher-status person brought the couple together and supplied a dowry, constituted a potent form of cross-class patronage and master/slave (or ex-master/ex-slave relations) and was central to the formation of clientage networks. It was also a significant nexus of power for older women, who were almost always the main marriage brokers. In Imperial Russia, too, especially before the dissolution of the elite women's quarters (the *terem*) by Peter the Great in the early eighteenth century, female marriage arrangers often acquired considerable authority and influence.[12]

One of the most famous shifts of the eighteenth century was the growing interest among elites in marrying for love (marriage for love had probably always been more prevalent at lower levels of society, because poor children tended to leave home early, and consequently parents had less pull). Love was rife in the newly popular novels (see Chapter 7), and marriage for love dovetailed nicely with the interest in emotion or 'sensibility' that swept Enlightened Europe in the second half of the eighteenth century. Love and marital choice struck increasing numbers of people as a more pleasant and rational way to organize marriage than dynastic concerns or families' greed for prestige and good connections. Oftentimes women were particularly enthusiastic about marriage for love, which seemed to give more power both to women and to men of the younger generation, while undermining the claims of families. It also seemed to promise greater marital happiness; perhaps even greater egalitarianism (whether it actually delivered was and is a matter of dispute). There was a similar trend at work in parts of the Ottoman Empire, with seventeenth- and eighteenth-century *muftis* (jurisconsults) issuing opinions that favoured women above the age of majority choosing husbands for themselves, and invalidating coerced marriages involving orphan or half-orphan girls, either before or after the age of majority.[13]

MARITAL RELATIONS

While the love match assumed at least a degree of companionship in marriage, a good many women did not view even marriage for love as a very good prospect. It is not hard to find eighteenth-century women expressing extreme ambivalence, even hostility, to conventional marriage.[14] Not surprisingly, one of their central criticisms had to do with the licence marriage gave men to control, abuse and exploit their wives. It is clear that a number of these women spoke from the heart. One of the favourite sayings of the novelist Belle van Zuylen (also known as Isabelle de Charrière, 1740–1805) was a line from la Fontaine, 'I've seen many marriages; none of them tempts me'; she once put off a prospective suitor with the words 'I have fortune enough so as not to need that of a husband; I have a sufficiently happy disposition and enough mental resources to be able to dispense with a husband, with a family, and with what people like to call an establishment . . .'[15] One of her novels is about a woman who chooses (she is not forced) to marry a perfectly decent man, only to find herself completely stifled by marriage: it is a 'story of desperate unhappiness in which there are no villains . . .' that bears comparison with Henrik Ibsen's much later play, *A Doll's House*.[16] Marie-Jeanne Riccoboni (1713–1792), one of the best-selling novelists of the eighteenth century, filled her novels with caddish men who take their wives' money and victimize them – mentally, physically and sexually – simply because law and custom say they can. Riccoboni herself endured an unhappy, though brief marriage, and eventually set up a life-long companionship with a former actress named Marie-Therese Biancolelli.[17] Though most of the people who voiced these kinds of sentiments were literate, there is no reason to think they were confined only to the better off; and, as we will see, there is some evidence of a new interest on the part of plebeian women in marriage avoidance as well, especially in Catholic countries (see below and Chapter 6).

Women feared being under the unpredictable authority of one man or his family, and they certainly feared dying in childbirth (see Chapter 3), but nevertheless the majority of women either chose marriage or acquiesced to it. Even in contexts where 'choice' did not loom large, many women yearned for greater economic security, companionship, sexual fulfilment, children, and a comfortable old age, and marriage promised, if it did not always deliver, all of these. Attaching oneself to a man did not make most women rich, simply because many men were still poor and episodically employed, and many were not prepared to share their earnings or other assets equitably with their wife or children. But ordinarily it helped, because men almost always made more money and controlled more revenue-producing assets than women did. Marriage was also the best route to greater economic security as one got older. Even an unhappy marriage might result in children, and children were, in the end, usually a profitable proposition (at least from the age of perhaps seven to eighteen) and a woman's best chance to look forward to a reasonably secure old age.

Another incentive was the enormous prestige advantage that married women *and women who had once been married* had over never-married women. Married women usually had more access to food and more lucrative jobs than never-married women, better seats in church and synagogue, and enhanced roles in religious processions. It was invariably matrons (wives or widows who had given birth), not spinsters, who populated the 'juries of matrons' that testified in the law courts on matters reproductive and sexual, or who took up more-than-merely-honourific town posts, like 'mayoress' or burgermeister's wife, not to mention far more powerful roles like queen mother or *valide sultan* (mother of the sultan).[18] Previously married women, especially if they were older women, generally also had more freedom of movement. Widows routinely lived in their own homes or apartments in European and Ottoman cities and rural areas; while unmarried women or, in the Ottoman Empire, younger divorcees, were banned or strongly discouraged, though not always successfully, from doing the same. Poor relief and even some criminal justice systems tended to distinguish between never-married women, who were often seen as suspicious, oversexed, prone to criminality, or even satanic, and married women or widows, especially if they were older and had children, who were somewhat more likely to be portrayed as honest and deserving. It is not a coincidence that widows and orphans were the charitable object of choice in all the major European and Middle Eastern religious traditions.

Though pressure to marry was sometimes great, and some marriages were entered into for cold-hearted motives, this does not mean they were all loveless. Early modern people recognized that love was an important cement for better family relations: 'love is, such a friend as is desired everywhere and without which a common weal, nay, a family would not subsist' wrote one late seventeenth-century Lancashire shopkeeper and would-be husband.[19] There are many cases of arranged marriages turning into loving ones (though also of marriages for love that turned very sour indeed). Women's ability to love both husbands and children – even when the former mistreated them – was particularly prized. There are some touching evocations of marital love and affection in the early modern period. Glikl bas Judah Leib, also known as Glückel of Hameln (1646–1724), the great German-Jewish memoirist and businesswoman, adored her first husband, and he felt the same; we get the impression theirs was a very egalitarian relationship. Tsar Peter the Great married the second time for love (after divorcing his first wife and consigning her to a convent) and his new wife, Catherine, the daughter of a Latvian peasant, was an important member of his council of advisers. He made her his co-ruler, and she succeeded him on the throne, though, as it turned out, she reigned only two years before dying. As is still the case today, husbands were more likely to predecease their wives than the reverse, but when wives died first we sometimes find husbands commissioning moving tomb-inscriptions or funerary poems, or even writing memoirs celebrating their wives' virtues and talents. Some men also published their wives' writings after their deaths, a tribute to their abilities as well as a way to immortalize their memories.[20] Men found other ways to affirm their devotion and respect for their wives.

One eighteenth-century *mufti* from Salonika (now in Greece) stipulated that his wife be the one to read the Qur'anic verses at his post-mortem endowment ceremony – and that they be dedicated to Fatima, the Prophet Mohammed's daughter.[21] Endearments were common in correspondence between husbands and wives, and while some of this, especially in the second half of the century, seems mainly to reflect the 'Cult of Sensibility' then lighting emotional fire-storms across literate Europe, in some of them the unaffected sincerity of feeling speaks across the centuries.

Undeniably though, one major difference with present-day views of marriage was that everyone accepted that some marriages never had and never would involve love. A loveless union did not, after all, always preclude a functional working relationship. Hester Thrale, the friend and patron of Samuel Johnson, was married to a brewer with whom she had little in common. The *philosophe* Montesquieu's marriage seems to have been solely a marriage of convenience; there must have been many marriages like these. Some communities and households actively discouraged open shows of affection between husbands and wives. Until at least the late nineteenth century it was considered inappropriate in some extended Balkan households for a husband to call his young wife by her own name; instead she was called *zheno*, a generic term for wife or woman, and endearments were frowned upon. Evidently this was intended to stop a new wife worming her way into her husband's affections before she had proved herself by working hard and bearing sons. In some of the very large Slavic *zadruga* households, which might contain thirty people or more, it seems that married couples who were too close were thought to undermine the larger harmony of the working group.[22]

MONOGAMY AND POLYGAMY

Montesquieu's best-selling *Lettres persanes* (Persian Letters) of 1721, the most influential Orientalist novel of the eighteenth century, and arguably of all time, makes a sharp distinction between Muslim societies and Christian societies on the matter of marriage. According to Montesquieu, who had not, at the time that he wrote the book, even visited a Muslim country, Muslim men practised polygamy, imprisoned their wives in harems, and turned them into sex-slaves, while Christian (or at least French) men endorsed monogamy, allowed their wives to move about and socialize freely, and probably gave them too much political and sexual rein. The *Persian Letters* conflated genuinely confining, but unique, royal institutions, like the household of the Shah of Persia (and, by extension, the Ottoman Imperial Harem) with all

Muslim marriages, while failing to mention the fact that the royal harems were important sites of political power (see Chapter 9). And it completely ignored non-elite women, the vast majority of the female population in Muslim as in Christian countries.

In reality the Muslim/Christian polarity was far less extreme than Montesquieu implies. For one thing, polygamy was a distinctly minority practice in Ottoman society in the early modern period (it remains very rare, and, in most cases, illegal, in former Ottoman lands to this day). Only about five per cent of the population was in polygamous marriages – or about two per cent of all marriages. Moreover, most polygynous marriages involved only two wives, not the bevy of nubile women conjured up by Montesquieu and other harem fantasists. Cost was the most important reason for this. Only well-off men could afford to pay a *mehr* (dowry) for more than one wife, especially since each wife was (in theory) supposed to have a separate dwelling or at least separate apartments, and a man's failure to treat his wives equally was an offence for which he could be taken to court. There was also the problem that women did not much like polygyny. Eighteenth-century Ottoman princesses refused to accept polygynous marriages, and since marrying a princess was often a condition of high office, men who married them had to divorce their first wife (in at least one case we know that this caused great heartache for the husband, and presumably the first wife as well). When Mary Wortley Montagu visited Istanbul in the early eighteenth century it appears that polygamy had become, at least temporarily, unfashionable, even among elites, perhaps due to the princesses' example. We also find some middle- or upper-middle-class women, as early as the sixteenth century, placing clauses in their marriage contracts that automatically dissolved the marriage if their husband took a second wife or concubine.[23] On the other hand, while overall polygamy was rare, there is some evidence that it was slightly higher in places with very imbalanced sex-ratios. Polygyny appears to have functioned in such communities both as a way to settle 'excess' women under patriarchal rule, and to encourage a more equitable distribution of wealth. Women who ended up as domestic servants, beggars or prostitutes in Christian communities could, at least in theory, be second wives in Muslim ones.[24]

Sex with slaves was almost certainly more common among Ottoman elites and sub-elites than formal polygamy. As we have seen, it was permitted by law and entailed certain advantages for the slave, though she only possessed actual 'rights' if she got pregnant. A slave concubine was less advantaged than a wife; she did not usually receive a *mehr*, and she did not automatically inherit from her master in the way a wife did from a husband. Some of the rights of wives clearly spilled over into concubinage, however, including, at least some of the time, the normative right to a separate domicile, and, of course, the equal treatment of legitimate and illegitimate children for inheritance purposes. Polygyny may not be an ideal system from the perspective of free women, especially first wives, but it undoubtedly gave more opportunities to slave women and their children. Few people could afford to own slaves, though, which meant that, outside the circles of the fairly well off, most men who were unsatisfied with their wives patronized prostitutes, preyed upon servants, beggars or other low-status women, men, or children, or put up with sexual frustration or deprivation – just like men in Christian Europe.[25]

Just as the prevalence of polygamy has been greatly exaggerated for the Ottoman Empire, monogamy is something of a misnomer for Christian Europe, at least if we mean by it sexual fidelity. An unknown and perhaps underappreciated proportion of men must have been faithful to their wives through thick and thin, but it is also very evident from rape and sexual assault prosecutions, divorce cases, paternity suits and other sources, including men's and women's diaries, that many were not. It was quite acceptable, even expected, in most, perhaps all, European countries for upper-class men to maintain a mistress. People further down the social scale liked to cast aspersions on this aspect of upper-class life, but there are enough recorded cases of middling men getting their servants with child, or catching syphilis or 'the clap' from prostitutes, to give us the distinct impression that, while they may have been greater hypocrites than other men, the middling were little more chaste.[26] In addition, though slavery was far less common in metropolitan Europe than it was in the Ottoman Empire, it was very common in Europe's colonies. There, as we have already seen, sexual intercourse with women slaves was an entrenched practice virtually across the slave-owning class. Most colonial settings also offered greatly enhanced opportunities both for colonial officials and for lower-class or non-elite men from the 'mother' country to enjoy sexual relations, generally without marriage, with local or indigenous women, either enslaved or at least nominally free. What one authority has called 'the dual marriage system' became institutionalized in some areas precisely because it allowed European men to carry on relations with local women while keeping themselves 'free' to enter later into formal matrimony of a more socially and financially advantageous kind with European women.[27]

In short, then, the overwhelming majority of Christian European, Muslim Ottoman, and Jewish men married or consistently cohabited with only one woman at a time. The main exception to this was upper-class men. If these men were Muslim they sometimes married more than one wife (though rarely more than two) or kept a slave concubine. Some very well-off Ottoman Jews also practised polygyny, but even more rarely than Muslims. If they were Christians or Jews, whether in the Ottoman Empire, Christian Europe, or Europe's colonies, they sometimes kept a slave concubine or mistress or had unformalized relations with local women – who enjoyed fewer rights than a wife and were easier to abandon.[28] In both Muslim and Christian societies and in Jewish communities too, the main prerequisite either to formal or informal polygamy was that a man had the financial wherewithal to maintain his other wife, concubine or mistress in a separate dwelling, which was why it was never common beneath the top stratum of society. Non-elite men made do with their wives or sought sex that was cheap or free and came with minimal responsibilities – in other words, coerced or semi-coerced sex with vulnerable and generally young people of low status. There is no evidence that this pattern differed appreciably according to religion, nationality or region. This is the larger reality that Montesquieu's *Persian Letters*, with its exaggerated and titillating view of the differences between 'Eastern' and 'Western' sexual and marital regimes, has succeeded in obscuring from view.

WOMEN AND THEIR PROPERTY

All European and Middle Eastern marital property/inheritance complexes disadvantaged women, but they did so in different ways and at different stages in the life cycle. And some systems offered them real advantages. In regions where inheritance of land tended to be vested in a single heir, usually male (the term for this is primogeniture or ultimogeniture), a woman unlucky enough to have brothers might get nothing except a discretionary dowry. Roughly speaking this was the case in most of England, much of France, parts of Germany, Northern Italy, and parts of the Balkans in the early modern period. It was also true of traditional Jewish law. It should be said, though, that moveable goods were usually more equitably distributed than land, and, in practice, families, especially intact families, often proved quite generous to daughters.[29] Girls or women who outlived their fathers tended to have a harder time in 'discretionary' regimes though, because brothers, stepfathers and guardians were often a good deal stingier and less accommodating. Another set of systems gave daughters half what their brothers got inheritance-wise. This was true of Denmark (which, in the eighteenth century, included Norway), rural Sweden, including what is now Finland, as well as Islamic *sharia* law. Girls got approximately what boys got in Portugal and Spain, Southern Italy, parts of France, Flanders, parts of Germany, Swedish and Finnish cities and towns, and some Hungarian towns.[30] Occasionally we find evidence of daughters being favoured over sons, as seems sometimes to have been the case on some Aegean islands, though probably primarily so she would be able to make a better marriage that might benefit the whole kin-group.[31] Throughout Europe it was common (though not universal) for a woman's dowry to replace any later claim she might have to a share of the inheritance, and inheritance practices among the aristocracy were often more miserly to women and subsidiary sons than those of commoners.

It was customary in most places for sons to get land while daughters got cash, goods (especially textiles), jewelry or domestic animals. Even in places where women did inherit land along with their brothers (as in cash-poor Sweden, at least on occasion), over time the tendency was for land, particularly agricultural land, to 'drift away' from women. A variant of this is that, in parts of Southern Italy and Greece, young women got a cottage or townhouse – that is, a house without farmland. In traditional Wales, women, even if they were heiresses (i.e. had no brothers), never inherited freehold land. It went instead to collateral male relatives, though widows did enjoy an unusually generous portion of their husband's moveable goods. In early modern Normandy, a famously inhospitable place from the perspective of women's legal rights, a large proportion of customary law (sixty-four per cent of the laws in one sixteenth-century redaction) was devoted to regulating, and usually excluding daughters, wives and widows from the ownership of real property. Certain types of land in both the Ottoman Empire and Russia could not be inherited by women at all, at least in theory, and across the European nobility numerous laws or lawyerly devices vested land and titles only in the male line, even in regions where the rules for commoner women were more generous.[32]

Most Christians and Jews assumed that the wife's property would come under the formal or informal control of her husband during marriage. For Christians this derived partly from pre-Christian laws and customs and partly from Matthew 19:3–9, 'For this reason a man shall leave his father and mother, and be joined to his wife: and the two shall become one . . .'[33] The principle of two becoming one was taken to its greatest extreme in England, where the ownership of all of a wife's moveable property, including wages she earned during the marriage, reverted permanently and absolutely to her husband. In addition, her real property (land) reverted to him during his lifetime, though he could not sell it without her permission. If she died he automatically inherited her land. Under ordinary circumstances, there-fore, a married Englishwoman could not own moveable property, could not administer or bequeath real property, and could not even make a will without her husband's consent.[34] Practice on the Continent (and, for that matter, in Scotland) was usually somewhat more advantageous to wives, though there were certainly places where wives enjoyed few rights. Wives' property rights were particularly weak in Florence (and Northern, but not Southern, Italy), parts of Northern France, among some Balkan ethnic groupings, and across a good proportion of the European nobility. In most of the rest of Christian Europe women's real and moveable property tended to come under the guardianship of her husband, but sometimes this was merely customary rather than legally binding, and husbands did not typically gain absolute ownership.

Sharia law contains an exceptionally strong defence of married women's (and indeed all adult women's, even slaves') separate property rights, and the Ottoman courts were generally prepared to back it up. Though there was less support for women's property rights among Orthodox, Jewish or Catholic minorities in the empire, there was some spillover effect here too, because, as we have seen, non-Muslim women were prepared to go to Muslim courts to fight for their rights. Muslim girls started out at a disadvantage, though, because, as in most of Scandinavia, they inherited half what their brothers did. However, they received an often substantial payment from their husband (the *mehr* is actually a requirement of marriage) and both their inheritance and their *mehr* were their property, which their husband was not allowed to use without their permission. The result was that many women began investing in real estate, money-lending, trade and so on very early in their marriages, and some were able to build up substantial estates which they used both to support themselves in the case of divorce and to cushion their widowhood. If they did give part or all of their *mehr* to their husband, and it was common both to give him some and allow him to defer payment of the full amount, it was considered a real debt and recoverable in the courts.

Muslim women, including married women, were thus extremely well endowed with property rights (at least they were if they had access to a law court: we may be sure things were less rosy in the remoter rural areas)[35] – the real disadvantage lay with inheritance, either as daughters or as wives. It is very revealing, therefore, that one of the 'growth' legal devices of the period was family trusts (*waqfs*), which *could* be used to get around women inheriting altogether (and may have originally developed for that purpose), but, in this period, seem more often to have been used to increase their share. In eighteenth-century Aleppo, in a pattern which was probably indicative of developments elsewhere in the empire, *waqfs* were founded by both men and women in increasing numbers from the later eighteenth century on. Men designated their wives or daughters as the major beneficiaries in eighty-five per cent of family *waqfs*, often giving the women a larger share than a strict interpretation of *sharia* law would dictate. Women who established *waqfs* were especially prone to split the proceeds equally among male and female beneficiaries. In particular, where a house or residence was involved, the *waqf* deed often explicitly stated that the rights of females to use the residence were equal to those of males. In the few cases where they were not, women were allowed equal rights until they married, and right of return to the residence if they divorced.[36]

The use of legal devices to get around women's legal disabilities was hardly confined to the Ottoman Empire. A good example comes from England where, as we have seen, married women's property rights were especially weak. In the early modern period married women, their families, and their lawyers began to chip away at this through increasing use of a legal device called the trust. Usually part of the marriage settlement or prenuptial agreement, a trust set aside assets under the control of trustees to be used solely for the benefit of the wife or widow or her children. The trust was a cumbersome and individualized solution to a serious structural asymmetry, and seldom robust enough to withstand a really avaricious and violent husband. It was also infantilizing: in theory the trustees and not the woman herself controlled the trust. But it often worked quite well for the narrow purpose for which it was intended. Initially largely an option for rich families, by the end of the eighteenth century the trust was being widely used quite far down the social scale.[37]

It may occur to the reader to wonder which early modern European women enjoyed the most advantageous legal position. To some extent it depended upon who one was. English law, so problematic for married women, nonetheless gave spinsters and widows quite robust property rights by comparison with some other European countries. By contrast, in most of the German-speaking lands and in much of the Italian peninsula, an unmarried woman, whatever her age, whether a spinster or a widow, had to have a male guardian who was legally entitled to control her financial affairs.[38] Proximity to a court made a major difference – though we sometimes find women going incredible distances to make a case or present a petition.[39] Class was often a more salient factor for both women and men than the letter of the law (though, as we have seen, sometimes the law was different for people of noble status). Noble status empowered some women legally, but handicapped others by comparison with commoners, especially when it came to inheriting from a parent. And race and religion worked to empower some, and greatly or fully disable others, at least in legal terms.

All that having been said, if one is talking broadly about legal systems the laurels probably go to Portugal and its colonies (Spanish law was also very hospitable to women). Portuguese women commoners, though not noblewomen, inherited equally with their brothers. Women retained the rights to half of the common marital property if their husband predeceased them (in rural Sweden, by contrast, widows got one-third, but widowers got two-thirds of the common marital property; in many parts of England widows had traditionally got one-third of their husband's estate, while the husband got all of hers, but in the late seventeenth century the laws were changed, so that the widow received what her husband chose to leave her, while he still got all of her moveable goods permanently, and her lands for his lifetime).[40] Portuguese women could, under some circumstances, acquire rights in the common marital property even if they lived with a man without benefit of holy matrimony, and, as we have seen (Chapter 1), at least some of the time this was extended to slave-concubines. Illegitimate children were bereft of inheritance rights in much of Christian Europe after the mid-sixteenth century, but in Portugal if a man could have married the mother of their children but failed to (in other words, there was no special impediment, like a prior marriage or clerical or noble status), the couple's natural children inherited equally with 'legitimate' children. This also applied (assuming the father recognized them) for the children of slaves. Divorced or abandoned mothers of young children, whether or not they were married, also had a right to be paid, by the father, for three years of wet nursing the child or children. Widows had strong rights to half the common marital property (see above) but also to the entire amount of their dowry, and there was a tradition of women, especially widows, managing estates and carrying on independent trades.[41]

TAKING AN INTEREST IN WOMEN'S LEGAL RIGHTS

Commentaries and *responsa* on women and the law were an ancient genre in all three major European and Middle Eastern religious traditions, but they inspired new interest in the early modern period. In the Ottoman Empire *muftis* began taking an increasingly expansive view of women's legal rights in the seventeenth and eighteenth centuries, influenced in part by the increase in the number of women litigants and by the real-life women's problems judges were encountering.[42] In Christian Europe and in Jewish communities as well, the migrating of law compilations and commentaries into print somewhat democratized knowledge of the law at the same time that it presented new marketing possibilities for publishers. Several of the earliest printed writings on women and the law came from Iberia or from around the Mediterranean. One of the first of these is the Portuguese jurist Rui Gonçalves' *Dos privilegios & praerogativas que ho genero feminino tem por direito commum* (The Privileges and Prerogatives of the Female Sex According to Common Law) of 1557.[43] During the seventeenth and eighteenth centuries, handbooks on the law of women also began appearing in England, France, the Netherlands, Italy, the German lands, and elsewhere, increasingly in vernacular languages (though many continued to be written in Latin, especially in the German-speaking lands), and they often included direct appeals to women readers. A Dutch book on marriage law from 1627 ostentatiously listed its publisher/distributor as 'de Weduwe' (the Widow), apparently using this as a way to signal that it was produced by and for everywoman.[44] A treatise on Jewish law from 1652, written in Italian with Hebrew elements, advertised itself as being 'for the benefit of God-fearing Jewish women'.[45] And *The Treatise of Feme Coverts, or the Lady's Law*, printed in England in 1732, asserted, with perhaps pardonable exaggeration, that 'the fair Sex are here inform'd, how to preserve their Land, Goods, and most valuable Effects, from the Incroachments of anyone'.[46] The last of these is especially interesting because it unhesitatingly appeals to women's putative desire for greater control over their assets. In time, handbooks and treatises began appearing in eastern Europe as well. Most of these date from the nineteenth century, but Cserey Farkas' *The Law of the Women of Hungary (Magyar) and that of the Hungarian Women of Eastern Transylvania (Szekely)* was published in Hungarian in 1800, and is said to have been penned some decades before.[47]

Law books are an acquired taste – some would say dull – and there were more exciting ways for early modern people to find out about women's relationship to the law. Just as they are today, the public was fascinated with the marital problems of the rich and titled, and the print media played to this shamelessly. Verbatim transcripts of divorce court proceedings were a perennial favourite, and specialists in shorthand were often employed to that purpose. Soon the different parties to family or marital disputes began using the pamphlet press proactively to air their cases, perhaps in the hope of influencing judges or public opinion or both. There are numerous seventeenth- and eighteenth-century examples of this from France, England, Holland, Sweden, and probably elsewhere and they look uncannily like what one sees today in the most scabrous celebrity divorce cases: domestic violence, prenuptial agreements abandoned, innocence supposedly betrayed, adultery, impotence, and accusations of the most sordid kind. In more than one case, these turned into full-scale pamphlet wars between the opposing parties, who sometimes used the occasion (or their lawyers did) to air larger concerns. Thus we find aggrieved husbands complaining that women in general are getting too much power in the law-courts, and wives (or their supporters) airing the sort of dirty linen about their husbands that would turn any woman off marriage, or, at very least, cause her to insist on an extremely good prenuptial agreement. These productions were all about women and men trying to make the law work instrumentally for them. And over and over again they drew attention to the disadvantaged position of women in the law.[48]

We lack sources like this for places without a popular print tradition, but that does not mean the law, and especially the law in relation to husbands and wives, was not talked about. A traveller to Istanbul and Anatolia during the closing years of the eighteenth century reported the following coffee house scene:

> . . . I once saw a party of [professional story-tellers] represent, with humour, disputants pleading before a Cadee [*kadi* or *sharia* court judge] the rights and privileges of a discarded wife; who, in reply to her husband's reproaches on account of her vexatious conduct, of which some ridiculous proofs were brought forward, retorted with great volubility and fury as to the inefficiency [inefficacy?] of his endeavours to prove agreeable. Such trash is highly amusing to the coffee-house loungers throughout Turkey, and may be met with in almost every village.[49]

This performer may or may not have been re-enacting a real case, but either way it suggests that questions about gender and the law were on people's minds. Moreover, as we will see, the 'rights and privileges of a discarded wife' were no means negligible. Coffee-houses were, of course, male spaces, but there were women story-tellers circulating about women's spaces (see Chapter 7), and some of them had outsize artistic reputations. If this really was such a common theme it seems probable that they would have had something to say about it.

Though most of the early books on women's law were written by male lawyers and jurisconsults, in the eighteenth century women also got into the business of commenting learnedly on the law – and some began calling for change. A landmark, at least in England, was *The Hardships of the English Laws in Relation to Wives* of 1735, a feminist critique of the English laws pertaining to marriage. *Hardships of the English Laws* was almost certainly written by

Sarah Chapone (1699–1764) of Gloucestershire. Chapone published at least one other feminist pamphlet, and carried on correspondences with many of the notables of the day, including the theologian and feminist Mary Astell, whose work she recommended to her friends, and the novelist Samuel Richardson who called her a 'great Championess for her Sex'. Chapone was not just a writer but an activist. Though not particularly well off herself and burdened with a large family (she bore five children), she raised funds to support the Anglo-Saxon scholar, Elizabeth Elstob, who was then in financial difficulties. She also assisted George Ballard, an antiquary and male 'champion of women' in putting together his book *Memoirs of Several Ladies of Great Britain Who Have Been Celebrated for their Writings* (1752), an important early work of women's history. Apparently she urged him to make the book more political, and helped find him patronage and subscribers.[50]

The Hardships of the English Laws contains critiques of, among other things, the existing legal remedies for wife beating, men's right to control their wives' mobility and whereabouts, fathers' automatic right to child custody and right to refuse their wives or widows access to their own children, widows' disadvantages in inheritance, women's loss of property rights when they married, and wives' inability to make legal wills. It often cites printed accounts of scandalous trials (see above) as evidence for the excessive power men have over women in marriage. Though Chapone professes to consider marriage 'the very Basis, Foundation, and Cement of Society, an Institution of God' she also shows no hesitation in equating it, in its present oppressive form, with slavery: 'Let every . . . Woman who is well treated, thank God and her Husband for the Blessing. At the same Time, she may reflect, that she is in the Condition of a Slave . . .'[51]

Considerably more staid and with a different kind of point to make was a treatise published in Latin in 1788 by Maria Pellegrina Amoretti (1756–1787), an Italian, on marriage in Roman law. Pellegrina Amoretti was the first woman to obtain a law degree, from the University of Pavia (1777), and the work was clearly intended, in part, to demonstrate that a woman could work in the more abstruse kinds of law, though, like Chapone's work, it must have been partially designed to show that neither the law nor the customs relating to women were immutable.[52] Books on women and the law (and perhaps even popular exposés about individual women's marital troubles), even when they were not explicitly feminist, undoubtedly taught some women to think in terms of legal rights, and they did so in areas (marriage and property rights) where the stakes were high. Demands for reform of the laws of inheritance and of women's property ownership

VOICES FROM THE PAST 2.1

A call to reform the law of marriage

Excerpted from Sarah Chapone, *The Hardships of the English Laws in Relation to Wives. With an Explanation of the Original Curse of Subjection Passed Upon the Woman. In an Humble Address to the Legislature (1735).* In the first passage Chapone provides a succinct discussion of the inadequacy of 'peace bonds' (instruments issued by Justices of the Peace that fined or imprisoned a violent husband if he persisted in his abusive behaviour) that would not be out of place in a modern discussion of legal responses to domestic violence. The second passage is an excursus into the comparative study of law. Chapone argues that married women's property rights are far more liberal in Portugal than in England, a view with which early modern historians tend to concur. This was part of a larger argument, that England, despite what was often claimed at the time, was not a 'Paradise of Women' in legal terms.

1. *Domestic Violence*

Obj[ection]. II. By the Law of *England*, a Woman who has been beat and abus'd by her Husband may swear the Peace against him, and if he can't find Security for his behaviour, send him to Jail.

To which I answer, *First*, that sometimes this Relief cannot be had, the Husband having it in his Power to lock up his Wife, and so prevent her Complaint, as in some Cases already cited.

Secondly, That the Consequences of this Relief (if it may be so called) bring great Hardships upon the Wife.

1. As it exposes her to the Resentment of her Husband at his Return Home, without abating his Power, which is so great, that he may revenge himself a thousand Ways not cognizable by Law.

2. That if he is a Tradesman, or a Labourer, she, and her Family depend upon him for Bread, and the Consequence of his lying in Jail must be, that she, and her Family must starve.

2. *Married Women's Property Rights in Portugal*

I have been informed by Persons of great Integrity, who have long resided in *Portugal* and consequently had Opportunities of knowing the Customs of the Country, that a Wife in *Portugal* if she brought never a Farthing [to the marriage], has Power to dispose of half her Husband's estate by Will; whereas a Woman by our Laws alienates all her own Property so entirely by Marriage, that if she brought an hundred thousand Pounds in Money, she cannot bequeath one single Penny, even if she left her own nearest and dearest Relations starving for want.

[Sarah Chapone], *The Hardships of the English Laws in Relation to Wives* (London: J. Roberts, 1735), 32, 29–30.

predated the demand for political rights for women in most countries. The reason, surely, is because women were in the courts, fighting these issues out, long before either men (most men anyway) or women were thinking in terms of more abstract rights like the franchise.

Writers on the law may have looked to relatively nearby countries and classical antiquity for legal comparisons, but most of them had no notion that there was anything to be learned from women further afield. Ottoman Muslim married women's property rights (and, after 1753, Russian married women's property rights) were, as we have seen, considerably stronger than those found in most Western or central European countries in the eighteenth century; moreover, Muslim women had much readier access to divorce. But this only very occasionally made its way into the eighteenth-century Western consciousness, and it is glaringly absent from most women's writing. To be sure, Lady Mary Wortley Montagu had talked about the extraordinary freedoms available to upper-class Ottoman women (see Chapter 1) but she did not go into any detail about the law. Voltaire, a considerable feminist, published a remarkable little satiric piece in 1765, ironically titled 'Wives Submit Yourselves to Your Husbands' (he was not recommending it), in which he pointed out that '[in Islam wives] are by no means slaves; they have property; they can make wills, they are able to request a divorce on occasion; they have their times for going to the mosque – and to their rendezvous: one sees them in the streets with their veils over their noses, just as you used to wear your mask some years ago . . .' but it was a mere squib.[53]

The pronounced Orientalist tendency in western European thought had a special resonance for writers on women because of its usefulness as a way to highlight the oppression of Christian European wives. Sarah Chapone was not alone in likening marriage to slavery; it was a commonplace of the period. But like most other writers of the day she tended to look East rather than West for her archetypal slave.[54] Sarah Chapone thought Englishwomen were possibly 'treated . . . better here, than the Grand Seignior [Sultan] treated his Slaves in *Turkey*'[55] but the whole point of the comparison was that the bar had been set so low. Though her own book was all about English wives' inability to make wills, their absence of real property rights, and their lack of custody over their young children, she clearly had no idea that Muslim women possessed all these rights.

From the perspective of women and the law one of the more remarkable changes to occur anywhere in Europe during the eighteenth century was the incremental improvement in Russian women's entitlements that culminated in the decree of 1753 granting married women absolute property rights. These reforms predated the various western European 'married women's property Acts' by a century or more. From 1730 on, and especially after the 1753 decree, there was a considerable increase in noblewomen's (and even free peasant women's) involvement in property transactions of every sort, though women were hampered by the fact that customary law gave them an unusually meager share of the parental estate, and they did not do especially well with respect to marital property divisions either. On the other hand, widows tended to have absolute control (instead of a mere life right) in lands they inherited from their husbands, a big advantage over, say, most English widows. The story of how this reform came about is a complex one, and solicitude for women's rights was not the most important factor.[56] Nevertheless, in Russia, and across Europe and the Middle East generally, the question of women's property rights was far more than academic. Where women had real rights they exercised them, and they used every device available to them, including litigation, to protect them. Then as now the law made a major difference in women's lives.

MARITAL FRACTURES

The last several decades of work on women's and family history has made it abundantly clear just how awful early modern marriage could be, but, as we saw in Chapter 1, it has also decisively laid to rest the old notion that no one ever intervened, that all husbands had a free hand, and that marriage was always a life-long prison sentence. Families, neighbours, the courts, the clergy, town officials, military officers, and other parties routinely, if inconsistently, intervened in troubled marriages, both to try to patch them up, and, more reluctantly, to work out some sort of permanent separation. Hundreds of thousands of marriages were formally (and much more often, informally) terminated in the eighteenth century. The fact that some respite was available for some couples in distress is important. But it remains true that one of the signal markers of women's subordination was that it was almost always harder for wives to leave than it was for them to be left. Women were strongly socialized to view themselves as 'virtuous' if they submitted to their husbands' wishes (including his beatings) and 'disobedient' – and selfish – if they objected, rebelled or turned to others for help. The routes to divorce, annulment or separation were highly gender asymmetric and women usually had to give up more than men did, financially, personally, and symbolically, in order to obtain a divorce or separation. In most Christian countries, though not in Muslim ones, they also lost custody of their young children. And it goes almost without saying that separation tended to increase the economic vulnerability of both women and children.

Overwhelmingly, the most common mode of ending a marriage was for the husband simply to walk out on his wife and children.[57] Men were usually much more mobile than women were. They had a wider array of jobs available to them, were safer on the road, and had more far-flung contacts (see Chapter 1). They were also apparently more willing to abandon their children. The problem was partly structural. Men's work was often episodic and paid barely enough to feed the worker himself. Devoted fathers in poor families almost always ate less than poor single men did, and chronic hunger would have been a major incentive for the less-devoted or weaker-willed simply to leave – just because they could do so much more readily.[58] And they did. In large numbers married men tramped to other towns or countries, joined the army, went to sea, or simply set up residence elsewhere and stopped contributing to their first family. It is difficult to say how many marriages ended in separation. One close study of the parish of Colyton in Devon, England in the eighteenth and early nineteenth centuries found evidence of separation for about ten per cent of marriages. In about forty-five per cent of these the husband initiated the separation, usually by going to work somewhere else or joining the military; in about eight per cent of the cases the wife left; in three per cent both parents left, abandoning their children; and in the remainder of the cases it is unclear who instigated the rupture.[59] Marital dissolution was a bit more formalized in the middle classes. Among the broad and growing class of literate city-dwellers many couples negotiated private separation agreements through lawyers. Often we know about these only because, much later on, one or another spouse went to court to enforce a maintenance agreement or try to get hold of the other's estate after their death. Mutually agreed-upon informal separations were also very common among the better-off nobility. These would often have been arranged marriages in the first place, and once their wives had borne an heir, and sometimes even before, many noblemen felt few compunctions about setting up with more attractive (and perhaps more tractable) lower-class mistresses. Emotional abandonment was often thinly concealed beneath the chilly forms of noble etiquette, but, as we have seen, both noble and upper bourgeois women were also sometimes forcibly 'retired' to convents or private madhouses. Still, better-off women must often have been relieved to retreat to a convent or, if they had the wherewithal, to one of their own properties. And they were not averse to running away themselves, like the Russian noblewoman who, in 1742, abandoned her adulterous spouse, returned to her ancestral lands, and gave her serfs instructions to kill her husband if he ever set foot in her village.[60]

The Catholic Church had long objected to divorce, though it was sometimes prepared to issue annulments, most often on grounds of the marriage being within the prohibited degrees of kinship or of non-consummation.

Generally, though not always, it was the powerful and well-off who managed to avail themselves of this means of escape, though, as we saw in Chapter 1, hundreds, perhaps thousands, of poorer women from minority communities, especially in Italy, Prussia and above all the Ottoman Empire, took advantage of the rule that conversion to the dominant faith annulled a previous marriage with someone of a minority faith. Most Catholic countries, as well as Anglican England, also permitted couples to petition for legal separation. Unfortunately though, the grounds were often quite narrow (few included marital violence, for example). Moreover, a legal separation did not allow either spouse to remarry during the other's lifetime. (Both women and men were liable for bigamy charges, a very serious and sometimes capital offence in Christian countries, though many couples, as well as people in authority, winked at the laws.)

The Reformation attack upon clerical celibacy, coupled with the elevation of scriptural authority, did lead some Protestant theorists to take a more flexible position on divorce. The grounds for this reconsideration were both the apparent scriptural support for divorce in case of a wife's adultery[61] and an emerging belief that marriage, a blessed state, required some meeting of minds, and should, therefore, be dissoluble in cases of extreme incompatibility. As a result some Protestant countries did permit very limited access to full divorce from the later sixteenth century on, though the grounds varied, and men often enjoyed the advantage. In England divorce *a vinculo* (that is, full divorce with the right to remarry) was, in practice, available only to men; the sole ground was the wife's adultery, and it could only be obtained by private act of parliament. As a result divorce *a vinculo* was both extremely rare and confined entirely to the rich and well connected. By contrast, in Norway, due to the availability of free legal assistance, divorce was available to poor people as well as rich ones. It was still very rare though: perhaps five couples a year obtained legal divorces in the whole country in the first part of the eighteenth century. The most common grounds were desertion and disappearance, followed by adultery. The Scandinavian countries – and Scotland – were unusual in that adultery tended to be interpreted symmetrically. That is, both women and men could obtain divorces if their spouse was unfaithful.[62]

Marital cruelty and physical abuse were not grounds for divorce either in the Scandinavian courts or the courts of most other Protestant countries (though in some places, like England, it could get a woman a legal separation by the eighteenth century). It also was not grounds for legal separation or annulment in Catholic regimes, or for unilateral annulment under *Hanafi* law, the official jurisprudential school of the Ottoman Empire. The fact that none of the faiths was prepared to attack spousal violence at its root (though all decried it rhetorically, and all were prepared to intervene in at least some of the most serious cases) should make us very sceptical about present-day 'competitions' for which faith system is intrinsically more enlightened when it comes to violence against wives. Thus, in the modern day, many Christians (and a good many Muslims) express shock and horror over the Qur'anic passage that appears to suggest that a disobedient wife may be beaten when all other methods have failed.[63] Certainly it is reasonable and right to argue that scripture should not be used to justify family violence. But the allegedly more merciful 'Christian' view reflects a very recent change of heart that is more indebted to secular agitation by women than to Christianity per se. Moreover, most of the writers who argue for a long tradition of Christian churchmen objecting to wife-beating simply ignore the fact that there is an equally distinguished, and indeed much more detailed, tradition within Islam. The fact is that, in the early modern period (and, indeed, well into the nineteenth or even twentieth century) all faiths assumed that men, as heads of the household, needed to have violence, or at least the credible threat of violence, at their disposal if they wished to keep their subordinates, including their wives, in line. It was especially necessary with respect to wives and daughters, because it was believed that, without the disincentive of painful punishment, many, perhaps most women (the daughters of Eve, after all) would be unable to resist sexual sin. People of all faiths undoubtedly disapproved of men who seriously injured their wives, or who abused them for unacceptable reasons: their clergy were prepared to say as much, and there were often devices like peace bonds at least theoretically available to moderate the worst excesses. In the end though, the fact that even the most brutal violence was hardly ever grounds for actually breaking up a marriage speaks louder than the rhetoric.

Sharia law enshrines an exaggeratedly asymmetric divorce system, in which men can divorce their wives for any reason simply by saying 'I divorce you'. This is the so-called *talaq* divorce, and if the man says 'I divorce you' three times (the 'triple *talaq*') the divorce is irrevocable. There were some limits on this ability, such as the rule that a man in his final illness could not divorce his wife. Less noticed by Western critics of this system, but crucially important in practice, was the fact that a man who divorced his wife had to pay back any part of her *mehr* that he had borrowed or that remained unpaid, support her for several months, and pay child support for any children while they were in the mother's custody. (In *Hanafi* jurisprudence she automatically got custody

– though not legal guardianship – of boys until the age of seven years and girls until puberty. After that, custody reverted to the father or his family.) The child support requirement was generous: it was supposed to be at 'a level commensurate with [the wife's] standard of living, enough to cover the costs of clothing, food, shelter, and even a servant if that were in keeping with her lifestyle.' All this meant that divorce was not a step most men took lightly. Rather often, in fact, men regretted speaking the words of the *talaq*, and tried to retract them, only to be met by their former wife insisting, in court, that the divorce stand and that she get the money she was owed. Women could also have their ex-husbands imprisoned if they failed to pay them back the *mehr* that immediately became due on the divorce or if they fell behind on child support, and this and related issues often came up in the early modern courts.[64]

Muslim women could also initiate divorce, but it cost them more, relatively speaking, than it did men. They virtually always had to give up their *mehr* and sometimes other monies or rights, such as their right to child support. This was called *khul* or *hul* divorce, and no specific grounds were necessary for her to do this, nor did she necessarily have to go to court, but she *did* need her husband's agreement (unscrupulous husbands would sometimes abuse their wives until the latter, in desperation, sought a *hul* divorce – thus giving up their *mehr* and their legal right to support). Women could also obtain annulments even without their husband's consent on various grounds, including if the marriage was deemed unsuitable on caste or class grounds. They could also petition to get out of a marriage if they had been married young and without their consent by someone other than their father or grandfather (e.g. by a guardian). In the early modern period *kadis* also routinely awarded women divorces on grounds of their husband's desertion or failure to maintain them, even though theoretically these were not grounds for divorce in the *Hanafi* school (in Jerusalem, Damascus and Nablus *kadis* would simply call in a colleague from another tradition of law where those were acceptable grounds).[65] As we have seen, *Hanafi* law did not consider cruelty grounds for a unilateral divorce initiated by the woman. However, it is interesting to note that, in the early modern period, *kadis* did sometimes bind over husbands not to beat their wives; if they did, the couple would be instantly divorced, which was a different way of achieving the same object. There are many cases of this kind in the Ottoman courts in the early modern period. As was also the case in Christian lands, law, custom and economic constraints made it easier for husbands to leave than wives. On the other hand, *sharia* law did give wives the right to initiate divorce, and also built in many more financial safeguards for women and children. As a result, in the Ottoman Empire both men and women availed themselves of divorce in fairly large numbers, and there was very little stigma attached to it.[66] The fact that Islamic law also permitted (indeed encouraged) remarriage for both parties was also crucially important, because it allowed women to start again from the beginning. Most did remarry, and sometimes the second or third time around they tried to negotiate better terms. In one sample of two hundred marriage contracts from seventeenth-century Cairo, thirty per cent of women had been married before, and women marrying again put many more conditions into their contracts. These included provisos like the following: the couple had to live next to her sister, the wife must be allowed to carry on her trade, she was to be allowed to go on pilgrimage, she was to be free to visit the public baths. Many women also added clauses forbidding the husband to take a second wife or a concubine (usually the penalty was that the woman would be immediately divorced if the condition was broken, and have her *mehr* returned intact). In Christian countries we also find that women marrying again were more likely to insist upon putting limiting conditions into their marriage settlements or prenuptial agreements, and on having a prenuptial agreement in the first place.[67]

Judaism permitted men to initiate divorce, though, as in Islam, a husband had typically to return his wife's dowry if he did. Notoriously, women could not obtain a divorce without their husband giving them permission (the *get*, or bill of divorce). If he would not agree (and it was financially in his interests not to, since, in theory at least, he would have to give her back her dowry and often other sums of money), his wife was left in a limbo state, unable to remarry, but also without the financial support of a husband. The *agunah* (abandoned woman who is unable to remarry) was a pathetic figure, often, in the early modern period, reduced to beggary or prostitution. Interestingly, significant numbers of women dealt with this by converting either to Christianity or Islam, which allowed them to start anew, though it could also cost them the support of their families and co-religionists. The advantages of this were particularly striking in the Ottoman lands, since, as we have seen, Jewish (and Christian) women who converted to Islam not only dissolved their marriage and regained their ability to marry, but, in accordance with *sharia* law, got back their dowries and could claim custody of their young children.[68]

Court records and other sources, from all over Europe and the Ottoman Empire, contain a wealth of information about why marriages broke down and how women coped. Abandonment, non-support, domestic violence, and adultery were all common. Both men and women committed adultery, but the pervasiveness of the double standard meant that men gained considerable advantages from claiming that wives were unchaste, while, with only a few exceptions, wives gained little advantage for making the same claim about their husbands. In both Catholic and Orthodox countries, allegations that a wife was unchaste were an excellent way to justify shutting her up permanently in a convent. Women said to be adulterous, even if the evidence was flimsy, also generally lost their right to their dowries and jointures, and were greatly disadvantaged in any divorce, separation or custody proceedings. In Normandy a family could strip a widow of her dower rights by claiming that she had 'behaved immodestly' during the period of mourning. In Hungary the adulterous wife lost all her property, both real estate and moveables. And in a *talaq* divorce, if the divorced wife was suspected of having committed adultery, she could lose her right to the return of her *mehr*. In many places both the courts and the public looked the other way if a husband killed his wife for adultery; some places actually permitted it, particularly if the killing was committed in the heat of the moment. By contrast, men's right to their property, much less their lives, virtually never, in any Christian or Muslim regime, hung upon their chastity.[69]

Much marital discord revolved around economic issues. Marriages foundered on the size of the dowry (and failure to pay it), access to job opportunities, a father-in-law's unwillingness to use his influence on his son-in-law's behalf, and disputes over the disposition of women's wages. Wherever women did have property rights these also came into the fray. In England, husbands routinely used violence to coerce a wife into agreeing to sell her real property (the wife's agreement was required to liquidate), to get hold of her separate estate, or to spend the monies set aside for her widowhood or her children's future. Consequently, sales of a wife's real property were sometimes preceded by her meeting alone with judges in order to swear that she really did agree to the sale. In Hungary contracts involving a wife's property might be annulled if it could be proved she had agreed under violent coercion. In Sweden, up until 1734, a husband could not sell his wife's lands without the permission *both of his wife and her relatives*.[70] French courts fairly routinely awarded women the right to administer their property separately for similar reasons. And the Qur'an explicitly forbids a man to threaten or use violence to force his wife to give up her property, and the *sharia* courts routinely ruled in accordance with this admonition.[71]

As these devices suggest, almost everywhere the man who sank the often carefully devised plans for a woman's widowhood, or intruded upon the future inheritance of their children, raised more hackles than the man who beat his wife senseless in order to pressure her into sex, because he disliked her friends, or because he thought she talked too much. Beating a woman up for her cash, lands or dower was also considered more heinous than other kinds of marital violence because it threatened to throw her and her children back on her kin – or on public charity – for support. As a consequence, women who went to court often focused much of their testimony around this kind of violence (there were also far more legal avenues for getting one's money or lands back than for getting a divorce, at least in Christian lands), and it is probable that the legal records overstate its prevalence by comparison with more quotidian and less actionable forms of cruelty.[72]

Going to court was only one of several ways to cope with a bad relationship. A different sort of alternative was magic. In a Castilian sorcery trial from 1701 it was revealed that one Zebriana de Escobar had consulted a magician about threats of violence from her lover, and about making herself more attractive to him, and such cases often turn up in the records of the Inquisition. Earlier we noted an English case where a battered woman was accused of visiting a fortune teller in Whitechapel to find out when her husband would die. A woman from Aleppo hired a geomancer to make her husband more affectionate toward her. When the spells failed to work, she successfully sued the magician in court.[73] There were also various places of refuge, especially in the cities. The houses of *kadis* were, as we have seen, popular places of refuge for women in the Ottoman Empire, and convents fulfilled much the same purpose in Catholic countries. In one rather well-documented case from Poland, the marriage of two nobles, Magdalena Czapska and Hieronim Florian Radziwill, foundered over his efforts, with copious resort to violence, to 'subdue her' and control her movements. In 1750 Magdalena, who showed little interest in being subdued, fled to the convent of Holy Sacrament Nuns in Warsaw and sued for divorce. In the seventeenth century, Venetian battered women went to the Casa del Soccorso, a kind of refuge for mistreated wives and 'fallen women', though husbands could also use it to confine their (allegedly) lewd wives. In eighteenth-century Madrid certain churches were expressly designated as places of refuge for women.[74]

In the very late eighteenth century, after the French Revolution, a number of European countries experienced a sudden and dramatic increase in women trying to obtain divorces. We will look at this in more detail in Chapter 9. But in some places this trend seems to have set in earlier. The case of Geneva, Switzerland is particularly interesting. For most of the eighteenth century Geneva saw approximately one divorce a year. However, there was a perceptible increase after 1765, largely due to a phenomenon that had rarely been seen before: women who deserted their husbands in order to run, often with their children in tow, over the border to France or Savoy where they could easily establish residency. Apparently this trend was precipitated by the fact that Genevan law asymmetrically favoured women: it banished men who deserted their wives, but did not banish wives who did the same thing, simply because no one had previously seen desertion as a woman's crime. This is evidently a case where an interesting piece of arcane legal knowledge spread among women in a border area, and some miserably married women seized their chance. It may not be coincidental that, by this point, Geneva had almost a one-hundred per cent female literacy rate, one of the highest in Europe.[75]

But high female literacy did not characterize the Ottoman Balkans, and both there and in other Ottoman regions (notably a number of the Mediterranean islands, including Naxos and Crete) it became very common in the late medieval and early modern period for Christian and Jewish women (and couples) to register their marriages in the *sharia* courts rather than with the Orthodox, Armenian or Jewish authorities, both because the *sharia* courts tended to be cheaper, and because the marriages could be relatively easily dissolved with the parties able to remarry. It was not just the ability to divorce that was at stake, however; some Armenian and Orthodox Christian women actually began demanding a *mehr*, just like Muslim women, that would be theirs to control.[76]

It is sometimes argued today that easier divorce hurts women, because it encourages men to leave. But the evidence from the eighteenth century suggests that men who could not divorce their wives simply abandoned them, had them locked up against their will, or negotiated private separations. And numerous men used the fact that women could not easily escape to make their lives and those of their children a living hell.[77] It is possible to find women writers, especially in France, advocating for easier divorce in the eighteenth century, though both men and women who wrote on the subject often found it necessary to do so anonymously.[78] But the more compelling testimony about women's need for divorce comes from the tens of thousands of Muslim women, and the far smaller number of Christian and Jewish women, who obtained (or tried to obtain) divorces or separations, or sought less formal solutions in this period. These women speak loudly across the centuries about how essential the right of women to escape a bad marriage was deemed to be to women themselves.

HOUSEHOLDS OF WOMEN

'The whole World is a single Ladys Family', wrote the English philosopher and feminist Mary Astell (1666–1731) expansively in *A Serious Proposal to the Ladies* of 1694, 'her opportunities for doing good are not lessen'd but increas'd by her being unconfin'd ... her Beneficence moves in the largest sphere'.[79] It was a remarkable thing to write at a time where spinsters were, as often as not, marginal people, more often associated with parasitism than generosity. In the sixteenth and seventeenth centuries, in many parts of Europe and possibly the Middle East, there had been new or renewed efforts to limit women's ability to live alone and be self-supporting (of course it is hard to know how well they worked).[80] But in the eighteenth century female-headed households, women living alone, pairs of women living without a man, and women living in groups all appear to have became either more commonplace or more acceptable. One study of ten early eighteenth-century Russian towns found an average of nine per cent (but in one town as high as fourteen per cent) of households headed by widows with children, as well as smaller numbers of abandoned or unmarried women with children. Such families took up a large proportion of the charitable rolls. In early eighteenth-century Rome, female-headed households made up over seventeen per cent of nuclear families in some parishes, while in Milan by the end of the century, in a parish near one of the city markets, the figure was sixteen per cent, but these families tended to live in dark, unhealthy cellars, suggesting that there, too, women living without a man were likely to be poor. Some relatively rural areas were also affected. By the mid-eighteenth century about twenty per cent of Spanish Galician households were headed by women; in some communities such arrangements characterized over a third of households – in part because single women, including unmarried mothers, had more legal rights than in many other parts of Europe. Less advantageously, it was a very poor area where many of the men had migrated away to find work.[81] In Istanbul and other Ottoman cities women often lived on their own in their own houses, and they can also be found in the courts, negotiating with, and sometimes suing, relatives (and especially in-laws) for their own space with its own entrance.[82]

Urban areas and proto-industrial regions (see Chapter 5) were especially likely to see heavy concentrations of single women. Large-scale silk, lace, thread and cloth production was spreading across Europe and the Ottoman Empire in this period. The women who worked in these industries often had relatively reduced marital options and strong incentives to economize by living in groups. Even before the rise of the factory system in the late eighteenth and early nineteenth centuries in England, and, a bit later, Belgium, large numbers of single women were living alone or in groups of two or more. The older sorts of women's jobs, for instance hawking goods in the street, also contributed their share of non-traditional living arrangements and continued to do so into the nineteenth century. Antoinette Corbières, a cheese hawker in Montauban in Southern France around 1800, was typical of many. She owned little or no property beyond, perhaps, a few household goods, and lived in a single, top-floor room with five or six unrelated women. We know this because she was close enough to her room-mates to testify on their behalf in a court case.[83] Members of the seamstresses' guild in eighteenth-century Paris routinely resided together and shared expenses. Some owned property in common and named each other as executrixes and heirs. A large percentage (between thirty-seven and forty-eight per cent, depending upon the sample), both in Paris and some of the provinces, never married.[84] Eighteenth-century English insurance records often show pairs of women living together, usually in towns, and insuring their household goods, including their book collections. Clearly these women were forming their own economic and cultural partnerships and support systems; some of them may well have been emotional and sexual relationships as well.

From at least the early eighteenth century, unmarried plebeian French women in some locales had begun, on their own initiative, pooling their worldly goods and, setting up group residences for themselves. Though these women's associations drew on the model of convents, most were fairly secular collective living arrangements (though members always had to stress their piety and commitment to celibacy). Some drew up elaborate contracts that tell us precisely whose goods were whose (in case someone wished to leave the community), and several also secured the explicit approval of the local mayor or village association, obviously a way to stave off the criticism that generally attached to unmarried women who did not live under the direct supervision of a higher status person. Others established their *bona fides* by offering needed charitable services, though not necessarily for free, such as a group in La Fouillouse from 1725 on, which ran little schools to 'instruct young ones in religion'. Other groups offered sick care in return for donations; some taught reading and catechism to poor young girls, instructed them in lace-making, and then absorbed their wages to support the whole group. Though many of these groups were, in time, absorbed into established women's tertiary religious orders (see Chapters 5 and 6), some resisted this, and instead sought to be completely independent.[85]

Poor women's living arrangements were escaping the control of the authorities at the same time that middle- and upper-class women were discovering the convenience, reduced costs and spiritual and other pleasures, of setting up households together. 'Romantic friendships', as historians call these relationships, were close, emotional, highly emotive and often physically expressive relationships between women that, for many, seem to have become the most important in their lives.[86] Very close relationships between women – both fictive and 'real' were not invented in the eighteenth century, nor were they unique to relatively elite women.[87] What *was* new was that, in this period, 'romantic friendships' among better-off, usually highly literate, women came, for some, to represent a viable and even relatively respectable alternative to marriage. They also began to be publicly performed in wholly unprecedented ways. There are numerous funerary monuments from the period that celebrate the love of one woman for another, reams of letters attesting to women's friendships; celebrations of female friendship written by both women and men; love poems between women; well-known literary and friendship networks; and, especially in Protestant countries (where there were no nunneries), a rash of proposals proposing, and novels celebrating, female educational and charitable communities (Mary Astell's *A Serious Proposal to the Ladies* of 1694 and Sarah Scott's *A Description of Millenium Hall* of 1762 are the most famous, but by no means the only examples).[88] There are also many known cases of noble and upper-middle-class women setting up households together, leaving their estates to beloved female friends, arranging to be buried with them, and so on. Some of these women were undoubtedly lesbian (see Chapter 3), but the phenomenon was clearly larger than that, and it enjoyed a degree of popular approbation that would have been impossible if the general public had thought these women were having sexual relations. Eleanor Butler (1739–1829) and Sarah Ponsonby (1755–1831), called the Ladies of Llangollen, became a tourist attraction for heterosexual as well as homosexual couples in the eighteenth and early nineteenth century; icons of true, because allegedly 'spiritual', devotion (though they did name their dog 'Sapho'). Their 'cult' even generated some of the earliest tourist kitsch: little porcelain figurines that featured the two of them in their distinctive garb. Less iconic, but also very well known, were the Dutch couple Betje Wolff and Aagje Deken, co-authors of a series of successful novels, and the French novelist Marie-Jeanne Riccoboni (in the running for the best-selling novelist of the eighteenth century) and her partner Thérèse Biancolelli. Alongside these kinds of relationships were the often genteel but fortuneless women who became companions to well-off women all over Europe in the early modern period. These relationships could be very complex: companions were depended upon but exploited, their class position hard to define, the connection often marriage-like in the best and worst senses. Co-residential arrangements between women were as unpredictable as those of husbands and wives, but they do testify clearly to the widening of lifestyle choices available to at least some eighteenth-century women.[89]

Less is known about women's households or friendships in eastern Europe, at least outside of religious communities (these are discussed in Chapter 6). There obviously were popular practices designed to celebrate and confirm women's friendships though. One eighteenth-century visitor to the Dalmatian Coast waxed eloquent about the rituals, common among South Slavic peoples, 'for solemnly conjoining two male friends, or two female friends, in the presence of all the people'. Male friends thus conjoined were called *pobratimi*; female friends were called *posestrime* (the Slavic root-words are for brother and sister). This observer, a typical man of the later Enlightenment, thought this a particularly pure example of a kind of unaffected and disinterested love that was (in his view) hardly any longer to be found in civilized societies. Perhaps the most interesting feature here is the joint involvement of clergy (these rituals were carried out in church) and kin in confirming and celebrating these fictive sibling relationships. This suggests that the institution of *posestrime* was linked both to genuine affection, and to other exchanges of a material and symbolic kind between kin groups; however, it is very difficult to find much additional information about them, or even to figure out when these rituals first began.[90]

WIDOWHOOD AND OLD AGE

Wifehood was the most prestigious of female states, and, for many women, the most comfortable materially speaking. Widowhood had its compensations – many women enjoyed the independence – but it was also fraught with uncertainty, peril and especially poverty, and it was often accompanied by a sharp descent in terms of status. A cautionary tale comes from the autobiography of the French Visitation nun and saint, Marguerite-Marie Alacoque (1647–1690, canonized 1920). When Alacoque's father was on his deathbed, he named his brother executor of the estate and guardian of Marguerite-Marie herself. As a result, according to Alacoque, 'mother ceased to have any authority in her house . . . She'd been forced to hand it over to others. With the reins in their hands we were neither of us little better than prisoners.' Left at the mercy of the uncle and a phalanx of hostile women, including a paternal grandmother and aunt and the uncle's mother, Alacoque and her mother were treated like servants, denied food and verbally and (it is implied) physically abused. The estate soon passed out of their hands too, and Alacoque's mother had neither the emotional fortitude nor the legal standing to resist.[91]

But European and Ottoman court records and family papers are full of widows who *did* resist; this was, after all, one of the few moments in a woman's life where a good portion of public opinion approved of her flexing her muscles. At least this was the case if she had children; one's impression from the sources is that women got a good deal less sympathy if they could not claim to be acting on someone else's behalf. And the widow was very likely to come under assault, not just from her husband's kin but from his creditors, who everywhere circled like vultures around a newly bereaved woman. In a typical case from the *sharia* court of Sofia, Bulgaria in the late seventeenth century, the administrator of a *waqf* (family trust) sued a widow, 'the Jewess Lola', for money allegedly borrowed by her late husband Samson and his business partner. However, Lola testified that her husband died bankrupt and swore on the Torah that she and her minor daughter Krala had inherited nothing from him. The *kadi* directed the *waqf* official to stop harassing them.[92] This was a relatively straightforward case; others often took years, especially if they involved in-laws. In Wales the gentlewoman Dorothy Mostyn fought with her deceased husband's family (and co-trustees of the estate) for almost twenty years to save her daughters' inheritance, in this case using arbitration, mediation and alliance-making in preference to the courts. The English equity courts, especially chancery, became famous venues for epic family battles, often pitting widows against their in-laws. Some of them lasted for decades.[93] Though many women went into legal battle at least ostensibly on behalf of their children (and if they did have children they loudly trumpeted that fact at every possible opportunity), throughout Europe and the Ottoman Empire, the central issue for many women was control over their dowries, *mehr*, jointure (widow's fund) or home, in short, their old-age or access to sufficient assets to marry again. Who today can blame them?

Poorer widows (who made up the majority) made their presence known in other ways. People felt sorry for widows and their children, and they were prime recipients of charity; indeed a good number of new widows' charities started up in the eighteenth century. There were even occasional efforts to help the widows of slain soldiers and navy sailors, primarily, it seems, because destitute or near-destitute women succeeded, through petitioning and demonstrations, in shaming early modern states into doing something on their own and their children's behalf.[94] The problems of widows were never-ending though. There were always more of them than willing charity could provide for, they were often clamorous in their need, and they and their children were prone to theft, prostitution, vagrancy and early death, none of them endearing qualities in a world where disorder already held too much sway. Poorer widows sued their in-laws too, but they almost always had smaller and more dispersed families than rich people did, and quite often when they went to court or appealed to higher authorities it was against entities such as guilds, which put up barriers to widows getting into (or remaining in) trade. We will examine this topic in more detail in Chapter 5.

Widowhood could be greatly complicated by minority status. In Swabia Christians placed strict quotas on the number of Jewish families who could reside in a given town (this was common throughout central Europe). 'Protected' status had to be paid for – it was a significant source of income for Christian rulers and local Christian elites – and because of the quota, every slot that was taken meant that some other Jewish family could not move in. Jewish communities would often initially support a widow by lowering her 'protection' tax (meaning others would pay it for her). But if she failed to remarry within a reasonable time after her husband's death, or proved unable to support herself or her family, she was likely to be expelled or forced to become a servant in someone else's house. Widows (particularly poor widows) did not have enough pull to retain a place in a context of scarcity and constraint.[95]

Old age is difficult at the best of times. In the resource-poor, survival-obsessed world of eighteenth-century Europe it could be desperately hard, especially for people without much status in the first place. Old people who were no longer capable of very much productive work were valued more in theory than in practice. Michal Kopczynski notes that inhabitants of Kujawy in northern Poland often showed respect for the elderly by doffing their caps, 'but they also did not hesitate to throw them out of the house and force them to go begging when it turned out they were no longer capable of earning their upkeep. Far from shocking anyone, this was regarded as something quite natural.'[96] This tendency was certainly not confined to Poland. As one poor old woman named Rachel Shoregh, from Bethnal Green in England, put it when she applied for parish relief: 'my children are all married and got familys which [in] these dear times they have as much as they can do to support and therefore are not able to assist me.'[97] Fearing that abandonment or poor treatment might be their lot in their declining years, many women (and men) tried, throughout Europe and the Ottoman Empire, to force their kin, and especially their offspring, to take care of them in their old age, often by tying bequests or inheritance to the provision of a separate room, fuel, and food allowances. Periodically we see older women and men appealing to the courts or the authorities to enforce such agreements. Sometimes the local authorities would force the billeting of old people on their families or even on unrelated people (often local poor widows). This was common in Russia, and apparently elsewhere. In England parish officials sometimes paid old people a stipend, which helped induce their relatives to take them in. In the Ottoman Empire the authorities often went to some trouble to identify distant kin in order to force them to take in elderly relatives.[98]

Many old people worked almost to the day they died. Alice Evans of London, a poor woman, was still selling fruit from a stall at the age of 107.[99] Old women with families probably worked especially hard to make themselves useful through offering childcare and other relatively 'easy' work (at least by the standards of the day). They also turned to conspicuous piety, both so as to be of greater value to their families (shrine visiting on behalf of a sick child, for example), and to take advantage of religiously based charity. Various sources imply that the position of old, sick, slaves or serfs was particularly dire; frequently bereft of family ties, they were often turned out of their homes just at that moment in their lives when they were in the greatest need of support. Periodically there were attempts to stop this practice, like a *ukase* of Catherine the Great which specifically forbade serf-owners to do this, but since it had few provisions for enforcement it probably did not change many people's behaviour. One does not imagine that the cast-off elderly lasted very long, especially in cold weather. And whether cast off or not, the elderly died in disproportionate numbers in famines, suggesting they often lacked sufficient social capital to warrant or insist on a share when food was scarce.[100]

DEATH

Women were often the managers of death in the early modern period. Despite the vicissitudes of their lives women did outlive their husbands more than the reverse. And throughout their lives, starting when they were very young, it was their job to take care of the sick, wash and lay out the dead and re-knit the social and familial fabric once they were gone (death was polluting, so lower-status people, such as women, tended to deal with it). Women also 'talked' to the dead more, or at least more openly, than men did; often one of their central duties was negotiating a particular family's relationship to its departed members through visiting or decorating graves, loud mourning rituals (everywhere associated with women), dreams, memento-keeping, household commemorations, memories and magic. To be sure, the work women put into death and dying was not always appreciated. Books on 'dying well' accused women of taking over the sickroom and distracting the dying person from coming to terms with his or her God.[101] Some found women's loud and histrionic mourning offensive and irreligious (see Chapter 6). Though they put much work into death and dying, in the general scheme of things women also tended to be remembered less than men. Partly this is because they died at more advanced ages, when the kin who might have taken care of (and paid for) arrangements to preserve their memories had either died or dispersed. The disparity also reflected the fact that women were deemed less important in life: it was harder to make a visible and individual imprint upon history when one was excluded from many of the activities by which men made their name.

Yet eighteenth-century women did not always submit easily to this regime of forgetting, especially if they had money. Rosa Farrugia of Malta put a lot of care, thought and money into preparing for death. In her will she bequeathed three houses to the Cospicua parish, the proceeds of which were to fund a total of eighty-nine masses a year to be said for her soul in perpetuity. They included:

> 2 high Masses with four torches on her grave and four candles on the altar
> 2 low Masses
> 1 high Mass with the exposition of the sacrament
> 1 low Mass every Friday
> 1 low Mass every first Monday of each month
> 7 low Masses on the seven days commemorating the Sorrows of Our Lady
> 12 low Masses during the Christmas novena
> 1 low mass on Christmas day.[102]

Farrugia was intent upon being remembered not just once or twice, but over and over throughout the year – and not just for a few years, but forever. Farrugia's vision was unusually expansive, but many women sought to immortalize their names in not dissimilar ways. Upper-class funerals, even for women, were often major public spectacles, with distributions to the local poor, funeral mementos, and impressive memorial stones. Women commissioned portraits for themselves that emphasized their most important achievements, such as good estate management, piety, their knowledge of science, their book collections, the number of children they had had or a particular body of professional knowledge and expertise they possessed (Plate 2). They also worked elaborate embroideries, built lavishly, or organized complicated charitable schemes. Sometimes their charitable acts speak volumes both about their own sense of identity and their notions about what other women were in need of. The 1701 last will and testament of Susannah Darnell of London, described as a 'singlewoman', meaning she had never married, includes the following clause:

> I give & bequeath to twelve young Maidens [that is, unmarried girls] that shall be borne and brought up with good virtuous honest and reputable parents living within the said parish of Giles [St. Giles in the Fields, London] the summe of twenty pounds a piece to place them out Apprentices to Sempstresses in London or Midd[lese]x.[103]

Darnell memorialized herself by helping provide for the economic independence of other women.

It is sometimes said that women's funerals focused on predictable feminine virtues but this was not universally the case. Some funeral sermons emphasized women's learning, or their influence among religious people. In Brunswick-Wolfenbüttel in Germany sermons for single women went out of their way to stress the exemplary service they provided for their natal families, which may seem condescending, but which struck at a central criticism of the never-married: that they contributed nothing to the public good. At least one sermon for a married woman focused on her numerous law-suits.[104] By the eighteenth century it was becoming common in some places to attach lengthy descriptions of a particular woman's achievements, complete with itemized lists of their charitable bequests on their memorial stone. Death also provided numerous opportunities for commemorating and celebrating the wide variety of family forms and institutions both women and men helped create in the early modern period. Women friends asked to be buried together. Nuns paid for memorial stones for other nuns. Close women friends who had never married endowed elaborate memorials for each other and wrote mournful commemorative poetry.

Death and its rituals also supplied the last chance (as it were) for playing out some of the less appealing features of early modern life. Litigation about burial costs was a common way for families to take revenge on a son-in-law whom they felt had mistreated his wife, sometimes all-too-clearly in belated compensation for interventions they failed to make when she was alive.[105] Death could also mark women's only partial assimilation into the cognate line (the family into which they married). In parts of traditional Hungary grave-markers show that wives were buried off to the side of burial grounds along with foundlings: outsiders in death as well as in life. Presumably this would have been especially true of women who had been childless.[106] Low or unfree status routinely translated into disrespect for people's mortal remains. Like anyone else, slaves wanted to be buried with dignity, with some sort of funeral service, in decent grave clothes, and either individually or with the people they felt closest to in life. In Brazil some owners tried to cut costs by simply leaving their slaves' bodies, naked and bereft of funeral rites, in swamps or on the beaches to be washed away in the tide. The Catholic Church, to its credit, objected strenuously to this, but the 'cheap' alternative was to bury one's slaves dishonourably in collective pit-graves, presumably with some underemployed padre mumbling who-knew-what over the bodies. Not unexpectedly, one of the central concerns of black confraternities in Brazil and elsewhere was to assure their members a decent burial.[107] Even Death, the great equalizer, registered status in the eighteenth century, and the tensions over that fact reached beyond the grave.

CONCLUSION

Given that so much was bound up with the forming and dissolving of families in the eighteenth century, they became a key locus for the exercise of authority as well as for strategizing, tension, insubordination, resistance, creativity and change. Women were rewarded in various ways for marrying and especially for bearing children; but they could also find themselves imperilled, in life, limb, purse and spirit, by the constraints and abuses of husbands, families and kin-groups. In this chapter we have been concerned to explore what women did in such situations, but we have also paid attention to context. Laws and customs affecting women and their property, divorce, and the like, were diverse, and some were demonstrably more favourable to women's (and often children's) interests than others. Enforcement was also very variable, dependent on convenience of access, commitment to the letter of the law, public opinion, the willingness of judges, *kadis* and the like to favour women over their male relatives, and an assortment of other factors. There are clear signs, especially from border areas like the Mediterranean, that some, perhaps increasing numbers of, women, both slave and free, were aware of this legal diversity, and tried to factor it into their plans. On the other hand, it is also quite evident that the laws, everywhere, were insufficient to overcome the real disadvantages of low status – indeed they were never intended to do so. People in trouble – slaves, abused wives, *agunah*, girls trying to escape arranged marriages, destitute single mothers and widows – took the drastic step of converting to Islam or Christianity from other faiths not primarily because of the intrinsic appeal of these religions, great though they might be, but because of the sheer lack of other options available to them.[108]

Three other concerns have animated this chapter. One, more a historio-graphical leitmotif than a real theme, is the way that slave or serf status affected key phases of the life cycle, and particularly the interplay of choice and coercion in relation to love, sex, companionship, marriage, childrearing (one's own and others' children), emancipation and death. Another concern is to examine and combat the allegations about the unusually low status of Muslim women that have been such a persistent feature of Christian European thought since the later seventeenth century, and which still have resonance today. This chapter does not argue that Muslim women's lives were in every way 'better' than those of other women. These societies were too complex, the problems of women too individual, to make such sweeping comparisons. By the same token there were some clear advantages for women in *sharia* law that were not, or were substantially less, available to women in much of Christian Europe. The most crucial of these were unusually robust women's property rights; the right of women to control their *mehr*, ready access to divorce and remarriage (albeit on asymmetric terms with men); custody rights over young children; and, at least for women in the cities and towns, unusually easy and cheap access to the law courts. If Christian women had known – if they had allowed themselves to know – how paltry their rights were in some of these areas by comparison with some of their near neighbours, would it have taken so long, especially in western Europe, to obtain access to divorce, child custody rights, and a wife's right to control her own money? It is a question worth pondering. The third concern is change over time. There is always a risk in a book like this of 'discovering' changes that any late medievalist will tell you actually happened centuries before. Nevertheless, there do seem to be some late seventeenth- and eighteenth-century shifts that were of real significance for the 'long' history of women and the family. Some of these are quite well-known, such as the new interest in tying romantic love and sensibility to marriage. Others are well known to specialists, such as the apparently new – or at least expanded – interest in 'romantic friendship' among women and the rise of *respectable* alternative living arrangements, in couples and single-sex groupings, for middle-class and elite women (they arose for other women too, but just not, for the most part, in association with respectability). Still other changes, such as the new preoccupation, enhanced by the print media, with issues to do with women and the law, and the dawning of the first calls for reform of the laws of marriage, are just now beginning to come to the attention of anyone other than a small cohort of legal historians.

Chapter 3

◆

SEXUALITY AND REPRODUCTION

Of all the cleavages that divide the lives and expectations of women of the twenty-first century from those of the eighteenth, the most funda-mental relate to death. In eighteenth-century Europe, the life expectancy at birth ranged between about twenty-five and thirty-five years, some four to five decades shorter than it is today. It was still shorter for poor people and slaves.[1] This did *not* mean, however, that most adults actually died aged thirty-five. In the eighteenth century the vast majority of deaths (two-thirds or more) occurred among children under the age of ten. This made childrear-ing a much more anxious and sorrowful enterprise than it tends to be today, but it also meant that, if one managed to survive past ten, one's likelihood of living a good deal longer was greatly enhanced, and the longer a person lived the more immunity she or he probably accumulated against lethal infectious diseases. People who survived to the age of thirty might well expect to live another twenty-five or thirty years, and most towns probably boasted a few people who lived into their eighties or even longer. Still, at any age this was a fragile and fearful demographic regime, one in which the deaths of teenagers, young adults and middle-aged people were much more common – and commonplace – than they are today. These groups were almost as susceptible as children to some kinds of epidemic diseases, and they were probably *more* susceptible simply to wearing out from hardship and toil.

The antidote in all times and places for death is, of course, reproduction, and before that, sex. Early modern people had little control over the voraci-ous appetites of death, but they could, and did, try to control the supply of new lives that came into the world. As has been true in many times and places, controlling and channelling women's sexuality was a major part of this larger project. However, such efforts gained in intensity in the sixteenth and seventeenth centuries, especially as a result of the Protestant Reformation and Catholic Counter-reformation. Protestant reformers zealously sought to import what they saw as biblical values into everyday life (then, as now, many of these involved sex), while Catholic reformers involved themselves in closer enforcement of the sacraments of the church, especially the sacrament of marriage. One result was more oversight of *male* sexuality, particularly of male homosexuals (sodomites) and, at least in Protestant countries, male adulterers and fornicators. But the heaviest impact, as we will see, was upon women, particularly women who had sex out of wedlock, and, by extension, their children.

THE DEATH OF CHILDREN

An infant born today has a considerably greater likelihood of living until aged sixty-five than an infant in the eighteenth century had of surviving its first year. Because death was so common among the young, having children was extremely physically and psychically fraught. To have a child, perhaps especially for women, is often to be drawn into an intense emotional connection, whether one wishes it or not. On average eighteenth-century mothers and fathers saw half their children die before they passed the age of ten. A single serious epidemic could carry off half, or even all, one's children in a few days.[2] The risks were great enough that some parents tried to shield themselves emotionally; this was one (though not the only) reason why many elite and middle-class people, and, in some places, even working people, sent out their children to wet-nurses – it meant that they barely saw, and hence, in theory, did not become attached to the baby during the period when it was most likely to die (the first year or so was especially dangerous). Some people were more successful at closing off their feelings than others, and it is certainly possible to find people (particularly, but not only, fathers) who appear to have been little affected by a son's or daughter's death. But we also find parents who were emotionally destroyed by the experience. One hundred and thirty-four people consulted Richard Napier, a renowned seventeenth-century English physician, in search of respite from uncontrollable grief. Fifty-eight of these people were mourning the deaths of children and, of that group, fifty-one (eighty-eight per cent) were mothers. Usually their deep sense of loss was reinforced by feelings of guilt. A mother named Joan Plotte contemplated suicide because, when her little son was dying and in terrible pain, she said of him, as many a parent faced with a visibly suffering child must have done, 'if he die, let him die'. She was obsessed with the thought that she might have 'caused' the boy's death by saying these six short words. As Napier put it: 'This thought troubleth her mind . . . [so she] careth not for her husband nor child but goeth into a corner to weep.' Another mother, Agnys Nueman, was still tormenting herself and in 'great grief' a year after her child's death because she felt 'she did not tend it well'.[3] In a lament from the island of South Uist in the Scottish Hebrides the grieving mother goes so far as to wish death on the children of a woman who blamed her for the death of her own:

> Yon woman who cast reproach on me, that I was losing my children I shall not ask for pain on thy soul, but that thou mayest know my affliction: That thy breasts be full and thy knee empty; I have buried five, Una and Jean, Morag and Anna, long haired Allan, which bereft me, which thinned my brown hair, and made slow my footstep.[4]

People did not necessarily experience death in a less complex way than we do today, even though it happened so often. And yet, there was also a good deal of callousness when it came to the deaths of children, especially those of other families. The deaths of children were *so* common that many people thought parents should simply submit to the will of God and 'get over' their grief. In a number of European folk traditions women who mourned too openly and too long over dead children were said to be inhibiting the child's passage to the other life, making it impossible for them to 'sleep peacefully', or even 'drowning' the child with their tears. The implication was that mourning too much was weak, self-centred, or even irreligious, especially if the baby was very young.

Official religious teachings did not necessarily offer much solace. Catholic (and, less consistently, Anglican) doctrine held that babies were depraved sinners, and unless the stain was washed away by Christian baptism they were forever cut off from paradise. This point was driven home by the rule that unbaptized babies could not be buried in consecrated ground (most other Protestant groups and the Orthodox were less rigid on this issue, while Muslims believed that babies were born in a state of sinlessness, and therefore went straight to heaven if they died).[5] For mothers and fathers who yearned for living children this doctrine must often have been deeply distressing, since many women bore stillborn babies or babies who died too soon after birth to be baptized. In effect it cut their dead children, to whom they were often already emotionally attached, out of their spiritual kinship system, and literally constructed the infants' bodies as polluting, akin to those of criminals or suicides, who were also buried on unconsecrated ground.

Women often sought ways to lighten the harshness of such teachings. We may imagine that many a midwife imagined – or claimed – that she had heard the baby draw a breath (baptism required that it be alive, even if only fleetingly) and that, in difficult births, some got very adept at administering the sacrament while the infant was still in the birth canal (baptism was the only sacrament that a lay-woman could administer, and even then it was only supposed to be performed if the baby was close to death). More spectacularly, the custom grew up in many parts of Catholic Europe (the Italian Peninsula, both rural and urban France, Trent, Bavaria, Flanders, and Savoy, and probably elsewhere) of staging 'temporary resurrections' of dead infants, who could then be baptized *en bloc* and reburied in village burial grounds near the rest of their lineage. There was, of course, much opposition to this from the religious hierarchy. In the mid-eighteenth century Pope Benedict XIV condemned the practice as a superstitious abuse, and it was still being denounced by French ecclesiastics as late as the early twentieth century. This is a particularly revealing example of the way the spiritual and emotional needs of mothers and fathers could, in practice, trump orthodox doctrine. In the modern day, ironically, bereaved parents won this argument – though not primarily out of concern for their feelings. The ancient doctrine of the unbaptized child or foetus as depraved and polluting due to original sin proved hard to reconcile with the anti-abortion movement's emphasis on the extreme innocence of the unborn. Consequently, in 1983, the Catholic Code of Canon Law adopted the originally Protestant position that 'the local ordinary can permit children whom the parents intended to baptize but who died before baptism to be given ecclesiastical funerals'.[6]

REPRODUCTIVE ACTS

Sex and the Single Woman

The best-known manifestation of what is sometimes called the 'new moralism'[7] of the sixteenth and seventeenth centuries was the mingled effort to define marriage more strictly (by insisting that couples get parental permission and marry in church, and by making annulments harder to obtain) and to crack down on sex out of wedlock. These initiatives were, of course, unevenly enforced across Europe, but nevertheless sufficiently widespread to constitute a cross-denominational trend. There is some evidence that the demands for church weddings initially had some success, especially in heavily Calvinist regions, but in many places that success was to be brief. So, for example, in

Scotland the kirk, by heavy use of shaming techniques directed against both male and female sexual delinquents, succeeded in getting the rates of illegitimacy down to about five per cent by around 1720; however, by the end of the century, at least in more industrialized regions, it had again become common for couples to move in together before they had their marriage solemnized by the kirk, or simply to have a layman witness their union.[8] Rising rates of informal unions and illegitimacy were, indeed, a feature of proto-industrial towns and villages virtually across Europe in the later eighteenth and nineteenth centuries, partly because young people were out of the direct control of adults and had a little bit of money to spend.[9]

In some other places the new notions of marriage never really took hold in the first place. In Orthodox Russia, which had its own, less systematic 'reformation', resistance to clerical oversight of marriage remained stiff throughout the eighteenth century, on the grounds that church weddings were costly and intrusive, and made divorce more difficult to obtain. In Lutheran Iceland, according to one historian, 'many (most?) rural Icelandic adults lived in *de facto* sexual unions for some period of their lives . . .'; meanwhile, Lutheran missionaries, come from the mainland, reported, in horrified tones, that most Icelanders considered it perfectly normal. In eighteenth-century Catholic Malta, couples and their families refused to view marriage as anything other than a personal matter. They often entered into clandestine marriages and separated at will. Courting couples usually had sex, and only married after the woman got pregnant, because neither partner was prepared to enter into indissoluble wedlock with a spouse who could not give them children (the last was a standard argument all over Christian Europe in favour of premarital sex). And these examples could be greatly multiplied.[10]

Attempts to 'shore up' or reinvent marriage focused a disproportionate amount of attention on women, particularly unwed mothers. From the sixteenth century on, especially in Protestant countries, they were increasingly subject to being whipped, turned out of their homes and jobs, stripped of honorific privileges (like the right to wear certain colours or types of ceremonial clothes), committed to workhouses, and treated like prostitutes. In early modern Sweden, women who bore children out of wedlock were supposed to pay a fine and perform public penance, and if they later married, they could not wear the bridal crown. Moreover, since the sight of them was alleged to cause children's diseases like rickets (rickets was called *höreskaver*, or 'whore's shingles'), they were sometimes required to wear a special 'whore's headdress', ostensibly so that people would know to keep their children away. In Baden-Baden, one of the German territories, the Margrave was insisting, as late as the 1750s, on savage beatings for women who became pregnant out of wedlock.[11] Catholic territories were, on the surface, less punitive: in the urban areas, though less in the rural ones, single mothers were encouraged to give up their child to foundling homes, and reintegrate back into society. But, increasingly, single mothers were kept track of, and, in time, *required* to give up their babies to a foundling home whether they wished to or not. In Russia rural priests called *zakashchiki* are said to have taken it upon themselves in the later eighteenth century to 'subject unwed mothers and women living alone to brutal inquisitions, punishments and fines', the latter, apparently, on the assumption that, if they were not already pregnant, they soon would be.[12]

The 'new moralism' undoubtedly brought misery and shame to many (which was, after all, part of the intention). It is more difficult to gauge how successful it was in permanently stigmatizing women who bore babies out of wedlock, had premarital sex, or entered into informal living-together arrangements. In eighteenth-century Sweden, bridal crown or no, most unwed mothers ultimately married, which suggests there was more sympathy for them than at first meets the eye. Or perhaps the shaming rituals backfired; after all, the women in question were people's daughters, sisters and sweethearts. A more sobering picture emerges from seventeenth- and early eighteenth-century Piedmont (now in Northern Italy). There, as in many parts of traditional Europe, a verbal promise to marry had long been considered sufficient to legitimize sexual relations. Many courting couples passed through more than one serially monogamous relationship before settling down into marriage with the person of their choice, and there were clear rules and norms for premarital sex which were enforced both by age-mates and families, and sometimes by the church courts. Usually when a woman got pregnant, marriage followed soon after. Even when it did not, children born out of wedlock were customarily recognized and supported by the father and took his name, which suggests that both mothers and babies were valued, whether or not a marriage had occurred. Though there was certainly a sexual double standard, and women's honour was more at risk than men's, fidelity seems to have been deemed more important to a woman's honour than virginity. Mothers of illegitimate children usually ended up married (often the dowry was provided by a former lover) and were integrated fairly seamlessly into society. So were their children. This is how things looked until around the end of the seventeenth century. But in the early decades of the eighteenth, the climate changed markedly and attitudes hardened. The Catholic Church stepped up the rhetoric on virginity for girls and church weddings for all, the sexual double standard became significantly more intense, oversight of morals turned more repressive, and women who bore children out of wedlock found themselves stigmatized in ways they had not been before. Fathers ceased either to acknowledge their out-of-wedlock children or support them, and illegitimate children were increasingly abandoned to foundling homes rather than being raised by mothers, fathers, or their natal kin. The vast majority of these babies undoubtedly died (see below).[13]

Still, there is much evidence that, over the course of the eighteenth century, many countries began to lose their appetite for punishing women for having sex and babies out of wedlock. Even in Protestant countries, almost always the most repressive, church penance was increasingly substituted for whippings, imprisonment and banishments. In Prussia fornication was decriminalized for pregnant women as early as 1765 (so as to remove what was thought of as an incentive to infanticide), and for everyone else in 1794. Most of the rest of the German territories either fully or partially decriminalized it between 1770 and 1830. Soon states were retreating from church penance as well. In Kurland on the Baltic, a ducal order of 1780 freed mothers of illegitimate children from church punishment also on the grounds that public shaming encouraged infanticide.[14] In many countries, both Catholic and Protestant, mothers of illegitimate children stopped being barred from receiving charity sometime in the late eighteenth or early nineteenth century, and many unwed mothers raised their illegitimate children through a combination of wage work, help from relatives (an understudied but crucial element when thinking about the status of unwed mothers and their children), and charitable relief. During the French Revolution there was even a short-lived effort to eliminate the legal disabilities on bastards, on the impeccably individualist, but religiously unorthodox, grounds that children should not have to suffer for the sins of their parents. It did not last, because both Napoleon and the Catholic Church opposed it.[15] More informal shaming and blaming practices continued of course, aimed both at unwed mothers and at their illegitimate children, but the tendency in much of Europe was to abolish or greatly diminish formal judicial or ecclesiastical punishments at least by the early nineteenth century if not before.

Illegitimacy in the Ottoman Empire

In the Ottoman Empire having children out of wedlock was associated primarily with slave concubines, who, as we have seen, gained certain rights by becoming pregnant, though fewer than would have accrued to a 'real' wife. There was little or no public anxiety about these women bearing children (at least if their master was the father) because they were seen as being under firm household and patriarchal control. The main opposition to a slave concubine having her master's children likely came from the man's 'real' wife, especially since the slave's children stood to inherit equally with her own. This would seem to be a formula for considerable conflict, and we know very little about how it worked in practice. It would be naïve to imagine, just because sex between masters and their concubines carried potential 'rights', that it did not sometimes bring down misery on the heads of women slaves and perhaps their children too.

Sex *outside* the domain of marriage and concubinage was a *zina* crime, which, if proved, theoretically carried the death penalty for both parties. However, the general trend in the early modern period was for *muftis* to remove sexual crimes like fornication, adultery and rape from the realm of *zina* (unlawful sexual intercourse, which might have resulted in execution by stoning or castration in the case of rape) and instead have the perpetrators pay an indemnity. Babies conceived out of wedlock or before marriage were generally readily legitimized, and even adulterine children were, in practice, considered legitimate. The notion of *zina* crime was also not deemed to apply either to prostitutes or their clients. There is only one known execution for a *zina* crime in Istanbul in the entire two-century span from 1600 to 1800: a couple who were stoned to death in 1680. The man was Jewish and the woman a Muslim and it seems probable that anti-Semitic prejudice, and the fact that this was a period of considerable popular and religious unrest, were the major contributing factors. Unmarried motherhood was never approved of in free women, however, and it sometimes resulted, from at least the sixteenth century on, in putting the woman under surveillance, or into the custody of provincial officials.[16]

Birth control and abortion

Attempts to control birth were probably widespread, and by the eighteenth century there is clear evidence from parish and other statistics that they were beginning to work. By the late seventeenth or eighteenth centuries declines can be seen among the French, Venetian, Milanese and Genoese aristocracies and the Genevan bourgeoisie; while by the early nineteenth century, large parts of France, two Danish provinces, Latvia, the city of St. Petersburg, Gotland, several Hungarian counties and a province in East Serbia were also showing pretty unmistakable signs of the use of fertility controls.[17] The main techniques that could actually be depended upon to work, at least some of the time, were *coitus interruptus*, where the man withdraws before ejaculation (it was, however, a sin, and some said a mortal sin); refraining from sexual relations most or all of the time; and prolonged breast-feeding. Condoms were also known, but seem largely to have been used by men who patronized prostitutes. There were some more fanciful methods. A recent study of fornication cases in the seigniorial courts of eighteenth-century Hungary yields such 'contraceptive practices' as burying the afterbirth from a previous birth in a pot in the ground; washing one's apron in the new moon and tying knots into its strings; wearing peas in one's boots; or serving one's husband the smoked genitals of a gelded horse.[18] These are probably typical of folk birth-control measures across Europe, useless, to be sure, but indicative of a widespread but unmet desire for greater reproductive control.

Early-term abortion was apparently quite widespread and likely more effective than attempts to inhibit conception. Prior to quickening, or the perceptible movement of the foetus in the womb, which usually occurs around the end of the fourth month, most people considered the foetus to be a part of the woman's body rather than a distinct person or soul. Abortifacient herbs such as savin, rue or pennyroyal, were viewed as legitimate ways to 'clear obstructions' and restore a woman's 'normal' menstrual flow. The resulting abortion was usually experienced, like many early miscarriages today, as a heavy menstrual period rather than as the termination of a pregnancy. This continued to be the majority view throughout the eighteenth century. In fact the term 'abortion' was most often confined to the post-quickening loss of the foetus, whether purposeful or as a result of a miscarriage. There *were* theologians in the early modern period who believed that ensoulment occurred at the moment of conception (or, more usually, a few hours after), and hence that abortion was sinful at any stage. One early modern legal system, the German Imperial Code, took this view and forbade abortion at all gestational stages. But in the eighteenth century the majority view, ratified by Protestants, by *Hanafi* Muslim law, and by most Catholic theologians, including most of the popes going back for centuries, held that the ensoulment of the infant occurred only at quickening. *Hanafi* jurists went so far as to grant a pregnant woman the right to an abortion up to the fourth month, even if her husband objected.[19] In sum, then, almost everyone agreed that abortion was neither criminal nor worthy of ecclesiastical sanctions *if it occurred before quickening*, a moment, of course, known best to the woman herself.[20]

Abortion post-quickening was much more problematic. It was also much more likely to be criminalized, and, in the early modern period, it increasingly carried the death penalty. As is true today, most of the women who found themselves resorting to post-quickening abortions (abortions after about the middle of the second trimester), were young, ignorant and unmarried. They probably also included a disproportionate number of raped servants or slaves. But they were not the only ones. Married women, especially after one or more particularly painful or debilitating birthing experiences, sometimes developed an overwhelming fear of undergoing another pregnancy. While death in childbirth was less common in the early modern period than used to be thought (see below), it was still much more common than it is today, and childbirth a good deal more painful, and often, more prolonged. It is not difficult to imagine any number of terrifying, and, in some cases, crippling, childbirth experiences that would put one off pregnancy for a very long time; and yet, all faiths considered it a sin for a woman to refuse her husband sex. It was a conundrum that drove some women – and couples – to desperate measures. Methods for inducing late-term abortions were diverse and harrowing. They included swallowing various kinds of poison, throwing oneself downstairs (or, a common technique of unwilling fathers, repeatedly punching or kicking a woman in the stomach), pushing a quill or other sharp object up into the uterus, massive bloodletting, and manual tearing of the placental membranes. Many women were left dead or permanently maimed as a result.

LOVE AND MURDER

Childbirth and midwifery

One can easily receive the impression from the older textbooks that pre-modern women routinely died during labour. They *did* die in childbirth in considerably larger numbers than modern European women do, but it was still a relatively unusual event. Even during the prime childbearing years only about one in five women's deaths came as a result of childbirth; women were far more likely to succumb to infectious diseases like smallpox, dysentery, typhus, malaria, tuberculosis and the plague. The number of mothers who died was also drastically out of proportion to the number of children who died. For every one woman who died in childbirth between twenty and a hundred babies perished in the first few years or so of life.[21] Some of the best evidence we have for the relatively low level of maternal mortality comes from eighteenth-century midwives' own case reports. Catharina Schrader (1693–1740), a Dutch Frisian midwife and surgeon, delivered between three thousand and four thousand babies over the course of her career, during which only twenty of the women died, a maternal mortality rate of five to seven per thousand deliveries. Childbirth in rural areas (like much of Friesland) was safer than urban areas, though. The maternal mortality rate in late seventeenth-century London was about twenty-one per thousand deliveries.[22] Today in the industrialized countries significantly fewer than one woman per thousand dies in childbirth, so the death-rate in childbirth in eighteenth-century Friesland (in Schrader's practice anyway) was over five times higher than it is in modern Europe (over twenty times higher in London). One hears a statistic like this and thinks 'most women died in childbirth'. But it is misleading to take the present as our comparison, because the base rate of maternal death today is so minuscule. Eighteenth-century women had more to fear from disease than from childbirth.

That does not, however, mean that women did not sustain other kinds of injuries. A recent report on maternal health in the developing world asserts that 'for every woman who dies [in childbirth] an estimated 30 to 50 women survive the same complications, but with short- or long-term disabilities', with the latter including infertility, uterine prolapse, depression and vesico-vaginal fistulas. Just to take the last of these, some estimates put the prevalence today of childbirth-related fistulas at 1 in 100 deliveries or higher in regions with particularly inadequate maternal health services. A fistula is a complication of prolonged and difficult childbirth where cut-off of blood supply to the mother results in holes in the vaginal wall, followed by chronic uncontrollable leakage of urine or faeces or both. In the developed world fistula is generally precluded by caesarian section or repairable after the fact by surgery. Where it is not preventable, or where surgery is unavailable or prohibitively expensive, as in some parts of the less-developed world today, fistula often results in the repudiation or shunning of women by their husbands, relatives, children and community. It can be the source of almost unbearable shame and incalculable misery for women.[23] There was no surgical intervention for fistula in the early modern world, nor were caesarians (other than post mortem) a real alternative. Women may not have died of childbirth in the numbers we used to think, but up to a quarter of them experienced other distressing, painful, and in some cases, devastating, *sequelae*. It was rational to be afraid.

Pictorial and other evidence from Europe and the Middle East suggest that early modern women gave birth surrounded by other women, often gathered in what look like enthusiastic celebrations (see the front cover of this book). Historians have often seen lying-in gatherings as evidence of female solidarity as well as of women's control of the birth process. Early modern childbirth undoubtedly *was* sometimes an occasion for networking and reaffirming secret or semi-secret married women's sexual and reproductive knowledge.

Lying-in gatherings complemented a larger system that often gave pregnant women greater access to charity than other women, as well as more nourishing food, and a greater right to good treatment both from their husbands and from the authorities; in short, it accorded women who were about to give or had just given birth special privileges and respect.[24] On the other hand, lying-in gatherings were more common among the better off than the poor, who in some places were lucky to be allowed a temporary place in the local poorhouse so as not to have to have their baby in the street. Russian peasant women often gave birth in the fields or woods, and because childbirth was considered polluting, they also regularly gave birth in bathhouses.[25] Lying-in gatherings could also be quite coercive. Midwives in many parts of Europe were urged to interrogate unmarried women at their time of greatest pain and fear about who the father of the baby was, and even to tell them they were going to die in order to get them to confess. And they were occasions for exclusion as well as inclusion. Often only married women attended them, and only people of the same religious group; failing to invite someone to a lying in, or failing to attend, were potent ways to indicate hostility or difference. Women who had visible deformities were sometimes banned from appearing in the streets where pregnant women might see them (reflecting the general theory, discussed in Chapter 1, that shocks to a pregnant woman's sensitivities would affect her baby *in utero*). It is most unlikely that these women would have been welcome at lying-in gatherings either. As Laura Gowing has rightly remarked, 'women's authority over the body divided them as much as it united them'.[26]

It is often said that the eighteenth century represented a period of decline for midwives, as man-midwives and physicians took over their practices and systematically undermined women's claims to special knowledge.[27] A general devaluation of women's own knowledge of reproductive matters, not to mention their phenomenological experience of illness, clearly was part of the rise of professional medicine.[28] However, at least where midwives are concerned, the decline thesis is probably wrong. The trend Europe-wide was rather for the regularization and professionalization of midwifery, a development which, on balance, seems to have benefited midwives, mothers and their babies. Midwifery was already quite a prestigious profession for women in some places, and some late seventeenth- and eighteenth-century practitioners did their best to enhance it further, in ways that look very like what male professionals were doing at the same time. Elizabeth Cellier (fl. 1670–1688), an Englishwoman, put forward a plan in 1687 for a Royal Midwifery Hospital, a corporation of 2,000 midwives, a sequence of instructional lectures in midwifery, and a system whereby poor women could receive obstetrical care.

A French midwife, Mme de Coudray (1715–1794), was behind a vast scheme of educating French midwives under royal patronage. She published a midwifery textbook, invented an obstetrical model for teaching about childbirth, and travelled indefatigably across France from 1751 to 1783, teaching thousands of young women how to be midwives. Luisa Rosada (fl. 1765–1771) used her post as midwife for the Spanish Royal House for Abandoned Children, a Madrid foundling hospital, to try to compete with local man-midwife-surgeons in the treatment of difficult births, and to publicize her own views on how to treat the problem of women unable to expel the afterbirth.[29] In Naples a midwife named Teresa Ployant wrote a midwifery manual, *Breve Compendio dell'Arte Ostetricia* (Short Compendium on the Art of Obstetrics) (1787) in which she urged other midwives to increase their scientific knowledge, become more professional, stave off the invasion of male doctors into the field of midwifery and so 'bring births to a happy outcome and at the same time save women's modesty'.[30] Often the state and male doctors were quite supportive of such efforts, part of a dawning pro-natalist movement that would become much stronger in the nineteenth and early twentieth centuries.[31] Johan von Hoorn of Sweden, a physician, instituted training courses for Stockholm's midwives as early as 1708, and later headed up a national midwifery school; the earliest effort of Ottoman reformers to offer professional education to women came in 1843 during the Tanzimat period, and consisted of setting up a training programme for midwives in the Imperial Medical School, sited in a former palace.[32]

Maternal and infant mortality did begin to fall perceptibly in a few countries in the later eighteenth century and even more in the early nineteenth, and it is very likely that some of it was owing to better and more consistent training of midwives, as Irvine Loudon has persuasively argued with respect to England.[33] Less positively, it has been argued that tying midwifery more closely to the state, and sometimes, as in Italy, the Catholic Church, made midwives less responsive to the needs and concerns of their clients. This took on added significance from the early nineteenth century on, as many European states began, for the first time, to criminalize pre-quickening (early-term) abortions as well as to police the use and availability of abortifacients, partly by keeping close tabs on the licensing of midwives.[34]

Love and daughters

Today most people assume that love is a birthright of all children, and that it should be shared out in a fairly egalitarian way. Though love was certainly an important feature of eighteenth-century adult–child relations, it was considerably less democratically distributed than it is today, and not all children were deemed to have the same right to it. This is particularly evident with slave children. It was perfectly legal in parts of Europe, and in many, though not all, of the European colonies, to sell young children away from their parents. Indeed, in some places it was common, a way to 'democratize' slave-owning, since children had a much lower market price than adults because they could not do as much work, and they were much more likely to die.[35] Obviously this practice is fundamentally inconsistent with the belief that all children have a roughly equal right to be loved and nurtured. Slave-children may seem an extreme case, but the assumption of a hierarchy of worthiness to be loved extended broadly across the population. Orphans or half-orphans, who made up between ten and thirty per cent of children under fifteen, were routinely 'placed' as servants in other people's homes at very young ages, or simply treated as servants by whomever took them in – even by their kin – which often translated into more beatings and sexual abuse and less access to food, warmth, decent clothes, an education and love.[36] They were also rather often turned out to join the tens of thousands of homeless and unwanted children found across Europe, semi-starved urchins who lived by begging, theft and early prostitution, and died young, mourned by few. Bastards of both sexes, and those with disabilities or obvious defects, were, in many countries, at the bottom of the 'love and nurture' hierarchy: a large percentage of them died of neglect or outright infanticide while still babies. Non-orphans did not always have it much better. Families sometimes sold their children, particularly their daughters, into debt-slavery (in Russia until about 1723; in the Caucasus into the nineteenth century) or indentured servitude (common in western Europe and the New World, and found in the Ottoman Empire as well) so as to realize some cash, erase a debt, and sometimes, for the truly destitute, in an effort to ensure the children got fed. They also pimped them. The 'eleven or twelve-year old' Venetian girl named Anzoletta, whom Jean-Jacques Rousseau and a friend 'bought' from her 'infamous mother' (Rousseau's words) around 1741 with the intention of sharing her between them sexually, could not have been so unusual. In eighteenth-century Paris, and, no doubt elsewhere, poor families with beautiful daughters often introduced them to prostitution, or, as they no doubt hoped, courtesan-ship, via a well-established system of contacts in the Opéra and other city institutions. One can deplore this in the abstract, but it was the only chance most of these girls and their families would ever have to move out of the semi-starved urban proletariat into something approximating comfort.[37]

Not all of this is inconsistent with love. But it does suggest that many people did not let themselves 'love' children – even their own – so much that it inhibited their ability to make hard-headed decisions about broader family interests. It also reflects the sad fact that parents often died young, leaving children who could not be easily integrated into other people's already crowded and often resource-deprived households. It is conceivable, too, that the high ratio (by our standards) of children to adults in all early modern societies – even with the high infant mortality rates – meant that the finite amount of available love simply attached 'naturally' (at least as early modern people would have seen it) to children to whom God had already seen fit to assign a higher status in terms of gender, birth-order, race, status or rank. Autobiographies, as well as numerous court cases, suggest that children (including orphans and slave-children) yearned for love, and often worked hard to try to love their parents or foster-parents, masters and even owners. But it was rather frequently the case that they did not receive it back in any form very recognizable to us today.

We might suppose that a mother would be her daughter's most important support, if that mother lived. But a natural sympathy between mother and daughter cannot be assumed, especially in societies where men monopolize much of the power. It was a commonplace of the time that mothers favoured their sons, because women's prestige and influence in the family she married into – and good treatment from her husband – depended heavily upon bearing male children and keeping them alive. Nadezhda Durova (1783–1866), the most famous Russian woman soldier of the Napoleonic War, had a mother who had passionately yearned for a son, and never could bring herself to love her daughter. She was both abusive and neglectful toward her infant daughter, once even throwing her out of the window of a moving carriage. As Durova matter-of-factly put it, 'my existence poisoned her life'.[38] Maternal neglect or dislike of daughters was, sadly, not uncommon. However, the seventeenth and eighteenth centuries did see a new interest in the rearing of both girls and boys, one that pointed in the direction of more modern conceptions of childhood, with their relatively egalitarian ethos and emotional/nurturant focus. New educational institutions proliferated, and so did children's books, and both reached out to girls (see Chapters 7 and 8). The end of the eighteenth century also saw a burgeoning humanitarian interest in the plight of slaves and serfs, and a new focus both on the inhumanity of breaking up slaves' families, and on the sexual abuse of girls and women. Still later, campaigns in some European countries to abolish child-labour sought to enshrine the principle that childhood should be a cosseted, preparatory time that allowed children to develop into individuals with their own needs and desires. But these moves in the directions of more egalitarian and individualistic conceptions of love and nurturance (and new demands upon poor mothers, who often had to work longer hours when their children could no longer contribute financially) were barely beginning in the eighteenth century.

Child-murder and abandonment

In many times and places girl babies have not survived infancy in the same numbers as their brothers, due either to outright infanticide or to differential neglect.[39] The natural human sex ratio at birth all over the world is about 1.03 to 1.06/1.0, that is, between 103 and 106 boys are born for every 100 girls, though because boys tend to be less robust and more accident-prone than girls, the sex ratio tends to even out by late adolescence. Local studies in regions as diverse as England, Tuscany, Bavaria, Ireland and Russia in the early modern period show sex ratios that are quite far off that mark. So, for example, in Willingham in East Anglia in the late seventeenth and first half of the eighteenth century, the sex ratio *at baptism* for babies born to couples married in the village rose as high as 1.49 to 1.50 (in other words, 149 boys were baptized for every 100 girls). Baptism typically took place a week or so after the infant was born, so the data suggest strongly that something had happened to a good percentage of girl babies in the intervening few days between birth and baptism. The most likely explanation is purposeful culling.[40] Similar patterns can be found episodically in other parts of Europe in the seventeenth, eighteenth and nineteenth centuries, though they tend to be less pronounced in urban areas. Other practices also likely affected child sex ratios. It was customary in many parts of Europe for girls to be weaned off the breast earlier than boys and they were also more likely to be sent away to a wet-nurse. Both practices would have disproportionately increased girls' mortality. Historians differ on how common the differential neglect or outright killing or abandoning of girls (or, for that matter, boys) was, and some point to other explanations, such as under-registration of girl children. There is even evidence from Spanish Galicia that some families there practised daughter preference. But this last must have been rare. It is pretty evident that some girls in eighteenth-century Europe never got a chance at life, just because they were girls.[41]

But the whole issue is complicated by the fact that child-murder or murderous neglect by married people was surprisingly widely condoned, virtually impossible to police, and rarely punished (the story for unmarried women was rather different as we will see). The evidentiary problems were real. Significant numbers of babies were stillborn or died of natural causes very soon after birth, and early modern forensic science, while it *could* tell if an infant had had its throat slit, could not plausibly distinguish between natural death and death by smothering, starvation, exposure or deliberate mishandling of the umbilical cord. The deliberate killing or abandonment of infants had long been frowned upon by pious people of all the main European and Middle Eastern religious traditions. Islam had (and has) a particularly strong antipathy to female infanticide and both the Qur'an and the *hadiths* condemn all infanticide, including when it is undertaken due to parental hardship. One famous and bitter passage in the Qur'an frames the issue in terms of a dramatic dialogue on the Day of Judgment in which the murdered infant herself is invited to speak as if in a court of law:

> When the sun is overthrown, And when the stars fall . . .
> And when the girl-child that was buried alive is asked
> For what sin she was slain
> . . . [Then] every soul will know what it hath made ready.

Medieval Muslim saints often demonstrated their sanctity by rescuing female infants slated for murder by their families.[42] Jews and some early Christians also condemned the practice (though the Bible never clearly does), and in medieval times the Christian clergy both periodically excoriated neonate killing from the pulpit and made its perpetrators do penance (usually a lengthy period on bread and water).

But it is far from clear how effective verbal condemnation was in practice. Indeed, the evidence suggests that a good proportion of the population saw infanticide as part of an arsenal of strategies parents used to save their other children from starvation, and that it was probably acceptable, at least to some degree, in less straitened circumstances as well. The right to kill one's offspring (or, more likely, just to let them die) was part of a kind of implied *patria potestas* that most people convinced themselves to overlook, largely because it was hard to think of an alternative. How widespread was such behaviour? Gregory Hanlon, who has made a rare effort to apply statistical techniques to the practice of marital infanticide in the early modern period, estimates that in early modern Tuscany in 'bad' (that is, food-scarce) years, from a quarter to a third of live births to married couples ended in infanticide, though we should stress that this was not under normal conditions.[43] Other estimates are more impressionistic, though based on a lot of anecdotal evidence. High rates of child-killing or murderous neglect are suspected for the Netherlands during the Napoleonic Wars, in nineteenth-century Bavaria, and in early modern Russia, among other places. Hardship was not the sole motive. Slave families seem to have been particularly prone to infanticide; it has been argued that Russian slaves practised it 'on a large scale'. New World slave-women were well known for practising both abortion and infanticide, attributed by historians today, and some observers at the time, to an unwillingness to bear rapists' babies, as well as reluctance to bring up children in a condition of bondage.[44]

Early modern people were faced with some horrible choices. Child-killing, fatal neglect and abandonment were undertaken in a real world of scant food resources, in which adding another baby imperilled the lives of older, healthier children. Parental love for the children with better chances sometimes trumped the natural desire to have all one's children survive, especially if an infant seemed sickly, underweight, in pain, or unlikely to live anyway. The survival of parents also sometimes hung in the balance, and parents had good reason to think that if they died their other children's chances of survival would be greatly diminished. This was not some rationalization either, as famine mortality patterns show. Chronic food deprivation, coupled with a high natural child mortality rate also seems, at least in some families, to have created a different and more ambivalent attitude toward sickly babies than is common today. Late nineteenth-century Russian doctors struggled with mothers who claimed that it was 'God's will' that a certain child should die. In the late eighteenth and early nineteenth centuries both poor people and elites often viewed the high infant mortality rate as a kind of 'gift' to poor parents, since it diminished the number of mouths to feed. The only real difference was that secularizing elites and the middle classes increasingly spoke the language of Thomas Malthus while poor parents continued to use the language of divine will. We also need to consider the other side of the coin. The same parents who decided to stop feeding or expose an already sickly child also loved their other children enough to starve themselves so the children could eat the little food there was. To parents it was not a question of love or absence of love, but a question of survival, a kind of child triage.[45] Those who are not faced with such impossible choices should not rush too quickly to condemn them.

Infanticidal single mothers

Though infant-killing was often condoned among married people, or at least deemed almost impossible to control by resort to the law, infanticide (or alleged infanticide) by unwed mothers became a locus of high anxiety in the early modern period, part of the more generalized effort to promote formal church weddings. Between the sixteenth and the eighteenth centuries many countries put in place punitive new laws designed to punish child-murder by single mothers. At first these were largely confined to Protestant countries or Catholic countries abutting on them, that is chiefly northwestern and central Europe. Later they spread more widely to other Catholic countries, to Orthodox Russia and, still later, to the Ottoman Empire. Typically these laws made infanticide a capital crime if it was not already, associated it closely with unwed mothers (many infanticide laws specified that *only* unmarried women could be convicted of the crime), and, most crucially, eliminated the need to prove that the mother had knowingly and wilfully done away with her newborn. The 1624 English infanticide law is typical. If a dead baby was found and it could be shown that an unwed mother had concealed its birth, execution was mandatory, even if the child had likely died of natural causes or been stillborn. Eliminating the need to prove that a woman had actually killed her baby greatly enhanced the likelihood of conviction. Of course, it also increased the probability of miscarriages of justice, but this could be and was rationalized by reference to passages like Deuteronomy 22:13–21 which directs that women found not to be virgins at marriage should be stoned to death. In some continental countries there was also increased use of torture against suspects (and usually only single women were suspects) which further contributed to convictions, since people routinely confess under torture to crimes they have not committed. The presumption of guilt led to a surge in executions of unmarried women, sometimes in exceptionally cruel ways, including burning at the stake (in Ireland, but only for a brief period); slow and agonizing death by impalement (parts of Poland); torture followed by execution (Belgium) and breaking on the wheel (Russia). It is not clear how many women died as a result of these laws, but it was certainly in the thousands, Europe-wide. The standards of evidence were so low that, in many places, women accused of infanticide were more likely to be convicted and executed than accused witches.[46] The presumption of guilt and disdain for due process generally did not apply in the case of married people. If a married woman or married couple did come under suspicion of child-killing or abandonment the usual stringent rules of evidence tended to be applied, which, given the high natural infant mortality rate, and people's unwilling-ness to testify against family members or delve into what went on in private households, meant that most were acquitted or the case never came to trial (see Voices from the Past 3.1).

Given the fairly informal attitudes of many Europeans toward marriage and premarital sex (see above), it is hardly surprising that there were many misgivings about this new and very selective form of judicial severity. Almost from the beginning there was discomfort with singling out unwed, often poor girls or women for conviction and execution when their seducers (or rapists), got off with fines, brief imprisonment or no punishment at all.[47] Moreover, whatever it might say in the Bible, a lot of people, even Calvinists, did not believe that women who had premarital sex deserved to die. For some time the opposition tended to be individualized however, with disturbances (presumably by relatives) at women's executions, pamphlet attacks on particular convictions deemed to be especially unjust, occasional jury nullification, and widespread use of reprieves and pardons.[48] However, in the eighteenth century distress at the treatment accorded to allegedly infanticidal women merged into a series of larger critiques. Enlightened *philosophes*, most notably the Milanese philosopher, Cesare Beccaria, launched a frontal attack on the use of judicial torture, and, in Beccaria's case, capital punishment, on the grounds that they made a mockery of the usual standards of evidence (especially the truth of confessions) and lacked both humanity and deterrent power. People began taking a new interest in legal consistency and due process, and regarding biblically based sex-crimes, and especially biblically based punishments for sex-crimes, with a newly skeptical eye.

Soon this began to affect conviction rates. In country after country, though at differing speeds, judges (and juries, where they existed) refused to convict, and sometimes to try infanticide cases in the first place, unless there was evidence of actual violence. And even when there was such evidence, accused women or their lawyers often successfully argued for extenuating circumstances, including postpartum dementia. By the second half of the eighteenth century many states had begun to replace the most draconian punishments with imprisonment, banishment or fines. Austria abolished the death penalty for infanticide (and other crimes) in 1787, replacing it with hard labour.[49] In England and some of the German territories, from an early date, pretexts had been found to acquit some women, even when the letter of the law said they should die. Conviction rates in London's Old Bailey, the central criminal court of London, took a dive as early as the 1710s and never really recovered. In many of the decades between 1710 and 1800 ninety to one hundred per cent of the accused were acquitted.[50] In the case of England the infanticide law was reformed in 1803 to make the standards of evidence closer to those for other kinds of murder (meaning there had to be some actual evidence that a wilful murder had occurred). During the late

VOICES FROM THE PAST 3.1

The unreformed infanticide law: two cases at the Old Bailey

The Old Bailey was the central criminal court of London. The infanticide law of 1624 mandated execution if a woman was unmarried, had given birth alone and in secret and the baby was found dead (see Case 1). Defendants who were married, on the other hand, were virtually never convicted either of infanticide or murder, even if the evidence (as in Case 2) seemed to point strongly to their having had a hand in the child's death.

Case 1. Trial of Joan Blackwell, Oct. 15, 1679

. . . The next [defendant] seemed to be an object of Compassion to most People present, a poor young Wench lodging about Thames street, betrayed (as she alledged) by a promise of Marriage and getting her with Child, which being perceived by the Woman that she lodged with, to whom she confessed the truth thereof, just when she came to fall in Labour about 9 or 10 a Clock in the Night, this . . . [landlady], fearing some charge or trouble might happen to her, who had entertain'd her, cruelly turned [Joan Blackwell] out of doors . . . In this sad condition in the street, and without any help was this poor Creature [the defendant] delivered, and being found lying as one half dead by the [night] watch, and her condition perceived; a midwife was called, who found the Child dead, but not separated from her Body, when she came to her; who asking her if it were still-born, the Prisoner both then and now said, it was not, for she heard it cry, but denied that she intended or used any wilful means to make away the Life of it nor did there any signs of Violence appear save only some little spots or marks of a Bruise or Pinch on the Throat, which some conceive might be occasion'd Involuntarily in struggling to Promote its Birth; by an ignorant Woman in her circumstances: however [it] being a Bastard Child, and the law making it death in that case for any woman to be delivered alone without calling help, she was thereupon found Guilty.

Old Bailey Online Reference: t16791015-2

Case 2. Trial of Alice Sawbridge, July 13, 1693

Alice Sawbridge, Wife of Thomas Sawbridge, of Islington, was tried for murdering her Male-Infant Child on the 20th of June last; the Child was found in a Clay-pit full of water swimming [i.e. floating] on the top of the Water by some Workmen that were at work in the Clay-pit; they thought it to be a dead Dog at first, but when they took it out of the water, it proved to be a Child, and the Child of the Prisoner, as she confessed in the hearing of several Credible Witnesses, who were sworn for the King [i.e. who testified in court]; and that she would not give any account why she so disposed of the Child, and none was present at the Labour; there was no proof against her that she murdered the Child, which the Law provides should be made appear; and the Child was no Bastard; so she was acquitted .

Old Bailey Online Reference: t16930713-11

eighteenth and first half of the nineteenth centuries a similar softening of attitudes occurred in France, the Netherlands, Ireland, Germany, Corsica and the Baltic lands. Most countries eliminated the more brutal punishments, along with torture, and a number explicitly abolished capital punishment for infanticide. This is a striking instance of the impact on the lives of young women of the secular retreat from biblically inspired punishments and the new preference for judicial consistency and due process. Child-killing continued to be seen as the crime of unwed mothers, however. And until birth control and abortion were legalized (most countries did this only in the twentieth century), it remained one of the commonest crimes of which single women were accused.

The foundling homes

Apart from singling out unmarried women for exemplary punishment the main response to infant-killing, whether by the married or the unmarried, was institutional rather than judicial. People were genuinely upset (and who would not be?) by the spectacle of dead, almost certainly unbaptized, babies cast upon trash heaps, thrown down the sewers, or floating by in the rivers, and the clergy and city elites soon hit upon an alternative. The first foundling hospital is said to have been established in Rome in the thirteenth century 'to end the scandal of women throwing babies into the Tiber River'.[51] They had spread to a number of Italian cities by the High Renaissance and into France and Austria by at least the sixteenth century. By the eighteenth century they had crossed over into Protestant countries, and soon all major Protestant cities had one, including London, Dublin (Ireland was under Protestant rule and so was the foundling hospital), Copenhagen, Stockholm, Berlin and Amsterdam and indeed most Dutch cities. So did Orthodox Moscow and St. Petersburg and by the first third of the nineteenth century they had also been established in (largely) Orthodox Romania and Greece and Muslim Cairo.[52]

Everywhere where there were foundling homes enormous numbers of children ended up in them. By the eighteenth century the numbers were staggering. The Milan hospital took in more than 73,000 children over the course of the eighteenth century, while the Spedale degli Innocenti of Florence took in over 25,000 in the last quarter of the eighteenth century alone. The Foundling Hospital in London took in more than 15,000 children in the late 1750s and early 1760s, though admissions were sharply curtailed after that. The Casa da Roda of Porto, Portugal admitted more than 60,000 in the eighteenth century. The Moscow and St. Petersburg foundling hospitals, founded in 1764 and 1770 respectively, had admitted between them over 80,000 children by 1800. By the middle of the nineteenth century, more than 100,000 babies were being abandoned to foundling homes every year across Europe. Though the rhetoric held that foundling homes mainly served unwed mothers, most hospitals took it for granted that a significant minority of the babies were actually legitimate.[53] We occasionally glimpse the human side of this. In the 1780s Jean François Bourgoanne, a traveller in Cadiz, Spain reported seeing (or hearing of) 'a poor widow [who] came to the Hospitium [an institution that was part hospital, part prison and part foundling home] to procure her five children to be received'.[54] A widow with five young and presumably not-yet-earning offspring would be a problem even in the event that she had had supportive and comfortably off kin. But the heavy resort to foundling hospitals also reflects the disintegration of family ties typical of many of the migratory poor in the late eighteenth and nineteenth centuries (and typical of propertyless people in all periods of history). Such people, whether married or not, often lacked the linkages, particularly to other female relatives, that would have made it possible to bridge the 'care gap', the period when the children needed care and feeding, but the mother had to work. The foundling hospitals soon became part of the survival calculus of the poor, whether married or not.[55]

Foundling hospitals were one of the great institutional tragedies of the early modern period. The reason is the staggering death rate, particularly of very young children (older children did a good deal better, and often their parents came back for them). In the early years foundling home babies may have had as good a chance as, and sometimes a better chance than, babies reared within their families, especially since the latter really were at high risk of being killed. But by the eighteenth century the story was much grimmer. Almost eighty per cent of babies taken into the Rouen hospital in the mid-eighteenth century died; by the end of the century the figure had actually risen, to almost ninety-five per cent, which is to say that hardly any of the babies survived. Between 1700 and 1800 the Madrid foundling hospital had a seventy-five per cent mortality rate. The London foundling hospital started off well: in the early years mortality rates were around twenty-nine per cent; but they rose as high as eighty-three per cent in 1760, before falling again in the later eighteenth century, largely as a result of narrower admissions policies. Between 1750 and 1799 the Dublin hospital had a mortality rate of eighty-nine per cent. Witnesses at mid-century described infants' bodies being 'stored' in vast coffins under the stairs, and then buried thirty-five at a time; the hospital is said to have reeked of death.[56] This is a level of horror that is hard to match, but there were hardly any eighteenth-century foundling hospitals with a mortality rate lower than sixty per cent before the end of the eighteenth century, and, as we have seen, in many the rate was much higher. Prospects did improve somewhat in the nineteenth century, probably because of more effective wet-nursing; still, as late as 1880 a report done on the Moscow hospital showed that nearly eighty-eight per cent of the 117,854 children admitted in the previous ten years, or over 100,000 children, had died.[57] The foundling death toll across Europe in the four centuries from 1500 to 1900 ran into the millions.

Much of the problem was institutionalization itself, or at least institutionalization under early modern conditions. In the eighteenth century institutional crowding was almost always associated with very high rates of infectious disease. Babies were an already vulnerable population with few natural defences. Many were brought in from rural areas, and people of any age moving from a rural area into a city were especially likely to succumb to infection. Sewage disposal was basic to nonexistent, thus encouraging the spread of killer diseases like infant diarrhoea. Vaccination for smallpox – one of the major infant killers – was still relatively uncommon in Christian Europe before the later eighteenth century, and, in any case, too dangerous to inflict upon infants.[58] But the foundling homes also brought out some of the worst aspects of human nature, and in a world that already took a pretty callous attitude toward the death of other people's children. 'Baby-merchants', both women and men, soon began circulating around rural areas, taking unwanted babies off people's hands for a small fee, and transporting them in baskets and carts to the foundling hospitals. Those who died were often dumped unceremoniously by the side of the road; the others might be half-gone by the time they arrived, and often died shortly thereafter. Hospitals, especially those with 'open' admissions policies, were overwhelmed. Usually there were not enough 'on-site' wet-nurses to meet the demand, and farming out babies to rural wet-nurses, as most eighteenth-century hospitals did, provided a sought-after source of income for women, but also encouraged numerous abuses (see Chapter 4). When no wet-nurses could be found, babies were 'dry-nursed' on pap or cows' milk – which, in the days before sterilization and pasteurization, was a literal formula for death.[59]

The carnage in the foundling hospitals had many contributory factors. There was the half-starved rush of both young men and young women to the cities and textile regions as jobs dried up in the rural areas; and the incessant efforts by church and civil officials to stigmatize unwed mothers, the main result of which was to damage their relationships to their families and to the fathers of their children – the 'care network' that, in most human societies, keeps infants alive. In the more immediate sense there was the drastic incompatibility between something that seemed like a good idea – putting unwanted babies into a hospital instead of letting them die in the streets – and the impossibility of keeping large numbers of babies fed and free from contagious diseases in early modern institutional conditions. One of the saddest things about it was that the foundling home represented not just a perverse incentive (though it was that), but a perverse incentive based upon a lie. Certainly many of these babies were at high risk of death if their parents kept them at home (in this sense the champions of the foundling homes were not wrong). But it is also the case that some hard-pressed parents, including a good many single mothers, who would not have killed or fatally neglected their children, were led to believe that their survival prospects would be better in the homes, when, quite clearly, the opposite was true. But it is only in retrospect that we can see these various elements melding into the human catastrophe most of these institutions proved to be.

Childrearing

Parental love is a wonderful, if not universally distributed, emotion that, then, as now, inspired many mothers and fathers to remarkable sacrifices for their children. It also complemented more purely economic motives. Out of necessity almost everyone viewed children explicitly as a source of labour and revenue. Early modern Europe suffered from chronic under-employment, erratic prices for staples (an especial problem in the cities, where most people were dependent upon the market for food), and fairly frequent climate-related and seasonal shortages. Most families needed the labour both of women and children to stay afloat. Often the one was played off against the other. Most mothers worked for pay when their children were young. When children grew old enough to work and contribute to the family finances, more mothers were able to forgo paid employment (most often they did not stop working; they just worked for their husband, but no longer for pay). Child labour also *complemented* women's labour. Poor mothers all over Europe and the Middle East used their children, and especially babes-in-arms, to enhance their begging prospects. As one London woman named Elizabeth Evans put it, when accused of infanticide in 1740: 'before she would have killed it [the baby], she would have gone a-begging with it'.[60] Foster-families may have been even more likely to do this – or just more likely to get caught at it. A 1790 report on the disposition of foundlings in County Wicklow in Ireland found that, in just one parish, seven had been sent off with strolling beggars; in short, foster-families were 'renting them out'.[61] Little girls began looking after still younger children at a very young age, allowing their mothers, who could do heavier work and also command higher wages, to spend their days in more 'productive' activities. Likewise in extended or complex families it tended to be when girls reached the age of (say) seven or eight, and could do serious work, or when young daughters-in-law came into a family, that a woman could retire from some of the heavier work and devote herself to the more managerial task of deploying the labour of others. This sort of trade-off is one reason why girls were always less likely than boys to go to school.

Childrearing was both less individualistic and less identified with actual mothers than it is today. It was, however, usually the work of females.[62] In many households, neighbourhoods or villages, one woman, probably elderly or for some reason less fitted for heavy work, or, alternatively, little girls, took care of the younger children so that mothers could go out to work. 'Collective' models of childrearing extended to fairly intimate processes like breast-feeding. The notion that a baby would only ever be breast-fed by its mother was probably fairly foreign to most Europeans in the eighteenth century and simply not feasible for women who had difficulty nursing, inter-mittent or inadequate milk supplies, or who needed to leave their children behind in order to work (see Chapter 4). Parents also did not automatically assume that they were the best people to bring up a particular child: one Russian noblewoman recalled that in her childhood (probably mid-nineteenth century) her parents had entrusted her to an aunt to raise 'because all the children before me had died, so they acted like peasants do in the country: when baby livestock die, they give the rest to another to bring up'.[63] Parents also routinely 'settled' their children with relatives, or 'apprenticed' them at very young ages (like seven or eight). Often this would permanently terminate the connection between parent and child.

Mothers supplied less hands-on childcare than we would expect, but, at least where families stayed together, they had a central role in ensuring the health and welfare of their children by magical and religious means. This is perhaps the commonest maternal activity we find reflected in the early modern records. Motherhood in the early modern period was ringed around with a good deal of guilt: mothers whose children died sometimes agonized afterwards about the fact that they had been unable (say) to breast-feed them or find them enough to eat, or had given them into the care of irresponsible people, or allowed people to wish ill upon them. And the fact that infant mortality was high did not preclude other people putting more blame on mothers than on anyone else. But guilt and blame were focused far less upon issues like spending time with one's children (the concept of 'quality time' was essentially nonexistent in the eighteenth century) than upon failure to fulfil, or follow precisely, an endless number of ritualistic and devotional duties and tasks thought to enhance one's children's well-being. Whole families, but mothers especially, were supposed to be perpetually working to interest God, the saints, the Virgin Mary, holy individuals, the local clergy, and the spirits of dead relatives in the welfare of their children (and husband), and to be constantly on the lookout for ways to avert supernatural attacks by evil spirits, djinns, restless souls, or the malevolent magic of other human beings. This formed a strong rationale for a lot of travelling about by women: to visit or consult holy men or women, worship at shrines, go on pilgrimages, search out magic springs, purchase lucky amulets, and the like. On the down side, there was infinite potential for wrecking or mistaking the formulas, confusing the benign and the malign, and offending both spirits and other people. There were also rich possibilities for a mother to discover her responsibility for (say) a child's crooked spine, mental slowness, epilepsy or death in her failure to perform some healing ritual correctly. Self-induced maternal guilt is certainly not a modern invention.

In the eighteenth century, female superstition (by which critics meant precisely the sorts of belief systems and practices we have been talking about) became a common target of attack both by the newly sceptical, and – though in more measured terms – some religious people as well. Late eighteenth- and early nineteenth-century reformers, who included a good many women, did a great deal to formulate a conception of motherhood that looks much more familiar to us today. It was not modelled on the majority of mothers and fathers, those who laboured in the fields all day, worked for a wage, begged, or starved themselves in order to sustain their families – but who also relied heavily on their children's labour and sometimes abandoned or even killed them if they felt they could not support them. Rather it was the far smaller number of comfortably well-off women, whose families had sufficient resources for them to stay home, who were the new ideal. The relative merits of this model for women and children are not for us to decide here; what is more important is that it was wholly unrealistic for the vast majority of eighteenth-century families.

SEX

The marital double standard

For centuries law and custom had permitted men to have multiple sexual partners but denied women the same freedom. The new Puritanism, most notably the famous Calvinist-inspired sex laws passed in, among other places, Sweden, Geneva, the Massachusetts Bay and Connecticut Colonies, and England during the Commonwealth period, did represent an attack upon the double standard, but only in a rather limited sense. In the Old Testament, the wife who commits adultery *and the man, married or not, who commits adultery with another man's wife*, both deserve death (their joint crime is the despoliation of another man's property and potentially his bloodline).[64] Husbands who had sex with an unmarried woman or a slave were not included in that mandate however: a man could only commit the sin of adultery against another man, not, as it were, against his own wife. Most of the countries that sought to be 'tough on adultery' in the early modern period, along with those that carried on as usual, accepted the double standard of Deuteronomy and Leviticus. Thus, in the notorious but short-lived English Adultery Act of 1650, passed by the ascendant Puritan party, the death penalty applied to an adulteress under all circumstances and the man who had sex with her, whatever his marital status. By contrast, a married man got three months in jail if he fornicated with a 'Virgin, unmaried [sic] Woman or Widow'. He only faced the death penalty if he had sex with a married woman. The fornication part of the law was undeniably embarrassing for those extramaritally sexual male householders who got caught, but since the main group that unfaithful married men had sex with was unmarried female servants, it was unlikely to cost men their lives; conversely, as we have seen, pregnancy might well cost the woman her life if the baby died.[65]

Still, it was a novel thing to propose executing men for adultery, and in the clear light of day most regimes lost their nerve. In the case of England the Adultery Act lapsed at the Restoration in 1660, and it seems that no one was ever executed under the statute. By the eighteenth century, across Europe, even the most rigid Calvinists had retreated from the notion of executing men for heterosexual crimes, often long before. It was simply too unpopular. The situation is less clear for women. There was far greater popular antipathy to adulteresses than to philandering husbands, and the fear of being cuckolded seems to have been one of the central masculine anxieties of the early modern period. There is a persistent literary trope of wives being killed for adultery, and a good number of actual cases of women being murdered by their husbands (this remedy was also widely accepted in customary law). Most adultery statutes punished women more severely than men. But it seems in the end that the majority of early modern adulteresses were banished or imprisoned rather than executed, though they were usually punished more severely than their male partner in crime.[66] However, the path of the adulteress and adulterer would soon diverge again. In the late eighteenth and early nineteenth centuries adultery for men was largely decriminalized, but, in a number of countries, men were handed new or strengthened powers to punish their adulterous wives. The Napoleonic Civil Code of 1804 provided that adulterous wives could be imprisoned for three months to two years *at the discretion of their husbands* (there was no comparable right for the wives of adulterous husbands); while the Penal Code of 1810 permitted husbands who caught their wives *in flagrante* with another man to kill them outright. This remained in the French penal code until 1975, and still later in some of the codes (such as the Italian code) that followed the Napoleonic Code. In Italy the right of a husband to kill his adulterous wife was only repealed in 1981. The French civil and criminal codes both had a huge impact elsewhere, particularly in Latin America and the Middle East: indeed the '*in flagrante*' provision was translated almost verbatim from the Napoleonic Code into Moroccan and Jordanian law; in the latter case it functions to this day to give the gloss of legality to (misnamed) 'honour killings'.[67] The Napoleonic solution was one of those classic compromises that punished a hated object (the adulteress), got the state out of private households, eliminated unpopular public punishments and preserved male dominance in the family – all in one stroke.

It remains to mention one other development on the adultery front – one that, at the time, hardly anyone noticed outside the Arabian Peninsula, though it would have far-reaching implications. There was no comprehensive 'Reformation' within Islam, but beyond the borders of the Ottoman Empire, deep in the Arabian desert, there were the first stirrings of an important new movement that had many parallels to the more rigid and puritanical forms of Calvinism. Mohammed Ibn Abd al-Wahhab (1702–1791) was the driving force behind what came, unflatteringly, to be called Wahhabism, a staunchly monotheistic form of Islam that – like Protestantism – objected to the interposing of any mediation (saints, shrines, whatever) between the believer and God. Ibn Abd al-Wahhab also resembled Calvin in his drive to translate ancient statutes to do with sex into punitive, modern forms. The Calvinists looked to the stern passages of Leviticus and Deuteronomy and tried to emulate the ancient Jews; Ibn Abd al-Wahhab looked to a selection of the *hadiths* and tried to emulate what he imagined to be the Prophet's example. In one of the most notorious episodes of his career, Ibn Abd al-Wahhab's efforts to recreate the 'perfect' morality of the early Muslim community in Medina inspired him to have a confessed adulteress stoned to death. At the time this was viewed as quite shocking, and to this day it is the act, arguably, for which Ibn Abd al-Wahhab is most notorious. In the seventeenth and eighteenth centuries, as we have seen, Muslim jurists went out of their way to avoid trying sexual deviancy as *zina* (sex crimes), and judicial execution for *zina* was almost unknown, though, as in Europe, husbands and fathers often enjoyed a licence to kill wives or daughters who were said to be sexually wayward. The judicial execution of women was vastly more common in early modern Christian Europe than in any of the Muslim lands. Still, this episode was, in its own way, a watershed because (like the various Calvinist experiments) it staked out a position on the relationship between the sacred past, sinful modernity and sexuality that became the benchmark for rigour and moral order.[68] Today judicial violence for fornication, adultery and sodomy (also a *zina* crime) remain, in practice, rare, even in the few Muslim countries where it is legal (chiefly Iran and Saudi Arabia) – though not rare enough. But its symbolic linkage to religious reform encourages vigilante killing by relatives to this day.

Coerced sex

Everywhere in Europe and the Middle East in the early modern period wives were expected to give their husbands largely unconditional access to sex and few women possessed the right to control their own bodies. This is very different from the view of most people today. Modern people, especially women, are deeply committed to choice and control when it comes to sex. This can make it difficult to draw the line between licit sex and rape in the early modern period: to us most of it looks coerced. And yet, even in those times, all coerced or reluctant sex was not the same. The trauma of the frightened young bride was different from the trauma of a young girl from, say, an insurgent Balkan province, or Benin on the West Coast of Africa, plucked violently from her own family and loved ones, transported under inhuman conditions to a foreign land, and forced to have sex with a man, or even many men, she did not know.[69] The rape of slaves was so defiling because the sexual intercourse was stripped of the community and kin support, rituals, protections and benefits that ordinarily accompany sex, marriage and motherhood in most societies, and which undoubtedly helped diminish or dissolve at least some of the psychic and physical pain associated with them. A slave woman in Christian European colonies not only had her body violated, but she was confronted by a racial regime in which she was not likely to be treated as a real wife, nor her children like a true family, in which her connections to her bloodline had been violently ruptured and might be again if her children were sold away. As we have seen, the rape of slaves by their owners in the Ottoman system (and, to some extent, Iberia and its colonies) had more potential long-term benefits for the woman than in the Dutch, French or English colonies. Nonetheless, it still involved a type of coercion that was different in kind from, and carried fewer benefits than, marriage among free (or freer) people and that could violate strongly inculcated beliefs about chastity and marital fidelity, as well as callously dispense with the usual rituals of marriage and sexual union.[70] Raped freewomen were in a somewhat analogous position. Not only did they get back nothing good in return for their chastity, but they lost part of their reproductive value, to themselves, to their families and to their present or future husband. Rape potentially destroyed their future, particularly if they ended up pregnant. It trampled permanently upon their sexual honour. This coerced and bitter exchange was very different from marriage, even in a regime where women expected to give up sexual control to their husbands.

Under normal circumstances, neither wives nor slave women could sue their husbands/masters for rape. Bringing a complaint in court was also out of the question for many, though not all, of the legally free girls and women who were forced, by men to whom they were not married, to have sex against their will. Shame, confusion, fear of punishment and the lack, especially among very young girls or lower-status women, of any strong sense of a right to bodily integrity, were potent barriers to coming forth with one's story. Sometimes we can see this in the very words they used. Women who, if we were using modern definitions, would be deemed the victims of violent rape, can be found referring to the experience using the language of seduction (as in variants of 'he hit me and threw me on the bed, and held my legs open and covered my mouth so I could not move or cry out and thus I was seduced and lost my virginity').[71] The fact that rape was usually a capital offence did not help matters; it both deterred women from coming forward (their rapists were usually people they knew), and it meant that people who might otherwise be allies denied rape victims their support. It also virtually guaranteed acquittal, especially in cases where the rapist was of a higher social status than his victim.

And yet, despite the impediments, thousands of eighteenth-century European and Middle Eastern women reported rape or attempted rape to the authorities, and a surprisingly large number also sought to prosecute perpetrators in court. Unfortunately, convoluted attitudes toward female sexuality and female agency combined with evidentiary problems to make successful prosecution of rape cases difficult to impossible, especially for adult women. This was because of the widespread belief that many, perhaps most women, and a lot of little girls, were sexually insatiable and prepared to perjure themselves – literally to lie away a man's life – rather than admit it. There were also almost insurmountable procedural problems. The fact that there were seldom any eye-witnesses to rape undermined women's efforts to get rapists punished in the *sharia* courts, since there was a rule that *zina* had to be witnessed by four Muslim men (the same rule also made it difficult to convict women of adultery or fornication, so it could work to their advantage). The same assumptions about the low credibility of women victims and women witnesses in general, especially with respect to matters sexual, prevailed in the courts of Christian lands, though usually in less codified form.

There *were* cases where women (or, more often, very young girls) successfully prosecuted their rapist. In a case adjudicated in Rotterdam in 1700, the head of the poorhouse for children of the Reformed Church, a man named Abraham de Herder, assaulted and raped twelve of the girls, who then brought suit. De Herder ultimately confessed (which was probably his mistake) and was sentenced to death.[72] Generally, though, especially when the penalties were severe (such as execution) most men were acquitted or convicted of far lesser crimes, unless they were foreigners, belonged to a minority group, or were of significantly lower status than their victims. A study of early modern Sweden found that cases for rape brought against common soldiers (who were often strangers, and almost always of a low status, thus fitting two of the above criteria) fairly often ended in conviction, and even, occasionally, execution. However, officers were usually either acquitted or freed on appeal, because it was much easier for them to impugn a girl's or woman's character and be believed.[73] In the Ottoman courts the combination of the high evidentiary standards for *hadd* crimes (of which rape was one), and the tendency in the early modern period to replace punishments like stoning or castration with fines, could work somewhat to women's benefit, as it led *kadis* to make rapists pay significant indemnities to their victims.[74]

Men who raped very young girls were more likely to be convicted than men who raped older girls or women. Clearly people felt particularly strongly about such cases. In a London rape case from 1699 involving a ten-year-old victim the court reporter notes that '. . . the Tryal . . . lasted very long, from between Nine and Ten in the Forenoon, till Five in the Evening; all which time the Court was crowded by a Multitude of People, among whom was a great many Women; who, though ordered to depart, would not stir till the Tryal was over, which being done, the Jury went out, and after some time they brought him in Guilty.'[75] In England the age of consent was ten, so if an eleven-year-old was raped the 'female sexual insatiability' principle meant she was likely to lose her case on the basis of her age alone. In the Netherlands only single women, and usually girls under the age of twelve, successfully prosecuted rape cases; married women never did, due to the belief that once a woman had tasted sex she could not be trusted not to want more. There was also a general suspicion that any girl or woman who was of a lower social status than the man who raped her was likely to be making false accusations of rape in order to extort money from the accused. For this reason few masters were ever convicted of the rape of servants, though they were occasionally convicted of much less serious charges or required to pay child support.

Extramarital sex was a crime, so women who brought an unsuccessful charge of rape risked being punished themselves. In a 1670 case from Delft in the Netherlands, a married woman named Chieltje Claes, who cleaned houses to support herself, was surprised and raped by a neighbour. But when the case came to trial the court decided that Claes had not been raped but rather had committed adultery (the theory seems to have been that, as a married woman, she should have known how to resist her attacker; since she failed to do so she must have been complicit). Adultery by a married woman was a far more serious offence in Holland than adultery by a man, so Chieltje was banished for fifty years and her rapist for ten. Most girls and women who reported rape were probably not banished, but it appears to have been fairly common to force rape victims to do public penance for fornication. Even lesser penalties would have been a significant disincentive to reporting rape.[76]

Incest cases were especially apt to result in punishment for both perpetrator and victim, on the assumption that both had participated in an especially heinous crime against God. In a fairly typical Dutch case from 1682 a girl named Maria had been raped by her father beginning when she was thirteen (he had told her: 'I have to do this to you. All fathers have to do it with their children.') When she got pregnant the father gave her potions to abort the foetus and locked her up. At the trial the testimony of her relatives focused not on Maria's violation but on the dishonour that the incest had brought upon the family. Both father and daughter were banished for life. It was rare for incest victims, unless they were very young (under the age of twelve), to escape additional punishment from the courts – most commonly banishment or imprisonment, though, at least in the Netherlands, they generally were not executed. In some other places incest victims could be executed along with the perpetrator.[77] Early modern people had such a highly developed conception of the taboo nature of some sex acts that concerns about who first initiated them, of the positioning of the participants, and even of whether the acts were forced on an unwilling victim, all faded into insignificance. For the same reason animals implicated in bestiality cases (often because the unlucky creature had given birth to vaguely human-looking offspring) were always solemnly executed, usually before the eyes of the person accused of having sex with it – who him- or herself was also executed. It was the only way to placate an angry God. Incest victims, people and animals accused of bestiality, and, as we will see, male homosexuals, would all benefit from the late eighteenth- and nineteenth-century retreat from biblically inspired notions of sexual crimes against God.

Homosexuality

Early modern people were not at all certain that female same-sex activity was a crime against God, or if it was even possible. This is in contrast with the view of *male* homosexuality – or at least the 'official' one. Let us, therefore, look briefly at the latter. In European and Middle Eastern history violent repression of male homosexual activity had virtually always been a byproduct of other concerns, namely: enforcing clerical celibacy; finding scapegoats for natural or military disaster; discrediting heretical or politically out-of-favour groups; and demonstrating one religion's moral superiority over all others. As a result prosecution was episodic to rare in the first millennium and a half of Christianity, and even rarer within Muslim polities, most likely because the latter lacked an institutionalized clergy sworn to celibacy.[78]

This began to change in the seventeenth century. Counter-Reformation fervour married to economic stress perhaps explain the unprecedented waves of executions for sodomy in 1611–20, 1641–60 and 1681–1700 in Lisbon, during which about 150 men were burned at the stake. Further north in Protestant England and Holland, Calvinist moral evangelists, perhaps frustrated by their inability to interest people in stronger punishments for adulterers, saw the opportunity to redeem their bedraggled popularity by attacking a new group of sinners. As a result, scores of sodomites were condemned to death in both countries, and hundreds more arrested, subjected, in some cases, to torture, and given lengthy prison terms. What sermons about Sodom and

Gomorrah accomplished in England and the Netherlands, newly rationalized police bureaucracies wrought in France, where thousands of men were picked up for sodomy using special entrapment methods (use of the death penalty for sodomy was far rarer in France than some other places, though).[79] At least in western Europe, extreme treatment of homosexuals in a sense replaced – and certainly outlasted – severe punishments for delinquent heterosexuals. Still, in the end, sodomites too benefited from the new secularism and declining enthusiasm for punishing private sexual expression. Sodomites ceased to be executed on the continent early in the nineteenth century, and the Napoleonic Penal Code of 1810, by failing to mention sodomy, largely decriminalized it, though executions lasted much longer in England.[80]

By comparison there was very little active repression of women who engaged in same-sex acts. Women, like men, routinely slept together anyway, and were expected to be physically and verbally affectionate with one another; this meant that their sexual activities were easy to conceal or overlook, especially since strong, even exclusive, mutual affection between women was deemed fairly normal. Female same-sex love also lacked spiritual urgency as a problem. The main motivation for attacks upon sodomites was the Sodom and Gomorrah story (Genesis 18–19) with its disturbing apparent warnings about collective punishment. By contrast, the most relevant Bible passage for female same-sex activity (Romans 1:26) is less than transparent, either in terms of exactly what sex acts it is forbidding and how God will punish them.

Same-sex love between women was not, however, so embedded in everyday life that it went unnamed or unrecognized. It used to be argued that genital sex between women was almost inconceivable, either as a practice or as a category of sexual behaviour, until the later nineteenth, or even early twentieth, century.[81] This has turned out to be untrue. Female same-sex erotic behaviour, in a complex that included stimulation of the genitals and other erogenous zones, vaginal penetration, strong emotional attachment, and setting up house together, was undeniably a known, if somewhat nebulous, domain of erotic/emotional practice in many parts of Europe and the Middle East in the early modern period. In Christian Europe the part involving genitals was often referred to as 'tribadism', though the terms 'sapphic' and 'lesbian' do appear and, contrary to what is sometimes claimed, they did not always refer to a poetic metre or to people born on the Greek Isle of Lesbos.[82] Efforts to find a lesbian 'identity' akin to modern ones are probably doomed to failure, though; for one thing it is very difficult to match the names writers gave to certain imagined practices to the 'real' things women did. Moreover, many of those imagined practices are more useful as evidence about men's anxieties than about women – such as the persistent claim that 'tribades' had huge clitorises that functioned like penises, or the belief, found across both Christian Europe and the Middle East, that lesbians required a penis-substitute in order to have anything recognizable as sex.[83]

There are some features of the discourse *about* same-sex love between women that look familiar to anyone who has studied later phases in the history of sexuality. So, for example, a large amount of speculation, fantasy and male pornography surrounded closed all-woman institutions. In the early modern period this meant a lot of attention to alleged same-sex activity in convents or harems. It does not seem only to have been western European men who associated same-sex activities with 'Oriental' female spaces, though it certainly is true that, thanks to Montesquieu, this became a particularly intense feature of Orientalizing discourses about Muslim women in the eighteenth century (in fact the 'lesbianism in the harem' trope had already appeared in Italian travel-writing about the Ottomans by the mid-sixteenth). Charges that a particular woman was engaging in same-sex erotic practices were also rather often used, both in Europe and the Middle East, to try to cut powerful women down to size. This was very evident in the realm of politics (see Chapter 8); it was also common in relation to women performers and intellectuals; witness the medieval belief that lesbianism was especially to be found among 'educated and elegant women, the scribes, Qur'an readers, and female scholars'. One of the common Arabic terms for lesbian was *zurefa*, which means 'elite'. Among the early modern Ottomans the wardrobe mistresses of women's music and dance troupes were routinely alleged to engage in same-sex activity, and in the eighteenth and early nineteenth centuries the charge of lesbianism also clung to some women poets, such as the well-known Leila Hanım (d. 1845).[84] Similar claims about women intellectuals, writers and actresses turn up in Christian Europe (see Chapter 7).

Occasionally real tribades do swagger across the stage of history. Henriette-Julie de Castelnau, Countess of Murat (1670–1716), was constantly in trouble late in the reign of Louis XIV for writing (or cooperating in the writing of) a critical pamphlet about the court, as well as for her open lesbian affairs ('a monstrous preference for people of her own sex'), impecuniousness and wild parties. Like a number of obstreperous French aristocrats she was kept under surveillance, and the police reports on her contain several breathless dispatches chronicling the progress of her love life. Later she was shut up for some years in a remote chateau where she wrote a collection of best-selling fairy tales.[85] Lower down the social scale, most same-sex activity simply faded imperceptibly into the woodwork. The main type that did *not* disappear without a trace involved transgender elements: these were cases where women dressed as men, married other women, and were imprudent or unlucky enough to get caught. It was fairly common for women to dress as men in the eighteenth century; indeed it was a standard way for lower-class women to travel, and also a way for women who could 'pass' to get better-paying jobs. Some of the latter group also seized the opportunity to marry. Maria van Antwerpen (1719–1781), going under the name of Machiel van Handtwerpen, officially married Cornelia Swartsenberg in Zwolle in the Netherlands in 1762. At the time of the marriage Cornelia was pregnant, and she later became pregnant twice more, while Maria represented herself as the father. One of the more intriguing features of this story is that Maria's own brother and his wife appeared as godparents for one baby's baptismal ceremony. Clearly Maria's family had come to terms with the couple's 'arrangement'. But the authorities were not so tolerant. Six years later Maria van Antwerpen was unmasked in Gouda and, after a lengthy trial, banished.[86] In a similar case from eastern Hungary, one 'Ferenc' Horvath was arrested in 1793 for having got a priest to officiate when she married her pregnant bride. 'Ferenc' testified forthrightly: 'I am a girl dressed up as a man and it has been three years since I married a gipsy girl. I have a man's and a woman's nature in me but I have never liked men, I have always loved women.' Witnesses testified that they thought she was a man because she served as a coachman (jobs linked to horses were marked male almost everywhere) and 'she smoked and sang songs for dancing just as any man would'. Maybe they really did believe she was a man, but it is also quite conceivable that, in the more fluid climate of the eighteenth century, especially in a traditional society like Hungary, a lot of people were content either to let her be a man if she could act the part, or imagine that she had changed her sex. On the other hand, both Ferenc Horvath and Maria van Antwerpen married women who were pregnant (and Ferenc married a 'gypsy girl' in a society where the Roma were stigmatized). This may signal that 'passing' women, or transgender people, depending upon what we wish to call them, circulated in the less sexually respectable wing of the peasantry and urban proletariat, a pattern that would last into the modern era.[87]

Sin, sex and erotic emancipation

It was not news to women of the early modern period that the discursive merger of sexual sin, female responsibility for the Fall, and the command-ment to Eve to be subject to Adam ('Your love shall be for your husband and he shall rule over you') was a potent weapon in the hands of men who wanted to keep women in a subordinate position in all things. Attacks upon (or at least attempts to moderate) the doctrine of Eve's sin would be the central plank in an enormous amount of female religious activism in the seventeenth and eighteenth centuries (see Chapter 6). The doctrine of women's responsibility for Original Sin bore especially heavily on women's sexual and reproductive lives, because it continually emphasized that women were sexually dangerous people, intent on snaring men into sin. It also associated women and women's bodies with pollution (menstrual pollution; birth pollution); it even ordained that they bear children in suffering – the other half of the punishment God, in his infinite wisdom, tailored especially to women. As we have seen, the belief that women were both sexually vulnerable and sexually insatiable also greatly undermined their ability to defend themselves in court against attacks on their sexual honour, and justified many of the constraints put upon their mobility and choices in life. Over the course of the eighteenth century, literal belief in the Bible and in the traditional teachings of the various churches went into at least partial retreat in much of literary Europe – by the 1790s Mary Wollstonecraft was calling the story of Adam and Eve a 'poetical story' invented by men to show that '[woman] ought to have her neck bent under the yoke . . .'.[88] But one did not have to be a deist like Wollstonecraft to see which way the spiritual winds were blowing. Already by mid-century many women had begun to shift their focus away from the question of Eve's sin, and whether modern women should continue to be punished for it, and instead were taking up the sexual double standard (a sort of secularized version of the same old debate). Why were women judged so harshly for the smallest sexual indiscretion while a man could have affairs, father illegitimate children, make advances to the servants and still enjoy the respect of his fellows, even be received in polite society? And why did the mere imputation of unchastity undercut a wife's rights in marriage (including, often, her rights to support, to community property, if any, and to her dower) while flagrant infidelity had no impact at all on a husband's legal entitlements? As Françoise de Grafigny (1695–1758) put it in her best-selling feminist novel, *Lettres d'une Péruvienne* (1747): 'How could [women] not revolt against the injustice of laws that tolerate men's license . . . ? . . . It seems that in France the marriage bonds are only reciprocal at the time of the ceremony, and that afterward only women are bound by them.'[89] Feminists sometimes exaggerated the extent of the double standard for effect; flagrant promiscuity did not, in reality, enhance every man's reputation, and there was a parallel movement by men, that went well beyond Protestant clerics, to encourage both masculine continence and an ideal of companionate marriage in which sexual double dealing was very problematic.[90] Nevertheless, women's views on the matter were, not surprisingly, always more barbed, and often took up the legal implications in a way that men's writing did not. Questions like these hit directly at the issues we have been discussing in this chapter.

They also raised some tactical dilemmas. It has always been a question for 'champions of women' whether women's interests are best served by stressing sexual restraint and constraint (ideally for *both* women and men) or by insisting that both women and men have an equal right to pursue erotic fulfilment. It was difficult in the sexually repressive and defensive climate of the early modern period to acknowledge openly the second of these possibilities and it remained extremely risky for quite some time after that. Nevertheless, in the later seventeenth and eighteenth centuries what one can only call female erotic self-determination did begin to make its way into some women's writing. It is at least implicit in the plots of most novels (see Chapter 7), and some authors also made it explicit, as in the Englishwoman Aphra Behn's scandalous *Love-Letters between a Nobleman and His Sister* (1684–87), one of the earliest English novels and the first known English epistolary novel. *Love-Letters* features explicit and transgressive sex scenes, serial non-monogamy, and an assertively sexual main character named Sylvia who is still alive and well at the end of the book (in other words, she is not killed off as punishment, like so many sexually knowing women in literature). Many women novelists in the late seventeenth and eighteenth centuries criticized marriage, or pointedly had their female protagonists refuse it, but few went so far as Behn, who has Sylvia insist at one point that:

> [Marriage is] a trick, a wise device of priests, no more – to make the nauseated, tired-out pair drag on the careful business of life, drudge for the dull-got family with greater satisfaction, because they are taught to think marriage was made in heaven . . .[91]

In other words, matrimony is not a divine institution but a clerical ploy, designed to paper over tedious lives and humdrum sex.

In the late seventeenth and eighteenth centuries we also find women penning erotic love poetry aimed both at male and female objects of desire, including such 'inappropriate' love objects as considerably younger men. The remarkable Swedish poet and feminist Hedvig Charlotta Nordenflycht (1718–1763), who deserves to be better known outside Sweden, wrote touching love poems, when she was in her forties, about the much younger man with whom she fell deeply in love.[92] Some women, once they were free to choose on their own, actually did marry much younger men; the historian and radical republican polemicist Catharine Macaulay (1731–1791), married at the age of forty-seven across class and generational lines to a twenty-one-year-old ships' surgeon's mate. The ensuing scandal shredded her reputation, but the marriage seems to have been happy.[93] Catherine the Great of Russia was notorious across Europe for her affairs with handsome, much younger men (see Chapter 8), and the well-known novelist and public intellectual, Madame de Staël (1766–1817), who once quipped, 'in matters of the heart nothing is true except the improbable', also married for the second time to a man half her age. Women who loved women were somewhat less open about their predilections, but the famous and forthright declaration about her sexual identity that the Yorkshire heiress, Anne Lister (1791–1840), committed to her diary in the earliest 1820s ('I love, & only love, the fairer sex & thus beloved by them in turn, my heart revolts from any other love than theirs'), not to mention her extraordinarily explicit descriptions of her erotic techniques and fantasies, owe much to eighteenth-century discourses of female erotic emancipation, even though Lister, no feminist and a terrible snob to boot, preferred to think she had got them from Jean-Jacques Rousseau.[94]

The displacement of the theological problem of the sin of Eve into quotidian social and family life presented one of the earliest 'universalistic' challenges to feminist or proto-feminist assumptions, one that, for the most part, 'champions of women' failed to meet. Whatever else one may say about it, the Genesis story suggests a quite universalistic conception of human origins. Most early modern Christians, Jews and Muslims believed that all human beings shared descent from Adam and Eve, and hence, many, perhaps most, also believed that all the daughters of Eve, regardless of race, religion or status, were, at heart, unchaste and sexually promiscuous. When European women writers attacked this belief, they usually did so in ostensibly universalistic language. But in practice, even as they sought to 'redeem' a group they called 'Women', they continued to tell themselves that poor women, servants, black women, Jewish women, Roma women, Irish women, etc. were so sexually immoral that they, in effect, forfeited their right to consideration. The sin of Eve (at least the sexual part) migrated out of their own souls and those of women like them, only to settle and lurk with especial vileness in the souls – and bodies – of women of other groups. Often this went unstated; at other times it took quite overt form, as can be seen from the malevolent dark-hued obeah women, Jewish and Gypsy temptresses, and sluttish servant girls who populate the work of female as well as male poets and novelists of the period.[95]

The ideological utility of simply refusing to see the humanity of other women is sometimes all too clear in the record. A standard tenet of colonial misogyny and of interracial sexual paranoia was the belief that European women became sexually inflamed and promiscuous when exposed to hot climates. When the Scotswoman Janet Schaw travelled to Antigua in the mid-1770s she put considerable effort into refuting this claim, insisting that the white women she met were 'modest, genteel, reserved and temperate' in their sexual behaviour as in much else. That left the problem of how to explain the large mixed-race population of the island – clearly someone was being sexually intemperate. To Schaw, who found the white men of the islands 'frank, open, [and] generous . . .', in short, very agreeable hosts, the answer to the conundrum was clear, and it had nothing to do with the fact that white owners could rape their slaves with impunity, or that black women had few economic opportunities and fewer legal rights. Instead she convinced herself (and tried to convince her readers) that the problem was those same men's understandable (she thought) difficulty resisting 'young black wenches' who 'lay themselves out for white lovers'. The fault lay with mercenary, hypersexual black women, and both white women and white men could be acquitted of blame. It was an all-too-common exculpatory gesture.[96]

Anatomy and destiny

As old faiths die or their powers wane, new ones take their place. The new religion of the eighteenth century was science, and just as the older faiths had made women's sexuality central to the order of things, so did many of the practitioners of the new science. Female pretensions to having more power and authority in the world were not high on the list of aims of either group. According to Londa Schiebinger, scientists in the later eighteenth century began paying new attention to (and often exaggerating) the differences in skeletal structure between men and women, and then using these differences to emphasize women's reproductive role as well as to justify their exclusion from higher education and public life.[97] According to Tom Laqueur, some time in the eighteenth century, a long-held view of men and women that emphasized the similarity, even homology, of their genitalia and which assumed that a person could change sex with relative ease (what he calls 'the one-sex model'), was largely replaced by a new emphasis upon sexual dimorphism and fixity of gender ('the two-sex model'). This shift reinforced the polemical claim that Nature had formed women for the function of reproduction and reproduction alone.[98]

Laqueur, in particular, has been taken up with real enthusiasm by people who work on the eighteenth, nineteenth and twentieth centuries. Many have come to see the alleged shift from a 'one-sex' to a 'two-sex' model as one of the constitutive transitions of Western modernity.[99] However, scholars who work on sex and gender in the sixteenth and seventeenth centuries have been more lukewarm towards Laqueur's theory, arguing, among other things, that attitudes toward gender, skeletal anatomy, the genitalia and sexual dimorphism were more diverse in the late medieval and Renaissance period than Laqueur allows, and, moreover, that many of the early anatomists were actually fairly warm toward the advancement of women.[100] Still, whether or not one accepts the one-sex to two-sex 'shift', it does seem that in the eighteenth century science *did* begin to be deployed to do more consistently repressive kinds of work than before, both with respect to gender and race. Indeed, as Schiebinger shows, new 'advances' in eighteenth-century botany, animal taxonomy, proto-anthropology, primatology, skeletal anatomy and 'racial science' had a strong tendency to confirm, instantiate and 'fix' the most retrogressive notions about racial and gender hierarchy, often through calling upon highly eroticized notions of women and persons of colour.[101] Scientists recycled much older themes, of course, from the tendency to view women almost exclusively in terms of their sexual and reproductive role, to the age-old belief in female sexual insatiability. But they also used the fashionable rhetoric of empirical science to reassure men that they should remain in control. By the end of the century, as we will see, the new science was being used not just to confine women's intellectual aspirations but to head off their political claims as well.

CONCLUSION

The battle between sex and death cast its shadow over almost every aspect of early modern life, but the hold of death was beginning to slip just slightly. Some time between the early nineteenth and the mid-twentieth centuries (it varied depending upon the country) a shift occurred that historians call the demographic transition. The demographic transition typically announces itself as a downturn, often quite steep, in the birth rate. Where previously women had perhaps five to eight children, of whom two to five grew to adulthood, they now started having only four, and then only two. The classic view is that, at a certain point, consciousness of rising life expectancy caused families to have fewer children than before, apparently because they could be fairly certain that the children they *did* have would survive. Whether the sequence was quite this simple is open to question,[102] but it is clear that, wherever it occurred, the transition both marked and helped create a different reproductive world. Women and children were the ones whose lives were most drastically altered by the demographic transition. Today most European women are pregnant, on average, fewer than three times in their lives and have two (or fewer) children. Birth control is widely used, and most people plan when and if they will have children. The whole psychology of childrearing has changed. As parents we assume, with good reason, that our children will outlive us. Because we have only a few children we invest heavily in their education and welfare, pushed, to be sure, by laws forbidding child labour and requiring that we send our children to school. Do we love our children more? Perhaps not, but because the ratio of adults to children is far lower than it was in the eighteenth century we *do* have a lot more love to spread around to fewer children. And because we have good reason to think that all our children will survive we give our hearts to them immediately, and with far fewer fears, reservations and emotional defences than eighteenth-century people did.

The eighteenth century was the last century in which all of Europe still lived and died under the old demographic regime. But it was by no means a static time. More and more people ceased to believe that God visited savage penalties on people who broke seemingly minor sexual rules, or even major ones, and governments' and churches' efforts to assist God in this punitive project gradually lost favour in the court of public opinion, though not quickly and never definitively. There was a distinct retreat from the doctrine of Original Sin, including the belief that women lived under a permanent burden of inferiority by virtue of being of the lineage of Eve. There was a new interest in education, and in science, which had potential that went far beyond whether women were naturally designed solely for childbirth. The professionalization of midwifery encouraged the belief that both maternal and child mortality could be controlled (as indeed it would ultimately be to a remarkable extent). Some people began to argue, late in the century, that it was immoral and unacceptable to drag some children away from their parents and sell them on auction blocks. The first efforts (albeit, at least in the case of the foundling homes, deeply problematic ones) were made to cope with the problem of unwanted children. And all of these, and other factors, helped create an environment in which some women began to think that they could and should have more choice and experience less coercion around sex and their own bodies.

Life in the old demographic regime had some heart-sickening features. It is not pleasant, even at more than two centuries' remove, to see people cope with children they, alternately, wanted desperately, and desperately wanted to get rid of, in a world where most people were perpetually hungry, and death was everywhere. We can also see many trends that point to the future. The details of the demographic transition are outside the scope of this study – we are just seeing the very beginning of it in a few places by the late eighteenth century. The reason it is, or should be, so interesting for women's historians, is precisely because exerting control over their bodies and sexuality and keeping their children alive, have both, historically, been extremely difficult for women. That reality is on display everywhere in the eighteenth century, from high infant mortality rates to the vicissitudes of marital sexuality; from rape, infanticide and incest trials to sexual slavery. Yet one also glimpses women refusing to succumb to nullity, and trying to exert control over the uncontrollable, through the courts, magic, religion, self-sacrifice and sheer will. The demographic transition is often represented as an almost mystical affair, where unwitting people somehow changed their reproductive behaviour and that changed the world. At one level it is mystical. But real women and men made the sexual and reproductive choices that brought it about (or dreamed of being able to make them), and that is an important milestone in the long history of women.

Chapter 4

◆

FOOD AND CONSUMPTION

WOMEN AND FOOD

Like us, women in the eighteenth century had a rich but conflicted relationship to food. But the terms of that relationship were different and the stakes far higher, because the supply of food was so much more precarious than it is today. In the early eighteenth century it still took, depending on the region, from sixty-five to ninety-five per cent of the population working on almost all the available farmland to feed everybody, and that often at a pretty minimal level.[1] In France today, to pick a famously food-loving nation, ninety-eight per cent of the population does *not* farm; as for the mere two per cent who do still farm, they cultivate or graze animals on a good deal less, though higher-quality, land than their predecessors, yet realize incomparably greater yields.[2] So in those times most people, whether they liked it or not, were farmers, and women, as we will see, had even more diverse and all-encompassing food responsibilities than men.

Famine

Most Europeans were well acquainted with hunger. Few winters went by without some people feeling the pinch; April and May were the cruellest months, particularly in northern Europe, because by that time the winter stores had run out, the livestock had almost all been slaughtered, and the late spring crops were not yet ready to eat. But most people were used to seasonal deprivation. What they really feared was famine. Famines generally began with a poor harvest or, more often, a series of poor harvests. These were the result of bad weather, crop diseases, the ravages of passing armies, soil-exhaustion, and sometimes of dramatic geological or weather events, like the massive Laki volcanic eruption of 1783–84 that deposited fluorine-contaminated ash over much of Iceland, poisoned fifty per cent of the livestock, starved up to a fifth of the human population, and affected European weather patterns and mortality as far away as Italy.[3] Once set in motion, famines were sustained and aggravated by speculative hoarding (designed to drive up prices), mismatches of supply and demand, and the tendency of hungry, panicked people to flock to the cities and towns in search of food. Trapped in the urban microbial swamp, these unfortunates competed with an often hostile – and famished – urban proletariat for handouts from local charitable and religious institutions or the city fathers, and succumbed in large numbers to the classic diseases of crowding, especially typhus, smallpox and dysentery. In the eighteenth century (and this is still true today) most victims of famines tended to die of infectious diseases, or, in some cases, of hypothermia, not, in the first instance, of hunger, though child-killing and parental suicide also tended to rise sharply, impelled by, in the words of one authority on modern famine, 'the mental fatigue that comes from hearing ceaseless cries for food that cannot be stilled'.[4]

In the most general terms, the 'hierarchy of suffering'[5] in famines started with the poor, particularly the landless or people living on very small plots. They always died in far larger numbers than any other group. Nineteenth- and twentieth-century famines, for which more accurate statistics are to be had, were generally associated with high mortality among old people and the young. There is some evidence that pregnant and lactating women were more vulnerable than other women, but, on the whole, adult women survived famines better than men of the same age group. It is not entirely clear why. Biological explanations such as adult women's higher percentage of body fat and smaller body frames, as well as supposedly greater immunity to some infectious diseases, are often put forward, but none has actually been proven. Some have also proposed more cultural explanations. Women's greater knowledge of famine-food foraging (see below) and 'control of the cooking pot' may make the difference, or the fact that they tend to migrate later than men, and thus are exposed less quickly to infectious diseases. Some have suggested that women survive because they are often prepared to prostitute themselves for food (though it turns out men do this too), because women are readier to seek help, or simply because, as some claim, they 'fight more tenaciously than men' to survive.[6] Babies at the breast also do fairly well (which, in historic populations, means their already very high mortality rates do not rise as much as one might expect), but children aged about one to nine die in hugely disproportionate numbers. Presumably this picture roughly reflects the situation in the eighteenth century as well.[7]

Famines had many ripple effects. If there was no crop to harvest farm labourers were thrown out of work; so were people in non-staple production. Hungry people often mortgaged or sold their lands at a pittance to richer neighbours in return for food or seeds for next year's planting. In seventeenth- and early eighteenth-century Russia (and likely in the Ottoman Empire too) it was not uncommon for people to sell themselves or their children into slavery in return for food. So famine, especially when combined with a fairly robust land market, could significantly alter the social environment, driving more people permanently into the city, or creating farm servants, day labourers or even slaves out of former small farmers. When the price of bread or other staples doubled or tripled, as it routinely did during famines, more elastic kinds of demand slowed or ceased, causing increased unemployment. Another effect of most famines was a sudden drop in fertility, probably due to stillbirths, famine-induced amenorrhoea, neonate infanticide, and increasing numbers of couples failing to marry because they lacked the resources. Modern research also suggests that intrauterine famine exposure can have deleterious effects upon a person's health later on.[8] Famines generally also led to significant out-migration, usually temporary, but sometimes permanent. During and in the years immediately following the Great Irish Famine of 1845–49, a million and a half people emigrated, and a quarter of a million smallholders and landless labourers were evicted from their homes, which were then often demolished. Women may have survived famines better than men, but that also must have meant that a disproportionate number of them saw their husbands, fathers, brothers or sons die or disappear, leaving them in a more disadvantaged position than before. There were places that did not experience serious famine during the eighteenth century. Italy had no famines, except between 1766 and 1768; France was largely famine-free between about 1710 and 1793, though the seventeenth century had been awful; and England sailed through the entire century without any significant famines, though some towns did see significant spikes in mortality in the terrible general crisis of 1740–42. Some historians consider the purely demographic effects of early modern famines to have been relatively small over the long term, meaning that usually they 'only' killed five to ten per cent of a given population (though famines in the Nordic countries seem to have had considerably higher mortality rates). Moreover, regions generally rebounded fairly quickly in population terms, though this did not prove to be true of the

Great Irish Famine. It is, however, impossible to quantify the psychological after-effects of seeing family members starve to death, including the crippling belief that, if one had sacrificed a bit more or prayed harder, one's children, husband or parents might still be alive. Food insecurity remained a feature of most women's lives well into the nineteenth century, and in some cases longer, an aspect of early modern life that one is deeply grateful not to have to experience.[9]

Excess female mortality

While adult women usually fared better than men in times of extreme scarcity, it is less clear that this was true under more ordinary conditions. A study of a group of sixty West German villages in the eighteenth and nineteenth centuries reveals that, at least in this area, married women were appreciably more likely to die than their husbands, especially in the food-scarce months. This differential is not accounted for by death in childbirth, since excess mortality was largely found among married women in the forty-five to sixty-five age bracket, most of whom would already have gone through menopause. Most of these women seem to have died in the late winter and early spring – the hungry months – of pulmonary diseases like tuberculosis, pneumonia or influenza, to which undernourished people tend to be more susceptible. It looks as if some husbands were simply starving their wives of food. The problem was probably made worse by some women's stinting on their food intake to feed their, by then, often teen-aged children. Unfortunately the incentive structure was against older married women: their death would allow their husband to remarry a younger, perhaps more attractive, still-fertile woman, who might come with a dowry. And indeed, in west German villages that showed high excess female mortality, it was very common for widowers to remarry within six months to much younger women, giving new meaning to the adage 'death is the functional equivalent of divorce'.[10]

Another dangerous stage for girls and women was adolescence. Good censuses were not done for much of the Balkans until the 1860s or later. But when they *were* done many regions, including Serbia, Bulgaria and Eastern Rumelia, Bosnia, Montenegro and Greece, showed significant surpluses of men (four to ten per cent and occasionally even more). Some of this could have been the result of female infanticide, but, at least for Serbia, it seems the culprit was differential mortality in adolescence, suggesting, perhaps, that girls (particularly, one suspects, female orphans) were particularly poorly fed or, as one historian has suggested, simply worked to death. One doubts that this was an entirely new phenomenon in the later nineteenth century, though it may have been exacerbated by modernizing trends, as seems have been the case in 1840s England, which also saw widespread excess mortality of pre-adolescent and adolescent girls.[11]

Food and the sacred

Food is charged with meanings that include, but go well beyond, taste or the assuaging of hunger. Food and food provision had, and to some extent still have, powerful sacral qualities, ranging from the ritual meal at the heart of Christianity ('Take, eat. This is my body') to speculations, common to many religions, about the kinds of foods people can expect to consume in Paradise. Women's role as mediators between the food supply and their own children probably meant that they had more power than men did over the life and death of their children. Indeed, several studies have shown that, in the early modern period, children whose mothers died were far less likely to survive than children whose fathers died, though exactly why this should be is less than clear.[12] This kind of power surely explains part of the combined fear of, and respect for, maternal power common to so many European traditions, as well as the prevalence of rituals that identify women both with food and with the sacred, particularly those aspects of the sacred that pertain to health and fertility. It is still true today, or was until recently, that when a Bosnian Muslim woman is married, she crosses the threshold of her husband's parents' home carrying a loaf of bread under her right arm and the Qur'an under her left – the one a symbol of nurturance and fertility, the other of piety and morality.[13] Women in the early modern period often took responsibility for identifying and distributing sacred or miraculous foods, and there are many European folk-tales about pious women who, by means of some sacred food, succeed in healing a sick person when the doctors have given up hope. During an outbreak of the plague in seventeenth-century Florence women banded together to organize a treatment regimen involving bread that had come in contact with a miracle-working nun – a transparent inversion of the main sacred ritual of Christianity, in which the distribution of sacred bread, the real or figurative body of the God/man Jesus, is presided over by an all-male clergy.[14] In Orthodox communities the communion bread was typically baked by a specially designated older woman, one who, because she no longer menstruated, was considered more ritually pure than other women. And in those days before clocks were common, women (or at least Catholic women) routinely timed their cooking by so many repetitions of the Ave Maria prayer.

To abstain willingly from food in a society where most people do not get enough of it is a dramatic act of sacrifice, and sacrifice itself had and has immense sacred and magical power in all the main religious traditions of Europe. Conspicuous self-denial with respect to food, in order to achieve religious transcendence, to placate God or the saints, or to benefit family members or neighbours in times of dearth, was greatly admired and could give rise to a kind of sanctification in one's own lifetime. It was also linked to early modern understandings of, and often genuine admiration for, motherhood, for almost everyone agreed that mothers were particularly prone to starve themselves in order that others might eat. This belief was powerfully metaphorized in numerous religious images and folk stories. Two examples are the oft-repeated image of the pelican who feeds her children with her own blood, and the heavy emphasis within Christianity and Islam (Sunni Islam especially) on the sacrifices of Mary or Maryam the mother of Jesus/'Īsā. Both mother pelicans and the mother of Christ connected women to food through a rich system of merging, overlapping and transmutating metonyms and metaphors. Breast milk was believed to be a decoction of blood, and blood the stuff of life, so a woman who suckled her child literally fed it with her own life-force. Motherhood turned her into food. Both the pelican and Mary also symbolized the still greater sacrifice of Jesus Christ who not only died for humankind but fed and continued to feed his body and blood to his followers. The everyday mother who denied herself food to keep her family alive was playing a part in a cosmic drama, which, we may be sure, was magnified in the hallucinatory state that often accompanies semi-starvation.

Women as food: coercive nursing and the commercialization of mothers' milk

In the early modern period women often breast-fed other women's children, and because there was almost always a high demand for this service, it could confer a variety of benefits on the woman herself, or her family. In parts of the Balkans, Anatolia and the Caucasus the wet-nurse's other children enjoyed an often prestigious and lucrative fictive kinship with the family whose child she had nursed. In the Ottoman system the children of the sultan's former wet-nurse were considered his 'milk sisters' and 'milk brothers' and the wet-nurse herself enjoyed a generous lifelong salary and a prominent position in the harem hierarchy. Things were not always quite so ideal outside the palace, however. Accounts from the nineteenth century suggest that some likely-looking women were bought along with their nursing child, only to have the baby taken away by a dealer so that the woman could be sold as a wet-nurse.[15] Similar horrors were visited upon New World slave-women. Few of them, particularly under the inadequate nutritional regime most were subjected to, had enough milk to nurse two babies at a time. In Brazil from the 1820s on, the children of African 'emancipadas' (women who were technically free, but still treated like slaves) were taken away from their mothers and placed in foundling homes or illegally made into slaves – so that the mothers could nurse white children.[16] It is not difficult to imagine the fate of slaves' own babies. In the face of this, women did what they could. One authority has suggested that the supposedly high rate of abortion among Brazilian slaves was part of a strategy to avoid being forced to become wet-nurses (when they would be likely to have to give up their baby anyway). Some women tried to capitalize on their temporarily enhanced value. One slave from Guayaquil, Ecuador, was asked by her owner to raise the child of a friend whose wife was unable to nurse. The slave complied on condition that her owner drop the price he was demanding she pay for her eventual manumission.[17] In the North American South, where much of the elite had their children raised by slave wet-nurses, all sorts of expedient and implausible theories arose about black women's unique maternal abilities, such as that they had a miraculous capacity to transfer their affections, entirely without resentment, from their own children to those of their masters or employers. And as late as the mid-twentieth century, North American textbooks on childrearing were claiming that black women 'invariably' produced more abundant breast-milk than whites.[18]

There had long been an elite market for wet-nurses. This has been especially well studied with respect to Spain, where women from certain villages in northern Spain were famous for the purity of their milk, and in high demand among the aristocracy in Madrid. There was an established migration route in the eighteenth century of Galician, Asturian and other women going south to take up jobs there, and the pay was high.[19] But most eighteenth-century wet-nurses nursed the children of middle-class or poor women, within what became a thoroughly commercialized mass-market. There was any number of reasons for this. Some women could not nurse, or were so debilitated after childbirth that it was considered imprudent for them to do so. Husbands often objected to their wives nursing, both because it 'ruined' their wives' breasts, and because of taboos against having sexual relations while a woman was nursing. In late seventeenth-century Leipzig, admittedly after a visitation of the plague, merchants encouraged the use of wet-nurses in order to enhance their wives' probability of conceiving. Poor women, and often middle-class ones, had to work, and usually could not bring their babies along, much less nurse them frequently enough to keep them quiet. In Lyons, the most important French silk city, seventy-five per cent of the population resorted to wet-nurses in the eighteenth century. In Paris, by 1789, between 90 and 98 per cent of new babies were being wet-nursed. By this time a good number of cities across Europe, among them Stockholm, Hamburg, Lyons, Marseilles, Madrid and Paris, had set up wet-nursing bureaus both to facilitate contacts between would-be clients and wet-nurses and to diminish the number of abuses concomitant to the 'trade'.[20]

Demand for wet-nursing was on the increase in the eighteenth century, due to a rising population, more women working in less-family-friendly jobs (like industry), and the increased demand from foundling hospitals (see Chapter 3). There is little question that the hospitals had an especially distorting effect upon the market. The London Foundling Hospital engaged some 620 wet-nurses from nearby Hertfordshire alone between 1756 and 1767 and there were comparable figures across Europe.[21] High institutional demand encouraged fraud. Some mothers took in a foundling, and then, when it died, substituted their own baby for it, in order to continue receiving wet-nursing payments. In Ireland and Sicily the hospitals instituted branding of foundlings as a means of deterring this. There was also the problem of disease. An infant with congenital syphilis can pass the disease on to the woman suckling it; the woman could then pass it to her own babies, husband, etc. And the direction of transmission could go the other way, a fact belatedly driven home after some municipalities hit upon the idea of punishing pregnant prostitutes by making them serve a term as 'captive' wet-nurses in the local foundling hospital. In some places the syphilis problem made it virtually impossible to find wet-nurses for foundlings.

The wet-nursing industry was subject to the usual economic stresses, as well as the vicissitudes of war and political unrest. Families who failed to pay the wet-nurse's bill often found themselves in court or debtor's prison. In the Ottoman Empire the ex-husbands of divorced women with young children were required to pay the women wages for breast-feeding the children – in line with the Qur'anic injunction that babies have a right to be breast-fed for two years. Here, too, women took their ex-husbands to court when they failed to pay.[22] During the French Revolution many hospitals stopped paying *their* wet-nurses. For women in dire poverty, whose own children were starving, and whose health was already undermined by too much nursing and too little food, this was the last straw. Some revolted, like wet-nurses in the vicinity of Montpellier who, in the 1790s, demonstrated in the streets and attacked foundling hospital officials. Many stopped feeding their nurselings. By 1792 the death rate for infants taken into the Montpellier Hôpital Général stood at eighty per cent and it subsequently got worse.[23]

Only women could breast-feed; indeed, only women who had themselves borne children. In a context of rising demand, that led both to opportunities and to exploitation. In a relatively 'free' labour market wet-nursing pretty consistently paid more than domestic service. Indeed, in the eighteenth century it became one way for mothers of illegitimate children to make a living – though often at the expense of their own children, who might be farmed out to a still cheaper wet-nurse, 'dry nursed' (which was very likely to kill them), or placed in a foundling home. In the context of slavery, coerced wet-nursing became one more way that women's sexuality and reproductive lives were appropriated to other people's ends, at great cost to their own well-being and that of their children.

Breast-feeding campaigns

In the second half of the eighteenth century, many elite and middle-class women (and men) in France, England, Spain and elsewhere, 'discovered' motherhood, both as a role they could reinvent for themselves, and as a form of charitable endeavour. This took several forms, including the setting up of new charities for mothers and children (especially lying-in charities and orphanages), pushing smallpox inoculation, and emphasizing the benefits of maternal breast-feeding for both rich and poor. One of the earliest champions of maternal breast-feeding (in fact she was a friend and, quite possibly, an influence on Rousseau[24]) was Marie-Angélique Le Rebours (1731–1821) who published a treatise in 1767 called *Avis aux mères qui veulent nourrir leurs enfans, avec des observations sur les dangers auxquels les mères s'exposent, ainsi que leurs enfans, en ne les nourissant pas* (Advice to mothers who wish to nurse their children, with observations on the dangers to which both mothers and children are exposed by failing to nurse). She had become a convert to maternal breast-feeding after putting out a succession of her own infants to wet-nurse and seeing them all die. But her argument ranged well beyond the usual complaint that wet-nurses were neglecting their charges or making them vicious, or that mothers who did not nurse their own babies were spoiled and indolent.

One of her central claims, in fact, was that *not* breast-feeding caused women to get pregnant again too soon after giving birth: 'What use is taking on wet-nurses, in order to have, as they say, some respite, and then becoming pregnant [again] although the body has not yet recovered? . . . In breast-feeding a long while, one conceives fewer children, but more of them survive.'[25] It was a succinct summary of the reproductive strategy that demographers would later associate with the demographic transition. And when it was followed, it probably did both save the lives of children and (quite likely) safeguard the health and lives of mothers who did not have to endure so many pregnancies. Le Rebours is also unusual for being one of the few middle-class people writing on wet-nursing who gave any thought at all to the plight of wet-nurses, whose own children were at a considerably higher risk of dying for lack of nourishment.[26] The maternal breast-feeding craze, always more successful as an ideology than as actual practice, particularly in France,[27] was one way that women tried to exert control over their bodies, reproduction and infant death. The 'indolent mother' stereotype notwithstanding, in real life it was often the husband who insisted on farming out babies, so that he could resume sexual relations with his wife, be able to command his wife's labour full-time, and not have to share his wife and his living space with bad-smelling, squally babies. Often it must have been over his wife's objections. Though it is hard to find people talking about it very explicitly, there are strong undercurrents in the pro-breast-feeding literature of discontent at men's sexual demands, especially where they interfered with breast-feeding (sex was believed to corrupt the milk), resulted in too frequent pregnancies, or were imposed on women who were ill or had recently given birth.

Women's efforts to rethink maternity are significant in another way. Infant and maternal mortality began to fall in some places as early as the eighteenth century and in many more in the nineteenth, and while there is little clarity about *why* they fell or about the order of cause and effect, it seems likely that nursing habits, mothers' diet, hygiene, expectations of children's future earning capacity, and smallpox inoculation were all factors.[28] So, most probably, was the gradual retreat from fatalism, which, in this context, could be characterized as the belief that babies and some parturient mothers have always died and always will die, and that it is probably God's will. Most mother-and-child charities sought to intervene in one or another of these areas, and they represented a particularly strong assault on fatalistic attitudes toward infant and maternal death; moreover, they were among the first groups to try to apply scientific reasoning and methods to public health. Women's charities have tended to be studied more as discursive formations than as results-based programmes (and certainly the former aspect cannot be ignored). But because the drop in infant and child mortality was such a central, if sometimes under-recognized, feature of modernization, and so significant for women's lives (see Chapter 3), the question of its success or failure in enhancing the survival prospects of mothers and children probably deserves more attention than it has received from historians. Some probing questions also need to be asked about the poorer women who consented to be part of initiatives like the Société de charité maternelle, founded in Paris in 1786 by one Mme d'Oultremont-Fougeret, wife of a royal financial official, and intended, like many such programmes, to encourage poor women to breast-feed their babies.[29] Did they put up with the condescension and intrusiveness because they could see some glimmer of hope that either they or their children might benefit?

The breast-feeding campaigns were also important as incubation chambers for what is often called 'maternalism'. This was a cluster of beliefs centred round the notion that motherhood was an extraordinarily powerful force that needed to be unleashed on the world at large.[30] We will discuss domestic feminism, the strain of thought from which maternalism grew, in more detail in Chapter 8. For now, suffice it to say that maternalism's champions tended to combine social and gender conservatism with a very elevated conception of women (the old emphasis on the sin of Eve seems very distant indeed), and a strong dose of sentimentalism,[31] and they had a considerable activist bent. Sarah Trimmer's discussion of breast-feeding (see Voices from the Past 4.1), published in 1787, is a striking early example. It also shows how readily maternalism could reinforce the ideology of women's separate sphere.

VOICES FROM THE PAST 4.1

Motherhood, breast-feeding and the world

For Sarah Trimmer (1741–1810), an influential English philosopher of charity and writer of children's books, breast-feeding by middle-class and elite women set in train a series of powerful social processes, all animated by emulation and sentiment. The mix of social conservatism (notably the opposition to class-mixing or to overt defiance of husbands) and enthusiasm for diffuse but strong female power is typical of her work.

> Little do many young mothers think to what miseries they expose their helpless offspring, by sending them from under the paternal roof to cottages where they frequently endure all the hardships of a state of poverty: little do they think that they are suppressing some of the most pleasing emotions that the female heart is susceptible of enjoying–emotions which would amply repay their utmost fatigues! that they are breaking one of the strongest bands of domestic happiness, by removing from view that dear pledge which was granted to increase conjugal love between them and their husbands, and attach them to their own homes. If pleasure is the object, where can a woman find one, in the whole circle of public amuse-ments, to compensate for the loss of that a fond mother feels while she nourishes her infant

with the food which is its natural right, and sees a succession of human beings thriving in their native soil under her own immediate culture? The maternal affections expand daily; filial love arises in the infant mind as an innate principle; the father is animated to sustain his toils by the sight of those dear objects which render them necessary; his cares are lightened by the hopes which their progressive improvement excites in his heart; and their innocent sports and prattle enliven his hours of leisure, and supply the most salutary recreation to his mind ... In short, if proper attention is likewise paid to the education of children, the mother's nursing them may prove the foundation of unanimity, peace, and prosperity; while her neglecting to do so may lead to discord and excesses which she had no idea of when she resigned one of her most important duties to a hireling.

I ... know that some gentlemen will not consent to their wives becoming nurses [i.e. breast-feeding their own babies]. I would by no means recommend disobedience to husbands; for unreasonable commands must be submitted to, rather than to make what are designed as the blessings of life occasions of domestic wranglings: but I think this is a cause which requires from a woman the full exertion of soft persuasion: and I cannot believe that a truly affectionate husband and father would tear his new-born babe from its fond mother's bosom, and banish it from the house, merely to save himself a little disturbance.

Source: Sarah Trimmer, *The Oeconomy of Charity; or, an Address to Ladies Concerning Sunday-Schools; the Establishment of Schools of Industry under Female Inspection; and the Distribution of Voluntary Benefactions* ... (London: T. Longman, G.G.J. and J. Robinson and J. Johnson, 1787), 94–6.

LIVING ON AND OFF THE LAND

Peasant food

Far from spending their time in the house, most women spent a good part of the day outside, in the fields, by the stream, on the commons, by the seashore, in the woods or (as was the case in towns and cities), in the marketplace, searching for fuel, water and food, both for animals and people. Women tended to be the ones responsible for small vegetable gardens, and in many areas they also had important responsibilities with respect to the staple food crop. So, for example, in some chestnut-growing areas their responsibilities seem to have been far heavier than men's. In the Cévennes in France it was estimated in the early nineteenth century that harvesting two hectares of chestnuts demanded a hundred working days a year for women and children and ten working days for men. Women and children did most of the heavy labour, gathering between 50 and 150 kilograms per day in up to ten-hour days.[32] The chestnut was a staple crop in many upland areas of France, Spain, Portugal, Corsica, Italy, and Turkey, and women's responsibility for it probably grew in the eighteenth and early nineteenth centuries.

Women and children also tended to take charge of pigs, goats and poultry. The meat, milk and eggs of domesticated animals provided a valuable supplement to all-grain (or, increasingly, maize or potato) diets, as well as supplying manure, skins, feathers, grease and the like. In many families the sale of farm commodities was also the main source of cash. However, the keeping of animals, unless there is abundant grazing land, diverts precious grains and forage foods away from direct human consumption. This is especially true of poultry, which tend to need grain. This explains why in poor regions and among less fortunate people the preferred poultry, if any were kept at all, were geese, which forage better than chickens (e.g. the much-prized parsley-fed goose) and are capable of being fattened on considerably less feed. For those with few resources and no religious objections the pig was probably the commonest animal of all, because it could eat all kinds of foods, including forest acorns. The other low-budget alternative was the goat, with its willingness to graze on terrain that sheep refused to consider.

In the early modern period most foods, whether purchased or grown or produced oneself, had to be processed, either to make them palatable or keep them from spoiling. Grains had to be ground, chestnuts hulled, skinned, fire-dried, and often ground, poultry killed and plucked, fish scaled and often dried, cream churned into butter, milk converted to yoghurt, meat and vegetables dried, pickled or smoked. Almost all of these were women's work, and most of them were both hard and time consuming. Take, for example, the grinding of grain. In the eighteenth century, in regions with few water- or animal-powered mills (which included much of eastern and southeastern Europe, as well as the poorer and more isolated or marginal parts of western Europe) it was still done with hand querns (handmills). The association of women, particularly low-status women, with the milling of grain is at least as ancient as the Old Testament (see Exodus 11:5). Eighteenth-century Turkish women used to tell a plaintive riddle that spoke to the endless daily grind of milling grain, and the way the hand-mill – figured, perhaps predictably, as male – seemed to rule their lives: 'What is it? It is short; its waist is thick/Oh why don't you ever get enough to eat/Oh Governor?'[33] In regions where water-, wind- or animal-powered mills were more prevalent, women had the job of carrying the grain to the mill or the dough to the common bake house to have it baked into bread (in many areas people could not afford the fuel to bake it in their own homes).

Most women spent little time cooking in the eighteenth century simply because home cooking consisted mainly of long-simmered grain- or (increasingly) potato- maize- or chestnut-based porridge or soup into which were thrown whatever other edibles – largely wild greens – were on hand. Often women *could* cook more complicated foods – festival foods or seasonal specialities, sometimes involved baking and other techniques – but they did not often have the time, the cooking facilities, the fuel or the ingredients to do so. The kinds of food most women were cooking, and that everyone was eating, was food that could be left to itself (or stirred by a child), while everyone else did more important jobs. Many of these dishes have survived in the European diet, but generally as breakfast food or side-dishes. In earlier times they were the main event at virtually every meal: Dutch hot pot (basically a soup of root vegetables, such as turnips and potatoes); Scottish oatmeal porridge; the various Mediterranean variants of cornmeal mush (polenta, millasse, mamaliga, etc.); rye bread or cracker soups; or Russian kasha (made of wheat, millet, barley or buckwheat groats). This would have been the diet year in and year out for a large percentage of the population, with only occasional seasonal variations.

The commons and its decline

Traditionally women, especially poorer women, had been extremely dependent upon common rights in forests, ponds, streams, grazing areas, peat-bogs and shore-lines. There they gathered mushrooms, wild greens, frogs, wild birds' eggs, berries, and, occasionally, insects (grubs and locusts were a good source of animal protein and fat for the very poor, at least in those areas – chiefly warmer climates – where the insects were large enough to make them calorically worthwhile to collect). They might also fatten a pig on acorns (this option was forbidden to Jews or Muslims by dietary law, but open to Christians), graze and water goats or a cow or two, collect animal dung for fertilizer or to sell, or keep geese. Peat-bogs and forests provided fuel. Beaches were a source of seaweed for food and fertilizer, shell-fish and drift-wood.

When a modern person picks up a shell on the beach, or catches and eats a fish from the sea, or goes out at dawn to gather mushrooms in the forest, she is exercising a kind of unspoken common right to the 'fruits' of that beach, ocean or forest. These are the pale vestiges of what used to be a large, complicated, and much-contested body of rights to forage, pasturage, hunting, gathering, fishing, fuel- and water-gathering, gleaning and cottage-building, thrown like a ragged patchwork over land and sea. Things have changed greatly since then. Most land and easily accessible water have been turned over to private ownership. Remaining 'commons', public parks, forests, and the like are hedged about, and for good reason, by environmental and hunting regulations. It would be impossible for any appreciable number of people to survive today on foraging in common forests, marshes and waterways, much less raise live-stock on common lands, not just because the knowledge of what is usable has been largely lost – though it has – but because that older style of living and resource exploitation could not possibly support the large populations of the modern era. The early modern period was a transitional one with respect to common rights. Depending upon where one lived, 'rights in the commons' might be quite extensive, but a rising population, overuse, deforestation (very advanced in large parts of southern and western Europe by the eight-eenth century), the advance of privatization measures, such as enclosure or anti-poaching laws, environmental pollution (especially of waterways) and urbanization had already denuded many places of usable resources, and put real or symbolic fences around a good proportion of the rest.

Desperation does not always go along with much generosity of spirit and common resources were a source of litigation, disputes, and hostile takeovers long before the eighteenth century. However, they came under far greater pressure in the great population rise of the period after 1700 and especially after 1750. The elimination of common rights occurred in diverse ways. In some cases landlords or seigneurs enclosed the commons for their own use or, probably more often, to lease or sell as private farms. In others, landholders in a given village, who might constitute anywhere from ten to sixty-five per cent of the householders, divided up the 'village commons' between themselves, excluding 'cottagers', people with a small house but no land to speak of. This was what generally happened in Denmark between 1776 and 1781, the result of a series of laws encouraging enclosure. In still others, lands were divided either legally or illegally among all households, or, in some cases, households with a male head. This left lots of people with very small individual holdings of not especially fertile land, as happened in the southern Massif Centrale of France, and women heads of household sub-stantially worse off than before.[34] As we have seen, famine often furnished an excuse to engage in mass evictions.

The pressure on, and gradual elimination of, common rights, affected poor people more adversely than better-off ones, and women more adversely than men. For older, poorer women the resources of the commons were often all that stood between them and total destitution. Advocates of enclosure were well aware of this. As one English 'improver' put it in 1787: 'to let four thou-sand acres of good land lie barren and desolate for about a dozen old women to pick up a scanty livelihood from cow-dung and goslings, is too great an absurdity to be seriously supported.'[35] Enthusiasts for progress could sometimes see with great clarity the world they were obliterating, but they were not bred to identify with those for whom older ways – in this case keeping geese and gathering cow manure to sell for fertilizer – bestowed a marginal advantage in the struggle to survive. And yet, some women clearly benefited from the redistributions of rights and resources. A distinct middle or middling class began emerging in many parts of rural Europe in the early modern period, especially from the late seventeenth century on. The women of these families often saw a greatly improved quality of life with respect to such basics as food, warmth and respite from hard labour – the latter because they could pass the labour on to poorer women, who, as their hold on resources slipped, became willing to take almost any work. In most areas in the eighteenth century, the various changes that go under the name of economic development, whether in town or country, resulted in some already better-off people getting richer, a genuine increase in the relative number of people somewhere roughly in the middle, and greater immiseration and declining living standards for landless labourers and other people who had to buy their food in the market on unreliable wages. People of the later eighteenth and early nineteenth were caught in the grip of a familiar feature of the modernization process. The old methods of cultivating the soil and utilizing the commons could not have fed the growing European population over the long range: its inefficiencies were real. But it would take several generations, in some cases much more, and a further, almost as wrenching, transition to industrialized factory production, for most Europeans to see the benefits of modernization. Those intervening generations saw an entire way of life sicken and die, with little confidence that anything would arise to replace it.

Revolutions in the garden

Food is not just what people eat. It can also define a way of life, a set of relationships to the land and other people, and a series of rules about who does what work. During the course of the eighteenth century the diet and the lifestyles of a large proportion of Europe's people, and particularly Europe's poor, were transformed by the widespread adoption of new or newly prominent staple crops. The two most important of these were potatoes and maize. Both had originally been domesticated by indigenous central and South Americans – maize in Mesoamerica; the potato in what is now Peru. And both were likely brought back to the Iberian peninsula in the late fifteenth or early sixteenth century. Maize appears to have taken early hold outside Europe, primarily in Africa and the Levant, and it was probably from the latter that it spread to the Balkans, Italy (where it is still sometimes referred to as 'granturco' or Turkish grain) and southern France. Unusually adaptable and fast-growing, maize delivered higher yields of calories and fat per acreage than most other crops. It was also, at least initially, resistant to disease, and some of its many varieties grew well under relatively adverse climatic and soil conditions. By the eighteenth century it was well established as peasant food and animal fodder in the dryer, warmer regions around the Mediterranean, including the Maghreb, the Levant, Turkey, Romania, Slavonia, Serbia, Hungary, eastern France, northwestern Iberia and Italy.[36]

As maize was to the South, potatoes were to the moister, colder regions of northern and central Europe, becoming a staple crop in parts of the British Isles (especially Ireland and Scotland), Belgium, the Netherlands, northern France, and parts of the German lands by the mid- to late eighteenth century. Potato-growing spread more slowly, but eventually very extensively in Scandinavia, North central Europe, Northern France and Russia, in many of these places crowding out most other foods from poor people's diets. The potato was less immediately popular than maize. The varieties first introduced in Europe were watery, bitter-tasting, strangely coloured and full of 'eyes'. They looked leprous, some thought, as well as inedible, and some of the names assigned to them ('earth's testicle', 'Eve's apple', 'the devil's apple' and the like) suggest an association with sex and sin as well as disease. Ordinary consumers also had their doubts. A lullaby from the Hebridean island of South Uist runs:

> What, love, will I do for you,
> for I have no breast milk for you?
> I fear that you will get the croup
> From the softness of the potatoes.[37]

Like maize, the potato recommended itself because it had an unusually short growing season and delivered a greater yield of calories per unit of land than any of the alternatives. One result was that landowners and territorial rulers began taking steps to encourage or force their dependants to switch to potato-growing as a kind of insurance policy against dearth. Frederick II of Prussia (r. 1740–1786) sent his soldiers into the fields to coerce peasants to plant potatoes; in 1765 the Russian *duma* encouraged their cultivation as a prophylactic against famine and plague; at one point Queen Marie Antoinette

(r. 1774–1793) was persuaded to wear potato flowers in her hair in a bid to encourage potato-growing in France.[38]

The introduction of these and other new crops profoundly affected the lives of women. The great advantage of potatoes and maize (and certain other high-carbohydrate foods, such as chestnuts and rice, of which cultivation was also expanding in the early modern period) was that they delivered a fuller feeling on less land than older staple crops or foraging had done. Early modern consumers were like most people in the sense that, when faced with few choices, they preferred a boring diet that minimized hunger cravings to a more exciting, more balanced, but less reliable one, that sometimes left them or their children feeling empty and desperate. Both maize and potatoes could grow in more marginal soil than their main competitors (wheat, rye, oats) and both could be cultivated with hand tools (the hoe), which made them ideal for poorer people who owned few or no draft animals. This also meant that much of the work of growing them devolved upon women, traditionally the kitchen gardeners, as well as the people typically assigned jobs that involved a lot of bending and stooping.[39]

Both maize and potatoes are nutritious as well as stomach filling. Potatoes are sometimes called the perfect food because of their high complement of essential nutrients, though to get the requisite protein it is said that labouring men in the eighteenth and nineteenth centuries routinely consumed between five and six kilograms of potatoes a day. A good source of vitamin C, potatoes are credited with having greatly reduced scurvy, common in the early modern period during the winter months, especially in northern Europe. A diet consisting solely of maize is more nutritionally problematic. By the 1740s poor people living in parts of Spain, Italy, Southern France, Romania, Austria, Southern Russia and Anatolia who were subsisting wholly on maize (foraging opportunities having by then been largely exhausted in many areas) began to manifest pellagra, a disease caused by niacin deficiency, and characterized by diarrhoea, severe skin rashes, dementia, and, in serious cases, death.[40] The perils of concentrating so exclusively on one kind of food were most powerfully demonstrated in Ireland. By the eve of the Great Famine of 1846–50 around three million people ate virtually nothing but potatoes and they were also the main fodder food for pigs and fowl, and significant for cattle as well. This left much of the food chain vulnerable to crop failure, which was exactly what happened in 1845, when the potato crop across Ireland and various other parts of Europe became infected with the potato blight *Phytophthora Infestans*. The resulting famine killed around a million people.[41]

The Great Potato Famine notwithstanding, in the eighteenth century potatoes and maize probably did blunt the effects of famines. They also had some more unexpected results. They probably made it possible to draft more men into the growing armies because the new crops could be grown with hand tools, and often delivered enough yield per unit of land for women and girls to feed whole families on it without much or any help from husbands or sons. In parts of the Balkans maize farming, coupled with political instability, seems to have encouraged greater local self-reliance and insularity from the market. Unfortunately it also reinforced some less-than-appealing aspects of local gender ideology. In Montenegro, into the twentieth century, women grew virtually all the food crop (largely maize, and some potatoes in the uplands), and indeed, did all the manual work, because dirtying one's hands and lifting burdens were considered dishonourable for men. Meanwhile, a good proportion of the men devoted themselves to banditry (primarily cattle-raids and preying on road traffic), blood feuds and war. It seems likely that, across Europe and West Asia, in the mountainous areas that were the traditional suppliers of soldiers (the Scottish Highlands, Switzerland, Albania, Bulgaria, the Caucasus, etc.) women took over more and more of the task of supporting families, sometimes setting in motion a pattern of hyper-exploitation of women's labour in subsistence agriculture that would survive into the twentieth century. It is not good for women when men have too much time on their hands.[42]

Agricultural modernization and declining living standards

The transition from a series of rural, agricultural, subsistence-oriented societies to a heavily urbanized, regionally integrated market economy occurred in several parts of the world in the early modern period, of which Europe was one.[43] Since then it has extended to most of the rest of the world. Europeans of all social classes, particularly in western Europe, benefited greatly over the long run from the commercialization of agriculture. In the short run it was a different story. Many historians now believe that the Agricultural Revolution (referring to the twinned processes of the commercialization and rationalization of agriculture) caused a good deal more pain, to more people, and over a longer period, than the Industrial Revolution, and that its benefits were concentrated for far longer within a narrower demographic. By contrast, industrialization usually led to some increase in real wages, though it is true that this did not always happen very quickly, and it had some less desirable side-effects such as crowding, occupational diseases and injuries, and increased pollution of the air and waterways.[44]

Virtually everywhere the commercialization of agriculture predated industrialization, sometimes by a century or more. It was enclosure, rural foreclosures and evictions, and low farm wages that first turned hundreds of thousands and soon millions of Europeans into landless rural labourers or urban proletarians in the eighteenth and nineteenth centuries. In eastern Europe, the commercialization of the grain trade was one of the key factors that led to the so-called 'second serfdom', where large swathes of the population of Russia, Poland, what is now eastern Germany, and elsewhere, were turned, from the seventeenth century on, into a captive labour force of serfs, tied to the land, and increasingly bereft of legal rights. In the West Indies, the South American mainland, and the southern portion of North America, the new global market in tropical and subtropical commodities, primarily sugar and tobacco (and later cotton), led to the enslavement of, first thousands, then tens of thousands, and ultimately some ten million west and west-central Africans. The impact of all of this in terms of people's food, and particularly their protein intake, was very marked. One of the most sensitive measures of nutritional well-being is stature. Where there is not much food, or it is of a low quality, people tend to be short; where there is plenty they tend to be tall, and this effect can usually be seen within a generation. Across much of Europe in the later eighteenth century stature fell, but in regions where agriculture modernized and reoriented to production for the market (including parts of the Netherlands, England, Belgium, Alsace and elsewhere) it fell, on average, a good deal more. In addition, there is a considerable amount of evidence that girls' and women's living standard (along with their stature) fell even more than men's, probably because of diminishing demand for female workers in agriculture (at least in England), falling wages, and the elimination of rights in the commons which, as we have seen, was especially significant for women.[45]

It was in the more economically dynamic areas, whether areas of commercializing agriculture or in the new industrial towns, and also in cities more generally, where poor Europeans' diets deteriorated most markedly. By contrast, people living in the remoter, less populous and more self-sufficient areas, tended, on the whole, to be taller, which almost certainly means that they were eating more and better foods, more protein, and fewer carbohydrates. Figure 4.1 is a reconstruction of the average diet of peasants in a village in Gévaudan, in the Cévennes region of France, in the latter part of the eighteenth century. The bread that made up ninety-six per cent of daily intake was probably made from barley and rye, and the diet would have been supplemented with cabbage and turnips, and a few wild greens. Meat was almost nonexistent.

Figure 4.1 Peasant diets in Gévaudan, France, in the eighteenth century

Percentage of total daily intake by weight in grams (Gévaudan, 1754–88)

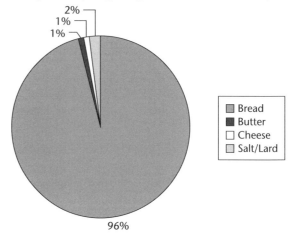

2%
1%
1%

96%

☐ Bread
■ Butter
☐ Cheese
☐ Salt/Lard

Source: R.J. Bernard, 'Peasant Diet in Eighteenth-Century Gévaudan', in Elborg Forster and Robert Forster, eds, *European Diet from Pre-Industrial to Modern Times* (New York: Harper Torchbooks, 1975), 19–46.

The apparent narrowing of food options seen in Gévaudan and many other places in this period was the result of growing regional specialization, an intensification of older patterns of labour exploitation, and an increasing gulf between rich and poor. Passing through Rhenish wine country in 1794 the Gothic novelist Ann Radcliffe remarked on the fact that, despite the richness of the soil, the peasantry was very poor, because 'the value of every hill is exactly watched by the landlords'. In the Rhineland common rights had largely disappeared, and much of the peasantry had been reduced to under-fed wage-serfs.[46] And almost everywhere the problems were exacerbated by rising populations and the fact that so many were moving to the unhealthy and relatively poorly fed cities.

The commercialization of agriculture presents one of the classic dilemmas of development. It played an indispensable role in creating the Europe of today, where almost no one starves (though food insecurity is still to be found, especially in eastern Europe). One can debate the relative role of welfare states and deplore some of the effects of present-day European food policies on the environment and on the developing world, but this still stands as one of the great achievements of human history, especially given the fact that the European population has more than quadrupled since 1750. But eighteenth-century people had to live with what they had, and the evidence suggests that by 1800, on average, the majority owned or controlled less land, competed with more people for what resources there were, ate less (though possibly more reliably, thanks to maize and the potato, as well as, in some places, improved market integration), and enjoying a diminished range of foods – notably less meat – than their forebears had done. Over the long run, these people's great-grandchildren would see the benefits of modernization, but, in many cases, only a century or more later. No one at the time could see ahead that far.[47]

SHOPPING

Locally self-sufficient or subsistence-oriented societies support very few or no shops and only the occasional, perhaps itinerant, seller of salt or metal goods. Few parts of Europe – except for some distant off-shore islands and a few of the remotest mountain ranges – were this self-sufficient by the eighteenth century. Almost everywhere the number of shops or market opportunities was on the rise, though in rural or more remote areas much buying was still off the back of wagons, from peddlers' packs, or from temporary stalls at fairs. The growth of retail outlets was especially pronounced in the economically robust northwest, though it was certainly not confined to that region – or, for that matter, unique to Europe. In 1785 a special census of English shops made for tax purposes found 23,083 shops, which considerably understated the true number, for it counted only shops that opened onto the street level, and did a less adequate count of shops in smaller towns. Larger French towns had long been famous for their retail shopping, and the same was true of the international entrepots of the Netherlands. Even in distant Russia a census of shops in the 1790s found 151 cities reporting some 14,060 retail stores.[48] There are fewer hard statistics for the Ottoman Empire, but Istanbul had been the largest city in Europe in the seventeenth century, with perhaps 600,000 to 750,000 inhabitants, and was drawing foodstuffs from hundreds of kilometres away, and other goods from much farther. Its famous *souk* had, by this time, been joined by a range of other shopping districts, including, from at least the seventeenth century, a special women's market.[49]

Everywhere shopping looked very different from what we are accustomed to today. In the first place most eighteenth-century towns were chronically short of cash. In this low liquidity environment 'buying' still often relied upon credit, barter, reciprocal gifting, appeals to others' good will or charitable instincts, and a certain amount of petty theft as much or more than it did on cash transactions. Shopping did not just encourage the formation of complex personal relationships and networks; it was inconceivable without them. Exchanging cash for, say, a dozen eggs, in the way we might do today is, or can be, both quick and largely anonymous. Everything has been established:

a general confidence in money as legal tender, the expectation that shoppers will generally carry cash or a credit card with them, the price of eggs, a high degree of assurance – due to careful packaging – that none of the eggs will be cracked, the manner and locus of the exchange, and how the purchases will be carried home (some vendors supply the bags; others, more environmentally conscious, encourage customers to bring their own). The buyer and seller may choose to exchange pleasantries, but this is certainly not necessary, and makes little or no difference to the transaction itself. In the eighteenth century, when none of these things was clearly set, petty buying and selling were the very opposite of anonymous, and women consumers in the marketplace spent a good proportion of their time managing the relationships upon which almost all transactions depended.

Because early-modern workers were fairly infrequently paid, many families lived on credit anyway, and suppliers, including retailers, were fairly accustomed to it. But 'credit' is a complex matter, woven together of reciprocal favours, fair promises, expectations of future return, bargaining, personal reputation, persuasion, and guilt. Women in the marketplace had an endless number of strategies. They might assert a moral right to credit based on some sort of 'connection': e.g. 'my husband used to work for your sister's husband'. They might 'volunteer' to carry a particular market-trader's goods, sweep his or her area or keep a lookout for petty thieves, or run about encouraging other people to buy from a particular stall-seller, perhaps in return for getting the semi-spoiled food at the end of the day. They might be available to contribute verbal support in case of some altercation, perhaps to loudly assert a particular stallholder's honesty or dishonesty. One gets the impression that many markets were quite factionalized, and people no doubt aligned themselves with one faction or another, partly in expectation of getting free or reduced-price food. Women also begged for food, often with a baby in their arms (an inducement to guilt in the hard-hearted), or sent their children out to beg; in general the division between asking for credit and begging was far less defined than it is today.[50] Some permitted hasty sexual favours: a kiss or a feel in return for some bread or vegetables. Many were prepared to swipe a piece of fruit, or to get their children to do it for them. Such complex social manoeuvres were a normal part of many early modern women's lives, particularly in the cities.

Food imports and other luxuries

Shopping both fed upon and fuelled the decline of subsistence lifestyles and economic localism. One way it did this was by encouraging the adoption of new foods that could not be locally grown. Unlike potatoes and maize, commodities like coffee, chocolate, sugar, tea and tobacco were tropical or subtropical and never could be produced on a large scale in Europe. Consumers who wanted them were reliant upon the market from the outset. The appeal of these goods, all of which were more or less habit-forming, helped both to accustom Europeans to buying, and to reconcile them to the notion that some foods had to be produced in far-away places under conditions they would have found abhorrent if they themselves had been subjected to them. It is not at all a stretch to argue that the sweet taste of sugar facilitated the process by which Europeans, women and men, rich and poor, justified slavery in their own minds.[51] Initially, of course, these foreign imports were purchased largely by the upper and middle classes. But by the first third of the eighteenth century in western Europe and much of the Ottoman Empire, and somewhat later in eastern Europe, they had also begun to filter down the social scale. It is one of the small ironies of women's history that, in the nineteenth and twentieth centuries, heavily sugared tea, initially a double luxury, became the appetite suppressant of choice for poor urban women across much of Europe.

The emergence of shops and shopping was in no way confined to western Europe, though it has been less studied elsewhere. In Russia, Peter the Great's insistence that the nobility of both sexes dress like the western European aristocracy, and that women and men socialize together, gave a major impetus to the growth both of shops (usually, at least initially, run by foreigners) and shopping. There were printed commercial directories in England, France and Germany by the end of the eighteenth century; less predictably, they were also to be found in Scandinavia, Hungary, and the American colonies. In Istanbul, long hospitable to a variety of kinds of craft and retailing endeavours, as well as an important international entrepot, guild control of shops was replaced in the eighteenth century by a much more flexible system, while the famous Balkan trade fairs continued to draw both buyers and sellers up to the end of Ottoman rule.[52] Marketing techniques such as demand creation and print advertising were not entirely new, but they became far more widespread, more 'populist' and more sophisticated in the eighteenth century. Fashion magazines with engraved pictures had become common by the later eighteenth century, especially in western Europe and in cities.

Shopping, especially shopping for 'luxuries', worried people, though. The promiscuous way that anybody with money could buy anything they wanted seemed dramatically to blur the class, racial and religious boundaries long shored up, at least in part, by regulating what sorts of luxuries the different ranks or other groupings were permitted to buy and display. Women were a particular problem. While it seems likely that men, who virtually always had more money than women did, probably consumed as much in aggregate, and certainly made the larger purchases,[53] women were almost universally deemed to be the more extravagant sex. In addition, though most women worked, they were already viewed, especially in the city, as the gender that 'consumed', while men 'produced'. This fictional division was well in place long before significant numbers of women actually left the paid or productive workforce, a nineteenth- or indeed twentieth-century phenomenon in many parts of Europe (see Chapter 5).

The other important association forged in these years (though it too had earlier antecedents) was between commerce and sexual immorality. It was widely claimed in the eighteenth century that women were more interested in adorning themselves than they were in family duties, and this claim was often buttressed with nostalgic comparisons to supposedly virtuous and frugal women of old. The allegedly 'new' passion for adornment was closely linked to sexual promiscuity, not just because it was so clearly designed to attract men (it was hard for early modern men to imagine that women might be interested in clothes, jewelry, etc. for any other reason), but because women would, or so it was argued, readily 'sell' themselves to men in return for fripperies. There was also a persistent belief that wives as a group were perfectly prepared to bankrupt their husbands in order to feed their shopping urges. The stereotype of the spendthrift wife became ubiquitous across Europe and the Middle East in the early modern period, turning up in divorce cases, plays (from Molière to Turkish *karagöz* plays), novels, popular proverbs and even old-style sumptuary laws. It was even used as an odd sort of justifications for colonialism and slavery, often represented as flowing from European men's need to feed women's insatiable desire for sugar, furs, tea, jewels, etc.[54]

There are several ways to read female shopping. A number of historians have stressed the way shopping handed women new forms of authority, both over taste and family finances, as well as, under some circumstances, a new degree of mobility (since they often had to leave their homes and neighbourhoods to pursue the best bargains). There is a good deal of evidence to support such an interpretation. Retailers everywhere sought to appeal to women – sometimes in the face of considerable disapproval from the pundits, the clergy and the state – by creating 'safe' and respectable spaces for women to shop. A famous example of this was Thomas Twining's 'Tea House for Ladies', begun in London in 1717. It is clear, moreover, that women seized the opportunity to accumulate goods that were highly fungible (meaning easy to exchange for other things). And they were, and probably becoming more so: there was a large market in old clothes, jewelry, snuff-boxes and the like throughout Europe and the Middle East in the early modern period. It seems likely that the new consumerism transferred some fungible assets from men, who always had more access to cash and other resources, to women. Women's consumer goods, clothes in particular, became, in effect, an alternative currency.[55] There is also a lot of evidence that women sought to impress their personality on, assert their ownership of, and enhance the value of consumer goods, especially textiles, by mixing their labour with them. This partially explains women's heavy involvement in embroidery, particularly but not only in the Ottoman Empire, for embroidered clothes and accoutrements were important prestige items for both men and women. All these complex negotiations with consumer goods may also have had a knock-on effect in the courts. It is surely not coincidental that suits for maintenance (i.e. suing husbands for failing to support their wives) became one of the most common forms of women's litigation in the early modern period and into the nineteenth. Moreover, the fact that, in a 'warming' economy, the luxuries of today are likely to become the necessities of tomorrow cannot but have bolstered women's maintenance claims over the long haul, even as it provided endless fodder for nostalgic fantasies about the virtuous, abstemious and undemanding women of old.

Food riots

In reasonable years it is thought that eighteenth-century urban labourers spent around half their income on food. But in years of dearth the price of staples routinely doubled or tripled as both growers and retailers sought to cash in on the panic. Poorer consumers, over much of early modern Europe (and, for that matter, early modern Asia, the Middle East and North Africa), responded with food riots, often either instigated by women, or involving heavy participation by them. Food riots could take a variety of forms including confrontations with bakers or other retailers, looting of shops, transport carts or granaries, efforts to stop the export of grain, or insistence on a 'just price' for needed foodstuffs. Food riots were, if not ubiquitous, then very common across Europe and the Middle East in the eighteenth century: there were at least 652 in France in the three decades before 1789; and thousands in England over the course of the eighteenth and early nineteenth centuries. They were also found in Ireland, Scotland, the Netherlands and Spain, though not, apparently, in Germany before the nineteenth. There were also thousands of small or large food riots in the early modern Ottoman Empire. Some of the largest episodes of civil unrest in the eighteenth century were related to food. A series of food-related riots convulsed thirty provinces across Spain in 1766, though it seems that most of the leaders (or at least those arrested) were men. The more famous and even more massive French 'Flour War' of 1775 was a response to bad harvests and the physiocrat Turgot's decision to eliminate price-controls on grain. It gave rise to more than three hundred riots in eighty-two villages and towns across Northern France during a three-week period, and 25,000 troops had to be sent in to restore order.[56]

No extensive first-hand accounts by food rioters have survived, but we do have a number of descriptions of food riots from the local officials whose job it was to pacify rioters. In 1709 an exceptionally cold winter drove up prices throughout northern Europe and caused a significant spike in mortality from the usual diseases that accompany starvation. On 24 March of that year, in Lyon, a crowd massed in front of a baker's shop to support a young man who had been refused bread. People began throwing rocks and, in response, the baker wounded the young man in the arm with a gun. The *prévôt des marchands* (superintendent of merchants), one Monsieur Ravat, succeeded in calming people down at first, but the next day the disorder grew, with angry crowds gathering in front of bread shops all over town. According to Ravat's report:

> I asked where the biggest crowd was, and, told that it was in the Rue de la Grenette, went there and discovered more than 1,500 persons gathered in front of a shop at which they were angrily throwing stones. I spoke to several women and told them that I would go in and give them bread if the baker had any. I searched his shop and sent others to search in other shops on the same street. We found one with bread. I told all the women who cried for bread that I would give them some.[57]

Ravat repeated this manoeuvre several times, essentially placating women by giving them bread, most likely at a price lower than what bakers were demanding. This was quite typical of the way early modern town officials dealt with food rioters, especially early in the eighteenth century: they took their side. Partly this was because they did not have the police power to put them down, or the stomach to shoot into crowds of women and children, but it was also because they often sympathized with rioters, at least to a degree. However, 1709 also demonstrates the limits of a policy of appeasement. A few months later officials were forced to raise the price of bread because they could no longer sustain their earlier policy of buying grain at hugely inflated prices from suppliers and selling it cheap to the bakers. This shifted consumer animus toward the *prévôt* and town officials: now the crowds massed in front of Ravat's house, and the confrontation grew increasingly violent, resulting in a number of arrests, though mainly of men.[58]

This whole episode is quite indicative of the way food riots were 'supposed' to work in a traditional economy. Groups of consumers, many, though not all of them, women, used violence or threats of violence to pressure grain merchants, middlemen and bakers to keep the price at what they were prepared to pay, and particularly to stop grain speculators making a killing on the backs of the hungry. Local officials either acquiesced or actively cooperated with rioters, as long as they did not get too violent or unruly; moreover, as long as city or parish coffers would permit it, city elites tried to keep prices down, and viewed that as part of the price of maintaining public order. When things started to get out of hand, they generally arrested men, even if, as in Lyon, only a few men had been involved in the original altercation. Clearly this policy encouraged women both to emphasize their role as nurturers and providers of food, and to believe that they enjoyed a certain licence to act provocatively in public. It is not uncommon to come across accounts that suggest that women were more violent and combative than their husbands, especially when it came to confrontations with authority.[59] Sometimes the latter belief could result in some fairly spectacular actions. Here is a description of a food riot that occurred sometime in the 1740s or 50s in Aleppo in the Ottoman Empire. The speaker is Alexander Russell, an English physician living there at the time:

> I remember an instance of dearth where a mob of women took possession of several of the minarets, and, preventing the [muezzins] from calling the people to prayers at noon, ascended themselves, and in a loud voice, from the gallery, exhorted all true Moslems to espouse the cause of their wives and children. Several granaries were broken open; the Mutsillem [deputy governor] . . . found it prudent to fly, and it was several days before the tumult subsided.[60]

We know few other details about this particular food riot, but it is clear that women took a very public role, and may even have initiated the unrest in the first place.

In Christian Europe, but possibly in the Ottoman Empire as well, food riots seem to have become much more common as well as more violent beginning around 1750. In part this was due to pressures no one could have foreseen and for which there were, at that time, no good solutions: the growing population concentrations in cities and textile-producing areas, regional specialization and diminishing subsistence farming created larger-scale food crises than before. And in part it was because old understandings broke down. In a number of countries eighteenth- and early nineteenth-century champions of *laissez-faire* began arguing that artificial interventions in the grain market, whether by well-meaning officials in the form of price and export controls and subventions, or by hungry crowds, were ultimately self-defeating – a disincentive to growers as well as a source of distribution bottlenecks.[61] After 1789 the new worker organizations (nascent trades unions), and Jacobinism, real or imagined, gave civil unrest a more terrifying aspect, at least from the perspective of the rich, the nobility and the established clergy. But there is evidence that attitudes were hardening even before the French Revolution. More and more one sees soldiers ordered to fire into crowds, as well as executions of the leaders of mobs – shooting into crowds sometimes killed women of course, but in the case of exemplary executions men seem disproportionately to have paid the price.[62]

A certain strain of thought, which began in the eighteenth century, has always seen food riots as atavistic reflex actions by people too benighted to realize that free trade was in their own interests. Conversely, historians on the Left have tended to view them as a heroic early form of opposition to the amorality of the capitalist market. Neither view is entirely satisfying, and the contexts within which food riots occurred (and still occur) may be too diverse to permit easy generalizations. Riots or fear of riots during famines forced municipal and provincial elites to exploit the capital, connections, coercive authority, administrative experience and bulk transport options they possessed in far greater abundance than poor people to find new sources of supply, and break through the bottlenecks. They must also have motivated merchants, intellectuals, local officials and rulers, not to mention rioters themselves, to think through the implications of free trade – both its undeniable benefits and its inadequacies – in a far more comprehensive way than they would otherwise have felt impelled to do.[63]

IN AND OUT OF THE KITCHEN

The politics of cookbooks

As we have seen, 'fine cooking' was not that common among the bulk of women, at least in the everyday. Nevertheless, recipes and remedies, passed down, gifted, kept secret, or strategically revealed, have been an important form of symbolic capital for women for as long as cooking has been a predominantly female domain. In the eighteenth century, literate women launched themselves decisively into cookbook writing, and their efforts are good indicators both of the ways some women sought to convert female knowledge and women's practical expertise into symbolic capital, and of emerging or expanding fissures between women. Recipes were powerful tokens of emotional and cultural continuity, connection and memory-making across the generations. Some eighteenth-century cookbooks registered this, such as Penelope Bradshaw's charmingly titled *Valuable Family Jewel . . . Containing All That Relates to Cookery, Pastry, Pickling, Preserving, Wine Making, Brewing, Bread Making, Oat Cakes, [etc.]*, an English cookbook from the 1740s.[64] And cookbooks were probably also the most successful women's printed genre of the eighteenth century. Many cookbooks went into multiple editions. Some continued to be published well into the nineteenth or even twentieth century. They were also routinely pirated (a signal marker of popularity in the eighteenth century), translated into other languages, and used until they fell apart.[65] Cookbooks grew out of a much broader commitment, common to many educated men and women of the seventeenth and eighteenth centuries, to the dissemination, for the general good, of previously secret or 'proprietary' knowledge. Cookbook writers, both female and male, were bringing information traditionally associated with the 'guild' of womankind into the public marketplace.

Cookbooks are a wonderful source for information about eighteenth-century food practices, particularly in the middle and upper classes; they also register a variety of more general social, cultural and economic trends. Transitional documents, many eighteenth-century cookbooks still have a certain amount of 'country' in them, in the sense that they often assume their readers will bring to table numerous wild birds, including larks, doves, plovers, blackbirds, thrushes, rooks, woodcocks, bitterns, widgeons, herons and puffins, as well as today's more familiar game birds (wild ducks, pheasants, partridges, grouses, pigeons, etc.). They also faithfully reflect the high cost of meat. Even though cookbooks were written for people who ate meat fairly often, and not for the increasingly vegetarian poor, they do register that larger world of dearth in that they assume that little or nothing of the slaughtered beast will be wasted. People with access to meat still ate and still had a taste for all kinds of cuts that most slaughterhouses today discard or make into pet food, including the brains, eyes, head, tongue, testicles, sweetbreads (thymus gland), intestines (tripe), spine, jowl, udder and feet. The recipe in Voices from the Past 4.2, which lavishes a good deal of care on a cut of meat (lamb stones) that has largely disappeared from European tables (except, it is said, in Spain), is quite indicative of eighteenth-century Europeans' broad-minded conception of food when compared with our own.

> ### VOICES FROM THE PAST 4.2
>
> *Waste not want not*
>
> #### A Fricasey of Lambstones and Sweetbreads
>
> Have ready some Lambstones blanched parboiled and sliced, and floure two or three Sweetbreads; if very thick, cut them in two, the Yolks of six hard Eggs whole, a few Pistaco [sic] Nut Kernels, and a few large Oysters: Fry these all of a fine Brown, then pour out all the Butter, and add a Pint of drawn Gravy, the Lambstones, some Asparagus Tops about an Inch long, some grated Nutmeg, a little Pepper and Salt, two Shalots shred small, and a Glass of White Wine; stew all these together for ten Minutes, then add the Yolks of six Eggs beat very fine, with a little White Wine, and a little beaten Mace; stir all together till it is of a fine Thickness, and then dish it up. Garnish with Lemon.
>
> *Source*: [Hannah Glasse], *The Art of Cookery, Made Plain and Easy* (London, 1747), 15.
>
> *Terms*:
>
> Lamb stones: lamb's testicles
>
> Sweetbreads: pancreas or thymus gland of calf or lamb

In fact, there were already real differences between cookbook writers' assumptions about food and those of the bulk of the population. Eighteenth-century printed cookbooks, essentially urban productions, include all sorts of (to us) unfamiliar foods, yet they still significantly understate the sheer diversity of field, forest, river, fenland and seaside products – mushrooms, wild herbs and greens, roots, buds, leaves, nuts, snails, frogs, eels, wild birds' eggs, berries, rabbits, seaweed, shell-fish – that went into rural diets, as well as the complex regional and seasonal variations on these themes. They did so because, by the eighteenth century, especially in western Europe, foraging, something almost all rural women did, had come to be associated with poverty and desperation. Sometimes the plant-names themselves show this. An old-fashioned French name for dandelion, '*l'or du pauvre*' (gold of the poor) advertises both the dandelion's bright colour and the fact that wild dandelion greens were a frequent addition to the poor woman's soup pot. In the eighteenth century several well-meaning writers actually published lists of wild foods in a bid to assist their poorer countrymen and women in times of dearth.[66] By the eighteenth century, foraging too had moved into the market, but it was a disreputable kind of market that tended to make better-off people nervous and embarrassed. Eighteenth-century travellers' accounts often report destitute women and children insistently trying to sell them baskets of berries or seagull eggs gathered off the sea-cliffs. They also describe women down on the beach or in the tidal pools picking the less saleable periwinkles, limpets and seaweed off the rocks for their own use. The last three were common famine food. But the prejudices of better-off people, who could concentrate on higher-status gardening rather than on foraging, who had the money to buy high-quality vegetables and meats in the market, and who never went hungry, were already beginning to blind them to the individual knowledge, inherited traditions and ingenuity that went into finding edible food 'in the rough'. The desperation, dirtiness and hard labour of it offended sensibilities; it seemed inconsistent with what was fast emerging as gastronomic art.

Cookbooks early showed signs of political and especially proto-nationalist aspirations, and women's cookbooks were no exception. The German writer Maria Sophia Schellhammer's popular cookbook was issued under various titles (Plate 3) including *Das Brandenburgische Koch-Buch* (the Brandenburg Cook-Book) and there were 'Piedmontese' cookbooks, 'Viennese' cookbooks, 'Swedish' cookbooks, 'Flemish' cookbooks, 'Parisian' cookbooks and endless variations on those themes. Some of these cookbooks actually made an effort to include local specialties; others just purveyed generic, or, more often, French recipes while draping their country's, region's or city's name over their title like a flag. Thinking about cooking and household management in terms of local or national identity offered an excellent opportunity for writers to explore fantasies of feminine inclusion in the emerging national and regional polities. Martha Bradley's *The British housewife, or, The cook, housekeeper's and gardiner's companion* (1756) and many more in this vein, celebrated a distinctly 'British' (or, as the case might be, 'French', 'Dutch' or 'Czech') woman, usually an idealized, but decisively managerial middling householder. This tendency would become much more pronounced late in the eighteenth century. As nationalist fervour spread across Europe and the New World, women, especially middle-class women, redoubled their efforts to try to find a place within the new polities and conceptions of 'nation' emerging almost everywhere, and food proved to be one important way to do this (see Chapter 9).

Food and drink innovators

Innovation in the realm of food and drink is often anonymous, partly because food is one of those realms that people take for granted and partly because low-status people (women, servants, slaves) are the ones who tend to oversee it. The central, and in many respects unrecoverable, story of early modern women and food is the story of the hundreds of thousands of nameless women who integrated novel food items such as potatoes, maize, peppers, aubergine, tomatoes, hazelnuts, coffee, tea, sugar and so on into their own and their families' diets and then swapped or passed on the recipes over the decades and centuries. In fact, partly because in the eighteenth century food (including prepared foods) became more commercialized than before, we can trace a few individual eighteenth-century women innovators, though there is considerable disagreement about what precisely they did. Several of these women are linked to cheese-making, a very old art, that, along with yoghurt-making, seems first to have been developed in the ancient Middle East, though independent discoveries of it in different places seem likely. Both cheese and yoghurt help cope with the problem of the swift spoilage of milk by using 'friendly' bacteria and moulds to crowd out undesirable ones. Cheese-making was closely associated with women in both the Middle East and Europe, both because milking was a tedious, hard-on-the-hands, everyday sort of job that men tended to avoid if they could, and because goats, the source of much cheese and yoghurt, were considered a 'woman's animal'.[67] Several new cheeses came to prominence in the newly robust commercial environment of the eighteenth century. Arguably the finest of English cheeses, Stilton, a luxury cheese (for it includes expensive cream), has been associated with a number of women. It may have been invented around 1720 by a woman called Elizabeth Scarborough who lived near Leicester and later at Little Dalby, though it is also said to be based on a seventeenth-century recipe by one Lady Beaumont, a relation of the family for which Scarborough worked. Better documented is the fact that another woman, Frances Pawlett (1720?–1808) of Wymondham, Leicestershire, a 'supreme cheese-maker', along with her husband William Pawlett, turned Stilton into a successful commercial cheese.[68] France's most popular cheese, Camembert, is said to have been invented – or at least significantly improved upon – by one Marie Harel, a Norman dairy maid, in 1791. The vague and disputed genealogies of these cheeses are typical of the challenges faced by food historians, though.

Urban women also developed new foods, new technologies, and, most prominently, new marketing techniques for food and drink. The most famous example was Nicole Barbe Clicquot, née Ponsardin (1777–1866) of Reims, who carried on and vastly expanded the champagne business she inherited at the age of twenty-eight when her husband of only six years died. La Veuve Clicquot, whose name still adorns an illustrious line of champagne (the real name of the line is Clicquot Ponsardin, incorporating both her maiden name and her husband's name), bought up the best Champagne vineyards, invented, in 1816, a new method of clarifying ('riddling') her wines, and managed to expand her international sales even in wartime, largely by having her supply-boats finesse the Napoleonic blockade of Russia. She was also an innovator in brand-name and personality marketing.[69]

CONCLUSION

Getting, preparing and overseeing the consumption of food took up a large part of women's lives in the eighteenth century. It was a source of artistic creativity, often overlapping with the supernatural, a gateway to power over life and death, a pretext for varieties of intimate coercion that have probably been too little examined historically – particularly forced wet-nursing – and a constant challenge to any woman's resourcefulness. If you had money to invest, something appealing to sell and marketing *brio*, the eighteenth century was a heady time, and some women prospered and made a name for themselves. The cookbook writers had a real vision, not just about food but about the place of the women who cooked it. Their public recognized and confirmed that, by buying their books in great numbers and, in time, by incorporating issues concerning food into an emerging ideal of rational domesticity (see Chapters 8 and 9). Domesticity was pretty meaningless to much poorer women though; for them the work of feeding themselves and their families grew more difficult in the late eighteenth century. The increasing pressure of population on the land, the decline of traditional methods and lifestyles, the growth in staple hoe crops, like the potato and maize, and the special challenges of trying to ensure an affordable food-supply in the early modern city must often have greatly taxed their ingenuity. Dietary vulnerability and unpredictability defined their lives in ways we can only glimpse today. Market transitions are still with us and they are still often miserable, in food and quality-of-life terms. Moreover, the environmental and resource challenges of the next thirty to one hundred years are likely to be some of the more extreme that human beings (not to mention other species) have ever faced. The experiences of eighteenth-century women speak to us because their time, like ours, was one of enormous technical, environmental, and social change. Those changes both defined their life choices and significantly affected their ability to sustain themselves and their families, often in ways that were distinctly gendered. The world is a very different place today, but, at least in those respects, we can probably expect interesting times ahead.

Chapter 5

◆

WORK AND MONEY

For a long time our view of pre-modern European women was built upon a myth. The myth was that, until the middle to latter part of the twentieth century, most European women devoted their lives entirely to their families, seldom worked for pay, and hardly ever left home. The fantasy of the non-working wife derives in part from a rather interesting historical misconception. In medieval and early modern Europe, and well into the nineteenth century (later in some countries), almost all women worked, and already by the eighteenth century large numbers of them (and the majority in most cities) worked for pay. However, some time between 1830 and the later twentieth century (precisely when depended on the country) a significant number of *married* women and a smaller percentage of unmarried women *did* leave (or never entered) the paid labour force, probably due to a sharp deterioration in the number and quality of jobs open to women, changes in the character of agriculture, a rise in real wages for men, and a heavy dose of propaganda about motherhood and domesticity. In England the 'trough' of women's workforce participation was about 1830 to World War II. In the post-World War II period the pattern reversed again and a large new influx of women, both single and married, re-entered the paid workforce. The chronology differed greatly from place to place. In most Western and central European countries (and also in Ireland and Scotland) married women left the paid workforce later and in smaller numbers than they did in England, and started returning in the second half of the twentieth century. In Russia and other parts of what became the socialist bloc, women dropped out of the paid workforce up to a century later (if they ever did), and for a briefer period. This phenomenon is sometimes called the 'U-curve' of women's paid workforce participation, meaning that it was historically high, declined for a period that lasted, depending on the country, between a few decades and a century, then rose again in the second half of the twentieth century to something close to what it had been before. The eighteenth century was at one of the high ends of the curve, meaning most women worked, either for pay or in subsistence agriculture.[1]

In the resource-poor, non-mechanized world of eighteenth-century Europe, leisure was not a viable possibility for any except a few nobles. Most girls started working around the age of six or seven, and most of the work was related in some way to agriculture, simply because that was the way of life of most of the population. Subsistence farming and unpaid work in commercial agriculture had long been important activities for women. In the early modern period paid farm service became the norm over much of Europe, especially for young women,[2] and wage-work largely took over in the cities too. For some urban areas historians have been able to compute women's work force participation with remarkable precision. In London in the period 1695 to 1725 at least seventy-two per cent of women worked for pay, and spinsters (at eighty-three per cent) and widows (at eighty-five per cent) were especially likely to do so. About sixty per cent of married women also worked for pay, and it is interesting to note that they were *most* likely to work for pay in their twenties, thirties and early forties, that is, the prime childbearing age.[3] By way of comparison, in 2004 the paid workforce participation by UK women – which is not, obviously, the same as London women – was around fifty-five per cent. High workforce participation by women – including married women – was not unique to London. In 1752, in Cardington, Bedfordshire, eighty-two per cent of married women aged twenty to thirty-nine worked for pay, many of them in the lace industry. And in Paris, among women availing themselves of the Hôtel Dieu in Paris in the late eighteenth century, seventy-four per cent of married women aged twenty-five to forty-four worked for pay and eighty-five per cent of Paris-born ones, and most of the ones who did not work were seeking employment but unable to find it.[4]

The most common jobs for women almost everywhere were as farm servants (more prevalent in rural areas), domestic servants (more prevalent in the cities), sewing, and carrying and selling things on the street. In addition to this, hundreds of thousands of women in Spain, France, England, Ireland, Flanders (now Belgium), the Netherlands, Switzerland, the German territories, the Czech lands, Austria, Italy, Russia, Bulgaria, Greece and Turkey worked in textile production for the market. Women also did a variety of other, usually low-level, tasks for pay, often work involving hard labour, like the Belgian *boteresses* (mainly coal-carriers), famous for their alarming physical strength, their odd gait – they walked leaning on two sticks – and their prematurely bent spines; the Swedish oarswomen who ferried people across rivers; or the many women who broke rocks at the heads of mines. Countless women made at least part of their living in less respectable ways, as thieves, smugglers (a very common activity for women), and manufacturers or retailers of illegal alcoholic drinks. One of the commonest illegal or semi-legal activities where women were concerned was prostitution.[5] Sometimes women perpetrated or were accessories to more serious crimes, including coining and, rarely, murder-for-gain. Over 750 women were indicted for coining in London between 1674 and 1834, and more than 150 women were condemned to death for it. In the murder-for-gain category, in Galata, a neighbourhood of Istanbul, a woman and two men were executed in the later seventeenth century for the murder of fourteen women. The woman had invited the victims to wedding feasts, and then, when they arrived wearing their jewels and best clothes, her accomplices murdered them for their finery.[6]

IS CAPITALISM GOOD FOR WOMEN?

For much of the twentieth century most women's historians were quite pessimistic about the effect of the market and especially industrial capitalism on women. Initially, at least, there was a tendency to idealize pre-industrial women's work and to argue (not unreasonably) that women's work lives became more constrained, less well-remunerated, and less fulfilling as women were slotted into the least prestigious 'segments' of the capitalist labour complex, such as low-paid service work, the non-union assembly-line, or unpaid work in the home – or joined the growing ranks of the totally destitute.[7] Over time this enthusiasm for the era before industrialization, and even before capitalism (capitalist relations always preceded industrialization, sometimes by a lengthy period) has waned considerably. Though women's work lives have changed greatly over the centuries, the evidence suggests that, both before and after the onset of capitalism and industrialization, women were concentrated in low-paid, less-prestigious kinds of work.[8] Historians of women have tended to explain this by reference to the continuity of violence and exploitation within the family, the ubiquity of laws (or ideologies) that seek to limit women's mobility, and the pernicious impact of the sexual division of labour within both pre- and proto-capitalist and mature capitalist societies. Most would agree that industrial capitalism, coupled with European expansion into much of the rest of the world in the eighteenth, nineteenth and first half of the twentieth centuries, exacerbated class and gender divisions and introduced new forms of race exploitation whose long-term effects are visible to this day.

In the last few decades some historians have grown more enthusiastic about the potential of market capitalism and industrialization for women. They argue that the free market and free (or freer) enterprise systems are intrinsically egalitarian, or at least more egalitarian than the alternatives, precisely because (it is argued) they work to undermine the vested interests that have traditionally held back women and other less powerful groups. The pro-market school concurs about the low status of women in pre-capitalist and pre-industrial economies, but it tends to view the culprits as trade-guilds, legal monopolies, licensing practices and closed professions (like those requiring a university degree), almost all of which historically excluded women, and often other groups, like Jews. Some historians have also grown more positive about the impact of early industrial capitalism on women, arguing that it offered women more opportunities than what it replaced, as well as, on the whole, higher wages and certainly a better standard of living.[9] An implicitly pro-market orientation has also informed much new work on early modern women as consumers. Historians argue that shopping and consumption increased women's mobility, allowed them numerous creative outlets, gave them more control of family finances, replaced some of their hard labour and gave them access to relatively liquid or fungible assets (material goods) that they could swap for money or use to accumulate social capital. Moreover, much of this new work also shows clearly that the proliferation of material goods did not just benefit elite women but powerfully affected both women and men of the labouring classes, often in ways that it is hard to interpret as anything other than positive.[10]

The 'anti-capitalist' women's history and the newer-style pro-market (or at least pro-consumption) women's history, have all contributed to our understanding of early modern and modern European women's history. Left-leaning women's historians have shown how the commercialization of agriculture sustained and reinforced oppressive conditions for many women. They have demonstrated the links between the exploitation of female and child labour within the family and the early factory system's heavy reliance on women and children as a cheap and easily manipulated labour-force. They have paid particular attention to the relationship between slavery, European expansion, and the rise of capitalist relations. And they have illuminated the way ancient beliefs about female inferiority, newer, mostly nineteenth-century, domestic ideologies, and functionalist biologism (the belief that women are 'made' for childbearing and that everything in their lives should be oriented toward that function) dovetails with and supports the inegalitarian workings of the market.[11] On the other hand, historians on the left have also fairly persistently focused on the losses rather than the benefits of markets and industrialization both for women of the capital-owning classes and for less advantageously situated women.

For their part, pro-market women's historians have been especially effective at showing how pre-modern organizations like guilds, 'closed corporations' like universities, and misogynist laws (especially those that constrained mobility) made it difficult for most women to sell their labour or the things they produced at a good price, obtain a practical education, or join the capital-investing classes on their own terms. The evidence is strong that early modern societies constrained competition in large part by limiting *women's* opportunities (and often, at the same time, the opportunities available to racial or religious minorities). Where women were the target, poor women and women who were not (or not any longer) married to a man were especially disadvantaged. This in turn suggests that lessening or eliminating constraints on the free play of competition had and may still have potential to improve women's lives.[12] But this approach still leaves, as a historical problem, the prolonged pain and suffering that the transition to a market society had for many, perhaps the majority of, early modern women, not to mention millions of slaves of both sexes (the main impetus for the expansion of transatlantic slavery having been the commercialization of sugar, tobacco and cotton production). And it also leaves some political problems. It has proven difficult for large parts of the world to realize the same kinds of benefits much of Europe has done from either capitalism or industrialization (much of Africa, for example, seems to be arrested in the 'pain' stage, with no respite in sight). 'Free market' rhetoric has often been a cover for resource extraction at the point of a gun, or, more recently, at the butt of a World Bank loan. And a whole new world of pain and suffering looms from the pressures of capitalist agriculture, mechanization and rising consumption on global climate, water supplies, fuel supplies and land. Issues and questions to do with early modern women cannot help but be seen within a larger trans-historical context.

CHANGING PATTERNS OF RURAL LIFE

When one lived on the land the margin of error was small. Crop failure, the untimely death of workers or future workers, war, a downturn in the price of grain, inflexible tax collectors, landlords or creditors, epizootic disease among domestic animals, and any number of other predictable or unpredictable events could mean misery, permanent loss of livelihood, or death. Partly for this reason, long before the eighteenth century, many people were seeking to diversify by participating in one way or another in the market. Wheat and other grains were grown for sale and often foreign export over large swathes of Europe; many people grew grapes to be turned into wine; women sold farm produce or did piece work (especially spinning) in proto-industries; and many women and men hired out as farm or domestic servants. Even serfs, who used to be viewed as uninterested in the market, can be found buying, selling and suing each other in the early modern period.[13]

In some places the commercialization of agriculture seems to have resulted in the shedding of more female than male jobs and in women's farm work becoming less diversified and prestigious. In England, from the later eighteenth century women farm-servants in some areas were confined almost entirely to weeding, stone-gathering, hoeing and spreading manure. The increased efficiency of crop-growing also led to a decline in dairying, one of the traditionally fairly high-prestige women's jobs.[14] But the pattern on the Continent seems to have been different. In most places between sixty and ninety per cent of the female labouring population continued to work in agriculture well into the nineteenth century and beyond, while in the great grain-exporting regions of eastern Europe it must have been closer to ninety-five per cent. The trend in many places was for agriculture to become more not less feminized. The combination of a rising population (and hence increased demand for food), a new quest for profits, and the lure of women's cheap labour kept them on the job. This was to last in most places until the onset of large-scale, mechanized industrialization in the mid- to late nineteenth century, and in areas that did not industrialize or did so only lightly, women's heavy involvement in farm work persisted at least until the middle of the twentieth century.[15]

DOMESTIC SERVICE

Domestic service was almost always the most significant single sector of female employment in the early modern period, especially for young, single women arriving from the country. Between five and fifteen per cent of the total urban population of western Europe were domestic servants and the percentage may have been still higher in parts of east-central Europe. Across both Christian Europe and the Ottoman Empire domestic service became more feminized in the seventeenth and eighteenth centuries. By the later eighteenth century it has been estimated that between seventy and ninety per cent of domestic servants, as well as a high percentage of domestic slaves, were women and girls.[16] In the very common 'life-cycle' type, a young girl went into domestic service around the age of fifteen, though servants could be found as young as six. Often she would have migrated from some rural area in search of a place. Ideally she saved part of her wages for a dowry and married sometime in her mid- to late-twenties. At marriage she and her husband often set up their own household by pooling their resources, and she ceased to work as a live-in servant, though she was likely to continue to work for money.[17]

When things went as planned this pattern had much to recommend it, and in some countries a good proportion of the population took this route. In England it has been estimated that up to two-thirds of the population worked at some point in either farm or domestic service. In much of Europe live-in domestic service (and in the Ottoman Empire both domestic service and domestic slavery) was the main way rural immigrants and orphans negotiated entry into urban life, adulthood and marriage. Service thus fulfilled an important social purpose (there were exceptions to this, a famous one being Southern Italy, where life-cycle service was rare).[18] On the other hand, almost everywhere servants tended to be very poor, and they were often quite vulnerable to exploitation, especially if they were very young. Servants were particularly prone to getting pregnant out of wedlock, and many prostitutes were former servants.[19] It did not help that their position in the household was often quite ambiguous. As we have seen, destitute parents or uncaring guardians often put out, sold or 'gave away' young girls as servants or slaves. Rather often these girls grew up and tried to sue their employers/guardians for overdue wages, their patrimonies and even for rape, only to find their exploiters representing themselves as foster parents who had taken them in as 'charity'. Child servitude, as Eyal Ginio has remarked, often 'blurred [the] line between charity and abuse'.[20]

Life-cycle servitude and slavery generally coexisted with a different pattern whereby some people entered life-long servitude, or, more often, fell back into it periodically, perhaps to stave off homelessness. In Poland an unusually large number of people seem to have defined themselves as servants, and a good number of these were life-cycle servants. But there were also fairly significant numbers of older women who had either remained in live-in service, or, more typically, returned to it in middle or old age. This pattern was more pronounced in regions with a surplus of women over men and in bad economic times. Poor single, widowed, abandoned or divorced women everywhere seem to have gone into domestic service. Often they simply moved in with relatives and received room and board but no wages in return for their work. Women with children, whether single mothers or destitute married women, put them into foundling homes or farmed them out to relatives and represented themselves as single to prospective employers. There were also efforts in various parts of Europe to force single women to become servants so that they would be under the supervision of a householder, while in Italy poor single girls often worked and lived in charitable institutions run by the church. This pattern has led some historians to argue that domestic service was as much a 'cover' for the structural underemployment of women, as it was a 'real' job.[21] If so, it was a perverse sort of cover; women often found themselves in the position of having only domestic service open to them, but being forbidden to bring their children along (almost no live-in situations permitted children). Eighteenth-century children may have been as likely to become 'economic' as actual orphans.

Still, because domestic service included room and board (often of far more value than any wage the person might receive) it could be a springboard to better things. Certainly servants sought to enhance their status. Research on late seventeenth-century Rotterdam shows that many servants owned gold jewelry and porcelain teapots (though little else in the way of personal property) and some went to considerable trouble to ensure that they had rather elaborate funerals. Servants in better-off households (not, however, the majority of servants) could sometimes do fairly well on tips; moreover, demand for domestic help was sufficiently high in many places that servants could fairly readily abandon a situation they did not like or where they felt mistreated, and find another – to the chagrin of employers.[22] Race clearly made a difference. The relationship of blacks (and, in parts of Southeast Europe, the Roma) to service was often more coercive than was the case for whites. France, Portugal, the Netherlands and England supposedly 'abolished' slavery within the metropole (though not in their colonies) in the early modern period, but in practice this was something of a cosmetic change. Rich whites liked the exotic look of black personal attendants, especially if the latter wore 'decorative' slave collars, as many were forced to do,[23] and many whites found it hard to conceive of black people doing anything except domestic service. They did not necessarily feel they had to pay for it either. In England, in the 1760s and 70s, the courts repeatedly held that black people *in England* – where whites liked to claim that the 'air was too free' for slavery to exist – did not necessarily have to be paid a wage, and had to serve their masters for life. Even fully emancipated blacks, whether male or female, had a difficult time getting any job except as a personal servant or, in the case of women, doing laundry.[24] In the Ottoman Empire African slave/servant-women, who were probably the majority of slaves by the later eighteenth century, tended to be assigned more menial jobs than either 'brown' (usually Ethiopian) or 'white' (usually Balkan or Black Sea) slaves. Black, brown and white slaves were all freed fairly quickly and, in theory, marriages were arranged for them, but the prevalence of black beggar-bands in Salonika and elsewhere suggests that black former slaves were less effectively assimilated into mainstream 'free' society than brown or white slaves were.[25]

STREET-SELLERS AND MARKET-WOMEN

Selling things at market, on the street, or door to door was among the most common jobs for women in the early modern period, throughout all of Europe and the Near East, as well as in the New World. As we have seen (Chapter 4), rural women were frequently heavily occupied in poultry-keeping, dairying, pig-rearing, gardening and foraging, and the choicest products of these labours often ended up for sale at one or another country fair or town market. By the eighteenth century, farm women who sold their own produce were being supplanted in many places by women employed as 'higglers' to carry to market and sell items produced by others. The ubiquitous milk-women were hired to carry heavy containers of milk to town, often starting out long before dawn so as to get their milk to market and sold before the warmth of the day caused it to spoil. There was also a very poor stratum of women who bought up perishable goods to sell at slightly higher prices in other villages or a different part of town.[26]

In many places women were confined by custom, and frequently by law, to selling perishable food items: milk, eggs, fruit, vegetables, fish or cooked food. Because there was no refrigeration, these items had to be unloaded quickly, so sellers were in a poor position to demand high prices for them. Often the arrangements, once they got to town, were quite informal: in the smaller towns of Europe and the New World people bought much of their food from women who set up 'shop' a few times a week, whatever the weather, with nothing but their baskets, on any space they could find. Food was always the main commodity, but in the eighteenth century women street-sellers also hawked some new or fairly new wares, among them newspapers, basically an invention of the early seventeenth century, and printed song-sheets or ballads, often sold by young women who actually sang them as a way to attract buyers. Even in places with very high rates of illiteracy, like

Hungary or Russia, street-sellers could be found hawking religious pictures, printed or written magic spells, and humorous and/or pornographic poems or pictures, often woodcuts.[27]

Most European cities regulated trading, especially in foodstuffs. Some of this was clearly related to health concerns (during epidemics cities tended to place bans on potentially contagious people selling food) or involved efforts to regulate weights and measures. Some of it was linked to efforts to supply towns during famines (see Chapter 4). A great deal of it involved limitations on women sellers. Typical regulations in early modern Portuguese towns included the following: requiring that milk only be sold by milk producers and their servants (an effort to undercut independent female entrepreneurs who were buying up large lots of milk, allegedly diluting the milk with water, and selling it at a profit); insisting that foodstuffs only be sold from the market or market stalls and not from people's houses (an attack on under-capitalized women's retail selling); and a rule that only married women and widows could sell things in the street (an effort to thwart singlewomen who preferred the freedom and quick returns of street-selling over the more 'appropriate' singlewoman's occupation of domestic service). In the French West Indies, and elsewhere in the New World, many slave-women sold vegetables or other comestibles in the so-called *marchés des nègres* (negro markets), often so as to accumulate funds to buy their own or others' freedom; not surprisingly, these activities too were hedged around by numerous regulations. In eighteenth-century Oxford, as in many other European cities and towns, the municipality doled out market licences to certain groups (often only men) and punished people (most of them poor women) who traded without one. There were also numerous efforts, disproportionately directed at women petty traders, to stop people selling on Sundays.[28] Polish cities often banned women from selling outside the market area and from their own homes. The municipal and church courts of German and Austrian cities prosecuted women who sought to sell in defiance of guild or other rules that tried to keep profits in the hands of men. Many Ottoman cities banned (or tried to ban) women street-sellers apart from those at the women's markets. Typical were the protests from the Istanbul candle-makers' guild about 'women and female slaves' making candles at home from beeswax and rendered animal fat, and then selling them for money (in spite of efforts like these, women peddlers called *bohcacı*, who sold goods door to door, remained an established feature of urban commerce, and essential to the workings of elite gender segregation). There were also, in that un-civil-libertarian age, numerous laws against selling subversive pamphlets, broadsides and newspapers, which often came down hardest on the women whose job it was to sell them. In Paris, in the 1750s, the authorities retained a spy, herself a 'reformed' thief, to police prostitutes and women who sold political pamphlets. She is supposed to have been able to imprison people on a whim, and was greatly hated.[29]

Hundreds, perhaps thousands, of regulations like these can be found across Europe and the Middle East, often the product of a close cooperation between municipal governments and guilds. Almost everywhere restraints on women selling things in the market were rationalized by the claim that women who sold things in the market were likely also to be selling themselves. As Madeline Zilfi has aptly put it, speaking of Istanbul (though it could be almost anywhere in Europe or the Middle East): 'Guild-initiated effort to curtail women's access to the marketplace ... appreciated that public consensus was more readily built on moral claims than self-interested economics.'[30] Almost everywhere these same restraints created a context in which sex was all many women had left to sell.

Free markets?

In the later eighteenth century many parts of Europe saw a lessening of the various constraints on who could trade, especially in food. The main reason for this was likely population pressures, and the fact that some cities had grown so large that efforts to police petty traders, never fully effective at the best of times, became prohibitively difficult. 'Free trade' sentiment also played a role. In Oxford in 1772 an old rule that higglers, cattle drovers and corn sellers needed to be thirty years old, householders, male, and either married or widowers, lapsed and was not renewed. On the Continent various 'enlightened despots' – not least some popes – decided to put their weight behind liberalization.[31] All this intersected with much longer-standing efforts by women to fight guild and municipal regulations across both Europe and the Ottoman Empire. There are many examples, and only two must suffice. In 1720 the Stambouli guild of sheep trotter sellers took to harassing the wives of blacksmiths, who, in direct competition with them, had been buying up lambs trotters from the slaughterhouse, cleaning and cooking them and selling them at the market, 'feeding their children with the proceeds'. The women's husbands petitioned the sultan, and eventually the sheep trotter sellers' guild was told to leave the women alone.[32] In 1799 Paula Llorens, a Barcelona widow, wanted to use the cart she owned to help her sons-in-law in their dry salting business. However, the carters' guild saw this as an encroachment on its business. Undaunted, Llorens petitioned the king, Charles IV, making the usual mother's claims (that she needed to make a living to support her children) as well as free trade arguments, and won her case.[33] The easing of regulations undoubtedly helped women sellers. However, counterbalancing them was a trend for more established markets to be set up in the larger towns and cities, sometimes with purpose-built shops and semi-permanent stalls. It is less clear that this was beneficial to women sellers. 'Established' shop-keepers, usually, though not always men, had both increased incentive and enhanced organizational clout to exclude petty traders – sometimes using the argument that the latter represented 'unfair competition' since they did not have to pay fixed costs like shop-rent – but more often arguing that allowing women to sell openly either brought down the 'tone' of the market, or would actually encourage public lewdness and prostitution.[34]

Still, in many places, despite the various impediments, women were too well-established, especially in the provisioning trade, to be dislodged. Significant market activity by women characterized most market towns in Portugal, Spain, France, Belgium, the Netherlands, Germany, Poland, and numerous Caribbean towns well into the nineteenth century and beyond, and was found in some parts of the Balkans and Anatolia as well. In Portugal *regateiras* (market-women) controlled bread-baking and fish-selling in many of the major towns and often worked closely with town governments to ensure the food supply. They also supplied foodstuffs like oil, vegetables and wine. They became synonymous with loudness and a propensity to insult officials, and were often in trouble with the law; but they were too essential to do without.[35] Market participation by Polish women, on the street and in stalls and shops, had been extraordinarily high in the seventeenth century, and though lower in the eighteenth it was still substantial. In Cracow in the late eighteenth century, thirty-nine per cent of single women were deriving their income from wholesale, retail or the sale of alcohol and women were also selling milk, clean water, tripe, oranges, hot food and cooking pots (Plate 4).[36] In Ottoman cities the emphasis on keeping the sexes separate and the concern to control female sexuality helped to tamp down female competition, as did the ubiquity of guilds; on the other hand, many women owned shops and other commercial property as investments, and at least some actually operated them. Moreover, by at least the seventeenth century, a separate women's market (*avrat pazari*) had been established in Istanbul, and apparently in other towns where both the buyers and most sellers were female and women could shop in comfort and safety.[37]

Unsurprisingly, some women tried to bolster their position either by capitalizing on their relationships to male guild members, or by setting up guilds of their own. In Warsaw and Cracow many of the market stalls had traditionally been owned and staffed by the mothers, sisters and wives of town craftsmen or lower-level office holders. Most of the women were married, but a good number (unusually) were spinsters, often co-running stalls with their mothers or sisters. Polish market-women also formed their own women-only guilds, which, in traditional fashion, sought to regulate or close down competition from hawkers and 'window-sellers' (women who sold goods from their own houses), as well as from middle-men. Poorer and less well-connected women were left to operate illegally.[38] The eighteenth-century Ottoman Greek women's guild featured in Voices from the Past 5.1 is probably fairly typical in that its members, having established themselves in the soap-making trade, were seeking to monopolize the market by charging

---

VOICES FROM THE PAST 5.1

Charter of the Women's Guild of Soap-makers in Trikki, Thessaly (1738)

Trikki, now Trikala, is an ancient town (it is mentioned in Homer), located in central Greece; in the eighteenth century it was part of the Ottoman Empire. This is a fairly formulaic guild charter; similar ones can be found across Europe and the Middle East. The only unusual thing about it is that the guild was women-only. The involvement of the Greek Orthodox Church reflects the Ottoman custom of devolving a good deal of local governance onto the religious leaders of the respective dhimmi communities (dhimmi were non-Muslim subjects of the sultan).

The women of the guild of soap makers – Stamoulo, Vassiliki, Margarona, Archonto, Veneto, Agnelo, Pagona, Triantafyllia, Chaido and Ekaterina – presented themselves in front of my humble self as chairman and the honourable clerics and dignitaries of our Metropolis of Trikke, and declared that it was an old custom that no men would be involved in this guild or practise this art. Thus, they unanimously agreed and begged us to ratify this agreement and enter it in the sacred codex; and should sometime in the future one of them wish to enrol in the guild a daughter or daughter-in-law so as to work in soap she would pay to the guild five *gurush*, as pay the other guilds. If any of the women should die, no one shall be permitted to take the tools of the trade which can only be dispensed by the women of the guild, while if any outsider attempts to practise the trade without permission by these women, in violation of the agreement and of the decree of the Church, they shall be liable to punishment by both the Church and the [Ottoman] Turkish authorities and pay ten *gurush* to the guild and fifteen *gurush* to the Church. We designate this guild as free of men, and it shall be under the care and assistance of the clerics and dignitaries. Whereupon this document was drafted, confirmed by my humble self and witnessed by the honourable clerics and dignitaries of our Metropolis of Trikke and entered in the sacred codex: 1738, July 27.

Source: G. Giannoulis, *Codikas Trikkis (Codex of Trikki)* (Athens: 1980), 45, quoted in Halil Berktay and Bogdan Murgescu, eds, *Teaching Modern Southeast European History: Alternative Educational Materials. The Ottoman Empire* (Thessalonikki: Centre for Democracy and Reconciliation in Southeast Europe, 2005), 115.

fines to competitors who were not part of the guild. They also tried to ensure female hereditary succession by allowing for the enrolment of daughters and daughters-in-law.

Femmes fortes of the marketplace

Almost everywhere market-women were associated with loud self-confidence, a tendency to speak their minds, and an unwillingness to be taken advantage of by men or anyone else. They were also supposed to be physically strong and to be much prone to quarrels and violence (some women actually staged prize fights as a way to make money). For reasons that are still not entirely clear, women who dealt in fish had a particularly vivid reputation, so much so that in France they spawned a whole genre of popular writing (*poissardes*) that tried to mimic their political plain-speaking, their fractured French, and their quick resort to violence (see Chapter 8). There are comparable, if less-developed 'literary' fishwives in England and elsewhere.[39] Almost everywhere market-women were very litigious – always a sensitive measure of at least partial female empowerment – and there are a surprising number of cases where they sued city officials and other powerful bodies, as can be seen in Portugal, the Netherlands, the Caribbean, and elsewhere.

Market women *did* cultivate the appearance of a high degree of personal and sexual self-confidence, though – and they played to their audience, partly, no doubt, because crowds are what every retailer wants. There was a vast interest throughout Europe in market women in general (not just fishwives) during the late seventeenth, eighteenth and into the nineteenth centuries, as evidenced in numerous pictures, songs, plays, tracts, satires, and efforts to imitate their street-cries. They were a plebeian version of the '*femmes fortes*', or strong, martial women, popular (though also often decried) in literate culture. This interest was especially pronounced in Spain. Eighteenth-century Spaniards, even aristocrats, became fascinated with *naranjeras* (orange-sellers), and other street sellers, who seemed, with their sharp practices, quick repartee and brazen sexuality, to epitomize the gritty élan of poorer urbanites. In Voices from the Past 5.2 is a speech by a fictional orange-seller from a sketch by the Spanish dramatist Ramón de la Cruz (1731–1794). *Majas*, as these women were called, were famous, like street-sellers and market-women every-where, for their quick tempers and easy resort to violence. They were also reputed to go about armed with daggers, an especially piquant variation on the market-woman's reputation for being hard to control, as well as an emblem of their ability to defend themselves against unwanted sexual overtures.

A Madrid street-seller reveals her technique

Don Ramón de la Cruz wrote some 450 comedic playlets, called 'Sainetes' that often featured Madrid working women. This is a speech from one such sketch, 'La Botillería'. Mariana, an orange-seller, is boasting about her sales ability to a less successful companion. She claims to have sold more than fourteen dozen limes and oranges in one afternoon and here she explains how:

> You girls merely walk up and down like town criers, yelling yourselves hoarse for nothing, because people who are strolling are not looking for oranges. Now I make for the ones who are sitting down, or I run to the carriages or to the men who are flirting with ladies, and, whether they call me or not, I begin dealing out oranges to them all and insist on their taking them. The women are naturally fond of sweets and accept the oranges; the men are vain and pay whatever I ask, without haggling. If you don't know this trick, my girl, learn it.

Source: Charles Kany, *Life and Manners in Madrid, 1750–1800* (Berkeley: University of California Press, 1932), 21 (translated by Charles Kany).

The general interest market-women inspired across Europe points to one of the real oddities of early modern attitudes toward women and work. Eighteenth-century people (unlike their late nineteenth-century descendants) assumed that all women of the popular classes – that is, virtually all women – should work. On the other hand, they always had mixed feelings about what this work should consist of, and where it should take place. And while they disapproved of mixing the sexes, they were also nervous about women gathering together in groups. Market-women in hundreds of European and colonial cities and towns, and some Ottoman ones, carved out a public space for themselves that was decidedly feminine. It was also boisterous, often political, frequently defiant of men, and at least some of the time sexual. Anxiety about women in the market is clear. And yet many people also found them endlessly interesting, and a source of transgressive pleasure. This ambivalence can be seen over and over in the eighteenth century.

ENTREPRENEURS, TRADESWOMEN AND WOMEN MERCHANTS

Widow and merchant

Most really substantial eighteenth-century women merchants got there by a different route than the market-square. One of these was Glikl bas Judah

Leib (see Chapter 2), who inherited a substantial international trade in precious stones and other goods when her husband died in 1689 and who carried it on with remarkable success. Glikl was a unique individual; her justly famous memoirs show an almost unsinkable enthusiasm both for trade and for life. But in terms of her business career she was fairly typical of women who became really substantial merchants. Unlike market-women, who often passed down their stalls from mother to daughter, or street-sellers, who might be spinsters, wives or widows, women merchants were almost always widows who had inherited the trade from their husbands. The reasons for this are not hard to find. While their husbands were alive, women often provided crucial assistance in the family business; in trading families they also routinely contributed to its capitalization, using their own money or *mehr* (in the case of Muslim women) and their dowry (in the case of Christians and Jews). Glikl boasted that her first husband, Haim, never made a business deal without her, and relied on her to write out his contracts. Given this kind of insider knowledge and commitment, especially if there were young sons who would eventually inherit the business, it was often deemed best for a knowledgeable widow to carry on rather than sell out. When Glikl's first husband Haim was asked, on his deathbed, about the disposition of his estate he is said to have answered 'I have nothing to will; my wife knows about everything; let her do as she has done up to now'.[40]

It probably made some difference that Glikl was Jewish. Across Europe and the Ottoman Empire, merchants, traders and proto-industrialists, both large and small, were particularly likely to belong to ethnic or religious minorities (French Huguenots, Quakers, Anabaptists, Jews, Vlach, Greek Orthodox, Armenians, Russian Old Believers, the Roma, etc.). In many cases the men of these groups were either denied access to the guilds or encountered other kinds of civil, economic or cultural disabilities. Without access to other social and political networks, family ties and ties with co-religionists or members of the same ethnic groups had to stand in for them. Women's contributions and networks were often crucial, especially in long-distance trade. All early modern distance-trading relied heavily on family connections, but minorities had to work particularly hard at marrying their children strategically, both so as to establish kin connections in places where they intended to trade and to bypass the hostility they often encountered while travelling or doing business. Glikl routinely travelled about Germany on business; she also went to Denmark, Holland, Flanders, and Northern France. She could do so because she had relatives with whom to stay, many of them her own children or in-laws. Often family and trade are so closely linked in Glikl's account that they are difficult to distinguish from one another. The excerpt from her auto-biography (Voices from the Past 5.3) shows her trying to use her business to reintegrate a scapegrace son back into the fold.

VOICES FROM THE PAST 5.3

Glikl bas Judah Leib, woman merchant of Hamburg

Here Glikl Leib (1646?–1724) describes her trading activities in the years after the death of her husband Haim in 1689. The excerpt shows the scope of her activities, their geographic breadth, and the way trading in the later seventeenth and early eighteenth centuries intersected with family concerns. We also see her using her connections to try to revive the economic fortunes of a son whom she had recently had to bail out of debt.

At this time [the 1690s] I was still quite energetic in business, so that every month I sold goods to the value of 5,000 or 6,000 reichstaler. Besides this I went twice a year to the Brunswick Fair and at every fair sold goods for several thousands, so that I could have recovered the [financial] loss I suffered through Leib [her son], if I had had peace. I did good business, received wares from Holland, brought much goods in Hamburg and sold them in my own shop.

I did not spare myself but travelled summer and winter and all day rushed about the town. Besides this I had a fine business in seed pearls. I bought from all the Jews, picked and sorted the pearls and sold them to the places where I knew they were wanted. I had large credits. When the Börse [merchant exchange] was open and I wanted 20,000 reichstaler, cash, I could get it. Yet all this availed me nothing, for I saw my son Leib, a pious young man, well versed in Talmud, doing nothing! I said to him, one day, 'Listen to me: I see no prospect for you. I am doing big business and it is beginning to be too much for me. I want you to help me and I will give you two per cent of everything I sell.' He accepted this offer with great joy. He was very industrious and had a chance of re-establishing himself if only his goodness of heart had not been his undoing. Through my introductions he became well-known among the merchants, enjoying big credit and everything of mine was under his care.'

Source: Glikl bas Judah Leib, *The Life of Glückel of Hameln, 1646–1724 Written by Herself*, trans. Beth-Zion Abrahams (London: East and West Library, 1962), 125–6.

Merchants and women in skilled trades

Despite the machinations of men and guilds there were scores, some-times hundreds, of substantial women traders to be found in almost every European town. Part of this is a testimony to women's willingness to fight for a niche; part to guilds' and town fathers' mingled guilt and unwillingness to see formerly middle-class women reduced to beggary or to drawing on poor relief; and part to the growth of new trades that did not have a strong guild tradition. Some towns (and countries) seem to have been more hospitable to women traders than others. In Stralsund in Swedish Pomerania (now North Germany), women merchants, all of them widows or spinsters, constituted eleven per cent of the 557 merchants resident in the city between 1755 and 1815. These women, some of them quite prosperous, handled large grain, malt and tobacco shipments to and from Sweden, the Netherlands, Northern England and the North American colonies, managed fleets of ships, and dealt with complex bills of exchange. Stralsund seems somewhat unusual in this respect, but in the Dutch Republic in the eighteenth century around thirty per cent of traders were women in many cities, perhaps because many of the retail guilds seem to have been relatively more open to them than in other places. Most of these women were engaged in local or inter-urban trading rather than long-distance trade; on the other hand, it appears that there were more opportunities for women entrepreneurs in the eighteenth century than there had been a century before.[41]

There were hundreds of women printers and publishers in the seventeenth and eighteenth centuries, virtually always widows or family members of printing dynasties. Women printers and booksellers are known to have operated in Britain, the Netherlands, Flanders, France, Switzerland, Germany, Austria, Denmark, Sweden, the Czech lands, Italy, Portugal, Spain, and the Ottoman Empire, as well as various European colonies, and women from minority communities, particularly Quakers, Huguenots, and Jews, were especially active. Women were also heavily involved in periodical and newspaper publication and distribution. A woman named Elizabeth Mallet briefly published the first daily newspaper in London in 1702 and two women, Elizabeth Nutt and Ann Dodd, often working in loose partnership, published and distributed a significant share of all the newspapers and political pamphlets in early eighteenth-century London, often coming up against the law in the process. Frau Struck, a widow, ran the only newspaper in Swedish Pomerania for some years. And the Widow Machuel, a bookseller in Rouen, did business between 1768 and 1773 with no less than fifty-six travelling salesmen.[42] Women printers, publishers and booksellers often ran into guild opposition, however. In England, new widows were under strong pressure by the Stationer's Company to auction off their stock and get out of the business. The widow of the bookseller Gabriele Piazzani of Rome had an injunction brought against her in 1735 by the Roman booksellers' guild to make her stop trading because she had remarried to a man who belonged to a different guild.[43]

Ottoman women entrepreneurs were often associated with the slave trade, and the Istanbul slave-dealers' guild, unusually, actually included some women in the eighteenth and nineteenth centuries. Moreover, other women are known to have traded slaves (all or mostly women and girl children) from their homes, as opposed to from the main slave market. One presumes that a good many of these slaves were actually distributed within women's social and investment networks, networks we still know very little about. On the other hand, there were efforts from at least the sixteenth century to squeeze women traders out of the Istanbul slave-trading guild or demote them to less prestigious positions on the grounds that they were fostering licentiousness, and a major reorganization in the mid-eighteenth century managed to get rid of a number of them.[44]

Several eighteenth-century women entrepreneurs have left a continuing mark. Nicole Barbe Clicquot's champagne business, which she inherited when she was in her twenties and made internationally famous, was discussed in Chapter 4. Eleanor Coade (1733–1821) was an English innovator in the sculpting of artificial stone. More than 650 pieces from the factory she owned are still extant today in the British Isles, Canada, the US, Brazil and the Caribbean (Plate 5). Coade never married and she lived most of her life with her long-time housekeeper to whom she ultimately left their home. Anna Maria Tussaud, better known as Mme Tussaud (1761–1850), held a job during the French Revolution, modelling the heads of guillotined aristocrats in wax, and came close, at one point, to being guillotined herself. She came to Britain with her four-year-old son in 1802, speaking no English, and having effectively abandoned her husband. By dint of extraordinary effort and talent she became a permanent part of the British cultural and touristic landscape. Mme Tussaud's in London still receives two million visitors a year. Johanna Borski (1764–1846) was an important Dutch banker. The daughter of an Amsterdam meat dealer, Johanna married her husband, Willem Borski, in 1790, and they had eight children, at least two of whom died young. When her husband died in 1814, she carried on his bank under the name 'the Widow W. Borski'. Through a string of judicious investments the bank became one of the three largest of the nineteenth century, and Johanna Borski one of the richest women in the world.[45]

TEXTILES

Since ancient times textile production has been associated with women, not just in Europe and the Middle East, but in Asia and the Americas as well. In Europe (and also in China[46]), spinning soon took on strong moral connotations. In the early modern period it was a mark of virtue for a woman to have a spindle or needlework almost perpetually in her hands, and even queens and princesses were pressured to conform. Spinning was prized primarily because so much thread was needed. In some branches of the early modern textile industry ten or more spinners were needed for each weaver. In England, on the eve of industrialization it was said that to make twelve pieces of woollen broadcloth required fourteen men, seventeen women and twenty-seven children, a revealing illustration of the age-based and gendered assumptions that pervaded the industry.[47] Unfortunately, the fact that almost all women were forced to learn how to spin, coupled with their exclusion from most other forms of work, meant that spinning paid poorly (economists call this phenomenon 'occupational crowding'). On the other hand, before mechanization, women could often support themselves by hand-spinning, albeit not at a high level – at least enough so that they did not have to go into service. Other kinds of textile production, especially at the early stages of the productive process, were similarly heavily feminized. In seventeenth- and eighteenth-century Lombardy (Italy) thousands of poor peasant women worked in a sort of share-cropper system, feeding the silkworms and reeling the silk. In Ottoman Bursa, in 1700, as many as half of the spinning implements were owned by women, and at minimum sixteen per cent of the female population was involved in artisanal production, mostly spinning. Both linen-making and lace-making were also traditional women's activities.[48]

Like most other 'old' trades, textile production and sales had been organized into guilds since medieval times and some medieval textile guilds had had women members, albeit with markedly fewer membership privileges than men. However, from the sixteenth century on, guildsmen increasingly sought to shore up their position by expelling women members or stepping up repression of guild-widows. In German-speaking lands, especially, male guilds tried to define 'proper' or 'respectable' women's work as work for home consumption, that is, outside the realm of the market (of course, this assumed that women who worked for cash were unrespectable). The purpose here was to put work that *was* for the market, and the profits accruing to it, entirely in the hands of guildsmen and their own immediate families.[49] The consequence of the numerous rules limiting women's ability to make a living was that many were driven on to the black market, a furtive economy of back-street shops and materials procured in secret or actually purloined. If they were challenged women claimed they were only producing cloth (or whatever the commodity was) for household use, not for sale. Poor women found themselves slinking about at night selling their handiwork, at great risk to their sexual honour. Remarkably, a few women were able to prosper in this inauspicious climate: in Lyon women formed an extensive underground economy based on their own and other women's labour and materials filched from larger workshops. But in most places (and even in Lyon) the difficulties of working under these conditions kept most women poor and marginal.[50]

The bigger Ottoman cities had many more guilds than most Christian towns, but while they were no more prone to admit women as active members, they seldom tried to keep women from owning shops: many guild-members paid rent to women owners. In addition, like male textile guilds elsewhere, they were usually not averse to women producing raw materials on the farm or getting involved in the early stages of the manufacturing process (for instance, retting flax – a, smelly, unpleasant job – or making silk or woollen thread). Sometimes we catch glimpses of women's involvement in these activities – or at least the marketing side, as in an account from 1779 by a traveller to Ottoman Bursa:

> It was a curious thing to see, while passing by the [market], women of all nations [he means of all religions], a large muslin veil on their heads, rushing en masse and obstructing the avenues. For today is market day. The women of the country side come down from their villages to sell their silk or wool, the proceeds of which are used to buy necessary things for the household for the entire week.[51]

Like their brethren in Christian Europe, Ottoman guilds did try to squelch female competition when it moved to higher stages in the manufacturing process or when women producers tried to sell their products directly instead of letting male guild members act as the middle-men. A 1682 case, also from Bursa, involved a group of eight silk-cord producers, all women, who sued the silk merchants' guild, which had apparently tried to stop them trading. In court the women argued, based on an old sultanic order, that they had the right to roam the city at will and sell in any market they liked. They won their case and then a subsequent one in which the silk merchants' guild counter-sued to force them to share in the payment of mercantile taxes.[52]

There were, of course, a few exclusively female guilds, especially in France, where, indeed, the growth of a consumer market in ready-made clothing seems to have led to an increase in the number and power of women's and mixed-sex guilds. By the mid-eighteenth century at least fourteen French towns and cities had tailors' guilds that admitted women, and at least three had independent women's guilds.[53] One of the two main Parisian women's craft guilds was the linen-drapers (*lingères*) which had been founded in the fifteenth century or earlier. By the 1780s there were about 800 'merchant-mistresses' and another 1,200 wage-earning members. The other, the seamstresses' guild (*couturières*) had been founded late, in 1675, and was both larger and somewhat less prosperous than the linen drapers, with a membership of perhaps 3,000, of which up to 1,800 were mistresses. Like the men's guild, they were thoroughly hierarchical and, when challenged, they appealed to ancient charters and privileges, as well as to the need for 'order' and the oversight of morality within the trade. But in other respects they were quite unusual. Unlike many women workers, they (or at least the *maîtresses*, who spoke for the guilds) had a very strong corporate and professional identity. They were also very aware of their status as women's guilds in a world where working women encountered many barriers. One of the standard arguments in favour of women's protected trades was that they offered women an alternative to prostitution (as well as 'saving' them from sexual harassment by male employers). To this the linen drapers, writing in a 1776 pamphlet, added another argument. The guild offered women a unique opportunity to be self-supporting, even to be their own person. Their profession was 'the only [trade] which women are allowed to manage themselves . . . the only one . . . which offers mature women the recompense of an authentic social standing . . . the only one where [women] do not need either to rent themselves out to an avaricious entrepreneur or to submit to a tyrannical associate disguised under the name of husband'.[54] This rather open distrust of male authority also displayed itself in the organization of the guilds. Both required that half the positions of leadership in the guild be filled by mature but never-married women (*filles majeurs*), clearly because they feared attempts by men to take them over. Not surprisingly, both linen drapery and seamstressing were heavily populated by spinsters and widows, a good number of whom set up in joint, long-term living arrangements with one or more other women. This was a real alternative to marriage, and one that offered women far more freedom than going into a convent. It was also an alternative that was on its way out. In the eighteenth century the women's guilds tenaciously held on to their privileges in the face of attacks by men's guilds and efforts by the state to close them down (one such effort generated the pamphlet of 1776, quoted above). However, when the Revolution came, the clamour for an end to corporate privilege proved irresistible. The French women's guilds, along with their far more numerous brother organizations, would be swept away forever in 1791.

Textiles and proto-industry

Proto-industry can be broadly defined as urban or rural manufacturing that takes place largely in rural cottages or urban dwellings rather than in factories, and is either un-mechanized or relies on very basic, and typically small labour-saving devices (e.g. the spinning wheel or, later, the spinning jenny, a multi-spindle spinning device). It is usually differentiated from 'cottage industry' by the fact that its products are destined not for use in the producer's own home or village, but for national, and even more distant, markets.[55] The distinction between industry and proto-industry was not as clear in practice as it was in theory, however. Proto-industries, especially in the eighteenth and nineteenth centuries, became extremely reliant on machines in some places, though, unlike the 'true' factory, they did not generally make heavy use of water power or steam. A good number of proto-industries had begun to gather workers together in factories or workshops by the eighteenth century. And it is clear that many early factories relied in part on women and men working in their homes in rather traditional ways. There were also numerous hybrids. One large cotton producer in Barcelona, from the 1770s on, actually invited his workers to live with their families *in* the factory, in part so that the women could both attend to daily chores and put in a good day's comple-ment of spinning – usually using spinning jennies.[56]

Textile production was never the only proto-industry but it was always a very important one, and virtually everywhere women made up the bulk of its labour force. In the Viennese cotton firm of Schwechat in 1752 there were 893 men engaged in distribution of raw materials, cloth finishing, and weav-ing, and 5,655 women spinners working out of their homes. By the 1790s there were said to be over 4,300 machines in use in and around Barcelona, mostly operated by women in their own homes. In the Gabrovo area of Bulgaria in the central Balkans, starting at least by the early nineteenth century, women made up the majority of textile workers, engaging in both spinning and weaving in their homes, while the men worked as itinerant tailors. A different kind of proto-industry had long occupied Ottoman *haremliks* (women's quarters of upper-middle and upper-class homes) which made, or directed lower-class women or slaves in the making of embroidery. The work was then sold either to dealers and wholesalers in the bazaar (often to order) or on an independent basis through other intermediaries. By the nineteenth century (and likely earlier) some of these women were also run-ning embroidery schools, some of which, like their counterparts in Christian Europe, were more akin to proto-industrial workshops.[57]

Most textile workers were poor, but there were usually some opportun-ities for women with capital or talent to enrich themselves. In the Ottoman Empire a few women, especially in the silk-city of Bursa, became major entre-preneurs, buying Persian silk, controlling large mulberry orchards, owning shops and looms, and investing in limited trade partnerships. In Le Puy in the

Haute-Loire (France), 30,000 women lace-makers, most of whom worked out of their homes, were a mainstay of the local economy. Sometimes they made more money than their husbands and brothers, who were typically agricultural or manual labourers. In this environment, too, a few women were able to parlay their skills or capital into still more lucrative activities. By the last quarter of the eighteenth century more than half of the lace merchants of Le Puy were women, the so-called 'Dames de Raphael' because they often sold from the Rue de Raphael. The lace industry, highly dependent upon fickle fashion, was very volatile though. When the Revolution of 1789 ushered in simple, 'non-aristocratic' fashions, the industry crashed, never to recover.[58]

Along with the risks, work in proto-industries *could* offer new opportunities for women and sometimes greater independence as well. In Colyton in Devon, as in Le Puy, women made up most of the workforce. These lace-workers were often self-supporting and groups of two or more lace-making women often formed independent households. The Colyton women were generally quite poor, but many were migrants from outside, and it seems clear that some saw their work as an opportunity to escape parental oversight and pressure to marry. On the other hand, in parts of Switzerland, Germany and the Balkans, proto-industry tended to hold young people (especially young women) at home and on the land longer, and, if anything, enhance the motivation of families and communities to control their mobility, earnings and sexuality. Families were not always wholly successful in this, though. The memoir of an eighteenth-century Swiss peasant named Ulrich Bräker records that his mother, 'would surreptitiously spin by lamplight' in order 'to earn a secret penny behind my grandparents' back . . .'.[59]

The industrial revolution

Beginning about 1760, the textile industry in the English midlands became one of the prime sites for a series of larger transformations that, in time, would powerfully affect every aspect of society. The sequence went as follows: 1. several branches of textile manufacture, initially and most importantly cotton manufacture, adopted new methods of organizing labour, most notably they began gathering more workers together in large workshops; 2. manufacturers in their new factories *and* local producers in their homes began utilizing labour-saving machinery to a far greater degree than before, both for early parts of the production process, such as carding and spinning (e.g. the jenny and the water frame), and for weaving (e.g. the flying shuttle); 3. factory machinery came increasingly to run on motor power (initially water-power; but in the nineteenth century, coal-fired steam) rather than human power alone. As we have seen, it was not uncommon for the ratio of spinners (usually women) to weavers (usually men) to reach ten to one or higher. In 1715, twenty-five worsted weavers (worsted was a type of wool cloth) had required thread from 250 spinners. The new spinning technologies made it possible, by the latter part of the eighteenth century, to reduce this ratio to one weaver to four spinners. The breaking of the spinning logjam in turn led to increases in production, though in the eighteenth century – and indeed, well into the nineteenth – these were confined almost entirely to the cotton industry and largely to Britain.[60] The Factory System led, over the next two centuries, to a thorough reorganization of the way all kinds of goods – not just textiles – were produced and consumed, and comprehensive changes in the kinds of work most people did.

As a result of industrialization one of the main jobs of women almost everywhere, and their main source of cash – hand-spinning – started down the road to obsolescence, followed more slowly by handweaving, and, at much longer remove, the home production of most clothing. Some of these processes happened more slowly than used to be thought. In some of the remoter parts of Europe women were still spinning and weaving for home use as late as the 1890s. But in most places, within a few decades or less, hand-spinning had sunk into a terminal depression, because it could not compete for cheapness with yarn from the new machines. Sometimes cheap yarn (and the resulting cheap cloth) became the basis for new or newly expanded industries like stocking knitting or new kinds of embroidery. Expanding trade and the growing consumer-base did float some new small boats. But often the new climate caused great hardship. Many of the traditional proto-industrial centres, like Northern Ireland, Suffolk in England, the Swiss highlands, German Silesia and parts of the Balkans and Anatolia, were devastated and did not recover, if at all, for over a century. Intensified rural impoverishment followed (in many cases these were areas where agriculture had never been particularly productive), along with increased migration and a diminished standard of living for women especially.[61] But while some women lost their livelihoods, other women's (and children's) labour was, from the beginning, central to the industrialization process.

In the English cotton factories women made up over half the workforce, and children a substantial proportion of the rest. Sixty-one per cent of workers in the Scottish cotton industry were women and girls. The story was substantially the same elsewhere. In Belgium, the first continental European country to adopt the factory system, seventy per cent of the Ghent cotton workers were women in 1800; presumably many of the rest were children. A few decades later, in 1837 in Eyoub, a suburb of Istanbul, a government factory that manufactured fezes (hats) for soldiers employed at least 500 women. In classic Ottoman style they had their own women's entrance, and congregated together each day to receive their wool, which they then knitted at home. By the 1860s the women silk-throwers of Bursa, 4,000-plus of them, mostly married women, had moved into factories.[62]

There were a number of reasons why employers preferred women and children to populate the new factories. The fact that women had been associated, often for centuries, with spinning meant that men often shunned it as unmasculine, even when it was mechanized. Some early manufacturing technologies were designed with women and children in mind and very awkward for other people to operate (there were complaints that some girls would be let go as soon as their fingers got too large). Employers also believed that women and children were easier to teach new skills to, and there was much talk of their allegedly superior manual dexterity and tractable dispositions. Women did not always turn out to be as submissive as entrepreneurs hoped though: they were among the Luddite crowds who smashed spinning jennies in 1790 in Somerset in England, some claiming that jenny spinners were earning only half the amount hand-spinners had done.[63] But disciplined or no, almost everywhere the main reason for the preference for women and children was the cheapness of their labour. Factory owners benefited from the abundance of women whose only saleable skills were in textiles, as well as from the large numbers of poor women who were so desperate for a job they were prepared to take starvation pay.

Industrialization represents a dilemma for social theorists and historians. Putting out industries and early factories both relied heavily on pre-existing gender stereotypes and occupational crowding to keep women's and children's wages low. Moreover, the living and working conditions for women factory workers were often horrific, particularly in states like Belgium, where there were particularly stringent rules against workers organizing, and a strong antipathy on the part of capitalists to any limitations whatsoever on working conditions. In an 1846 study of one thousand Belgian women factory workers, 194, or almost one in five, had had at least one serious accident, usually involving extremities being crushed in the spinning gears.[64] Clearly the transition was painful: there is continuing debate about how painful for how long, and whether women had it worse than men.[65] On the other hand, many longer-term improvements in the standard of living flowed, at least in part, from industrialization and the spread of a market economy, including far cheaper consumer goods and, for many people, higher real wages. The early history of women and factories does point up the complexity of the relationship between pre-existing gender inequalities and major shifts in the organization of work. The western European model of economic expansion had a great deal to offer to some women, but its benefits were extremely unevenly distributed. Moreover, some of the classic problems of 'dependent' and uneven development at the regional and national level, with their attendant social problems (migration, broken families, rising crime rates), were already beginning to be visible by the later eighteenth century in, among other places, the Balkans, parts of Ireland and some of the German lands. In some cases they have lasted to this day.

OTHER SERVICE JOBS

Medicine and healing

Midwifery, discussed in Chapter 3, is one of the few pre-modern women's health-related occupations most people today have heard of. But there were many others. A study of French medicine in the eighteenth and early nineteenth century found scores of women medical practioners, including, among others: an early nineteenth-century dentist's widow from Limoges who carried on her husband's profession dressed in men's clothes and wearing a false beard; women urinoscopists, who examined people's urine to diagnose disease; women who claimed to have miraculous cures and preventatives for rabies; women oculists; women who purveyed salves and ointments for cancer; women somnambulists (who claimed to be able to heal while in a trance state); women désensorceleuses (unwitchers – many illnesses were thought to be caused by magic); and others. These women came to light through police records or legal suits, which explains some of the more bizarre elements, but it is likely that there were thousands who practised more unobtrusively, and this is just in France. It is no stretch to imagine that the situation was fairly similar across the rest of Europe and the Middle East. Some medical specialties, such as bone-setting, were widely associated with women. Sarah ('Sally') Mapp, the Epsom bone-setter (1706–1737), became briefly famous in England, both because of her skill and because she first came to public attention in the aristocratic and horse-racing resort town of Epsom (such was the route to fame in the eighteenth century). We also hear of female bone-setters in eighteenth-century France, such as Mme Thevenet in the Nièvre, said to have set to her work like 'the boldest of men' (setting broken or dislocated bones before anaesthesia and x-rays took both strength of arm and courage of intuition and will). And as far away as Ottoman Aleppo, the Englishman Alexander Russell, himself a physician, remarked disapprovingly that '[t]he reduction of dislocations and fractures, is less practised by the surgeons, than by persons who make a distinct profession of it, and who very often are self-graduated [that is, not university- or apprentice-trained] old women'.[66]

As should already be clear, there was little unanimity in the European or Near-Eastern population at large as to what constituted 'proper' medicine in the eighteenth century. It was really only in the nineteenth century, and in some cases the twentieth, that physicians succeeded in fully establishing themselves, and even then their hegemony was never complete. Some of these women healers were clearly greatly respected, like Madame Lany, from Champagne, who attracted patients from twenty-five miles away, or the woman hernia surgeon from Languedoc who charged one family from the minor nobility 790 *livres* – a staggering sum – for curing their daughter. Women healers seem to have been especially common in eastern Europe and the Ottoman Empire, presumably because of the high level of gender segregation (though Ottoman women did sometimes consult male doctors), and the informal nature of most doctors' training, whatever their gender. Regina Salomea Rusiecka (1718–ca. 1760) was a woman physician who thrived in this environment. Originally from Poland, Rusiecka learned ophthalmology from her first husband, a Lutheran physician, and after he died she travelled all over eastern Europe curing people (she was especially well known for her work with cataract sufferers). When she finally settled down it was in Ottoman Istanbul, presumably because she found both a large and well-heeled female clientele and a vibrant women's medical culture.[67]

In a number of Catholic countries healing (or at least nursing) was linked to tertiary orders of women who took temporary vows of chastity. The most famous of these were the Daughters of Charity, founded in France in the 1630s by Vincent de Paul and the pious noblewoman, Louise de Marillac (both were subsequently sainted). By 1700 this body, made up of single-women from largely rural peasant backgrounds (country girls were preferred because city girls were deemed to be enervated and impure), was already running around two hundred hospitals and other charitable institutions across France. The order spread widely, first to Poland and then to other Catholic states, such as Bavaria, and to the colonies, including French Louisiana. In the course of the eighteenth century most French hospitals (as well as orphanages and poor-houses) came to be run either by the Daughters or similar women's organizations. It was a very hard life. Close and constant contact with the sick poor (the sick rich did not frequent hospitals) was not only dispiriting but dangerous. Especially in the early years, a good many of the 'Grey Sisters', as they were called, succumbed to infectious diseases. But on the positive side the Daughters received a steady wage (for most of the eighteenth century it at least kept even with the wages of an upper servant, and when it did not the sisters were quick to demand raises), room, board and clothes, considerable authority for the more talented, a supportive community, the chance to travel, and the right to medical care and a decent burial. Moreover, unlike in regular religious orders, there was the possibility of resigning and returning to 'lay' life, since women took only annual and not perpetual vows. The Grey Sisters and their many imitators earned enormous prestige. Some historians credit them with having halved the mortality rate in French hospitals over the course of the eighteenth century, and they made themselves so indispensable that even the French Revolution could not permanently dislodge them (see Chapter 9). They also succeeded in creating a truly viable and, at least for some, attractive alternative career path for poor to middling women who could not or did not wish to marry.[68]

INVESTMENT AND PROPERTY OWNERSHIP

Early modern moralists made it clear that, while men operated in the world of money and markets, women were supposed to invest a more emotional and spiritual currency in the well-being and affection of husband and children, especially their sons. In time their care, love, self-abnegation and prayers would bear abundant interest in the form of a comfortable and respected old age, an honourable death and assured salvation. While some women had to be content with this, many others sought more tangible returns. Let us look first at women's investments and property ownership in the Ottoman Empire. In Islamic law, as we have seen, marriage was not primarily conceived of as a melding of the assets of the two partners. Each spouse owned her or his own property, and each could buy and sell that property without the other's permission (see Chapter 2). It is clear that many women used part of their *mehr* to invest in property or other assets, and to do so at an early stage in their adult lives. In addition, anything a woman inherited during marriage was legally hers to hold and control, and so were any funds she obtained by gift, piece work, sales or investment. *Sharia* law is also very clear that women do not have to contribute their own funds to household upkeep (though in practice many women did), and the Ottoman courts were prepared to attach a man's assets on behalf of his wife if he refused to support her – even if she was already well off in her own right. One result of the separate property regime was a very high rate of home-ownership by women. In seventeenth-century Bursa a third of the women in one middle-class sample individually owned a house or share of a house, and this pattern probably held true for many Ottoman cities, though it is likely to have been less prevalent in rural areas.[69]

Ottoman women often started investing in their teens, when they married, and continued across the lifespan. In Aleppo in the mid-eighteenth century women made up one-third of buyers of commercial property, and one-seventh of buyers of agricultural property. They often bought shares in bath houses and orchards, and both large and small collections of shops. Both married and widowed women, and rich and poor, got involved in money-lending to both men and other women. And because women owned real property on their own, and the law guaranteed their rights to it, women had little trouble obtaining credit. One businesswoman, Imhani bint Mehmed Çelebi of Bursa, was worth almost a million *akçes* when she died in 1682. She owned a large farm, several houses and had put out more than a quarter of a million *akçes* to loans. She also had debts herself, having borrowed from eleven different individuals and *waqfs* (family trusts) to the tune of around 50,000 *akçes*.[70]

When we turn to Christian Europe we find a similar enthusiasm for invest-ing, and, as time went on, more opportunities to do so, but also somewhat more legal impediments. The rules and customs to do with marital property meant that in some Christian lands women did not really control their own money unless they were widows or spinsters who had reached the age of majority, and even then their freedom of action was often limited by law or custom because of the belief that their money belonged more to their children than it did to them. Still, many women, particularly older women, did actively invest. The main areas, as in the Ottoman Empire, were money-lending (to individuals, charitable foundations, towns or states); buying property and collecting rents; and investing in various trading or manufactur-ing ventures. Like Ottoman women, women in Christian Europe were heavily involved in the first and second of these, and to a lesser extent in the third. In Catholic countries, especially, numerous upper-middle- and upper-class women 'invested' in large charitable institutions, often using them as a way to store up patronage for use by relatives, or to establish annuities for them-selves or others. Thus, in 1771, the Turin widow Caterina Ferri gave a major bequest to the local hospital in which she also established a life income for her mother and sister.[71] In some Protestant countries 'projectors' began reaching out to women anxious about supporting themselves in their old age – especially given the fact that they ordinarily had no control of any of the marital assets during their husband's lifetime. One English widow's insurance scheme from 1696 began its pitch: 'Experience Informs us every Day, of the Misery and Calamity of Women after the Death of their Husbands . . . who, tho' they [the women] may bring considerable Fortunes to their Husbands, are often times left in a very mean Condition', and promised to deliver a £500 benefit to women whose husbands died more than six months after they subscribed.[72] In addition, growing (though seldom very large) numbers of women, including women of quite humble means, invested in shipping ventures, including the commodities trade, the spice trade, the slave trade and various other colonial or commercial projects, helped by the fact that shares were often broken into fractions (1/16, 1/32, etc.) so that smaller investors could get involved.

Since many women in Christian Europe did not control their own money until they were widows (if even then), they often only began actively investing quite late in life, and so were not in a position to enjoy long-term gains. This is ironic, because in the early modern period the epicentre of trade, industry and investment shifted away from the Mediterranean and toward northwestern Europe, which led to some very enticing new investment opportunities both in trade and in government securities. Women's limited ability to take advantage of them is reflected in a recent study of a sample of women who invested in Bank of England shares during the South Sea Bubble of 1720 and the years immediately after. Married women constituted a mere five per cent of active women investors (that is, those who bought and sold shares, as opposed to those who simply passively owned them) while widows and spinsters together made up almost ninety-five per cent. In fact the real figures are even more unbalanced, for several of the married women investors were elite Dutch or Polish women investing from abroad. Still, another interesting recent finding is that several English widows were very substantial dealers in stocks in the early eighteenth century, buying and selling both for other women and for men. One of these, Johanna Block, a broker and dealer, was the thirteenth-largest purchaser of Bank of England shares during the South Sea Bubble, selling shares with a book value of £36,230. She also bought and sold East India Company shares in large blocks, and was a major player in the London financial market.[73]

But whatever the character of the property laws, there were ideological impediments that all women would-be investors faced to one degree or another. Everywhere the identification of women with families and sacrifice, and the tendency to assume that men were more deserving of money and especially real property than women, made it difficult for them to become the possessive individualists so beloved of eighteenth-century political and economic theorists. Clearly there were places where women were more active (one would like to know about Portugal for instance). But even in countries or regions where women, and especially wives, did have fairly robust property rights, it would be naïve to think that they enjoyed equality with men. Even in the Ottoman Empire very few women, even women of property, ended up, on average, as rich, or owning as much property as did men.

MAKING DO AND FALLING THROUGH

Coping with debt

In the early modern period most of Europe decisively turned the corner from a partially barter-based society to a largely cash-based one. This shift occurred against a backdrop of fluctuating money supplies, under-employment, rural indebtedness and the lack of an established tradition of paying people quickly for their work. As a result, most of the population was chronically in debt to landlords, seed-suppliers, millers, grocers, bakers, tax collectors, business partners, money-lenders, suppliers, their employees, the local clergy and their own relatives. High debt-burdens, in turn, created an environment in which up to a half of the population was almost constantly on the verge of destitution.[74] People dealt with this through judicious management of credit networks, begging, resort to institutional charity, and a variety of other measures that hovered on the border between theatre and fraud. Especially in the cities, women were usually the ones delegated to negotiate credit relationships with crucial agents like the landlord or the baker, because they were thought to be more skilled at appealing to creditors' charitable instincts than men. That is why we so often see eighteenth-century women arriving at their creditors' doors with a babe in arms – or ideally several – to beg for time or another advance. Women with hungry children embodied the stark reality of need and it was their job to play that role to the hilt. The Swiss peasant-proto-industrialist Ulrich Bräker describes in his autobiography an episode in which he tried and failed to seize a family's household goods in lieu of an unpaid debt. Arriving with the court officers at the house, he found a scene of high desperation:

The woman pleaded, pointing her fingers at the tattered bed and the few pots in the kitchen; the children in their rage were howling away. The sooner I get out of this, the better! I thought, [so I] paid off the broker's men and the sergeant-at-arms and stole away empty-handed after receiving promise of payment in fixed instalments, payment which is still due.

Afterwards Bräker claimed to have heard rumours that, in anticipation of his arrival, the family had hidden away their most valuable possessions and hired rags to wear so as to look more pathetic.[75]

But there is no question about the stark reality of widespread misery, and, even in families where there was still a man about, it often fell to women to do what needed to be done. So, for example, women were often the ones in charge of pawning household goods and clothes, an important survival strategy of poor people throughout Europe and the Middle East. Women were thought to be able to extract a better price from the pawnbroker; and many of the things they were pawning (pots and pans, clothes, bedding, etc.) were within women's domain. A number of cities, mainly in Catholic countries, actually ran small loan institutions (the *mons pietatis*, or *monte de pietà*) intended to offer poor people no- or low-interest loans or opportunities to pawn their possessions, and the registers of these institutions show that it was often women who negotiated the loans or pawns.[76] At the local level, many poor and middling neighbourhoods had well-developed small-scale lending networks, often controlled by women pawnbrokers, money-lenders, old-clothes dealers, or financial intermediaries.[77]

Begging and charity

Women and children made up a significant proportion of beggars in the early modern period. A rather well-executed census done in 1796 on a sample of 2,000 London beggars found 198 adult male beggars and 1,802 adult female beggars. Between them they claimed to be responsible for 3,096 children, most of whom, presumably, also begged or acted as begging props for adults. In short, women made up about ninety per cent of adult beggars and women and children combined made up about ninety-six per cent of all beggars. We do not have figures as precise as this for other parts of Europe, but it is hard to avoid the conclusion that women beggars were very common, and usually in the majority. They certainly made up the bulk of recipients of charity almost everywhere, a product of the disadvantaged position of women in the labour market, the large number of women who had been abandoned, divorced, widowed, or had husbands in the military, and the fact that husbands tended to die before their wives.[78]

Charity is never only about succouring the desperate. It always speaks to other issues: theories about who does and does not belong (the Roma, Jews, blacks and 'strangers' could hope for little Christian charity in the early modern period unless it was in the context of an attempt at religious conversion); hopes of future reciprocity either in this world or the next; calculations about deterrence and incentive; and the need to display and vindicate extreme differences of status and entitlement. In the eighteenth century, social hierarchy was often enacted and confirmed by higher-status people theatrically extending charity to their inferiors. The nobleman flinging coins for his inferiors to scramble for, or peasants or charity children thanking their lord or lady (or other benefactor) on bended knee, were not just literary devices but real scenes of daily life. The early modern period was famous for its charitable institutions, often ostentatious monuments to the piety and generosity of the better off. There were the soup kitchens linked to mosque complexes in the Ottoman Empire; refuges for the *malmaritate* (the 'badly married', often women who had separated from their husbands) in some Italian cities. There were also many attempts to improve the declining years of the pious and respectable elderly: the antique almshouses of Britain and the Netherlands (*hofjes*, as they are familiarly known in Dutch) are a still-visible reminder of this agreeable impulse. From about the turn of the seventeenth century in the Dutch Republic and Protestant parts of Germany, and later elsewhere, there was a rage for workhouses (*tuchthuizen* or *rasphuizen* in Dutch; *Zuchthäuser* in German), in which inmates (mostly women and children who would otherwise beg for their bread) worked instead at spinning or far more onerous tasks like 'rasping' coloured wood for the dye industry, beating hemp, picking oakum and even dry-grinding glass. Sixty-three of these were set up in German territories in the seventeenth century alone.[79]

Much debate has swirled around these institutions, especially those, like workhouses, madhouses and venereal disease hospitals, that relied heavily on incarceration, a trend that Michel Foucault famously called the 'Great Confinement'.[80] Most historians today argue that the vast majority of the poor did not end up in such institutions, and many of them were used strategically by the people they were supposed to be confining. Thus, the lock hospitals for diseased prostitutes were sometimes resorted to willingly by syphilitic women because they were the only place where they could get free care; they also turn out, at least until the later eighteenth century, not to have been very well 'locked'.[81] However, there is also no question that, especially in the later eighteenth century, provision for the poor often turned to provision *against* the poor. Homeless people could be summarily removed to workhouses, *maisons de charité*, and the like, and many of these institutions grew quite punitive. It is also true, though this did not happen everywhere, that poverty began increasingly to be viewed as a sort of crime or a mark of bad character, rather than a bad turn of the wheel of fortune – ironically just at the time when population pressures, war and rural displacement – in short, structural problems – were causing perceptible increases in rates of poverty. And then there were the special problems of women. The common eighteenth-century spectacle of homeless women crowding into garrison towns to sell sex, or into cathedral towns to take advantage of the more abundant charity often found there, seeking shelter near charcoal or lime kilns because of the warmth, or trudging in small, miserable bands from town to town in search of work, all testified to the desperation that was so many women's lot across Europe and the Middle East. In the end, charity was palliative at best.[82]

War and women

The massive increase in the size of armies that occurred in the later seventeenth and eighteenth centuries imposed new hardship on both women and men. It also offered some women new opportunities. In some of the places where warfare was endemic or military service was extremely common, women, children and old men sustained the economy and family life. Having men go into the military was functionally much like having them migrate away to work, although the percentage who failed to return home was certainly higher. Women in British seaports from the later seventeenth century on developed complex financial networks organized around 'sailor's tickets', promissory notes generated by the navy. They also took major responsibility for dealing with the navy bureaucracy, so much so that some women carved out a profession for themselves representing men as well as other women who were having trouble getting paid. In some places legal devices arose to ensure that women had the authority to deal with property and other issues in the absence of the men. In Hesse-Cassel women occasionally inherited in preference to their brothers, while in England the power of attorney, which transferred a man's authority in financial and business affairs over to his wife or female kin while he was away at sea, became common in seaport towns. In the Ottoman Balkans, *kadis* often bent the rules in an attempt to give women whose husbands had gone missing (and who were probably dead), enhanced rights over the man's estate.[83]

Women often congregated around armies, not least because staying at home was likely to land them and their children in the workhouse. Travelling with an army clearly became a quasi-acceptable, if not precisely respectable, way for some women to see the world. In 1736 an observer campaigning with the Russian army counted 80,000 troops and 8,000 sutlers (or provisioners), of whom a good many, presumably, were women. During the Seven Years' War one French army had 30,200 men and 12,000 camp followers of both sexes. The Gibraltar garrison in 1777 had 4,000 men, 500 women and 1,000 children. And in 1777 the army with which Burgoyne invaded North America consisted of 7,200 troops, accompanied by a 'train' of 2,000 women.[84] The women 'on the strength' (that is, officially allowed to be there, usually as laundresses) were in the minority. Much more numerous were the 'unauthorized' women', the wives or lovers of soldiers who had paid their own way to join their men, and the women (and children) that armies tended to collect around them while on campaign: war refugees seeking food and protection, petty traders, part-time prostitutes, beggars, etc. Most of these women did not draw rations, so they were in a pretty desperate state much of the time, reliant on their own wits, entrepreneurship and ability to attract the pity or sexual interest of one or more soldier. Of course they worked. They did laundry, fetched water, foraged for and prepared food over and above the standard rations, mended clothes, provided nursing care, supplied sex, and took care of the children (Plate 6), both their own and the orphaned children of dead comrades-in-arms (the 'daughter of the regiment' is not just an operatic conceit). They were often summarily dropped when the campaign was over, especially if they were foreigners. When Wellington's troops left the Iberian peninsula in 1814, at the end of the Peninsular War, 'the poor faithful Spanish and Portuguese women, hundreds of whom had married or attached themselves to our soldiers and who had accompanied them through all their fatigue and dangers, were, from stern necessity . . . abandoned to their fate'.[85] One can only imagine these women's state of mind as they stood on the beach, many of them pregnant, watching the troop-ships sail away into the horizon.

Prostitution

'Simply put', Richard Symanski has remarked, 'men are willing to pay more for sexual access than for almost any other forms of female labour'.[86] Men were not prepared to pay very *much* more for it in the early modern period, but it was enough to ensure a significant number of prostitutes (or, more likely, women who periodically sold sex) in most European and Middle Eastern towns and cities, and even in rural areas. In the late medieval period many towns across Europe had had their own municipal brothels, but this sort of thing was largely gone by the eighteenth century. Both the Protestant and Catholic Reformations had resulted in crack-downs on the most visible kinds of vice. Still, prostitution continued to be legal (though regulated) in eighteenth-century Seville, Amsterdam, and a number of Polish and German cities, and tacitly accepted as a necessary evil in many other towns, large and small. Even where it was illegal, local authorities usually contented themselves with only periodic repression of the most flagrant offenders, or with picking up women who, say, combined prostitution with theft or were visibly diseased.[87]

Prostitution was highly socially differentiated. At the top of the profession were courtesans, fashionable and often very beautiful women who had sex with elite men, usually in a serially monogamous fashion, in return for being kept in a style to which they were happy to grow accustomed. They were an accepted stratum in almost all of Europe's great cities, and, while generally unwelcome in the gatherings of respectable women, they were nevertheless widely admired for their fashion sense, their hostessing abilities, their often high level of culture, their liberated love lives, and their sometimes meteoric ascent up the social ladder. Many seventeenth- and eighteenth-century courtesans were able to accumulate both money and considerable cultural capital. Ninon de Lenclos (1620–1705), courtesan, writer, salonnière and free-thinker, refused ever to marry, had affairs with some of the most famous men in Europe, and was good friends with many other powerful people of both sexes. She died very rich in her early eighties and bequeathed money for books to the son of her accountant – who grew up to be Voltaire, the most celebrated *philosophe* of the eighteenth century.[88]

A middle group worked and often lived in brothels or taverns, and sometimes even moved in travelling bands. Some eastern European prostitutes followed the fairs or, as in Poland, turning up for meetings of the Sejm or diet, occasions for large numbers of free-spending nobles and their retainers to congregate. Episodically, prostitutes could do fairly well financially. In early modern Poland a particularly generous mark could net a woman as much as a servant would make in three months, or even a half-year. Their conditions of work depended very much on whether they could retain their independence, and, if not, whether the woman or man who managed them was a bully, criminal or worse. In many places it *was* women who managed prostitution, probably because it involved deploying the labour of other women and was only semi-legal. Ironically, this made it a relatively 'free' trade in a world in which almost all the best-paid work was monopolized by men. In early modern Polish cities around sixty per cent of procurers are said to have been women. Most of these, unlike the prostitutes themselves, were married women. One historian has gone so far as to say (speaking both of Polish procuresses and brothel-owners, and prostitutes themselves) that 'in no other group of urban marginals did women occupy a position as important and as independent as in the world of professional prostitution'.[89] That may be, but this was a trade where 'independence' often flowed from the ability to exploit others. In Paris, dressmakers were sometimes accused of trying to pimp their female employees to men. In 1776 one Mme de Brossard, a Paris dressmaker, was accused by one of her employees of introducing her to various men who 'wanted to take liberties with her' and beating her and threatening her with arrest if she refused to cooperate. Women slave-dealers in Ottoman cities were periodically accused of 'repeatedly selling young women to bachelors' (in other words, forcing slaves to be prostitutes, which was a crime and forbidden in the Qur'an). The incidence of this sort of thing may be exaggerated in the sources, because the slave-dealers' guild often charged irregular women dealers with channelling young women into immoral ways so as to cut women out of the guild. But it is unlikely that the charge was entirely fictional.[90]

While women who lived mainly by prostitution are the easiest to spot in the records, it is likely that most prostitution was more casual. For a lot of women, selling sex was just another of the things one did when one was out of a job, short of money or food, living on the street, about to be evicted for non-payment of rent, or on the verge of being sent to debtor's prison. Contemporaries realized this to some degree, and the need to keep women from prostituting themselves by giving them more and better-paying job opportunities was already part of the arsenal of feminist argumentation by the eighteenth century – as we saw in the case of some women's guilds. Whether 'professionals' or not, there were too many prostitutes for most policing and justice systems to cope with. No one knows now, or knew then, how many there were, though unprovable estimates like 40,000 (London), and 100,000 (Paris) were occasionally bruited about. Clearly there were enough of them that punishing, much less incarcerating, all or most of them would have been prohibitively costly, as well as very socially disruptive of poor communities. In early eighteenth-century London several evangelical moral reformers were beaten to death by outraged locals when they tried to make citizen's arrests of prostitutes: presumably these women were significant players in the neighbourhood economy. As this suggests, another reason for tolerating prostitution was the fact that it was a staple activity for poor women, orphan girls and the like, many of whom would otherwise have had no source of income at all. These girls and women were at high risk of becoming a drag on public funds or charity, or simply of dying, with their children, in a ditch by the side of the road. Periodic resort to prostitution allowed them partially to support themselves, though it also fed the stereotype that all poor women were sexually immodest. Early modern people may not have known much about economics but they could see that women had few occupational alternatives; consequently, even amid the constant criticism of sexual women, the prostitute was often allowed to ply her dishonourable trade relatively freely and most people pretended not to notice that a lot of other women occasionally engaged in prostitution when they or their children ran short of other options.

This ambivalence is nicely exemplified by the treatment of prostitutes in Ottoman Damascus. Damascene neighbourhoods routinely sent delegations to complain about women who committed the crime of 'facilitating association with strangers', a euphemism for prostitution, and sometimes succeeded in getting them banished from the quarter (though some women simply refused to leave). But the complainants or the court refrained from using the term *zina* (fornication) which could, at least in theory, have carried a heavier penalty – clearly no one wanted these women to die. Moreover, probably because Damascus was a major garrison town, some officials actually courted their favour, perhaps as a way to reach their janissary protectors (the janissaries were Ottoman infantry units who, by the eighteenth century, often controlled a good proportion of the economy, especially in highly militarized areas). In 1743 one high official went so far as to put on a lavish public celebration during which he hosted and gave rich gifts to different urban interest groups, including prostitutes. But there is also evidence that sympathy for prostitutes went deeper. There was, for example, a widespread desire to avoid offending prostitutes, reflected in the popular saying 'since prostitutes bear the guilt of mankind, God out of sympathy to them accepts their appeals'. Perhaps this is why, in 1748, some Damascus prostitutes were bold enough not only to stage a public celebration, but to '[walk] unveiled while chanting and dancing in fulfilment of a vow made by one of them to celebrate the recovery of her boyfriend from his illness'. This kind of behaviour suggests a group that, though unrespectable, did not feel particularly under attack.[91]

Prostitutes did not go unpunished either in the Ottoman Empire or elsewhere. They clearly were a stigmatized group, especially if they manifested symptoms of disease. English prostitutes were routinely consigned to 'bridewells' (houses of correction), where the prurient could pay to come and watch them beat hemp and receive whippings for not doing it industriously enough. Sometimes there were crackdowns on prostitutes for religious reasons, as happened in England during the reign of the Societies for Reformation of Manners in the early decades of the eighteenth century.[92] In Poland they were tolerated most of the time, but punished and banished during visitations of the plague, presumably as part of a bid to placate the deity. During the 1708–09 Warsaw epidemic, prostitutes were forced into work-details and given the job of interring plague victims. It is unlikely that many survived this assignment. The Bicêtre prison in Paris, the dumping ground for prostitutes with syphilis from 1750 to 1792, may represent the nadir in the eighteenth century for prostitutes. At times it had up to eighty women sleeping in shifts in a 30- by 35-foot room on ancient and filthy mattresses impregnated with faecal matter and pus. A picture from earlier in the century shows Parisian prostitutes being transported to prison in open carts, while onlookers jeered.[93] This sort of thing was not standard practice, though, either in France or across the rest of Europe or the Middle East. In fact, as we saw in Chapter 3, more laissez-faire attitudes toward sex and, by extension, prostitution were already starting to emerge in many European towns and cities by the later eighteenth century. These were given considerable impetus by the wide pro-mulgation of the Napoleonic Code, which made no mention of prostitution, and which therefore effectively decriminalized it. Punitive treatment of prostitutes did not, of course, end with the Napoleonic Code. There were continued efforts almost everywhere to identify and confine women who were suspected of infecting soldiers with venereal disease. But eliminating prostitution entirely struck very few people as a viable proposition and by the late eighteenth century a distinct unwillingness to interfere in other people's sex lives (especially the sex lives of single men) was clearly gaining ground.[94]

CONCLUSION

In the eighteenth century everyone assumed that most women would work. No one was interested in having even more women and children relying partially or wholly on charity than there already were. Women's traditional labour, paid (as farm or domestic servants) and unpaid (doing much the same things for free) formed one of the bulwarks of family life. Women workers also supplied a disproportionate amount of the labour for many of the most important, 'modernizing' sectors of the market, especially proto-industries, and, eventually, the factory system proper. And yet, women's work had also to be controlled if men were to hold on to the better jobs, more of the capital, and most of the prestige. In juridical terms this was done through laws and customs that sought, not always successfully, to keep women out of certain professions and away from control of their own money. In cultural terms the most effective weapon was attacks on women's sexual reputations, and these always came to a crescendo when women began to pose a competitive threat. None of these actually kept women at home, but they were a very effective rein on them mixing too freely with men, particularly in business settings, and a powerful justification for excluding them from 'honourable' jobs, usually synonymous with the best-paid jobs. Women's vulnerable sexual reputation built the fence within which the gendered division of labour – meaning men's monopolies – could flourish.

But it is a mistake to expect male unanimity on the subject of women or their work. Poor men also suffered from the constraints upon their female kin. And not everyone was appalled by the spectacle of women in public. In fact, the eighteenth-century fascination with market-women, rural women's work gangs, women doing laundry, and factory-girls, as well as 'public' women such as prostitutes and courtesans, suggests an enduring ambiguity about what people thought women really should be doing. Daily necessity, with which all women and men had to live, confounded every prejudice, every custom and every law.

Chapter 6

◆

PATHS OF
THE SPIRIT

Masculine religions

Judaism, Christianity and Islam all worship the God of Abraham, a masculine God who is generally quite hostile to other deities. Goddess-worship was apparently common in the second and first millennium B.C.E. when Judaism was being consolidated, and consequently God's ire tended to fasten upon it, and perhaps (some scholars think) inspired Him or His people further to emphasize His masculine attributes. Christianity further reinforces the masculinity of God by positing the existence both of a Father God and a divine Son, and putting their relationship and complex oneness at the very heart of its message. There is somewhat more hesitation in Islam to assign God a definitive gender; still, like the other two faiths, Islam includes explicit and repeated endorsements of male supremacy and derives its authority from a string of almost exclusively male prophets. The eighteenth century is closely associated with some of the earliest fairly widespread secular and secularizing movements, notably the clutch of movements and trends, some of them explicitly anti-religious, usually referred to as the 'European Enlightenment'. It might have been expected, given the masculinist focus of the various faiths, that women would reject them in large numbers and sign on, so to speak, to the Enlightenment. Some clearly did, particularly toward the end of the century. But the bulk of the evidence suggests that most women of the time were more powerfully drawn to religion than men were, and that, on the whole, they tended to side with faith and 'irrationality' over secularism and 'reason'. Why should women have shown such a lot of what Ruth Harris, perhaps tongue in cheek, calls 'resistance to the promises of progress',[1] especially when many of the 'traditional' ideologies on offer explicitly relegated them to an inferior position?

Part of the answer is that all of the European religions co-existed and intertwined, usually ambivalently, with many other supernatural beliefs and customs that tended to give women a more central role.[2] The various eighteenth-century faith-systems did include a set of more or less deeply held convictions about God, saints, spiritual forces, right and wrong, hierarchy, and the origins of things that derived, for the most part, from orthodox tradition and writings. But they were also made up of countless individual and collective ritual acts, sometimes indebted to older pagan religions, and sometimes more recent inventions, that aimed to ward off trouble, attract good luck, and ensure that the cycles of the cosmos, nature, and the afterlife would continue to function as they should. Almost everywhere women were at the heart of that project.

Apotropaic ritual and syncretism

Apotropaic practices are spells, prayers, good luck charms, invocations to patron saints or spirits, collective songs, dances, food practices, processionals, feast days and death, burial and commemorative practices whose main purpose is to ward off evil. Life lived at the mercy of nature bred a good deal of insecurity about whether basic cycles and transmutations involving food, animals, crops, birth, sex and death would turn out for good or for ill. They were likely *not* to turn out because of the power and ubiquity of evil in the world – not some disembodied concept of evil but a host of malign forces, spiritual, human or animal, actively working to visit bodily pain, accidents, death, impotence, barrenness, mental illness, poor harvests, epidemic and epizootic diseases, bad marriages, monster births, dried up wells or streams, house fires, soured milk, bread dough that failed to rise, spoiled food, floods, erratic prices, tax collectors, military recruitment parties, and war, upon oneself or one's relations.

The power of all ritual practices aimed at warding off evil lay in the way they reproduced older associations and linked past, successfully completed cycles to present-day ones. Women appealed to spirits that had a traditional association with a particular activity, family or locale. They retailed spells and invocations learned from previous generations, useful because they had (or were said to have) worked in the past. They scrupulously observed ritual practices in order to judge their efficacy for future use. And they invented new rituals that spoke to new problems: the early modern expansion of the military draft, new kinds of taxes, the growth in both rural and urban indebtedness, ever-longer and more complex trade networks, new civil entities like police forces, and new and unfamiliar diseases. Women's power was tied closely to their ability competently to deploy ritual, magic and religious devotion to support the everyday round of creating and sustaining life and managing and neutralizing deterioration and death. And they capitalized upon the general anxiety that surrounded transformations of all kinds. Most women did not rule their own households, and their 'public' secular power was much more limited than that of most men. However, as a group, they presided over a liminal space, the metaphorical threshold of a world alive with supernatural forces and pregnant with the possibility of turning out either way: growing healthy, lucky, fertile and strong, or withering, souring, or metastasizing into something dangerous. This was a world of creativity as well as of risk, beside which Enlightenment secularism could seem both pedantic and barren.

Popular devotion was often syncretistic, which is to say that it had a tendency to mix together beliefs and practices drawn from a wide variety of traditions. Established religions, or more especially their clergy or learned men, had a vested interest in preserving the key articulations of the faith (Scripture, the Talmud, the Qur'an, church decretals, canon law, *hadiths*, legal commentaries, theological treatises, etc.) in written form, and 'purity' often meant being quite clear about the canonical beliefs and writings. By contrast, most other traditions, whether 'popular' forms of the established religion, survivals of earlier animistic or folk religions, or new religious or occult movements, relied in good part on oral transmission. Their practitioners were largely unconcerned with establishing a canon, and much more likely to view faith in highly functional terms. If the rituals of one tradition failed to cure her husband's impotence or make her hens start laying again, a woman was likely to turn to those of another – or mingle several traditions together on the theory that this would increase their force. Women's rituals routinely combined appeals to (say) the Virgin Mary and to pagan spirits. Or a woman might pray at a Muslim saint's shrine on one day and purchase a lucky amulet from a Jew on the next, while insisting that her child wear something blue to ward off the evil eye. Jesuits seem to have had a reputation for being especially good at expelling demons, so that even Muslims and Jews called upon their services. And couples afflicted with childlessness were famous for being willing to try any faith's rituals or healers.[3]

Blaming other women

The power women had was perilously close to pollution, which may partially explain why they often blamed other women for their problems. It was part of women's job to be especially attuned to the power of envy – particularly envy on the part of other, less fortunate, people who might wish them or their family ill (see Chapter 1). Women's daily participation in rituals of transmutation, from cooking, grinding grain and doing laundry to watching children grow up, meant they constantly rubbed shoulders with other women, and had numerous opportunities to watch out for correlations between the behaviour (or simple presence) of a particular person and some crucial transmutation gone awry. So, for example, in parts of eighteenth- and nineteenth-century Sweden there was a belief that 'whores' (here meaning women who had had extramarital sex, whether or not they took money for it) could cause diseases in children merely by looking at or touching them. The following dialogue between two women, noted down by a folklorist, must have taken place in the 1860s but it reflects much older ways of thinking about the world. The first woman was concerned about her son who was manifesting the symptoms of rickets, a common and potentially crippling childhood disease we now know to be the result of vitamin D deficiency. The second woman, a tailor's wife named Stina, clearly considered herself something of an expert on childhood diseases:

> Stina: Well . . . the boy obviously has 'whore rickets.' He's been sitting on the lap of a 'secret whore', you can be sure of it.
> Mother: That's impossible . . . I'm sure there hasn't been anybody else here [other] than Blomgren's sister Tilda. And she couldn't be a 'secret whore!'
> Stina: But you can see for yourself that the boy's got rickets. And you haven't been near anybody dead [contact with a dead body was thought to be another cause of rickets]. Tilda has got to be a 'secret whore.' No use doubting it. This illness here proves it. If Tilda had been 'honest' [i.e. chaste], this boy wouldn't have rickets. It's hard to tell how many men she's had but you can't trust her.[4]

This dialogue exhibits several of the standard features of pre-modern magical and mythopoeic reasoning. Largely ignorant of the true causes of illness, people looked instead for malevolent forces swirling about in the world. They routinely confused correlation with cause (Tilda had had contact with the afflicted child, so she must have been the cause). They often linked pollution to sexual deviance. In Stina's imagination Tilda was surrounded by a sort of toxic aura. It also shows the paranoid side of some women's (and men's) thinking. 'Good' mothers had to be constantly aware of hidden

Plate 1 *Ottoman women in a park* (detail) (1787). Istanbul's public parks were an innovative new development of the eighteenth century, and they were extremely popular with women who could often be seen socializing there in same-sex groupings (from Ignatius Mouradgea d'Ohsson and Constantin d'Ohsson, *Tableau général de l'empire othoman, divisé en deux parties, dont l'une comprend la législation mahométane; l'autre, l'histoire de l'empire othoman*, Paris, 1787) (Amherst College Library and Collections).

Plate 2 *A Dominican nun pharmacist with the accoutrements of her profession,*
Stefano Ghirardini (1723). Convents often provided charitable medical care and
this larger than life-size portrait suggests that this nun took considerable pride in
her abilities (Museum of Fine Arts, Budapest).

Plate 3 *The ideal cook and kitchen in the early eighteenth century.* This utopian scene from a well-known German cookbook shows a well-dressed upper-class woman with a key in her hand (the mark of her authority) looking confidently down into the kitchen where servants are preparing a meal. Behind her, guests are arriving: the event will be a success (Frontispiece of Maria Sophia Schellhammer, *Der wohl-unterwiesenen Köchin zufällige Confect-Taffel* (The Well-instructed Cook with her Incidental Confectionary), 3rd edn, Berlin, 1723, originally published 1699) (Schlesinger Library, Radcliffe Institute for Advanced Study, Harvard).

Plate 4 *Polish woman street-seller*, Jean-Pierre Norblin (late 18th century). Street-sellers, many of them women, were ubiquitous in many European cities. In many early modern Polish cities almost all the trade in perishable food was in the hands of women, though they sold all kinds of other commodities as well (Princes Czartoryski Foundation).

Plate 5 *Trade card for Eleanor Coade's Artificial Stone Manufactory*, designed by John Bacon, R.A. (late 18th century). Eleanor Coade's firm was the premier modelled stone manufactory of the late eighteenth and early nineteenth centuries, and she worked with all the best architects of the day, largely in the neoclassical style. Very durable, her work can be seen to this day in many parts of the British Isles. She also exported to Canada, the United States, Brazil, Russia, Poland, South Africa and the Caribbean (John Johnson Collection, Bodleian Library).

Plate 6 *British Light Dragoon's barrack room* (by T. Malton and Thomas Rowlandson after Thomas Rowlandson, 1788). Both women and children were a common sight in early modern army barracks, and regiments also sometimes 'adopted' the children of former comrades. The death rate among soldiers was high though (mostly from disease) and there were often legal impediments to soldiers marrying, so these informal arrangements were often the only experience of fatherhood they were likely to have (courtesy of the council of the National Army Museum, London).

Plate 7 *Bektashi woman dervish's grave-marker from Istanbul.* The Bektashi Sufis were relatively egalitarian (though also quite religiously heterodox) and permitted women to participate in various ritualistic activities. The stone commemorates dervish Fatma Hanim (d. 1812) and it combines Bektashi symbolism with the tac, a man's head-gear, even though the deceased was a woman. On the stone is a lengthy poem that includes the following verses: 'my eyes are directed towards the beloved, the world appears as nothing to me/For the sake of Yûsuf in the Egypt of the heart I have given up being the woman Zelikha [this is a reference to a story from the Qur'an]/My place is now placelessness, I have given up being a woman of this world' (photographer: Klaus Kreiser, German Archaeological Institute in Istanbul; thanks to Irvin Schick for the translation).

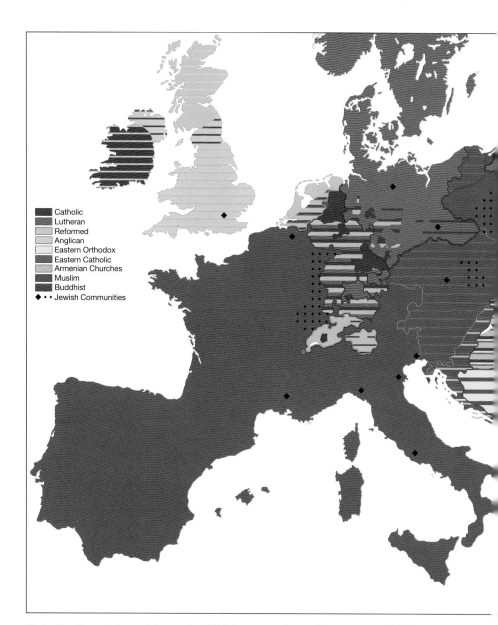

Plate 8 *The religions of Europe in 1750.* Large sections of Europe were fairly religiously homogeneous in the eighteenth century, though in many cases only because of prior expulsions or forced conversions of religious minorities. Other regions remained quite diverse in their religious composition. In 1750 this was especially true of parts of what is now Germany (split between Protestants and Catholics, with some Jews); the Balkans (mixed Orthodox, Catholic, Muslim and

Jewish, with a few Protestants); Austria-Hungary (predominantly Catholic, but with newly conquered Orthodox regions); Poland-Lithuania (Catholic, with significant numbers of Orthodox, Jewish and 'Eastern Catholic' populations; the Black Sea and Caspian Sea regions of Russia (largely Orthodox and Muslim, with a Tibetan Buddhist enclave); and Anatolia (with Muslims, Greek Orthodox and members of the Armenian churches).

Plate 9 *Catherine II on horseback, wearing the uniform of the Preobrazhensky Guards,* Vigilius Eriksen (after 1762). This portrait, copies of which Catherine liked to confer upon visiting dignitaries, commemorates her *coup d'état*, when, dressed in military uniform, she rode at the head of some 14,000 troops to confront her husband, Tsar Peter III, and force him to abdicate the throne in her favour. It plays deliberately both to the popular admiration for cross-dressed women warriors, and to a long tradition of equestrian portraits and statues of kings and victorious generals (Photograph © The State Hermitage Museum, St. Petersburg).

Plate 10 *A Society of Patriotic Ladies, at Edenton in North Carolina*, Philip Dawes (1775). This disapproving cartoon of the Edenton ladies engaged in signing their petition deliberately imitates brothel scenes by Hogarth and others. In addition to suggesting that the Edenton ladies are over-sexed harpies and bad mothers, it also sounds the alarm that, if privileged women are allowed to have 'rights', other groups (African Americans, plebeian men) are likely to follow (Library of Congress, LC-USzC4-4617).

Plate 11 *French Women at the National Assembly*, Jean-François Janinet (1789).
This drawing, of events to which Janinet may have been an eye-witness, depicts
the Women's March to Versailles on 5–6 October 1789, and specifically women's
efforts to convince the National Assembly to accede to their demands for bread.
The next day the women brought Louis XVI and Marie Antoinette back to Paris,
thus putting them under the control of the revolutionaries. It was a key turning
point in the French Revolution (© RMN/Droits reserves).

or secret pollution, as well as that which walked about openly. And it clearly demonstrates women's willingness to indict other women on grounds of sexual immorality, real or imagined. In both Serbia and Istanbul the plague, which struck repeatedly in the eighteenth century, was personified metaphorically as an outcast woman, a kind of wraith, who wandered from town to town casting her deadly spells. During outbreaks people often claimed actually to have seen her and many towns apparently had specific rituals designed to neutralize her power – rituals which, one suspects, involved extremely unpleasant treatment of itinerant beggar-women.[5] Again there is the linking of illicit female sexuality (why else would she have been cast out?) and toxic danger. Witch-trials, often the result of accusations against women by other women, and almost always involving a range of bizarre sexual claims, are another variant of this. They lasted in parts of Christian Europe, most notably Hungary and Poland, well into the eighteenth century: the last witch was judicially executed in Switzerland in 1782, a servant named Anna Göldi, accused of bewitching the daughter of her employer. But vigilante killings of reputed witches lasted far longer.[6]

Seventeenth- and eighteenth-century women and men were still, for the most part, open to the possibility of miracles; they were people for whom the mysteries of faith were real. This aspect of their lives has continued appeal even in more rational, but perhaps more spiritually arid, times. The tragic side is that this was also still a world in which evil was believed to be an actual physical force, a living, albeit supernatural entity that could reside in, take possession of, and work through real people. Belief in witchcraft and diabolism is not egalitarian; it almost always finds the devil in already vulnerable groups, typically strangers, poor people, slaves, women, the elderly, occasionally children, and racial and religious minorities – particularly, in the early modern period, Jews, the Roma and people of African descent. Well over 100,000 people died between 1450 and 1800, often horribly, as the direct result of such beliefs.[7]

THE RELIGIONS OF EUROPE

Catholicism

In the sixteenth century and thereafter, under pressure both from Protestantism and from purists and reformers within its own ranks, the Catholic Church committed itself to a renovation of the established clergy and church hierarchy, a reassertion of clerical control of the holy sacraments, and a 'purification' of popular religious practice. This 'Catholic Reformation' came at the expense of many other, less regularized forms of devotion, many of them especially associated with women. There were many efforts to suppress or limit processions to 'holy' places (such as 'sacred' springs or grottos); veneration of local *beatas* (holy women who often lived independently); and some of the more colourful death and burial rituals both in Europe and the colonies. Local saints, many of them never officially canonized, were 'replaced' by officially approved ones.[8] At the same time, whether because of or in spite of the Catholic Reformation, there is much evidence, across Catholic Europe (see Plate 8), of a renewal of faith, especially in the cities. This had major implications for women. Across Europe the number of Catholic women's religious orders and congregations more than tripled in the later sixteenth and seventeenth centuries. There grew up a robust new interest in female literacy, accompanied by much expanded distribution of devotional books. And the worship of the Virgin Mary and female saints took on a new intensity and new institutional forms.

Catholicism had always accorded a powerful role to female saints. In popular belief (and at least in part ratified by the church hierarchy), these saints often oversaw or had the power to remedy problems of everyday life, such as childbirth, infertility or illness, or marital conflict. The most powerful woman in the Catholic pantheon was and is the Virgin Mary, mother of God. Devotion to the Virgin has waxed and waned in the history of Catholicism, but it reached one of its peaks in the eighteenth and nineteenth centuries, culminating in 1854 in the promulgation of the dogma of the Immaculate Conception (that is, freedom from original sin) of Mary. Mary symbolized many things to early modern women. As 'Queen of Heaven' she was a model for the influence women could have over even the most powerful men. There were many popular tales of Mary intervening successfully with her son Jesus to save a sinner or otherwise alter someone's destiny, and we may be sure that countless prayers were directed to her by women desperate for more control over their own lives. Less positive, at least from a modern perspective, was the way Mary's extreme sexual purity tended to strengthen the equation of female sexuality – and mortal women in general – with sin.[9]

In the eighteenth century, Marian devotion (that is, prayer, meditation, music, art, reading and so on, centred around the sacred heart, immaculate conception, nativity, holy name, maternal grief, or other aspect of the Virgin) became an important rallying point for women to come together to pursue religious and charitable projects. Hundreds of thousands of Catholic laywomen joined Marian sodalities or confraternities, many of them Jesuit-initiated, in both Catholic Europe and the colonies. The confraternities often had elaborate organizational structures, gave women a new licence to move about and intervene in the public sphere, especially in charitable affairs, and built solidarity between women. And while the church hierarchy was often ambivalent about them (and in fact, in the later eighteenth century, closed or colluded in closing large numbers of them down), these groups could, in some cases, create powerful ties between the clergy or municipal authorities and women. Less agreeably, some of the confraternities (or their successor organizations) helped push a heavy dose of wifely obedience and maternalist ideology, especially from the later eighteenth century on, and this became even more pronounced after the French Revolution as the whole church lurched to the right and a Europe-wide backlash against political women set in (see Chapter 9).[10]

Since early medieval times convents had served to concentrate and preserve the salvific and apotropaic power of holy virgins. In the elaborate spiritual division of labour of Catholicism 'brides of Christ' were supposed to devote themselves to prayer and ascetic practices on behalf of their families, communities and Christendom. By the early modern period convents had also become an important part of the dynastic strategy of well-off families. Families placed one or more daughters in convents both for the spiritual profit a nun's life of prayer would generate for her kin, and because, by the early modern period, convent entry fees were generally substantially lower than a regular dowry would have been. Moreover, putting a daughter or daughters in a convent (and, often, younger sons into the priesthood) usually kept them out of the inheritance stream, making it possible to concentrate assets in one son (see Chapter 2). Traditionally convents wielded a considerable amount of temporal as well as spiritual power, and up to around 1600 it was not uncommon for nuns to engage in numerous activities outside the convent. However, the Council of Trent, the great 'Reforming' council that sat intermittently from 1545 to 1563 to respond definitively to the challenge of Lutheranism, imposed significantly greater restrictions on nuns and convents, abolishing mendicancy (begging) and public charitable or evangelistic work for women religious, insisting on nuns' total and permanent enclosure and segregation from men, and enforcing the vows of poverty more strictly than before.

Closing the lid on convents clearly had intellectual and spiritual implications, but there has been some disagreement as to what they were. It has been argued that seventeenth- and eighteenth-century cloistered nuns were deliberately denied opportunities to engage in advanced theological study to which earlier generations of nuns had had readier access. Local bishops are said to have discouraged nuns from publishing, from engaging in theological debate and from some mystical paths.[11] The silencing in 1693 of the great Mexican nun, poet, playwright, theologian, and feminist, Sor Juana Inés de la Cruz (1648–1695), is often seen as emblematic of this trend. So is the active repression, especially in France, of Jansenist nuns. (The Jansenists emphasized a rather severe, Augustinian conception of sin and predestination, and were often accused of being Protestants – specifically Calvinists in disguise. They also accorded important roles to women.)[12] It has also been argued that nuns, far more than most male religious, were channelled more and more narrowly into ascetic and disciplinary practices like self-flagellation, the wearing of hair-shirts and celices, and sensory and food deprivation, that were supposed to mimic the suffering of Jesus Christ. On the other hand, it is clear that practice differed greatly depending upon the religious order, the country and the local bishop. Some convents were deeply involved in music and theatre. Many supported their members in intellectual activities, including writing and publishing (see below and Chapter 8). A recent study of one eighteenth-century Portuguese convent in Braga, which may or may not be representative, shows that many of the nuns moved around between orders and houses, there was considerable flexibility as to religious practice, and some nuns clearly lived a very rich spiritual life. However, there is also evidence, in some places, of far more sustained efforts at control and containment of women's bodies and spirituality than was true for men, and a somewhat disturbing (from a modern perspective) emphasis on self-inflicted pain.[13]

Certainly many seventeenth- and eighteenth-century nuns and other Catholic women continued to write mystical or devotional works. Well over a hundred *printed* spiritual autobiographies have survived from the early modern period by Spanish, Portuguese, French, German, Austrian, Belgian, Polish, Canadian and Latin American nuns, nun-missionaries, Catholic lay activists, and pious women. Hundreds more lie unpublished, often in local or convent archives. Women also wrote and dictated religious poetry, visions, sacred drama, theological works, and histories of their orders. Sister Maria Jesus de Agreda of Spain (1602–1665)'s controversial *Mystical City of God*, composed between 1637 and 1645, was a passionate defence of the Immaculate Conception of Mary, with sections said to have been vouchsafed to Agreda by the Virgin herself. It went into more than 89 editions in the next three hundred years, and certainly contributed to the spread of Marian devotion outlined above. The lay mystic and theologian Jeanne Marie Bouvier de la Motte Guyon, usually known as Mme Guyon (1648–1717), defied bishops and wrote a commentary on the Bible as well as best-selling books on numerous religious topics; she also produced some remarkable auto-biographical writings, and was imprisoned repeatedly for her beliefs. The illiterate Spanish *beata* Sor Beatriz Ana Ruiz (1666–1735) dictated religious visions to a male amanuensis, including a lively and influential description of purgatory. Benedikta Gradić (1688–1771), a Benedictine nun from Dubrovnik, wrote a Christmas pageant in Croatian for the nuns to perform.[14] There were many others like them.

Even as the older orders became ever more tightly cloistered, 'third orders' of nuns (tertiaries) began to appear whose members took only temporary vows, devoted themselves to charity, and often were not enclosed at all. In Chapter 5 we looked at the activities of one of these groups, the Daughters of Charity, famous for its nursing and social work. All in all, the impression one gets of the burgeoning 'third orders' is of tremendous spiritual excitement. And when one combines that with the lay women's confraternities, eighteenth-century Catholic women's spiritual and organizational life seems in a flourishing state indeed. As least part of this was missionary fervour. As women's historians have often noted, women tend to excel in work that defends corporate, ethnic or religious 'purity' in the face of real or imagined external attack, undoubtedly because they sense that this is an area where they are likely to be given an unusual amount of creative scope.[15] There is no question that the militant faith of the Counter-Reformation inspired women with a burning zeal to save lost souls. The rise and persistence of Protestantism, the continued presence of unconverted Jews on European soil, the conquest by the (Catholic) Austrians of formerly Muslim-dominated lands in Hungary and the Balkans, continued tension between Catholics and other groups in and around Poland and Ukraine, and the European expansion into the Americas, Africa and Asia, massively increased the number of candidates with potential to be claimed or reclaimed for the True Faith, and numerous women rose to the challenge, often overcoming the skepticism of male ecclesiastics to do so. Some of the most formidable women of the early modern period were nun- or in a few cases, lay-missionaries.[16]

Catholic missionaries of both sexes undeniably perpetrated much spiritual and bodily violence upon the people they sought to convert. Simple fellow feeling was often singularly lacking, as is demonstrated by the long-lived practice of taking away other people's children by force to rear them as Catholics (see below). Conversely, they also seem to have been more successful, much earlier, than Protestants, both in assimilating non-European women into the faith and, at least in some cases, allowing them to forge significant spiritual and institutional roles for themselves. Ignacia del Espiritu Santo (1663–1748), a mixed-race (Filipina/Chinese) woman, founded the first indigenous Philippine women's order (the Religious of the Virgin Mary) in Manila in the late seventeenth century. Four different Indian women's convents were founded in Mexico in the eighteenth and early nineteenth centuries (the first in 1724 for Indian women of noble descent), though the 'top-down', grudging and racialist fashion in which at least two of them were established would cause lasting tension. The first black women's Roman Catholic religious order, the Oblate Sisters of Providence, devoted to educating black children, was founded in 1829 by Saint-Domingue-Haiti-born mulatta Mary Elizabeth Lange (ca. 1780–1882) in the slave-state of Maryland in the United States.[17]

In the eighteenth century some Catholic women – better-off laywomen especially – began taking up what they saw as a more 'rational' and 'modern' approach to the faith that emphasized morality, charity, education, and a more disciplined, inward, and individualistic faith. Numerous Catholic women wrote didactic or moralizing works (or patronized other women who did), encouraged new women-centred religious foundations, and joined devotional gatherings, like the seemingly ubiquitous rosary confraternities, described by one authority as: 'a disciplined form of prayer recitation . . . that fostered an interiorized and individualized spirituality'.[18] They also committed themselves in large numbers to good works, most of them 'out in the world.' Some of these women were among the most remarkable people of their time. Maria Gaetana Agnesi (1718–1799), a Milanese mathematician and writer of an important early calculus text, considered taking the veil, but ended up consecrating herself to charitable activities on behalf of the poor. Honora Nagle, known as Nano Nagle (1718–1784), from an Irish-Catholic gentry family, founded a series of schools for children, at a time when it was still illegal in Ireland to run a Catholic school. Ultimately she founded a new order of unenclosed nuns who would be 'devoted solely to works of charity among the poor'.[19] Josefa Amar y Borbón (1749–1833), a physician's daughter from Spain, sought charitable and educational reforms, and also wrote several tracts intended for women. In the following passage she lays out her views on the kind of Christianity mothers should be trying to inculcate:

> [R]eal devotion and virtue consist not in the exterior formula of visiting numerous churches and reciting many orations, a vice more common to women than to men . . . what is important is to cement in them that true and solid virtue consists in practising good and abhorring bad, in controlling one's passions, in mortifying one's appetites, in practicing charity, and above all in complying with one's obligations.[20]

As Amar y Borbón makes clear, 'rational piety' was not easily reconciled to older, and still very popular, forms of female piety which were noisier and more corporate, more comfortable with traditional magico-religious practices (including belief in miraculous healing and witchcraft) and far less oriented toward the written word. This divide would follow Catholic women into the nineteenth-century and beyond, on the face of it, a weakness, but, at another level, testimony to the enormous diversity and versatility of women's commitment to Catholicism, not just in Europe but across the globe.[21]

Eastern Orthodoxy

In the eighteenth century Eastern Orthodoxy was the dominant religion in Russia (Russian Orthodoxy), much of the Balkans and Western Anatolia (Serbian Orthodoxy; Greek Orthodoxy, etc.), and was also heavily represented in Poland, the Ukraine, Hungary and other Eastern and Southeastern European and middle Eastern regions. Orthodoxy and Roman Catholicism had split apart in the eleventh century, but continued to share a great deal in theological terms. In the early modern period, among the key differences where women were concerned were: somewhat greater tolerance on the part of most branches of Eastern Orthodoxy for popular religious practices than was the case in the Catholic Church; more diffuse and decentralized structures of authority, a less developed female monastic and confraternity tradition, and the fact that parish clergy (though not monks and nuns) could marry (in Roman Catholicism both parish priests and monks have to take a vow of celibacy). The Orthodox Church's willingness to countenance a fairly high degree of local diversity of religious practice, coupled with the relatively low literacy and slow progress of urbanization in some of the Eastern lands, meant that Orthodoxy at the village level sometimes looked more 'medieval' than Catholicism did. Ecstatic pilgrimages and widespread belief in miracles remain popular among many of the Orthodox even in the twenty-first century. So does belief in the power of religious icons. And the Orthodox priesthood retains an important role in healing and apotropaic rituals to this day.

The tolerance of the church hierarchy for popular belief did have its limits, especially in Russia. Unhappiness with the so-called 'excesses' of popular devotion began to grow during the reign of Peter the Great (r. 1682–1725). A spiritual directive of 1721 sought to discredit as 'superstitious' a wide range of practices, from 'false' miracles and making claims for unapproved icons to votive offerings at streams and stones popularly believed to be holy. Over time, church and secular courts were given wider powers to investigate such practices, as well as to police blasphemy and magic. But what one historian has called 'Russia's version of the Counter-reformation' was never as thorough-going as the one that roiled the Catholic Church. There was far less support for it either at the elite or popular level, and numerous practical problems. How, for example, was a 'false' icon to be distinguished from a 'true' one? Heavy-handed efforts to decide such questions were still causing discord in the church on the eve of the Bolshevik Revolution of 1917.[22]

Icon-veneration was extremely important for women. The whole process of identifying a powerful icon played greatly to women's traditional strengths, in addition to magnifying the influence of lay-people of both sexes. Usually icons gained fame because ordinary people were healed by them, often after having been urged to pray to a particular icon in a dream or vision. The history of an icon popularly called the 'Kaluzhka' Mother of God from the diocese of Kaluga, southwest of Moscow, is probably quite indicative. According to legend, in 1748 two women serfs were cleaning out the attic of a local landowner, and came upon the icon wrapped up in dirty sackcloth. The two got into an argument about what it was and one of the women, Evdokia, lost her temper and spat upon the image. Instantly she fell into convulsions. That night the Virgin appeared to Evdokia's parents in a dream, complaining that their daughter had blasphemed against her, and demanding restitution. After prayer, offerings before the insulted icon, liberal applications of holy water, and the like, Evdokia was restored to normalcy. Others were subsequently healed by praying in front of the icon, which was soon moved to the village church, and in 1771 it was said to have saved the town of Kaluga from a visitation of the plague. In 1812, it was supposed to have played a role in the victory of the Russians over Napoleon and, in later years, to be efficacious in warding off cholera.[23]

A significant part of the devotional life of Russian believers in the later eighteenth and nineteenth centuries revolved around often elaborate 'visitations' by and processions involving icons of this kind, the vast majority of them representing the Virgin Mary. The fact that apotropaic miracles were part of the everyday, and the miraculous could be in one's own house (both in Russia and in the Balkans the miracle-working icon was as often to be found in a private household as in a church) helped settle a mantle of exciting mystery and sanctity about daily life. It also accorded women, who usually tended household icons, an important spiritual, and even quasi-political role, since rivalries between households and villages about the relative strength of 'their' icon by comparison with those of other people, debates about what particular icons were good for, and decisions about what religious acts would enhance a particular icon's 'willingness' to look out for families' or localities interests, necessarily relied heavily upon the evidence women could bring to bear.[24]

More than western Europe, eastern Europe continued to be afflicted heavily into the eighteenth century by doctrinal conflicts, heavy-handed attempts at 'top-down' religious reform (especially in Russia), and a series of destructive and lengthy wars. In addition, a good number of Orthodox believers in the Balkans and Turkey, and smaller numbers in what is now Southern Russia, Georgia and the Ukraine, lived under Muslim rule. All this made for a good deal of bitterness and zealotry within the various movements for spiritual renewal that, in eastern as well as western Europe, characterized the period. Religious martyrdom had fallen somewhat out of favour in western Europe by the late seventeenth century. But it continued to flourish in Russia and the Balkans, and, as in other faiths, the spectacle of the church under attack provided a powerful enticement to women's participation. This was very evident in Russia in the doctrinal chaos and schism that characterized the second half of the seventeenth century. A number of Orthodox nuns supported the Old Believers (dissidents who opposed certain seventeenth-century liturgical invocations), and several noblewomen, most famously Feodosya Morozova (1632–1675), withstood torture and imprisonment and died martyrs' deaths for their refusal to conform to the official view.[25] Communities of Old Believers, who, in the eighteenth century, scattered to Poland, the Caucasus, Siberia, the Ottoman Empire, and even as far as Canada, often took on some of the classic features of persecuted sects, including giving an enhanced role to women. This was especially true of the so-called 'priestless' Old Believers.[26] As early as 1706, in a female Old Believer community established near the river Leksa in Russia, women fulfilled virtually all liturgical and administrative functions, including supervising and acting as music directors, leaders of church services, and readers. In the eighteenth and nineteenth centuries many priestless Old Believers also permitted women to baptize, and some also allowed them to administer the sacrament of Penance, confess other women (and, less often, men), and even act as 'spiritual fathers [sic]' to communities, especially during periods where the groups were suffering under heightened state repression. The Old Believers placed considerable emphasis upon lay celibacy, and while this remained an unsettled issue, and some groups ultimately abandoned it, it proved a way for some women to abandon unhappy marriages or avoid marriage altogether, assert their spiritual equality with men, and bypass the numerous real and symbolic associations between wifehood and submission. Under the religiously tolerant regime of Catherine

II (r. 1762–1796), several large Old Believer communities were established in Moscow and other cities, where they built an array of chapels, almshouses, hospitals, and single-sex dormitories. Almost immediately these became important magnets for female migration to the city, in part because they offered women jobs in Old Believer-owned textile manufactories and in the sects' many charitable institutions. The communities also helped rural women get residency papers, in some cases furnishing runaway female serfs (often women escaping abusive husbands) with 'recycled' passports from deceased former members.[27]

Female monasticism had never been as prevalent in Orthodoxy as it was in Catholicism, and in the eighteenth century it was reduced still further. In 1764 Catherine II, in line with many 'enlightened despots' of her day, suppressed many Orthodox monasteries and the vast majority of convents. With far fewer opportunities than before to enter a convent, pious Russian women reverted to more informal models of sanctity. Eighteenth- and nineteenth-century Russia was rife with women hermits, mystics and holy-women, both Orthodox and Old Believers, living dramatically austere lives in the forest, embarking on long and difficult spiritual pilgrimages (like the 900-mile journey Matrona Naumovna Popova (1769–1851), a Russian mystic, took on foot around 1800 to visit the Solovetsky monastery), effecting miraculous cures, and imparting religious advice. It was not uncommon for young peasant women to eschew marriage, set up small cottages for themselves, often on their parents' land, and devote themselves to prayer and good works. Soon other pious women would join them and a small religious community would form. The growth of women's religious communities *after* the 1764 decree that closed most 'official' convents was at least as remarkable as anything seen in Catholic Europe. The number of convents grew from 68 to 475 between 1764 and 1917, with the number of nuns and aspirants rising from a little over 5,000 to over 73,000 by the time of the Bolshevik Revolution.[28]

That other great seat of Orthodox belief, the officially Muslim Ottoman Empire, also saw considerable turmoil around issues of religion in the eighteenth century. Though the Ottoman Empire was one of the most religiously tolerant polities in Europe this did not mean that all faiths were treated equally or that all faiths had comparable access to political power. Islam was clearly the favoured religion, and there were all sorts of ways, from sumptuary laws and rules governing the height of churches and synagogues, to limitations on marriage, inheritance and witnessing in court, that advertised and confirmed Islam's favoured position. Unsurprisingly, these policies caused resentment, and in the eighteenth century, as Ottoman military strength began to weaken, some regions that had long considered themselves disadvantaged began to grow restive. Not unexpectedly, religion formed one of the main focal points around which these nascent insurgencies coalesced. A good example is St. Kosmas of Aitolos (1714–1779), who circulated around the Balkans in the 1750s, 60s and 70s, prophesying, performing miracles, trying to win converts to Islam back to Eastern Orthodox Christianity, founding schools, emphasizing the Greek language, disparaging the Jews, and prophesying an apocalyptic defeat of the Turks.

Women, in particular, seem to have flocked to see and hear St. Kosmas. This certainly had something to do with the man's message. St. Kosmas did not hesitate to speak warmly of the heavy influence upon him of his mother, and he had a quite egalitarian message where women (at least Christian women) were concerned, encouraging nuns in their vocation, arguing that God had created woman to be equal to, not inferior to, men, urging husbands to treat their wives as companions not as slaves, and giving voice to inscrutable but provocative prognostications such as 'a time will come, when one woman will drive away the Turks with a distaff' (it is very possible that he had Catherine the Great in mind). He is also reputed to have given out some 40,000 head-scarves to women in accordance with the verse in First Corinthians 'Every woman that prays or prophesies with her head uncovered dishonours her head', and to have stressed the need for women to dress simply and without ornaments. Apparently some of his female devotees took both to veiling and to dressing themselves entirely in black.[29] The Ottoman authorities finally had St. Kosmas murdered in 1779, apparently for what would today be called 'political' reasons: he was said to be aggravating ethnic divisions by allegedly preaching hatred of another religious group (the Jews) which, in turn, undermined loyalty to the tolerationist Ottoman state. But to his followers he was a martyr to the faith, one who, like Jesus Christ, was turned in to the authorities and 'crucified'. He has ended up a saint in the Greek Orthodox Church. The study of women and eighteenth-century Balkan Orthodoxy is, as yet, in its infancy, but some of the themes of St. Kosmas' mission suggest that the region was not as distant from developments in other faiths – notably the growing tendency to make special appeals to women – as we might at first imagine.

Protestantism

The Protestant assault upon Catholicism begun by Martin Luther in 1517 aimed to replace an emphasis on the intercessory power of clergy and saints with a new reliance on faith, scripture and the individual believer's direct connection to God. It ended by splitting western and central Europe apart, with, roughly speaking, the northern third disavowing its allegiance to the pope, and the southern two-thirds, as we have seen, endorsing a 'purified', more disciplined, and newly expansionist form of Catholicism. By the middle of the seventeenth century the broad outlines of the denominational map of western and central Europe were largely fixed. However, Protestantism, lacking a single spiritual head such as the pope provided for Catholicism, and without that religion's pretensions to be a universal faith, had a pronounced tendency to fission into new denominations. As early as the 1530s, several 'wings' of Protestantism had emerged, variously taking their inspiration from Martin Luther, John Calvin of Geneva, Ulrich Zwingli of Zürich, 'top-down' initiatives like that of King Henry VIII of England, or radical and often anticlerical initiatives like those associated with the various Anabaptist sects.

One of the most significant differences between Protestantism and Catholicism (and Orthodoxy, which, in some places, like Hungary and Transylvania, also lost goodly numbers of souls to the new Protestant religions), was the demotion of the Virgin Mary and the saints, as well as many of the traditional devotional practices that had involved them. Much of early modern Protestant militancy, especially in the Calvinist wing, was devoted to savage attacks on what were pejoratively called 'works', understood as any human activity that purported to speed one's own, or someone else's progress to salvation. These included: pilgrimages of any kind; 'worshipping' a statue or icon (Protestants had a particular antipathy to anything that smacked of polytheism or idol-worship); beseeching a saint for help in times of trouble; getting a priest to sprinkle holy water on a sick child; or having masses said for a person's soul. Protestants also objected to the doctrine of transubstantiation: the belief that, at the climax of the mass, the bread and wine is turned, through the mediation of the officiating priest, into the literal, though invisible, body and blood of Christ. The objection to 'works' explains why sixteenth-century Calvinist rioters or armies often went to some trouble to break, or even urinate on statues of the Virgin, as well as to smash altars, communion rails and stained-glass windows.[30] All were seen as, in effect, insults against the prerogatives of God, who alone would decide – without help from humans, inferior supernatural entities, statues, etc. – who was to be saved and who was to be damned. Protestants did not immediately abandon the old practices of apotropaic magic or clerically mediated healing; competitions as to which side's holy men were better at exorcising demons were an important feature of denominational manoeuvring for power well into the eighteenth century.

But the momentum of Protestantism almost everywhere was in the direction of phasing out apotropaic forms of faith, because they so often relied on idolatrous 'props' like religious statues, they used a similar transformative (and magical) logic to discredited doctrines such as transubstantiation, and they manifestly involved numerous non-scriptural elements. For women, who often derived considerable power and influence from precisely these kinds of rituals, this was a major shift; many must have experienced it as a loss. Apotropaic practices never entirely disappeared from Protestant regions, but they were rendered more marginal and far less respectable.

Another feature of Protestantism that had a major impact on women was its opposition to monasteries and convents. The basic theological premise of monasticism was, as we have seen, that whole communities could benefit from the existence of distinct groups of people (celibate men; holy virgins) who could devote their lives to prayer. Protestantism rejected both the notion that another person or group could have much, if any, influence on any-one else's salvation (the purists said none), and the emphasis on the special power of virginity. As far as most Protestants were concerned – and they were not shy about saying it outright – convents were prisons in which sexually frustrated old maids spent useless lives engaged in futile prayer. Martin Luther and later Protestant reformers were emphatic that the proper role for women was to be useful and committed wives and mothers, and they insisted that monks and nuns leave their monasteries and convents and marry like other people (Martin Luther himself married a former nun). For a long time Protestantism's virulent opposition to convents extended to virtually all women's organizations. As late as the early nineteenth century in some Protestant states (notably many of the German lands), and well into the eighteenth in most others, any effort by Protestant women to form per-manent charitable, religious or, in some extreme cases, educational institutions was met by charges that they were trying to set up 'Protestant nunneries'. This largely explains why the associational life of Protestant women was so stunted – and belated – in the early modern period by comparison with that of Catholic women. On the other hand, when Protestant women did take up charity-work they sometimes more than made up for lost time (see Chapter 9).

What did Protestantism offer to women? Many religious movements are very hospitable to women at first, but tend to sideline, or even seek to dis-credit women leaders once the movement is fairly well established. There were numerous Protestant women martyrs in the sixteenth century and important Protestant women patrons as well, mostly from among the aristocracy. For the most part this did not last. The better-established Protestant denominations – Lutheranism, Calvinism, and Anglicanism – soon put women in their place by emphasizing the authority of the male clergy, calling for wifely obedience, stressing the Apostle Paul's call for the Corinthian women to be silent in church, and impugning the modesty and chastity of women who stepped out of line.[31] They could never sideline women completely, however. First, there is a real, if muted, strain of spiritual egalitarianism in the New Testament *and* in the Protestant message ('the priesthood of *all* believers'). Secondly, especially in the later eighteenth century, Protestant women became heavily involved in charitable activities which greatly enhanced their prestige (see Chapter 8). Thirdly, Protestantism kept sending out new, often more egalitarian shoots, or, to put it less kindly, falling into schisms. Quakerism (established in England in the 1650s and 1660s), Labadism (which flourished, especially in the Netherlands, from the 1650s until 1732) and Methodism (a series of movements within English and American Anglicanism that began in the 1730s and finally split off into several independent sects in the late eighteenth century) were just three of the *hundreds* of new Protestant sects or movements that started up in the sixteenth, seventeenth, eighteenth and nineteenth centuries. Virtually every one of those sects offered an opportunity for some women, even if only briefly, to think anew about their relationship to God and their fellow men and women.

From the beginning, Protestantism's strong emphasis on coming into direct, intellectual contact with the word of God, as vouchsafed in the Bible, encouraged both literate people to join, and the illiterate to try to learn to read. As a result Protestant women were probably more literate on average than Catholic, Orthodox, Muslim or Sephardic Jewish women, though not, perhaps, quite as literate as Ashkenazi Jewish women (see below). Many scholars believe that this emphasis on reading and praying encouraged a more individualistic faith; some think it encouraged more individualistic attitudes in general. This is hard to prove, though, because women were also subjected to a heavy dose of tracts and sermons about female subordination, sacrifice and duty; moreover, there was a long tradition of self-focused devotional reading and writing in Catholicism as well.[32] It is, however, true that, between the second half of the seventeenth century and the early nineteenth, a surprising number of independent Protestant women prophets, mystics, writers and itinerant evangelists began to appear, particularly in England and Holland. These women were diverse as to their beliefs, but a number of them were associated with some quite subversive views about sin, salvation, the Trinity, the role of women in religion, and even the nature of the divine.

Antoinette Bourignon (1616–1680), originally from Flanders, was opposed to the anthropomorphic image of God conventional among Christians at least in part because it was so uncompromisingly male. She liked to argue that, instead of thinking of God as 'Old man, Young man, and Dove' (an irreverent play on the Holy Trinity), the deity should be thought of as Good, Justice and Truth.[33] Jane Lead (1624–1704), an English mystic, published numerous books in English, German and Dutch, and, with another woman mystic founded the Philadelphians, what Sylvia Bowerbank has described as 'an ecumenical and millenarian movement whose main aim was to work together to build a culture of peace, receptive to the coming of Virgin Wisdom'. By the 1690s Lead was one of the most famous mystics in Protestant Europe. She, too, was bothered by the 'maleness' of contemporary notions of God. Here is how Lead describes the promise of 'Divine Wisdom' in one of her writings: 'She would be my Mother . . . For if I would apply myself to her Doctrine, and draw my Life's Food from no other Breast, I should then know the recovery of a lost kingdom.'[34] The mysterious M. Mersin (fl. 1696–1701), publishing in England, put out more than a dozen tracts in which she developed a theology centred around the women of the New Testament (notably, somewhat unusually for a Protestant, the Virgin Mary), argued that, at the Second Coming, 'women will be delivered from the bondage [to men] which some has found intolerable', and asserted that, due to men's failure to understand His Word, God now preferred to speak through women prophets. A number of the more radical German Pietists argued that the third person of the Trinity was female, and even went so far as to call 'Her' the 'Mother of Believers'.[35]

In several cases the draw of the female divine gave rise to full-fledged messianic movements that prophesied the imminent coming of a feminine incarnation and even, in some cases, claimed She had already arrived. Such tendencies were especially common among English Protestants. At least four secessionist sects were started in England by women in the late seventeenth and eighteenth centuries, and three of those four posited either some version of the female divine, or an actual female messiah. The least radical of these was the Methodist evangelical movement led by Selina Hastings, Countess of Huntingdon (1707–1791), which ultimately became known as the Countess of Huntingdon's Connexion. It was fairly conservative theologically, though the Countess's thorough-going control of the purse-strings, personnel, clerical training, and even church architecture of her movement gave rise to analogies between her and a 'Mother in Israel'.[36] Three much more radical movements were Jane Lead's Philadelphians, with their emphasis on the Goddess Wisdom and preparing the world for the reign of Peace (see above), the Shakers, a pacifist and celibate sect begun by Mother Ann Lee (1736–1784), who was later proclaimed by her New World followers to be the female messiah, and the movement begun by the spectacular female messiah (or at least self-proclaimed mother of the future messiah), Joanna Southcott (1750–1814), who at the height of her fame is said to have had ten thousand followers.[37]

Protestant women mystics and theologians also took up one of the other burning issues of the day, the question of who would be saved. There was a distinct retreat among many Protestants from the Calvinist belief that hardly anyone would be saved; indeed some sped in the other direction, arguing that God was easily great enough to save everybody, and merciful enough to want to. The German pietist theologian, Johanna Eleonora Petersen (1644–1724), who published fourteen books on religion, including the first autobiography by a woman in German, argued strongly for the principle of universal salvation, as opposed to one in which God picks and chooses who will be saved. This theology did not necessarily eliminate the concept of original sin, but it certainly made it seem a good deal less fearful. It also demolished the claim that only members of one faith would get to heaven, while everyone else would be consigned to hellfire.[38]

Though a number of Protestant women evangelists circulated around Europe in the late seventeenth and eighteenth centuries, organized mission-ary work outside Europe came much later for Protestant than for Catholic women. Most of it is no earlier than the early nineteenth century, and there was far less independent women's missionary work (most Protestant women missionaries accompanied their husbands, as they still do today). The major exception to this was the Quakers, or Society of Friends. The Friends had no ordained clergy, and all believers were thought to manifest the spark of the Divine. Quakerism proved to be a very gender egalitarian creed. As George Fox, one of the founders of the Society, put it, '. . . the light is the same in the male, and in the female, which cometh from Christ . . . and who is [he] that dare stop Christ's mouth?'.[39] Women were heavily involved in Quaker proselytizing, especially in the early decades of the movement, and this continued, albeit in somewhat more subdued form, into the eighteenth century and beyond. In Voices from the Past 6.1 is a brief but touching testimony to the life of Elizabeth Ashbridge (1713–1755), a Quaker minister, born in England, who immigrated to America in her late teens, and died while in Ireland on a preaching tour. It speaks both to the abilities of a successful Quaker minister, and to the esteem a spiritually accomplished woman preacher could inspire.

VOICES FROM THE PAST 6.1

Elizabeth Ashbridge, Quaker minister

Early estranged from her father, a ship's surgeon, Elizabeth embarked for America as an indentured servant while still in her teens. Her employer turned out to be sexually abusive, and she bought herself out of her remaining time. A few years later she married a violent alcoholic ('I had got released from one cruel servitude, and then, not content, got into another for life'), and around that same time she found her way to the Society of Friends. Her husband greatly disapproved of this, mainly because other men harassed him about having a 'preaching' wife. But after he died Elizabeth began devoting much of her time to preaching and missionary work. She married again in 1746, this time apparently happily, to another member of the Society of Friends. But after only seven years of marriage she travelled to England and Ireland to preach, leaving her husband at home. While abroad she visited a number of Quaker meetings, but soon fell sick with what proved to be a fatal illness. She never got back to America. Among Elizabeth Ashbridge's last recorded words were 'Dearest Lord, though thou slay me, I will die at thy feet; for I have loved thee more than life'. She died 'in a quiet frame', in the Spring of 1755.[40]

Testimony from the National Meeting of Ireland . . . Concerning Elizabeth Ashbridge

. . . Thus our dear Friend finished her [life] course. It remains briefly to add our testimony concerning her.

She was a woman of an excellent natural understanding; in her conversation cheerful, yet grave and instructive; she felt the afflictions of others with a tender sympathy, and bore her own with patience and resignation.

As a minister, she was deep in travail, clear in her openings, plain and pertinent in her expressions, solid and awful [i.e. reverential] in her deportment, and attended with that baptizing power, which is the evidence of a living ministry; and which so evidently attended her, in the last testimony she bore in a public meeting, (in great bodily weakness,) that most or all present were reached and deeply affected thereby, and a young woman was, at that time, convinced of the truth; which was as a seal to the finishing of her service in the work of the ministry; and, in which, being so owned to the last, we have no doubt, but she now receives the reward of the faithful servant, and is entered into the joy of her Lord.

Source: Elizabeth Ashbridge, *Some Account of the Early Part of the Life of Elizabeth Ashbridge* (Dublin: Christopher Bentham, 1820), 57–9.

Judaism

The Jews of Europe and the Ottoman Empire were as diverse in linguistic, cultural, religious, and political terms as any religious groupings of the early modern period. The three main European groups, based on language and region of origin, were: (1) the Sephardim, the peoples expelled from Spain and Portugal in the late fifteenth century, who scattered to the Ottoman Empire, the Netherlands and Italy, primarily, and also Morocco, and who generally spoke Ladino or Judeo-Portuguese; (2) the Ashkenazi, who largely settled in eastern Europe, especially Poland and Bohemia, with smaller groups in Germany, and who generally spoke Yiddish; and (3) the Romaniots, who had settled in Greece in Roman times, later spread more widely in the Balkans and into Anatolia, and who spoke a form of Greek. These groups differed among one another in almost every possible respect, from marriage law (especially the rules about divorce) to liturgy, from the ritual slaughtering of animals to the treatment of *Marranos* (Jews who had been forced to convert outwardly to Christianity), and there were also many other internal divisions.[41] Often the differences made it difficult for people to intermarry or worship in the same synagogues.

It is not easy to figure out where women fit in to this kaleidoscopic picture. However, Jews (or many Jews, anyway) had some characteristics which make such study a little bit easier. One was that they tended to have a somewhat higher rate of literacy than people of other faiths (though literacy was not, as is sometimes claimed, universal, even among Ashkenazi Jews).[42] Another was that Jews got involved quite early in printing, so they were in a position to publish work by and for other Jews; this would, in time, open up exciting new opportunities for women. The first printing press in the Ottoman Empire was started by Sephardic Jews in 1493, only a year after the expulsion of the Jews from Spain, and the 1590s saw the first Jewish woman printer, Reyna Nasi, who opened up two different presses near Istanbul. By the seventeenth century there were Jewish-owned presses in Poland, Italy, Switzerland, Bohemia, the Netherlands, and several German states, and in the early eighteenth century one opened in London. Initially such presses specialized in Hebrew religious books. However, especially in central and eastern Europe, they soon began publishing books in Yiddish, the vernacular language of most Ashkenazi Jews. These books were often set in a form of type, revealingly nicknamed *Vayber Taytsh*, or women's Yiddish, that was intended to be more accessible to the non-learned reader. Quite early these books began reaching out explicitly to women readers, like the 1544 Yiddish translation of the Jewish prayer book, the *Sider*, which opens: 'Come here you pious women here you will see a delightful thing'. In this climate it was not long before a few brave women began trying their hands at authorship. Rivkah Tiktiner bat Meir (d. 1605) of Prague, a *firzogerin* (woman prayer-leader), a common role for educated Jewish women, is one of the first published Yiddish woman authors. Her posthumously published book *Meynekes Rivke* (Foster mother or Wet-nurse Rebecca) (1609) focused on women's obligations with respect to the proper rearing of children. Tiktiner, who knew Hebrew, also published a

Yiddish translation of a medieval Hebrew work entitled *Duties of the Heart*, which became widely popular.[43]

A second development that helped open up new spiritual and authorial opportunities for women was the translation of a number of Hebrew and Aramaic religious texts into Yiddish including the *Tsene Rene* (a Yiddish translation of the first five books of the Hebrew Bible, often called the 'Women's Torah'), parts of the *Talmud*, and sections from influential mystical kabbalistic texts like the *Zohar*. This had a powerful effect upon women (and presumably lower-class men), because it meant that they now had access to sacred texts that had previously been available almost exclusively to a narrow band of fairly elite, or at least linguistically adept men. The growing availability of kabbalistic texts in Yiddish proved to be especially important. Kabbalah was a mystical and esoteric tendency within Judaism with roots that went back at least to the medieval period. Some strains of Kabbalah placed considerable emphasis on the 'feminine' side of the divine, or the *Shekhinah*, variously understood as the divine bride, the in-dwelling presence of God in his Creation, Israel (most often in the sense of the collectivity of Jews), the Peace of God, and mystical ecstasy. It also tended to attribute evil more to an eternal demonic potency than to human sin, and it stressed an old kabbalistic belief in the power of human effort to alter the human condition and 'repair the tear in the world' (*tikkun o'lam*). Kabbalistic thought became considerably more popular, and began to gain something like a mass following, in the aftermath of two extremely traumatic mid-seventeenth-century events. The first was the Chmielnicki massacres in Poland/Ukraine of 1648–54, in which between eighteen thousand and thirty thousand Jews died at the hands of rampaging Cossacks and Ukrainian peasants. The second was the meteoric rise and ignominious fall of Sabbatai Zevi (1626–1676), a Romaniot Jew who claimed to be the Jewish messiah, gathered a massive following across Europe and the Ottoman Empire, and then, in 1666, was forced by the Ottoman authorities to convert to Islam. In the unsettled and insecure atmosphere that followed these events Kabbalah, with its complex but ultimately hopeful view of the relationship between humanity, God and the world, its emotional and ecstatic approach to faith, its occultism, its emphasis upon the *Shekhinah*, and its rather non-specific messianism and millenarianism, seems to have struck a chord. By the early eighteenth century, kabbalistic texts were being printed in cheap editions (often pastiches or excerpts) and in both Yiddish and Ladino. Some of the translators were women, like Ellus bat Mordecai of Slutsk, who published a book of translations of kabbalistic writings in 1704.[44]

Kabbalistic thought would have a major impact on popular Jewish piety in the late seventeenth and eighteenth centuries. Among other things it influenced the genre most widely associated with women, collections of tkhines or supplicatory prayers, some of them old but translated, some new-composed. *Tkhines* collections were never an exclusively female genre, and many were written for men. However, a number of them focused on concerns important to women, such as childbirth, ritual cleanliness, children's sickness, dietary rules, visiting cemeteries to pray or weep over the graves of one's relatives, and the like. This does not mean that they only spoke to individual issues or problems though. For one thing, they often reflected collective crises, like this moving supplicatory prayer written by a woman named Toybe Pan during the great plague epidemic of 1680 in Prague:

> Every gate is locked except the gate of tears
> Beloved Lord God, hear our prayers
> Collect our tears in Your vessel
> And rescue Your people, Israel.

During the epidemic, as was common, the Jews were locked into the ghetto, so the first line is literally true. At the same time it is metaphorical; in that it refers to the common belief (also found in kabbalistic thought, as well as in other non-Jewish mystical and pietistic traditions) that tears, perhaps especially women's tears, have special power to move God (see Voices from the Past 6.2).[45]

VOICES FROM THE PAST 6.2

A Jewish girl's prayer-colophon

By Gele, daughter of Moyshe the Printer

This autobiographical prayer was inserted into one of these tkhines collections by the person who set the type for the book. Gele was eleven years old, the daughter of a printer from Halle in Germany. Her mother had died. Not only does the poem describe Gele's own contribution to the process of book production, but it also takes up the theme of women's tearful petitions to God ('we cry out and implore Him'), and probably reflects the heightened messianic enthusiasm so common among Jews in the late seventeenth and eighteenth centuries. Gele also uses the poem to point out to God that, at least of late, He has not been paying much attention to His people's prayers (in fact, she puts it more diplomatically: 'our Prayers do not seem to reach their destination'). Some have seen this tradition of 'arguing with God' about issues of justice, often as if in a court of law, as an especially unique and powerful feature of Jewish piety and Jewish conceptions of the Divine.[46]

From beginning to end
Of this beautiful new prayer book

I, Gele, daughter of Moyshe the printer
And Madam Freyde, daughter of Yisroel Kats of blessed memory
Have set all the letters with my own hand.
I who was born one of ten children
Am a maiden less than twelve years old.
But do not be shocked that I must work
For we daughters of Israel
Sit long in exile.
One year ends and another begins,
But the Messiah does not come.
Year after year
We cry out to God and implore Him
But our prayers do not seem to reach their destination.
And I must stay silent
For I and my father's house
Cannot speak too openly
As it is with all Jews
As the verse says:
Those who have known the destruction of Jerusalem
And have suffered in bitter exile
Will know great joy again
With the coming of the Messiah.
Amen and so may it be.
Beloved Sirs, buy this prayer for a small sum of money
For there can be no greater delight in the world
Than to please God, blessed be He, as much as you can.

Source: From *Tkhines* (Halle, 1710), quoted in Devra Kay, ed. *Seyder Tkhines: the Forgotten Book of Common Prayer for Jewish Women* (Philadelphia: The Jewish Publication Society, 2004), 19–20. © 2004 by Devra Kay, published by the Jewish Publication Society, with permission of the copyright holder.

Yiddish religious books, particularly the *tkhines* collections, are not the first or the only early modern religious genre designed for a mass audience. But they are among the first explicitly and repeatedly to include literate women. Given that men's domination of the great monotheistic religions up to that time had been predicated in part upon a monopoly or near monopoly of sacred texts, the question naturally arises as to what happened when women in significant numbers began to gain access to some of these texts. Did the content of the religious message start to change? It seems that this did happen with respect to some early Yiddish religious writing by and for women. Jewish tradition, like that of many other faiths, contains some quite misogynist material. Take the issue of death in childbirth. The Mishnah, the first (early third century C.E.) written redaction of Jewish customary law, argues that women who die in childbirth are being punished by God because

'... they are not meticulous in the observance of the Niddah [menstrual taboos and post-menstrual purification], Hallah [a ritual involving a blessing and burnt sacrifice of a piece of bread dough] and lighting the [sabbath] candle'. As in Christianity, there was much emphasis on the association between the sin of Eve and female spiritual or bodily impurity. As one rather undiplomatic, though widely read, male writer put it in 1604:

> Therefore [because Eve caused the spiritual death of Adam] the woman must also ... suffer torment and misfortune. And therefore she must have her period every month, and must fast once or twice [a month], so that she will remember her sin and remain in a constant state of remorse. Just as a murderer continuously does, who must all his days fast and regret his sin, so must the woman do as well. Every month she immerses herself in the ritual bath, so that she will remember her sins and be pious ... Therefore, it is fitting for her to recite the prayers for a repentant sinner...[47]

But other contributions to the genre, written both by women and by men, dilute these kinds of beliefs in various ways. It could be argued that the very fact of there being special prayers written for women to recite while in midst of childbirth implies that there are ways to stave off death other than dwelling perpetually upon one's biological impurity and ancestral sin. And in fact, some *tkhines* explicitly seek to deflect the blame away from the female petitioner, by, in effect, asserting her individuality, as opposed to her connection to the sin-soaked lineage of Eve. The *Tsenerene* ('Women's Torah'), first published around 1600, was written by a man, Jacob ben Isaac of Yanov. But periodically ben Isaac ventriloquizes the voices of women, as in a prayer for women in labour that runs: 'Lord of the world, because Eve ate of the apple, all of us women must suffer such great pangs [in childbirth] as to die. Had I been there, I would not have had any enjoyment from the fruit...'[48] (I interpret this to mean: had I been in Eve's place I would not have succumbed to temptation.) Did ben Isaac come up with this intriguing theology himself, or did he hear it from the women in his family? One suspects the latter. Sabbatai Zevi, the False Messiah, is reputed to have promised that he would 'lift the curse of Eve' from women, which suggests that this was a topic of general discussion in the 1650s and 1660s; it was certainly a common feature in Christian millenarian thought around the same time.[49] One late eighteenth-century or early nineteenth-century *tkhine*, attributed to a woman named Shifrah Segal of Brody (formerly in Polish Galicia), rejects the notion of Eve's sin entirely, suggesting instead, in a complicated, Kabbalistic argument, that women light the sabbath candles not to expiate or symbolize their sin, but in order that the whole community may be brought close to the *Shekhinah*, which is the light of God.[50]

Tkhines writers also sought to elevate the reputation of women by emphasizing the power and virtue of the Biblical matriarchs, and seeking their help as mediatrixes with God. Sarah Rebecca Rachel Leah Horowitz (fl. 1720–1790) was born in Polish Galicia and became well known for her Talmudic scholarship, her knowledge of Kabbalistic sources, and her book, *Tkhine of the Matriarchs* (1780s or 90s). As its title suggests, Horowitz's book deals with Biblical women like Leah and Rachel, and it has a particularly powerful representation of Rachel, rising from her tomb to plead with God to have mercy on His chosen people. The book is also influenced by Kabbalistic mystical practice, which had long seen Rachel as an embodiment of the *Shekhinah*. A *tkhine* by a Serle bas Jacob Kranz from the late eighteenth century calls upon 'our mother Sarah [the wife of Abraham] to plead for us in this hour of judgment . . . And especially, pray for our little children that they may not be taken away from us.' In the nineteenth century it became common for *tkhines* writers and women poets to call upon Rachel for help and inspiration, and in the early to mid-nineteenth century Rachel's tomb, located near Jerusalem, developed into an important pilgrimage destination for Jewish women, as it remains to this day.[51]

Hasidism was the most powerful of the new pietistic Jewish religious movements of the eighteenth century, and its relationship to women has long been controversial. Some have viewed it as a fundamentally egalitarian movement, because it emphasized prayer, love, a close, emotional relationship with God, mystical experience and miraculous healing over Talmudic study, ancient languages, or *halakhic* observance. It does seem that the miracle-working *zaddiks* (*zaddik* means 'righteous man' or, as some say, saint), played to female and family concerns. One critic says of the *zaddiks*: 'this one heals the sick; that one expels ghosts; this one frees *agunot* [women whose husbands refuse to give them a divorce]; that one finds what is lost; this one cures barren women; that one reads minds; this one predicts the future . . .' Many of the miracles attributed to the Baal Shem Tov (1700?–1760), who is usually thought of as the founder of Hasidism (or at least its best-known figure), look very similar to the ones performed by Sufi dervishes or Catholic beata, or that we see attributed to icons, and ..nts' tombs and statues.[52] We also see women (and men) embarking on pilgrimages to seek the assistance of famous *zaddiks* or make votive offerings at their tombs. The question of women and Hasidism grows more heated over the issue of whether women miracle workers and visionaries could acquire anything like the sort of prestige that attended certain charismatic men.

Mystical movements, even as they seek to commune with the *Shekhinah*, the divine beloved, the female essence, the divine Sophia, the Virgin Mary (or

Maryam) or the various other feminine incarnations, avatars or principles, have frequently been very uncomfortable with real women, and particularly real women's bodies. That is one reason why mysticism so often goes along with celibacy and sexual self-denial, both in faiths like Catholicism and Russian Orthodoxy, which revere holy celibacy, and, less predictably, those like Islam, Protestantism and Judaism that command almost everyone to marry. Many mystical traditions also view women as purposefully trying to distract men, and hence as people actively to be avoided or shunned by those who truly want to walk the mystic's path. Both Kabbalistic thought and Hasidism (and, as we have seen, popular belief within most faiths) had a tendency to identify women, and especially female sexuality, with the demonic.

The career of the one well-known female *zaddik*, Hannah Rochel Verbermacher (1806?–1888?), the famous 'Maid of Ludmir', falls in the nineteenth century but it is worth a brief mention in this context. Hannah Rochel is often thought to demonstrate the limits of Hasidic 'egalitarianism'. She was very well-educated and extremely pious, and, around 1825, she used her inheritance to build her own study house (*beys medresh*) in Ludmir in the Ukraine, just as a male *zaddik* would. There she gave lectures, received petitioners, and used to pray wrapped in the *tsitsit* (fringed shawl) and wearing the *tefillin* (phylacteries), traditionally required of men only.[53] She is also thought to have gone to other towns to preach to women, and was renowned for her ecstatic praying as well as for her healing miracles. She drew a substantial following, but within a few years male *zaddiks* began uniting against her and saying she was possessed by a *dybbuk* (a malign spirit). A good many of the details are lacking, but as a result of the furore and the pressure brought to bear upon her, Hannah Rochel came to feel that she had lost her powers. This was not the end of the Maid of Ludmir's story, however. Some decades later, around 1859, Hannah Rochel emigrated to Jerusalem. Once there she seems to have resumed her public religious activities, attracting numerous adherents, most of them older Ashkenazi, Sephardic and even Muta'rabi (Arab-speaking) women, receiving supplicants, holding court on Sabbath afternoons 'according to the custom of the *rebbes* from Poland', studying daily, and leading popular pilgrimages to Rachel's Tomb, where she would recite *tkines* and sometimes hold all-night prayer vigils. She is also said to have attracted Muslim women devotees, which would not be all that odd, given the ecumenical nature of this kind of apotropaic and petitionary faith. Though it is still not known exactly when Hannah Rochel died, women were still praying and making supplications over her grave (thought to be on the Mount of Olives) as late as 1936, almost a half century after her death.[54]

The Maid of Ludmir was part of a larger opening out of opportunities for Jewish women that began roughly in the seventeenth century and greatly expanded in the eighteenth and early nineteenth centuries. As we have seen, *tkhines* and other women's literature often focused on important biblical women. By the late eighteenth century, Jewish women had begun to translate the notion of *tikkun o'lam*, 'healing the tear in the world,' one of the central ethical injunctions of the Kabbalah, into charitable and other 'associational' activities. At least in the German lands, they formed women's organizations earlier than Protestant women. As individuals and as members of organizations some of them would also be among the first women in Europe and the New World actively to campaign for an end to religious discrimination. When Reform Judaism in its various guises came onto the horizon in the early nineteenth century the spiritual emancipation of Jewish women and a secularized adaptation of *tikkun o'lam* were both central, albeit controversial, parts of the programme, and they remain so to this day.

Islam

The five pillars of Islam, in order of importance, are:

1. The Testimony of Faith (Shahadah) ('I believe there is no God but God and Mohammed is his messenger')
2. Ritual Prayer five times a day (Salat)
3. The Paying of Alms (Zakat)
4. Fasting on Ramadan (Sawm)
5. The Pilgrimage to Mecca if it can be done without undue hardship (Hajj).

These are required equally of all believers regardless of gender, race or social status; in Islam, as in Christianity, there is a strong imputation that women and men are equal before God. However, where Christianity is rather vague about how this is to work in the everyday (and one could easily receive the impression that it is *only* before God that women are, in any sense, equal), early Muslims worked quite hard to operationalize a relatively strong position for women. The Qur'an and *hadiths* (oral traditions, mostly about the Prophet and the community he built around him) consciously bolstered women's property and inheritance rights, insisted they be party to their own marriage contract and retain control of their dowry, and inveighed against female infanticide (Chapter 3). A number of Mohammed's companions and counsellors were women, including his first wife, Khadija bint Khuwalid, a wealthy woman merchant, who is considered his first disciple.

Mohammed's later wives also played important roles both during and after Mohammed's life. Most of them outlived him, they were considered important and holy personages in their own right, and they are also the sources for a lot of the information about Mohammed and the early community that passed into the *hadiths* which are second only to the Qur'an in terms of their religious authority. At least two thousand *hadiths* are traceable back to over one hundred and fifty early Muslim women. Hundreds are attributed to Mohammed's favourite wife 'Aisha (also spelled Ayisah, 'Aṣiya or Aïcha). There is no other major faith so dependent upon the witness of women whose names we actually know, and *hadiths* continue to be crucial sources for defining Islam to this day.[55]

Despite the prominence of women in its early history, Islam, like Christianity and Judaism, clearly favours men. All the Abrahamic faiths make efforts to limit women's access to social capital, usually by undermining their ability to interact freely or speak to men, and in all faiths, the most 'virtuous' women have traditionally been those who were either entirely sequestered away from men (e.g. nuns) or who seldom stirred from their homes. Constraints on female mobility and ability to communicate with the other gender are, however, especially codified in Islam. The most significant religious limitations on early modern Muslim women derived from three passages in the Qur'an, one that calls upon male visitors who ask questions of the wives of the Prophet to do so from behind a curtain or screen (note the apparent onus on the male visitors rather than the wives); another that enjoins 'believing women' to dress modestly, and especially to cover their bosoms when in the presence of men who are not close relatives; and a third that asks free Muslim women to differentiate themselves from slaves, including Muslim slaves, by covering themselves with their cloaks when they are on the street; the aim here is to make them less vulnerable to verbal and sexual harassment.[56] The Qur'an does not mention veiling in the modern sense of covering the head or face. These passages were contextualized, glossed, complicated, debated and contradicted in numerous *hadiths*, some of which do mention various kinds of veiling; they were also discussed and ruled upon by many later interpreters running up to the present. Some of this is not at all unique to Islam. As we have seen, women of many faiths and conditions throughout Europe and the Middle East wore 'head-clothes', and were still doing so in the eighteenth century. Women wore veils or head-clothes to advertise elite, free or sexually respectable (usually married) status, to mark their membership in particular religious orders (either Catholic or Orthodox), to attend religious services, to show that they were especially pious, or to make it easier to travel.

The bigger question is what these confusing revelations meant for women in the early Muslim community. We know that Mohammed's wives and the women among the Companions attended mosque (indeed the Prophet's wives essentially lived in or immediately adjacent to the mosque), prayed with men, contributed to discussions about doctrine and social ethics, memorized Qur'anic passages, were signatories to early allegiance pacts, and even went to war (one woman, 'Umara Nusayba bin K'ab, fought in the Battle of Uhud with sword and bow in hand, and, at a crucial moment, helped shield the Prophet Mohammed from attack).[57] However, many Muslim feminists and women's historians think the new screening and cloaking revelations marked a shift away from the early Muslim movement's openness to women and it certainly reflected a more repressive view of female sexuality and personal vulnerability. Moreover, the men who succeeded Mohammed to the leadership of the community added even more restrictions on women after the Prophet's death, in part, some argue, in order the limit the power of his wives, especially the formidable 'Aisha.[58] Still greater constraints, at least on elite women, followed Muslim conflicts with and ultimate conquests of Zoroastrian Persia and Christian Byzantium, both of which practised elite female seclusion. Elite female seclusion in Muslim lands, like the practice of placing Catholic nuns in locked convents, did not extend to most women. Nevertheless, in both traditions it formed the basis for a powerful anxiety about female sexuality that affected even non-elite women to some degree, and certainly encouraged a high degree of surveillance of women's social interactions. As we have seen, these strictures did not keep Muslim women – even elite women – from using the law-courts, from engaging in extensive business and charitable activities and from socializing with other women – nor, as we will see, did it stop them from becoming artists, musicians or intellectuals (see Chapter 7) or wielding political power through their male relatives (Chapter 8). But segregation and surveillance, and the obsession with female sexuality that inspired them, made these activities more difficult, hampered women in the accumulation of social capital, and disadvantaged them by comparison with men.

They also affected female religiosity. After the Prophet's death, during the reign of Caliph Omar (r. 634–644), possibly as part of the bid to constrain the power of Mohammed's wives, the view arose among some powerful men that it was indecent for women to go to mosque, ironically in direct contravention of a statement to the contrary by the Prophet himself.[59] Though practice shifted back and forth on this issue, by the early modern period it had become well established that, when women did inhabit sacred space, they did so differently and separately from men. They conducted their own individual or small-group devotions near or in saints' shrines and used female prayer leaders (for which there is a long tradition in Islam), rather than praying along with a male *imam*. Some women clearly were bothered by this. In the seventeenth century at least one Istanbul mosque seems to have been endowed by a prominent member of the Imperial Harem specifically for the use of women, but it did not remain that way. Whether it was taken over by men, or there were not a sufficient number of women interested in that form of worship, history does not relate.[60] Early modern women did participate in a variety of ways in religious festivals, such as those associated with circumcision, with Ramadan, and perhaps above all with ceremonies associated with the birthday of the Prophet. The latter were later particularly important for women, because, at least as performed by Turkish women, the *mevlûd* recital (the declaiming of a poem about the life of the Prophet) lays great stress on motherhood and childbirth, though it is not clear if that was also true in the eighteenth century.[61] Some older women did go to mosque, but it was not incumbent upon them in the way it was for men. Women clearly had powerful spiritual lives, but they ran them on their own and with other women. They were the ones – not men – who decided which shrines to visit, how to perform the rituals, which holy women or men were worth consulting, and who was holy in the first place.

There was, however, a somewhat more heterodox form of Islam that does seem to have had some institutional appeal for women. 'Sufism' is a blanket term for an ancient and diverse set of traditions of organized Islamic mysticism that were extremely popular in the early modern period, indeed undergoing a considerable revival. There were more than thirty different Sufi orders active in Istanbul alone by the early nineteenth century. In Sufism the usual Muslim practice of daily prayer and attendance, at least for men, at the mosque, was supplemented (or, in a few heterodox orders, replaced) by efforts to achieve transcendence and community through such meditative and devotional practices as repetition of the name of God, dancing or twirling, musical performance, or commensality. The main locus of activity was the lodge or *tekke*, where Sufi dervishes (people initiated into the order) could live, sometimes work if they had a trade, or, if they were itinerant mendicants, obtain temporary lodging. The *sheik* (leader) of the *tekke* also lived there, along with his family, and typically presided over the spiritual, apotropaic and healing concerns of a much larger community of sympathizers or people in need. His very considerable spiritual charisma probably often extended to and may have been enhanced by his wife or wives. Many *tekkes* also engaged in extensive charity, particularly distribution to the poor, and some orders also had extensive involvements in trade, manufacture, mining and the military. Most orders observed the rules of gender segregation common in the society at large, but several of the sects, most famously the Bektashis, who were especially popular, though also controversial, in Anatolia and the Balkans, eschewed segregation and admitted women on a relatively equal basis to men (though exactly how equal seems to be hard to determine). The Bektashis, very unusually, also had rituals that required the involvement of both a husband and a wife, and some *tekkes* had quarters for women dervishes who wished to live a celibate and pious life.[62] Another more socially elevated order, the Mevlevi, was associated with musicians and intellectuals. There were several prominent Ottoman women poets linked to the Mevlevis, including Leila Hanım (d. 1824) and Şeref Hanım (1809–1861), a composer of *methiye* (Sufi hymns of praise) as well as poetry (see Chapter 8).[63]

Part of the promise of Sufism for women lay in its diversity and flexibility, theologically and devotionally, and the way it absorbed, coexisted with and helped strengthen thaumaturgic and apotropaic saint and shrine-devotion. In the Balkans and Anatolia there were a number of terms for women members of Sufi orders, most of them derivatives of the Turkish term '*baci*', meaning 'older sister'. Gravestones for eighteenth-century and early nineteenth-century Sufi women, of which there are a number in Ottoman cemeteries, sometimes refer to them as dervishes, just as they do for men, and advertise the woman's order in the design of the stone. One gravestone, for a Bektashi woman dervish named Fatma Hanım (d. 1812), has male headgear carved on the top of it which may suggest that she dressed as a man, took on typically male roles in the order, or was especially respected (Plate 7).[64] At least one Sufi women's lodge is thought to have been established in the late seventeenth century in Bosnia, under the aegis of the Turkish/Serbo-Croatian poet Sheik Hasan Kaimija (d. 1691/92). Like many sheiks he transformed his house into a lodge but in his case he appointed his wife to be *vekil* (sheik's representative) there. After Sheik Kaimija's death the lodge was moved to Sarajevo and it continued, well into the 1750s, to be led by a woman. Not surprisingly it is said to have become an important women's spiritual and educational centre. Cults organized around women dervishes and *babas* lasted in Sarajevo area at least until World War II.[65]

Sheik Kaimija's women's lodge adds to our impression that lodges were reaching out to women in this period. One reason we know this is because later eighteenth-century pictures of Sufi lodges (*tekkes*) around Istanbul often prominently display the latticed sections within which women sat. The instinctual response of many modern readers is to see this as indicative of second-class status, but it is unlikely that that was the first thing that came to people's minds in the eighteenth century. Many of these *tekkes* would have been newly built in this period, a time, as we have seen, of great ferment and enthusiasm in Sufi circles, so considerable thought must have gone into their architecture.[66] The women's sections were not insubstantial either. Some of them were deep galleries extending along one, two or even three sides of the upper regions of a particular lodge, as can be seen in late eighteenth-century engravings as well as in later paintings, photographs and ground-plans. They were most likely seen as inviting, even as an advertisement that this *tekke* welcomed women believers and allotted them important space. For example, in one major *tekke*, the Hasirizade Tekke (Sa'di order) near Istanbul, the family (women's) living area was larger than the sheik's receiving room, and led via a semi-enclosed walkway to a gigantic women's gallery around two-thirds of the upper story of the *semihane* (the large room where ceremonies took place).[67] A spatial layout of this kind would also have offered opportunities for other, more informal kinds of cultural and religious activity. There was a robust salon culture of poetry, musical performance and discussion associated with many of the Sufi orders, and it seems very likely that some of this was organized by sheik's wives on behalf of women. It is likely not coincidental that grave-markers of the wives and mothers of Sufi sheiks (and sometimes ordinary dervish women) from the eighteenth century proudly display the symbol of their order, and, in the former case, make sure to lay out their family affiliations, suggesting that they identified closely with what was, often, a kind of family business. Both sheiks' wives and ordinary woman sympathizers also made large donations to *tekkes*. In one prestigious Salonika *tekke* between the years 1741 and 1767 half of the twelve charitable endowments were established by women, including two of the largest.

Like that of most early modern women, Muslim women's piety probably inclined heavily toward supplicatory devotion and vows directed at various inter-mediaries (shrines, sacred trees, local holy men and women, etc.) and oriented toward the usual familial and apotropaic concerns. It is generally assumed that Sufism's emphasis on the shrines of famous persons, the way it tries to enhance individual holiness in the here and now, and the fact that adepts/dervishes were often associated with supernatural healing and miracles, played to this kind of female piety. But we do not actually know how consistently true this was. It seems unlikely that all orders, especially the more prestigious ones, were open to or supportive of the everyday spiritual practices of local, often poor, women. Women's stereotypic focus on individual problems – infertility, children's illness, love, marriage, alleged demonic possession and the like – would have been easy to caricature, and male Sufis were just as capable of casual misogyny as other men. On the other hand, many shrines, tombs, etc. were actually in or near people's houses, and eighteenth-century sources mention (without seeming to view it as at all odd) women acting as shrine caretakers, a role that is still a common one for women today.

The whole process of determining who was a 'saint' or holy person was extremely informal in Islam, even more so than in Eastern Orthodoxy. This owed much to the fact that there was no real Muslim clergy, or at least no clergy with recognizably sacramental responsibilities. Someone was considered a saint if they were associated with extraordinary piety, military or other feats, or miracles, either during their lifetime or after it. A Sufi dervish or sheikh could end up a saint, but so, at least in theory, could a local holy woman with no particular institutional affiliation. It was a very populist conception of sanctity, and one in which women's opinions, rumour, and so forth counted.[68] Some of these women were clearly quite formidable characters (see Voices from the Past 6.3).

VOICES FROM THE PAST 6.3

A Bosnian holy woman confronts an Ottoman pasha

This is a story about Gülbacıı, a Bosnian holy woman from Sarajevo, which shows both her miraculous powers, and the influence saintly individuals were thought to have (note that it made sense to people to represent a holy woman as being able to intimidate an Ottoman official).

. . . A new pasha was appointed to the Bosnian *sançak* [an administrative unit]. He intended to oppress the Bosnian population. However, while traveling to Bosnia by the sea, he dropped his *tesbih* [prayer beads] into the water. After he arrived in Sarajevo, a multitude came to show their respects to him. Gülbacıı sent a courier who was to present the pasha with a gift, wrapped in a handkerchief. Seeing that his *tesbih* was in the handkerchief the pasha inquired who sent it to him and eventually learned that it was Gülbacıı. He ordered her to visit him, but she refused and replied that he should come to her if he needed anything. Indeed, the pasha sought her out and demanded to know how she obtained the *tesbih*. Gülbacıı responded: 'I showed you a *keramet* [miracle] so you must reject the intention you came with. Here in Bosnia there are many good people and therefore you should behave yourself.'

Source: Told to me by Tijana Krstic and reproduced here in her own words. She based the tale on Muhamed Hadžijahic, 'Badžijanije u sarajevu i bosni – prilog historiji duhovnosti u nas' [Female Sufi Saints in Sarajevo and Bosnia – a Contribution to the History of Spirituality], *Anali Gazi Husrev-begove Biblioteke* 7–8 (1982): 109–33.

As we have seen, women played an unusually prominent role in early Islam. Did this have any effect on eighteenth-century women's piety? The evidence is meagre, but we do find some women appealing explicitly to that tradition. A recent study of *waqf* (charitable trust) endowments in eighteenth-century Salonika found several women who, when endowing sacred recitations, stipulated prayers on behalf of 'Aisha, the most beloved of the Prophet's wives, and Fatima, his daughter. Clearly the intention was that these historic figures would, in turn, intercede on their behalf. The only man who mentioned these early women, a *mufti* (jurisconsult), stipulated that his wife be the one to read the sacred texts.[69] It is possible that Sufism offered an outlet for women interested in forging a connection to distinctly 'feminine' forms of spirituality, even more androgynous notions of the divine. Some Sufi mystical traditions place considerable emphasis upon the figure of the creative feminine, upon contemplation of the characteristics of the 'perfect' woman in order to understand aspects of the divine, upon spiritual marriage or spouseship, and upon female miracle workers and saints, including the Virgin Mary (or Maryam as she is called in the Qur'an), the mother of Jesus/Isa. There is actually a shrine to Maryam in Selcuk, near Ephesus in Turkey, which is still visited by both Muslims and Christians.[70]

Going to Mecca is one of the five pillars of Islam, a religious duty enjoined upon all believers, male and female, to perform once in a lifetime if they possibly can. In the eighteenth century it took about two-hundred and sixty days (with lengthy layovers) to make the round trip by foot, camel and, for better-off women, litter, from Istanbul to Mecca and back. Women did not make the trip anywhere near as often as men did; but women *hajjis* were not a negligible group either. An early nineteenth-century visitor to Mecca counted at least two thousand women pilgrims, many of them, he thought, rich older women 'who wish to see Mecca before they die'.[71] The pilgrimage to Mecca was both dangerous and gruelling. To get there overland the camel train had to pass through empty, dry desert, in constant peril of Bedouin attacks. In 1757 a tribe called the Banu Sakhr attacked the caravan on its way back from Medina to Damascus, plundering it mercilessly, killing many people on the spot and leaving others to die of their wounds, thirst and exposure in the desert: 20,000 pilgrims are said to have perished, including numerous Ottoman notables and the sultan's own sister. With danger on every side, almost the only succour was to be found from the cisterns, reservoirs and fortified rest-stations endowed over the centuries along the pilgrimage routes by Abbasid, Safavid and Ottoman princesses, busy enhancing their own or their dynasties' reputation for piety.[72] An even more prominent feature of the *hajj* was the women of early Islam, Mohammed's powerful wives, his daughter Fatima, his mother Amina and many others, all of them associated with miracles and *baraka* (spiritual power, blessings and charisma); their tombs all pilgrimage destinations in their own right. There was more to the Hajj than saints' tombs, of course, but women who made it back from Mecca would do so with renewed confidence in Islam as a religion notable both for its powerful women and for the generosity with which they shared their spiritual power with those who made the effort to come. The woman pilgrim would be marked for the rest of her life as a holy person, not to mention someone who possessed courage and moral strength well beyond the ordinary. Such women were now entitled to use the honorific 'hajji' in front of their name and some sources suggest that they became essentially equal to men.[73]

RELIGIOUS TOLERATION AND BEYOND

The sixteenth and seventeenth centuries stand out as a time of extraordinary religiously inspired violence. The witch trials were very much about the belief that 'good' religion was under threat from the religion of the devil. There were the Spanish and Portuguese Inquisitions' cruel persecutions of alleged crypto-Jews and crypto-Muslims; Ottoman massacres of Iraqi Shi'ites; the St. Bartholomew's Day massacre of 1572 (it actually lasted for months) in which thousands, perhaps tens of thousands, of French Protestant were slaughtered; the long and dreadfully destructive Thirty Years' War, begun over religion, the Chmielnicki massacres of the Jews; Oliver Cromwell's 1649 massacres of Irish Catholics at Drogheda and Wexford; the Savoy massacres of Waldensian Protestants in 1655; the 'Montenegrin Vespers' of Christmas, 1702, when much of the Muslim population of Montenegro was put to the sword, and many more. Often this was violence of the most barbarous kind. During the Savoy massacres of 1655 (to pick one almost at random) women were gang-raped and then had sharp rocks thrust up their vaginas until they died. Fathers were forced to parade in front of their tormentors carrying the severed heads of their own children slung around their necks.[74] No group escaped unscathed from the ravages of the sixteenth and seventeenth centuries and rare was the faith that did not have blood on its hands.

There is no evidence that women were any less susceptible than men to the belief that faiths other than their own were satanic, though it is true that at least some women's (and men's) preoccupations were turning to conversion rather than outright killing (and it *is* an improvement, though persecution and killing sometimes followed for those who refused to cooperate, or wanted later to change back again). The Mariavites were a special women's religious order founded in Poland in 1737 by a Jesuit priest with the express purpose of converting Polish Jewish women to Catholicism. There were a number of convents across Europe whose members specialized in kidnapping, baptizing and indoctrinating Jewish and Protestant children (similar tactics would later be adopted by American Protestants as a way to assimilate Native Americans, and Australians of various faiths to assimilate Aboriginal peoples). And both lay and religious groups of both sexes, and especially a good number of women aristocrats, made a business of identifying poor or desperate people of the 'target' faith, whatever it was – often orphans without protectors or abused and runaway wives – and either bribing or brow-beating them into converting.[75] Apparently it was a bracing business dragging souls back out of the grip of Satan, and there were many refinements, often focused on girls and women in trouble. The Vienna foundling home refused to take the children of Jewish single mothers unless their mothers would consent to have them baptized as Catholics. The Dublin foundling home, run by Protestants, tried to stop Catholic women from having their babies baptized in their own faith.[76] In both institutions virtually all the infants died, but at least their souls had been saved.

The history of the rise of religious toleration is often told primarily with reference to intellectuals like Pierre Bayle, John Locke and Voltaire, or 'Enlightened' heads of state like Frederick II of Prussia, Joseph II of Austria and Catherine II of Russia. More attention should probably be paid to the growing revulsion of more ordinary people, who, in increasing numbers, thought about the evidence of their own lives and began questioning the claim that people of other faiths were servants of the devil and consequently deserved to be persecuted, shunned, excluded from political, economic and social benefits, raped, or killed. No doubt some people had always had their doubts. There is a long tradition in Turkish and Balkan folklore of tales by or about the Bektashi Sufis in which they 'chide intolerant religious dogma, [and] attack the idea of a God who punishes dance, music, drinking, and other worldly pursuits'.[77] Most Christians did not – and could not – read the Bible, yet even illiterates could quote a passage like Luke 6:35, 'Judge not lest ye be judged; condemn not lest ye be condemned', because it had long before been transformed into vernacular proverbs. But there seems to have been an upswing in this sort of thinking in the last quarter of the seventeenth century, especially in western Europe; by contrast, the Ottomans, long famous for their tolerance for, if not equal treatment of, 'People of the Book' grew *less* tolerant in the later seventeenth and eighteenth centuries, especially with respect to Jews, who often bore the brunt of popular riots, many of them fomented by the Janissaries (traditionally converts to Islam from Christianity).[78]

A number of the women we have encountered in this chapter believed in religious toleration. Antoinette Bourignon (see above) argued that a Lutheran was no less likely than a Catholic to be saved. Jane Lead, the leader of the Philadelphians, also believed in universal salvation, and so, as we have seen, did the pietist theologian Johanna Eleonora Petersen. Elizabeth Ashbridge seriously contemplated converting to Catholicism but drew back from the brink when told she would have to swear to the proposition that 'whosoever died out of the pale of the church were damned'. This struck Ashbridge as both uncharitable and unfilial: '. . . I had a religious mother who was not of that opinion [Catholicism], I therefore thought it would be barbarous in me to believe she should be damned.'[79] The Catholic mystic Mme Guyon had friends and correspondents who were Protestants, and was appalled when fellow-Catholics tried to draw her into a project to convert Protestants by force.[80] There were also plenty of more ordinary women who socialized with women of other faiths in spite of edicts and rules forbidding this; indeed, the fact that such edicts were so common across Europe and the Middle East (and came both from the authorities and minority communities themselves) suggests they did not work very well. Rates of intermarriage varied enormously, though they seem to have been rising in at least some places in the eighteenth century (some Dutch, German and French cities, Transylvania and Ottoman Bosnia and Crete) often despite dire warnings that it was a terrible sin. Some mixed Protestant/Catholic couples actually went so far as to divide their children between the two faiths, with the girls following the mother's faith and the boys the father's faith, or simply alternating child by child.[81] There were other accommodations, like the practice, in parts of the Balkans and the Caucasus, of Muslims and Christians forming fictive 'blood brother' and 'blood sister' relationships with each other, practising inter-ethnic breast-feeding (which created a fictive kinship bond, and, handily, a taboo against marrying 'milk-sisters' or 'milk-brothers') and arranging other kinds of reciprocal sponsorships that militated against ethnic violence.[82]

Another recurring theme of this chapter has been efforts by seventeenth- and eighteenth-century women and men to soften or revise many of the more patriarchal aspects of the monotheistic faiths by emphasizing women believers, female aspects of the divine, female spiritual headship, new female monastic or lay orders, female ministries, traditionally 'feminine' styles of worship (such as the emphasis upon tears and emotion found in many mystical and revivalist movements of the day), female religious figures from the past, and even female messiahs. This naturally raises the question whether there is any relationship between more 'feminine' forms of spirituality and the rise of religious toleration. If there is, it is likely to be an indirect one. People were most repelled by religious intolerance because it so often turned violent (many also resented the amount of surveillance it involved). In the sixteenth and seventeenth centuries religious intolerance led repeatedly to warfare, with its attendant economic dislocations, property damage, high taxes, epidemics, refugee problems, political disintegration, massacres, broken families, and sustained psychological trauma. As war-weariness grew (and by the later seventeenth century it was widespread), some people began to rethink the original premises. One premise a surprising number of people seem to have been prepared to reassess was the insistent masculinist emphasis of most mainstream religion. Why should this have happened? Much as one might like to think otherwise, it is most unlikely that women are naturally 'nicer', more tolerant or more peaceful than men. Nor is it the case, looking across history, that devoté(e)s of goddesses are notably more peaceful than those who follow male gods. However, it does seem to be the case that, from the later seventeenth century on, a good many people thought or hoped that a greater emphasis upon more stereotypically 'feminine' styles of spirituality might have some generally pacific effect. Most eirenic[83] movements of the period touted a combination of (a) religious toleration; (b) world peace, sometimes linked to messianic or millenarian expectation; (c) a retreat from the concept of Original Sin; and (d) some sort of interest either in the female principle or in an increased role in religion or society for actual women. Jane Lead's quest for an ecumenical culture of peace that could welcome in the Virgin Wisdom was more radical than some, but it had many contemporary parallels, particularly within Judaism. Conceivably, her and others' efforts to rethink the nature of God spoke to larger emancipatory impulses: there were plenty of these about in the late seventeenth century. Or perhaps, as people looked around for what had gone so terribly wrong, the balance of the universe simply seemed to them to have tipped over too far. The impulse to create more feminine forms of faith and spirituality, while far too inchoate, miscellaneous and scattered to qualify as a programme, was an important, and probably too little recognized, tendency within early modern religion that pointed toward more modern notions of faith, social ethics and spiritual diversity.

Healing and spiritual power

Partly as a result of the rise of religious toleration (and its close cousin, religious scepticism), organized religion saw both its political power and its power to define and control followers' intimate lives and religious expression decline sharply by the end of the eighteenth century. This meant conflicting things for women. On the one hand, religion *was* one of the central ideological props for male supremacy, and especially for the view that women were sexually dangerous. Moreover, church officials were almost always deeply ambivalent about women having too much spiritual power. On the other hand, as we have seen, religion and religious movements offered much scope for women, and as the power of ecclesiastical authorities to coerce (at least) outward conformity diminished (this happened more quickly in some countries than in others) this scope actually expanded. Now that believers had to be lured in rather than forced, women became a more valued constituency than before, not least because they proved to be more devoted church-goers than men. Most faiths ended up allowing, even encouraging, women to take active roles out in the world, particularly in the form of religious charities.[84] In many faiths women found new liturgical opportunities opening up to them, though they moved into positions of substantial authority only in a few, usually splinter, denominations and in some of the occult movements that gained popularity in the late eighteenth and early nineteenth centuries.[85] The fate of apotropaic devotion is especially interesting. The Catholic Church, for one, had spent much of the seventeenth and eighteenth centuries trying to moderate what it saw as its excesses. As the Church's temporal power slipped it shifted course yet again, and sought new accommodations with women's traditional apotropaic and healing interests. The most remarkable example of this is Lourdes. In 1858, only four years after the Holy See proclaimed the doctrine of the Immaculate Conception, the Virgin Mary made a series of miraculous appearances at Lourdes in the Pyrenees Mountains to a former shepherdess named Bernadette Soubirous. In time, Lourdes became a major locus for Marian worship, miraculous healing (complete with syncretistic elements, such as the association of miraculous cures with water sources) and spiritual pilgrimage. The nineteenth, twentieth and twenty-first centuries have seen thousands of 'apparitions' (appearances) of the Virgin Mary, many of them to women and girls – far more than was the case in the seventeenth and eighteenth centuries.[86] The old styles of devotion, toward which the Church had long been ambivalent, have been transformed into a modern, approved and extremely popular form of lay (and especially female) piety.[87] Other faiths made similar accommodations. As we have seen, Protestants had tended to be especially critical of traditional forms of apotropaic devotion. But eighteenth- and nineteenth-century Protestant pietistic and evangelical movements like Methodism and its many later offshoots often took up faith healing as one of the 'proofs' of their aliveness to God. Neither Russian nor Balkan Orthodoxy ever gave it up. And Balkan and Anatolian popular Islam is still organized in good part around apotropaic devotion, often focused on the tombs of holy people, and in large part controlled by women.[88] The various faiths' willingness both to rethink women's role and to accommodate their concerns may have been a product of desperation, particularly in western Europe. But it was, nevertheless, of tremendous significance in the creation of new forms of faith in a modern world.

```
┌─────────────────────────────────────┐
│                                     │
│          Chapter 7                  │
│        ──────◆──────                │
│                                     │
│          CULTURES                   │
│          OF WOMEN                   │
│                                     │
└─────────────────────────────────────┘
```

POPULAR CULTURE

How does one even begin to recover the cultural world of non-elite European women? Many of these women were illiterate or could read but not write. Their thoughts, sayings, poetry, songs, stories, jokes, dramatic performances and daily rituals were only very occasionally described at the time, and usually to criticize not celebrate them. The bulk of their art has not survived, they wrote few letters, and they did not have a way to notate music. Few publishers were interested in what they had to say, even when they did know how to read and write. It is true that a few popular writers (especially poets), musicians and other performers were 'taken up' by their social superiors, and that included several women.[1] During the eighteenth century a scattering of people, the first folklorists, began taking an interest in writing down old songs, stories or customs. And in the nineteenth century state builders and nationalists often sought to recover an idealized and (where women were concerned) sanitized version of 'folk culture' as part of the project of inculcating love of country. Nevertheless, researching the cultural and aesthetic lives of non-elite women in the early modern period often seems like picking through the potsherds at a much-looted archaeological site.

We do know that popular and oral cultures almost never offered women the same opportunities as they did men. Here is the great Serb folklorist, Vuk Karadžić (1787–1864), writing about his own peasant childhood in the late eighteenth century:

I was born and brought up in a house where sometimes my grandfather and uncle, sometimes various men from Hercegovina (who would come almost every year to spend the winter with us), would sing and recite songs the whole winter through . . .[2]

For Karadžić the songs that counted, and those for which the singers were remunerated with gifts, money, food, a job, or a place to sleep, were those composed and performed by men. Ironically, Karadžić later became interested in women's songs and collected many, including a possibly unique body of early nineteenth-century peasant women's erotic songs.[3] Moreover, like many other folklorists in his own time and since, he soon discovered that some of his best informants, even for 'men's genres', such as epic songs about *hajduk* (outlaw) heroes, turned out to be middle-aged and old women, many of them blind (the association between blindness and singing, for both sexes, is an ancient one). Still, the performative universe he describes in his childhood memoir was one in which higher-status performances were the province of men, particularly men on the move.

Accounts like Karadžić's are rare. The most abundant evidence about women and popular culture comes not from the eighteenth or early nineteenth century, but from modern folklorists' and anthropologists' descriptions of parts of Europe and the Middle East where 'traditional', and largely oral, cultures survived into recent times – or, in a few places, up to the present. There are obvious problems with using these data to talk about the early modern period; when one is relying largely on recollection one can never be sure how far back the continuities stretch. And even if we could establish a direct connection we would still get a moving target. Cultures are always changing, hybridizing, and evading our attempts to 'fix' them at a particular place and time. This is true of predominantly oral cultures (which, by the eighteenth century, in all but the most remote places, were already being affected by – and affecting – print culture), heavily literate or technologized cultures (which can also have large oral elements), and all the many mixtures in between. Insofar as we *can* cautiously generalize backward from the recent past, it would seem that pre-modern popular cultures were never especially egalitarian. One of the longest-lived sites of European oral culture is Hungary, and here gender hierarchy suffused the popular performance arts. The case of Hungarian storytelling looks much like that of Serbian epic song. Male storytellers circulated around, tended to perform in all- or largely-male occupational settings, and sometimes enjoyed considerable renown. Women, by contrast, told low-prestige stories, mostly to children and to other women in gender-segregated settings. Occasionally they told stories for mixed groups of adults if they came from a storytelling family in which all the men had died. However, they generally did so in a more restrained and less 'performative' way than men did, and there was anxiety about their telling stories to people outside the family circle. The constraints on women storytellers functioned to undermine the degree to which their artistic contributions could function as cultural capital and hence accrue them prestige, power, money or geographical mobility.[4] In short, then, the popular arts mirrored the kinds of exclusions and impediments that dogged women's work and family lives more generally.

Gendered restrictions

There were also numerous restrictions on the *kind* of art women were allowed to pursue. In many European regions, both rural and urban, women were not permitted to play solo instruments such as the violin. Women *were* generally allowed to sing, to play instruments such as the lute or harp, used largely for the purposes of accompaniment, to play the castanets, tambourine or other simple rhythm instruments – drums in the Middle East, though not, usually, in Europe – and to play background instruments if they were needed for a family band. One of the latter is the Hungarian gardon, a cello-like instrument ideal for rhythmic accompaniment and bass lines, which tended to be played by the wives of rural fiddlers – a musical version of the sort of ancillary tasks women were so often confined to. The prohibition against women performing on solo instruments, and sometimes on any instruments, rose to the level of a taboo. As one elderly Hungarian woman reported to a twentieth-century musicologist, '[a female solo instrumentalist] would have been scorned out of the village'.[5]

What happened to women who defied the taboos? There must have been a lot of variation. In parts of the Balkans some women appear to have become sworn virgins (taking on men's clothes and men's occupations and social status) in order to be able to exploit their musical talent. On the island of Malta, on the other hand, well into the twentieth century, women who became professional singers in the traditional *bormliza* style were categorized as prostitutes. This did not necessarily prevent them from becoming quite well-known members of coteries of professional musicians. Nor did it actually require that they be prostitutes in the modern definition of that term; some formed stable relationships with men of their choice. However it did mean that respectable women would not greet them in the street; nor could they visit respectable women's houses. They 'bought' their right to support themselves as musicians by giving up the sphere of women's solidarity and sociability.[6] Similarly exclusionary tactics, inflected as well with racism, met gypsy women who sang or danced for money: all over Europe the grudging admiration for their skill tended to go along with the assumption that they were prepared to sell their bodies as well. Often they were shunned as degraded people even by their own families.[7]

Power and ecstasy

Still, what early modern communities took away with one hand they gave back with the other. In many societies the performance arts have a significance that goes far beyond whether one can swap a song for a night's lodging or elicit some nobleman's coin in return for performing a dance. In eighteenth-century Istanbul, music was performed in both men's and women's asylums to calm down or cure mad-people. During the outbreak of bubonic plague in 1713 in the Jewish ghetto of Prague, women sang 'plague songs' to lull the sick and dying to sleep. Up until recently, Maltese women could insult one another by making up songs and sending their children to sing them over a rival's wall. Throughout Europe and the Middle East love songs were thought to have a magical ability to 'incite' love; dances to enhance fertility, both of humans and of animals; and some dramatic performances and theatricalized rituals to elicit divine blessings or have salvific power.[8]

A number of recent studies of gender and music have focused on fairly remote, usually mountainous, regions in Europe and the Middle East, such as Southern Spain, Yugoslavia, Albania, and Northern Morocco, where village women still perform, or fairly recently performed, 'sung poetry' as part of their everyday lives. One genre that has recently been the subject of sustained analysis is a northern Moroccan women's genre called *'ayoua. 'Ayoua* was (and, to a limited extent, still is) almost always performed outside, to accompany women's activities such as carrying water or searching for fuel, herding animals, washing clothes, harvesting, and making pilgrimages to nearby saints' shrines, in addition to weddings, funerals, circumcisions and calendrical festivals. It often takes the form of a dialogue between two singers, and it relies heavily for its emotional impact upon audience participation (often exhortations of one sort or another). It is also quite competitive, with a strong emphasis on volume, stamina in holding out long melodic lines, and intricate vocal ornamentation. The subject matter of such songs includes: praise of saints or of much missed people from one's community or family; the vagaries of love; laments; songs about nature (especially about birds); and songs about the pain of emigrating to the city. It might also include more morally and politically complex topics, such as a song about a woman obliged by the death of family members to become a prostitute and live apart from and shunned by her village, or songs that advertise the bad, undutiful or unchaste behaviour of family members. Older women, especially, who do not wish to, or cannot any longer do heavy work, may spend whole days at a nearby shrine, singing songs, and drawing in blessings and sacred power (*baraka*) into their bodies, which they can then 'convey' back to their relations. '*Ayoua* is clearly a women's cultural form. It also had and has a spiritual potency that, while it enhances the value of the singer, does not translate readily into modern exchange value, or even modern conceptions of cultural or performative prestige.[9]

'*Ayoua* is anything but unobtrusive, and the same was probably true of women's performances in many other places in the early modern period. Albanian, Yugoslav, Bulgarian and Ukrainian women's call and response and choral singing was intended to be sung, if possible, at a high volume, probably because loud singing was associated with strength, health and capacity to work hard and bear numerous children. Fine singing was also an attribute of beauty. Women's generally higher and more penetrating voices are a powerful instantiation of gender difference, and singing was often a way to express or display sexual yearning, physicality, and individual and collective pride in femaleness.[10] It also communicated things that were hard to say to a person's face, such as criticisms of family members or social superiors, or opposition to arranged marriage. All societies where arranged marriages are common, or where whole groups are forbidden to other groups – usually by religious differences – seem to support a repertoire of songs about star-crossed lovers who die of love or actually commit suicide rather than be parted.[11] Clearly early modern women's singing, participatory, but with opportunities for individual competition and display, linked to daily spirituality, drenched with feminine emotion and power, and audible at some distance, was a major locus of artistic creativity, social commentary, power and ecstasy for women and their audiences.

Women's noise

The most noticeable and public arenas for popular women's expression in the eighteenth century were religious and life-cycle rituals, particularly childbirth, circumcision of sons (in Jewish and Muslim communities), marriage, and death. The descriptions we have of such activities make it very clear that these were a powerful aspect of women's identities as women. One of the more perceptive western European observers of eighteenth-century Ottoman life, the Scottish doctor Alexander Russell, gives an unusually detailed description of women's ritual life in the Ottoman city of Aleppo. The scenes he describes reflect the more highly sex-segregated cultures – both then and now – that surround the Mediterranean. They are also recognizably urban. But the kinds of events being celebrated by these women were echoed in many parts of Europe and the Middle East in the early modern period. In Aleppo women put on very loud parties in the bathhouses and in their quarters to celebrate births and reintegrate postpartum women back into the community. They formed part of circumcision processions (this involved women picking mock fights all along the route: in effect a kind of street theatre). Poorer women gathered to greet travellers, for which they expected or hoped to receive a 'gift', and they often formed crowds around popular religious figures, such as Sufi dervishes, or Christian or Jewish holy men.

Women took up a lot of the aural space in Russell's account: their faces might be covered (Muslim, Christian and Jewish women all went veiled in Aleppo) but they could certainly be heard and seen about town. Women often staged events, with hired musicians, dancers, and other performers, in *hamams* (bathhouses) they had rented for the day. They went through the streets in groups, often on their way to all-day events in the gardens or countryside, either singing themselves or, in the case of more elite women, preceded by groups of paid singing-women. On certain holidays, groups of women engaged in choral dialogues with male singers in the Muezzin's tower. And women's loud Ramadan parties went on long after the men had gone to bed, a strong reminder that, especially in these crucial life transitions, women's presence could not be got around or minimized.[12]

Laments for the dead

Almost everywhere in early modern Europe and the Middle East, women were associated with a stylized and highly theatrical form of mourning that combined song, poetry, weeping, and often self-mutilation, such as the tearing of clothes or hair. Professional mourners, who were almost always women, were well known for their extemporaneous poetry, their dramatic power, and their ability – supposedly because of their own sad life experiences – to inhabit, or at least vocalize, other people's grief. Today this ancient aspect of women's culture survives only in a few places among very old women. In the eighteenth century professional or semi-professional women mourners could still be found in Corsica, Malta, Italy, Sardinia, Spain, Portugal, France, Ireland,

Scotland, Wales, Germany, Poland, Russia, across Scandinavia, throughout the Balkans and the Greek Isles, and all over the Ottoman Empire.

Women were thought to have unique powers when it came to dealing with death. Older rituals sometimes demanded that women stay awake by the corpse – often while making a loud noise, singing and the like – so as to ward off evil spirits that might otherwise interfere with the safe passage of the dead person's soul or invade the lives of the rest of the household. Women's tears and declamatory laments were also widely believed to have a salvific effect (see Chapter 6); to die 'unwept' by one's female relatives is a misfortune in parts of Greece to this day.[13] The result was both some remarkable extemporaneous poetry, and a form that women could sometimes turn to their own devices. Laments were culturally powerful: an opportunity for a woman to express unbearable loss on her own behalf and that of others, to personalize the dead, to draw attention to her or her children's own social and economic peril – an especial problem for widows – and to take up a great deal of aural space. Sometimes they had a more malignant purpose. In Corsica, and presumably other places, women sometimes used laments to shame their male kin into taking violent action against vendetta foes, often by bitterly mocking their sons', brothers' or husband's masculinity.[14] Unlike most other 'popular' forms, laments tended to talk a good deal about inward feelings – loss, pride, anxiety, hatred, the urge to merge physically with the dead person, etc. In many countries they also testify to distinctly supernatural aspects of the female body: rituals that involve women displaying or tearing their hair or clothes, or drawing, or occasionally drinking blood, only make sense in a world in which hair, blood and clothes are saturated with spiritual potency.

VOICES FROM THE PAST 7.1

Caoineadh Airt uí Laoghaire (lament on the death of Art O'Leary) (1773) (excerpts) by Eibhlín Dubh Ní Chonnaill (1743–1800)

The lament of Eibhlín Dubh Ní Chonnaill (in English-language anthologies she often appears as Eileen O'Connell) for her dead husband, Art O'Laoghaire (Art O'Leary), is one of the most famous of all Irish laments.[15] Eibhlín's husband was outlawed and then shot because he refused to sell his horse to a local Protestant landowner after it had won a race (by law Catholics were only permitted to own horses worth five pounds or less). His wife, as she relates, had the first intimation of his death when his riderless mare turned up at their home covered in blood. This lament contains some touching references to the couple's children, as well as to Eibhlín's unborn child, which, she prophesies, she will miscarry from grief. She also takes the opportunity to curse Morris, her husband's murderer.

My love and my delight
The day I saw you first
Beside the markethouse
I had eyes for nothing else
And love for none but you.

My mind remembers
That bright spring day,
How your hat with its band
Of gold became you,
Your silver-hilted sword,
Your manly right hand,
Your horse on her mettle
And foes around you
Cowed by your air;
For when you rode by
On your white-nosed mare
The English lowered their head before you
Not out of love for you
But hate and fear,
For, sweetheart of my soul,
The English killed you . . .
My love and my darling
When I go home
The little lad, Conor,
And Fiach the baby
Will surely ask me
Where I left their father,
I will say with anguish
'Twas in Kilnamartyr;
They will call the father
Who will never answer.

My love and my mate
That I never thought dead
Till your horse came to me
With bridle trailing,
All blood from forehead
To polished saddle
Where you should be,
Either sitting or standing;
I gave one leap to the threshold,
A second to the gate,
A third upon its back.
I clapped my hands,
And off at a gallop;
I never lingered
Till I found you lying
By a little furze-bush
Without pope or bishop
Or priest or cleric
One prayer to whisper
But an old, old woman,

And her cloak about you,
And your blood in torrents –
Art O'Leary –
I did not wipe it off,
I drank it from my palms.
Grief on you, Morris!
Heart's blood and bowels' blood!
May your eyes go blind
And your knees be broken!
You killed my darling
And no man in Ireland
Will fire the shot at you.

Destruction pursue you,
Morris the traitor
Who brought death to my husband!
Father of three children –
Two on the hearth
And one in the womb
That I shall not bring forth.

Source: This translation from the Irish is by Frank O'Connor, and is reprinted from his *Kings, Lords & Commons: An Anthology from the Irish: Irish Poems from the Seventh Century to the Nineteenth* (Dublin, London: Gill and Macmillan, 1989), 109–19.

Subversive humour

Many of women's cultural expressions were far less serious, of course, though even witticisms can shade over, at times, into something like social critique. Here is a Turkish riddle, deriving from one of women's most exhausting and unending tasks, milling grain with a mortar and pestle. It is clearly a send-up of masculine sex-talk and also suggests a distinct lack of enthusiasm about a wife's duty to submit to the sexual demands of her husband – since it likens heterosexual sex to tedious, repetitive, pounding and grinding. It runs: 'My navel to your navel, my handle into your hand, let me put it in your blessed hole. What am I?' The 'real' answer is not, of course, the importunate husband, or his sexual equipment, but the humble handmill. A number of jokes from the period seem, like this one, to have revolved around the inadequacies of male sexual performance, though they do not always presume that women dislike sex. Indeed, this seventeenth-century English jest, reproduced here with its original spelling, suggests quite the reverse:

A gentleman lay with a very pretty wench, and never so much as toucht her all that night; in the morning she riseth, pisses the chamberpot almost full, opens the Bed cloathes, and poures it in upon him: He began to sweare and curse; nay faith sayes she, though you'l none of the flesh, you shall have some of the Broth.[16]

· 259 ·

The popularity of the theme of male impotence may have to do with the fact that a husband's inability to perform sexually could sometimes be the basis for annulling the marriage. It also reflects women's fears that their future reputation and economic well-being will be compromised should their husband be unable to father a child. But the impotence theme also clearly struck at men's inordinate (and, it is often suggested, ridiculous) pride in that part of their anatomy that most clearly marked them as superior to women. 'May his hands fall off, if he doesn't lift my legs/May the flocking crows crap on his prick' runs one early nineteenth-century Serbian woman's song cursing an impotent young husband.[17] Obviously there is sexual frustration here, but it may not be far-fetched to see this genre as also expressing a yearning for greater female sexual, reproductive and bodily control.

A good number of tales, both comic and otherwise, from the early modern period focus on unreasonable husbands or masters, and at least some of the time these men get what they deserve. That is certainly the case in the folktale 'Something Unusual for Dinner' (Voices from the Past 7.2). Tales like this one may have been performed strategically by women (or, for that matter, by men) as an indirect rebuke to someone who actually *was* acting unreasonably.

VOICES FROM THE PAST 7.2

Something unusual for dinner

The tale: a man whose wife can do nothing right in his eyes refuses to reveal how he wants her to prepare the large fish he has just brought her. Hoping to satisfy him anyway, she cooks every piece in a different way. When he rejects the boiled piece, she brings the baked one, then the steamed one, then the fried one, etc. All are rejected, until finally, in desperation, she asks him 'My dear, what do you really want?' To which she receives the angry reply: 'Why don't you just serve me shit?' As it happens, her child had soiled the table cloth shortly before, so she dexterously places the results on a plate and serves them to her husband.

This tale captures the desperation of an abused and put-upon wife, who, having been set up to fail, nonetheless does everything she can to anticipate her husband's wishes. In the end though, she gets her revenge. The husband asks for shit for dinner not, obviously, because that is what he really wants, but because he wants to cast aspersions on the food he has already been served and on which she has worked so hard. But literal reality catches up with him, and deservedly so. He has been unreasonable; his wife has been scrupulously obedient. The joke is on him. Eighteenth-century toddlers, at least in peasant households, mostly went around naked, because cloth was too valuable to be used as nappies. Women simply cleaned up after them. The tale's power comes from the way the husband is suddenly forced to face the kinds of disgusting substances that it is usually the woman's job to keep out of sight and smell-range. We should probably imagine this tale told with all due theatricality: simulated gagging, the miming of awful smells, and groans of disgust from the audience. Versions of this comic tale have been found in France, Italy, both north and south Germany, and Kashmir, and there are analogues in the Middle East.

Source: Albert Wesselski, *Versuch einer Theorie des Märchens* (Reichenberg: F. Kraus, 1931), 175. Thanks to Bogdan State for the translation. Adapted by Margaret Hunt. Aarne-Thompson Tale type J1545.3.

Though a tale like 'Something Unusual for Dinner' probably owed some of its popularity to women's identification with the put-upon wife, women often had little sympathy for the travails of other women. The following English joke, told to a seventeenth-century joke-compiler by his mother – which surely qualifies it as a woman's joke – is a case in point:

A plain Country Wife, her daughter being ravisht [i.e. raped], came to complaine to a Justice of [the] Peace, that such an one had newly Raveld her daugh[t]er, and she would crave his worshipps warrant [for the perpetrator's arrest]. [A]nd another complaind that one had Refresht her Daughter.[18]

This joke is at the expense of two uneducated country-women who had come before a local magistrate to seek justice against the men who had attacked their daughters. The humour lies in these women's ignorance of the 'proper', that is legal, term for rape, which the joke knowingly informs us, is 'ravished'. Not only is it devoid of sympathy either for these women or their daughters, but it seems to be suggesting that uneducated (and therefore lower-class) women should think twice before burdening the court with trivial problems they do not even know how to name. While women *could* identify with other women (and there are examples of them doing so), their differences and their other loyalties often seemed more salient, just as they frequently do today.

Societies where people generate culture because it is deemed to be an essential part of everyday life look different from ones in which culture is monopolized by professionals, and almost everyone else 'consumes' what they produce. The former have a special intensity of emotion, of creative energy, and of aesthetic commitment that it is hard to recapture after the fact. Eighteenth-century Europe was not an ideal world for women, but the passing away of old and much loved cultural forms and styles, some of which did constitute a form of female empowerment, is something to be mourned.

LITERACY

Over the course of the later seventeenth and eighteenth centuries it became quite widely accepted that some education for girls – at least for middle-class and elite girls – was on balance a good thing, not least because women themselves battled to make it acceptable. The results were world changing. In the sixteenth century less than five per cent of women Europe-wide knew how to read, and in many rural areas female literacy was virtually unknown. By the end of the eighteenth century parts of Scandinavia had a literacy rate (at least for reading, if not writing) of close to ninety-eight per cent for both men and women, the highest in Europe, and literacy was also quite high in a number of Protestant cities like London, Edinburgh, Amsterdam, and Geneva. In England, in the middle of the pack for Protestant countries, women's literacy rose from about ten per cent in 1600 to fifty per cent by 1840 (it drew even with men just as the nineteenth turned into the twentieth century). In the countryside around Turin, a rural and Catholic region, in 1710 only six per cent of brides were able to sign their names; eighty years later, in 1790, thirty per cent could.[19] In general, literacy rose more slowly in rural and more remote areas of Europe, in eastern Europe, in the Ottoman Empire, and around the Mediterranean (with the partial exception of the more cosmopolitan port towns).[20]

Eighteenth-century people took a great interest in reading, and more and more of them seemed to think this should extend to girls as well. Much of this happened at the local level. In extremely low-literacy regions, like parts of eastern Europe, where even many noblewomen could not read, it became commoner over the course of the eighteenth century for noble families to engage governesses and tutors to teach their daughters as well as their sons. In western Europe there arose a whole new industry of proprietorial and (in Catholic countries) convent-based girls' schools for the middle and upper classes. Across Europe larger numbers of girls were allowed into local village schools, where they existed, and many religious minorities – Irish Catholics in Ireland, Muslims in the Volga Region, Ashkenazi Jews in Poland and Germany – also set up schools for girls, or paid more attention to tutoring them at home.[21] Even in quite humble families – the sort of families where girls worked rather than going to school – daughters were sometimes taught to read by relatives, though in many areas poorer girls, especially, encountered opposition when they wanted to learn to write. Long after letter-writing and a graceful writing-hand had become markers of status for middle and upper-class women, lower-class women with that skill were thought to be prone to pridefulness and immodesty. Moreover, it was often their mothers who tried to stop them learning, on the grounds that people would suspect their chastity, and they would be unable to marry.[22]

Some of the more famous educational projects of the day were state-run enterprises. A number of monarchs, among them Catherine the Great of Russia and Maria Theresa of Austria-Hungary (and earlier, Louis XIV, at the behest of his mistress, Madame de Maintenon), oversaw the establishment of schools. Maria Theresa, not known for her tolerant attitudes to non-Catholics, was even prevailed upon to set up schools in Eastern Orthodox Serbia and Romania; about a quarter of Serbian girls are said to have attended at least for a time.[23] Both education and literacy were far less prevalent in poor, remote, war-torn or non-dominant language-speaking areas though; many of these saw little improvement in either men's or women's literacy during our period. Only about five per cent of the population of Greater Hungary in the eighteenth century knew how to read (and most of these were men or members of the nobility); while as late as 1870 Transylvanians were still seventy-nine per cent illiterate and Croatians and Slavonians eighty-four per cent. Women's literacy rates remained low in much of the Ottoman Empire until well into the twentieth century, though it was always higher in the cities, in professional families and among Jews.[24]

Over the long run, the great migration into the cities, the homogenizing effect of mass education and new pastimes, genres and preoccupations combined to make storytelling, competitive singing, female mourners, popular healing, peasant women's erotic songs, and (doubtless) many other genres and practices largely obsolete. Women's literacy made its own contribution to this process. As it moved from being a prestige acquisition, to being de rigueur for the urban middle classes, and then the rural middle classes and the urban poor, and then virtually everyone (a process which took until the twentieth century in most of Europe), the older expressive forms associated with women, virtually all of them orally transmitted, fell to the bottom of the cultural prestige hierarchy. But that was much later. In the eighteenth century, the older world of women's popular culture (largely, but never totally rural) and the new world of reading, writing, books, newspapers, commercialized concert going, opera, fine art and the like (largely, but never totally urban), existed side by side, influencing but also competing with one another in ways that cultural historians are still struggling to understand.

A CULTURAL MARKETPLACE

The sophisticated cultural marketplace we enjoy today first began to form in the early modern period. The printing industry, dating from the second half of the fifteenth century, was orientated from the start toward the market. So were many of the new artistic or literary genres of the day, from small religious prints to broadside ballads to cheap chapbooks, to novels. Seventeenth- and eighteenth-century people promoted new commercial ventures and venues (concert rooms, purpose-built opera houses, theatres, dance halls, bookstores, print shops) within which music, drama, dance, literature and art could be experienced not just by the special invitees of nobles, but by anyone prepared to pay for it. One result is that, in contrast to the situation for 'popular' or at least rural cultures, we know an extraordinary amount about women and 'high-' and 'middle-brow' culture in the eighteenth century. Tens of thousands of women's letters survive – along with thousands of others by men that talk about women artists, especially actresses. There were thousands of women poets and journalists, and hundreds of women published novels, or wrote dramatic works, and a great deal of their work has been preserved either in print or in manuscript form. Women also worked in – and read – genres that are unfamiliar or seem somewhat marginal or specialized today: spiritual autobiographies; collections of prayers or hymns, 'historical letters' (fictional letter collections intended to illuminate a particular set of historical events); political ballads; collections of biographies of 'virtuous women'; embroidery; and much more. And much of that has also survived, though it is seldom read today.

The culture market offered greatly expanded opportunities for women to participate in culture and the arts in good part because the various venues and genres were new and less hidebound than some of the older ones (universities for example). Women were able to capitalize on the fact that men were not united on a policy of exclusion. Conservatives objected of course, but then as now audiences, including many men, found brilliant and talented women captivating and were willing both to celebrate them and pay money to read their work, view their art and see or hear them perform. There was a down side to this of course. Particularly in the performing arts, the culture market also made possible new modes of exploitation of women, especially lower-class and unfree women, because promoters quickly recognized the market draw of sexuality on display. We will deal with both of these aspects in this chapter. It must also be admitted at the outset that there is so much that has survived from this world that one cannot begin to survey it in such a brief compass. Therefore in what follows we will talk about only a few of women's most characteristic or enduring contributions to the cultural marketplace broadly construed.

Missives from the world of women: letters, didactic literature and autobiography

In the early modern period, for the first time, a number of new print genres began to be marketed that came, or purported to come, out of the 'world of women'. Publishers took fairly acceptable elite and middle-brow female literary or oral genres or practices, such as letter-writing, advice-giving, and recollections about one's own or one's family's past, and transformed them into print forms that could then be sold. Often this was not a case of dragging women or their words from the private sphere out into the public (though sometimes that was the rhetoric). In reality all these forms already circulated in manuscript or as persuasive practices in a larger world of kinship networks, literary coteries, religious movements and politics. But publication did give women a considerably larger sphere of influence, and it also raised the possibility of making a living from writing, as a good many women, particularly in England and France, succeeded in doing in the later seventeenth and eighteenth centuries.

Letters (or purported letters) and didactic books were among the earliest women's writings to be published in significant numbers, because they could easily be represented as 'useful': seventeenth- and eighteenth-century women authors often justified appearing in print by emphasizing that their desire to help others outweighed their 'natural' feminine aversion to publicity. Often women mixed the two genres, further stamping them as being within women's proper sphere. Such was Christiane Mariane von Ziegler's *Moral and Miscellaneous Letters* (*Moralische und vermischte Send-Schreiben*) (1731), a collection of didactic letters in which she called for better education for women and reflected on why men so often discouraged women from pursuing intellectual endeavours (von Ziegler suspected hidden jealousy).[25]

Many of these books focused on traditional female skills, such as cookery (see Chapter 4) and midwifery (see Chapter 5). Eighteenth-century women also wrote books on education, manners and morals, mathematics, embroidery patterns, gardening, dying well, legal issues of special interest to women (see Chapter 2), and a host of other topics. Though ostensibly a 'traditional' and hence conservative kind of female activity, this genre quite often had a reformist bent, and it also served to display and dignify women's skills, secrets and knowledge sets and show that they were just as rational as those of men. Of course didactic books also sometimes encroached on masculine spheres of influence. Thus, in 1678 an anonymous London woman, presumably a small shopkeeper, wrote a book, *Advice to the Women and Maidens of London*, urging them to lay aside their sewing and embroidery and learn double-entry bookkeeping, so as to be able to keep better track of their families' expenses and run the family business should the need arise. In a similar vein, but at a very different social stratum, the Polish noblewoman and politician Anna Jablonowska (1728–1800) published a book entitled *Dobra gospodiny* (The Good Landowner) (1784), intended to teach, as the subtitle has it, 'the 'fundamentals of estate economics to young people'. She was in a position to know about estate management, for she owned eleven towns, over one hundred villages, and thousands of serfs.

Late seventeenth- and eighteenth-century diaries and autobiographies, both published and unpublished, also revealed women's secrets, but in a far more personal way. The Danish Countess Leonora Christina Ulfeldt (1621–1698) spent twenty-one years, from 1663 to 1685, as a political prisoner, during which she wrote her great prison memoir, *Jammers minde* (Memory of Woe), considered one of the great Danish prose works of the seventeenth century. In 1751 the Polish noblewoman Anna Radziwill née Mycielska (1729–1771) wrote a rhymed autobiography-lament for the husband she adored. On the other end of the social scale we have the autobiography of Ann Candler (1740–1814), an English 'peasant poet' and abused spouse who spent a large part of her life in the workhouse, and Charlotte-Élisabeth Aïssé (c. 1694–1733), a Circassian former slave-girl turned courtesan.[26] Early on, many women struggled with guilt over the ego-centred focus of the diary and memoir; these forms coexisted uneasily with the lessons most women received about subordinating their desires to others' needs (or at least looking like they were doing so). Over the course of the eighteenth century, though, women became perceptibly more comfortable with the prose display of self. Thus the French high-society portraitist and later Royalist refugee, Elisabeth Vigée-Le Brun (1755–1842), could write in her memoirs, seemingly without the slightest self-consciousness: 'when I ponder on the quantity of good, kind people I have met because of my talent, I am pleased that my name is well known . . .'[27]

Still, the subversive power of the memoir was and is somewhat vitiated by the fact that the form is unabashedly individual. Memoirs often convey advice, but unlike didactic writings it is hard for them to feign disinterestedness. Women, like men, commonly used memoirs, and to lesser extent diaries, to argue a case before the world, God or posterity – to try to right, if only symbolically, an injustice to which they had fallen victim. For women this often meant airing their marital troubles. One of the autobiographical writings of the aged English gentlewoman Elizabeth Freke (1642–1714) is titled 'Some few remembrances of my misfortunes which have attended me since I was married', and it details her husband's callous, violent and mercenary behaviour toward her. The Dutch freethinker Isabella de Moerloose (fl. 1661–1712), several times shut up in a house of correction for her heterodox beliefs, worried in her memoir (among other things) about the religious implications of having submitted to oral sex with her by then-deceased husband. The French aristocrat and adventuress, Hortense Mancini, Duchess of Mazarin (1646–1699), sought in her memoir to justify her abandonment of – and later law-suit against – her pathologically controlling and spendthrift husband. And Mary Robinson (1756?–1800), actress, novelist, feminist and courtesan, tried to show how her husband's neglect had pushed her into an adulterous affair with the then Prince of Wales.[28]

Other women wrote upon a larger canvas. The German pietist Johanna Eleonore Petersen (1644–1724) sought, in her autobiography, to recover her good name: like many women religious reformers, she had been subjected to wounding gossip, in her case the slanderous rumour that she was the mother of an illegitimate child. The Girondin strategist, Mme Roland (1753–1793), in prison and, as she well knew, soon to face the guillotine, sought, somewhat inconsistently, *both* to claim that she was a virtuous wife and mother, *and* to demonstrate that she was a truer and smarter patriot than any of the men in the French revolutionary government. And Catherine the Great of Russia (r. 1762–1796) in her numerous autobiographical writings aimed above all to justify her seizure of power by putting her unique personality, intellectual abilities and achievements as a monarch all on display.[29]

Poetry

Poetry was always the genre in which women were most readily accepted. Thousands of women composed and published poetry in the late seventeenth and eighteenth centuries, in English, German, French, Danish, Dutch, Italian, Latin, Polish, Spanish, Russian, Portuguese, Greek, Croatian, Serbian, Yiddish and other languages; and many others wrote poetry that was never published, and often never meant to be. Just for England, admittedly the nation with the most robust publishing industry of the day, a modern anthology of the work of *contemporaneously published* eighteenth-century English women poets includes over one hundred names.[30] Even in places that lacked a developed printing industry in the official language, such as the Ottoman Empire, about half a dozen women poets, writing in Ottoman Turkish and various Balkan languages, became well-enough known in the eighteenth and early nineteenth centuries to have their poems circulate orally or in manuscript among poetic coteries and to feature in literary anecdotes. The most famous of these, Fıtnat Hanım (d. 1780), despite being yoked to a boorish husband, enjoyed a successful career as a poet, writing elegant verses about love, nature, cruelty and stoicism (see Voices from the Past 7.3).

VOICES FROM THE PAST 7.3

An Ottoman poet writes of love

Fıtnat was a pen-name meaning 'natural wit'. Fıtnat's given name was Zübeyde, and she was the daughter of a sheyhülislâm (a high judicial official). Like many daughters of intellectuals she received an excellent education. There were many stories and anecdotes about Fıtnat, suggesting both that she enjoyed literary friendships with male poets, and that she was a great mistress of repartee. Fıtnat was also linked anecdotally both to lesbianism and to homosexual men, which may reflect truths about her or her coterie, but may also simply be an effort to explain her success by identifying her with other forms of gender and sexual boundary-crossing.[31] This poem is written to, or at least about, a woman (Fıtnat addressed love poetry both to men and to women), and it evokes the ambivalence both of the lover (Fıtnat herself) and of the beloved in a sophisticated marketplace of objectification, obsession, deferred pleasure, power and loss. 'Kays . . . wandering in the desert of madness' refers to the epic of Layla and Majnun, in which the protagonist, Kays, the possessed one (majnun), his love for Layla thwarted, wanders off to the desert and over time ceases to be obsessed with Layla and instead becomes obsessed with obsession itself. The legend of Layla and Majnun was a favourite of Sufi mystics.

> In a heart that bears the image
>   of the life giving lip
> Lies the divine nurturer of the soul,
>   speaker of colored words
>
> That alluring one never glances at the one
>   who would buy union
> In her quarter, a thousand addicts of desire
>   offer their souls in the palms of their hands
>
> With all his wisdom Plato was content
>   to live in a cask
> While Kays took his pleasure wandering
>   in the desert of madness
>
> For tyranny and torment, there is love and faithfulness,
>   for separation there is union
> Oh my heart, for every sorrow in this world
>   there is a cure

Oh Fıtnat, the Beloved has her way of treating
    the lover; she knows what to do
She offers faithfulness in one hand,
    absolute cruelty in the other

Source: *Ottoman Lyric Poetry: An Anthology*, edited and translated by Walter G. Andrews, Najaat
Black, and Mehmet Kalpaklı (Austin: University of Texas Press, 1997), 144, 256–7. I am
grateful to Jamal Elias for discussing with me the epic of Layla and Majnun.

Poetry offered considerable freedom in terms of subject matter. Eighteenth-
century women's poems range from praise of nature to erotica, from protests
against inhumanity and injustice (such as the slave trade or the poor treatment of illegitimate children), to celebrations of other women's intellectual
achievements, from calls to revolution to defences of the social hierarchy,
from praise of science to musings on the divine. A number of women wrote
poetry on feminist themes, dealing with such issues as the sexual double
standard, the civilizing power of women (this was the topic of a series of
poems by Ekaterina Sergeevna Urusova, perhaps the greatest eighteenth-
century Russian woman poet);[32] the inability of some people to take women's
scholarship seriously; and the vanity of men.

The fact that early modern people – perhaps especially poets – delighted
in coded language and double meanings, makes it a continuing challenge to
understand one of the commonest types of women's writing: poems about
their deep friendships with and often love for other women. An early generation of scholars laboured hard to argue that these women could not possibly
be articulating anything other than a completely chaste love, while others
interpreted almost all romantic poetry written to other women as evidence of
homosexuality. Today the pendulum has swung to the middle. Clearly some
women were deeply committed to elevating the 'spiritual' over the 'carnal', in
their relationships with women as well as men. Conversely, some women
wrote considerably more 'carnal' poetry than others and we know more than
we did about Sapphic coteries in the eighteenth century. Moreover, there
is good evidence that some women fell in and out of love, 'broke up' with
each other (and not always especially gracefully), and concealed actual lesbian
relationships beneath the conventions of female romantic love.[33] The most
reasonable approach to the whole genre of women's love/friendship poems
written to other women is probably to think of them as excellent sources for
exploring the *variety* of kinds of relationships early modern women could have
with each other, realizing both that people routinely put things into poetry that

they were reluctant to put into regular letters, and that literary productions have an extremely complex relationship to 'real' life.[34] We also need to be cognizant of the fact that many, and likely the majority of, more subversive or sexual poems by women were probably destroyed, either by the poets themselves or by their relatives; it was very hard for most eighteenth-century people to imagine that posterity would care more about a woman's poems than about her reputation for chastity, piety and religious conformity.

Novels

Fiction was always more controversial for women readers and writers than didactic work, autobiographies, and poetry. Novels concerned love, intrigue and adventure, and they often dealt with dangerous matters like adultery or, especially in early novels, women protagonists who avoided marriage altogether. Moreover, they gave impetuous youthful desire priority over the more sober, dynastic aims of parents and kin-groups. Novels frequently featured cross-class love-alliances, and novels by women (and even some by men) typically included less-than-demure and very adventure-prone female protagonists. Most also focused unashamedly on the challenges and rewards of this world and not of the next. For all these reasons a good deal of worry coalesced around the form: conservatives became convinced that novel-reading was addictive, especially for girls and women, and that impressionable and already over-sexed female readers would almost inevitably try to act out what they read, by engaging in love affairs, defying their elders, disobeying their husbands, neglecting their household duties, and forgetting about God.

Conservative anxieties failed to deter a critical mass of French or English women novelists from publishing, or hundreds of thousands of women and men from buying their books; but they did affect women intellectuals in much of the rest of Europe. Germany furnishes a telling example. In the later seventeenth century several pioneering novels were written by women, including one, by Maria Katharina Heden, later Stockfleth (1634?–1692), that contained a striking feminist-utopian message about courtship, equality of the sexes, and literary self-improvement. But German women's active contributions to the new genre dried up for some time after that, apparently due to an onslaught of moral disapproval and anxiety over excessive French cultural influence.[35] The next German novel by a woman did not appear until 1771. Similarly, no novels by women appeared in the Netherlands or Russia until the 1770s and 1780s, while most Spanish and Italian novels date from the early nineteenth century.[36] Novels emerged even later in some eastern and east central European states (the 1850s), and the first Ottoman novel by a *man* appeared only in 1872. The first two novels by Ottoman women were both by feminists though. First was the Istanbul-born Armenian activist and *salonnière* Srpouhi Dussap's *Mayda*, written in Armenian and published in 1883; the second was Fatma Aliye's *Muhâderât* (Virtuous Ladies), written in Ottoman, which appeared in 1892.

Women novelists began almost immediately to centre their work on female protagonists, often organizing their plots not just around stories of love, but around women's heroic adventures, often while dressed as men. As we have seen, transvestism was still a real-life practice in the eighteenth century, especially for women who wished to travel unmolested, take up men's jobs, or even, as the brilliant physicist and mathematician Émilie du Châtelet (1706–1749) once did, to get in on a discussion of higher mathematics in an all-male coffee-house. As a plot device it allowed female protagonists to be every bit as noble, creative, and erotically adventurous as male ones. But with or without cross-dressing, women novelists, and a few male novelists as well, succeeded in putting women's thoughts, dreams, problems, successes, and failures at the centre of the fictional universe. In itself this was a considerable achievement, especially when we compare the novel to some other prose genres. History writing, for example, routinely proceeded as if there were no women in the universe apart from the occasional persecuting queen or evil mistress to a king; so did the bulk of political or religious writing, though more so among Protestants. Just featuring women does not, of course, automatically make a work 'feminist'. Novels were often used in the eighteenth and nineteenth centuries to celebrate feminine retirement, domesticity, self-sacrifice, and companionate marriage. Moreover, their heroines were quite capable of mouthing support for female subordination. On the other hand, the misused heroines and caddish men who populate the wildly popular novels of Marie Jeanne Riccoboni (1713–1792), the overtly feminist and sexually unorthodox heroines of the German author Sophie Merau (1770–1806), the deistic and put-upon heroines of Ann Radcliffe, the martial women of a number of post-revolutionary novels (on both the revolutionary and counter-revolutionary side),[37] even the explorations of female genius in the French-Swiss author Mme de Staël's *Corinne* (1805) suggest that this was never a form that was easy to control.

Children's literature

The first women to take a serious interest in children's literature were a group of late seventeenth- and early eighteenth-century aristocratic French women novelists who began embedding fairy tales in their fiction; around two-thirds of the literary tales that appeared between 1690 and 1715 were written by women. Some of these writers clearly saw the writing of fairy tales as part of a campaign to elevate the status of women's discourse. A collection of tales by Marie-Catherine, Baroness d'Aulnoy, that appeared in 1698, are set not in a peasant-woman's cottage (the setting of Charles Perrault's contemporaneous – and more famous – *Tales of Mother Goose*) but in an upper-class salon, where female eloquence is prized, and women can both talk and write at a very sophisticated level.[38] For d'Aulnoy and others the fairy-tale genre became a vehicle for exploring female empowerment, sexuality, the body (especially pregnancy), and what is sometimes referred to as the 'rational uses of fantasy'. Children's literature would be enormously important for children, of course, but from the first some women used it to show that communication between women, as well as between women and children, could and should happen on an elevated plane. Over the long run women's contributions to the genre aimed (it has been argued) to emphasize female agency, rationality, expressive control, and intellectual complexity, rather than the rote, passive, brute unfolding of biological necessity.[39]

Before mid-century the centre of gravity of children's literature shifted to Britain, where the publisher John Newbery and then, from 1780, his nephew's widow, Elizabeth Newbery, between them virtually 'invented' the genre. Elizabeth Newbery, in particular, seized the opportunity to engage at least eighteen female children's book authors.[40] Somewhat earlier Sarah Fielding (1710–1768) published what is often thought of as the first children's novel, The *Governess, or the Little Female Academy* (1749). It is also the first girls' school novel, and, like many subsequent contributions to the genre, it emphasizes girls thinking for themselves, and working together in pursuit of virtue and reason. Women were involved early in the mechanics of teaching children to read and acquire useful knowledge quickly and effectively: Anna Laetitia Barbauld (1749–1825)'s *Lessons for Children* (1778–79) is one of the first to try to make literacy more attainable through graded lessons, large print and wide margins. The novelist Sarah Scott (1720–1795) and her life-partner, Lady Barbara Montagu (c. 1722–1765), planned a series of 'teaching cards' for children, designed to introduce them to history, among other topics. Women also wrote a number of books on science for children. Sarah Trimmer, one of the most prominent English domestic feminists, wrote children's natural histories, and was especially committed to humane treatment of animals. Her very popular writings on animals, particularly on wild birds, both anthropomorphized animals and sought to stop naughty boys from torturing and killing them ('civilizing' little boys is a leitmotif of much children's literature by eighteenth- and early nineteenth-century women; the larger motives are not difficult to detect).[41] In Trimmer's many writings women, especially mothers, are represented unapologetically as moral exemplars; the seventeenth-century world of women fighting to be seen as virtuous seems a distant bad memory. In the best-selling natural history books for children by the Quaker author, Priscilla Wakefield (1750–1832), mothers have been turned into natural scientists. In Wakefield's books lessons are generally conveyed through cosy conversations between women, or interchanges between parents (especially mothers) and their daughters. In her *Domestic Recreation, or Dialogues Illustrative of Natural and Scientific Subjects* (1805) a mother explains to her daughters the anatomy of the human eye, the physics of rainbows, and the biology of sea anemones. Wakefield's *Introduction to Botany* (1796) introduces the Linnaean taxonomic system through the medium of an exchange of letters between two sisters.[42] Women are positioned in these works as well educated, up to date on the latest scientific research, and actively engaged in the dissemination of useful knowledge to the rising generation.

Finally, a number of women authors wrote books specifically for young girls and young women, often seizing the opportunity to encourage mothers to take just as strong an interest in their daughters as in their sons. An early example can be seen in the work of French governess to the English elite, Jeanne Marie Le Prince de Beaumont (fl. 1748–1782). Her *Young Ladies Magazine* (1760) recommends heavy involvement by elite women in the upbringing of their daughters, and defines the rearing of girls as a rational, highly skilled enterprise of major social significance.[43] In France, Stéphanie Félicité, Countess de Genlis (1746–1830), also a governess to the great, contributed many writings on children, from special 'moral' plays intended to be acted out by the young (especially young women) to her *Adèle et Théodore* (1782), a feminist riposte to Rousseau's ideas on the education of girls. Middle-class feminists were just as involved in the children's literature genre as elite feminists were. Thus Mary Wollstonecraft put together an anthology of useful readings for young women, called the *Female Reader* (1789); while Anna Letitia Barbauld did her one better in 1811 with a literary anthology provocatively titled *The Female Speaker*. By this time, as we will see (Chapter 9), the rush of political events had made it seem possible, at least for liberals and those who continued to see the Revolution in largely positive terms (of whom Barbauld was one), that women *could* speak in the public sphere and should be trained to it from childhood.

WOMEN AND THE PERFORMING ARTS

Dramatic arts

Professional actors and actresses had an extremely equivocal reputation in the early modern period (see below), but this did not usually extend to the writing of plays. Indeed, plays were the second most common women's literary genre after poetry. The range was extraordinary. The writing and performing of plays was common in eighteenth-century Spanish, Italian and Polish convents, and likely in convents all over Catholic Europe. The great Mexican nun-intellectual, Sor Juana Inés de la Cruz (1648–1695) wrote six full-length dramas, of which three were secular, and numerous shorter dramatic pieces.[44] As we have seen, for a long time German women writers shunned novels as French and hence immoral, but they nevertheless wrote plays; some of these, like Luise Gottsched's *Die Pietisterey im Fischbein-Rocke* (Pietism in Petticoats) (1736), a German adaptation of a French satire on women's learning and religious pretension, were anything but feminist, though. By the second half of the eighteenth century some women playwrights had begun to rival male playwrights in popularity. For a period in the 1760 and 1770s the Danish playwright Charlotta Dorothea Biehl (1731–1788) was the most performed playwright of either sex in Denmark (she was also a notable translator and writer of fictional letters). She was especially famous for her comedies, which often featured women who chose friendship with men over marriage to them (which was also true of Biehl herself), but which also celebrated sensitive husbands who had a sincere commitment to companionate marriage.[45] As Biehl's career suggests, women were quick to exploit the potential of drama as a vehicle for commenting on social issues. Catherine the Great wrote a number of plays notable for their verve if not for their high literary quality; several of them, as befitted a friend of Voltaire, are designed to satirize and discredit superstition. The Spaniard, María Rosa Gálvez (1768–1806), wrote at least thirteen original plays, often featuring female protagonists, and dealing with such topics as incest, rape, and domestic violence. Seven of them were produced on the Madrid stage.[46] In France, Olympe de Gouge (1748–1793) wrote a number of highly political plays that attacked chattel slavery, examined divorce, adultery and the rights of illegitimate children, and protested against the confinement of women to convents.

Traditionally, professional actresses, if not amateur ones, had been identified with prostitution, for what other kind of woman would flaunt herself on a public stage? This was one part of a more general hostility to the theatre that stretched back to the early Christian Church. In France, professional actors and actresses remained under a ban of excommunication right up to the Revolution. Some rigidly Calvinist regimes (like the city-state of Geneva) allowed no theatres at all. But by the eighteenth century such attitudes were increasingly at odds with the realities of the market and public taste. Across Europe there was a mounting passion for the performing arts, and as a result the best actresses, singers and dancers were greatly in demand. Work in the performing arts also became extremely lucrative. By the 1770s the *starting* salary for French and German actresses was some four times what a successful lace worker could command and six times more than what most female servants could earn.[47] During the second half of the eighteenth century, actresses often made as much or more money than actors, even in the provinces – a powerful indicator of public tastes. As a result, thousands of women became professional actresses, dancers and musicians in the eighteenth century, and hundreds became nationally, and in some cases internationally, famous. With the possible exception of queens and the Virgin Mary, no women were more talked about, written about, or obsessed about than women performers. By the second half of the eighteenth century in Madrid, a city famously in love with theatre, a good portion of the urban population was divided into factions affiliated with famous actresses of the day. People wore their colours, paraded them about the streets in festive litters, gossiped about their affairs, and fought street brawls in their honour.[48]

It became common for women performers to be taken up by aristocratic or even royal patrons who promoted their careers, set them up in some style, and expected, in return, to enjoy their sexual favours. Affairs with elite men could be extremely profitable; proximity to the well born also gave women political power, including the pull to demand better roles and higher salaries. Clearly some actresses were shrewd businesswomen and fully in control of their own choices in life. The innovative Belgian-born dancer Marie Anne de Cupis de Camargo (1710–1770), one of the inventors of modern ballet, took up with Louis de Bourbon, the Count of Clermont. Clermont insisted that she retire from the stage, but La Camargo soon got bored, resumed her career, and ended up retiring a decade later with a handsome government pension. But, just as clearly, some were thoroughly exploited by theatre producers and patrons. In Russia and Poland it was fashionable in the eighteenth century for the nobility to build up acting companies consisting of their own serfs, some of whom were educated in special schools. More than one aristocrat was said to have bankrupted himself subsidizing their education and training, paying for their costumes, and building private playhouses. Some of the serf actresses, women like the Russian actress and singer Praskovya Kovalyova (1768–1803), became extremely famous. Kovalyova was part of the serf company of the Sheremetev family, and she was given the stage-name 'the Pearl' (all the Sheremetev actresses were named after jewels). Kovalyova in the end discreetly married Count Nicholas Sheremetev, who proved very devoted to her in the face of wounding rumours about his having married a servant. But this was a rather unusual outcome. Serf actresses were extremely vulnerable to sexual exploitation and physical abuse – some serf theatres stocked whips – and the capacity for self-determination displayed by a number of French, English, German, Italian and Spanish actresses seems largely to have eluded them.[49]

Women performers modelled lifestyles, attitudes toward luxury consumption, and approaches to marriage, sexuality, professionalism and public display of self that were profoundly at variance with the standard expectations for women of the time. Some of them also made a great deal of money. As a result they became the focus of much anxiety. Religious leaders routinely condemned the theatre in general and actresses in particular. The popular press was forever retailing lurid stories about female performers' sex lives (male performers were far less interesting to readers), commenting upon their disputes with management or other actors and actresses, and representing them as women with too much power. However, over time their cultural prominence began to tell. Due to the runaway popularity of the theatre, the traditional social exclusion of actresses could not be comprehensively sustained. The *philosophes,* particularly Voltaire, were almost always great champions, while the more 'enlightened' *salonnières* helped by welcoming actresses and musicians (though less often dancers) into their salons. A further blow to traditional attitudes came in the late eighteenth and early nineteenth century, when some less-well-heeled Polish noblewomen became professional actresses themselves.[50]

Actresses could hardly have missed the ambiguity of their position and some were quite active in efforts to improve the status of the theatrical profession, and of actresses in particular. In Leipzig, Germany, Caroline Neuber (1697–1760), an actress and theatre director, patrolled the morals of her actresses, sought to improve the quality of acting programmes (by, among other things, insisting that people memorize their lines instead of simply declaiming them extemporaneously), and tried to purge the repertoire of the cruder popular comedy, much of it extremely misogynist. Neuber also penned a number of theatrical preludes and similar short pieces, using them as a platform to articulate her ideas about the future of the theatre.[51] Some have credited her with creating the first 'German school' of acting. Claire Josephe Hippolyte Legris de La Tude (stage-name, Mlle Clairon) (1723–1803), one of the great French tragic actresses of the day, worked tirelessly in the 1760s to try to end the Catholic Church's policy of automatic excommunication of actors and actresses. In 1761 she arranged for the publication of *Libertés de la France contre le pouvoir arbitraire de l'excommunication* (French Liberties Contrary to the Arbitrary Power of Excommunication), complete with a prefatory letter in which she talked about what it was like to be a pious Catholic (arguably something of an exaggeration in her case), who, solely because she acted in the theatre, was forbidden to marry in the church, to have her children baptized, or to receive last rites. Presumably because of its outspoken anticlericalism the Parlement of Paris ordered that the pamphlet be publicly burned by the city executioner.

The theatre company to which Mme Clairon belonged, the Comédie-Française, had originally been Louis XIV's own theatre troupe, and despite its absolutist origins it had a surprisingly egalitarian system of self-government. Actresses participated fully in the weekly general assembly, and voted just like the men in the collective decisions about what plays to put on, the distribution of parts, etc. They also met in judgment on labour disputes generated by dozens of provincial theatres in France and elsewhere. Women's influence at the Comédie-Française did not go unchallenged. Actresses were often subjected to scurrilous attacks in the periodical press and pamphlet literature, including, in Clairon's case, accusations of lesbianism. There were also several attempts to undercut their power, including, in 1766, a royal decree that confined the job of preliminary screening of scripts to male actors only. By this time top actresses had also begun writing plays, both as vehicles for themselves, and to make larger cultural and political points. Mademoiselle Raucourt (1756–1815) of the Comédie-Française, a famous *tragédienne* and reputed lesbian, wrote and starred in a drama called *Henriette* (1782) that featured a cross-dressing woman soldier. According to Pamela Cheek, Raucourt was '[playing] deliberately . . . with the homosexual and heterosexual eroticization that rumor and the scandal sheets had built around her'.[52] Paris in the later eighteenth century is one of the first places where we can identify fairly open sapphic coteries, specifically in the circles around some actresses (Raucourt was one of them); *Henriette*'s opening night must have been quite memorable.[53] There is no question that at the Comédie-Française and other theatre companies some women wielded a degree of power far out of proportion to that accorded most other commoner women of their time, and they did so while insisting on a very different standard of sexual morality than was the norm.

Musicians and composers

Some of the most celebrated musicians of the eighteenth century were women opera singers. As we have seen, it was more difficult for women to become instrumentalists; nonetheless dozens of them did, particularly on the harpsichord and in the later eighteenth century, on the new forte-piano, the predecessor of the modern piano. There were other more unexpected opportunities for women. Venice, especially, was famous for the 'daughters of the Ospedali', girls' music schools affiliated with the major philanthropic organizations of the town. For much of his career the noted Baroque composer Antonio Vivaldi taught violin and acted as choir director at the girls' school linked to the foundling hospital (this is a striking exception to the usual reluctance to teach bowed instruments to women). His famous concerto cycle, *The Four Seasons* (1723), was first performed by these girls, undoubtedly in one of the concerts whose admission fees helped fund the institution.[54]

Hundreds of eighteenth-century women also tried their hands at composing music. As with male composers, the majority of these women's works do not stand the test of time. Some do, though, and musicologists are even now in the midst of trying to untangle the truly great Baroque, rococo, classical and early romantic women composers from the merely good to mediocre ones. Several of the most talented early modern women composers were nuns, including Isabella Leonarda (1620–1704), an Ursuline religious from Novara in North Italy. Leonarda published more than 200 works, largely, but not entirely, sacred vocal compositions. She was greatly esteemed during her lifetime, and her works are widely scattered across the early modern archives and libraries. There are a number of modern recordings of her work, which is tuneful, technically complex and deeply spiritual.[55]

Women composers, like their male counterparts, often relied on aristocratic or royal patronage. Elizabeth-Claude Jacquet de la Guerre (1659–1729), a virtuoso harpsichord player who also wrote chamber music and an opera, came, like many other eighteenth-century women composers, from a family of professional musicians. A child prodigy, she first came to fame in the court of Louis XIV, who greatly admired her playing. Her work compares favourably with that of François Couperin, often considered the greatest composer for harpsichord. Maria Antonia Walpurgis (1724–1780), a member of the highest aristocracy and married to the Prince Elector of Saxony and heir to the Polish throne, wrote two operas including one entitled *Talestri, Regina delle amazoni* (Talestri, Queen of the Amazons) (1760). This work, which has recently been recorded, artfully reverses many of the gender conventions of eighteenth-century opera. Almost all the characters are women, the male lead has to disguise himself as a woman in order to win the queen's love, and he is the one who sings the stereotyped 'lasciami morire' (let me die) aria, more often sung by women and emblematic, in eighteenth-century opera, of hyperemotionality and enslavement to love.[56] Women also benefited from the rise of public concert-going (essentially an eighteenth-century phenomenon) which meant that they did not have to rely so heavily on a single patron. Elisabetta de Gambarini (1730–1765), who was of Italian ancestry but lived her entire, unfortunately short, life in England, was able to take advantage of her multiple talents (she was a singer, harpsichordist, organist and composer), and the common practice in England of publishing by subscription, to put out several collections of her own compositions. Her six sonatas for harpsichord included 213 subscribers, among them Georg Friedrich Handel. All the sonatas have modern recordings. Austrian-born Maria Theresia von Paradies (1759–1824), though blind from the age of three, became a virtuoso pianist and travelled all over Europe, giving public concerts and enjoying the patronage of various European nobilities. Mozart and Haydn both composed concertos in her honour. In the early nineteenth century she founded a music school for girls in Vienna. Polish-born Maria Szymanowska (1789–1831) was an early romantic composer, performer and musical *salonnière* with a European-wide reputation. Her virtuosic writing for piano, her appropriations of Polish folk dances and her unusual key changes are believed to have influenced her fellow Pole, Friedrich Chopin.[57]

A different tradition of music making is represented by Panna Czinka (1711?–1772), a violin prodigy who became the most famous Roma woman musician of the eighteenth century.[58] Panna Czinka came from what is now Slovakia, from a family of musicians with links both to the Ottoman and the Austro-Hungarian empires. She was, by all accounts, an electrifying performer and from about 1725, and thereafter for almost the next half century, she led her own gypsy band. She was also a composer, though no music definitively attributed to her has survived. She always performed in a man's military outfit and she is also said to have been buried in the same garb, with her violin beside her. In Panna Czinka's case the costume – both masculine and military – probably helped give her licence to play an instrument traditionally associated with men. It may also have made her feel and seem more inviolable in the face of sexual propositions. Panna Czinka was extraordinarily popular among central and East European aristocratic audiences, but her disinterest in their amorous proposals was legendary. As one poem, supposedly by a rejected admirer, puts it: 'Czinka Panna, you play beautifully/But your heart is made of stone . . . /And your lips made of ice/They say that love cannot conquer you'. In fact Panna Czinka was married to one of her band-members, a blacksmith, and they had five children together. The coupling of surely genuine admiration of the artistry of women musicians with a powerful tendency to eroticize them was common in the eighteenth century, just as it is today. In Panna Czinka's case this was compounded by contemporary stereotypes of Roma women as sexually available, by the fact that she was performing for men who were unaccustomed to being rejected sexually by lower-class women, and by a complex mixture of idolisation of her talent and fixation upon her dark skin and hair and white teeth: 'Dark beauty of the Gypsy peoples, where can I begin the praise of your deeds?' asks an elegy written in the year she died.[59] Women negotiated public musicianship in very diverse ways in the eighteenth century, assisted by the addictive emotional power of the medium (and of performance more generally), and probably by its increasingly commercialized character, but restrained by the close association between music, public performance and sensuality. Extraordinarily talented women sometimes made this system work for them, but they were made to pay in ways that were both obvious and subtle. The larger purpose, one assumes, was to keep most women from taking that route, but we get the distinct impression that in large parts of Europe, the barriers began falling in the eighteenth century, and in many cases it was impossible ever to erect them in the same way again.

The Ottoman performance sphere

Music was extremely important within the Ottoman system, both symbolically and aesthetically; indeed it was considered to have a close and almost mystical connection to the continued health of the Ottoman dynasty. Consequently, both freeborn elite women and slaves were trained in music and dance, often with the best musicians of the day (traditionally an exception was made to the practice of elite female seclusion in order for girls to go for lessons). Some aristocrats were well known for their musical ability. One of these, Dilhayat Kalfa (Lady Kalfa) (1710–1780), is considered one of the great Turkish instrumental composers of the early modern period.[60]

Professional women performers were organized into all-female dance/music/acrobatic troupes, usually consisting of six to twelve performers each, overseen by a manager and her assistant. Most of the performers in these troupes were slaves, usually Gypsies, Armenians or Jews. Some of the most talented women would have experienced some upward mobility via marriage or concubinage, akin to what awaited the best western European actresses and musicians. On the other hand, musical performance, especially if it was for pay, was clearly an unrespectable occupation, because women performers performed for men as well as for women. It seems likely that the association between performance and minority religions and ethnicities (not to mention slavery) would both have intensified the imputation of unrespectability and undermined professional performers' control of their own careers and sexuality. There were also older traditions that suggested deep disapproval of performance, and performances by women in particular, and that tended to link them to sexual deviance or excess. The counterpart to the Catholic excommunication of actors and actresses was that *Hanafi* law did not accept court testimony from wailing women (that is, professional women mourners), singing-women, or people who sang to the tambur (a stringed instrument like a lute) or who sang in public. And one of the stock figures in Turkish Karagöz (shadow) plays is the lesbian dance-troupe manageress or wardrobe mistress. Some may well have been lesbian, of course; however, as in western Europe, this is usually impossible to prove one way or the other. We are on firmer ground in saying that rumours of this kind were a way to question these women's talents (or at least the 'purity' and 'naturalness' of their talents) by casting aspersions on their virtue or suggesting that their preferences were odd or eccentric. Whether such ploys worked is, at least in the eighteenth century, rather less clear, either for Christian Europe or the Ottoman Empire. Cross-dressing was certainly a common way to fend off sexual advances; conversely, rumours of unusual sexual practices may simply have made these women seem more fascinating as artists. It is hard to know.

One side effect of women controlling their own money in a gender segregated society, was that they could support a female performance sphere. Though clearly not representative, the entertainments for which we have the most evidence were staged by extremely powerful and opulent women, some of whom had their own permanent staffs of musicians. One of the fullest contemporary descriptions is of a spectacle put on by the Princess Esma Sultan, sister of Mustafa III (r. 1757–1774), in the garden of her palace sometime during her brother's reign. It featured troupes of women musicians and dancers, as well as a separate troupe of twelve women dressed as men who put on a kind of joust. Boat women, also disguised as men, rowed guests around an artificial lake. Most performances must have been smaller-scale entertainments, though, held in bathhouses, in private homes or in public parks (to which women often went), involving musical performances both by slaves and freewomen, and usually consisting of singers accompanied by a plucked instrument, such as a lute (*ud*).[61]

Istanbul clearly supported a culture market – music, dance and other kinds of performances were done for money, there was a sophisticated system of grooming professional musicians and other performers, and specialized performers circulated around between performance venues. However, in contrast to the western European cities, at least, this was still primarily an oral culture, illiteracy was relatively high, and there was no popular press. Poetry circulated around in manuscripts and in people's memories (it was a culture that placed a high emphasis on memorization), there were traditions of dramatic performance (especially the shadow theatre), and in place of the novel there was storytelling. This was not, however, the storytelling of peasant huts, though, as with most high culture forms, there must have been some cross-fertilization. Rather, it was a sophisticated, largely urban form: complex, multivalent, improvisatory, and filled with social satire, politics, philosophy, religion, history, interesting characters, and great plot lines. Many professional storytellers were women, and the best of them were very famous. The *masalcı*, as she was called, was often old (this was a job where age may actually have enhanced one's reputation, in addition to allowing greater mobility). And her performances involving refined poetics, rich metaphors, the ability to inhabit different characters, split-second timing, and so on.[62]

Precisely because this was an oral form, it is difficult to reconstruct the content of the eighteenth-century *masalcı*'s repertoire. Most tales were only written down in the nineteenth or twentieth century, if at all, and they were intended for live performance, not to sleep silently on a printed page. Still, it seems clear that there was a good deal to interest women. One common theme (also found in the tales of other countries) is women who are falsely accused by their husbands or male relatives of being unchaste. In some of these the truth is revealed by magical means, or by virtue of the woman's quick thinking.[63] In others the result is tragedy. In a Bosnian tale from Sarajevo a man leaves his native land and has a number of magical adventures. When he finally returns evidence is produced to suggest that his sister has committed a (presumably) sexual sin, and he has her killed. Having second thoughts about this, he has two large oak trees pulled out of the ground and planted over his sister's grave. He prays to God to show him whether she is innocent or not. If she is innocent the trees will take root; if she is guilty the trees will die. Both trees take root, and (the storyteller concludes) are still the most impressive trees in the cemetery. This is a tale about the tragic consequences of jumping to conclusions about a women's chastity, an ancient theme in

Islam, and it contains an at least implicit critique of so-called 'honour crimes'.[64] It is also a tale of revenge, literally from the grave, since it was common in the Balkans to believe that oak trees, because of their deep roots, could reach down into the underworld and be a conduit for communication with the dead. A lengthy cycle of Turkish tales, indebted to the medieval Arabian tale anthology, *Thousand and One Nights*, and first collected in the nineteenth century, revolves around Dellé, the female master thief, who haunts the souks, cheats merchants of goods and money, and perpetrates a variety of creative scams, all while hiding behind the anonymity of her veil. When it suits her purpose, Dellé is also prepared to cross-dress. In one story she disguises herself as a *kadi* and renders verdicts advantageous to her interests.[65] Both performance and the patronage of performers was clearly an important area of Ottoman women's subjectivity, and likely also one that permitted them to comment on their world. Hopefully it is one we will hear much more about in the years to come.

WOMEN AND THE VISUAL ARTS

In the early modern period professionally executed art became a widespread form of domestic display. In some countries, such as England and the Netherlands, cheaper forms of art (notably prints) also penetrated into the middling or trading classes. As art came to be seen as a polite accomplishment, and people saw that there was money to be made from it, it became fairly common for women to take it up. As in the case of music, the patronage of royal and aristocratic women played a significant role in many women artists' careers, particularly portraitists, in part because many women seem to have preferred being painted by female artists. Rosalba Carriera (1675–1757), though from a fairly humble background (her mother was a lace-maker from Venice), pioneered pastel portraits and became very popular across the European elite. She influenced numerous other artists, helped establish the rococo style, and was admitted to the Roman Accademia di San Luca in 1705, and later the French Académie Royale de Peinture et de Sculpture. She was one of the first woman artists to succeed despite not having come from an established artistic family and she never married.

Rosalba Carriera notwithstanding, normally women artists were even more likely than women musicians to come from families already engaged professionally in the field, both because the fine arts required a long period of specialized training and because fine artists relied even more heavily than musicians and actresses on elite patronage. The Swiss Neoclassical painter,

Angelica Kauffman (1741–1807), the most famous woman artist of the eighteenth century, was carefully nurtured by her artist father, who saw her from the start as a major talent. Kauffman went on to have a brilliant career in both Italy and England, and in the latter country she became a founding member of the Royal Academy of Arts. Unusually, she executed a number of history paintings, the most prestigious eighteenth-century artistic genre and one usually deemed more appropriate for male artists. Many of her works deal with women and classical antiquity, such as a series of paintings she did on the theme of women mourning the deaths of their loved ones in war, and a number of paintings about Penelope awaiting the return of Odysseus. Her work shows an enduring preoccupation with finding ways to represent motherhood and the power of female virtue in history.[66]

The ownership of paintings always remained something of an elite privilege. By contrast, the proliferation of printed books, and especially the growing use of woodcuts and engravings within books (and engravings separately sold), brought art before a wider spectrum of the population, in addition offering a new outlet for a good many women artists. This was especially true in the field of scientific illustration, a largely new, or at least greatly expanding, genre of the later seventeenth century. Some of the best scientific illustrators of the early modern period were women, apparently an offshoot of women's traditional association with flower gardening, herbal medicine, and the painstaking detail of flower embroidery. The greatest of these were scientists in their own right, women like the German-born Marian Sybilla Merian (1647–1717), sometimes called the mother of entomology. Merian travelled to the Dutch colony of Surinam when she was in her fifties and produced the first really accurate artistic renderings of many insects, of processes like metamorphosis, and of numerous tropical plants. Her fascination with biological processes unfolding over time, and her efforts to convey them on the page, often lend her pictures a surreal and almost pantheistic quality. At least twenty published scientific illustrators of the seventeenth and eighteenth centuries were women, and their influence carried on into the nineteenth.[67]

Today many academies of the arts, museums, galleries, arts funding organizations, and the like, deliberately exclude textile arts from their purview; they have been relegated to the category of 'women's decorative crafts'. In the eighteenth and early nineteenth centuries these distinctions were not yet quite so fixed, or at least some women thought they might not be. The Stockholm Royal Academy of Fine Arts, as revived by Queen Lovisa Ulrike (r. 1751–1771), both included embroidery in its collections and appointed women embroidery artists as regular members. Clearly Lovisa Ulrike, who was herself no mean embroiderer, wanted to support and dignify the artistic endeavours in which she and her own court engaged.[68] An even more overtly political intervention came in 1800 when an enterprising needlewoman named Mary Linwood (1755–1845) opened a gallery in London devoted entirely to displaying embroidered fine art. An early nineteenth-century pamphlet about the gallery, presumably by Linwood, indicates that she opened it in part to protest 'a law of the [British] Royal Academy, absolute as that of the Medes and Persians, which forbids the admission of any species of needlework', and she makes it abundantly clear that she considers herself equal to anyone working in any medium. An accompanying poem by one Miss Aickin maintains that needlework and weaving were the first arts, long predating sculpture and painting, even though, in recent times, science and learning, together with 'manly arts' have 'rent . . . the aged tape'stry from the wall' (she makes it sound like rape). Now Linwood, whom she compares to an Amazon, has come forward to create a new needlework that can take its place with the other arts on a ground of equality.[69] Although Linwood did not achieve her larger goal of winning equal treatment in the Royal Academy for the art of embroidery, her gallery was extremely successful, one of the great tourist sights of London, and it stayed open for almost half a century.

Embroidery probably came closest to being considered fine art in the Ottoman Empire. It is said that virtually all Turkish women learned to embroider; the skill was certainly very widespread, and went back to nomadic times. There were both men's and women's embroidery workshops in the eighteenth century, as we would expect with a highly respected art form, and art historians are still untangling what the relationships were between the two. As we have seen (Chapter 5), many middle- and upper-class households specialized in embroidery, and women of all social classes must have sewed or embroidered for money. In elite, and often even in non-elite, households, almost every piece of cloth – handkerchiefs, clothes, napkins, pillow covers, cradle covers, table mats, turbans, prayer mats, and so on – was covered with fine embroidery; this was a major aesthetic commitment that seems to have been sustained for centuries across virtually an entire society. It also offered women a way to project their art out into the world, as well as to accumulate social capital, because embroidered items were a central item of gift exchange. Some of the most technically sophisticated embroidery ever executed came out of Ottoman embroidery workshops, and Ottoman stitching, flower representation and colour schemes influenced embroidery styles and aesthetics across Europe. Not only were samples of Ottoman needlework avidly sought after in the eighteenth century, but women from Christian Europe supposedly tried, on occasion, to acquire Ottoman women as slaves in the hope that they would teach them new embroidery techniques.[70]

CONCLUSION

In the *Observations on the Feeling of the Beautiful and Sublime* (1763) the philosopher Immanuel Kant wrote: 'laborious learning or painful pondering, even if a woman should greatly succeed in it, destroy the merits that are proper to her sex . . .'; and, more snidely, 'A woman who has a head full of Greek, like Madame Dacier [a prominent seventeenth-century classicist], or carries on fundamental controversies about [Newtonian] mechanics, like the Marquise de Châtelet [who did the definitive translation of Newton's Principia into French, and taught Voltaire all he knew about physics] might as well even have a beard; perhaps that would express more obviously the mien of profundity for which she strives.'[71] Kant's great inspiration, Jean-Jacques Rousseau, wrote that the theatre should be banned, in part because he thought actresses were so immoral (he also wrote several operas, but consistency was never Rousseau's strong suit). Both men convinced themselves that women could never make an independent cultural contribution and should not even try; Kant, in particular, helped flesh out the influential argument that, while women existed to inspire male genius, they could never be creative geniuses themselves. If one did not know how many active women writers, actresses, musicians and artists there were in eighteenth-century Europe, it would be easy to assume that Kant, Rousseau and men like them were registering an actual historical absence of talented women. As this chapter has shown, neither was the case. Women did experience impediments on account of their gender, and sometimes their race and religious affiliation too. But women had long had an important place in the art and performance of the everyday. And in the new culture-market growing up across Europe and the Middle East, they won admirers of both sexes, and found numerous opportunities to make great art as well as to carve out social power for themselves. By no stretch of the imagination could women be considered marginal to the cultural life of eighteenth-century Europe.

Chapter 8

◆

CIVIL SOCIETY
AND THE STATE

It used to be conventional among historians to distinguish between the 'Private Sphere' (the sphere of the household, of women and of family life) and the 'Public Sphere' (the sphere of men, politics, the market, etc.), and the implication was strong that the two were pretty radically separated from one another, at least in the modern period (a good deal of women's history writing in the 1970s and 1980s was, in fact, devoted to historicizing this supposed separation).[1] Today most historians of women reject the notion that 'home and family' and the world outside them are, or ever have been, distinct in practice. Influenced by feminist and post-modern theory, by the German social theorist Jürgen Habermas (and by Habermas's feminist critics),[2] and by a growing body of evidence about real women's lives, historians these days tend to argue instead that the boundaries between family and household and the rest of the world are vague, always in flux, and constantly being crossed.[3] As this book has repeatedly shown, in the early modern period women, like men, tried to forge connections across households and, if they could, with more distant bodies – village or town councils, faraway kin, governments, markets, religious bodies, guilds, law-courts, military bodies, and even the dead. It is true that women and other lower status groups almost always encountered far more constraints when they sought to enter into the public arena, precisely because connections make for social and political power. The supposed need to separate the 'public' world from the 'private' household was, in fact, part of the ideological edifice that held women back.

For many women *and* men civic opportunities – the ability to form connections that confer social power – expanded in the eighteenth century, as a result of new political concerns, new media (such as printed books and newspapers), greater ease of travel and communications, new relationships to government, and the rise of societies, academies, salons and clubs, some of which were relatively hospitable to women. There were also forms of power available to women in the eighteenth century that were subsequently lost. As long as monarchies and nobilities had significant cultural and constitutional roles, a few women enjoyed extraordinary amounts of political power, and some others enjoyed it by virtue of their close connections to men with power.[4] Maria Theresa of Austria-Hungary and Catherine II of Russia, both of whom are discussed below, were two of the most powerful women who ever lived; moreover, like several other female monarchs of the day, they openly sought to bolster the reputations of other women (especially women artists and intellectuals) as well as to offer women more educational opportunities. Half a century later, 'crown' feminism, as we might call it – opportunist, perhaps, and certainly top-down, but quite characteristic of the times – was largely gone, both because hardly any monarchs of either sex were still that powerful, and because, by that time, even women rulers were coming under heavy pressure to present a more 'domesticated' image.[5]

WOMEN IN PUBLIC

Justifying a public role for women

Many times in this book we have encountered women trying, successfully or unsuccessfully, to exercise agency, by mobilizing social or family contacts, through magic or religion, by various economic endeavours, and by exploiting others – particularly other women or girls. Openly pushing beyond the household, by, for example, gathering together with other women to agitate for some sort of common concern, was potentially very risky. One of the traditional ways for women to justify actions like these was by appealing to their status as a special-interest group, essentially the corporate body of women, or, more often, some subgroup of women – noblewomen, mothers of children, wives of a particular group of men, women of a particular faith, women who pursued a particular occupation. Women used 'corporatist' arguments to assert their right to hold on to female knowledge monopolies, especially to do with sex, childbirth or traditional female tasks like needlework. And women often used such arguments to stop men from interfering with or trying to dominate activities they thought they had a right to control themselves. Women in some eighteenth-century German villages and towns took to the streets to insist that they – and not the local burgermeister or provincial governor – be able to choose the village midwife.[6] In 1699 English women packed the courtroom during the trial of an alleged child-rapist and refused to leave (see Chapter 3). Stambouli blacksmiths' wives argued that they had a 'traditional' right to sell certain foods on the street so as to feed their children. Women cookbook writers tried to rally their readers to oppose male chefs (see Chapter 4). And French women's guilds lobbied the government to support their monopolies against incursions by men (see Chapter 5). Female corporatist arguments tended to appeal to conventional notions about the gendered division of labour, particularly the association of women with childbirth and childrearing, textiles or cooking. When no such association existed someone generally made one up, a nice example of Eric Hobsbawm's 'Invention of Tradition' in the day to day.[7]

The second justification for women's civic action sprang from the assumption that gender hierarchies and exclusions, though not wrong in themselves, simply could not be sustained in crisis situations. Essentially it was an argument from necessity, and it was often used to rationalize militant women's actions during epidemics or food shortages, or when the men were absent, more vulnerable to retaliation than women were (e.g. in conscription riots, see below), or simply reluctant to do what needed to be done for the moral or physical survival of the community. These 'emergency powers' arguments thrived in time of war, where they often became transformed into highly emotive arguments about group integrity, community defence, the survival of families, threats to female chastity from invading armies, and the like. The necessitarian argument generally assumed that women stepped out of their traditional roles reluctantly, temporarily and for the good of others, and it tended to emphasize ineluctability ('we can do no other') rather than rational choice or free will. It was a position that allowed a speedy return to the status quo *ante bellum* once the war or crisis was over.[8]

From about the middle of the seventeenth century feminist arguments for greater female opportunity began to proliferate. The two main issues were a call for greater access to education for women; and a critique of the way the heavy emphasis on the sin of Eve was used to impugn women's honour and deny them both secular and spiritual opportunities. In the eighteenth century some feminists (whom we will call, for the sake of argument, 'egalitarian feminists') also embarked on a series of pointed critiques of the sexual double standard and of male tyranny within the family (one feature of this was an explicit interest in both the theme and the practice of marriage avoidance for women). They also took an interest in women's inclusion in previously all-male learned academies and professions. At this point a word is in order about the word 'feminist' and its various derivatives. Many historians of the nineteenth and twentieth centuries (though less often historians of the early modern period) prefer to reserve the term 'feminist' or 'feminism' for the post-1800 period, and to use terms like 'proto-feminism' for feminist philosophies and philosophers that emerged earlier. This seems faint-hearted to me; it also assumes a rather narrow conception of what feminism is (often, for example, it includes a belief that feminism must be secular or staunchly gender-integrationist in order to be worthy of the name). For purposes of this discussion, if a strain of thought calls for a permanent (as opposed to simply temporary) expansion of women's role, for improving women's status or for increasing women's access to something (e.g. education, or spiritual leadership) we will call it feminist. This is in line with the usage of most historians of sixteenth-, seventeenth- and eighteenth-century women.[9] This does not mean one must agree with all eighteenth-century feminists, just as they did not agree among themselves. For one thing, as we will see, some feminists were extremely socially conservative, and few were very universalist in their conception of the category of 'women' whose status they wished to improve.

One of the more successful 'new' kinds of arguments for women's civic activism in the eighteenth century and beyond was, in fact, a conservative type of feminism which some historians call 'domestic feminism'. The ancestress of the nineteenth-century 'Cult of True Womanhood', eighteenth-century domestic feminism was essentially a hybrid.[10] It shared with egalitarian feminism the call for female education – though almost always with a strong preference for it being single-sex and oriented almost entirely toward religion and motherhood – and an interest in defending women against the imputation that they were far more sinful and dishonourable than men, though domestic feminists tended to make this argument somewhat more decorously than some egalitarian feminists, and, in fact, they almost never directly criticized men. From the corporatist and necessitarian traditions domestic feminists took an exaggeratedly conventional image of women's 'traditional role', and, quite often, a belief that families, homes, nations, religion and values were under attack. Almost everywhere its champions were deeply religious in their outlook and loud in defence of traditional hierarchies, including gender hierarchy (this last made some of them quite critical of more egalitarian feminist strains). Let us take this opportunity to look in more depth at these two kinds of feminist thought, realizing that, in practice, all such broad-brush typologies tend to blend together; individual women's views changed over time, some people dipped into both, and women soon learned to express more acceptable positions in public, whatever they might believe in private.

Eighteenth-century feminisms

Feminist ideas are not unique or original to Europe, much less western Europe or North America, though the claim that they are has, ironically, been useful *both* to those who want to claim that the West is always best, *and* to those elsewhere who want to stave off feminist demands by claiming that they are foreign imports. The great Ottoman poet, Mihrî Hatun (fl. 1470–1515), who refused marriage, devoted herself to her art and won praise and gifts from Sultan Bayezid II, is a clear example of someone fully prepared to voice sentiments recognizable to any feminist. She once made the following spirited riposte to an attack upon her by a competing poet:

> You say women have little understanding and that you do not listen to them for that reason. Yet Mihrî, who prays for you [and wishes you well], explains – and clever and mature people confirm it: a talented woman is better than a thousand untalented men, a woman of understanding is better than a thousand stupid men.[11]

Scholars are just beginning to discover some of the ways early modern Ottoman women projected themselves physically or symbolically into the public arena, and the jury is still out on whether any of this constitutes an effort to work for 'a permanent expansion of women's role, to improve women's status or increase women's access' (to use the definition adduced above). Scholars looking into these issues have fewer sources available to them than people who work on urban western Europe. The Ottoman Empire not only had no popular printing industry, but women's literacy rates were low, and record survival has been poor. Consequently, historians have recently been looking much more at material culture (women's memorial tombstones, embroidery, sartorial display) and the history of spatiality (especially women's and men's behaviour in Istanbul's public parks and garden) in an effort to find out how Ottoman women exercised agency in the public sphere, and, so to speak, 'resisted the dominant paradigm', if indeed they did, on which the jury is still out.[12] We will take up these issues, especially the last, in due time.

In western Europe feminism appears to have emerged partly out of efforts to push the egalitarian tendencies within Christianity. Thus Marie Le Jars de Gournay (1565–1645), one of the most influential early feminists, staked her argument primarily on a pithy gloss on Galatians 3:28–29, to wit, that 'the soul has no sex', and went on from there to deliver a stinging critique of the way male intellectual monopolies held back women. François Poulain de la Barre (1647–1723), a French male egalitarian feminist who was influenced both by the philosopher René Descartes and (most likely) by de Gournay, went farther, arguing that the apparent gulf between men and women was the result of socialization, not innate superiority or inferiority. It followed, he thought, that women were fully capable of taking up positions as university professors, leaders of armies, judges and heads of state.[13] As indicated above, egalitarian feminists soon moved from critiquing the doctrine of women's responsibility for Original Sin (often by arguing that the issue should be left to God to deal with, not man) to the sexual double standard. They were also prepared to criticize what they saw as excessive male power, within institutions such as universities, within the family, by virtue of men's right to use coercive power against their wives, and because of unjust laws (see Chapter 2). The Portuguese poet Paula da Graça's 1715 feminist attack was called 'The Goodness of Women Vindicated and the Malice of Men Revealed', and it deplored both male brutality and misogynist propaganda against women.[14] As we saw in Chapter 2, English law reformer Sarah Chapone likened marriage to slavery, and thought that the laws did not suf-ficiently protect women against marital violence (Chapone's correspondent and inspiration, Mary Astell, recommended that women seriously consider avoiding marriage altogether, as had a number of later seventeenth-century French women writers).[15] Later feminists deplored the poor treatment of both mothers of illegitimate children and the children themselves (Olympe de Gouges); made men's machinations against their wives' persons and property a major plot feature (the best-selling French novelist Marie Jeanne Riccoboni among others); and used the stage to examine the effect of rape and incest on women (the late eighteenth-century Spanish dramatist, María Rosa Gálvez) (see Chapter 7).

The issue of breaking down male monopolies, especially in matters intellectual and professional, went well beyond the printed page. There was, for example, the lengthy campaign, beginning in the 1650 or 60s, and periodically renewed over the course of the eighteenth century, to have women authors admitted to the prestigious Académie française.[16] More successful was the epic decade-and-a-half-long campaign by the remarkable Dorothea Erxleben (1715–1762) to be allowed to take her degree in medicine at the University of Halle in Prussia. Along the way Erxleben wrote a lengthy book defending women's right to study (1742),[17] petitioned Frederick the Great, pursued a successful career as an unlicensed healer, actually wrote a medical thesis in Latin (later also translated into German), passed the university exams, and raised nine children, five of whom were her own. She finally obtained her degree in 1754 at the age of thirty-nine.[18] The Spanish feminist Josefa Amar y Borbón (1749–1833) was a vocal supporter, in 1786, of a campaign to admit women to the Madrid Economic Society.[19]

Egalitarian feminists openly proposed real structural change, which guaranteed that their ideas would always be controversial. Their suggestion that men were prone to abuse their power and should be stripped of their right to 'tyrannize' their wives and daughters was especially disturbing because critics were convinced that women who were free of coercive male oversight would almost instantaneously abandon their chastity or marry unwisely – thus wrecking their own lives, their families' honour and their potential children's future. It also seemed to contravene Scripture, which is why, in practice, a good number of otherwise egalitarian-sounding feminists, especially early in the century, tip-toed around the issue of a husband's right to lead. Both the English feminist Mary Astell and the Portuguese feminist Paula da Graça were prepared to argue that female subjection in marriage had to be retained, because it was ordained by God. On the other hand, both asserted that this was for reasons of social utility alone, not because women were actually inferior. The more radical Sarah Chapone implied strongly that if women had sinned it was up to God, not man, to discipline them for it. It would take a wholesale retreat from biblical Christianity (and biblical Judaism) to solve that problem comprehensively, and it is not coincidental that most egalitarian feminists of the eighteenth century, both female and male, at least after about 1740, embraced Enlightenment anticlericalism and argued either for a 'rational' Christianity (by which they meant one that did not take the strictures of Genesis and Leviticus on women as binding in the present) or for deism. They also used the Enlightenment emphasis on socialization (what is sometimes called the doctrine of the 'blank slate') as ammunition in their campaign to bypass the doctrine of Original Sin and show that, if they were given a decent education, women could achieve anything men could. Still, in the meantime, even feminists of the late seventeenth and early eighteenth centuries agreed that there was no requirement for adult female submission *except* within marriage, obviously a strong argument for staying single.[20]

Like egalitarian feminism, domestic feminism had seventeenth-century antecedents, but during the first two-thirds or so of the eighteenth century its best-known champions were men. The British journalists Joseph Addison and Richard Steele presented an early variant in their highly influential journal the *Spectator* (1711–12), calling for improvements in women's education while offering fulsome praise for women who selflessly stayed out of public life, guarded their purity, and devoted themselves to smoothing out the 'rough' natures of men. At the same time they were quite critical of women who spoke or dressed in too hearty and 'masculine' a way, and who insisted on prenuptial agreements rather than handing their money unconditionally over to their husbands when they married. The *Spectator* was influential both in Britain and on the Continent (and, indeed, in the colonies), and in Catholic countries its emphasis on education and powerful but indirect feminine influence fused readily with the Catholic Reformation's renewed interest in the sacrament of marriage as well as with the growing trend of devotion to the Virgin Mary (see Chapters 3 and 6). The Catholic apologist Pierre-Joseph Boudier de Villemert's *l'Ami des femmes* (The Friend of Women), first published in 1758, is thoroughly indicative. In this sustained paean to Woman's divinely ordained civilizing mission, Boudier de Villemert argues for women's education but against anything that would confuse what he views as the distinctive and complementary roles of the two sexes. He is particularly repelled by women religious leaders like Madame Guyon or Antoinette Bourignon (see Chapter 6) and by any and all egalitarian religious sects or movements. Women's true mission is, quite clearly, to be found in marriage, and, like Addison and Steele, Boudier de Villemert explicitly opposes expanding married women's property rights.[21] *l'Ami des femmes* would be translated into German (1759), into Russian (1765), twice into English (1766 and 1802), and into Spanish (sometime before 1779), and it went into numerous French editions. Boudier de Villemert's ideas were probably a good deal easier to swallow, especially for women, than Jean-Jacques Rousseau's rather eccentric non-sectarian version of the domestic feminist ideal in Book V of his didactic novel *Emile* (1762).

While it is tempting to see domestic feminism as a rear-guard attack by men on egalitarian inclinations among women (and in some respects it was, especially in the early years), there is no question that large numbers of women were attracted to it. This was especially the case once it became associated with reforms having to do with children and with the notion that motherhood could be an important force in history and society, a philosophy often referred to as 'maternalism'.[22] Among the earlier male domestic feminists motherhood was only a subsidiary theme – far less important than the theme of women as supportive companions to men. But the most influential women theorists of domestic feminism, people like Marie-Angélique Le Rebours (who probably influenced Rousseau) and Sarah Trimmer, seem a good deal more interested in being mothers than in being wives; indeed at times they were somewhat impatient (though of course in a very oblique fashion) with the way men put their own needs before those of their offspring, especially when it came to mothers breast-feeding their own children (see Chapter 4). This was even truer of Hannah More (1745–1833), one of the great English domestic feminists. After an early broken engagement she made a vow never to marry, but this did not stop her from devoting much of her life and writing to the education of girls.[23] Domestic feminism's belief, shared with other feminists, that women were at least as moral as men, also had real appeal and was, in truth, quite subversive given what had preceded it. Conversely, its stress on conventional gender values, and especially on female sacrifice and obedience, even in the face of masculine tyranny, meant that it incurred less opposition than egalitarian feminism had done, and many women must have seen it as more strategic. After all, most of them had to live with the men they were trying to win over. Domestic feminism also played well to the pro-natalist sympathies of most modernizing states (see Chapter 3). Across western and central Europe and, slightly later, eastern Europe and the Middle East, domestic feminists found powerful allies both among government reformers, and, to a lesser extent, in the various religious establishments. Domestic feminists *did* encounter opposition at times. Teréz Brunswick (1775–1861), often called Hungary's first feminist, a disciple of the Swiss educational reformer and arch-domestic feminist, Johann Heinrich Pestalozzi (1746–1827), set up well over a hundred woman-run kindergartens, in the teeth of criticism by conservatives who claimed they were too empirical and hence irreligious. And during the July Monarchy French officials would investigate the huge women's Society for Maternal Charity on suspicion of subversive activities.[24] It is easy to caricature domestic feminism, especially in its early years, but maternalism gave it a much larger vision than the one it started out with, and its champions had an inexhaustible appetite for public activism that belied their supposedly exclusive focus on domesticity and the home. Moreover, in practice many women alternated between the two positions, or situated themselves somewhere in the middle. Thus egalitarian feminists learned to lay more rhetorical emphasis on women's duties as mothers than on women's right to cultivate their intellectual or artistic talents; while domestic feminists were sometimes prepared to critique the sexual double standard and even to countenance creative reinterpretations of the Bible, at least in private.

Feminism and Orientalism

The various justifications for women's public action did not generally extend to women from racial or religious minorities, to status inferiors, or to women in distant lands. Corporatist appeals by women, though at times emphasizing common female experiences like childbirth, focused in practice on the 'rights' of fairly narrow and distinctive groupings (the wives of army officers; or women fish-sellers from a particular market; or women from a particular neighbourhood who were unhappy with the price of bread; or members of a women's trade guild). The rhetoric of defending traditional privileges and entitlements was usually inconsistent with extending the argument to competing groups. It was essentially the same with necessitarian 'emergency powers' arguments, except that, because they tended to arise in times of crisis, and especially in time of war or threat of war, they were usually violently hostile to anything conceived as threatening to the collectivity. Arguments from necessity certainly justified some remarkable public actions by women, as we will see. But the paranoid rumour-mongering that accompanies most public crises, then and now, could also turn easily into attacks on innocent people. Historically women have shown themselves no less willing than men to participate in massacres and pogroms directed at people of other religions, ethnicities, nationalities, or political viewpoints, and it is usually some sort of argument from necessity that licenses this kind of behaviour.

The various feminisms, with their more explicit rhetorical commitment to the broad category 'woman' would seem better candidates for developing an expansive vision. But in practice this proved elusive. Most feminists we know about, at least before the early 1790s, were middle class or higher, because those were the people who tended to be able to write well, and who had the connections to get published. Some of these women were quite interested in charitable initiatives on behalf of poorer women (see Chapter 3 and below), but they were typically not in favour of expanding the latter's authority. Some feminists did take up the issue of slavery but, especially in the case of the domestic feminists, it tended to be in a cloyingly sentimental way that retained racial hierarchy (see Chapter 9). Both domestic feminists and egalitarian feminists were quick to adopt Orientalist claims about the allegedly extreme oppression of women in foreign and especially Muslim lands (see above, Chapter 3) and to put them to various opportunistic uses. Their motives were not the same of course. Domestic feminists, especially the men, believed or claimed to believe that marriage in Christian lands was fundamentally quite sound, and certainly not notably exploitative. When a marriage turned bad it was usually because women had forgotten their duty to submit with grace, or, alternatively, succumbed to luxury and dissipation. Thus, Boudier de Villemert jumps upon the 'harem slave' stereotype explicitly so as to show what paragons Western Christian husbands are. In his view 'the people of the Orient' (he means the men) are polygamous, sexually insecure tyrants who lock up their women but can never find true satisfaction with them (the influence of Montesquieu's *Persian Letters* is strong). By contrast, Western men are true friends to their wives, while the latter, blessed with freedoms of which their 'Oriental' counterparts can only dream, need only commit themselves fully to their womanly destiny to make themselves and their husbands blissfully happy.[25]

At first sight it is more difficult to see why egalitarian feminists would be drawn to orientalist arguments; after all, they were often quite critical of men and marriage in their own societies. But they routinely used exactly the same tropes of sexual enslavement in the harem to dramatize the argument that Western men were just short of, and indeed gaining on, 'Eastern potentates' in their propensity to tyrannize and sexually objectify women. This was, in essence, the view of the great late eighteenth-century English feminist, Mary Wollstonecraft (1759–1797), but it turns up in the writings of many eighteenth- and nineteenth-century feminists from across Europe.[26] Eighteenth-century feminists seldom attributed independent thoughts, agency, or capacity for self- or group-determination to non-Christian women; nor did they see them as people from whom they might have something to learn.

CIVIL SOCIETY AND SOCIABILITY

Academies

Jürgen Habermas's conception of the public sphere laid enormous stress on the ways that voluntarist societies, clubs, salons, coffee-houses and the like, disseminated news and information, engaged in deliberative discussion and put pressure, directly or indirectly upon the state. His original formulation stressed that these organizations and venues were, in effect, 'open to all', a claim which has not held up to feminist scrutiny.[27] Still, Habermas's meditations on what clubs and voluntarist societies actually did in the early modern period, and the way they helped ideas to evolve, social connections to grow, identities to form, and politics to become more accessible, has been of enormous interest to European women's historians. For change was very much in the air. By the later seventeenth century secular and single-sex women's cultural organizations had begun to emerge (women's religious organizations were, of course, much older, though largely confined to Catholic countries) and a few mixed-sex institutions were beginning to look more kindly on women's participation as well. This was especially true on the Italian peninsula. Some of the earliest permanent mixed-sex intellectual groupings in Europe were found there in the form of academies (*accademia*), membership institutions devoted to the common pursuit of literature, science, philosophy or the arts. The first to let in women was apparently the Accademia dei Ricovrati of Padua which, in 1669, inducted Elena Lucrezia Cornaro Piscopia (1646–1684), who, in the same year, became the first woman to earn a doctorate from a European university (the University of Padua). Another academy that inducted women was the Arcadia, formally established in Rome in 1690, but growing out of an earlier circle that had met under the patronage of ex-Queen Christina of Sweden (1626–1689). In the eighteenth century not only did other Italian academies admit women, but at least three different Italian women formed their own. The academy phenomenon had European-wide ramifications, because, in the increasingly expansive and cosmopolitan cultural world of the late seventeenth century, some Italian academies began inviting notable foreign women intellectuals from France, Britain, the German lands, Switzerland, the Netherlands, Scandinavia, Poland and other countries to take up membership, and scores of women accepted. At least twenty French women of letters were inducted into the Ricovrati, though the women did not enjoy equal membership rights with men. Still, many of these women would not have been permitted to join comparable institutions in their own countries, so the Italians not only extended an important form of symbolic recognition to women artists and intellectuals, but helped make the famed cosmopolitanism and internationalism of the Enlightenment into a more gender-inclusive phenomenon than it would otherwise have been.[28] The academies also offered another kind of recognition. With the printing industry growing apace in the eighteenth century, they became important clearing houses for journals and other kinds of publications, with the result that a surprising number of eighteenth-century Italian women edited literary journals, and many more published in them. Italy was also unique or almost unique, in that women could receive university degrees and a few even taught at the university level, all of the latter at the University of Bologna.

The prominence of Italian women intellectuals and the policy of relative inclusion did spark conservative opposition, including some early and influential claims that women's biology made them presumptively unfit to pursue intellectual endeavours. These efforts soon became detached from the confining prison of empirical fact. In the 1770s an anatomist named Petronio Zecchini, predictably, perhaps, a man with links to the University of Bologna, floated the claim that, while men thought with their brains, women actually thought with their uteruses (he called this the phenomenon of the 'thinking uterus' or '*l'utero pensatore*'). He went on to assert that because the uterus, unlike the brain, was such a volatile and unpredictable organ, women actually could not think in the conventional sense. This explained, to Zecchini's satisfaction anyway, why it was so essential that they relinquish intellectual pursuits and subject themselves to men.[29] Still, conservative hysteria aside, as Rebecca Messbarger has remarked, 'eighteenth-century Italian women more and more frequently defended the integrity and the rights of women from inside recognized centres of intellectual exchange: the academy, the university, and the pages of respected publications'.[30] In this sense the Italian peninsula was truly unique.

There was no cultural scene anywhere else in Europe that was as open to women as eighteenth-century Italy; nevertheless the climate was shifting. By the late seventeenth century several local German literary societies had begun opening their doors to women members; more would do so in the eighteenth.[31] Outside Italy and Germany most other academies, especially those founded under royal aegis, tended to be open only to men. The Royal Society, founded in London in 1660 for the promotion of science, did not have women members, though in the eighteenth century its *Transactions* occasionally published women's scientific observations. There were, as we have seen, repeated efforts in the later seventeenth and eighteenth centuries to nominate women to the Académie française, but all were rebuffed, despite the fact that some of the most famous writers of the day were women (the Académie française, like a number of other all-male institutions, did periodically award women literary prizes, though). Academies that were founded relatively late or were established by women monarchs tended to be more inclusive. So, for example, Queen Lovisa Ulrike of Sweden formed or revitalized several academies and made sure they admitted women.[32] Catherine II of Russia would actually appoint a woman director of her two royal academies (see below). The Académie Royale de Peinture et de Sculpture in France let in several women artists in the 1780s, but in at least one case only because of the active intervention of Queen Marie Antoinette. The British Royal Academy of Art, started in 1768, had two women as founding members, Angelica Kauffman and Mary Moser, but much of the rest of the membership resisted Kauffman's efforts to get them to induct more.

Salons

In the seventeenth century French women's salons had been a crucial locus for a variety of literary, rhetorical, and philological endeavours.[33] In the eighteenth century a somewhat altered variation on this theme became one of the central social institutions of the French Enlightenment. Salons tended to be run by charming, brilliant and well-off women in their own homes (in that sense they were different from the academies, though the lines sometimes became blurred). Part of their appeal was that the *salonnières*, as these women were called, succeeded in creating an intellectual atmosphere very different from the antagonistic style of the universities where much intellectual activity had previously taken place. The new deliberative climate set up by women like Marie-Thérèse Geoffrin (1699–1777), Suzanne Necker (1737–1794) and others allowed the *philosophes*, most of them men, to converse, make contacts, and cultivate the 'spirit of critique' for which they became so justly famous.[34] The notion, common to most of the salons and some of the academies, that women should be given a place at the intellectual table clearly reflects the seepage of feminist ideas into elite and sub-elite patterns of sociability. To be sure, mixed-sex sociability did not become axiomatic as a result of the salon, and quite often it was not very egalitarian (the belief, more common to domestic feminists, that it was women's job to 'civilize' the rough nature of men was often at least as salient as the egalitarian feminist belief that women were just as able as men). But it was never quite as easy after that to argue for women's total exclusion from cultural and intellectual endeavour; indeed, in many circles it came to be seen as old-fashioned and intellectually short-sighted.

In the eighteenth century all or largely women's salons also became a good deal more common and expanded their social purview (seventeenth-century women's salons had been largely aristocratic in composition). As intellectual ability turned into the coin of social prestige, it became very much more worthwhile to cultivate connections to other intellectual women by meeting together, corresponding with one another, and publicizing one another's work (often this meant translating it into the local language – a very common women's activity in this period). In university towns across western and central Europe small salons and gatherings were organized by the wives and daughters of lawyers and college professors. An all-women's scientific academy, the Natuurkundig Genootschap der Dames (Women's Society for Natural Knowledge), was founded in 1785 in Middelburg in the Netherlands; it would meet regularly for almost a century.[35] Circles and epistolary networks – indeed veritable cults – sprang up around certain female couples, such as the best-selling co-novelists Aagje Deken and Betje Wolff in the Netherlands. The English Bluestocking circle benefited greatly from the promotional zeal and charm of Elizabeth Montagu (1718–1800) and Elizabeth Vesey

(1715–1791), two well-heeled admirers of literature, the arts and other women intellectuals. Long-lived cliques also formed around certain actresses and women musicians. Many of the latter were mixed-sex; however, the Duchesse de Villeroy (1731–1816), a great theatre aficionado and well-known lesbian, put on all-women dinners in the 1780s, and is even alleged to have staged sapphic theatrical entertainments.[36] Dozens of royal and princely courts also ran ongoing musical, literary, artistic and theatrical salons in the seventeenth and eighteenth centuries, and women artists, musicians and intellectuals were often quite prominent, especially in courts headed by women.[37]

As both mixed-sex and single-sex cultural opportunities became common the rules began to change. At the height of the Enlightenment salon, in the middle decades of the eighteenth century, famous men like Buffon or d'Alembert or Diderot took up much of the conversational space while women tended to put in a few well-chosen words and set the tone (though they also wielded real patronage power, and launched many a young *philosophe* on his career). By late in the century it was not uncommon for the novelist, Madame de Staël (1766–1817), the daughter of Suzanne Necker, and literally reared in her mother's salon, to hold forth for an hour or more at a stretch. Her champions, both male and female, thought she was one of the most brilliant thinkers of her day; some others thought it immodest for a woman to talk so much.[38] By this time some of the salons were working almost as hard at including a diverse array of talented women as they were talented men; which often meant bringing in women traditionally viewed as 'unrespectable', such as actresses. The fact that, at the end of the eighteenth century, Rahel Varnhagen (1771–1833)'s Berlin salon drew both Christians and Jews has somewhat overshadowed the fact that it also included actresses, a number of whom she considered personal friends – at the time this was almost as innovative as the mixing of faiths, not to mention dangerously French and libertine.[39] Warsaw's extraordinarily vibrant salon culture, both before and after the various partitions, featured numerous women performers, and, at least the music salons, if not the literary ones, are said to have been remarkably socially mixed.[40]

The mixed-sex salon sent a shot across the bow of the old, almost reflexive, belief that women were sexually dangerous and so intellectually inferior that they had nothing to add to men's conversations; all-women salons conveyed a different kind of message: that women were worth talking to and cultivating by other women as well as by men. Together they added up to a real, if inconsistent, commitment, especially among the 'enlightened', to a sort of intellectual meritocracy, and even the belief, among some people of both sexes, that progress required a more-or-less ostentatious support of female intellectuals. Of course, both within and outside the world of the salon, many men (and some women) remained quite ambivalent about female intellectuals. As 'précieuse' became a term of abuse in the seventeenth century, so 'bluestocking' (the name that stuck to a prominent group of eighteenth-century English-women intellectuals) did in the eighteenth. In Russia, the term 'Zhemanikha' was coined to describe ridiculously affected aristocratic women, who emphasized their preference for French literature and manners.[41] Further down the prestige scale girls never stopped being told that they should not seem too learned, for fear of putting off suitors, and even established women intellectuals sometimes felt they needed to stress their ability to do domestic tasks, lest their unnatural interest in scholarship undermine their claim to be women.[42] Still, the salon, a mixed-sex or all-woman artistic or intellectual gathering that meets in a private home, has never, since then, disappeared from European cultural life.

Freemasonry

Freemasonry, that quintessentially eighteenth-century institution, played an unusual role in the development of mixed-sex sociability. It also provides evidence of the way – just as Habermas predicted – sociability could shade into politics. Fairly consistent themes of Freemasonry were (and, to a degree, still are) the championing of 'Reason'; a broad commitment to religious toleration; a high-minded conception of friendship; egalitarianism within the lodge (hence the iconic phrase 'all brothers meet upon the level'); and a tendency to replace notions of inherited sin with a somewhat mystical, this-worldly utopianism and humanitarianism. In Britain, where the movement began, it was not at all hospitable to women. However, it looked quite different on the continent, especially in the Netherlands and France. Beginning as early as the 1740s, the tolerant, mystical and relatively egalitarian ethos of Freemasonry led some lodges to open their doors to women. The earliest lodge known to have initiated women (ca. 1751) was in the Hague, and the membership included both the wives of male Freemasons and actresses from the local Comédie-Française. For some decades integration occurred rather discreetly however, and most of the growth, at least in France, seems to have occurred in the 1770s and 80s. By the time of the Revolution of 1789 there were at least thirty lodges of adoption (the name for mixed-sex lodges) in France, and at least six in Paris alone and hundreds of women had been initiated into Freemasonry.

What did this rather odd, occult movement have to offer to women? Undoubtedly some were drawn to the emphasis on virtue and egalitarian friendship both with other women and with men. The inclusion of actresses in some of the early mixed-sex lodges was an especially emotive emblem of women 'meeting upon the level'. Freemasonry's larger vision, which emphasized peace and reconciliation between warring factions, particularly warring religions, took up some of the eirenic themes so popular with radicals from the later seventeenth century on (see Chapter 6). Women were also drawn to the doctrinal and ritualistic side of Freemasonry. Adoptive Freemasonry included women in its rites (and, as time went on, allowed them to officiate), but its decidedly eclectic, opportunistic and non-literal attitude towards holy texts offered numerous opportunities for rethinking problematic doctrines. So, for example, some Freemasons were not only prepared to rethink original sin, but actually to perform radically alternative versions of the story of the Fall that exonerated women. In some eighteenth-century Masonic rituals women initiates re-enacted the eating of the apple from the Tree of Knowledge, but only after the seeds had been removed. The accompanying catechism made it clear that the seeds had constituted the evil. In effect this ritual released women from responsibility for Eve's sin, but left them in the role of transmitters of Wisdom and Knowledge, an old Kabbalistic and mystical trope. In other Masonic rituals women were urged to 'slay the serpent', thus symbolically purging the world of evil, the opposite of what Eve was alleged to have done. By the 1770s women were voting on key issues of lodge governance and performing their own rituals, and the decision to admit women was being represented as akin to 'Light [being] finally introduced into spaces that were occupied by shadows'.[43] This kind of inclusion, which redefined women as active citizens within a mystical republic of Virtue, almost certainly helped pave the way for women's participation in the republican clubs of the revolutionary era, and it may not be coincidental that some of the most active women's clubs come from areas where there was already a strong presence of lodges of adoption (see Chapter 9).

Evidence of eighteenth-century women's attraction to Freemasonry is still turning up. In Portugal the movement was extremely popular in the 1730s and 40s, with 312 known lodges before 1738 (Pope Clement XII excommunicated Freemasons in that year, and the movement consequently went underground on the Iberian peninsula). It is not clear whether any of these lodges initiated women. But the first Portuguese feminist novel of the eighteenth century, Teresa Margarida da Silva e Orta's *Aventuras de Diófanes* (The Adventures of Diofanes) (1752) is full of Masonic elements, including a powerful and theatrical heroine, a female mage who represents the two faces of the eternal feminine, a utopian republic, and a woman's initiation into a secret society devoted to esoteric and Kabbalistic knowledge and to the pursuit of Virtue.[44] In Poland, the noblewoman and holder of theatrical salons, Anna Potocka née Ossolińska, was also founder in 1768 of a lodge of adoption called the 'Virtuous Sarmation'[45] and an important Masonic activist. And in late eighteenth- and early nineteenth-century Russia, the noblewoman and memoirist Anna Labzina, who had a strong spiritual and intellectual interest in the problem of human sin, forged her own unique Masonic spirituality through her connection to the Dying Sphinx lodge in St. Petersburg.[46]

Hammams and public gardens

When Lady Mary Wortley Montagu wrote that the Turkish *hammam* or bath-house was '. . . the women's coffee house, where all the news of the world is told . . .' she was invoking, *avant la lettre*, one of the iconic civil society institutions of the Habermasian public sphere. Montagu was, presumably, acquainted, at least by repute, both with English and Ottoman coffee houses (neither were welcoming to women), and she was clearly trying to convey the *hammam*'s centrality to the 'public sphere' of Ottoman women. Of course, Montagu also implied that women spent a good deal of their time lounging about in an unclad state, gossiping and having their hair done, and it has proved difficult to recover a more high-minded picture of the kinds of things that went on there.[47] We do know that the dressing room (*camekân*) of the *hammam* was a prime venue for musical and theatrical performance, as well as for life-cycle celebrations, that female herbalists and medical practitioners set up there, and that it was central to deal-making around marriage and property-sales, and probably other kinds of buying and selling – all major arenas of influence for women. Some women even had it put into their marriage contracts that their husbands could not forbid them to go to the *hammam*. The *hammams* had another trait that Habermas and others often fasten upon in relation to eighteenth-century male sociability in western Europe: they were, at least to some extent, cross-class in character, though the implications of this have been relatively little theorized in the Ottoman context. As with coffee houses, the reputation of a particular *hammam* was closely tied to the woman at the top: the bathhouse manageress, who often was also the owner (bathhouse ownership was a common form of women's investment in the eighteenth century) and many of these manageress/owners were clearly major social and cultural entrepreneurs not very different from some *salonnières*.

One of the newer social and cultural venues of the eighteenth century, especially in Istanbul, were the public parks and gardens, many of them former palace gardens recently given over to the public. These became hugely popular, and, like parks in western Europe (mostly established somewhat later), they had a measurable effect upon practices of public sociability. Almost all accounts of Stambouli parks and gardens, as well as numerous pictures, emphasize the sheer variety, in class, gender and religious terms, of the crowds who frequented them. They also became venues for cultural activity (dance, music, storytelling) as well as for conspicuous sartorial display (Plate 1). Contemporary images (not to mention frequent snorts of disapproval from clerics) show that women were experimenting with a variety of new outdoor dress-styles: including daring décolletage or thin muslin tops that left almost nothing to the imagination, 'ethnic' clothes (that is, styles associated with other religious groups) and various kinds of head-gear, including flimsy, see-through veils. While most park sociability continued to be single-sex (men congregating in some areas, women in others), both men and women also used these new public spaces to flirt and otherwise flout the rules against mixed-sex sociability.

This in turn inspired a stream of edicts and prosecutions aimed at controlling the mixing of the sexes and of women from different religious communities. These included periodic bans on women visiting certain gardens, only allowing women to leave their homes on certain days of the week (rather common in Ottoman cities); and sumptuary rules, mostly aimed at ensuring that *dhimmi* (non-Muslims) did not wear clothes that would make people mistake them for Muslims, but also (as in one edict from 1760) forbidding 'shameless [Muslim] women' from wearing provocative fashions that made them look too much like Christians.[48] As noted earlier, we have very few written sources from Ottoman women from this period, and none that reflect upon their condition, so we must tread carefully in interpreting their response. On the other hand, it is hard to imagine women submitting easily and without a good deal of grumbling to these heavy-handed attempts to control when and where they socialized and what they wore. Mobility and sartorial issues like these, perhaps combined with unhappiness over the inferior quality of the separate and unequal public accommodation sometimes offered to women, as well as (of course) women's activities in the law-courts, are all places to look for a break in the façade of total acceptance and passivity that is so often the superficial picture one is given of early modern Ottoman women.[49] After all, regimes seldom bother promulgating edicts or passing laws of this kind unless someone is doing something the authorities view as potentially subversive.

Ironically, one group that had no difficulty convincing themselves that feminism (or something very like it) was on the march among Ottoman women was conservative men. The conservative backlash in the early 1730s against Grand Vizier Ibrahim Pasha's liberalizing policies, which had included making entertainment parks more accessible to women and (or so it was claimed) greater tolerance for gender-mixing, asserted that his reforms had poisoned relations between husbands and wives and encouraged wives to steal money from their husbands and demand divorces (which brow-beaten *kadis* supposedly keeled over and gave them). Supposedly it had also caused an epidemic of illicit sexual relations.[50] These were, of course, precisely the kinds of criticisms Christian European conservatives were trotting out at almost the same time about the slippery slope of egalitarian feminism; indeed these anxieties still have resonance among religious conservatives to this day.

THE STATE: CONFRONTATION AND COLLUSION

Neighbourhood women confront the state

In 1697 Margaret Mortimer, a middle-class London widow, was the victim, along with about twenty others, of a fire that burned down Derby Court in Westminster.[51] After the fire the group successfully applied for official permission to have their designees gather charitable contributions on their behalf – only to have the trustees of the charity botch the collection and abscond with the money. In the face of this double catastrophe, Widow Mortimer and her neighbours put in a petition to the House of Commons for redress. They also probably hired a lobbyist to deliver the petition first to the Lord Chancellor and then to the House of Commons (no doubt it helped that the Houses of Parliament were a short walk from Derby Court). And Mortimer, who had emerged as the main spokesperson for the group, took advantage of the thriving press in the capital city to write up and publish the facts of the case. The pamphlet she wrote makes it clear that she had all along been one of the prime movers in this local action: 'I did take the names of all the Trustees [of the charity]'; 'I did leave written Summon's [sic] at each Trustees House', 'I prevailed with Dr Oldys to give them a meeting'; 'I drew up a Writing, that if the Major part of the sufferers would join me in an humble Petition to my Lord Chancellor, I hoped his Lordship would grant us some Relief'; and so on. Widow Mortimer possessed confidence, connections, a sense of how the system worked and the ability to lead. So much so that she published at least two additional pamphlets addressed, again, to Parliament, recommending the setting up of a national board of charitable collections so that what had befallen her and her neighbours would not happen to other people in distress. This is a classic case of the way an emergency could license a very extensive female role – in this case including lobbying the national government for a significant administrative change.

Fifty years later, in 1750, a rumour swept through Paris that the police were abducting children, perhaps for transportation to the colonies; perhaps for more nefarious purposes. The most sensationalistic version of the rumour – that some prince or princess desired to bathe in human blood as a cure for leprosy or some similarly distasteful disease – was a figment of some people's overheated imaginations. However, it *was* true that the Paris police had recently grown unusually zealous in picking up young people they accused of being vagrants. And there is evidence that some mothers had had to 'buy back' their offspring from gaol (probably the police were running some kind of extortion racket). In May of that year the anxiety and resentment turned violent. The first riot, in the rue des Nonnains d'Hyères on the evening of May 16, was touched off when a woman 'holding a child by the hand', verb-ally assaulted a passing group of archers and a constable, exclaiming loudly that 'these rascals were only looking for a chance to abduct people's children'. A brawl ensued, the archers had to be rescued by the Watch, and one person died. Several days later, anger blazed up again into at least six different con-flagrations, in one of which a constable named Labbé was chased by a large crowd, cornered, and finally beaten and stoned to death, after which his bloody corpse was dragged victoriously about the streets. Women were quite prominent in these disturbances; indeed, some later commentators claimed that the whole uprising was instigated by women who had had their children taken or were worried they would be. As one man remarked, 'Even in the animal kingdom the mildest female becomes ferocious, wild and completely unrecognizable in defence of her young.'[52]

Some Parisians would undoubtedly have felt more comfortable if all politicized women could be represented as working 'in defence of their young', an image that falls squarely within the purview of women's special corporate interests and expertise. However, women's political action was not always so easy to categorize. The Parisian fishwives (*poissardes*), who soon entered, albeit only indirectly, into this story, are a case in point. Since medieval times they had enjoyed special royal favour, and by the early modern period this had developed into annual ritual meetings with the king during which they would toast him and speak to him candidly about the welfare of his subjects.

As a result the fishwives became known for their loud and uncompromising political pronouncements, and the *poissarde* became a recognizable oral and literary genre featuring frank language about political and other issues, exaggerated versions of popular oral sayings, deliberate use of lower-class mispronunciations and street argot, and a comic adopting of a lower-class woman's supposed point of view. According to Carla Hesse, 'The market women of Paris . . . acquired a kind of popular political legitimacy and a privilege to free political speech enjoyed by no other group in French society under the Old Regime.'[53] So it is not surprising that only a few days before the riots of May 1750 broke out, with the capital seething with poisonous rumour, someone in a tavern was overheard to say: 'our women of Les Halles [where the fish market was] will all get together and go to Versailles to dethrone the King and tear his eyes out, then they will come back to Paris and kill the Lieutenants of Police and Crime . . .'[54] In the event nothing this revolutionary occurred (though it is oddly prescient of the Women's March to Versailles in October of 1789). Rather, when things calmed down, the government dealt with the situation in the customary way. Several men were executed for their roles in the riots (usually it was men who were punished for participating in riots, even ones that women instigated) but there was no chance of identifying or punishing the hordes of ordinary women and men who had also taken part. Efforts were also made to suppress subversive speech, like the tavern remark about dethroning the king, cited above, which we know about because it turned up in a spy report. And the police somewhat modified their arrest procedures. These mothers' interventions, clearly reliant upon the doctrine of emergency powers (what could be more compelling than attacks upon their children?) were, in the end, met with appeasement. In that sense these political actions worked.

Women and war

Between the first third of the sixteenth and the early eighteenth century there was an approximately ten-fold growth in the size of Europe's armies, along with a vast increase in weapons expenditure, battleships, barracks, and all the other accoutrements of war. The 'Military Revolution', as it is often called, was accompanied both by higher taxes, and by a significant expansion in the size, scope, and power of state bureaucracies. There were, of course, social consequences as well. During the long eighteenth century (from the 1690s through the Napoleonic Wars) perhaps sixteen million people died in combat in Europe and its colonies, and many more perished from the epidemic diseases that were rife in all militaries.[55] Eighteenth-century war-making inhibited young people's ability to form families, both because of the high death rate among young men and because so many militaries refused soldiers the right to marry (see Chapter 2). It caused severe refugee problems, especially in eastern Europe and in and around the Balkans. And it spread killer diseases: the bubonic plague epidemic of 1768–71, which killed 120,000 people in Russia alone, was one of many introduced by soldiers on the march. The military revolution also created a large class of men and women – soldiers, their female kin and their children, plus refugees – who were marginalized, sexually suspect, often homeless, and heavily reliant on charity.[56]

Naturally all this affected war's popularity. Beginnings of wars, then as now, were often accompanied by a burst of popular enthusiasm, but this tended to wane quickly as the casualties, the destruction, and the tax demands increased, the epidemics began, the bands of begging women and children swelled, and the recruiting parties stepped up their activities. Forced conscription was a particular source of resentment, and for obvious reasons it tended to bring out women (conscriptable men generally fled). Here is a member of an English navy press gang describing a foray, in the mid-eighteenth century, to a port town in search of victims:

> We secured 17 of them [impressed men], and guarding them along the streets, several hundreds of old men, women, and boys, flocked after us, well provided with stones and brickbats, and commenced a general attack; but not wishing to hurt them, we fired our pistols over their heads, in order to deter them from further outrage; but the women proved very daring, and followed us down to low water mark, being almost up to the knees in mud.[57]

Recruitment and conscription drives all over Europe and the Ottoman Empire met public hostility, and the simmering opposition to high prices, corruption, tax hikes and the levees of sons and husbands not infrequently degenerated into local riots and even full-scale revolts. Troops who overstayed their welcome could also come in for popular attacks. An account from eighteenth-century Aleppo notes that 'during the war with Nader Shah [mid-eighteenth century], certain troops, who on their way to the frontiers halted some days in the city, refusing to quit their quarters at the appointed time, were fairly driven out by a mob of women, armed with distaffs and stones'.[58]

Many people today like to imagine that women are intrinsically less warlike than men. This view was common in the early modern period as well. From at least the seventeenth century, as we have seen, dissident religious sects, including Anabaptists, Quakers, some Pietist groups (most notably, the Moravians), and some Russian Old Believers had linked pacifism in various ways to feminist and socially egalitarian beliefs or practices (see Chapter 6). Several of the Enlightenment philosophes, most notably Voltaire, also combined opposition to most wars with a fairly thoroughgoing feminism. It might have been expected that this pairing would flourish and develop some practical political expression in the years that followed, especially as more and more women broke into print. Certainly there were some women who worked this vein. The most interesting was Madame de Beaumer, editor, from 1761 to 1763, of the Paris-based *Journal des Dames*. Under de Beaumer's leadership the *Journal* began calling for an end to all wars, celebrating famous women, deploring male oppression, recommending republics over monarchies – partly on the surely specious grounds that republics were less militaristic – and claiming that the whole world was on the brink of a feminist millennium. De Beaumer was unusually forthright about her pacifism – too forthright, as it turned out – and she had, depending upon your view, either a brilliant or a dismal sense of timing. The Seven Years' War (1756–63) was in its final throes, it had gone badly for France, and it was proving a major embarrassment for the already unpopular regime of Louis XV. The censors, who had been caught napping, were outraged by de Beaumer's effrontery and she stayed out of prison only because, like many radical publishers, she had aristocratic protectors. Thwarted there, the censors first interfered with the content of the journal, then suspended publication, and finally, in 1763, refused de Beaumer permission to publish at all unless she would agree to turn the journal into a fashion magazine (she refused). In the end, ill, exhausted and heavily in debt, she admitted defeat, passed the paper on to a less incendiary colleague, and moved to the Netherlands, where she died three years later in 1766.[59]

Female patriots

While there was certainly hatred of war, particularly from those who suffered at its hands, most public pronouncements by women (with a few notable exceptions like de Beaumer) suggest vocal support for it. Eighteenth-century wars had diverse causes: the push for territory, both in Europe and abroad; defence against other nations' attacks; dynastic and succession disputes; competition for trade; tension over religion; independence and proto-nationalist struggles; and, late in the century, efforts both to propagate and to resist revolutionary attacks on monarchy and other *ancien régime* institutions.

But, whatever the pretext, women soon discovered that the atmosphere of heightened alertness, busy preparation, cross-gender solidarity, sacrificial rhetoric and state-approved xenophobia (and sometimes outright racism) that tended to accompany war was particularly conducive to an expansion of women's role. Wartime created the ideal environment for a wide variety of necessitarian arguments, many of which took up the claim, dating from classical antiquity, that women needed to bolster men's fighting spirit by demonstrating their own superior valour and capacity for sacrifice. Early modern war propaganda was replete with images of martial goddesses, and it was not just feminists who searched for warrior princesses in the chronicles or oral lore of the Visigoths, Celts, Britons, Picts, Anglo-Saxons, Romans, Etruscans, Greeks, Vikings, Huns, Scythians, and so on. Some of this may have inspired some of the several score women who donned men's attire and formally enlisted in one or another military in the century or so prior to the French Revolution – women soldiers would become far commoner after 1789 – though it is notoriously difficult to untangle the motives of individual women combatants.[60] Allusions to war goddesses, Spartan mothers, and the like, certainly helped to legitimate some very discomfiting female displays, at least when seen from a soldier's perspective. In 1707 in Boston, in the Massachusetts Bay Colony, crowds of women shamed soldiers returning from the abortive siege of Port Royal, Nova Scotia (we are in the War of Spanish Succession) by presenting some of them with a wooden sword – to replace their real ones, which they had not used to sufficient purpose – and threatening to drench them with their chamber-pots ('Is yo[u]r piss-pot charg'd neighbor? So-ho, souse the cowards').[61]

Obviously the last was not the sort of patriotism respectable women were likely to want to be associated with, and the trend over the course of the eighteenth century was for women's public patriotic expressions to become much more respectable, more decorous, and a great deal more common. In time, and especially during and after the revolutionary climacteric, they would come to form an important part of the ideological apparatus of the military state. Patriotic societies and displays also turned into an extremely important venue for women acting politically. This process has been particularly well studied for Britain where, from at least the 1740s, women had become deeply involved in celebrations and adulation of military heroes, as in the cult of Admiral Vernon, the hero of Porto Bello. By at least the 1750s women were contributing heavily both to patriotic associations and soldiers' and sailors' charities. By the later eighteenth century they were organizing subscriptions and campaigns to clothe soldiers, making flags and banners (usually presented publicly to the soldiers in large open-air ceremonies, which could include a woman addressing the crowd), and establishing themselves as patriotic poets. They also injected some traditional feminine (and potentially feminist) themes into patriotic discourse, including an emphasis on ancient Anglo-Saxon women warriors, and a tendency to argue, as the English poet Anna Seward did in her famous 'Elegy on Captain Cook' (1780), that female grieving for the loss of husbands and sons in war was the most authentic expression of national loss.[62]

Just as some women plighted their troth to established states, others devoted themselves to trying to unseat them. Even before the era of revolutions (usually thought of as the final quarter of the eighteenth century) the participation of women in political riots and rebellions was conspicuously high. During the Fronde (1648–53) in France, a revolt that sought to limit monarchical power, noblewomen as well as women of the people had been extraordinarily active, as politicians, military leaders, neighbourhood rabble-rousers, and at the barricades.[63] In the Netherlands women had been heavily involved in Orangist (which usually meant pro-war) demonstrations and riots in 1653 and 1672; they would be again in 1747 and in the 1780s.[64] Various sixteenth- and seventeenth-century Hungarian or Slovak women, among them the famous noblewoman warrior, Maria Széchny, resisted the Austrian or Ottoman armies.[65] And there were probably women members of *hajduk* bands, those irregular Balkan bandit groups that harried both the Ottoman and the Habsburg forces and made life miserable for travellers, because the tradition of the Balkan sworn virgin made it politically acceptable for some women to adopt life-long male dress and social roles.[66] A number of women were involved in the Jacobite rising of 1745, primarily in raising troops, though in a couple of cases leading them. There were also several women leaders of anti-colonial rebellions including Josefa Gabriela Silang (1731–1763) of the Philippines who, in 1762, inherited the leadership of an anti-Spanish revolt when her husband was assassinated. The forces she was leading were defeated in battle, and she was captured and executed along with about a hundred of her followers.[67] Back in Europe proper, the Polish Revolt of the Confederation of the Bar (1768) was conceived by Princess Anna Jabłonowska and launched from her country estate. She later funded it and sent soldiers. And Ottoman women were involved in several insurrectionary street actions in the eighteenth century, including the Aleppine revolt of 1775 which drove out the sitting governor.[68] These feminine insurrectionary activities would be dwarfed by the events that followed 1789.

Women, war and the origins of the welfare state

War and militaries put heavy new burdens on both men and women in the seventeenth and eighteenth centuries. It also gave women, in particular, a new kind of claim on the military state. Everywhere we find women putting pressure on militaries, over the drafting of sons or husbands, officer graft, compensation for the loss of a male wage-earner through death or disability, problems over pay, promotions for their male kin, widows' benefits, military confiscations and requisitions, and theft or rape by soldiers. They also tried to use the military command structure to cope with other kinds of problems, such as spousal abandonment, alcoholism or non-support, or domestic violence. Even rebel armies found themselves responding to petitions from women.

VOICES FROM THE PAST 8.1

Women petition the military

The English Royal Navy: a mentally ill husband (1702)

This woman's profoundly depressed and suicidal husband had been put off his boat, HMS Neptune, and into sick-quarters. Then it was decided that he was unlikely to recover so he was provisionally discharged. Mrs. Moody made unsuccessful attempts to get him into a hospital in London. Then she petitioned the Navy in person for money to bring her husband up to Newcastle so that his family could take care of him. England was at this point just a few months into the War of Spanish Succession. The Commissioners agreed to her request.

Wed. 26 August 1702

The Wife of Francis Moody late belonging to the [ship] Neptune and sent from sickquarters at Portsmouth for Melancholy, was refused to be taken into the Hospitals at London, and being subsisted at 2 shillings per diem to this Day in Order to his Cure at home, the Woman desiring the Board to allow her something for the charge of carrying him to Newcastle where they have Relations, there will take Care of him.

Resolved that he be allowed the said 20d, giving a Rec[eip]t to the Treas[urer] for the same, as in the case of 2s per diem while in the Hospital.

Source: National Archives at Kew, ADM 99/2 Royal Navy, Commissioners of Sick and Wounded.

A widow tries to safeguard her property in the midst of a revolt (1705)

In 1705, the town of Astrakhan, at the mouth of the Volga River in Russia, raised a revolt against Peter I's demands for more soldiers and higher taxes. At one point the rebels formed a provisional local government that, among other things, ordered the redistribution of property belonging to local landholders loyal to the tsar. This petition came from the widow Anna

Gavrilova, probably as soon as the news spread around the city that property would be redistributed. It seems that Gavrilova was afraid that her own land would be taken away. It is written on a small scrap of paper without a date or signature (Gavrilova may well have been illiterate and had someone else write the petition). It was clearly written in haste and it is in a colloquial style that probably closely mimics Gavrilova's own way of speaking.

> Fair Judges, Messrs. Iakov Ivanovich, Gavrili Larionovich, Antip Ermolaevich and all the guards and troops I [am] the poor widow, Anna Gavrilova, daughter of the garden, of the cabbage and the pepper. You found it within yourselves, did you not? to spare [others] their garden plots? Gimme the same – a poor lady – take pity, so I can feed myself or, if only to protect your own health and honor your ancestral fathers! Sirs, be gentle, take pity!

Source: Quoted in N.B. Golikova, *Astrakhanskoe vosstanie 1705–1706* (The Astrakhan Uprising of 1705–1706) (Moscow: Moscow University Press, 1975), 156–7. Thanks to Anya Zilberstein for providing the translation.

One of the key developments of the eighteenth century was the rise, in some states, of basic social welfare entitlements for soldiers and sailors and, at least some of the time, for their kin.[69] These were the result of sustained campaigns, in which women played a major part. The wives of officers mobilized their connections endlessly and often with considerable skill. Women without many connections showed up in force, usually with their children, intent on shaming the state into meeting their needs. In the seventeenth century, Swedish military widows succeeded in winning the rights to special land grants; and English naval widows also gained some limited widows' bounties.[70] Because states were often slow to pay, not just pensions but basic military wages, women often got involved in noisy and sometimes violent altercations. There were already demonstrations over pay and stipends for the families of English navy sailors by the 1660s, when, during the Second Anglo-Dutch war, the diarist Samuel Pepys, then a Navy bureaucrat, encountered numerous women's demonstrations, including one by 'above 300 [women]', wives of prisoners of war in Holland, '[who] lay clamouring and swearing and cursing us . . . laying down the condition of their families and what they have done and suffered for the King, and how ill they are used by us'.[71] By the late seventeenth century, officers' widows were clubbing together to pay parliamentary lobbyists to push money Bills; and, in the early eighteenth century, women formed a conspicuous part of demonstrations over pay and officer graft in front of the English Houses of Parliament. Similar demonstrations, by 'distressed seamen and their wives and children' occurred in Copenhagen in 1718.[72] Women loudly emphasized the fact that they and their children were starving while their men sacrificed (or had already sacrificed) their lives for the state. Bands of begging soldiers' wives were a familiar feature of war: we can imagine that some of this begging was very pointed indeed.[73]

The welfare state as we know it today was still far in the distance, but we can already see localities and national states trying to plot a response. Some regimental commanders started allowing the homeless wives of soldiers to 'camp' in the barracks when the regiment was out on campaign. In the early eighteenth century, Peter the Great of Russia began requiring Orthodox convents to offer nursing and other services to disabled or impoverished veterans and their wives and orphans, and we may be sure that this, too, was the result of popular pressure.[74] Britain increased its widows' pension system and partially rationalized hospital care for disabled soldiers and navy sailors. Prussia developed a rather extensive system of 'garrison schools' and orphanages.[75] Over time most Christian European states and the Ottoman Empire came to offer benefits to soldiers and their kin, though it took until the nineteenth century in some places. Intermittent and inadequate as they were, these various measures clearly improved women's lives, and certainly they came in response to women's individual and collective agitation. They also had decidedly equivocal implications: not only were they based upon a formula of first taking away most women's options and then representing them as, in effect, wards of the state, but they tended to focus attention on the struggle for public entitlements, to the exclusion of other kinds of political rights. Nevertheless this was an important early arena for women's public activism, and a key part of the rise of modern conceptions of the state.

PRIVATE VOLUNTARISM

Charities and empowerment

Virtuous women were supposed to be charitable, and charity prudently deployed could significantly enhance a woman's power both within and outside her family. Older women were often particularly prominent in this regard. In the Ottoman Empire the older woman who devoted her declining years to acts of piety and charity was an established social type, who enjoyed considerable standing in the community. Sometimes she dispensed individual charity; though a goodly number of these women also set up special charitable foundations on behalf of the neighbourhood poor, widows, their children, or their present or former slaves.[76] It is easier to be generous if you have something to give away, but across Europe and the Middle East many relatively poor people also routinely engaged in individual charitable acts, often making personal sacrifices to do so. And while they may not have left many marks in the historical record, such people must have been an important part of local support networks, as well as the jockeying for power and influence within poor communities. Sometimes they turned themselves into veritable local saints, like the remarkable Matrona Naumovna Popova (1769–1851) of Zakonsk, in Russia, a poverty-stricken orphan who began sheltering pilgrims and the poor and caring for the sick, orphans and foundlings. Her piety and selflessness gradually acquired Popova a following and the esteem even of the highest ecclesiastics.[77]

One of the most visible kinds of 'good works' in rural areas consisted of noble or propertied women offering free medical care to local peasants, who might or might not be their own tenants or serfs. Some women accumulated considerable local reputations as a result of such activities. When the pious and charitable noblewoman Madam Iakovleva, of the Ural Mountains in Russia, died in around 1771, there was an outpouring of mass mourning. Her body was paraded about the town; inmates in the local prison where she often made charitable visits fainted and wept aloud; and crowds of wailing beggars ringed the family's home declaiming 'Forgive us, our nurturer and mother! . . . You have abandoned us poor folk, left us orphaned!'[78] Clearly some charitable women became very significant local celebrities. From the later seventeenth century, women who sought this kind of role had additional encouragement in the form of handbooks of 'charitable medicine for ladies' like the one published in 1675 by Madame Fouquet (Marie de Maupeou), wife of the French controller general. In the ensuing seventy-five years the book went into dozens of editions in French, Italian, Portuguese and Spanish.[79] Some of these purchasers probably got it for household use; nevertheless, the publication history of this book alone suggests that there were thousands, perhaps tens of thousands, of literate (which probably means middle-class or higher) women in the late seventeenth or eighteenth century who fancied the idea of becoming charitable healers.

Women had long used charity to promote their religious views (see Chapter 6), and they continued to do so in the eighteenth century. However, there was a growing tendency to form charities that melded religious and secular objectives. Many eighteenth-century women took up charity school work: these institutions' remit was to teach saleable skills (almost always in textiles) to poor young girls and women while simultaneously subjecting them to a strong dose of the prevailing religion, whatever it was. These schools were supposed to keep women off the charity rolls, enhance their marriage prospects, give them an alternative to prostitution, and teach them patient acceptance of the station to which God had assigned them. In the mid-eighteenth century, Rosa Govona managed just such a poor house in her hometown in Piedmont (now part of Northern Italy), with such success that she was made the first superintendent of a new spinning school/workhouse (founded 1755) in Turin, where she employed destitute girls and young women as spinners, weavers and makers of gloves, stockings and ribbons. She or her successors soon opened a number of satellite schools, which were enthusiastically promoted as being able fully to sustain themselves on the profits of their inmates' labour. They were also represented as the 'modern' solution to the perverse disincentives of traditional charity. In reality the schools were receiving preferential treatment in the awarding of military contracts and were also given exemption from guild regulations that controlled the quality of the product and the pay and treatment of the workforce. Moreover, they enjoyed a huge competitive advantage because they ran on what was essentially slave labour: inmates were forced to work for nothing, the buildings in which they lived and worked were set up like prisons, and they were not allowed to leave either to take up another job or marry.[80] In England, middle-class women lobbied to be able to participate in local charities that served women, and there are several examples of 'ladies' committees' either taking over their management entirely or doing the day-to-day direction. Their arguments were an amalgam of 'corporatism' and domestic feminism. In the 1780s a group of middle-class women from York took over the local charity school for girls, partly on the grounds that they were better qualified than men to deploy poorer women's labour and teach them virtue. Their first act was to dismiss the old Master, as a man 'unfit for the trust reposed in him'.[81] Like Rosa Govona's poor houses, the York institution was essentially a factory, and the women who ran it were as entrepreneurial as any manufacturer.[82]

Women's charitable endeavours often aimed oblique attacks at the way men (or the world) treated women. In Chapter 4 we spoke about women's involvement in charities that aimed to help mothers with children – especially charities that encouraged breast-feeding or smallpox inoculation, that set up orphanages, or that were otherwise intended to encourage the survival of babies. Women (and not just women who were mothers) also attracted the attention of the charitable. The homes for the *malmaritate* (unhappily married) in Italy are good examples of this: at least initially, they sheltered battered women as well as women who were at risk in other ways.[83] Noblewomen dispensed much charity to other women of gentle birth brought down in the world by the 'great indiscretions' of their husbands, and the begging letters found in large numbers in some elite women's family papers regularly rehearse this theme.[84] The frequent bequests from all over Europe and the Middle East to feed, clothe or house old women (and sometimes 'old maidens', or spinsters) were, if nothing else, a rebuke to a world that demonstrably did not provide adequately for such women. Marriage charities were also important: the *valide sultan* (mother of the sultan) Kösem was well known for seeking out poor orphan girls and endowing them with a *mehr*, a home and furnishings; and women of all religious persuasions, across both Christian Europe and the Ottoman Empire, bequeathed money to provide dowries for poor women, including special funds for noble girls whose families had come down in the world.[85] Women were also much involved in the various hospitals and homes for penitent prostitutes, transparently a bid to control the sexual habits of men – and their capacity to infect their wives with venereal disease – by containing the sexuality of less respectable women (some of the dowry funds, which aimed to get women into lawful marriage rather than be forced to rely on prostitution, served a complementary purpose).[86]

Not all charities were top-down, and not all women's organizations were composed only of middle-class or elite women. A census done in 1803 of English friendly societies found extensive involvement of textile workers in female friendly societies (these were essentially member-run insurance schemes that provided sick pay or burial expenses out of membership dues). In Lancashire, Middlesex and Devon, three important textile-producing areas, there were 193 such organizations with well over sixteen thousand members. Most of these organizations apparently dated from the final decades of the eighteenth century.[87] Friendly-society-like organizations could also be found in some early modern Ottoman cities, where African women, both slave and free, had a complex and quite politicized associational life. The organizations these women founded (often, at the time, called lodges; later sometimes called Negro Associations) were found in Istanbul, Smyrna (now Izmir) and probably some other Ottoman towns, and were an amalgam of charity, friendly society, support network, political organization, guild, refuge and religious cult. Most of the evidence about them comes from the early nineteenth century, though it is pretty clear that they were already established by then; indeed there is some evidence for festival activity by displaced Africans as early as the sixteenth century. The lodges included both freed persons and slaves of African origin, and were invariably headed by a former slave-woman called a *kolbaşı* who held her position for life. It was the responsibility of the *kolbaşı* to purchase the freedom of black slaves who were maltreated by their masters, put up unemployed or sick freed women, and find work and arrange marriages for refugees and members. Each *kolbaşı* was also the head of a religious cult or lodge that included a variety of African-derived and perhaps Sufi elements. The lodges clearly were 'civic' entities. The members, and especially the leaders, negotiated with owners and sometimes with the authorities; and they also staged very public outdoor celebrations, usually in May of each year, that included dancing, singing, other ritual activity and special foods. Presumably these were, at least partly, fundraisers for the various lodges, and it seems likely that the eighteenth-century expansion of park activity and entertainment enhanced their success (in the nineteenth century they blossomed into major public spectacles, attended by thousands). As might be expected, the *kolbaşı* and lodges were unpopular with slave-owners because they were said to make slaves unreliable (meaning, of course, that they gave abused slaves a means of escape), and with the authorities because of the pagan elements evident in their religious practice. Though the societies were never closed down, there are several cases of *kolbaşı* being exiled to other cities (usually Bursa on the Anatolian coast). A case from 1804 involved a *kolbaşı* named Saliha and four other black women who were accused of 'assemb[ling] forty or fifty black females and commit[ting] shameful acts in Üsküdar [a suburb of Istanbul]' (presumably these were rites that struck the authorities as polytheistic). A *kolbaşı* who went by her African name, Tunbuti, was exiled in 1817 for 'disobedience to the authorities' (unfortunately we have no idea what the circumstances were).[88] The eighteenth-century history of these organizations is tantalizingly difficult to uncover, but they do greatly widen our sense of the spectrum of possibilities for Ottoman women's public visibility and politicization.

AFFAIRS OF STATE

Removing women's right to vote

In a number of medieval and renaissance polities women (though almost exclusively propertied widows, and usually noblewomen) had held the right to a vote at the parish, village, town and national level, because they were seen as representing their family's or deceased husband's or father's interests, because property itself conveyed deliberative rights, or some combination of these two principles. However, during the seventeenth through the early nineteenth century, often thought of as the seed-bed of modern conceptions of politics, these rights (which we must stress were only available to a small percentage of women) largely disappeared, and were in some cases explicitly legislated away. Sweden is instructive in this regard. After 1718 significant amounts of power were transferred from the monarchy to the Riksdag (deliberative assembly) and elections became more significant, because they translated into real power for the winners. Initially, presumably reflecting medieval practice, propertied widows were permitted to vote in church elections, civic elections (for town councils and mayors) and even national elections for Riksdag members. Between 1726 and 1742 widows participated in about fifty-three per cent of mayoral elections, and the percentage actually increased to about seventy-eight per cent from 1743 to 1757. In 1758, however, a confusingly worded decree probably intended to stop proxy-voting in mayoral elections was seized upon by town councils to stop women voting in them and this had a knock-on effect on other kinds of electoral contests. Until 1757 propertied widows had participated in all Riksdag (national) elections, but their involvement dramatically declined after 1758, apparently due to a combination of women being actively refused the right to vote (there are several documented cases of this), and some women simply quietly refraining from doing so due, one presumes, to more diffuse kinds of pressure. The burgher corporations (the all-male body of townsmen of the higher tax-brackets) now began searching high and low for new rationales for excluding women altogether from the civil franchise. Popular arguments around 1758 were: that widows had not taken the burgher oath, that the deceased men the widows claimed to be representing 'bear no association with the now living burghership'; that no one who could not themselves serve in office should be able to vote; that no other country allowed women the vote; and that allowing widows to vote would encourage them to try to participate in other public deliberations, which would 'cause great disorder and less taciturn conduct among the public'. In 1772, a national decree finally excluded all burgher widows from voting in Riksdag elections.[89] It proved generally to be the case in Europe that, as civic rights were extended to more men and the notion of citizenship became more individualistic, women tended to be explicitly excluded (see Chapter 9).

Women and political power

Early modern women did occasionally take public note of the fact that they did not have very many political rights. During the mid-seventeenth-century English Revolution a large women's petition called for women having a 'proportional share in the freedoms of this Commonwealth', and deplored efforts to stop them from petitioning. It also asked rhetorically: 'Have we [women] not an equal interest with the men of this Nation, in those liberties and securities, contained in the Petition of Right, and the other good laws of the land?'[90] Shortly after, we find the subversive claim by the seventeenth-century natural philosopher Margaret Cavendish, Duchess of Newcastle (1623?–1673), that, since women could not serve in Parliament, they owed it no loyalty.[91] Explicit calls for women's right to vote or serve in government office are rather rare before the French Revolution, though. The Spanish feminist Josefa Amar y Borbón's remarkable 1786 essay, 'A Discourse in Defense of the Intelligence of Women and their Aptitude for Government and other Positions Occupied by Men', was one.[92] The Marquis de Condorcet, a male egalitarian feminist, also mounted an important and influential call for women's access to all the offices of governance in 1788, though five years later, when he was in a position to put these ideas into practice, he and his revolutionary colleagues lost their nerve.[93] But these are unusual. On the other hand, a very large number of women and men before the revolution, including Amar y Borbón herself, compiled dictionaries of famous women and they often included examples of effective women rulers; the not-so-hidden message was that women could do anything men could do, including govern states.[94] The main reason why few women or men called for the vote for women is that no *ancien régime* states were based upon mass political rights for *either* men or women. In those countries where there was a franchise only a minority (often a tiny minority) of the population enjoyed it (as we have seen, that sometimes included a few widows). With rare exceptions, heads of state got there because of ancestry, not individual merit or someone's vote, and so did delegates to most assemblies. 'Politics' was a mixture of protocol, factions, payoffs, and knowing or being related to the right people.

This did mean that while neither commoner men nor commoner women had much formal political power, at least at the regional or national level, noblewomen virtually had it handed to them, just by virtue of the fact that their male kin monopolized almost all truly influential positions. Only noblemen gained provincial governorships and other plum administrative positions. They held all the top judgeships in most states, and they had a stranglehold on the officer corps (by the eighteenth century this was being achieved by the simple expedient of excluding all non-noble boys from most military academies). The various parliaments, diets, senates, etc. either were confined to the nobility or gave the nobility significantly more power than other groups. Even high ecclesiastical offices (bishoprics, cardinalates, etc.)

went almost exclusively to nobles, often at ages that were absurdly incompatible with the gravity of these offices' spiritual responsibilities. Though there were fewer formal positions for noblewomen, there were some: the position of lady-in-waiting for queens could carry both influence and a generous pension. 'Princess-abbess' was a rather common appellation, especially in the German lands, and frequently such women enjoyed both spiritual and secular governance powers. People in the top tier of eastern European nobles, which included some women, sometimes owned dozens of villages, and hence could control the lives of thousands of serfs. In Spain the invariably noble abbess of the large, ancient and extremely rich Cistercian Monastery of Santa Maria la Real de las Huelgas in Burgos exercised an unlimited secular authority over more than fifty villages, administered her own law-courts, preached, and issued licences authorizing priests.[95]

The result of all this concentration of power in bloodlines is that the personal papers of eighteenth-century noblewomen – like those of noblemen – are full of letters from people seeking to mobilize their influence to get themselves recommended for jobs, to win patronage for new inventions or soon-to-be-published books, to get introductions to people who might later be useful in their careers and to get help in contracting marriages, with property disputes, with court cases, and the like. Noblewomen who knew how the system worked, and who were persuasive, could, over time, build up a significant constituency in the endless exchange of favours that constituted so much of upper-class life. They could also further the careers and marriage prospects of their own kin, as well as people loyal to their particular faction, and there is much evidence that they did.[96]

Some noblewomen also became embroiled in more formal political activities. English noblewomen often got involved behind the scenes (and occasionally quite openly) in parliamentary electioneering, which took on much more importance after the establishment of a constitutional monarchy in the Revolution of 1688–89. There are many known cases of noblewomen throwing their influence to one side or another, contributing money to favoured candidates, and persuading or buying off voters (noblewomen landowners sometimes actually 'owned' or to all intents and purposes controlled a certain number of votes). They even ventured into political 'dirty tricks', as the English noblewoman, Lady Susan Keck (1706–1755) apparently did in the 'Rag Plot', a successful attempt to influence the Oxfordshire elections of 1754 by associating the Tories with Jacobitism and political disloyalty.[97] Polish noblewomen also had prominent roles in politics. The seventeenth century had already seen Polish noblewomen participating occasionally in the debates at the Sejm (noble senate), and playing pivotal roles in both domestic and foreign policy, especially during the reign of Marie-Louise, wife of King John Casimir Vasa in the middle decades of the seventeenth century. During the eighteenth century Polish noblewomen had considerable influence at court, and influenced the debates both in the provincial dietines and General Sejms. Only a few examples out of many must suffice. Elzbieta Sieniawska (c. 1669–1729) was closely involved in the diplomacy around the Great Northern War, helped support an uprising in Hungary, and was known to change sides when it was to her advantage. One of the first women's political salons in Europe was established in 1736 in Warsaw by Izabela Czartoryska née Morsztyn (1671–1758), and was an important meeting place for politicians. Unlike in many French salons, Polish noblewomen participated openly in political discussions. As we have seen, a Polish noblewoman fomented the Revolt of the Confederation of the Bar. And Polish women were on both sides of the debates surrounding the election of Stanislaus Poniatowski; one of the women hostile to him probably penned political treatises in the 1770s. We will have more to say about Polish women during the Age of Revolutions, but it was already clear, well before the dawn of the last and most dramatic phase of the eighteenth century, that they played a more open political role than women in virtually any other country in Europe.[98]

Women who were close to the monarch by virtue of birth (such as the king's or sultan's mother, sisters or daughters), marriage or sexual relations (queens and mistresses), or having been his wet-nurse or the wet-nurse of his children, had even more opportunities to accrue power, and hence expectations were even greater that they would help to promote their own and their relatives' (or faction's) interests. Diplomats, throughout the early modern period, routinely reported on or speculated about the political, factional or religious loyalties of royal women because they were assumed to, and often did, have real influence. Marriages were virtually always political: they frequently 'sealed' treaties or realignments of alliances, and they were treated as significant affairs of state. Even in the Ottoman Empire, which did not marry its royal women away into foreign lands, marriages of princesses or women from the retinue of the *valide sultan* (mother of the sultan) to high officials of the empire were a key means of ensuring support for a particular sultan (or the *valide sultan*'s faction – not always the same thing).[99]

Since royal women's power was linked to the reputation of their dynasties they often used their personal fortunes to add to their own and their family's lustre. Some of this survives into the present day in the form of their public building projects, which often had a religious or charitable bent. *Valide sultans* and sometimes other prominent harem women as well, had a venerable history of building: they endowed many of the most famous mosque and charitable complexes in Istanbul and elsewhere. Natalia (1673–1716), the sister of Peter the Great of Russia, was closely involved in his decision to move the Russian capital to St. Petersburg, and she personally supervised some of the building plans, particularly the plans for cultural institutions. Later she founded a home for the sick, the elderly and abandoned children. Many monasteries, convents, religious orders, schools, hospitals, medrassas, and soup-kitchens, throughout Europe and the Middle East, owe their origins to royal women, busy burnishing the reputation of their royal lines.[100]

Finally, royal women – mothers, sisters, wives, mistresses – did advise rulers, and often to considerable effect. Peter the Great is said to have greatly esteemed the counsel of his sister-in-law, Praskovia Saltykova (1664–1723), and both she and Natalia supported him by adopting the new, more 'European' clothing styles he sought to get the Russian nobility to wear – styles that were frighteningly revealing for women schooled in older ways and only recently emerged from seclusion. It is hard to imagine that he would have embarked on that policy in the first place without their support.[101] Peter also relied heavily upon his second wife, Catherine (1684–1727), born Marta Skavronskaia, the talented daughter of a Lithuanian peasant. She accompanied him on campaign, and was part of his inner circle of advisers. After his death she succeeded him on the throne (as Catherine I) and tried to carry on his policies of Westernization.[102] There was a venerable tradition in the Ottoman Empire of the *valide sultan* being one of her son's main advisers. She often acted as his regent, and during the so-called 'sultanate of women' (1530s–1660s) a succession of royal wives and *valide sultans* either exerted powerful influence over political affairs, or, in later years, actually ruled the empire from the harem. When Turhan Sultan, mother of Sultan Mehmed IV, died in 1683 a contemporary wrote: 'Alas, the strongest prop of the state is gone.' Queen Maria Josefa von Habsburg of Poland (1699–1757), in addition to bearing fourteen children to her husband Friederich-August of Saxony (he was also King August II of Poland), participated actively in the negotiations in the Reichstag, pursued numerous diplomatic initiatives, and, in 1756, organized the defence of Saxony against the aggression of Prussia, her husband having fled to Poland.[103] There are hundreds of similar examples of this sort of female influence – or outright rule – the product of a time when almost all politics had to do with personal connections.

Like commoners, royal women were very dependent upon good relations with the men in their lives for the exercise of power. At the same time they were vulnerable to attack for misusing that power, and often simply for having it. It was almost an axiom of popular belief that royal women used their sexual power to control men and divert them away from policies that would have been truly in the kingdom's interests. Moreover, since royal women were expected to model the behaviour expected of all other women, people worried that, if they gained too much power, the 'natural' gender hierarchy would be threatened. Even so, the viciousness of the attacks upon them can be shocking, even from more than two hundred years' remove. Almost always the focus was on sex – the more perverse the better – or the abuse or killing of children. Louis XV's brilliant mistress and close adviser, Mme de Pompadour (1721–1764), was routinely represented as a social-climbing whore who drew the king away from governance and from his religious duties. In addition to rumours that she was organizing the kidnapping and killing of children so that the king could bathe in their blood (see above), she was also said to be masterminding 'famine plots' – conspiracies to starve the populace by interfering with the availability or price of grain.[104] Turhan Sultan (1627–1682), one of the most powerful of the *valide sultans* during the Sultanate of Women, was accused of having a lesbian relationship with Meleki Hatun, a slave-woman who was one of her main political aides, and, later, of having an incestuous relationship with one of her stepsons.[105] Virtually identical claims would later be made with respect to Marie Antoinette of France (see Chapter 9). Nervousness about women who publicly asserted their views, and particularly a tendency to fixate upon their sexuality, was hardly confined to aristocrats or royal women. But because royal women (and the high aristocracy) did live a more 'public' life than most other women, and because politics is always war by another means, they were particularly vulnerable to attack.

Some women heads of state

Political rights in the modern sense may not have been very meaningful to most eighteenth-century women, but they were *very* interested in female heads of state, closely followed the progress of their reigns, and often tried to interest them in reforms on behalf of women, particularly in the realm of education and law reform. Part II of Mary Astell's *Serious Proposal to Ladies* (1697), proposing what was, in effect, an English women's university, was dedicated to the soon-to-be Queen Anne, in hopes that she would bring the project to fruition, while the French egalitarian feminist Olympe de Gouge's famous 1791 *Declaration of the Rights of Women and the Citizen* (see Chapter 10) was addressed, considerably more ambivalently, to the not-yet-deposed Queen Marie Antoinette. Women in distress often petitioned queens in hopes that (presumed) fellow-feeling among women would help their case. In some places this could include women very far down the status hierarchy. In 1704 and 1705 respectively two Brazilian women slaves, one named Custodia Telles and one named Maria do Pilar, petitioned Queen Maria Sophia of Portugal asking for their freedom so they could escape the sexual advances of their masters. Both were successful. In do Pilar's case, her master was a prominent man who had been able to thwart her attempts to get the colonial courts to intervene, and she did not have enough money for a proper legal appeal. Going straight to the queen over this man's head won her her freedom.[106]

As a general rule most states preferred to avoid vesting official sovereignty in females if they possibly could. All royal succession policies favoured males over females, and several of the surviving monarchies (e.g. Britain, Luxembourg and, as of this writing, Spain) still do. Some countries passed over women entirely, even if there was no male heir (this was the case in France, where the succession was confined to men only and justified by a conglomeration of flimsy precedent, forgery and appeals to nature called the Salic law).[107] Elective monarchies, such as the Holy Roman Emperorship, or semi-prerogative monarchies, such as the Ottoman Sultanate, never went to women. And yet, women did hold power in Europe in their own right in the eighteenth century. They held power on a temporary basis as regents for their sons or absent husbands and they held proxy power by virtue of the incompetence, illness, absence or disinclination to rule of the men they married. They sometimes inherited thrones because there was no male heir, as did Maria Theresa of Austria (r. 1740–1780); or no male heir of the right religion, as did Anne I of Britain (r. 1702–1714). They sometimes presided over transfers of power, as when Rabia Gülnüş Sultan, mother of both Mustafa II and Ahmed III, was petitioned to approve the deposing of one son and the enthronement of the other in 1703, because, as head of the harem, she was the only one with sufficient authority both in the inner world of the imperial residence and the outer world beyond it to permit a change of regime to proceed.[108] And occasionally, most famously in the cases of Tsarinas Elizabeth (r. 1741–61) and Catherine II of Russia (r. 1762–1796), women seized power themselves by coup d'état.

As with men, not every woman who acceded to a throne, whether as a regent or in her own right, was up to the demands of the job. There were, nevertheless, some extremely able women on the thrones of Europe in the eighteenth century, and this is significant because it was a time when monarchs still wielded real power. Maria Theresa, Archduchess of Austria, Queen of Hungary and Bohemia and Empress Consort of the Holy Roman Empire (r. 1740–1780), is a famous example. Few monarchs have had so unprepossessing a start to their reign. When Maria Theresa's father, Charles VI, died suddenly in 1740 she found herself, as she later commented, 'Without money, without credit, without an army, without experience and knowledge of my own and finally, without any counsel, because [everyone] at first wanted to wait and see how things would develop.'[109] Within five months three different European rulers had laid claim to her throne or parts of her territories; Frederick II of Prussia actually seized part of her empire by force. The treasury was empty, and the army demoralized by a long series of defeats. The nobilities of her various dominions were reluctant to help and unwilling to contribute monies for what they saw as a lost cause. Most people thought the Austro-Hungarian Empire was in its death-throes. But Maria Theresa, twenty-three years old, was handsome, charismatic, certain of her divine right to rule, and far more competent than her late father and she would not concede defeat. She speedily taught herself how to lead (her father had 'shielded' her from politics) and embarked on an extraordinary campaign to rally support. Less than a year later she appeared before the Hungarian Estates, not, as is sometimes supposed, as a young, beautiful queen in distress with her infant son in her arms, but as a stateswoman. She delivered a speech in Latin, offered a serious deal in exchange for military and financial assistance, and presented her infant son a few days later, 'not as an appeal, rather as a pledge' as one biographer puts it.[110]

In her long reign Maria Theresa achieved a great deal. She regularized the collection of taxes to some degree, and taxed nobles and clergy, not just peasants as had been the case in previous reigns. She attracted a succession of highly competent advisers and statesmen, and seems to have known how to use their talents. Though a zealous Catholic, she dissolved most of the contemplative religious orders in order to fund a major new educational initiative that, for the first time, educated both males and females up to about the age of ten. She founded technical colleges and academies to train up young aristocrats for government service, reformed the military, balanced the books, and bore sixteen children. Maria Theresa also initiated a major reform of criminal law and procedure, one aspect of which was the virtual abolition of witch-trials (and certainly of executions, since, in the new code, all convictions had to be appealed to Vienna, where they were invariably quashed). Witch-trials lasted later in the Hungarian part of the Austro-Hungarian Empire than almost anywhere else in Europe (they were still going strong in the 1750s when they had largely ended in most other places) and about ninety-two per cent of those executed were women, so this was quite a significant reform.[111] She also patronized numerous literary and musically talented women, including some important women composers.

There were also some considerably less appealing features of Maria Theresa's reign. Though she was prepared to and did appeal to Enlightenment notions of rationality to suppress witchcraft trials, she was appalled by many of the other ideas of the Enlightenment, and especially by calls for religious toleration and freedom of the press. She was perfectly prepared to work with Catherine II (see below) and Frederick of Prussia to dismember Poland. She was also extremely religiously bigoted. She sent in troops to control Protestant Moravians and, literally, force them into Catholic churches, and, in 1745, she expelled the Jews from Prague, and was still trying to limit their ability to live freely in Vienna as late as 1777, when much of the rest of Europe was finally abandoning such tactics.[112] By the time of her death her regime was considered not just old-fashioned but politically and religiously retrograde by much of Enlightened Europe.

Catherine II of Russia (r. 1762–1796), often styled 'Catherine the Great', was born a minor German princess and sent at the age of fourteen to Russia to marry the heir to the Russian throne. It was a typical political marriage. But Catherine was far from being a typical person. In swift succession she learned Russian, converted from Lutheranism to Russian Orthodoxy, to the distress of her own relatives, and set about making herself popular. For his part, when her husband acceded to the throne in 1761 as Tsar Peter III, he swiftly antagonized almost everyone, and within months plans were afoot to replace him with his much more prepossessing wife. On 28 June 1762 the thirty-three-year-old tsarina slipped away from her husband, who was staying at one of his country estates, and went secretly back to St. Petersburg. There, with her co-conspirators, she sought and received the support of the four main St. Petersburg guard regiments and of the church hierarchy. When the city was secured she dressed in the uniform of one of the regiments and, mounted on a dappled grey stallion, set off at the head of fourteen thousand troops to confront her husband (Plate 9). After some ineffectual attempts to rally support, Peter signed the abdication letter. A week later he was strangled, probably not on Catherine's orders, though she certainly participated in the cover-up that followed.

The image of Catherine II has been greatly affected by the peculiar lens with which women rulers tend to be viewed. Like any number of male monarchs before and after her, Catherine fairly openly took lovers – twelve of them – over the course of her sixty-seven years, all of them male as far as we know. She was also unfailingly gracious and generous to her ex-favourites and retained several of them as close friends. In many senses her love-life seems rather modern. But that was not how contemporaries, or, for that matter, an older generation of historians saw it. The association of women wielding power with excess sexuality was very ingrained, and so was the notion that any woman who had sex outside of marriage had to be deeply flawed in character. One result is that, until very recently, many historians applied a quite perceptible double standard of judgement to her and her reign. Catherine was a patroness of several of the *philosophes* (notably Voltaire and Diderot) and a strong supporter of arts and letters (particularly of women artists), of education and of religious toleration. But because she did not follow the 'full' enlightenment programme to the letter, and became, like every other European monarch, more repressive in the face of the French Revolution, many historians dismissed her as a self-publicizing opportunist. She is also frequently criticized for not freeing the serfs, even though it is quite impossible that she could have done so and still kept her throne.

Like Peter the Great, Catherine II aimed to turn Russia into a European nation. She wished to increase its population and wealth, assure its security, educate its people and change its culture. Much of this she did. In economic terms she ended most monopolies and controls (she was an early admirer of Adam Smith) and engaged in various projects intended to bring in new trade and encourage exports. She also established a system of land surveying that regularized village ownership of land and encouraged more cultivation. Administratively, she created provinces that were reasonably uniform in size, and she encouraged urban development. She founded a primary education system for both boys and girls, which, though not universal, was far more extensive than anything seen in Russia up to that time. She also set up a school for noble girls and appointed the Countess Ekaterina Dashkova (1743–1810) to be the head of the St. Petersburg Academy of Arts and Sciences as well as the Russian Academy – the first woman so honoured in all of Europe. Dashkova, a woman of considerable energy, immediately embarked on a reform of the beleaguered St. Petersburg academy, while at the Russian Academy she initiated a vast Russian dictionary project and started a monthly magazine. For her part, Catherine II interested herself in public health, founding hospitals in St. Petersburg and Moscow and setting up a college of medicine. She also encouraged smallpox inoculation, having herself inoculated in 1768 and then setting up inoculation programmes. And she fairly consistently supported greater toleration of religious minorities across Russia; including Old Believers, Jews and Muslims (she is one of the few Christian rulers of Europe ever to endow a mosque – in her case two).[113]

Catherine II is most criticized today for her willingness to be a party to the dismemberment of Christian Poland (along with Frederick the Great and Maria Theresa), something that was only accomplished with considerable loss of life and by crushing the fledgling liberal constitutional monarchy of Thaddeus Kosciusko (see Chapter 9). Conversely, she tends to be praised for her military successes and territorial acquisitions at the expense of the Muslim Ottoman Empire, a fine example of the unacknowledged biases that often creep into the writing of European history (it is bad to seize territory from Christians; but European historians applaud if a monarch seizes territory from Muslims). Even though she could not have freed the serfs, many historians continue to believe, probably with reason, that she could have done more to improve their lives. She also had an ego as big as Siberia, but that is hardly unusual among successful leaders. The most revealing illustration of how intimidating contemporaries found Catherine came after her death in 1796. There is absolutely no question about how and where Catherine died: she suffered a stroke in her state apartments in St. Petersburg and died in her bed; dozens of people witnessed it. But a rumour soon surfaced, probably invented by a French revolutionary propagandist, that she had been crushed to death while having sex with a horse. As we have seen, it was common across Europe and the Ottoman Empire to impute perverse sexual proclivities to women with political power. In Catherine's case her undoubted self-mastery and success, as a ruler and as a lover, seem to have demanded an even more than usually extreme response. One of the most able rulers of the eighteenth century is still primarily remembered, at least outside Russia, not for her achievements, or even for her very real shortcomings, but for this titillating fable about her death.[114] There were also more local slights to her memory. When Catherine's son Paul I acceded to the throne in 1796, one of his first acts was to promulgate a Fundamental Law of Succession that, for most intents and purposes, barred women from the throne. Paul and Catherine had detested one another; still, it was a powerful repudiation of the principle of female sovereignty, and a vindictive attempt by a far less able ruler to symbolically erase his mother's long and illustrious reign. Russia has not had another woman head of state to this day.

CONCLUSION

It is very difficult to deliver an overall judgement about the extent to which women's public sphere opportunities expanded or contracted in the eighteenth century. No women rulers after the late eighteenth century wielded the kind of power some eighteenth-century queens did; and the nineteenth century also saw something of a decline in the power of noble-women, though perhaps not as quickly as used to be thought.[115] Some of the apparent softening of male monopolies proved a false dawn. After Dorothea Erxleben successfully won her medical degree from the University of Halle, no woman received a degree from a German university until 1901. Even though Mary Moser and Angelica Kauffman had been founding members of the British Royal Academy of Arts, thereafter the organization refused to extend membership to any other women, and only did so in the 1860s as a result of a well-orchestrated feminist campaign. The Swedish academies opened to women by Queen Lovisa Ulrike were closed to them again in the early nineteenth century. Some of this seems to have been as a result of a resurgence of anxieties about women in the public sphere that accompanied the conservative reaction to the French Revolution, and some of it derived from newly 'biologistic' and functionalist notions of women drawn from the new science.[116] It is also pretty evident that the rise of broader-based conceptions of citizenship for men tended to go along with a narrowing of political opportunities for some women, at least in relation to voting. The successful mid-eighteenth-century move to divest Swedish woman heads of household of the vote had echoes in other countries, including England, France, and the young United States of America.

On the other side, it is indisputable that middle-class and elite women's charitable activities, both religious and secular (or semi-secular), expanded enormously in the eighteenth century and that a wide range of new public sphere opportunities arose for women of all ranks, especially in relation to health and social services (the work of tertiary religious orders, especially in France, is especially striking) and to the military. By the late eighteenth century, even outside revolutionary France, evidence also begins to turn up of organizational activity by non-elite women – freed black women and black slaves in the Ottoman Empire; textile workers in England. Arguably, though, some of the most significant eighteenth-century achievements where women were concerned were ideological. There is much about eighteenth-century feminism that foreshadows what was to come in the next two centuries, and the fact that a good deal of it appeared in print form meant that it did not sink into oblivion quite as quickly or thoroughly as it might otherwise have done. Many nineteenth- and twentieth-century women and men would take up the torch for women's education, women's inclusion in hitherto male institutions, alternative all-women's academies or colleges, law reform, civic action, and, ultimately, women's right to participate in government via the vote. Especially in the relatively arid early decades of the nineteenth century, it is clear that some continued to be inspired by their eighteenth-century predecessors. The thing that stands out above all others (and it is one that feminists across the ideological spectrum could claim some credit for – though more secular attitudes also helped) was their success in largely retiring the notion that all the daughters of Eve lived in a permanent state of incipient sin. There is little question that this was the main ideological justification both for gender hierarchy – including male coercion within the family – and for excluding women from civic and political activity in the pre-modern period. Of course, women had always had ways to get around the prohibitions on public actions; moreover, the lifting of the curse was not comprehensive and many women were left out. It was also not a panacea; new more secular justifications for excluding and dominating women (and other groups) were rapidly found. But it did create, even in the face of the early nineteenth-century backlash, a base upon which later women activists could build.

The revolution that began in the thirteen North American colonies in 1775 proved, to most Europeans' amazement, that the combined power of republican virtue, strong military leadership and domestic antiwar sentiment could bring an ancient monarchy, at least temporarily, to its knees. Other revolutions were born, at least in part, from the Thirteen Colonies' example, and women had a part in all of them. None of them was strictly democratic, despite the misleading term 'Age of Democratic Revolutions' that is sometimes used to refer to the last quarter of the eighteenth century. But all of them stood for a significant expansion, or at least a shift in the composition, of the political class. Several of them, mostly notably the French Revolution and the Haitian Revolution, abolished slavery and 'feudal' tenures. And because eighteenth-century women were already participating fairly extensively in politics, publishing, the arts, etc., the question arose more insistently in these than in earlier revolutions whether they too should benefit as a group.

THE REVOLUTION IN AMERICA

In the tense time that preceded the American Revolutionary War (1775–83) American women patriots refused to drink imported tea and dusted off their spinning skills (or those of their servants or slaves) to replace British cloth imports with American-made homespun. Women were involved in street actions against British soldiers, they participated in the tarring and feathering, and quite possibly the lynching of loyalists, and they were prominent in the mass funerals that followed the so-called Boston Massacre of 1770 when

British soldiers fired into a hostile mob and killed five people. In October of 1774, in the so-called 'Edenton Tea Party', a group of fifty-one women in Edenton, North Carolina, resolved to drink no more tea and buy no more English cloth, and sent a petition to George III signalling their intentions. This petition was probably not as shocking to British public opinion as some have assumed, and it was certainly not the first ladies' petition. Nonetheless, it did give rise to a satirical print, Philip Dawes's 'A Society of Patriotic Ladies' (1775) (Plate 10), which stakes out a position we will encounter repeatedly in this chapter. The *mise en scène* of Dawes's picture is intended to suggest a brothel. We are shown the Edenton women, ugly, with ridiculously big hair and low-cut gowns, engaged in officiously signing their petition. A man at the centre of the picture is either fondling or about to kiss one of the signers, who looks at him lasciviously. To the side, working girls are flirting with a misshapen, clearly lower-class white man who seems to be trying to get in the door. A black servant or slave is shown looking on, as if she too might sign the petition. Down on the ground, unnoticed, a young child is being licked by a dog. The none-too-subtle message is that the women of Edenton are luxury-loving, over-sexed harpies who do not know where their children are. Moreover, their intrusion into the political sphere is likely to open the door both to poor white men and black people trying the same thing; in short, to the complete disintegration of the 'chain of hierarchies' with which this book began.

Even before the Thirteen Colonies actually declared their independence, it was becoming clear that the notion of liberty from oppression would be a difficult concept to control. In 1773 the African-American poet, Phillis Wheatley (1753–1784), aged about eighteen, published a poem 'To the Right Honourable William Legge . . .' which draws an explicit connection between the experience of enslavement and the 'tyranny' that oppressed the North American colonists. Wheatley wrote the poem when she was still a slave, and though she does not explicitly call for slave emancipation – it is hard to imagine that her owners would have let her publish it if she had – the implication is hard to miss (see Voices from the Past 9.1). The question 'liberty for whom?' also occupied Abigail Adams, wife of John Adams, a delegate to the Continental Congress that was then meeting in Philadelphia. In a famous letter of March 1776 she urged her husband not to allow the Congress to give the benefits of liberty to men alone: '. . . in the new Code of Law which I suppose it will be necessary for you to make I desire you would remember the ladies and be more generous and favourable to them than your ancestors . . . Remember all Men would be tyrants if they could.' She also remarked, half in jest, 'If particular care and attention is not paid to the Ladies we are determined to foment a Rebellion, and will not hold ourselves bound by any Laws in which we have no voice or Representation.' She is not specific, but it is likely that she was interested in an expansion of married women's property rights. But her husband John quashed this overture by return post, likening woman's desire for rights to children, apprentices, students, Indians and slaves being insolent and disobedient.

Abigail was obviously angry at this rebuff. She complained to a friend about her husband's 'saucy' response and talked about organizing a woman's petition to Congress. And in her next letter to John she pointedly emphasized the inconsistency of 'proclaiming peace and good will to Men, Emancipating all Nations, [yet] you insist upon retaining an absolute power over Wives'.[1] Abigail Adams did not win this battle. All of the American colonies' law codes drew heavily upon the English model of minimal rights for married women, and this remained true well into the next century. Moreover, with very few exceptions, no one other than white men (and, initially at least, no one except property-owning white men) got 'voice or representation' in government. The ideal in the new United States was marriage and mother-hood for most white women, slavery for most black women and men, and a position somewhere between deadly enemy, distrusted ally and neglected ward for most Native peoples. And so things would long remain.

VOICES FROM THE PAST 9.1

A slave poet reflects upon the meaning of liberty (1772)

Phillis Wheatley (1753–1784) was probably born somewhere along the Gambia River in West Africa. She was captured by slavers when she was about eight years old and brought to Boston, Massachusetts where she was sold. Her owners renamed her Phillis, after the slave-ship that brought her across the Atlantic. In this poem Wheatley movingly contrasts unfreedom ('injur'd Rights', chains, 'bitter Pangs', separation from loved ones) with freedom and asserts her right to pronounce upon what these concepts really mean because of her own tragic history of having had her liberty forcibly stolen from her. The third stanza of the poem suggests that Wheatley saw herself as writing a kind of political petition in poetic form. William Legge was the recently appointed British Secretary of State for the Colonies.

   To the right Honourable William Legge, Earl of Dartmouth
   By Phillis Wheatley
   HAIL, happy Day! When smiling like the Morn,
   Fair *Freedom* rose, New England to adorn:
   The Northern Clime beneath her genial Ray

Beholds, exulting, thy paternal Sway;
For, big with Hopes, her Race no longer mourns;
Each Soul expands, and each Bosom burns:
While in thy Hand, with Pleasure we behold,
The silken Reins, and *Freedom's* Charms unfold!
Long lost to Realms beneath the Northern skies,
She shines supreme; while hated *Faction* dies:
Soon as appear'd the Triumph long desir'd,
Sick at the View, he languish'd and expir'd.

No more, of Grievance unredress'd complain,
Or injur'd Rights, or groan beneath the Chain,
Which wanton Tyranny, with lawless Hand,
Made to enslave, *O liberty*! Thy Land. –
My Soul rekindles, at thy glorious Name,
Thy Beams, essential to the vital Flame. –
The Patriot's Breast, what Heavenly Virtue warms,
And adds new Lustre to his mental Charms!
While in thy Speech, the Graces all combine,
Apollo's too, with Sons of Thunder join.
Then shall the Race of injur'd Freedom bless,
The Sire, the Friend, and Messenger of Peace.

While you, my lord, read o'er the advent'rous Song
And wonder, whence such daring Boldness sprung;
Whence flow my Wishes for the common Good,
by feeling Hearts alone best understood?
From native Clime, when seeming cruel Fate
Me snatch'd from Afric's fancy'd happy Seat
Impetuous – Ah! What bitter Pangs molest,
What Sorrows labour'd in the Parent Breast?
That, more than Stone, ne'er soft Compassion mov'd
Who from its Father seiz'd his much belov'd.
Such once my Case – Thus I deplore the Day,
When Britons weep beneath Tyrannick Sway.
To thee our Thanks for Favours past are due;
To thee we still solicit for the new:
Since in thy Pow'r, as in thy will before,
To sooth the Griefs which thou di[d]st then deplore
May Heav'nly Grace the sacred Sanction give,
To all thy Works, and thou for ever live;
Not only on the Wing of fleeting Fame,
(Immortal Honours Grace the Patriot's Name,)
Thee to conduct to Heaven's refulgent Fane;
May feiry Courses sweep the ethereal Plain,
There, like the Prophet, find the bright Abode,
Where dwells thy Sire, the Everlasting GOD.

(Written in Boston, 10 October 1772; published *New-York Journal* for 3 June 1773.)

Source: Reprinted in *The Collected Works of Phillis Wheatley*, John C. Shields, ed. (New York, Oxford, Oxford University Press, 1988), 217–19.

REVOLUTIONARY POLITICS IN THE 1780S

Up to that point when the young, upstart American Republic disturbed the calm, the Enlightenment had, in many ways, been an armchair programme. Republicanism was more akin to a series of intellectual debates about classical antiquity than it was a political programme.[2] All this changed with the American Revolution. Now, suddenly, a group of former colonists, claiming to act on the authority of 'the people', had shattered the chains of monarchical authority and formed a nation without an established religion or a hereditary nobility and based on recognizably enlightened principles such as free speech, freedom of the press, the separation of church and state, *habeas corpus*, an end to torture, and the right to a judicial trial. True, the new nation retained chattel slavery – this was already seen as inconsistent by European onlookers. But if you were white, and especially if you were white and male, America looked far freer and more egalitarian than anything seen in Europe up to that time.

Poland

Liberal Europe was soon firmly in the camp of the Americans, and many educated Europeans, including numerous nobles, wiled away the late 1770s and 1780s reading the writings of the American revolutionaries. In Poland, still reeling from the first partition of 1772, George Washington was lionized, and the short-lived Constitution of 3 May 1791 incorporated a number of ideas drawn from the Americans. Noblewomen like Anna Teresa Potocka (1746–1810), Izabela Czartoryska, née Fleming (1746–1835) and Rozalia Lubomirska (1768–1794) were fervently active around the Four-Year Sejm which drew up the new constitution, and they lobbied for numerous reforms, including a scheme of universal education for both boys and girls that was, at least on paper, the most comprehensive in Europe. At the Sejm women often sat with the male delegates and they directed much of the political theatre that accompanied the deliberations. At one point Izabela Czartoryska, the head of what can only be described as the women's wing of the Patriot party, with drums rolling, publicly cut off the powdered locks of the marshal of the Lithuanian confederacy, who thereafter found it expedient to switch to national dress. The loud involvement of women from the galleries of the Sejm, cheering, catcalling, voice-voting along with the delegates, and so on, set an example that soon would be repeated in France. Women were active outside the Sejm too, in heavily politicized cultural interventions like the staging of a play called *The Spartan Mother* in which Izabela Czartoryska played the mother of heroes.[3] It would all be swept away by the Russian occupation of Poland in May of 1792, and the failure, two years later, of Kosciuszko's Rebellion. The second and third partitions of Poland, and the demise, in 1815, of Napoleon's short-lived 'Duchy of Warsaw', wiped Poland off the map of Europe for over a century.

The Netherlands

In the United Provinces of the Netherlands conflicts between 'Orangists' (supporters of the Prince of Orange, the traditional Stadhouder, or head of state) and 'Patriots', a more liberal party, partly inspired by the American example, led to the polarization of the citizenry, and ultimately, in 1786–87, to a series of municipal and provincial 'coups' and electoral takeovers that left the Patriots in control of most of the country. Women affiliated themselves with both sides of the conflict, but women of the popular classes particularly distinguished themselves on the Orangist side. Catherine Mulder (1723–1798), better known under the name Kaat Mossel, was a seller and inspector of mussels, who was arrested in 1784 for inciting and leading an Orangist riot in Rotterdam. Her trial and her behaviour in prison (for instance throwing raucous celebrations for the prince's birthday from her prison cell) made her the toast of the Orangists. When amnestied in 1787 she refused to leave prison unless she was officially acquitted and received financial compensation, and she got both. Much higher up the social scale, the Stadhouder's wife, Wilhelmina of Prussia (1751–1820), proved much more forceful than her husband in combating the Patriots. Disobeying her more faint-hearted husband's express command, she manoeuvred her brother, the King of Prussia, into invading the Netherlands and restoring Orangist hegemony. On the other side of the conflict, 'Patriot' women signed petitions, gave money, and wrote numerous pamphlets. Well-known novelist and champion of education for women, Betje Wolff (1738–1804), openly threw her support to the Patriot party, even though, in calmer times, she had argued that women should refrain from getting involved in politics.[4] All over Europe, women of all social backgrounds – market-women like Mulder, middle-class intellectuals like Wolff, and noblewomen, like the Poles and Wilhelmina of Prussia – were beginning to reassess their relationship to citizenship.

Brabant/Belgium

The tumults of the 1780s also threw up some more disturbing reminders of the risks political women faced. The Brabantine Revolution of the late

1780s was a bid for independence for Belgium from the Austro-Hungarian Empire. Two of the best-known revolutionaries were women. Anne Thérèse Philippine, the Countess d'Yves (1738–1814), a liberal noblewoman, was the main intellectual of the movement. She wrote pamphlets and corresponded with sympathizers all over Belgium, appealing to natural rights doctrine to protest the Austrians' violation of Belgian liberties and calling her compatriots to their sacred duty to cast off 'the yoke of despotism'. D'Yves herself did not focus much attention on the rights of women (though she never submitted to the 'yoke of matrimony'), but one of her admirers dedicated a pamphlet to her in which he asserted that 'the Belgians . . . have maintained their liberty throughout the centuries because women no less than men have worked continuously to guard it'.[5] A different sort of revolutionary was Jeanne Pinaud de Bellem, often called 'La Pinaud'. At the outbreak of the revolution Jeanne de Bellem, like d'Yves, was in her early fifties and had, for several decades, been the established mistress of one of the main instigators of the Revolt. Her home quickly became a gathering place for would-be revolutionaries. De Bellem herself wrote revolutionary verse, and she and her daughter tirelessly passed out her own and others' writings, often under the noses of the Austrian soldiery. In 1788 she was jailed for distributing subversive pamphlets. She, too, came out of prison a national celebrity, especially when, after the defeat of the Austrian troops in 1789, her long-time lover, Henry Van der Noot, became the effective head of what was to be the short-lived United States of Belgium (its name was, of course, modelled on the Americans).

Unfortunately Van der Noot's enemies and rivals soon came to see the benefits of undermining him by maligning de Bellem. A concerted campaign got underway to paint de Bellem as a social-climbing prostitute who wanted to destroy the nation. Bellem's social origins were humble and she had borne a child out of wedlock, so she was very vulnerable to attack. Typical of the sort of thing hawked around the streets is an obscene picture of de Bellem and Van der Noot making love on a couch, with one of Van der Noot's close associates slinking off in the background. The implication was that de Bellem was having sex with all the men of the Statist leadership (the 'Statists' were Van der Noot's party) and had thereby made all of them slaves to her will. Belgium was deluged with such images, attacks not only on de Bellem personally (though they were that), or even just on her party, but on the very idea of a woman playing a significant role in politics.[6] The United States of Belgium would last less than a year before Austrian troops, capitalizing on the new nation's internal divisions, recaptured control.

THE FRENCH REVOLUTION OF 1789

At the dawn of revolution

Women were political players from the earliest days of the French Revolution. First there were the *cahiers de doléances* (registers of grievances) that poured into Paris in the run-up to the fateful meeting of the Estates General in May of 1789. Though the majority came from men, women also seized the opportunity to publicize their concerns. Groups of working women complained about attempts to suppress women's guilds, claiming that they had led to widespread immiseration of women workers, and were causing desperate women to turn to prostitution. Several petitioners wanted schools to be established to allow women to learn new vocational skills. One Mme B. submitted a lengthy petition decrying the law's injustices to women, particularly in the realm of daughters' inheritances. She also thought women should be admitted as deputies to the Estates General ('women cannot be represented except by [other] women') and she buttressed her claim that women were fully capable of intelligent governance by citing the example of effective female monarchs, including Catherine II of Russia.[7] One colourful petition from the Sisters of St. Vincent de Paul of Hondtschoote in Northern France objected to having been assigned by town notables to do nursing care – the activities of groups like the Grey Sisters (see Chapter 5) were apparently giving rise to the belief that all nuns could be pressed into social services, whether they felt called to it or not. This group clearly did not. 'Being born free' wrote the mother superior, who knew her Rousseau, her nuns had chosen a convent where they could lead a strictly contemplative life. If, when they were taking their religious vows, someone had told them they were signing up to be nurses, 'every [nun] without exception would have responded: 'if I had wished to be a nurse I would have chosen a hospital'.[8]

Very quickly the focus shifted from petitions to the streets. Women were present at the storming of the Bastille on 14 July 1789, and several women later asked to be rewarded for their patriotic behaviour on that day. They had a much more central role in the Women's March to Versailles of 5–6 October 1789, one of the turning points of the revolution, because it brought the king and the royal family to Paris where it was much harder for them to resist the revolutionaries' demands. September and October of 1789 had been punctuated by growing fears about food shortages. The rumour shooting across Paris was that Louis XVI and Marie Antoinette were deliberately starving Paris in preparation for setting the troops against the National Assembly and rolling back the revolution. On the morning of 5 October the market-women of les Halles and others began gathering, and by noon around four thousand women and four or five hundred men had set off for the palace at Versailles, twenty-one kilometres (thirteen miles) away. When the procession reached Versailles, women went first to the meeting place of the National Assembly. There they tried to engage the delegates in a discussion both of the food situation and the problem of the excessive numbers of troops stationed in and around Paris. They spoke through their elected representative, a man, but a contemporary drawing of the event suggests that the women also fanned out and lobbied delegates on their own account (Plate 11). In the meantime, other women had succeeded in getting an audience with the king, during which they extracted from him a written promise to provide Paris with adequate provisions. But it was not enough to pacify the demonstrators. Early the next morning women invaded the royal apartments once again and insisted the king return with them to Paris. Amid the tense negotiations in and outside the royal chambers at least one of the king's guards fired into the crowd and two of the guards were subsequently killed. At length the whole group set off back to Paris. The royal family rode in coaches, surrounded by National Guard; the rest marched back bearing the severed heads of the two murdered guards on pikes. As the procession passed into Paris proper, one woman famously called out to the crowd lining the streets 'We no longer lack bread and we bring you the baker, the baker's wife and the baker's son.'[9]

Feminism in revolutionary times

Feminist ideas did not spring into being in 1789. However, the revolution did give female and male feminists more outlets and a greatly expanded audience, and it multiplied hopes for real change. Already in 1789, *Citoyenne* (Citizeness) Desmoulins, in 'Motions Addressed to the National Assembly', was calling upon the delegates to 'respect the laws of nature' and redress the many ills that had been visited upon women. She urged the Assembly to abolish the dowry system and called for women to be educated for economic independence, not simply to be dependent wives. Convent-educated herself, Desmoulins deplored the notion that there was anything 'religious' about enclosing women, many of them for life, behind thick walls and iron grilles. As she put it: 'If we are all born free, if you propose to break the chains of servitude, you cannot abandon these expiring captives, equally born for liberty.'[10]

As we have seen, a number of egalitarian feminists had been willing to criticize men and marriage as tyrannical, but feminists of the Revolutionary era went quite a bit farther. They began claiming that men's traditional relationship to women was close kin to the discredited relationship of kings to subjects, and therefore fundamentally despotic. Because despotism infringed upon the natural right of human beings to be free it had to be rooted out in all its forms before a more just society could be established. *Citoyenne* Desmoulins likened the oppression of women to 'another despotism'. In an address to the National Assembly in December 1790, Etta Palm D'Aelders spoke of prejudice against women as 'the most difficult to uproot of any of the despotisms'. And Olympe de Gouges spoke in 1791 of how man 'wants to command as a despot a sex [woman] which is in full possession of its intellectual faculties'.[11] It was an electric claim and an important moment: the revolution saw, for the first time, the firm linkage of women's rights to the radical assertion that women were born with the same 'natural right to be free' as men.

Women presented numerous petitions and sent many delegations to the National Assembly and its successors,[12] and several, including Etta Palm D'Aelders, Pauline Léon and Claire Lacombe (who reportedly turned up 'dressed as an Amazon') actually addressed the group. Many more women spoke before largely or entirely male clubs or in the Section meetings.[13] New women's journals began appearing, and scores of women's rights pamphlets were published, written both by women and by men. Women seized upon the new patriotic form of address '*citoyenne*' (female citizen) as a kind of badge, claiming it for themselves in preference to honorifics like '*madame*' and '*mademoiselle*' (or, for that matter, the plebeian term '*femme*', as in '*Femme* Dubois', the woman/wife Dubois). Some of the appeal, we may be sure, lay in the way '*citoyenne*' advertised female citizenship and women's relationship to the state, not their marital status or social rank.

By 1791–2 a recognizably feminist programme had begun to emerge, and it picked up a number of traditional concerns (see especially Chapter 8). Activists wanted to reform women's education, because they saw illiteracy (and, at least in the eyes of some, the control of women's education by the church) as among the main forces holding women in subjection. They also wanted an end to the sexual double standard. Another speech by Palm D'Aelders in the summer of 1791 objected strongly to a proposed law that permitted a husband to charge his wife with adultery but not vice versa. There were a number of calls for more occupational opportunities for women (see Chapter 5). Some women also wanted to reform the laws of marriage and permit divorce. It was clear to the author of *Griefs et plaintes des femmes mal mariées* (Grievances and complaints of unhappily married women) (1789), that indissoluble marriage was especially disadvantageous to women, and that it had essentially become a way for husbands and families, with the collusion of priests, to retain despotic control over women's property and person. Soon groups of feminists were lobbying and petitioning the French National Assembly on the divorce issue.[14] When the right to divorce was actually achieved in September of 1792 – arguably the first case of a major legal reform won, at least in part, through feminist activism – the irreverent journal *Mère Duchesne*, mimicking the speech of a market-woman, crowed:

> Be proud of yourself, Mère Duchesne, for bloody hell you should be. In the past when we wanted to speak, our mouths were shut while we were told very politely, 'You reason like a woman'; almost like a goddamn beast. Oh! Damn! Everything is very different now; we have indeed grown since the Revolution . . . Bloody Christ! How liberty has given us wings![15]

As we have seen, demands that women be permitted to vote were relatively rare before the Revolution (they are also late; most of them date from the 1770s and 80s). In the new polity the franchise suddenly mattered (or, at least, seemed as if it would in future matter) and in response to the times dozens of individual women or women's organizations called for the vote and the right to participate equally with men at all levels of government.[16] The most powerful feminist manifesto of the day, and arguably the first in history, was Olympe de Gouges' 'Declaration of the Rights of Women and the Citizen' of September 1791. It argued for the equality of women to men on natural rights grounds ('Tell me [you men], what gives you sovereign empire to oppress my sex?') and called for women to be granted the same rights that men had been given in the Declaration of the Rights of Man and the Citizen, that great 1789 hymn to natural rights. De Gouges wanted all political rights and all 'honours, positions, and public employment' that were available to men, including the right to elective office, to be opened to women as well. She was aware, though, that mere formal equality was unlikely to solve all women's problems, and she was particularly concerned about women's sexual vulnerability. For this reason she wanted men who seduced women – especially upper-class men who seduced lower-class women – to be required to support their children and to pay 'an indemnity equal to his [the seducer's] wealth' to the mother. Inheritance laws were to be changed to permit all a man's offspring, whether legitimate or not, to share equally in his estate. She also imagined a society in which a woman could forthrightly say 'I am the mother of a child which belongs to you, without being forced by a barbarous prejudice to hide the truth.' De Gouges appended to her Declaration a 'Form for a Social Contract between Man and Woman', essentially a secular marriage contract, which provided for joint jurisdiction over common property, and for equitable division in case of separation or divorce. This was the most comprehensive attack upon the sexual double standard anyone had yet made – even though, somewhat inconsistently, de Gouges also demanded more rigorous treatment of prostitutes.[17]

Feminist thought in the 1789–93 period went beyond recommending changes in the law. The widespread interest in women's education, for instance, reflected recognition of how few trades or occupations were open to women, a problem greatly compounded by women's constricted education. Accordingly, the very practical Mme de Bastide proposed to the Assembly to set up a school of typography for women: 'Men have free schools of design, lecture courses in languages, the sciences, the arts and vocations, just for them. [Women have none]. Yet no one is unaware that the ordinary work of women is inadequate to support a family.'[18] De Bastide thought that printing, because it was relatively sedentary and required patience and good manual dexterity, would be especially appropriate for women, and would even draw in respectable but impoverished women who might otherwise believe themselves incapable of paid work. Several feminists, including de Gouges, asked for equal rights for women in government employment. But the main revolutionary response to this problem, driven by desperate women appealing for work, was a series of factory-workshops (the so-called *ateliers patriotiques*) set up to employ the poor and (usually) to produce uniforms and other necessities for the military. These would soon become important loci for plebeian women's organizing.[19] There was also attention to subsistence issues. In Year III of the New Revolutionary Calendar (1794–5) one of the few cookbooks of the eighteenth century oriented toward a plebeian or at least lower-middle-class audience appeared. Madame Merigot's *La Cuisinière républicaine* (The Republican Woman Cook) was, appropriately enough, a book of potato recipes, and its author obviously strove for easy but tasty dishes based upon cheap and wholesome ingredients. She also argued for the superiority of the potato over wheat on the grounds that it was an anti-scorbutic (that is, it prevented scurvy, a poor person's disease) and that an experiment on foundling home children had showed that potatoes made them feel more full than wheat-based dishes. This was far indeed from the world of the aristocratic chef, but it was also a considerable departure from the preoccupations of middle-class women cookbook writers.

VOICES FROM THE PAST 9.2

Cooking potatoes in year III of the revolution

The name of this recipe for potato meat-balls or croquettes, published during the most radical and anti-aristocratic phase of the French Revolution, 'Steward's Potatoes', suggests that this is a very economical way of cooking them. Madame Mérigot's is the first known French potato recipe book, though a few individual recipes had been published earlier. The publisher's Foreword advertises the book's 'simplicity and economy', and makes a point of the fact that it omits what it calls (with some irony), 'patisseries and ragouts recherchés' (pastries and exquisite ragouts), in other words, aristocratic cuisine.

Steward's Potatoes

When the potatoes are cooked and peeled mash them well with a wooden spoon. Make a mince of all kinds of meat, boiled or roasted, put in a little butter, salt, pepper, parsley, chives, minced shallots, one or two eggs; add your potatoes in as large quantities as you have mince-meat; mix everything together, form meatballs of medium size, dip them in a little white of egg that you will have previously reserved, flour them, and fry them: serve them garnished with parsley or with a sauce.

Source: Madame Mérigot, *La cuisinière républicaine, qui enseigne la manière simple d'accomoder les pommes de terre; avec quelques avis sur les soins nécessaires pour les conserver* (The Republican Woman Cook, Showing the Simple Manner of Using Potatoes, with Advice on Conserving Them) (Paris: Chez Mérigot jeune, Libraire, Veuve Hérissant, Imprimeur, An III [1794–5]), 30–1. Thanks to Ronald Rosbottom for assistance with the translation.

Women and political clubs

Between 1789 and 1793 political societies and clubs proliferated, both in Paris and in the provinces. The most politically influential clubs offered full membership only to men; however, women crowded the galleries as spectators and participated in the debates that spilled out into the halls, streets, theatres and cabarets. Mixed-sex political clubs soon began to appear. One of the earliest, known as the Fraternal Society of Patriots of both Sexes, Defenders of the Constitution, probably began meeting in February of 1790. Members discussed politics and read the decrees of the National Assembly; they also addressed each other as 'brother' and 'sister', likely in imitation of a Masonic lodge (see Chapter 8), and called for the legalization of divorce and more educational opportunities for women.[20] Women-only patriotic clubs and societies also made an appearance, apparently first in the provinces. By 1793 there were scores of them, some of them very large. The Dijon women's patriotic society had 400 members, while the Bordeaux one claimed

800 members, and was said to be capable of bringing out more than 3,500 women to its outdoor rallies.[21]

Women's patriotic societies were one part school of citizenship, one part charity (favourite causes were setting up girls' schools and, after war broke out, making clothes and bandages for soldiers), and one part staging area for increasingly theatrical displays of patriotism. A women's political club that met in Marseilles from 1790 was probably fairly typical of these early efforts. It was committed to the 'public demonstration of our civic virtue ... and fidelity to the Constitution', and the members, who included the wife of the mayor, pledged to 'march under the standard of Liberty, toward the altar of the fatherland, there to swear, with their citizen-husbands, their children and their brothers, to be faithful to the Nation, to the Law and to the King'.[22] In their early stages women's clubs took up traditional feminine themes: education, charity, and, at least at first, religion (several engaged in collective prayer on behalf of the nation). But in April of 1792, after months of mutual sabre-rattling, France declared war on Austria and Prussia and within months fidelity to the king was obsolete and collective prayer the object of ridicule. The new patriotism demanded an entirely different level of commitment – and from men *and* women. As one patriotic catechism for girls – one of many from the period – put it: 'You must love your elders and friends, but you must love your country more.'[23]

But what did it really mean for a woman to 'love her country more' than she loved her family? One answer came from a group of women activists closely allied with the radical 'sans-culottes'[24] movement: women should take up arms and fight. In March of 1792 Pauline Léon (see above) and three hundred and sixteen other *citoyennes* put in a petition to that effect to the Legislative Assembly, asking not simply to be allowed to bear arms but to practise public manoeuvres with them. It is true that the petitioners tried to finesse the problem of women's duties in the home by arguing that they needed arms to protect their families and their chastity in case of enemy invasion. But at its heart the petition was grounded on the natural right to defend one's liberty and to resist oppression, recognizably revolutionary demands, and doubly so in a society where, for centuries, only aristocratic men had been permitted to bear arms. The implications were enormous. All over Europe bearing arms in the service of one's country was linked in the public mind – if, less often, in the minds of generals or heads of state – to special rights and benefits that often came to look like a species of citizenship rights. The fact that men rather than women went to battle, even if it was only a small proportion of the men, was also one of the traditional secular justifications for male supremacy. The link between bearing arms and women's freedom from oppression was spelled out a few weeks later by Théroigne de Méricourt (1762–1817), another well-known woman activist, in a speech to one of the male political clubs. She called on women to form army corps, and finished with the rousing words: 'Break our chains; it is finally time that women emerge from their shameful nullity, where ignorance, pride, and [the] injustice of men have kept them enslaved for so long.'[25]

One result of this incessant glorification of female martial spirit was that, during the Revolutionary period, more women than ever before donned uniforms and joined the military. Women fought on all sides of the many conflicts that were to follow, but they were especially prevalent among the French and their allies. At least forty women are thought to have fought in the front lines during the French Revolutionary Wars and there may have been many more.[26] A number of women also served under Napoleon. Virginie Ghesquière (1768–1867) reached the rank of sergeant fighting in the Napoleonic Wars, and was decorated for bravery. Joanna Żubr received the Polish Virtuti Militari medal for bravery (from the Duchy of Warsaw), and also achieved the rank of sergeant. She participated with her husband, an ensign, in Napoleon's invasion of Russia. Marie Schellinck (b. 1757) of Belgium served in the military for seventeen years, saw action in twelve battles, and was wounded three times. She was promoted to the rank of Lieutenant and was awarded the French Legion of Honour and a pension by Napoleon.[27] Half a dozen and probably more women would die at the Battle of Waterloo in 1815, some of them water-carriers or camp-followers, and some of them in uniform.

By 1793 the vicissitudes of war and the ever-worsening food situation helped push the balance of power in the Legislative Assembly (and the Convention that succeeded it in September of 1792) toward an especially militant faction called the Montagnards. This aggravated an already widening split among the women revolutionaries. Many of the more feminist revolutionaries, among them Olympe de Gouges and Théroigne de Méricourt, were most sympathetic to the Girondins, or moderate wing in the Assembly, who also had as one of their main political strategists Mme Roland, the brilliant wife of the Girondin Minister of the Interior (see below). On the side of the Montagnards (increasingly referred to as the Jacobins) was a new women's political club called the Society of Revolutionary Republican Women, which had been officially created on 10 May 1793, and which stood for 'prompt and vigorous measures to save the country' and the 'extermination [of] all villains'. The Society of Revolutionary Republican Women (hereafter SRRW) called not only for women to bear arms but for the creation of 'companies of Amazons' committed to fighting the 'enemies within' (that is, domestic counter-revolution) just as men were fighting the 'enemies without' (the Austrians and Prussians). Like its Montagnard allies, this new women's society nurtured an implacable hatred of the Girondins.[28]

Arguably the SRRW was more Jacobin than it was feminist, though it is true that the source material about their inner workings is not very abundant. The Society stood for direct action (street demonstrations, patriotic processions, and occasionally brawls with political rivals) and its members took little interest (at least as far as we know) in issues like women's education or the sexual double standard (its members did, however, weigh in on work for poor women and on the matrimonial code).[29] Moreover, the SRRW's disillusionment with representative institutions meant that women's political rights were never especially meaningful for its membership. Other women's organizations protested the failure of the Montagnard Constitution (never, in the event, actually implemented) to extend the vote to women; indeed, several provincial societies actually took it upon themselves to 'vote' solemnly to accept the Constitution, and then to forward the results to the Convention, accompanied by written protests at the Constitution's failure to give women political rights.[30] But we see little of this sort of thing from the SRRW; there is some evidence that the membership discussed women's capacity to govern at one of their meetings, but the authenticity of the account has been questioned.[31] It was certainly not a central part of their programme. But in the summer of 1793 direct action was what counted, and during those hectic few months of factional conflict, street violence and assassination the SRRW emerged as the most celebrated women's organization in the country.

Girondin women

Let us take a moment to look at two of the Society of Revolutionary Republican Women's enemies. Jeanne Manon Roland de la Platière (1754–1793), better known as Mme Roland, was a pillar of the more moderate Girondin party. A talented politician and a superb writer, Mme Roland had more in common with the *salonnières* of the Old Régime than with feminist theorists like Olympe de Gouges or, still less, Jacobin militants like the women of the SRRW. Along with her husband, an important Girondin, she had attended some of the meetings of at least one of the mixed-sex clubs, but she never showed much interest in women's rights, and she evidently preferred being the sole woman among a cadre of men. She also claimed to want to work only behind the scenes and wrote that she thought this the most appropriate role for women. This strategy was to prove somewhat self-defeating though. In the first place, the men she associated with were, in most cases, less able than she was, and, in the second place, her enemies seized upon her reticence to fashion her into the classic 'Old Régime' scheming female who manipulated men through sex.

In the summer of 1793 one more last-ditch effort was made stop the onward march of the Montagnards, and it took the form of the political assassination of Jean-Paul Marat, the most influential Montagnard, stabbed to death in his bath. The assassin, Charlotte Corday (1768–1793), was a twenty-five-year-old Girondin sympathizer who admitted, during her trial for murder, to having read more than five hundred political pamphlets – clear evidence, to some, of the dangers of letting women read whatever they wanted. The first modern political assassination by a woman: it was a milestone of a strange kind. Unfortunately Corday only played into the hands of the Montagnards. Soon after Marat's death, amid street demonstrations and brawls in and around the Convention, to which the SRRW made no small contribution, the last remaining Girondins were ejected from the Convention. Those who could do so fled; the rest, including Mme Roland, were imprisoned. It was from prison, while she awaited execution, that Roland wrote her remarkable revolutionary memoir, *Appeal to Impartial Posterity*, to be published after her death.

The reign of Terror

Beginning in September of that same year the Jacobins greatly increased their use of repressive security procedures originally drawn up under the Girondins, and added some innovations of their own. The bloodiest phase of the Revolution was about to begin. The Terror was a concerted effort to suppress a series of revolts in the provinces, especially in the region in and around the Vendée, eliminate political competition, quell real or suspected royalist plots, rid the country of refractory priests (that is, priests who had refused to swear an oath of loyalty to the Revolution), and generally to annihilate people opposed to the Jacobin regime. Almost seventeen thousand people were shot or guillotined at the behest of the various tribunals between March 1793 and August 1794, and at least as many may have died in prison of dysentery, typhus and the like (more than 300,000 people were imprisoned for longer or shorter periods). In the insurrectionary Vendée, up to a quarter of a million people died. Perhaps half of these succumbed to disease and the other half, including thousands of women and children, were shot, drowned, bayoneted, cut to pieces or buried alive in an orgy of killing often accompanied by rape.[32]

The Terror seemed, and to this day continues to seem, a profound betrayal of the great hopes with which the Revolution began. It was also, in some respects, business as usual. It was quite standard for early modern states (as it would be for modern ones) to respond to insurrection with large-scale killing, and the Terror was by no means the bloodiest of these. But the Terror has retained its hold on the macabre imagination of posterity, first because the *philosophes'* revolution was not supposed to be business as usual, and second because the Terror killed royals, aristocrats and members of the clergy alongside the unglamorous groups (peasants, proletarians, rank-and-file soldiers, slaves, etc.) about whom journalists, novelists and many historians have more difficulty working up an outrage. And even in the Terror, contrary to myth, the vast majority of victims of the Terror were not aristocrats but commoners: insurrectionary peasants and lower-class rural and town-dwellers who agitated against military conscription and the high price of food. More than seven times as many peasants and labourers died as did nobles, and of the total noble class less than one per cent went under what Jacobins liked to refer to as 'the avenging power of the knife'.

By far the largest group of women (around 760) to go to the guillotine was peasants, labourers, small tradeswomen and shopkeepers, laundresses, market-women, textile workers and the like. Their crimes included, among other things, making remarks against the Revolution while drunk, hanging on to royalist or Catholic mementos, and being married to or in sexual relationships with accused men. Some of them, it seems, were simply in the wrong place at the wrong time.[33] Still, women of all classes died for recognizably political activities too. Several women workers from the *ateliers patriotiques* came under suspicion essentially for having organized workers to demand better working conditions, and narrowly escaped death; some of the shop supervisors did go to the guillotine.[34] Olympe de Gouges was executed on 3 November 1793, accused of being a royalist, though her real crime was having suggested a system of secret balloting by which people could choose whether they wanted to have a republican, federalist or monarchical government. One newspaper remarked piously a few days later: '[Olympe de Gouges] wished to be a statesman and it appears that the law [has punished] this conspirator for having forgotten the virtues appropriate to her sex.'[35]

Mme Roland went to the guillotine only a few days after de Gouges, not before a number of pamphlets and flyers had appeared accusing her of sleeping with half the Girondin leadership. She is reported to have exclaimed, as she passed the statue of Goddess Liberty on her way to the guillotine: 'Ah Liberty! What crimes are committed in thy name!' The Polish noblewoman, Rozalia Lubomirska, one of the enthusiastic supporters of the reforming Polish Four-Year Sejm (see above), came to France in 1792 and got involved in a Girondist 'counter-revolutionary plot' which sent her to the guillotine in June of 1794, aged only twenty-six.

About one hundred nuns were also executed (there were perhaps fifty-five thousand women religious in France before the Revolution, though by the time of the Terror many had fled the country). Nuns had always been prominent critics of the ecclesiastical policy of the Revolutionaries. They actively championed convents in numerous written addresses to the National Assembly, emphasized their manifold services to the nation as nurses and teachers, and tried to combat efforts to vilify them by redefining themselves as citizens of the *patrie*. Some of them also angrily protested the calumnies spoken against them and the religious life; in 1792 one Benedictine abbess, in the midst of fighting off attempts to appropriate the property of her convent, went so far as to publish a defiant pamphlet likening local revolutionary officials to drinkers of blood.[36] The 'crimes' of the nuns who went to the guillotine included receiving communion from refractory priests, hiding them or their papers, corresponding with émigrés (generally relatives) and owning royalist tracts.

No victim of the Terror caused more international outcry than the former queen, Marie Antoinette (1755–1793), the daughter of Maria Theresa of Austria (see Chapter 8). A rather imprudent woman, she had been a consistent foe of the Revolution. Well before 1789 she had been vilified in the gutter press as a promiscuous schemer whose only loyalty was to her natal land, and who, by her 'execrable counsels', had supposedly influenced the king to pursue policies harmful to France. The remark she was supposed to have made when told that people were starving on account of the high price of bread ('let them eat cake') was the invention of a Jacobin propagandist. But it is an apt, albeit unfair, illustration of her reputation on the street, and it also links her to the tradition of the 'famine plot', the implicating of aristocratic women, royal mistresses, queens, etc., in alleged diabolical schemes to starve the people (see Chapter 8). During the Montagnards' surge to power, attacks on the former queen intensified, and the accusations against her grew increasingly pornographic. She was said to have slept with dozens of men and to have had lesbian affairs with two of her court ladies, the Princess de Lamballe and the Duchesse de Polignac. She was even alleged to have had an incestuous relationship with her eight-year-old son.[37] At her trial, confronted by accusations so lurid as to be almost unanswerable, she was often reduced to monosyllables. To the claim of incest she roused herself to retort that '. . . Nature herself refuses to respond to such a charge laid against a mother', and more pathetically, 'I appeal to all mothers who may be present . . .' – but she was unable to continue. On 16 October 1793 she went to the guillotine. One of the many congratulatory statements sent into the Revolutionary Tribunal afterward exulted: 'It is fallen at last, the head of the haughty Austrian woman gorged with the blood of the people.'[38]

The abolition of women's societies

By September of 1793 the Jacobins had turned against their erstwhile friends, the Society of Revolutionary Republican Women, because the society was too difficult to control, and its vocal support for the most radical delegates had started to grate on the more centrist Convention leadership. The Jacobins also glimpsed an opportunity to bolster their waning popularity by playing to what was, by this time, a growing popular backlash against political women. The rumour going around Paris was that the 'Jacobin women' were set on convincing the Convention to make all women wear their hair short, draft mothers into the army, permit women to vote in assemblies, and invalidate all marriages celebrated under the Old Régime.[39] Wild stories began circulating, like the one about a woman who was constantly running off to the galleries of the Jacobin club (or, in some versions, actually delivering speeches there) and who returned home one day to find her child burned to death. Consequently, '[her] poor [husband] has left her, wishing to live no longer with someone who believes that, for a woman to be a good Jacobin, it is necessary to be a bad mother'.[40] Meanwhile, a police spy reported ominously in late September of 1793 that

> Malevolent people . . . inspire women with the desire to share the political rights of men [and] seek to persuade them that they have as many rights as men in the government of their country, that the right to vote in the sections is a natural right that they should demand, that in a state where the law consecrates equality, women can claim all civil and military jobs.[41]

Casting about for what to do, the Convention commissioned a report on whether or not the SRRW should be closed down on grounds of being a threat to public security. Instead of confining itself to the SRRW, however, the commission took up the bigger question of whether *any* women's political societies should be allowed to exist. By late 1793 there were women's patriotic clubs in around sixty provincial towns, and they were quite diverse. The biggest had seven to eight hundred members, but could turn out double or triple that number for major events. Some had become involved in projects on behalf of the Constitutional church (the revolutionary alternative to the old Catholic Church). Many devoted time to patriotic festivals, to helping war widows, and to running workshops where poor women made bandages and the like for soldiers. Many groups were self-consciously run like political assemblies, with members voting officers in and out, passing 'laws', debating motions, and the like. A number of them had submitted memorials supporting the 'Montagnard' Constitution, and, as we have seen, some of them also explicitly asked the Convention for the vote for women. Few groups were as extreme as the SRRW, though it is true that some women's societies had taken it upon themselves to police price controls on staple foods or made themselves obnoxious to local male Jacobins by opposing them on controversial questions and having the temerity to get involved in political lobbying. Undoubtedly some were both more feminist and more committed to representative institutions than the SRRW was.[42]

The commission's report actually spent most of its time focused on something the SRRW had seldom expressed much interest in: women's participation in rational political discourse and in deliberative government. The report used two interlinked strategies to undermine any claim women might have to active citizenship. First, it argued that 'Nature' had only vouchsafed to men the extensive knowledge, unlimited attention, moral fortitude, capacity for profound and serious thought, and physical strength needed to act politically. Women not only lacked the requisite mental abilities, but would be forced 'to sacrifice the more important cares to which nature calls them', namely, marriage, household management and childrearing, if they became embroiled in politics. Second, it appealed to classical Athenian notions of female modesty and chastity: '[I]f, among ancient peoples, [women's] natural timidity and modesty did not allow them to appear outside their families, then in the French Republic do you want them to be seen coming into the gallery to political assemblies as men do? Abandoning both reserve – source of all the virtues of their sex – and the care of their families?'[43] Clearly the answer was a resounding no.

When the report was presented one or two delegates protested, but to no avail. The Convention voted overwhelmingly to shut down all women's societies. When the residue of the SRRW protested several weeks later at a meeting of the Paris Commune they were mocked as 'denatured women' and 'viragos'. Moreover, the man chairing the meeting took it upon himself to lecture them on natural law, and to observe that Nature had given women breasts as a clear sign that they should spend their time at home nursing babies, not haranguing men from the galleries. He also made a point of reminding them of the guillotining, only two weeks before, of Olympe de Gouges, 'the first to set up women's clubs', and of Madame Roland 'who thought herself fit to govern the republic and who rushed to her downfall'. The message was brutally clear.[44]

The Thermidorian reaction and beyond

In July 1794, during the month of Thermidor in the Revolutionary calendar, Maximilien Robespierre, architect of the Terror, was deposed and hastily guillotined. The women who had supported the Jacobins and, increasingly, any women who sought to get involved in politics, whatever their views, became targets of attack. The 'Gilded Youth,' the reactionary street-gangs of Thermidor, started beating up and sometimes raping women suspected of being Jacobin-sympathizers, concentrating especially on women who wore revolutionary cockades, carried weapons, or had short hair.[45] Meanwhile the food situation continued to deteriorate. By May of 1795 people in some Paris neighbourhoods were living on an ounce of bread per day. There was a spike in suicides, mostly starving people drowning themselves in the River Seine. Some mothers threw themselves in with their famished children in their arms. One of the last major instances of female activism was the insurrection of Prairial, Year III (20–24 May 1795), largely instigated by women. When it failed, the Convention passed a law banning women spectators in the galleries, and prohibiting them from attending political gatherings or gathering in groups of more than five in the street.[46] Jacobin women began being figured in contemporary media as cannibalistic hags, as in a play from 1795 entitled *Tactic of Cannibals, or the Jacobins* which featured horribly ugly 'Jacobines', ironically named 'Beauty, Youth, Virtue, and Sweetness'; all crying out for blood.[47] Even more lurid rumours were passed about in the streets, as is reflected in an account by a rather credulous Englishwoman who passed through Paris in 1796. Ostensibly she is simply describing the women she sees on the street, but the imagery is of housewifely and maternal duties gone dreadfully awry:

> . . . [F]ear gave way to curiosity [she writes] and made me more than ever attentive to the fierce and horrid countenances of the women, which were worthy [of] the savage devourers of the hearts of the murdered; an act of horror they certainly performed more than once, during the massacres. The very sight of the children made one shudder, on recollecting what I have been assured is true, that the scattered limbs of those murdered by their parents, had served them to play with in the streets.[48]

By this time the activist women of the former SRRW and the Paris Sections were in full retreat, but so too were those feminists in Paris and the provinces who had hoped for law reform, a greater role in governance, the vote, better treatment of unwed mothers and illegitimate children, more job opportunities, and improvements in girls' education. All political women were lumped together in an onrushing wave of reactionary conservatism. The new orthodoxy was that women who attended meetings or talked about starting societies were defying nature and neglecting their real duties as mothers and wives. The most influential contribution of the post-Thermidor period to the question of women and politics, Charles Guillaum Theremin's *De la condition des femmes dans les républiques* (On the Condition of Women in Republics) of 1799 used a mix of Rousseauism, biological and psychological determinism, and domestic feminist gender-mysticism to attack political women *en bloc*. Theremin claimed that no real women ever tried to invade the sphere of men: 'women are happy to be our co-sovereigns, and they never demand to be the generals of an army of women, [or] presidents of a feminine legislative body . . .' Women who did demand such things (one reminds oneself that he is writing only six years after Olympe de Gouges went under the guillotine) were not real women. In Theremin's words they were 'hideous androgynes', 'divided beings who belong to neither sex . . . and can fulfill neither the functions of men nor those of women'. Predictably Theremin was opposed to women possessing a vote or participating in politics, on the grounds that they already exercised a far more comprehensive sovereignty, 'their imperishable power over the hearts of men'.[49] Theremin married traditional themes of domestic feminism (including the coupling of fulsome praise of women with a suspicious attitude toward any who asked for legal or political rights) to emerging conceptions of the 'republican man', figured as rational, independent, in command of his own household, and fully capable of acting politically both on behalf of himself *and* his dependent wife. Behind the republican man was a masculine deliberative assembly whose independence and high standard of disinterested republican virtue were defined and confirmed by their separation from the world of women.[50] Egalitarian feminists both in France and in England published pamphlets refuting Theremin, and calling for a larger role for women than being votive goddesses for men, but by that time the backlash against political women, across the political spectrum, was too massive for them to have much impact.[51]

Napoleon Bonaparte staged his *coup d'état* on 9 November 1799, and around the same time the title '*citoyenne*', borne so proudly by women revolutionaries of all stripes, began to fall out of favour. The elements that made up Napoleon's Consulate and then empire thought it sounded vulgar, and it came increasingly to be reserved for servants, and then dropped away altogether. The preferred term of address for a respectable woman reverted to either '*madame*' or '*mademoiselle*'; the effect, no doubt welcome to men like Theremin, was to insert women symbolically back into the family, define them primarily by class and marital status, and distance them from the very name of citizenship.[52]

The émigrées

The Revolution created a permanent rift between the revolutionaries and those who had profited from or identified with the Old Régime, not to mention the many who had once lived well and now found their property confiscated, their names dragged in the mud, their priests executed or turned out, and their brothers, sons and husbands sent off to die in quixotic efforts to regain what they had lost. Only a minority of the émigrés were actually noble (between sixteen and seventeen per cent), though it was these who inspired the greatest sympathy and who naturally took the lead in the émigré communities established in England, the Netherlands, Prussia, Austria, Switzerland, Spain, Portugal, Italy, Russia, the Ottoman Empire, and even as far away as New York and Venezuela.

The émigré(e)s began by trying to live as they had done in France, but many were soon reduced to poverty because the revolutionaries confiscated and sold their estates. Numerous aristocratic women found themselves working for a living for the first time in their lives, often doing fine embroidery, though the Comtesse de Flahaut supported herself writing novels, and one Mlle Mérelle tried and apparently failed to fashion a career for herself as a harpist. Foreign governments distrusted the émigré(e)s as possible revolutionaries themselves, and, in any case, French and therefore likely libertine.[53] Stéphanie de Genlis (1746–1830), novelist, educator, children's book writer (see Chapter 8), and author of what is arguably the first book of feminist literary criticism, *The Influence of Women on French Literature* (1811), was able to get a permit to reside in Prussia, but the printers were ordered not to publish her works unless they obtained special permission from the Department of Foreign Affairs, and ultimately she was asked to leave. Accustomed to being able to wield a certain amount of influence, some noblewomen tried to confront this new crisis head on. The Archduchess Maria Christina of Belgium, sister of the executed Marie Antoinette, had had to flee to Bonn in the face of the advancing French army. There she is reported to have passed the time marking the positions of the various armies with coloured wax markers on a military map and she was said to know more about troop movements than most men; rumour had it she had also fired cannon.[54] In a similar vein, in 1814 a group of French monarchist noblewomen joined forces to publish the memoirs of Renée Bordereau (b. 1770), a *guerillera* of the Vendée, who had joined the revolt to revenge the massacre, at Republican hands, of most of her family. According to the preface 'history offers no example of a woman who has given her sovereign more constant proof of her fidelity, who has shown more bravery and steadiness in the field of battle'. The Bordereau memoirs also offered an opportunity to show their heroine saving innocent women from would-be Republican rapists, protecting children, old people, and priests, giving away all her booty for the relief of refugees, and killing numerous Republican men, including one who was allegedly carrying around an infant spitted on his bayonet.[55] The French revolutionaries with their ceaseless praise of female martial spirit and real-life female brigades had set an example, and even monarchists found themselves following suit.

The largest single émigré occupational group was the clergy, and they came not just from France but from places threatened by the French armies. The English gothic novelist Anne Radcliffe, travelling through Northern Europe in 1796, describes groups of refugee nuns 'driven from some convent in Flanders', living miserably on barges near Dort, partially open to the elements, still wearing their habits, and occupying themselves with needle-work, which, presumably, they hoped to exchange for food.[56] The most miserable émigrés tended to be old servants whose former employers could no longer afford to keep them on, seamstresses, who had to cope with a market flooded with women whose only skill was sewing, widows, and people with much pride but few resources and even fewer saleable skills. Homegrown aristocracies mobilized to help the émigré nobility, but far less attention was paid to commoner refugees of either sex. For many of these women and men the Revolution was an unmitigated disaster. Even before the end of Napoleon's reign, nine-tenths of them had returned to France.[57]

THE AFTERMATH

Gains and (mostly) losses

Women did not gain the vote from the Revolution or the right to sit in the Legislative Assembly or National Convention. However, they did benefit tangibly from several legal reforms. The divorce law of 1792, a remarkably egalitarian document for its time, permitted both women and men unilaterally to initiate divorce on grounds of incompatibility as well as other grounds, including cruelty. It has been estimated that 30,000 divorces occurred during the period 1792 to 1803 and in some towns up to two-and-a-half times more women than men petitioned for divorce, most often citing domestic violence against them or their children.[58] A series of laws passed between 1791 and 1794 established equal inheritance regardless of gender or birth order, benefiting not only many women, but younger sons, and even illegitimate children; it also fixed the age of majority for women at twenty-one, a considerable improvement. The new inheritance laws aimed above all at eliminating the material basis for aristocracy (particularly primogeniture in the male line), and it sent many newly empowered women to court to demand their rights from fathers, uncles, and particularly brothers who had never thought they would have to share the family patrimony with a woman.[59]

As we saw, revolutionary feminists had often identified men's oppression of women with despotism and this theme was also taken up by women in their court cases and associated petitions. However, now the targets were much more personal: fathers who sacrificed the well-being of daughters to concentrate resources on one son; husbands who deliberately removed to towns whose legal regimes would allow them to have enhanced power over their wives' dowries; and brothers who failed to pay their sisters' patrimonies. Court cases speak of 'unnatural brothers', who had 'usurped' women's rightful property; and even of 'marital despotism', showing that the revolutionary feminist rhetoric was having a wide influence. Similar language can be found in the many individual and group petitions that showered down on the Convention when it looked like the equal inheritance laws might be scaled back. A petition from forty *citoyennes* of Calvados in Normandy in 1793 complained that single women 'lack the bare necessities of life while their brothers, living in abundance, stubbornly deny them not only humanitarian aid but even [the] small share that the old custom accorded'. A petition from forty women of the district of Falaise asserted: 'At birth nature gave us equal rights to the succession of our fathers.' And one *Citoyenne* LeFranc from Caen wrote with pardonable exaggeration to the men of the National Convention: 'you have only passed one law beneficial to women, the law of 17 nivôse [that is, the equal inheritance law]. If you destroy this law of equality that has converted to the Republic an infinity of women and girls led astray by the fanaticism of priests, they will say with good reason that you are unjust and that you have taken advantage of the fact that we are not represented at the Convention. . . . They will say to you that men have made the laws and they have made them for themselves.'[60]

After Thermidor, the Convention began edging away from these earlier reforms, and few of them survived the enacting of the Napoleonic Code in 1804. The code did not, as is sometimes asserted, eliminate women's right to divorce, but it did narrow the grounds and make it considerably harder for a woman than for a man to obtain a divorce (even that equivocal benefit did not last long, because in 1816 the restored Bourbon monarchy *did* abolish divorce, and it was not legalized again until 1884). The Napoleonic Code also divested illegitimate children of inheritance rights, and, while keeping aspects of the equal inheritance law, gave parents more discretion over bequests than the Jacobins had done. It swept away customary (and pre-revolutionary) laws and practices that, in some areas, had permitted married women to control their own property. And it stripped single women of most legal rights. In the long run, therefore, women gained little in legal terms from the Revolution, and at least some of them lost badly, especially on the marital property front.[61]

And what of the revolutionary women activists? As we have seen, the Revolution briefly offered unprecedented opportunities for women to enter the world of politics. It may have been even more significant in terms of their entry into the Republic of Print. Women published more than two hundred and fifty political works between 1789 and 1800, scores of them recognizably both egalitarian and feminist. Along with this there was a significant upswing in the number of women publishing works of all kinds, including novels, books of history, plays, memoirs, songs, letters, religious tracts and legal treatises. Women also founded and edited more than twenty journals. Moreover, the publishing trend – unlike the women's political clubs – survived into the nineteenth century.[62] Still, it seems likely that, if she had managed to survive the Terror, Olympe de Gouges would have been dispirited by what she saw. By the late 1790s misogynist sentiment seemed to be everywhere. Political women in general were being demonized for the excesses of the few, and it proved easier to blame 'blood-drinking Jacobin hags' for the Terror than the men who actually allowed it to occur. Domestic feminism did emerge stronger than ever from the Revolution, thanks to men like Theremin, and even more to the Catholic Church, but it was very much at the expense of more egalitarian strains. It was to be a very long time before there was a significant liberalization in the position of French women, either in terms of law reform or political rights. French women finally voted in their first national election in 1945, a quarter century or more after most other European women gained the suffrage, and fifteen years after Turkey and much of central Asia.

Slavery and its critics

Abolitionist and anti-slavery movements[63] were, like the various revolutions, partly a product of the Enlightenment focus on natural rights, though in practice they were often more indebted to the rise of sensibility. In the eighteenth century 'sensibility' referred, among other things, to the capacity of refined people to empathize with the feelings and particularly the pain of others. Women were supposed to be especially capable of this sort of deep feeling, and a number of humanitarian movements, including concern for destitute children, opposition to the slave trade, and the prevention of cruelty to animals grew out of this (relatively) novel interest in vicariously experiencing others' pain while at the same time participating in attempts to salve or diminish it. Slaves had, of course, long been involved in efforts to win freedom for themselves. As we have seen, they used religious conversion, the courts, appeals to various monarchs, self-purchase and flight, and in some places (Brazil; some Ottoman cities; London) slaves and free blacks also formed political and religious organizations that tried to help other people win their freedom. There were some connections between slaves and former slaves and British abolitionists, most of them involving efforts by members of London's black community and sympathetic whites to keep individual slaves from being transported to the West Indies and resold. But blacks were not, on the whole, welcomed as equals into European abolitionist or anti-slavery movements, even though some slaves or former slaves, most famously Mary Prince (b. 1788?), publicly voiced opposition to slavery, in Prince's case in a powerful memoir, published in 1831, about her life as a slave.[64]

In the 1760s, even as the political situation heated up in the thirteen American colonies, graphic accounts of the mental, physical and sexual abuses of slavery began appearing in sentimental novels and poetry. Most of the early anti-slavery polemics also date from this period.[65] White European women, particularly English and French women, did contribute to this project, though it is also true that many of them were slow to abandon meliorism with respect to the institution of slavery. English feminist and novelist Sarah Scott's *Sir George Ellison* (1766), set partly in Jamaica, calls for slaves to be educated, converted to Christianity, and allowed to marry and own small plots of land. Rather radically, it also advocates ending the use of the lash. And it asserts that the power of the slave-owner is 'merely political' and that slavery, while it might be functionally necessary, is neither divinely ordained nor a natural right (the similarities with feminist arguments about women's subjection within marriage are striking). But Scott did not envisage actually ending slavery as an institution, at least not at that point in her life.[66]

The most radical woman critics of slavery all emerged after 1780, amid the atmosphere of anticipation that accompanied the American and later the French Revolution. In Olympe de Gouges' play *L'Esclavage des noirs* (Black Slavery) (1786, revised 1792) the hero, an educated slave named Zamor, murders a white official (referred to by Zamor as 'that barbarian') who had been trying to rape his love, Mirza. The play attributes slavery purely to colour prejudice and greed, and Zamor looks forward to 'Enlightened men' returning 'this precious liberty [freedom], man's primary treasure, of which cruel ravishers have deprived us for so long.' In the course of the action Zamor saves the life of a white woman and Mirza befriends the woman as an equal. Finally Zamor is pardoned, despite having killed a white man (an issue that made the play extremely controversial at the time) and both he and Mirza gain their freedom, though general emancipation must await the coming to power of 'Enlightened men', presumably seated in one or another French legislative assembly.[67]

As it was in so many other areas, the French Revolution proved to be a watershed in the history of discrimination on the basis of religion and race. Though it involved a considerable struggle, in September of 1791 it was finally agreed that Jews would enjoy all the privileges of French citizens. In April 1792 full civil rights were extended to free men of colour in all French colonies, and on 4 February 1794, in response to the rebellion in Haiti (Saint-Domingue), slavery was abolished in the French Colonies (this was reversed in 1802 under Napoleon, though, and only made permanent in 1848). Black activists in France and in the Caribbean played important roles in both the latter two decisions. In fact, two men of colour sat as delegates in the French National Convention in the mid-1790s, Jean-Baptiste Belley, a free black, and Jean-Baptiste Mills, a free mulatto, both from the French colony of Haiti.[68]

The sequence of events, and, at least to some extent, the motives that, in 1807, led Britain to become the first major slave-trading nation to permanently abolish the slave trade (Portugal had done so earlier, though incompletely), were somewhat different. In Britain, for many, if not all, of the white activists, Christian humanitarianism was far more salient than (say) a natural right to be free of bondage, much less a commitment to racial equality. English abolitionists deplored the cruelties of slave-traders and white women activists were often drawn into the movement by their genuine horror at the sexual and physical abuse of slave-women. But many of them, especially those associated with the Evangelical movement, also believed in the racial inferiority of Africans, and were not above suggesting that, distasteful as it was, at least slavery offered these 'savages' exposure to Christianity.[69] This is clearly on display in 'the Sorrows of Yamba, or the Negro Woman's Lamentation' (1795), a poem co-written by Hannah More, which ventriloquizes the slave-woman, Yamba, immediately after her conversion by a local missionary, as follows:

> Now I'll bless my cruel capture,
>   (Hence I've known a Saviour's name)
> Till my Grief is turn'd to Rapture,
>   And I half forget the blame.

This after having been torn away from her husband and two children, had her baby die during the middle passage, been half-starved, 'mangled by whipping', and driven to attempt suicide.[70] A surprising number of the more conservative abolitionists, moreover, were, at best, luke-warm emancipationists; they sought to end the Transatlantic *trade* in slaves but were less committed to and sometimes opposed eliminating slavery as an institution (this partly explains the thirty-year gap between the 1807 abolition of the British slave trade and the emancipation of slaves in the British colonies).

Nevertheless, especially in Britain, abolitionism and anti-slavery agitation was one of the other major routes through which many white women moved into politics, with huge numbers of women, from the late 1780s on, participating in boycotts of slave-produced goods (especially sugar), organizing petition drives, and the like. It is also true that many white abolitionists never abandoned the belief that people of colour should remain in permanent tutelage to whites. The ending of slavery – earlier or later, depending upon the country – was important and necessary, and European women, especially British women, made a real contribution to it. But it also ended up as one element in a set of claims about the superior sensibility and humanitarianism of western Europe in general and Britain in particular, proof of Europe's duty and destiny to 'save' the allegedly monstrously oppressed and helpless women of other races and nationalities. One result was that western Europe sailed smartly into the era of high imperialism with a good many feminists aboard.[71]

The Revolution outside France

France in 1789 was one of the largest, most powerful and most culturally influential countries in Europe and the Revolution was the major news event for a generation. For liberals and reformers everywhere it seemed, at least at first, the harbinger of a new and far better world. It was also a challenge to rethink old assumptions about privilege, even among some of the privileged themselves. In Denmark the Countess Louise Stolberg, sister of one of the country's most influential men, burned her family tree in the drawing room fireplace in a symbolic repudiation of hereditary nobility.[72] In many parts of Europe there were calls – usually, but not always rebuffed – to free serfs, curtail the power of the clergy, and institute equality before the law regardless of rank.

There is no question that the very visible participation of women in the early years of the French Revolution inspired many women in other lands. The revolutionary form of address for women ('*citoyenne*') was widely imitated, and some of the time so was the feminism. In Saint-Domingue-Haiti and Guadeloupe former slave-women freed in the emancipations of 1793–94 began to be called '*nouvelles citoyennes*' (new citizenesses) or sometimes '*citoyennes noires*' (black citizenesses).[73] Thaddeus Kosciuszko's 'Appeal to Polish women' of April 1794, part of the general mobilization of Poland against Russian occupation, referred ringingly to the 'citizenesses' he hoped would support the effort. Gioseffa Cornoldi Caminer, who had edited the first Italian journal explicitly for women, *La donna galante ed erudite*, turned up ten years later as *la cittadina* (citizeness) Cornoldi Caminer, a translator of pro-Jacobin pamphlets. Carolina Lattanzi, from Mantua, who also described herself as '*cittadina*', presented a public address on 'Schiavitù delle donne' (the Slavery of Women) in 1797, dating it, in Jacobin fashion, 'Year I of the Liberty of Italy': 'you [men] hate one despot; we [women] detest the aristocracy of men, under which we have suffered for so many centuries...'[74] An anonymous Italian oration from the late 1790s argued that, apart from breast-feeding, men should share all household tasks, including cooking and childrearing, and called for 'women's right to participate in all public assemblies and in the ratification of all laws and to hold all public offices'.[75]

In London, popular debating societies had been debating questions about women and political rights since 1780, but in the 1790s, despite a significant increase in government intimidation, some began taking up the topic in a more pointed way, usually by way of debating the ideas of Mary Wollstonecraft. In an ad from 1795 two 'female citizens', partisans of Wollstonecraft, proposed to defend the topic 'Would it not be advantageous to the liberty and happiness of the world that women should equally partake [of] all the rights and privileges of man?' And in 1797 the Westminster Forum debated the question 'In the present Association of the Sexes is not Man a Tyrant and Woman a Slave?'[76] Feminist pamphlets, articles and novels, both by women and by men, appeared in Britain, Spain, Sweden, several of the German States, the Italian Peninsula, the Netherlands, Hungary and no doubt other places. A group of 'Hungarian Mothers' published a pamphlet in 1790 arguing that Hungarian noblewomen should enjoy the same rights as noblemen – including the right of election to the Hungarian diet. The next year noblewomen (perhaps the same group) scaled back their demands and requested the right to attend debates when the diet met. Another Hungarian tract from the period deplored the 'subjugation of women' and argued that since queens could wear crowns women should be able to hold other sorts of government offices as well.[77] Feminist tracts also appeared in some of the European colonies. Judith Sargent Murray (1751–1820), of Gloucester, Massachusetts, had written her 'On the Equality of the Sexes' earlier, but it was in the heady year 1790 that she actually published it. Like many she turned against the French Revolution during its Jacobin phase, but in her 'Observations on Female Abilities' (1798), a tract full of female sacrifice on behalf of chastity, nations and the public good, she commended the heroism of Charlotte Corday, and argued that Mme Roland 'not only dignified the [female] Sex, but human nature in the aggregate; and her memory will be held in veneration, wherever talents, literature, patriotism, and uniform heroism, are properly appreciated'.[78]

Several revolutions followed the French Revolution, but the Haitian Revolution of 1791–1804, an incendiary combination of anti-imperial struggle, slave revolt, and Jacobinism, may have had the most long-lasting significance, especially in the New World. One of the pivotal moments in that struggle was the unilateral abolition (later ratified by the French National Convention) of the slaves of Saint-Domingue by Commissioner Legé Félicité Sonthonax in 1793. This was primarily a military manoeuvre, designed to win support for the Republic against a counter-revolution by royalists supported by the British. However, the act was preceded by considerable agitation, and

Sonthonax is supposed to have been pushed to it by a petition signed by 882 field-workers, presented in a formal ceremony during which, as a near contemporary account describes, 'women, carrying their children or holding them by the hand . . . , threw themselves at his feet, while calling for the triumph of the Republic and liberty'.[79] In 1804, after much bloodshed, Haiti became the second independent nation in the New World (the first being the United States). It was, however, the first black republic, and the first led by former slaves or the children of slaves. The fact that black troops defeated European armies and that blacks and mulattos proved capable of forming a functioning government played the kind of inspirational role among slaves and the colonized in the Caribbean and across the Americas that the American and French Revolutions had in Europe. And yet, when the Haitians came to write their constitution in 1805 it contained the line 'no one is worthy of being a Haitian if he is not a good father, a good son, a good husband, and above all a good soldier'. In Mimi Sheller's words '[it] foreshadow[ed] the militarization of the state, the marginalization of women, and the depiction of citizens as male protectors of family and nation'.[80] Moreover, as in Europe, the post-revolutionary regime both demanded that 'respectable' women take up a primarily maternal role, and painted market-women and other women with public roles – the same women who, before the revolution, had often used their trading profits to purchase their own and others' freedom – as promiscuous women who consorted with the colonial oppressor and dishonoured the republic.[81]

Women also played a role in the Irish Rebellion of 1798, which was also partly inspired by the other revolutions. Women formed associations (the United Irishwomen, an auxiliary to the United Irishmen), swore oaths of secrecy like the men, and were involved in spying and trying to undermine the morale of the loyalist (pro-British) forces. As in many nationalist struggles, insurrectionary rhetoric was highly gendered. Claims were made that loyalists were engaged in the systematic rape of Irish women (and certainly, especially during the 1797 and 1798 counter-insurgency, some rapes did occur), and this was accompanied by a more figurative image of Ireland 'raped' by British rule. Opposing it was the familiar trope of the patriot mother who, in the words of Nancy J. Curtin, 'urges her boy to choose death with honour' rather than betray his comrades and his country.[82] As in other revolutionary contexts, some women sought a more permanent expansion of their public role. Mary Ann McCracken, sister of Henry Joy McCracken, leader of the insurgency in County Antrim, was an admirer of the English feminist and republican, Mary Wollstonecraft. Writing to her brother in prison, she exclaimed: 'Is it not almost time for the clouds of error and prejudice to disperse and that the female part of the Creation as well as the male should throw off the fetters with which they have so long been mentally bound?' And she expressed a hope that the new Irish nation would extend more generous rights to women than any nation had done before.[83] As it turned out, the rebellion was brutally crushed, and Henry, along with Mary Ann McCracken's fiancé, Thomas Russell, were executed. Mary Ann spent the rest of her long life engaged in charitable endeavours on behalf of women and the poor – a very different future than the one of which she had dreamed.[84]

Jacobin-inspired revolutionaries also tried to establish a republic in the former Kingdom of Naples (now part of Southern Italy). There, as in many parts of Europe, invading French armies found homegrown radicals prepared to help them bring freedom to their own countries. In Naples one of the most dramatic carriers of the revolutionary flame was Eleonora Fonseca Pimentel (1752–1798), of Portuguese origin, but raised in Italy. A true daughter of the Enlightenment, Fonseca Pimentel once engaged in a public exchange of verses (in a literary journal) with the then aged Voltaire. Inspired by the events of 1789, she soon became a fervent revolutionary. She was closely involved with the setting up of the short-lived Neapolitan republic (declared in January of 1799) and was appointed director of the fledgling republic's first political periodical, the *Monitore Napoletano*, which she filled with impassioned editorials. Unfortunately for her and her comrades, the Catholic Church proved better at winning hearts and minds than the republicans. In the summer of 1799, an army of 17,000 Catholic peasants, the Santafede (armada of the holy faith) led by Cardinal Fabrizio Ruffo, marched on the fledgling republic, and when Napoleon abandoned his Neapolitan allies the die was cast. Facing impossible odds, the republicans surrendered in July. Many would be massacred in the streets as 'enemies of God'; Fonseca Pimentel escaped that fate but was brought to trial by the restored Bourbon monarchy a few weeks later, accused of 'public speech in the streets, speech on platforms, and the drafting of a sordid newspaper'. In her defence she stated that she acted '. . . so that Neapolitan ground could become free'. She was executed by hanging on 20 August 1799.[85]

By this time public opinion in many places had turned against the Revolution. Certainly there were still holdouts. In Philadelphia and New York, pro-Jacobin women were known for dressing ostentatiously in French fashions, wearing the *tricouleur* and singing French revolutionary songs. As late as 1800, a group of New Jersey women celebrated the Fourth of July (America's Independence Day) by toasting 'the female Republicans of France' and 'the rights of women – may they never be curtailed'.[86] But even in the distant American Republic reaction had set in. It is not coincidental that it was New Jersey women drinking to the rights of women, for New Jersey was the only state where some women and free black had the vote. The New Jersey state constitution of 1776, promulgated in the same year as the American Declaration of Independence, had set forth the right to vote of 'all free inhabitants' who met residency and property requirements. More than likely, this did not reflect any burning desire to include women or free black men; it was probably a case of careless drafting. Be that as it may, in the 1780s both white women and free black people who met the property and residency requirements did successfully exercise their right to vote in local elections, and in 1790 a new election law actually acknowledged what was, by then, the status quo, and referred to voters as 'he or she'. For the next seventeen years women of both races and free black men who met the property require- ments voted freely and openly in New Jersey elections. Moreover, in at least one election for the state legislature, that of 1797, a bloc of women rather ostentatiously tried, and almost succeeded, in swinging the vote in one of the state's largest cities against a man named John Condict. Not a man to forget a slight, in 1807 Condict retaliated by putting in a Bill to 'restore the safety, quiet, good order and dignity of the state' by disfranchising women and black people. The main rationale was that both groups lacked the intellect to reason politically, and could be easily manipulated by their lovers, husbands, parents, and employers. In other words, unlike propertied white men, they could not really be virtuous (that is, independent) voters. There was also a strong implication that voting was incompatible with 'female reserve and delicacy', that women and black people were especially prone to corruption, and that allowing such people to vote would expose the state of New Jersey to ridicule. The Bill passed into law, and as a result black men did not vote again in New Jersey until 1870 and women of any race until 1920.[87]

The Ottoman Empire

Istanbul had a large French population, a good number of whom sided with the revolution. By 1793 republican clubs had sprung up in Izmir, Aleppo and Istanbul, presumably started by French expatriates. There is also said to have been a 'formidable' movement in favour of the revolution by Turks who were resentful over the tendency of Louis XVI's government to favour Austria and Russia. Turkish republicans wore the revolutionary tricolour cockade, and addressed one another as friend ('*dost*') and brother ('*kardache*').

In the Istanbul suburb of Pera both French and Turkish 'patriots' danced around a tree of liberty and sang revolutionary songs. There was also considerable support for the Revolution at court, especially within the pro-reform faction that came to the fore under the Ottoman sultan Selim III (r. 1789–1808). It is likely that some of this support was concentrated in the harem, because Selim III's mother, Mihrişah, and her *kethüda* (the woman official who looked after her extensive political and financial affairs) were both strong supporters of Selim's reforms. Ultimately Selim formed an alliance with the French National Convention, though there was soon a cooling of affections, and Napoleon's invasion of Egypt (1798–1801) was the *coup de grâce*. Still, during Selim's reign and that of his successor, Mahmut II (1808–1839) we hear a great deal about Ottoman royal women (particularly princesses, who always had more freedom than other members of the royal family and who often maintained their own palaces) entertaining foreign women, talking in public to foreign men, riding around town in their carriages, and even, in one case, that of Hatice Sultan, Selim's sister, visiting a foreign dignitary's villa to observe the work of an Austrian landscape architect whom she later employed to beautify her own palace.[88] The Tanzimat reforms, which began in 1839 but had numerous antecedents in the reigns of both Selim III and Mahmut II, would pick up several revolutionary themes, most notably an interest in women's education, patriotic motherhood and famous women from the past.[89]

The French Revolution had a powerful influence in the Balkans where it provided inspiration to several generations of nationalist revolutionaries intent on throwing off Austrian or Ottoman rule. The contradictions of female politicization were very much on view. Rushing fearlessly into the arms of death has always had a certain iconic appeal for patriots, perhaps even more when those rushing were women. Thus, there was a persistent association of women of the Souliote Confederacy (an area of persistent Greek resistance to the Ottomans) with battle, but they were most famous because a group of them hurled themselves and their children over a steep cliff in 1803 to their deaths rather than be taken alive by the Turks.[90] Suicidal actions by women in war, often merged (as in this case) with the ancient trope of women killing themselves in defence of their chastity, would become a favourite theme of romantic nationalism. It also made its way into women's writing. The first modern Greek woman playwright, Evanthia Kairi (1799–1866)'s play *Nikiratos* (1826), about the siege of Missolonghi by the Ottomans in that same year, is indicative of the mood. Kairi was a strong advocate of Greek women's rights, and, like her famous brother,

Theofilus Kairis, a secularist. She was deeply committed to the Greek War of Independence, and in 1825, along with thirty-one other women, had published *Letter of Some Greek Women to the Women Philhellenes*, describing the enormities perpetrated against Greek women by the Ottoman armies. The play itself focuses upon a group of Greek women who are prepared to (and ultimately do) sacrifice their lives for their country: they declaim in chorus at one point: 'We prefer death/over indecent and dishonourable slavery . . . /We, too, will die free.'[91] Rape of Christian women by Turks would become a central trope of anti-Ottoman propaganda throughout the nineteenth century. It also won an enduring place in pornography, giving rise to a robust and long-lived pictorial genre consisting of extremely explicit scenarios of 'dark skinned' Turkish men raping naked 'white skinned' Christian women. This persistent trope both fuelled religious division and helped to justify 'retaliatory' rapes of Muslim women into the modern period.[92]

Conservative reaction and religious revival

The French Revolution's major unintended consequence was the creation across Europe of a powerful and long-lived party, vested in the churches, the old aristocracy, and the more hidebound monarchies, that viewed 1789 as anathema, democracy as a plague, secularism and religious toleration as a modern heresy, and feminism as a crime against nature. The émigré aristocracy and a substantial portion of the Catholic Church formed the bitter nucleus of this tendency, but they were joined by many aristocrats and churchmen of other lands and faiths, both shocked at the enormities perpetrated in France and worried that their own lower orders, not to mention their wives and daughters, would get out of hand.

The change in the Catholic Church was especially striking. Before the Revolution many Catholic clerics of both sexes enthusiastically championed the expansion of women's sphere, in at least some cases going well beyond calling for women's access to education.[93] The more liberal among them also supported religious toleration and an end to clerical celibacy, and welcomed the notion of a more ethical church that put ordinary parishioners' needs ahead of currying favour with the nobility. A number of French men of the cloth initially joined the Revolution, and in other countries clerics – in a few cases even bishops – supported republican initiatives right through the 1790s.[94] However, as it turned out, the French Revolution took an extremely radical, anti-clerical and ultimately anti-Christian turn, and there were efforts to export this to some of the countries France conquered in the wars of the

1790s. As a result, most of the more activist Catholic clergy – at least those who stayed in the church – gravitated toward counter-revolutionary movements and even military actions. This was true in the insurrectionary Vendée, in French-occupied Italy, in southern Germany and in Spain. And in the early nineteenth century the church turned significantly more intransigent on a number of social and political questions, including religious toleration (they usually opposed it) and on questions to do with women.[95] In the next two centuries the Vatican would become the strongest single international force opposing women's suffrage, married women's property rights, the liberalization of divorce and women's reproductive freedom, including the right to abortion and birth control. Would the church have turned so decisively against women's rights had it not been for the Revolution? It seems unlikely.

It was not just the church hierarchy that turned conservative, nor was it just Catholics. Beginning in the 1790s and lasting well into the nineteenth century, Europe (and many of its colonies and former colonies) experienced a wave of popular religious revivals. In Catholic countries, as we have seen, there was a massive growth in Marian movements, which especially appealed to women, and an upswing in sightings of the Virgin, saints' miracles and the like (see Chapter 6). Large popular evangelistic and often millenarian movements arose or intensified in virtually all the Protestant regions too, including England, Scandinavia and some of the German-speaking states. A number of these viewed the Enlightenment, with its emphasis on the pursuit of freedom, equality and happiness in this life, as the teachings of the devil and the French Revolution as a judgment from God. And yet, the more radical sects also incorporated aspects of the revolutionary programme, such as fairly 'democratic' sect governance structures, an emphasis on lay preaching and a relatively prominent role for women. Several of the newer religious sects and denominations permitted women to preach, and there were a number of female mystics and messianic figures, the two most famous being Joanna Southcott in England (see Chapter 6) and Julie, Baroness de Krüdener (1764–1824), whose millenarian prophecies convinced Alexander I, Tsar of Russia, at least for a time, to join the Christian revivalist band.[96]

Further south, in the Balkans the Orthodox revivalism that began with Saint Kosmas (see Chapter 6) expanded further, and in time blended with the various anti-Ottoman and anti-Austrian nationalist movements of the nineteenth century. But in the short term, fear of the spread of revolutionary ideas inspired both the Ottoman authorities and the Greek Orthodox church (whose hierarchy was often pro-Ottoman) to crack down on dissent, or at least to worry about it in ways they had not done before. So, for example, there were anxious reports from Orthodox churchmen in 1798 that Maniot Greek women were burning candles before a portrait of Napoleon 'the Great Liberator', just as they did before household icons. And a report to the Ottoman Grand Vizier in the same year warned darkly of the spread of subversive works in France by 'known and famous atheists' like Voltaire, and that heresy was 'spreading like syphilis' even to young people and women. The fear clearly was that the contagion would spread to the empire, and indeed, the following year, the government, in typically Ottoman poly-denominational fashion, began making proclamations in Syria and elsewhere warning people away from French ideas, because the latter 'assert that the books which the prophets brought are clear error and that the Qur'an, the Torah and the Gospels are nothing but lies and idle talk'.[97]

Meanwhile, in heavily Muslim parts of Southern Russia, beginning around 1800, a series of movements got underway, in defiance of the Russian Orthodox establishment and Russian law, to win back lapsed Muslims to the faith. It is not clear whether this was the product of Sufi revivalism washing West from central Asia or French revolutionary or millenarian themes washing East from Europe – or both. What is clear is that Muslim women took enthusiastically to missionary activities, especially educational projects and the distribution of Sufi tracts and pamphlets. Interestingly, a number of these featured powerful, miracle-working women and Sufi seekers. In one of them Fatima, the prophet's daughter, works miracles; another, The Tale of Joseph, features a central feminine character, Zuleikha, who becomes a Seeker of God. In another tract a woman uses prayer to stave off a giant from raping and eating her. And in the book of St. Mary, Maryam rises from the dead to comfort and fortify her desperate son, Isa/Jesus.[98]

After the final fall of Napoleon in 1815, conservatives tried to turn back the clock to the time before 1789. This meant often savage repression of democratizing, lower-class or anti-colonial movements, policing of the press and all kinds of organizations (even, as we have seen, some domestic feminist organizations), trying to reinstate the repressive power of the various churches, re-establishing monarchies (in some cases where there had been none before) and preaching a version of feminine domesticity that was far more thorough-going than anything seen in the previous century. Earlier it was argued that the real winner in the post-revolutionary period was domestic feminism. But in fact it was, in some ways, even more conservative than its eighteenth-century predecessors. Caroline Pichler (1769–1843), a Viennese salon woman with close links to the Habsburg monarchy, exemplifies the trend. Pichler's mother, Charlotte Greiner, had been the Empress Maria Theresa's secretary and close associate, and toward the end of Maria Theresa's reign and into the 1790s, Greiner ran a salon much frequented by Viennese poets and musicians, including Wolfgang Amadeus Mozart. Presumably she endorsed the conservative, Catholic maternalist-feminism of her friend and employer. But Caroline Pichler proved to be significantly more conservative than her hardly radical mother, especially on the women's issue: 'The opinions of my mother herself on the unjust situation we [women] find ourselves with respect to man . . . even the pretended rights of women, raise no echo in my soul' she wrote. Pichler believed that nature had been right to assign women a subordinate role, and that men were superior to women even in 'properly feminine' activities such as cooking and embroidery. Moreover, she confessed that she never felt at ease with intellectual women like Madame de Staël, whom she thought too masculine, and she seems to have viewed actresses as degenerate symbols of a type of libertinism that had come in with the French Revolution. On the other hand, she was a great believer in chaste and patriotic women wielding their femininity to unite their countrymen against external military and cultural threats – especially French threats.[99]

During the nineteenth century many European women monarchs and aristocrats would loudly endorse domesticity for women, at least partly in acknowledgement of their own greatly diminished political power. They also drew ever closer to the various churches, especially the Catholic Church, which, as we have seen, also grew much more conservative after 1800 (though it also enjoyed less political power; in prestige terms the church never fully recovered from the drubbing it had received at the hands of the Enlightenment *philosophes*). In later years even quite personally powerful noblewomen often opposed political rights for women. For this class of women it seems feminism had come to be so linked to democracy that it was seen more as a threat to their class position than as a route to their emancipation as women.[100] On the other hand, though there was a wholesale retreat from women's and democratic politics there was no comprehensive resurgence of Old Testament-based misogyny. Domestic feminists like Sarah Trimmer and Hannah More were virulently opposed to the French Revolution and none too approving of egalitarian feminists, but they were steeped in sentimentalism, Christian meliorism and the belief that mothers would save the world. They blamed social ills on democrats, the Godless, and libertines, not on Mother Eve and her posterity.

The republican revolutions of the later eighteenth century, with the exception of those in the United States and Haiti, were all beaten back. But new movements would succeed them, in the Balkans, in Latin America, in Russia, and in western Europe, and again women would join the fray. Soon new movements would spring up, and some of them featured both strong outreach to women, and a very egalitarian message. In this group one might include the English Owenites, the French Saint-Simonians, with their belief in a female messiah, some of the Old Believer and Sufi sects in Russia, and others.[101] Most European women did not win comprehensive citizenship rights, or indeed full marital property rights or ready access to divorce, before the twentieth century. On the other hand, almost everywhere they became vastly more involved in nationalist, patriotic and charitable endeavours. This was true even in places with very little tradition of organized female voluntarism. Thus, in both Prussia and Russia women's patriotic associations sprang up during the Napoleonic period, in both cases with strong encouragement from their respective crowns, and with royal women prominently involved. Many other women's organizations would follow. The first Ottoman women's organizations would also be orientated explicitly toward service to wounded soldiers and the nation.[102] Similar tendencies can be seen within proto-nationalist and nationalist movements, particularly in eastern and southeastern Europe, where women often oversaw a kind of 'female' sphere, which, though identified symbolically or actually with motherhood, was by no means confined to the home. It encompassed vernacular language movements, poetry, cooking, maternal charities, nursing (especially of soldiers) and children's and girls' education, but could and often did extend to the realm of politics as it is more traditionally understood.[103]

CONCLUSION

The Age of Revolutions, because it overturned so many ancient verities about hierarchy, religion and politics, allowed women across Europe, albeit temporarily, to envision a future in which 'masculine despotism' no longer had free rein. In this brave new world of seemingly infinite possibility, many older feminist themes moved more into the mainstream – at least for a time – than they had ever done before. The Age of Revolutions also saw the first overt claims by groups of women activists, gathered into clubs and societies, for inclusion in the body politic, and not just in France but in many places across Europe. On the other hand, the various revolutions also signally failed to deliver many permanent benefits to most European women. Even for freed slaves, the most obvious long-term beneficiaries of the Revolutionary era (at least in part thanks to women's political activism), the process of liberation was very protracted, and often, as in Haiti, and later, in the United

States, extraordinarily bloody. Moreover, few 'general emancipations' anywhere compensated former slaves for the lives that had been stolen from them – which ensured, almost everywhere, that freed slaves and their descendants would long remain at the bottom of the social ladder. For many women, slave and free, rich, middle-class and poor, noble and commoner, lay and religious, the Age of Revolutions brought chaos, war, repression and the death of almost everything they valued. Moreover, it featured some very traditional methods for marginalizing political women, including imputations about perverse sexual practices, literal blood-thirstiness, and fundamental unfitness for the ethical wielding of power that would not have been out of place in a seventeenth-century witch-trial or an anti-Semitic pogrom. Still, the sin of Eve never did stage a comprehensive comeback and part of the credit for this must go to domestic feminists who, while they made it difficult, perhaps impossible, for women to aspire to real equality with men, nevertheless offered a strongly positive view of female worth (especially mothers' worth) and numerous opportunities for women to wield social and political power 'out in the world'. The diverse and remarkably public roles women played in most of the Revolutions, as well as the reaction that followed, go far toward explaining why the process of turning women into real citizens has proved so long and so arduous. The remarkable thing is that, even amid the avalanche of propaganda for motherhood and subordination that smothered Europe and the New World in the early nineteenth century, the sense of egalitarian possibility the Revolutions bequeathed to women never entirely went away.

CONCLUSION

———— ◆ ————

'Ilove my sex; I am determined to support and to vindicate its honor and its rights'. So wrote Mme Beaumer, pioneering feminist and journal editor, in her *Journal des Dames.*[1] There is much to love about eighteenth-century women: their creativity, their courage in the face of forms of adversity most of us today can barely imagine; the ability of some of them to love and make themselves loved, their defiance of men, masters and fate, their energy, their self-sacrifice, their faith, both intense and, at times, intensely strange. Of course there is also much about them that is neither pretty nor lovable. For one thing we do not kill, neglect or abandon our children in anywhere near the numbers they did, or view them in such mercenary terms; but then most of us do not have to bear child after child in pain, fear and unhygienic conditions. If we were suddenly transported to those times would we do much better?

When I began my career as a historian twenty-five years ago the study of early modern women was in its infancy. Most of the questions one wanted to ask about women's lives were met with unsatisfactory answers which usually boiled down to 'we will never know, because there are no sources'. In the years since then our knowledge of things we thought we would never know has become ever more clear and distinct. Researching and writing this book has given me an even greater appreciation than I had before for the women and men who have made this underappreciated historiographical revolution. Their work is everywhere on display here.

My main aim in writing this book was to contribute to a project with which many people are now involved, that of rethinking the history of Europe and its surround in a way that de-centres western Europe, particularly Britain and France. Women's historians have been very committed to this project, but even the wonderful work that has been done in the last couple of decades to give early modern European women's history a more global focus has tended (often for understandable reasons such as availability of sources and language facility) to follow traditional trade and colonization routes, with British historians focusing on the old British Empire, French historians focusing on the former French colonies, Dutch historians focusing on former Dutch colonies, and so on. In the meantime, marvellous work (including a good deal of women's history) done in and about regions or communities that were not colonies of Western powers in the early modern period, or whose records are in languages few outsiders know (Portugal, Hungary, Poland, Russia, the Balkan peninsula, the Scandinavian countries, European Turkey, and also some minority communities) often has not had the readership it deserves.

In order to reorient the story one has to think about why that story is as it is, and this is especially challenging with respect to the Ottoman Empire. The people of Christian Europe, including its historians, have found the Ottoman Empire, both as a European and as a Middle Eastern polity, enormously difficult to come to terms with, and much ideological effort has been devoted to sequestering it off in its own distant corner of the intellectual map. To this day many historians of early modern Christian Europe know far more about North and South American colonial history, or the history of distant South Asia, than they know about the Ottoman Empire. Hardly any broad surveys of European history in English or French cover it in any detail; indeed a surprising number of accounts of early modern Europe, by tacit agreement, simply stop at the military border of the Ottoman Empire – wherever that happened to be in any given year.

The ethical implications of all this are great, especially where women are concerned. The image of the sexually enslaved Ottoman woman which emerged first in the sixteenth and early seventeenth centuries, and was widely popularized in the eighteenth, not least by feminists, was a crucial part of efforts to make the Ottoman Empire seem radically 'other', the 'Evil Empire' of its day. One result has been a very long-lived inability to grapple with the humanity of either women or men in the Ottoman context, particularly if they were Muslim. Another has been numerous missed opportunities, on all sides, to engage in truly comparative discussions of the way different social, political, legal and religious systems impinge upon women. Such discussions are not easy at the best of times, but they are even harder when one group assumes that another consists solely of empty ciphers. I have relied heavily in this book on the work of Ottoman women's historians, partly because they speak languages I am unable to, and partly because they treat early modern Ottoman women as real people living in a world both of opportunity and constraint – not the same ones as their neighbours to the north or west, but nevertheless recognizable as being within the purview both of women's history and of humanistic inquiry. I only hope that I have done their work justice, and that it will encourage other non-Ottoman European historians to think about European religious and cultural diversity in both the past and the present as an inspiration to generosity, collaboration and intellectual openness.

A volume that proposes to cover a whole century, especially a century poised, as the eighteenth-century is, between what most people think of as 'old' and what many think of as 'new' or 'modern', must at points weigh in on what it all means. In this volume I have tried to tread carefully between the Scylla of eternal decline and the Charybdis of constant progress. Inevitably my own likes, dislikes and prejudices have played a role here. I happen to believe that rising female literacy is more likely than not to empower women. To the extent that female literacy was, most of the time, curving upward in Europe in the eighteenth century, particularly in western Europe, this is likely to have been a good thing for women, and I think the many eighteenth-century 'women's' genres (which would include novels, feminist writings, women's journals and children's literature, among others) are evidence for that. On the other hand, I do not think it is romanticizing the past to shed a few tears for forms of aesthetic expression that, unlike, say, the book trade, were more embedded in local village or peasant cultures than in the market; or that *were* very much in the market (like the Ottoman urban performance sphere) but have left few traces.

I also believe that women's lives improve when they have greater control over their own sexuality and reproduction. One form of control that most readers of this book are so accustomed to that we barely think about it is signalled by the strong confidence we have that our young children will survive. Of course parents worry, but it is one thing to worry when children are dying all around, and quite another to worry when a child's death is a very rare occurrence. To the extent that children's survival rates began to improve in some countries in the late eighteenth century – and organizations were established, mostly by women, which had that as their main aim – I think that probably constituted an advance for women; it certainly did for children. In saying that, I do not want to seem to understate the awful dilemmas created for eighteenth-century women by the fact that most birth control methods were either worthless or very uncertain. This lack of control, coupled with economic stress, spousal desertion, draconian punishments for unwed mothers (though these, thankfully, were on the decline) and, perhaps, the exhaustion of love, made for very large numbers of unwanted children, as well as far higher rates of infanticide, child abandonment, and sheer reproductive misery than we are accustomed to today. The tragedy of the foundling hospitals stands out because it was so spatially concentrated, but even without the foundling hospitals the situation was dire. Modern churchmen who seriously argue that banning birth control would be good for society should pay a bit of attention to the desperation that was the lot of countless women and children in the eighteenth century.

There are other things that seem obviously positive, such as the beginnings of the movement to abolish chattel slavery, though it is a tragedy of world historical proportions that it took until the late nineteenth and even the early twentieth century for it to reach fruition in all of Europe and her various colonies and former colonies.[2] It is also one of those sad ironies of history – and of very great long-term significance – that the anti-racialist element in the critique of slavery, epitomized by the more radical feminists like Olympe de Gouges, played such a minor role by comparison with the high con-descension and anti-egalitarian 'sensibility' of evangelicals. And yet, clearly, all reformers, whatever their stripe, were affected to some degree by the cult of sensibility and the rise of humanitarianism. Translated, at least some of the time, into fellow-feeling, humanitarianism would fuel a great many move-ments in the nineteenth and twentieth centuries whose impact, in terms of civil rights, disability rights, children's rights, women's rights, and the rights of victims of torture (among other things), are still with us. Though one can and should criticize aspects of these movements, the claim that the world would have been better off without them is, frankly, a pretty hard sell.

In some other realms the story seems more equivocal to me. I love food and I believe it is often not given its due (nor, often, are the food-preparers). Clearly some people's food options changed over the course of the eighteenth century; moreover, there is a good deal of evidence of a greater degree of choice and innovation – some of it the result of the market in commodities. On the other hand, the evidence is very strong that food consumption fell and the general standard of living of many, perhaps most, Europeans deteriorated in the later eighteenth and early nineteenth centuries. Some of this was the result of the disruptions of war; a good deal of it came from the combination of rural overpopulation, a growing gulf between rich and poor – partly brought on by the commercialization of agriculture – and migration. This is one of many areas where life improved for some and probably got worse for the majority. The standard of living would, it is true, improve greatly over the long run; industrialization does usually have that effect, though not necessarily immediately (and of course industrialization, at least as it has evolved so far, poses other problems in terms of worker health and damage to the environment). But in the eighteenth century all many people saw was their present misery. More positively, it seems generally to be the case that the range of types of income-producing activities available to women – from working as actresses, to market selling (at least in some regions) to investing in government bonds – increased over the course of the century, and at this point most historians seem to be of the view that the greater access to a range of material goods provided by the market *on balance* improved rather than diminished most women's status and economic power.

Religion, feminism, and charity were all connected in the eighteenth century. Women's high comfort-level with religious expression (also, typically the area in which they were allowed the greatest public scope) meant that spirituality was everywhere an important locus for female activism, including on some issues, like women's right to study religious works, and even to preach, that are recognizably feminist. The centuries-long effort to exculpate women as a group from the inherited guilt of Eve's long-ago sin was finally largely successful in the eighteenth and early nineteenth centuries, and this victory has had consequences, most of them positive, to this day. We are, perhaps, accustomed to attributing this to the Enlightenment retreat from religion, and certainly the *philosophes* and their friends (including the Freemasonic movement) bore some responsibility for it. But in the final analysis it was women who effected this change.[3] Moreover, whatever one may think about domestic feminism as a political programme, there is no question that its supporters were just as involved in this effort as egalitarian feminists were. Indeed, since domestic feminists tended to remain within a faith tradition, this was an issue that was especially dear to their hearts.

Women's role in politics is also a complicated story, and its trajectory is, in some ways, the inverse of the story of food: some success in the eighteenth century, followed by years in the nineteenth-century political desert. Obviously the eighteenth century was a great age for women monarchs, but just as clearly women monarchs with real power were about to exit the stage, and Joan Landes and Lynn Hunt are surely right to argue that elite women more generally lost out to the new late eighteenth-century 'masculine' politics of parliaments and assemblies, though in many countries (and arguably even in France) this happened quite late.[4] At a very different level of women's political activism, it still thrills the heart to see the flowering of women's publishing, speech-making and organizing, a good deal of it feminist, that accompanied the French Revolution and its many daughter revolutions. Not only did the *citoyennes* take up many older themes in feminist thought, but the French Revolution also witnessed the first known instances in Europe of collectivities of women committed to improving women's status in the law and increasing their purchase on citizenship. Historians differ on how effective and comprehensive the post-revolutionary conservative reaction was. Clearly women's organizing did not go away; but for a very long time (well into the twentieth century in some countries) it stayed very much confined to the 'women's sphere', as newly defined by domestic feminists like Charles

Theremin and Hannah More: the world of motherhood, faith, cooking, charity and education for young children. The most compelling evidence of the power of reaction is the fact that it was not until more than a century *after* the final deposing of Napoleon in 1815 that most European women actually achieved basic political rights, and it took an especially long time in France. The trajectory of change is indeed both strange and unpredictable.

Obviously I believe women do possess some agency, and that, while attempts to actualize that potential can be (and, in the eighteenth century, often were) a cruel exercise in futility, they can also, under the right circumstances, be a force in history. I also think it is probably wrong to imagine that, in the vast majority of cases, the exercise of agency, especially individual agency, can rise much above its social surround. To paraphrase every social scientist's favourite line from Karl Marx (readers should pay due attention to the seamstressing imagery): 'woman makes her own history, but she does not make it out of the whole cloth, she does not make it out of conditions chosen by herself, but out of such as she finds close at hand.'[5] I have gone to some trouble in this book to show that the '[materials] close at hand' and social conditions women, for most intents and purposes, did *not* choose, often predisposed them to think of and practise agency at the expense of those weaker than themselves, particularly other women and girls. What was true of families and work relationships was also true of the sphere of civic action. It is (and was) the case that women are often given far greater rein to participate openly, even vociferously, in civic life if they devote themselves either to loudly touting 'traditional' values for women or to belligerent defences of the threatened communal body of Christians, or Britons, or the French, or whatever the group *de jour* happens to be. This is still true in our own time. There is also the problem of who is exercising, or trying to exercise, agency. Agency was – just – possible for those at the very bottom of the social ladder and real historical women exist to prove that this was occasionally so. But it is surely important to acknowledge that for people in that position the 'materials close at hand' were that much more pitiful, even soul-destroying, the risks that much greater, and the rewards, when and if they came, often barely worth the effort. We can and should celebrate the exceptional, and there were some remarkable interventions by women in the eighteenth century, some of which probably did set in motion developments from which both men and women still benefit today. But we should never delude ourselves that 'individual agency' really can, in the vast majority of cases, triumph over entrenched and institutionalized poverty, enslavement, abuse or neglect. For activist societies and groups, and for larger mobilizations (like those of the early movement of women and men opposed to the slave trade) one can, perhaps, be a bit more optimistic; but if the story of eighteenth-century women teaches us anything it is that the outcome of collective interventions is often very difficult to predict, either in the short or long range.

In this book I have tried to bring eighteenth-century women out of the archives, the printed books and the pages of specialized history journals, and show them as the imperfect, unpredictable, and full-blooded people they actually were. I have found these women immensely entertaining to study. They are different from us in so many ways, pushed and pulled by forces that have, to a large extent, ceased to operate on modern people, or which do so in very different or less visible ways; full of prejudices and hatreds we no longer feel, or conceal if we do; and embedded in a universe of spirits and other supernatural forces most of us today greet with scepticism. Though they have turned to dust, these women still speak, and if we are lucky we can catch snatches of what they have to say.

NOTES

---◆---

Introduction

1 See Bibliography.
2 See esp. Wiesner 2008. But see also the older and more chronologically ambitious Anderson and Zinsser 2000 (originally 1988) which worked hard to include Russia, among other places.
3 A very partial list of recent studies on women, gender and the law-courts includes: Ågren and Erickson 2005; Buturović and Schick 2007; Desan 2004; Gerhard 1997; Marrese 2002; Peirce 2003; Sonbol 1996; Sperling and Wray 2009; and J.E. Tucker 1998. The term 'Big Europe' is from Judith Bennett.
4 There is a vast literature on the subject. I have found the following to be especially useful: Campbell, Miers and Miller 2007:II; Butler and J. Scott 1992; N.Z. Davis and Farge 1993; Ko 1994; W. Johnson 2003; and Theiss 2004.
5 Mahmood 2005.
6 Campbell, Miers and Miller 2007:II, 15–17.
7 Key sources on bargaining and resource distribution within families include Agarwal 1997; Alter and Oris 2000; Derosas and Oris 2002; and Kandiyoti 1988. See also Peter 2005.

Chapter 1: Hierarchy and Difference

1 'Compound family' and 'complex family' are technical terms that refer to two different types of extended family households. The first is used to refer to a household that houses more than two generations (e.g. young couples move in with one or the other of their parents); the second is used to refer to a household that houses more than one married couple from the same generation (e.g. a family where two brothers live together with their wives and children, and perhaps also their parents). Compound and complex families are often contrasted to the 'nuclear family' which consists only of the married couple and their children.
2 Da Molin 1990; Fairchilds 1984; Ginio 2003; Kandiyoti 1988; Karpinski 1996.
3 Wetherell, Plakans and Wellman 1994.
4 On the diversity of treatment of bastards compare Lee 1977 with Ransel 1990, esp. 37 note 25.
5 Evans 1998:18.
6 Lewin 1992; B. Lewis 1990:91, 159.
7 Rosman 2005:42–5, 48, 53–4.
8 This famous phrase is from Patterson 1982.
9 Amussen 2007; Blackburn 1988; C. Brown 1995; Campbell, Miers and Miller 2008; Drescher 1994; Paton 2001; Postma 1990.

10 Erdem 1996:49–53, 152–7.

11 A *hadith* is a report of the sayings or actions of the Prophet Muhammad or his companions, accompanied by an indication of the chain of oral transmission. Many of these originated with the Prophet's wives. Together with the Qur'an, which they supplement, clarify, and occasionally confound, they are the most important sources of Muslim spiritual and ethical direction.

12 J.E. Tucker 1998:171–2.

13 Qur'an 2:221 and 24:33 See also 2:221, 4:92, 5:89, and 58:3–4.

14 Erdem 1996:19, see also 49–53; 152–7, 165; Faroqhi 2000:99. On upward mobility for women slaves, see Fay 1998; and Zilfi 2004:24.

15 Toledano 1997:163. For the differential treatment of domestic slaves (as opposed to harem slaves) and the concentration of African women in the former group see 13–14, 57, 131.

16 A rather positive view is Soulodre-La France 2001.

17 Chaves 2000:111; McAlister 1984:396–8, 418–21; Conrad 1983:245–67. I am grateful to Konstantin Dierks for introducing me to the Chaves article and to J. Celso Castro Alves for introducing me to the Conrad book.

18 Campbell, Miers and Miller 2007:II, 16–17; Peabody 2005; Chaves 2000.

19 Hoch 1986; Jespersen 1995; Kahan and Hellie 1985; Ogilvie and Edwards 2000.

20 Gray 1987.

21 Azevedo 2003.

22 Hay 1980; T.J. Davis 1985.

23 Paton 2001; Gavigan 1989–1990. On the possibly diminishing appetite for punishing women in these ways, see Pushkareva 1997:177 and Shoemaker 2004:92–5.

24 Peters 2005:47. I am somewhat simplifying a complex system.

25 Peters 2005:33.

26 Quoted in Conrad 1983:260. Emphasis mine. The town was Itapemirim, Espírito Santo.

27 Anna Clark 1995:63–87.

28 Dickie 2003; Dekker 2001; Görög-Karady 1985; Dysa 2001; Evans 1988; Hsia 1988; Felsenstein 1995.

29 Farrow 2004:180.

30 Turniansky 1988. Though see B.J. Kaplan 2007:317–18 who argues that the ghettos played an at least partially beneficent role by protecting Jews' personal safety and culture.

31 For efforts to discipline uncontrollable noblewomen – including by means of forced institutionalization in convents – see d'Argenson 1891:10–18, 88–98, 252–3.

32 Pushkareva 1997:102, 174; Foyster 2005:28, 126–7, 208–9, 228–9, 249.

33 Pushkareva 1997:56; Salve 1997. See also Bächtold-Stäubli 1930:III, 1239–88.

34 Gaite 1991:19.

35 Engel 1994:65; Hitchcock 2005; R.C. Davis 1998.

36 J. Blum 1961:552; Hoch 1986:183. I have also benefited from discussions on this issue with my colleague, Peter Czap. On gender and slave escapes, see Norton 1996: 209–12 and Campbell, Miers and Miller 2007:II, 9–10.

37 Travellers' descriptions of early modern Venice (some of which are detailed in R.C. Davis 1998) are almost identical in tone to descriptions of Istanbul. As Davis

shows for Venice, one reason for this was that travellers were basically blind to about eighty-five per cent of the female population. They simply did not see them even when they were in plain sight, and when they did they dismissed them as prostitutes or old women.

38 Seng 1998 is an important discussion of the contrast between travellers' accounts and the reality of urban women's lives.

39 Stowasser 1996:28; Aravamudan 1995:69; E. Thompson 2003:54–6.

40 See E. Thompson 2003:56–7, though there is debate about how comprehensive such strictures were in practice, especially for lower-class women.

41 Zilfi 1995.

42 Göçek and Baer 1997; Cichocki 2005; Seng 1998.

43 Barnai 2002:43.

44 A. Russell 1794:I, 141.

45 Khoury 1997a:125–6.

46 Montagu 1965:I, 406, 328; Aravamudan 1995.

47 Peirce 1993:134–6.

48 Cynarski 1968; Lorence-Kot 1985:59–60; Bush 1983–1988:II.

49 On the question of enforcement, see especially Somerville 1997.

50 K. Wilson 2004 has a perceptive discussion of the promiscuity issue.

51 Smith did this by claiming that people worked more efficiently if they were better paid, from which it followed that slavery was the least efficient system of all. See A. Smith 1937:80–1, 365–6 (originally published 1776).

52 Goldenberg 2003. The curse of Ham was still being invoked to justify slavery in the mid-nineteenth-century United States. See Haynes 2002.

53 Grellman 1787:84–5; Görög-Karady 1985.

54 Roper 1994:198–225 and Roper 2004:69–103.

55 Boggs 1930:87. On the other hand, Jesus had clearly favoured the disabled and stigmatized. On this issue, see Stiker 1999, esp. 34–8. There is a large historical literature on the topic of the 'maternal imagination'. Roodenburg 1988 outlines the issues and supplies numerous citations.

56 Aarne and S. Thompson 1981:428–9 (Tale types 1475–99 'Jokes about Old Maids').

57 Maloney 1976 makes clear how widespread this belief system was. On the 'Judenblick' see Berliner 1980:102.

58 Maloney 1976; Roper 1994; Vukanović 1989.

59 Schaw 1921:129.

60 B. Lewis 1990:5–6; Zilfi 2004:8.

61 Engel 1994:20.

62 See among others, Ailes 2006; Boulton 2000; M.R. Hunt 2004b; Outhwaite 1999: 497–510; Russell-Wood 2000; Zarinebaf-Shahr 1997.

63 The literature on women in Muslim law-courts in the early modern period is vast. See esp. Sonbol 1990 and Zilfi 1997b.

64 Jennings 1975:114.

65 E.S. Cohen 1992; Dean 2004; Gowing 1996.

66 M.R. Hunt 2000; Horwitz 1998.

67 Baer 2004b:426, 445.

68 Baer 2004b:22–4.

69 Peabody 1996:41–56.

70 A perceptive account of breach of promise suits and female honour is Cavallo and Cerutti 1990.

71 Frost 1994:182. The case dates from the 1730s.

72 Shoemaker 2004:229–30; Hurl-Eamon 2005.

73 Jennings 1993:16–18. For the later period, see Saint Cassia 1986.

74 Landers 1999:136–46, 150–3, 252, 256–7; C. Brown 1995.

75 Quoted in Clancy-Smith 2005:79.

76 B.J. Kaplan 2007:276–82, though Kaplan may exaggerate the degree of agreement on what an 'un-baptized' person was for purposes of invoking the 'disparity of cult' impediment to marriage in canon law. It is also my impression that, in practice, those eager for converts were prepared to collude in *de facto* divorces in order to prevent perversion from the faith with respect to either the woman or her children. For marriage dissolution involving Old Believers who converted to Orthodoxy (albeit later) see Paert 2004:569, 571–2.

77 Baer 2004b.

78 Landers 1999:24–35, 75–9.

79 Quoted in Vanzan 1996:330.

80 M.R. Hunt 1995:90.

81 Hardwick 2006.

82 For the complicated roles played by servants, see Bailey 2003:32–5, 115, 122, 157–8 and M.R. Hunt 1995:97–100.

83 Hardwick 2006:23–4; Bogucka 2004:18; Peabody 1996:41–8.

84 M.R. Hunt 2004b.

85 For a London case, see *Old Bailey Proceedings Online* 7 July, 1779, trial of James Barrett accused of raping Anne Lowther (t17790707-49).

86 Campbell, Miers and Miller 2007:II, 9.

87 C. Brown 1995; Landers 1999; Mott 1989; Peabody 2005; Schiebinger 2004.

88 Peabody 2005; Wong 1996.

89 For slave and free black women in the courts, see Chaves 2000; Landers 1999; Peabody 2005; Townsend 1998.

Chapter 2: Families

1 'Matrimonio y mortaja, del cielo bajan'. Quoted in Reher 1997:194, 219n.

2 Ferrer i Alòs 1993; Livi-Bacci 1986:183–5; Hurwich 1993:707–10.

3 On the marriage policies of the early modern Dutch East India Company and comparable colonial bodies, see Stoler 2002:29–34, 47–8, 51–5.

4 Pol 1994:78–9.

5 Livi-Bacci 1968:219; Poska 2005:42; Sharpe 1991:56.

6 P.K. Taylor 1994:213.

7 Burić 1976:132; Skendi 1976:16; Hammel and Gullickson 2004.

8 P.H. Wilson 2005:54–5. See also Rublack 1999:260; Hacker 1981 and Sharpe 1996:130–3.

9 Farnsworth 1990; Kahan and Hellie 1985:149–50; Lindenmeyr 1996:38.

10 Lokken 2001. See also Russell-Wood 2000:314–15. For marriage strategies among Ottoman slaves, see Baer 2004b.

11 V.A. Aleksandrov, *Sel'skaia obshchina v rossii (XVII-nachalo XIX v.)* (Moscow, 1976), 304, cited in Czap 1978:115; Plakans 1975:634.

12 F. Davis 1986:36–7, 250; Findley 1989:119–30; Kollmann 1983.

13 J.E. Tucker 1998:46–52.

14 Astell 1700; Sol 2002.

15 Boswell and de Charrière 1952:399 (Belle van Zuylen to James Boswell, Utrecht, 16 February 1768).

16 Joan Hinde Stewart and Philip Stewart, 'Introduction' in de Charrière 1993:xiv.

17 Sol 2002.

18 Froide 2005:15–43. See also J.M. Bennett and Froide 1999.

19 Lowe 1938:24 (entry for 13 July 1663).

20 See, e.g., Ashbridge 1820; Baxter 1681; Godwin 1798.

21 Ginio 2001:126n.

22 Sapurma 1997:38; Balikci 1965.

23 Faroqhi 2000:103.

24 McCarthy 1979:320–3.

25 Ginio 2003.

26 See, e.g., Merians 1996; Tóth 1991:44–7, 54–5.

27 R. Smith 1987.

28 Baer 2004b:443; Ghosh 2006:23, 25, 28–30.

29 Diefendorf 1995.

30 Ågren and Erickson 2005; Sperling 2004; d'Eszlary 1962; Hurwich 1993. Thanks to Jutta Sperling, Maria Ågren and Amy Erickson for endless help in untangling the complexities of early modern European inheritance and property law.

31 Kasdagli 1999:261–313.

32 Swett 1996; Schneider 2000:8; Diefendorf 1995:170; d'Eszlary 1962:432; Rosa 1995.

33 On Jewish law, see Levine 1968.

34 Prior 1990; Erickson 1993.

35 Zilfi 1997a.

36 Meriwether 1997.

37 Davidoff and Hall 1987:209–10; Staves 1990; Erickson 1993:102–55; M.R. Hunt 1996:140–1, 157–62, 275n–6n.

38 Palazzi 1990; Holthöfer 1997. There were many complexities, however, for which see esp. 436–7.

39 See, e.g., Peabody 1994.

40 Erickson 1993:26–8, 169–71.

41 Sperling 1992.

42 J.E. Tucker 1998: see esp. 179–86. As Tucker points out (67–70), reform-minded *muftis* did not always win the battle over entrenched patriarchal customs and interests.

43 I am grateful to Lisa Baskin for help with sixteenth-century legal treatises.

44 F. Criep, *Uanden Keyser, Ghemaeckt inden Jare Noopende't Contracteren van Huwelicke van Persoonen Zijnde Beneden Hare Jaren* (The Hague: de Weduwe [the Widow], 1627); it is very odd for a widow publisher not to say whose widow she is and the likelihood is that it was purposeful.

45 Slonik 1652. I have not seen this tract, but it is said to include information on marriage law alongside the more traditional focus on the halakhic duties of women. Thanks to Paola Zamperini for translating the Italian title for me, and to Susan Niditch for help with the Hebrew.

46 *Treatise of Feme Coverts* 1732:vii quoted in Erickson 1993:105. Elizabeth Nutt, one of the co-publishers along with her son Richard, was one of the most active London publishers of the early decades of the eighteenth century.

47 Cserey 1800. Thanks to Stephanie Reitter for translating the title for me (see bibliography), and to David Schneider for help on the orthography.

48 Discussions of this phenomenon include Daumas 1988; Maza 1989; Goldsmith 1995; and Ågren 2009. I am grateful to Maria Ågren for allowing me to read her manuscript in progress. Bérenguier 1995 argues that this kind of literature does not lend itself to a more far-reaching critique of women's legal position, but I disagree.

49 J. Griffiths, *Travels in Europe, Asia Minor and Arabia* (London: T. Cadell and W. Davies, 1805), 111, quoted in And 1963:25.

50 *Selected Letters of Samuel Richardson*, ed. John Carroll (Oxford: Clarendon Press, 1964), 340 quoted in Keymer 2004, from which this account of Chapone's life is drawn.

51 Chapone 1735:45–6.

52 Pellegrina Amoretti's treatise was *De Jure Dotium apud Romanos* (On the Law of dowry among Romans).

53 Voltaire 2002:138.

54 Ferguson 1992; Andrea 2007.

55 Chapone 1735:45–6.

56 Marrese 2002:40–59, 101–45.

57 The classic discussion of this is Hufton 1975, to which this account is greatly indebted.

58 One study finds that eighteenth-century married men with children had higher mortality rates than men without them. See Klasen 1998:455.

59 Sharpe 1990:67.

60 Foyster 2005; Marrese 2002:98.

61 Matthew 19:9 and 5:32.

62 Phillips 1988; Johansen 2005; Leneman 1998.

63 Qur'an 4:34. Not surprisingly, there is a wide range of views about what this notorious passage actually means. Some liberals and Islamic feminists hold that the passage is deliberately written in such a way as to preclude – even forbid – a man ever actually resorting to violence against his wife, and almost all commentators, even conservatives, emphasize the many statements, in the Qur'an and *hadiths*, that either prohibit or severely limit a man's ability to beat his wife.

64 Quoted in J.E. Tucker 1998:125–6. See also Zilfi, 1997a and Sonbol 1996.

65 J.E. Tucker 1998:83–5.

66 Imber 1997; Jennings 1993; Zilfi 1997a.

67 Hanna 1995.

68 Baer 2004b:441–3; C.M. Clark 1995:92, 99. The *agunah* has not gone away. See, e.g., the website of the Jewish Orthodox Feminist Alliance which 'sees the agunah issue as a community problem and believes there is a critical need for a systemic, halakhic solution to the plight of agunot': http://www.jofa.org/about.php/advocacy (accessed 8 August 2008). At the very end of our period Jewish women also began seeking civil divorces. See Dubin 2007.

69 Schneider 2000:12–13; Marrese 2002:87–94; d'Eszlary 1962:433; Hardwick 2006: 16–17.

70 Ågren 2003:273–4.

71 Qur'an 4:19. See also 4:20–1.

72 d'Eszlary 1962:431; M.R. Hunt 2000. On verbal and sexual cruelty in early modern marriage, see especially Foyster 2005:32–9.

73 Vollendorf 2005:163–5; M.R. Hunt 1995; Marcus 1989:226.

74 Kany 1932:385; Bogucka 2004:19. Though Poland was a largely Catholic country the nobility seems to have had little difficulty obtaining divorces.

75 Monter 1980:195–6. Cott 1976:592, writing on the eighteenth-century Massachusetts Bay Colony, also finds a striking *pre-revolutionary* increase in divorce cases.

76 Ivanova 2007; Laiou 2007.

77 For the impact on children, see especially Foyster 2005:129–67.

78 Francini 1997 discusses several of them.

79 Astell 1701:129–30. Thanks to Amy Froide for drawing this quotation to my attention.

80 A variety of reasons have been put forward for this including: Reformation teachings on women (for Protestant countries); The Council of Trent and the Catholic Reformation (for Catholic countries); the new prominence of proto-Islamist groups and movements (in parts of the Ottoman Empire), new worries about sexuality (almost everywhere); new guild-related exclusions of women's work; and gathering attacks on women's property rights. For a good account of some of these, focused especially on Germany, see Wiesner 1986. There is considerable doubt as to how consistently any of these strictures affected women below the elite.

81 Kaiser 1992:65–6; Palazzi 1997:180–1; Poska 2005:38.

82 Zarinebaf-Shahr 1998; Khoury 1996.

83 Darrow 1989:171–3.

84 Crowston 2001:356–75.

85 Turin 1989:14–24.

86 The classic discussions of 'romantic friendship' are: Smith-Rosenberg 1975 and Faderman 1981.

87 On the literary tradition, and its enormous complexity, see especially Traub 2001.

88 Hill 1987.

89 Lanser 1998; B. Rizzo 1994. I am grateful to Lisa Baskin for introducing me to the world of 'Ladies' memorabilia.

90 Alberto Fortis, *Viaggio in Dalmazia* (1774), quoted in Wolff 2003:96.

91 Alacoque 1961:5–7,105.

92 Boéskov, Epstein, and Andreev 1990:31.

93 Swett 1996; Erickson 1993.

94 M.R. Hunt 2004b; Ailes 2006; Wagner 2007:100.

95 Ullmann 2000:102–3.

96 Kopczynski 1998:83.

97 Quoted in Sokoll 2000:42. See also Wales 1984.

98 Sokoll 2000:37–42; Marcus 1990.

99 Boulton 2000:51.

100 Dirks 1993.

101 Helt 2003:43–4, 50–3.

102 Ciappara 2005:295.

103 National Archives at Kew (Great Britain), PROB (11/461 Dyer quire number 137, Prerogative Court of Canterbury, Last will and testament, Susannah Darnell (1701).

104 M. Arnold 2003:60–3.

105 M.R. Hunt 2000.

106 Zentai 1979.

107 Soares 2007:83–4. On tensions over burial in other slave states, see Jamieson 1995.

108 I am grateful to Jutta Sperling and Shona Kelly Wray for allowing me to read the introduction to their forthcoming volume (Sperling and Wray 2009). For some additional reflections on this issue see Minkov 2004.

Chapter 3: Sexuality and Reproduction

1 Livi-Bacci 2007:121–2.

2 Dresch 1990; Knapp 1998; Knodel 1970; Walle 1986.

3 Quoted in MacDonald 1981:82–3.

4 Quoted in M.F. Shaw 1977:243, lament collected in 1948 from Mrs Iain Campbell, South Lochboisdale, South Uist, Scottish Hebrides, trans. M.F. Shaw.

5 Cressy 1997:114–17. I am grateful to Jamal Elias for discussing Islamic conceptions of sin and childhood with me.

6 Cavazza 1994; Harris 1999:295, 416n. For the 1983 reforms, see *Codex Iuris Canonici* (1983 revision), c. 1183 § 2 .

7 Scribner 1996:I, 254.

8 Leneman and Mitchison 1988; Boyd 1980:55. I was sent off in this direction by Anna Clark 1995:45–6.

9 There is an extensive literature on rising rates of illegitimacy in the later eighteenth century and early nineteenth century. See, among others, Adair 1996; Blayo 1975; Fairchilds 1978; and Ingrao 1982.

10 Ciappara 2001; Paert 2004; Tomasson 1977:424. See also Poska 1998:101–26.

11 Lövkrona 2002:12; Hull 1996:109.

12 Kertzer 1993:40; Ransel 1988:39.

13 Cavallo and Cerutti 1990.

14 Hull 1996:115n; Plakans 1975:634.

15 On Catholic unwed mothers keeping their children, see especially Poska 2005. On bastardy and the law, see Traer 1980:156–60.

16 J.E. Tucker 1998:160–7; Ze'evi 2001; Kohbach 1986; Duben 1985.

17 Coale and Watkins 1986:441–2; Livi-Bacci 1986:184–6; Andorka 1971.

18 Tóth 1991:48–9.
19 Hatem 1997:72.
20 Rublack 1996:92; Schiebinger 2004:115–18, 177–93.
21 The comparison is adapted from Loudon 1992:162, 164–5.
22 Schrader 1987; Loudon 1992:160.
23 Millennium Project Task Force 4 2004:51; Loudon 1992;159–60.
24 Rublack 1996.
25 Ransel 1988:267.
26 Rublack 1996:91; Gowing 2003:51.
27 Ehrenreich and English 1973. Though influential, this account is now very dated.
28 Duden 1991.
29 Cody 2004; Gelbart 1993; Ortiz 1993:103–7.
30 Quoted in Filippini 1993:166–7.
31 Davin 1978.
32 Romlid 1997:38–9; Ulman 2006. The Tanzimat period (1838–76) saw a number of modernizing reforms in the Ottoman Empire intended, among other things, to make it more competitive with Western European powers.
33 Loudon 1992:160.
34 Schiebinger 2004:190–1; Richter 1998:546.
35 Mott 1989.
36 Ginio 2003:173–4; Sonnino 1994; McCants 1997.
37 Rousseau 2000:313–14; Kushner 2001; di Simplicio 1994:53.
38 Durova 1988:19, 28.
39 Hrdy 1992.
40 Reynolds 1979.
41 Ransel 1988:131; S. Wilson 1988:777. For evidence of possible daughter preference, see Poska 2005:54.
42 Qur'an 81:1–3, 8–9, 14 quoted in Giladi 1990:186. The translation of the Qur'an is by Pickthall.
43 Hanlon 2003.
44 Schulte 1984:92–3; Hellie 1982:448–9; Schiebinger 2004:139–49.
45 Scheper-Hughes 1992.
46 Crawford 2004:159; Dülmen 1991; Jackson 2002; Kamler 1988; J. Kelly 1992; Kertzer 1993; Naess 1990:370; Ulbrich 1988.
47 Lövkrona 2002; Gowing 2003; Lynch 2000:137; T. Rizzo 2004; Tinkova 2005.
48 Hull 1996:69n, 115; Jackson 2002.
49 See Tinkova 2003 on the Czech lands, then under Austrian control; and Tinkova 2005 on the other Habsburg lands.
50 Statistical function, *Old Bailey Proceedings Online*.
51 Quoted in Ransel 1988:5.
52 Ener 2005; Gallant 1991.
53 Kertzer 2000; Levene 2005; Sá 2000; Viazzo, Bortolotto and Zanotto 2000.
54 Bourgoanne 1790:II, 67.
55 On the 'care gap', see Hrdy 2001; Viazzo, Bortolotto and Zanotto 2000:72.
56 Robins 1980:20.

57 Levene 2005:88; Ransel 1988:257.

58 It is hard to say how common vaccination was in the Ottoman Empire though the practice was known there considerably earlier. See Dinc and Ulman 2007. Variolation was supposed, by some, to have been introduced to Turkey from Central Asia in the sixteenth or seventeenth century by Circassian harem women, but this story seems a bit too good to be true.

59 Sá 2000:30–1; Kertzer 1999.

60 Quoted in Hitchcock 2005:498. 'Before she would have killed it' is meant in the sense of 'rather than killing it'. See also *Old Bailey Proceedings Online*, 16 April 1740, trial of Elizabeth Evans for infanticide (t17400416-24).

61 Robins 1980:32.

62 Simonton 1998:25.

63 A. Unkovskaya, *Vospominaniya* (Reminiscences) (1917) quoted in Roosevelt 1995:275.

64 Leviticus 20:10; Deuteronomy 22:22.

65 Firth and Rait 1911:II, 387–9. See also Kingdon 1995.

66 Kingdon 1995:117; d'Eszlary 1962; Mezger 1948.

67 *Code civile* (1804), articles 308–9; *Code pénal* (1810), article 324. Early modern Muslim jurists were ambivalent about honour killings on humanitarian grounds and because they contravened the very strict rules for proving a *zina* crime. In Judith Tucker's words *muftis* 'felt [families] should not judge or punish sexual transgressions' (J.E. Tucker 1998:176). On the other hand, honour killings had considerable warrant in customary and tribal law in many parts of Europe, Central Asia and the Middle East. This made them difficult to combat. On jurists who acquiesced to them, albeit unhappily, see Peirce 2003:365–6.

68 DeLong-Bas 2004:24–9.

69 W. Johnson 1999; Postma 1990:243; Toledano 2006.

70 Faroqhi 2001a:122.

71 Chaytor 1995; G. Walker 1998.

72 Heijden 2000:626.

73 Jansson 2002:324.

74 J.E. Tucker 1998:162–4. See also Ze'evi 2001.

75 *Old Bailey Proceedings Online*, 13 January, 1699, trial of William Pheasant accused of raping Deborah Wise (t16990113-1).

76 Heijden 2000:628–9.

77 Heijden 2000:631. See also Egmond 2001; and M. Jónsson 1998.

78 Greenberg and Bystryn 1982.

79 Huussen 1987; Rey 1987; J. Meer 1989; Boon 1989; Merrick 1999.

80 Harvey 1978.

81 Faderman 1981.

82 Donoghue 1995:3–5, 261–3.

83 Traub 2001; M.R. Hunt 1999.

84 Göçek 2003:I, 74; And 1963; S.O. Murray 1997:99. I am grateful to Selim Sirri Kuru for guidance on issues to do with the history of sexuality in the early modern Ottoman Empire.

85 d'Argenson 1891:11–12, 89, 94.

86 Dekker and Pol 1989:64–7.

87 Tóth 1991.

88 Wollstonecraft 1988:26.

89 Quoted in DeJean 1991:154; see also 243–4.

90 A nuanced account of the complexities of male sexual incontinence is Shepard, 2003:152–85.

91 Behn 1987:108–9. I have benefited greatly from Gardiner 1989.

92 Nordenflycht 1924–1938. I owe my acquaintanceship with Nordenflycht to Offen 2000:40.

93 Hill 2004.

94 Lister 1988:145, entry for Monday 29 January 1821. See also Lister 1992.

95 Ferguson 1992:233–4.

96 Quoted in Coleman 2003:177. This view of Schaw is drawn entirely from Deirdre Coleman.

97 Schiebinger 1986.

98 T.W. Laqueur 1990.

99 *Making Sex* is sometimes read in a more reductionist fashion than its author appears to have intended. For one thing Laqueur goes to some trouble to show that the 'two-sex model' has never completely carried the field, or at least in no simple, uncontested or predictable way. See T.W. Laqueur 1990:233–43.

100 An account of the debate is to be found in Stolberg 2003.

101 Schiebinger 1993.

102 For some of the causal and chronological complexities, see Chesnais 1992.

Chapter 4: Food and Consumption

1 England was exceptional in this regard. The percentage of the population engaged in agriculture began dropping sharply in the late eighteenth century. By 1800 it is thought that about thirty-six per cent of the population was engaged in agriculture, but this was far lower than anywhere else in Europe. See Wrigley 1985:700, 704.

2 *Pocket World in Figures* 2007:146.

3 Steingrímsson 1998.

4 Dirks 1993:160. See also Sen 1981.

5 The phrase is from Ó Gráda 2004:16.

6 Macintyre 2002. Though compare Hufton 1971:104–5.

7 A. Blum and Troitskaya 1997:138.

8 See especially the large literature on the delayed medical after-effects of the 'Hunger Winter' of 1944–5 in the Netherlands.

9 Ó Gráda 1989:55, 63; Watkins and Menken 1985.

10 Klasen 1998. This saying comes from Lawrence Stone.

11 Todorova 1983:63–4; Humphries 1991; Ginsburg and Swedlund 1986.

12 Derosas and Oris 2002.

13 Bringa 1995:158.

14 Calvi 1989:228–9.

15 Peirce 1993:131; Parkes 2004; Tugay 1963:306.

16 Conrad 1973:55, 62. *Emancipados* were Africans confiscated from illegal slave traders after the abolition of the slave trade (but not slavery as an institution) in the early decades of the nineteenth century.

17 Mott 1989; Townsend 2000:192; Fildes 1988:250.

18 Haug 1992; J.M. Johnson 2005.

19 Fildes 1988:10; Sarasúa 2001.

20 G.D. Sussman 1982:19–23; Fildes 1988:210, 229; Wunder 1998:19–20; Hafter, 1995b:52–3.

21 Fildes 1988:174.

22 Zilfi 1997a:286. Qur'an 2:233 'Mothers shall suckle their children for two whole years; [that is] for those [children] who wish to complete the suckling. The duty of feeding and clothing nursing mothers in a seemly manner is upon the father of the child . . .' (trans. Pickthall).

23 C. Jones 1982:192–4.

24 In *Emile*, Rousseau had made a strong appeal for maternal breast-feeding.

25 Le Rebours, *Avis aux mères qui veulent nourrir* (3rd ed., rev. 1775), 14, quoted in Théré 1999:553 ; see also Théré 554–6. This discussion is indebted to Théré and to Senior 1983:esp. 376–7, 383, 387.

26 We now know that nursing depresses both menstruation and ovulation, at least for a time. Le Rebours did not know the precise mechanism, but she was perfectly familiar with the result.

27 G.D. Sussman 1992:31. Sussman argues that, in some places (e.g. eighteenth-century Rouen), the breast-feeding campaign was fairly successful among the lower middle classes; but he is skeptical about it having a lasting impact among elite women.

28 For a sense of just how complex the question of causality is, see Moring 1998. On smallpox see Razzell 2003.

29 G.D. Sussman 1992:30.

30 For 'maternalism', see especially Michel and Koven 1990.

31 On the popularity of the trope of maternal weeping, especially from the 1780s on, see Penny 1975.

32 Fauve-Chamoux 2000:I, 361.

33 Başgöz and Tietze 1973:474, entry no. 479.1.

34 P. Jones 1983:121–51.

35 Alexander Croke, *A Short View of the Possibility and Advantage of Draining, Dividing and Enclosing Otmoor* (London, 1787) quoted in Thwaites 1984:41.

36 J. Andrew 1993.

37 M.F. Shaw 1977:143, tune and words collected from Mrs. Agnes Currie and Miss Peigi MacRae, North Glendale, South Uist (no date). Potatoes were actually a good weaning food, because they were high in vitamin C and therefore a prophylactic against infant scurvy.

38 R.E.F. Smith and Christian 1984:199.

39 Simonton 1998:27–36.

40 McNeill 1992:89–90.

41 Ó Gráda 1989:24–5, 55–6, 70.

42 Palairet 1997:147–150; McNeill 1992:20; Boehm 1984; Simonton 1998:30, 114, 117–18, 130, 209.

43 China was another, along with parts of Japan. See Rozman 1973; Pomeranz 2000.

44 Steckel and Floud 1997.

45 See especially the work of John Komlos and his many collaborators, e.g. Komlos 1989. For women, see Humphries 1990:17–42; and Humphries 1991; and compare with Nicholas and Oxley 1993.

46 Radcliffe 1795:51.

47 Allen, Bengtsson and Dribe 2005.

48 Mui and Mui 1989; Kahan and Hellie 1985:274.

49 Inalcik and Quataert 1994:493–9, 584–96. Compare Palairet 1997:357–70.

50 Hitchcock 2005:478–98.

51 Mintz 1986.

52 Ruane 1995; Yıldırım 2000; Palairet 1997:68, 73–5.

53 Vickery 1994.

54 L. Brown 1993.

55 See especially Lemire 2005; Fontaine 2003; Styles 2003.

56 Rodríguez 1973; Bouton 1993:xix–xx.

57 Quoted in Monahan 1990:657.

58 Monahan 1990. See also Hufton 1974:252–3.

59 Beik 1997:36–7 gives several examples. See also N.Z. Davis 1978.

60 A. Russell 1794:I, 328.

61 Hufton 1975; Monahan 1990; Thwaites 1984; Tilly 1983; Sadat 1972.

62 Bohstedt 1990. Bohstedt argues that the majority of food riots actually were organized by men, but the authorities' tendency, almost everywhere, to single out men for punishment, makes me a bit skeptical.

63 Rashid 1980; Walton and Seddon 1994.

64 Bradshaw and Lambart 1749.

65 One should not always trust the claims of publishers about multiple editions, however. Some of these are ploys to make it look as if a particular book is more of a runaway bestseller than it really is.

66 Sibbald 1709.

67 The rationale for this association was not complimentary either to women or goats – it was that both were devious, hard to control, hypersexual and devilish.

68 Hickman 2005:22–6.

69 Etienne 1994.

Chapter 5: Work and Money

1 Boserup 1970; Tilly and Scott 1978.

2 Davies 1960; Engel 1994; Kussmaul 1981; Palairet 1997; Sabean 1990; Simonton 1998; Snell 1985.

3 Earle 1989:337–40. Sixty-one per cent of married women aged 25–34 worked, and sixty-nine per cent of married women aged 35–44.

4 Saito 1979; Juratic 1987:882, Table 1.

5 Hilden 1993; Hufton 1975; Simonton 1998:27–30, 38–45, 67, 106–8.

6 Powitz 1995 (thanks to Dagmar Powitz for allowing me to read this thesis); Hufton 1975; Faroqhi 2001b:157.

7 Clark 1919. See also Pinchbeck 1977, though Pinchbeck argued that, while women experienced deskilling, on balance, the Industrial Revolution was good for women because it freed them to be housewives and mothers. For more recent discussions, see Valenze 1995:esp. 42–5, 128–30; and Sharpe 1996.

8 Bennett 1988. See the critique of Bennett by Hill 1993; and Bennett's rejoinder in Bennett 1993.

9 Hafter 2001; Nicholas and Oxley 1993; Ogilvie 2004; and Ogilvie 2003.

10 See, among others, Berg 2005; Fontaine 2003; Jianu 2007; J.M. Jones 2004; Lemire 1988; Ruane 1995; Styles 2002; Vickery 1994.

11 See, e.g., Valenze 1995. On slavery, see Amussen 2007; Ferguson 1993; and Sussman 2000. On ideologies of domesticity, see especially Davidoff and Hall 1987.

12 See especially Ogilvie 2004.

13 Ogilvie 2001; Peabody 2005:58–9.

14 Snell 1985.

15 Simonton 1998:112–25, 207–13.

16 Dubert 1999:218–21; Momsen 1999; Sarti 1997:125–63; Zilfi 2004:25–6.

17 Arru 1990; Carlson 1994:87–96; Fairchilds 1984; Fauve-Chamoux and Fialova 1997; Karpinski 1996; Meldrum 2000; Zilfi 2004.

18 Da Molin 1990.

19 Fairchilds 1984; Hill 1996; Karpinski 1996; Kussmaul 1981; Sogner 1997.

20 Ginio 2003:173–6.

21 Kuklo 1997; Carlson 1994; Sarti 1997.

22 Carlson 1994.

23 Dabydeen 1987; Amussen 2007:191–217.

24 Nadelhaft 1966; Blackstone 1770:I, 127, 423–5; Fryer 1984:67–8, 72–4, 230–3.

25 Ginio 2003:171. Compare Findley 1989:122–3, 129.

26 Dekker 1987; Dias 1995; Karpinski 1989b; Özgüven 2001; Thwaites 1984; Heuvel 2006 (I am grateful to Danielle van den Heuvel for allowing me to read a copy of her work in progress); Wong 1996.

27 Tóth 2000:92; Farrell 1983.

28 Abreu-Ferreira 2001; Peabody 2005:58; Thwaites 1984.

29 Bogucka 1989; Wiesner 1997a; Ogilvie 2004; Faroqhi 2001b:56, 58; M.R. Hunt 1984:41–68; Farge and Revel 1991:45–6.

30 Zilfi 2004:10.

31 Thwaites 1984:31; Groppi 2002:50; See also the large literature on the liberalization of the grain trade, which, however, was more likely to be controlled by men than was the trade in perishables. See, among others, Grab 1985:186–210; and Bouton 1993.

32 Faroqhi 2001b:155–6, 158. See also Yi 2004:155–7; and Khoury 1997b:138, 184.

33 Vicente 2003:183.

34 Thwaites 1984:30–5.

35 Abreu-Ferreira 2001.

36 Kuklo 1998. In the seventeenth century, women seem to have almost entirely mono-polized selling in some Polish towns. On this, see Karpinski 1989b.

37 Özgüven 2001.

38 Fontaine 2002:22; Karpinski 1989b. It is not clear whether the women's guilds lasted into the eighteenth century, however.

39 For France, see Hesse 2001:3–30. For England, see D'Urfey 1700:44–55, 'The fish-wives' dialogue'.

40 Leib 1962:108. See also N.Z. Davis 1995:5–62.

41 Rabuzzi 1995; Heuvel 2007. Thanks to Danielle van den Heuvel for advising me on proportions of Dutch women traders.

42 Wunder 1998:92–3; Fontaine 1996:74–7; M.R. Hunt 2004a.

43 Groppi 2002:44.

44 Faroqhi 2001a:128–34.

45 Wiersma 1998.

46 Bray 1997.

47 Berg 1994:138.

48 D. Quataert 1991:161; J. Quataert 1985; Sharpe 1996:31; Sweets 1995; I. Jonsson 1995.

49 J. Quataert 1985.

50 Hafter 1995b; See also Guenzi, Massa and Caselli 1998; Wunder 1998:85–9.

51 Lowry 2003:57. I am grateful to Madeline Zilfi for this reference.

52 Gerber 1980:237–8.

53 Crowston 2001:173–4, 199.

54 Truant 1995:57; see also Crowston 2001:217–93.

55 Ogilvie and Cerman 1996:1–11, 227–39. On gender and proto-industry, see Simonton 1998: 37–47.

56 Vicente 2000:18–19, 21.

57 Moch 2001:II, 135; Vicente 2000; Lampe and Jackson 1982:245; Krody 2000:30–1.

58 Gerber 1980:237; Sweets 1995.

59 Sharpe 1991; Bräker 1970:56.

60 Berg 1994:236.

61 Sharpe 1996:36, 147–8; Gullickson 2001; Moch 2001.

62 Thomson 1992:237, 256; Hilden 1993:19–20; Pardoe 1838:III, 177–81; D. Quataert 1991:161–76.

63 Berg 1994:136–65 is the source for much of this discussion.

64 Hilden 1993:64.

65 Nicholas and Oxley 1993; Burnette and Mokyr 1995. Compare Horrell and Humphries 1992.

66 Ramsey 1988:138, 169–73, 195–6, 220, 265, 308; T.A.B. Corley 2004; A. Russell 1794:II, 141.

67 A. Russell 1794:I, 245, 254; II, 123, 141; Konczacki and Aterman 2002. Regina Salomea Rusiecka's autobiography, 'Proceder podrózy i zycia mego awantur' ('The Conduct of my Life's Travels and Adventures'), written down about 1760 in Istanbul, will soon be published in English translation by Wladyslaw Roczniak and Lynn Lubamersky.

68 Hufton and Tallett 1987; C. Jones 1989:esp. 89–154.

69 Gerber 1980:233. See also Ze'evi 1995:167.

70 Marcus 1989:54, 192. Gerber 1980.

71 Cavallo 1995:169–72.

72 Friendly Society for Widows 1696. Despite the name this was an insurance scheme, not a true friendly society.

73 Carlos and Neal 2004:205–11; Todd 1999. I am grateful to Barbara Todd for allowing me to read the paper.

74 Ginio 2003; Hufton 1974; Robert Jütte 1994; Marcus 1990:171–9; Muldrew 1998; Wales 1984.

75 Bräker 1970:173.

76 Lemire 1998; Lemire, Pearson and Campbell 2002; Muldrew 1998; Wijngaarden 1998; Carbonell-Esteller 2000.

77 Lemire 1998; MacKay 1999.

78 N. Rogers 1991; Hitchcock 2005; T.B. Smith 2001.

79 Harrington 1999:312n. I am obliged to Anne McCants for information on Dutch charities.

80 Foucault 1973:38–64.

81 Siena 2004.

82 D.T. Andrew 1989; Ener 2005:504; Sharpe 1996:131–3, 137.

83 M.R. Hunt 2004b; P.K. Taylor and Rebel 1981:371–3; Zečević 2007.

84 Hacker 1981:655; St. John Williams 1988:39.

85 Lieutenant Gratton, quoted in St. John Williams 1988:59–60.

86 Symanski 1981:3.

87 See among others Frykman 1989; T. Henderson 1999; Hufton 1974:306–17; C. Jones 1978; Juratic 1987; Rafeq 1990; Semerdjian 2003; Pol 1996.

88 There have been, as of this writing, surprisingly few good modern studies of eighteenth-century courtesanship in its social context. An exception is D.T. Andrew 1994a. I am grateful to Donna Andrew for letting me read this unpublished paper. Biographies of courtesans abound, and many of them are historically almost worthless. A happy exception is Duchêne 1984. An interesting autobiography of an eighteenth-century courtesan is Robinson 1994 (originally published 1784).

89 Karpinski 1989a:24–5, 39.

90 Crowston 2001:103; Erdem 1996:33–7. See also Qur'an 24:33.

91 Rafeq 1990.

92 Mowry 2004; Simpson 1996.

93 Karpinski 1989a:724–5.

94 Dabhoiwala 2008. Thanks to Faramerz Dabhoiwala for allowing me to read this work in progress and also for some illuminating conversations. See also Hull 1996:esp. 314–22, 349–53; and Walkowitz 1980.

Chapter 6: Paths of the Spirit

1 Harris 1999:xiii.

2 A good overview of that ambivalent relationship is Levin 1993.

3 Tóth 2001:83; Elias, 1988:218.

4 Frykman 1989:201 (I have slightly streamlined the dialogue).

5 Curzon 1955:271; D. Wilson 1970:22.

6 Ankarloo and Clark 1999.

7 Ankarloo and Henningsen 1990; Levack, 1995; Behar 2001; Dysa 2001; Hsia 1988.

8 Ahlgren 1995; Christian 1981; Voekel 2002:106–22. I am grateful to Pamela Voekel for discussing this issue with me.

9 On the social implications of the virginity cult for real women, see Strasser 2003.

10 Hufton and Tallett 1987; E. Clark 1997; Terpstra 1995; Voekel 2002.

11 Caffiero 1999.

12 Kostroun 2003; F.E. Weaver 2002a.

13 Bellini 2005.

14 Fališevac 2001:38.

15 See, e.g., Chaudhuri 1992; Sarkar and Butalia 1995.

16 Choquette 1992; N.Z. Davis 1995:63–139.

17 Schumacher 2002; Lavrin 1999; Morrow 2002.

18 Luria 2001:V, 254.

19 Quoted in Raughter 2004.

20 Josefa Amar y Barbón, *Discurso sobre la educacion fisica i moral de las mujeres* (Madrid: 1790), 150 quoted in Voekel 2002:144; see also 145–50. My treatment of Amar y Borbón is drawn almost entirely from Pamela Voekel.

21 T.A. Smith 2003; Voekel 2002; Mazzotti 2001; F.E. Weaver 2002b.

22 Worobec 2006:336. Worobec is here discussing the work of E.B. Smilianskaia, *Volshebniki, bogokhul'niki, eretiki: Narodnai religioznost' i 'dukhovnye prestupleniia' v Rossii XVIII v* (Magicians, Blasphemers, and Heretics: Popular Religiosity and 'Religious Crimes' in 18th-Century Russia) (Moscow: Indrik, 2003).

23 *Appearance of the Kaluzhsk Icon* 2001.

24 Shevzov 1999; Kenna 1985. As Kenna and others point out, the icon is supposed to *channel* grace rather than be divine in its own right. That is why believers are said to 'venerate' rather than 'worship' icons. However, these theological distinctions were sometimes difficult to sustain in daily practice.

25 Michels 1995.

26 The Old Believers were roughly divided into the *priestly* Old Believers, 'who retained ordained ministers and major sacraments', and, if necessary, bribed Orthodox priests to perform the rituals in the old way, and the *priestless* Old Believers, who had lay ministers who could administer the sacraments of Baptism and Penance. Paert 2003:30–1.

27 Paert 2003:40–1, 45–9, 63–85, 162–71.

28 Meehan 1998:11–15; Worobec 2006:345.

29 Cavarnos 1971:32–5,45–6,52–3. The information on St. Kosmas' activities and teachings comes largely from Sapphiros Christodoulidis' *Life of Saint Cosmas* first published in Venice in 1814 and translated in Cavarnos' book (25–43). Christodoulidis was one of Kosmas' disciples.

30 N.Z. Davis 1975:152–88.

31 Wiesner 1997b. The key scripture passages are 1 Corinthians 14:34–5 and 1 Timothy 2:11–12. Compare Wunder 1998:44–62.

32 See, e.g., Mücke 2000:5,16, 33–5; and compare, among many such works, Cholakian 2000.

33 Irwin 1991:307.

34 Bowerbank 2004.

35 Hitchcock 2004. I presume she was some sort of Protestant, perhaps, given her name, a French Huguenot. But she could also have been Catholic. See also Mack 1992; Jung 1998:51–5; and Fogleman 2007.

36 Hammond 2006; Tyson 1995. For Methodist women preachers, see Chilcote 1991.

37 Hopkins 1982; B. Taylor 1983.

38 Petersen 2005; Mücke 2000:22.

39 Shea 1990:123.

40 Ashbridge 1820; Shea 1990.

41 S.J. Shaw 1991:46.

42 Parush and Brene 1995:185–6.

43 N.Z. Davis 1995:24; Weissler 1998; Kay 2004:16; Ramos-González 2005:220.

44 Ramos-González 2005; Rosman 2002; Weissler 1998:12.

45 Kay 2004:236–43, esp. 242.

46 Laytner 1990.

47 Mishnah, *Shabbat*, 2, 6 quoted in Marienberg 2003:7; R. Benjamin Aaron Solnick, *Seder Mitsvas ha-noshim* (Basel, 1602), 3b–4a, quoted in Weissler 1998:69.

48 Jacob ben Isaac of Yanov, *Tsenerene* (Amsterdam, 1703), 4b, quoted in Weissler 1998:73. My discussion of *tkhines* literature is heavily indebted to Weissler.

49 Gershom Gerhard Scholem, *Sabbatai Sevi, the Mystical Messiah, 1626–1676* (London: Routledge & Kegan Paul, 1973), 403–6, cited in Taitz, Henry, and Tallan 2003:197.

50 *Tkhine imrei Shifre* (n.d., n.p.p.) quoted in Weissler 1998:61–2; 93–4.

51 Serl bas Jacob ben Wolf Kranz, 'Tkine of the Matriarchs for the Blowing of the Shofar', quoted in Weissler 1998:145; see also 104–25, 136–7, 141. For pilgrimages to Rachel's tomb, see Deutsch 2003:199–202.

52 Mordecai Wilensky, *Hassidism Umitnaggedim: Letoldot Hapulmus Beneihem Ba-Shanim* (Jerusalem: 1990), quoted in Hundert 2004:202. On the content of the miracles, and especially the emphasis on curing barrenness, see 142–53.

53 For the debate on women and the *tsitsit* and *tefillin*, see Deutsch 2003:129.

54 Deutsch 2003:125, 138–40, 143, 175–6, 185, 190–210.

55 Kabbani and Bakhtiar 1998:xxxii. It has also been argued that, on balance, Islam represented a diminution in women's status compared to what it had been in pre-Islamic Arabia. See Ahmed 1992:41–78.

56 The key passages in the Qur'an are 33:53 (male visitors must speak to the Prophet's wives from behind a curtain or screen); 24:30–31 (women should not display their adornments or their bosoms or other private parts to unrelated men); and 33:59–60, (free Muslim women, but not Muslim slave women, must cover themselves with cloaks or mantles on the street). This discussion is indebted to Mernissi 1991:85–101; Ahmed 1992:53–5; and Stowasser 1994:90–4.

57 Mattson 2008:21n, 68, 86.

58 Mernissi 1991:141–60; Ahmed 1992:60–1; Stowasser 1994:85–103, 180–8.

59 The Prophet's words, recorded in various *hadiths*, were variations of 'do not prevent your women from attending mosque when they ask to do so'. See Khoury 1996:176

for an interesting eighteenth-century rendering of the issue of early Muslim women going to mosque.

60 Peirce 1993:265.

61 Tapper and Tapper 1987.

62 H.P. Laqueur 1992; Raymond Lifchez, 1992b. The other fairly egalitarian orders were the Khalwati and the Jarrahi. For this, see Elias 1988:223.

63 Kefadar 1992:309.

64 H.P. Laqueur 1992:292–3.

65 Hadžijahić 1982. There had been a number of very active Sufi women's convent-lodges in medieval times, particularly in the Levant.

66 Ginio 2001; Ginio 2006.

67 See d'Ohsson 1787 for engravings of Sufi *tekke* and Lifchez 1992b:88, 92–3, 97–9, 109 for building schemes.

68 Filipovic 1954; Hadžijahić 1992; Zhelyazkova and Nielsen 2001.

69 Ginio 2001:126. For women and *waqfs* in the early modern period, see Fay 1997; Meriwether 1997; Filan 2007.

70 Elias 1988:118.

71 Burckhardt 1968:195–8.

72 Tolmacheva 1998.

73 An illuminating dervish's memoir of the *hajj*, with a strong focus on tomb-visiting and on the early women of Islam, is Edib 1825:esp. 110, 119–20, 142–3, 153, 155, 165. Mehemmed Edib appears to have made his pilgrimage in or around 1779. The *hajj* is very different today.

74 Stoppa 1655. Modern inter-religious and inter-ethnic violence also tends to be aimed at the integrity of families and lineage, and this often takes the form (as in the Savoy) of the hyper-violation of women and the humiliation of men by raping and killing their wives and children. See Stiglmayer 1994; Green 2002; Helie, Naqvi, and Mischkowski 2003.

75 Teter 2003:274n; Hundert 2004:67.

76 Staudacher 2002; Robins 1980:48–50.

77 Başgöz 1971:101.

78 Baer 2004a; Shaw 1991:119–46.

79 Ashbridge 1820:4, 8–9.

80 Bruneau 1998:154–8.

81 Shaw 1991:82, 137–8; B.J. Kaplan 2007:267–8, 276–93; Ivanova 2007; Šolić 2007: 325–6.

82 Parkes 2004:347–9.

83 'Eirenic' movements are movements that promote peace and reconciliation. In this period they often sought either to reconcile diverse faiths into a simplified creed that most people could agree upon, or to emphasize religious toleration, or both.

84 Caffiero 1999 has an especially lucid discussion of this process.

85 Darnton 1968; Garrett 1984:67–81; B.J. Gibbons 1996; Leask 1992.

86 The 'apparitions' phenomenon is covered in some detail in Luria 2001:V, 255–6.

87 Harris 1999.

88 Lozanova 2001.

Chapter 7: Cultures of Women

1 Kord 2003; Waldron 1996.
2 D. Wilson 1970:23.
3 Karadžić 1992.
4 Dégh 1969: 90–3, 97–100.
5 Tari 1999.
6 Pettan 2003:293–5; McLeod and Herndon 1975:84–7.
7 Silverman 2003.
8 Turniansky 1988; McLeod and Herndon 1975:91; Bohlman 2003; Gouk 1999.
9 Curtis 2001.
10 Petrovic 1990.
11 See, e.g., Englezakis 1995:240–41 on the Song of Emines and Christophe, about the impossible love between a Christian boy and a Muslim girl, which, of course, ends in both their deaths. Except it does not end because 'The girl's grave grew a lemon tree and the boy's a cypress/And every Sunday they would turn and kiss each other'.
12 A. Russell 1794: I, 141, see also I, 75, 131, 137–8, 140, 157, 202, 254, 256.
13 Holst-Warhaft 1992:30.
14 Bithell 2003:42–4.
15 For issues of transmission, see Buttimer 2006: I, 320–71 esp. 331–4.
16 Le Strange 1974:98–9.
17 Karadžić 1992:33.
18 Le Strange 1974:19.
19 Graff 1987:191.
20 Cassar 2001; Earle 1989; Houston 1988; Johansson 1981; Monter 1980; Stephens 1990; Tóth 2000; J.Ij. Meer 2002.
21 Kefeli 2001; Petschauer 1989; Raughter 2004; Roggero 2001; Skedd 1997.
22 Karsch 1990:133; Roggero 2001:922.
23 Adler 1974.
24 Tóth 2000.
25 K. Goodman 1999:114; Watanabe-O'Kelly 2000:49–51,56.
26 Nielsen 2004; Bogucka 2004:141; Aïssé 1787; Humphreys and Leonard 2004.
27 Vigée-Le Brun 1989:47.
28 Freke 2001; Roodenburg 1985; Mazarin 2008; Robinson 1994.
29 Petersen 2005; Roland 1990; Catherine II 2006.
30 Lonsdale 1989. Lonsdale only includes those poets whose work he considers to be of lasting value.
31 Gibb and Browne 1963:IV, 150–9.
32 Vowles 1994:44–50.
33 Donoghue 1995; M.R. Hunt 1998.
34 Gemert 1995. My treatment of this issue is especially indebted to Lia van Gemert.
35 Brandes 1991:56; K. Goodman 1999:217n. My thanks to Ute Brandes for her help on all things to do with German literature.
36 Sullivan 1990.

37 Grenby 2001; Ty 1993.

38 Harries 2001:46–72. I am grateful to both Betsy Harries and Jill Shefrin for discussing with me the issue of the early tales' intended audience.

39 Seifert 1996; P. Brown 2000; Harries 2001; H. Tucker 2003.

40 Shefrin 2004; Roscoe 1973.

41 Ferguson 1998:7–26.

42 Shteir 2004.

43 Shefrin 2006:191–5.

44 Arenal and Schlau 1989; E. Weaver 2002; Bogucka 2004:151.

45 Alenius 2004:78–80.

46 E.F. Lewis 2004:97–152.

47 Clay 2005.

48 Kany 1932:301–4.

49 Roosevelt 1995:129–55; Stites 2007.

50 Bogucka 2004:151.

51 K. Goodman 1999:127.

52 Cheek 2003:61.

53 Berlanstein 1994; Clay 2005; Goncourt 1890.

54 E. Arnold and Berdes 2002.

55 Bowers 1986:127–8, 146–8, 164–7; see also Letzter and Adelson 2001.

56 López 2000.

57 Noble 2004; Ullrich 1946; Golos 1960.

58 There is some evidence that the reluctance to have women learn bowed instruments was less extreme among some Central European Roma, though that may be a later development. See Silverman 2008:120–2.

59 Waigand 1970:306. Thanks to Dagmar Powitz for translating the German.

60 *Kadın Bestekârlar* 2001.

61 F. Davis 1986:157, 160–1.

62 B.K. Walker 1990:I, xxiv, xxxv–vii.

63 See, for example, the tale 'The Chastity Wager on a Faithful Wife', B.K. Walker 1990:II, 248–54; storyteller: Esat Söylü, Yozgat, date: 1974.

64 Öztürkman 2002:179–80; storyteller: Abdurrahman, described as 'a 36-year-old Bosnian born in Montenegro', date: before 1894; see also Qur'an 24:4–25.

65 Decourdemanche 1896:83–160. Decourdemanche has an equivocal reputation among modern Turkish scholars, especially those who work on images of Ottoman women. On this see Schick 1998:89–90.

66 Roworth 2003.

67 N.Z. Davis 1995:140–202; Lindkvist and Werkmäster 1998. I am grateful to Maria Ågren for translating the title for me.

68 Lindberg 1998.

69 *Linwood Gallery*, n.d. I am grateful to Lisa Baskin for introducing me to Miss Linwood. See also Myrone 2004.

70 F. Davis 1986:227–9. Krody 2000:30–76.

71 Kant 1960:78.

Chapter 8: Civil Society and the State

1 Smith-Rosenberg 1975; Davidoff and Hall 1987.
2 Habermas 1989; Benhabib 1992; N. Fraser 1992.
3 J.W. Scott 1988:178–98; and Vickery 1993.
4 Landes 1988. But compare Hesse 2001.
5 Darrow 1979; Schulte 2005; Weisbrod 2005.
6 Lindemann 1996:205–9.
7 Hobsbawm and Ranger 1983.
8 I am indebted here to T. Kaplan 1982.
9 See, e.g., Stuurman 1998; Sullivan 2001; Vollendorf 2001.
10 The term 'Domestic Feminism' was coined by D.S. Smith 1973; the 'Cult of True Womanhood' comes from Welter 1966. For the latter term's application to Europe, see LeGates 1976.
11 Quoted in Faroqhi 2000:122.
12 See, among others, Eldem 2007; Hamadeh 2007; and Peirce 2007.
13 This section is indebted to Stuurman 1998.
14 da Graça 1715. For a discussion of this poem, see Lopes 1989:30–32. My treatment of da Graça relies on Lopes.
15 DeJean 1991:21–2, 89–90, 239n, 251n. See also Maclean 1977.
16 DeJean 1991:67–70, 231–35n; Schroder 1999:376–82.
17 Leporin 1742.
18 Markau 2006.
19 Sullivan 2001:142.
20 Astell 1700; da Graça 1715. The main sticking point was Genesis 3:16. A useful discussion of feminism (by which she means egalitarian feminism) and the retreat from religion is K.B. Clinton 1975, though she focuses more on male than on female feminists.
21 Williams 1980:41–3, 47–51. My treatment of Boudier de Villemert is heavily reliant upon David Williams.
22 On maternalism, see especially Michel and Koven 1990.
23 Skedd 2004.
24 Gárdonyi 1984; Adams 2007.
25 Williams 1980:45–6.
26 Andrea 2007. On the persistence of such ideas, see R. Lewis 2004.
27 N. Fraser 1992:77–83.
28 Storer 1947; Messbarger 2002. This section is greatly indebted to Rebecca Messbarger.
29 Messbarger 2002:66–8.
30 Messbarger 2002:8–10, quotation 10.
31 Brandes 1991:54–5.
32 Laine 1998.
33 Beasley 2006.
34 D. Goodman 1994. My discussion of the salons is greatly indebted to Dena Goodman's work.
35 Jacob and Sturkenboom 2003.

36 Toepfer 1990.

37 See, among others, Algrant 2002; Bogucka 1999; Dianina 2004; Laine 1998; Rice 2003; Strobel 2005.

38 Robert 1933:329.

39 Hertz 1978:106.

40 Goldberg 1999; J.Ij. Meer 2002.

41 C. Kelly 2001:39.

42 Thomas 1992.

43 Burke and Jacob 1996:515n. My treatment of Freemasonry is based upon this source and upon numerous discussions with Margaret Jacob.

44 da Silva e Orta 2002. On Portuguese Freemasonry, see the editor's introduction, 25–31.

45 Bogucka 2004:174.

46 Marker 2000:370–4, 382, 387–90.

47 Montagu 1965, quoted and discussed in Aravamudan 1995:80–1. See also F. Davis 1986:133.

48 Hamadeh 2007:302. My treatment of Stambouli parks and gardens is drawn entirely from Shirine Hamadeh.

49 Though it comes much later, it is worth noting that the earliest known explicitly feminist writings by Ottoman women, dating from 1868, focused on women's inferior (and often filthy and cold) public accommodation, especially on the Stambouli ferries. See Altınöz 2003:10.

50 Gürtuna 2000; Zilfi 1995.

51 Mortimer 1702. I am grateful to Cynthia Herrup for drawing this broadside to my attention.

52 This account and quotations from Farge and Revel 1991:9, 16, 98.

53 Hesse, 2001:17, see also 3–30.

54 Quoted in Farge and Revel 1991:127.

55 For the statistics, see Clodfelter:2002. Thanks to Bogdan State for adding up the estimates.

56 Hacker 1981; Lindegren 2001; Sućeska 1982; P.K. Taylor 1994; P.K. Taylor and Rebel 1981; P.H. Wilson 2005.

57 Spavens 1998:21.

58 A. Russell 1794:I, 295.

59 Gelbart 1987:95–132, 170–206.

60 Among the more useful contributions to the question of women warriors (or would-be warriors) are Dekker and Pol 1989; Dugaw 1989; Noé 1986; Wheelwright 1989.

61 Quoted in A.F. Young 1990:193.

62 Colley 2003:260–1; K.Wilson 1995:50, 164, 172; Guest 2000:258–60.

63 Carrier 2003.

64 Brake 1990:128. Orangists favoured greater power for the Prince of Orange, traditionally the Stadhouder (head of state) of the Dutch Republic.

65 Bogucka 2004:178.

66 A. Young 2000. There were women border fighters on the Polish-Ottoman border in the sixteenth and early seventeenth centuries, and at least two band/clans headed by women (Bogucka 2004:120).

67 For an earlier and more successful woman rebel leader, see Thornton 1991.

68 Bogucka 2004:171; Marcus 1989:88. Women also *opposed* such insurrectionary activities, for which see A. Russell 1794:I, 295.

69 Woloch 1976; Lin 2000; M.R. Hunt 2004b.

70 Ailes 2006.

71 M.R. Hunt 2004b:29.

72 Rockstroh 1932. Thanks to Jan Lindegren for drawing this to my attention and translating the relevant passage.

73 P.H. Wilson 2005.

74 Wagner 2007:200, 203.

75 Dorwart 1971:174–6

76 Ahmed 1992:122; Fay 1997; Meriwether 1997; Peri 1992.

77 Lindenmeyr 1996:15.

78 Lindenmeyr 1996:22.

79 Ramsey 1988:36.

80 Cavallo 1995:229–33.

81 Almyra Gray, *Papers and Diaries of a York Family, 1764–1839* (London: Sheldon Press, 1927) quoted in M.R. Hunt 1996:169; Lloyd 2002.

82 Similarly exploitative 'charitable' projects were to be found in France, England, the Netherlands and Belgium, especially in the second half of the eighteenth century.

83 S. Cohen 1992.

84 D.T. Andrew 1995:289.

85 Peirce 2007:227; Hufton 1995:67–8, 246; Tikoff 2008.

86 S. Cohen 1992:35; Hufton 1995:318–19; C. Jones 1978:7–28. English women were more reluctant to get involved in these sorts of charities. See D.T. Andrew 1989: 63–4.

87 Reader 2004.

88 Erdem 1996:173–6; Toledano 2007:204–54. On confraternities outside the Ottoman Empire, see Gray 1987:54–7.

89 Sjögren and Lindström 2004:252 (quoting a source from 1759) and 254 (quoting a burgher proposal of 1770). For similar developments in England, see Hirst 1975: 18–19, 24; Fieldhouse 1972. See Chalus 2005:45–7 for a lucid reconstruction of how electoral politics actually worked in eighteenth-century England.

90 'Humble Petition of Diverse Well-affected Women' (second Leveller women's petition of 1649), in H.L. Smith, Suzuki and Wiseman 2007:II, 36.

91 Cavendish 1997:25 (Letter 16). I am grateful to Hilda Smith for drawing this letter to my attention.

92 Sullivan 2001.

93 Condorcet 1788.

94 There were many biographical dictionaries of women. See, e.g., Ballard 1752; de Froes Perym 1736; *Rittrati e vite* 1775; Schønau 1753; Wichmann 1772.

95 Escrivá 1944.

96 D.T. Andrew 1995; Bogucka 2001; Chalus 2005; Kettering 1989.

97 Chalus 2003.

98 Bogucka 2001; Bogucka 2004:161–175.

99 Algrant 2002; Peirce 1993; Orr 2004.

100 Pushkareva 1997:178; Ruggles 2000; Thys-Senocak 2006; Peri 1992.

101 Pushkareva 1997:125–7; Hughes 2001:22.

102 Hughes 2004.

103 Quoted in Peirce 1993:239; Watanabe-O'Kelly 2004:265–75.

104 Algrant 2002:103; S.L. Kaplan 1982.

105 Peirce 1993:282.

106 Russell-Wood 2000:313–14.

107 Hanley 2003.

108 Wunder 1998:153–62; Peirce 1993:265.

109 Quoted in Beales 1987:I, 24.

110 Crankshaw 1983:79.

111 Klaniczay 1992; Klaniczay 1990.

112 Wangermann 1977.

113 Fisher 1968.

114 This section relies principally upon de Madariaga 2002. See also Meehan-Waters 1975; Alexander 1989.

115 Cannadine 1999; Bush 1983–1988.

116 Cherry 1993:56–7; Schiebinger 1989.

Chapter 9: Age of Revolutions

1 A.F. Young 1990.

2 Whelan 2004:219–20.

3 Butterwick 2005:698, 714–15, 727; Bogucka 2004:150.

4 Dekker 1987: 352–3; Brake, Dekker, and Pol 1990.

5 Quoted in Polasky 1986:90.

6 Polasky 1986.

7 Rebérioux and Duhet 1981:34.

8 Rebérioux and Duhet 1981:66.

9 Quoted in Roessler 1998:34; see also 7–48.

10 Rebérioux and Duhet 1981:105.

11 Palm D'Aelders quoted in Rebérioux and Duhet 1981:100, 108; de Gouges quoted in D.G. Levy, Applewhite, Johnson 1979:89.

12 From October 1791 it was called the Legislative Assembly, from September 1792 the Convention, and from 26 October 1795 the Directory.

13 In 1790 Paris was divided into forty-eight 'Sections', which were supposed to be the main local administrative units of the city. Each Section also had a general assembly where people assembled to discuss both local and national issues, and where the men voted on issues of concern. They were often the headquarters for sans-culottes demonstrations or insurrections.

14 Francini 1997:103; Traer 1980:105–19.

15 Quoted in Godineau 1998:100. See also Kates 1990:166–8.

16 Rebérioux and Duhet 1981:31–42, 131–46.

17 Olympe de Gouges, 'Declaration of Rights of the Woman and Citizen', quoted in D.G. Levy, Applewhite and Johnson 1979:87–96.

18 Rebérioux and Duhet 1981:83.
19 DiCaprio 2007:26–30; 96–109.
20 Godineau 1998:103–5.
21 Godineau 1998:102; Desan 1992.
22 'Lady Citizens of District 7' (Marseilles), 7 July 1790 quoted in Rebérioux and Duhet 1981:80. At this point in the Revolution Louis XVI had not yet been deposed.
23 Quoted in Harten and Harten 1989:341.
24 'Sans-culottes', literally 'without breeches', referred to the fact that urban workers wore pantaloons (long trousers) rather than the knee-length breeches and stockings associated with bourgeois and elite men. The sans-culottes tended to be considerably more militant than the bulk of the middle-class revolutionaries.
25 Godineau 1998:109.
26 Andress 2006:157–8.
27 Bielecki 2001; D.E. Jones 2003:193.
28 Godineau 1998:119.
29 DiCaprio 2007:95–6; Godineau 1998:174.
30 Godineau 1998:135–8.
31 Cole 1998.
32 Greer 1935:25–37; Andress 2006:244–51.
33 Andress 2006:96.
34 DiCaprio 2007:109–45.
35 Quoted in Vanpée 1999:49.
36 Choudhury 2004:167–9, 176.
37 L.A. Hunt 1991. The charges of lesbianism were circulating before the Revolution.
38 Quoted in A. Fraser 2001:528.
39 Godineau 1998:165–6.
40 Quoted in Godineau 1998:274. See also Germani 1990:39.
41 Quoted in Godineau 1998:172.
42 Desan 1992. My treatment of the provincial clubs is entirely drawn from Suzanne Desan's essay.
43 National Convention Session of 9 Brumaire, Year II (30 October 1793) quoted in D.G. Levy, Applewhite, and Johnson 1979:213–17.
44 Pierre-Gaspard Chaumette, in a speech at the City Hall on 27 Brumaire, Year II (17 November 1793) quoted in D.G. Levy, Applewhite, and Johnson 1979:219–21. Olympe de Gouges did not, so far as is known, ever set up a woman's club.
45 For attacks on women, see Gendron 1993:25–9, 40, 42–3.
46 Hufton 1971:105–6; Godineau 1998:316–64; Roessler 1998:170–94; Gendron 1993:128–36.
47 Germani 1990:217.
48 A. Douglas and Mrs. M. Douglas 1797:33.
49 Theremin 1799:62–4, 69, 74, 83.
50 L.A. Hunt 1992:81–2, 90, 98, 122–3.
51 Pipelet de Leury 1800; Robinson 2003.
52 Godineau 1998:368.
53 Carpenter 1999b:68–9, 72, 87–99, 141–3, 186. See also Carpenter 1999a.

54 Radcliffe 1795:122.

55 Bordereau 1814:3. For her noble patronesses, see 8. Other women warriors of the Vendée are discussed in Andress 2006:248.

56 Radcliffe 1795:358.

57 Carpenter 1999b.

58 Traer 1980:188n; Phillips 1980:108–24.

59 Darrow 1989; Desan 1997.

60 Quoted in Desan 1997:597, 614, 624.

61 Desan 1999:81–121.

62 Hesse 2001:37–78.

63 In eighteenth- and early nineteenth-century Britain 'abolitionism' usually meant efforts to abolish the transatlantic slave trade. Abolitionists were *not* necessarily committed to ending slavery as an institution.

64 Midgley 1992:12, 86–92; Prince 1997.

65 Ferguson 1992:162–3.

66 Stoddard 1995:382–4.

67 de Gouges 1994. I have also benefited from Cowles 2007.

68 Useful primary sources on this and other issues of discrimination and emancipations (e.g. the emancipation of the Jews) are compiled in L.A. Hunt 1996.

69 Midgley 1992:20–2.

70 E. Smith and More 1795. On the poem's authorship, see Richardson 2002. Richardson argues that More superimposed the Christian material on top of and somewhat at cross-purposes with Smith's more tragic and sentimental tale.

71 Midgley 1992; Midgley 2007:41–64. See also Chaudhuri and Strobel 1992; Burton 1994; Hall 2002; and Stoler 2002.

72 Jespersen 1995:II, 68.

73 Peabody 2005:66–7.

74 V.R. Jones 2000:126. The quotation is from Messbarger 2002:133.

75 Giuli 1997:274.

76 Thale 1989:82–3; see also D.T. Andrew 1994b:357–8, 377–8, 392.

77 Király 1969:167. See also Fábri 2001:47.

78 J.S. Murray 1995:23, 37.

79 Ph. Garran-Coulon, *Rapport sur les troubles de Saint-Domingue* (1797–99), quoted and discussed in Peabody 2005:65.

80 Constitution of Haiti (20 May 1805), quoted in Sheller 1997:244.

81 Scully and Paton 2005:11; Garrigus 2003.

82 Quoted in Curtin 1991:137; see also 134–6. My treatment of the 1798 Rising is drawn entirely from Nancy Curtin's essay.

83 Quoted in Curtin 1991:138.

84 Curtin 1991:134, 142.

85 Buttafuoco 1977; Noether and Coppa 1989; S.J. Brown 2006:588. Thanks to Amanda Collins for helping me with the Italian.

86 Quoted in Branson 2001:143.

87 Norton 1996:191–3.

88 Jamgocyan 1990; Clogg 1969. See also F. Davis 1986:10–11, 15–16.

89 Somel 2001:57.

90 Gerolymatos 2002:140–1.

91 Constantinidis 1998.

92 Schick 2007.

93 See, e.g., de Froes Perym 1736. De Froes Perym is said to have been the pen-name of Fr. João de S. Pedro.

94 Robertson 1999:19.

95 S.J. Brown 2006.

96 S.J. Brown 2006.

97 Quoted in Clogg 1969:93–4.

98 Kefeli 2001:259–60.

99 Robert 1933:314–16, 325–6, 328, 333.

100 See especially Darrow 1979 and Macknight 2007.

101 Moses 1982; B. Taylor 1983.

102 On the Russian Women's Patriotic Society (Zhenskoe Patrioticheskoe Obshchestvo) (1812) and its offshoots, see Lindenmeyr 1996:111, 271n. On the German lands, see Hagemann 2004; on the Ottoman groups, see Os 1999:95–100.

103 There is a large literature on this topic, though it has had a rather strong western European and American focus. For some correctives to this, see the articles in Hawkesworth 2001; Hawkesworth 2000; and Iggers 1995.

Conclusion

1 Quoted in Gelbart 1987:118.

2 Brazil only abolished slavery in 1888; French Madagascar did so in 1896; the Ottoman Empire suppressed the slave trade in 1880 (though it continued to some degree clandestinely) but there continued to be a few slaves, mainly women domestics and harem slaves, right up to the end of the Empire in 1922–23.

3 This is likely to have been primarily a Christian and Jewish effort. In Islam the issues are somewhat different since Islam does not have a concept of original sin for women to be responsible for; nor is there a need for a saviour to redeem humans due to their inherent sin. See the interestingly altered Qur'anic version of the story of the first couple in the Garden of Eden, Qur'an 7:19–55.

4 Landes 1988; L.A. Hunt 1992.

5 The correct quotation is to be found in Marx 2005:1.

FURTHER READING

◆

GENERAL TEXTS

Lisa DiCaprio and Merry E. Wiesner, *Lives and Voices: Sources in European Women's History* (Boston, MA: Houghton Mifflin Co., 2000). A collection of primary sources with very good coverage of the early modern period.

Olwen Hufton, *The Prospect before Her: A History of Women in Western Europe 1500–1800* (London: Fontana Press, 1997).

Merry Wiesner, *Women and Gender in Early Modern Europe*, 3rd edn (Cambridge: Cambridge University Press, 2008).

NATIONAL HISTORIES

Maria Bogucka, *Women in Early Modern Polish Society, against the European Background* (Aldershot: Ashgate, 2004).

Amila Buturović and Irvin Cemil Schick, eds, *Women in the Ottoman Balkans: Gender, Culture and History* (New York: I.B. Tauris, 2007).

Mary O'Dowd and Margaret MacCurtain, eds, *Women in Early Modern Ireland* (Edinburgh: Edinburgh University Press, 1991).

Mary Prior, *Women in English Society, 1500–1800* (London: Methuen, 1985).

Natalia Pushkareva, *Women in Russian History from the Tenth to the Twentieth Century* (Armonk, NY: M.E. Sharpe, 1997).

Samia I. Spencer, ed., *French Women and the Age of Enlightenment* (Bloomington: Indiana University Press, 1984).

Heide Wunder, *He Is the Sun, She Is the Moon: Women in Early Modern Germany*, trans. Thomas Dunlap (Cambridge, MA: Harvard University Press, 1998).

Madeline C. Zilfi, ed., *Women in the Ottoman Empire: Middle Eastern Women in the Early Modern Era*, The Ottoman Empire and Its Heritage, 10 (Leiden: Brill, 1997).

CHAPTER 1: HIERARCHY AND DIFFERENCE

Simon Dickie, 'Hilarity and Pitilessness in the Mid-Eighteenth Century: English Jestbook Humor', *Eighteenth Century Studies* 37 (2003):1–22. Why did eighteenth-century people think cruel jokes at the expense of disabled or maimed people were hilariously funny? Europe before the 'rise of humanitarianism'.

Eyal Ginio, 'Living on the Margins of Charity: Coping with Poverty in an Ottoman Provincial City', in Michael David Bonner, Mine Ener and Amy Singer, eds, *Poverty and Charity in Middle Eastern Contexts* (Albany: State University of New York Press, 2003), 165–84. Down and out in Ottoman Salonika; excellent on begging, institutional charity, and the position of orphan girls.

Shirine Hamadeh, 'Public Spaces and the Garden Culture of Istanbul in the Eighteenth Century', in Virginia H. Aksan and Daniel Goffman, eds, *The Early Modern Ottomans: Remapping the Empire* (Cambridge: Cambridge University Press, 2007), 277–312. Sophisticated discussion of Ottoman women in the public gardens and parks of Istanbul and the interplay of freedom and constraint.

Michal Kopczynski, 'Old Age Gives No Joy? Old People in the Kujawy Countryside at the End of the 18th Century', *Acta poloniae historica* 78 (1998):81–101. The equivocal position of old people in a peasant society.

Sue Peabody, *There Are No Slaves in France: The Political Culture of Race and Slavery in the Ancien Régime* (New York: Oxford University Press, 1996). The position of people of African origin in eighteenth-century France, with particular attention to efforts by slaves to obtain their freedom in the French courts.

CHAPTER 2: FAMILIES

Primary sources

The Memoirs of Glückel of Hameln, (New York: Schocken Books, 1977). A deservedly admired memoir by a German-Jewish woman merchant, with attention to religion, family life, trade, folkways, and anti-semitism.

Elizabeth Freke, *The Remembrances of Elizabeth Freke, 1671–1714*, ed. Raymond A. Anselment, Camden Fifth Series, 18 (Cambridge: Cambridge University Press, 2001). An old woman reminisces about her tempestuous life and difficult marriage.

Secondary sources

Maria Ågren and Amy Louise Erickson, eds, *The Marital Economy in Scandinavia and Britain, 1400–1900* (Aldershot: Ashgate, 2005). An innovative set of essays on the comparative history of the law and practice of marriage covering England, Scotland and all the Scandinavian countries.

Elizabeth A. Foyster, *Marital Violence: An English Family History, 1660–1875* (Cambridge; New York: Cambridge University Press, 2005). A fine country-based study based on numerous case studies.

Allison M. Levy, ed., *Widowhood and Visual Culture in Early Modern Europe* (Aldershot: Ashgate, 2003). An unusual perspective on (largely) upper-class widowhood through art, 'word-paintings' in funeral sermons, architectural patronage, charity and the memories of those they left behind.

Michelle Lamarche Marrese, *A Woman's Kingdom: Noblewomen and the Control of Property in Russia, 1700–1861* (Ithaca, NY: Cornell University Press, 2002). The road to, and implications of, the 1753 decree granting married women control of their own property.

Amira El Azhary Sonbol, ed., *Women, the Family, and Divorce Laws in Islamic History* (Syracuse, NY: Syracuse University Press, 1996). A classic collection that covers much more than divorce. Essays on family violence, minority (*dhimmi*) communities, female property ownership, charity, child custody, and more.

Jutta Gisela Sperling and Shona Kelly Wray, *Across the Religious Divide: Women's Property Rights in the Wider Mediterranean (ca. 1300–1800)* (New York: Routledge, 2009). Essays that cross the Ottoman/Christian European divide and open up a whole new world of women litigants.

CHAPTER 3: SEXUALITY AND REPRODUCTION

Primary sources

Vuk Stefanović Karadžić, ed., *Red Knight: Serbian Women's Songs* (London: Menard Press, 1992). A possibly unique early nineteenth-century collection of Serbian peasant women's erotic songs.

Anne Lister, *I Know My Own Heart: The Diaries of Anne Lister*, ed. Helena Whitbread (New York: New York University Press, 1992). A Yorkshire gentlewoman's diaries detailing her same-sex erotic adventures, mostly carried on under cover of romantic friendship.

Justina Siegemund, *The Court Midwife*, trans. Lynne Tatlock (Chicago: University of Chicago Press, 2005). The first midwifery text written by a German woman, and full of detail about the practice and politics of obstetrics in the early modern period. Excellent editor's introduction.

Secondary sources

Nina Rattner Gelbart, *The King's Midwife: A History and Mystery of Madame du Coudray* (Berkeley: University of California Press, 1998). An unusual and exhaustively researched biography of the most famous eighteenth-century French midwife.

Abdul-Karim Rafeq, 'Public Morality in 18th Century Ottoman Damascus', *Revue du monde musulman et de la Méditeranée* 55/56 (1990):180–96. The place of prostitution in a military town, with interesting details on neighbourhood attitudes.

David L. Ransel, *Mothers of Misery: Child Abandonment in Russia* (Princeton: Princeton University Press, 1988). The social and familial context of infanticide, child abandonment, and foundling home mortality.

Ulinka Rublack, 'Pregnancy, Childbirth and the Female Body in Early Modern Germany', *Past & Present* 150 (1996):84–110. An influential essay on the privileges accorded to pregnant women, with many details on the birth process.

Londa Schiebinger, *Nature's Body: Gender in the Making of Modern Science* (Boston: Beacon Press, 1993). Enlightenment Science, evolving notions of race, gender and 'European superiority', and the ways they all interact.

István György Tóth, 'Peasant Sexuality in Eighteenth-Century Hungary', *Continuity and Change* 6 (1991):43–59. 'Folk' birth control methods, abortion, magic, transvestism, women married to women – all gleaned from Hungarian court records.

CHAPTER 4: FOOD AND CONSUMPTION

Primary sources

Margaretta Acworth, *Margaretta Acworth's Georgian Cookery Book*, ed. Alice Prochaska and Frank Prochaska (London: Pavilion/Michael Joseph, 1987). Excellent introduction and some rather good recipes.

Secondary sources

Cynthia A. Bouton, *The Flour War: Gender, Class, and Community in Late Ancien Regime French Society* (University Park: Pennsylvania State University Press, 1993). Gender in the wave of food riots that swept parts of France in 1775.

Kate Macintyre, 'Famine and the Female Mortality Advantage', in Tim Dyson and Cormac Ó Gráda, eds, *Famine Demography: Perspectives from the Past and Present* (Oxford: Oxford University Press, 2002), 240–59. Explores why women are more likely to survive famines than are men.

George D. Sussman, *Selling Mothers Milk: The Wet-Nursing Business in France 1715–1914* (Urbana: University of Illinois Press, 1982). The organization of the wet-nursing trade, and its implications for urban women's work and infant mortality, plus eighteenth-century maternal breast-feeding campaigns.

Joan Thirsk, *Food in Early Modern England: Phases, Fads, Fashions 1500–1760* (London: Hambledon Continuum, 2007). Fascinating material on changes in diet as a result of new crops and new preservation techniques; also spells out the demographic implications.

CHAPTER 5: WORK AND MONEY

Maxine Berg, *The Age of Manufactures 1700–1820: Industry, Innovation and Work in Britain*, 2nd edn (London: Routledge, 1994). Influential study that explores the role of women and ideas of gender in the British industrial revolution.

Clare Haru Crowston, *Fabricating Women: The Seamstresses of Old Regime France, 1675–1791* (Durham, NC: Duke University Press, 2001). Illuminating study of the seamstressing industry in eighteenth-century France, with attention to women's guilds, guild politics, working conditions, fashion and sexuality.

Suraiya Faroqhi, 'Women's Work, Poverty and the Privileges of Guildsmen', *Archiv Orientalni* 69 (2001):155–64. Brief but informative article on work opportunities for women as well as the gendered politics of work in the early modern Ottoman Empire, with a focus on Istanbul.

Olwen Hufton, 'Women and the Family Economy in Eighteenth-Century France', *French Historical Studies* 9 (1975):1–22. Influential essay on how poor women 'made do' in eighteenth-century France, with attention to marriage and spousal desertion, female criminality (especially salt-smuggling), migration and begging.

Anne E. McCants, 'Petty Debts and Family Networks: The Credit Markets of Widows and Wives in Eighteenth-Century Amsterdam', in Beverly Lemire, Ruth Pearson and Gail Grace Campbell, eds, *Women and Credit: Researching the Past, Refiguring the Future* (Oxford: Berg, 2002), 33–50. Women's money-lending and other revenue-producing activities with attention to gender, life-cycle and credit-worthiness.

Sheilagh C. Ogilvie, *A Bitter Living: Women, Markets, and Social Capital in Early Modern Germany* (Oxford: Oxford University Press, 2003). The many ways women who wished to sell their labour or their manufactures were disadvantaged, especially by male-run guilds, town corporations and the law.

Deborah Simonton, *A History of European Women's Work, 1700 to the Present* (London: Routledge, 1998). The best general book on European women's work, with unusually strong coverage of the pre-industrial era, of women and farming, of domestic service, and of proto-industry.

CHAPTER 6: PATHS OF THE SPIRIT

Primary sources

The Life of Lady Johanna Eleonora Petersen Written by Herself: Pietism and Women's Autobiography in Seventeenth-Century Germany, ed. Barbara Becker-Cantarino (Chicago, IL: University of Chicago Press, 2005). A journey of faith by a radical pietist visionary. Excellent introduction on women and pietism.

The Memoirs of Glückel of Hameln, trans. Marvin Lowenthal (New York: Schocken Books, 1977). A deservedly admired memoir by a German-Jewish woman merchant, with attention to religiosity, family life, trade, folkways, and anti-semitism.

Elizabeth Ashbridge, 'Some Account of the Fore Part of the Life of Elizabeth Ashbridge', in William L. Andrews, ed., *Journeys in New Worlds: Early American Women's Narratives* (Madison: University of Wisconsin Press, 1990), 117–80. The epic worldly and spiritual journeying of a Quaker woman minister in England, Ireland and America.

Secondary sources

Marc Baer, 'Islamic Conversion Narratives of Women: Social Change and Gendered Religious Hierarchy in Early Modern Ottoman Istanbul', *Gender & History* 16 (2004):425–58. Why late seventeenth-century Jewish and Christian women converted to Islam, with a lot of attention to individual stories.

Luis R. Corteguera, 'The Making of a Visionary: The Life of Beatriz Ana Ruiz, 1666–1735', in Marta V. Vicente and Luis R. Corteguera, eds, (Aldershot: Ashgate, 2003), 164–82. An illiterate Valencian *beata* who had both political and religious visions and was listened to at the top levels of the Spanish government.

Brenda Meehan-Waters, 'Popular Piety, Local Initiative and the Founding of Women's Religious Communities in Russia, 1764–1907', *St. Vladimir's Theological Quarterly* 30 (1986):117–42. The spiritual depth and organizational creativity of Russian Orthodox women in the eighteenth and nineteenth centuries.

Irina Paert, *Old Believers: Religious Dissent and Gender in Russia, 1760–1850* (Manchester: Manchester University Press, 2003). The doctrine, sociology and diversity of the Old Believer heresy in the eighteenth and nineteenth centuries, with considerable attention to the centrality of women and gender.

Chava Weissler, *Voices of the Matriarchs: Listening to the Prayers of Early Modern Jewish Women* (Boston: Beacon Press, 1998). Classic study of vernacular literature for Jewish women in the early modern period, with a lot of attention to women writers, religiosity and efforts to expand spiritual opportunities.

Antonina Zhelyazkova and Jorgen Nielsen, eds, *Ethnology of Sufi Orders: Theory and Practice*, The Fate of Muslim Communities in the Balkans, 8 (Sofia: IMIR, 2001). Pathbreaking collection of articles on Islam, Sufism and folk religion in the Balkans.

CHAPTER 7: CULTURES OF WOMEN

Primary sources

Jeannine Blackwell and Susanne Zantop, eds, *Bitter Healing: German Women Writers from 1700 to 1830: An Anthology* (Lincoln: University of Nebraska Press, 1990). A well-chosen collection that includes memoirs, dramatic sketches, letters, and excerpts from novels from a diverse group of German-language writers spanning the entire eighteenth century.

Françoise de Grafigny, *Letters of a Peruvian Woman*, trans. G.J. Mallinson (New York: Oxford University Press, 2009). The best-selling novel of the first half of the eighteenth century, it features critiques of the sorry state of women's education, of the sexual double standard and of the inequities in the law of marriage. In the end its heroine refuses marriage.

Sumru Belger Krody, *Flowers of Silk and Gold: Four Centuries of Ottoman Embroidery* (Washington, DC: Merrell in association with The Textile Museum, 2000). A very thorough history of Ottoman women embroiderers, including information on flower and other symbolism and beautiful reproductions.

Roger Lonsdale, *Eighteenth-Century Women Poets: An Oxford Anthology* (Oxford: Oxford University Press, 1989). A luminous collection of poems by Englishwomen on love, religion, friendship, the deaths of dearly loved children, female scholarship, feminism, views of the French Revolution and much else.

Louise-Elisabeth Vigée-Lebrun, *The Memoirs of Elisabeth Vigée-Le Brun*, trans. Sian Evans (Bloomington: Indiana University Press, 1989). Vigée-Lebrun was Queen Marie-Antoinette's favourite artist, and this lively memoir is full of information on how to make it as a woman artist at the very end of the Old Régime.

Barbara K. Walker, *The Art of the Turkish Tale*, trans. Helen Siegl (Lubbock, TX: Texas Tech University Press, 1990). The definitive book in English on the Turkish tale, this collection leaves no doubt that it was an important genre for both men and women, as well as a vehicle for playing out family and gender politics.

Secondary sources

Lauren Clay, 'Provincial Actors, the Comédie-Française, and the Business of Performing in Eighteenth-Century France', *Eighteenth-Century Studies* 38 (2005):651–79. Illuminating essay on the gendered economics and politics of the theatre, both in Paris and the provinces.

Melissa Lee Hyde and Jennifer Dawn Milam, eds, *Women, Art and the Politics of Identity in Eighteenth-Century Europe* (Aldershot: Ashgate, 2003). Eighteenth-century women artists (Angelica Kauffman and others) and upper-class women's patronage.

Andrea Immel and Michael Witmore, eds, *Childhood and Children's Books in Early Modern Europe, 1550–1800*, Children's Literature and Culture, 38 (New York: Routledge, 2006). Distinctive features of early children's literature in England, France and Germany.

Tullia Magrini, ed., *Music and Gender: Perspectives from the Mediterranean* (Chicago, IL: University of Chicago Press, 2003). Important collection of essays on gender, ethnicity, religion and sexuality in relation to female dancers, singers and instrumentalists, both historically and in the present. Strong coverage of the Balkans.

Wendy Rosslyn, *Women and Gender in 18th-Century Russia* (Burlington, VT: Ashgate, 2003). Articles on literature, reading habits, religion, autobiography and the theatre.

CHAPTER 8: CIVIL SOCIETY AND THE STATE

Primary sources

Mary Astell, *A Serious Proposal to the Ladies: Parts I & II*, ed. Patricia Springborg (London: Pickering & Chatto, 1997). English feminist Mary Astell's plan for a women's research college where they could devote themselves to scholarship instead of having to marry.

Elisabetta Caminer Turra, *Selected Writings of an Eighteenth-Century Venetian Woman of Letters*, trans. Catherine M. Sama (Chicago: University of Chicago Press, 2003). Caminer Turra was one of the most important journal editors in eighteenth-century Italy, a feminist, and an important publicist for Enlightenment ideas.

Mary Wollstonecraft, *A Vindication of the Rights of Women* (New York: W.W. Norton, 1975). The most famous late eighteenth-century English feminist work, by a woman who was also an important 'English Jacobin'.

Secondary sources

Tjitske Akkerman and Siep Stuurman, eds, *Perspectives on Feminist Thought in European History: From the Middle Ages to the Present* (London: Routledge, 1998). Particularly strong on early modern egalitarian feminist trends, with attention to learned women, utopian thought, the Enlightenment, royal patronage, and specific feminists, including François Poullain de la Barre and Mary Wollstonecraft.

Sandra Cavallo, *Charity and Power in Early Modern Italy: Benefactors and Their Motives in Turin, 1541–1789* (Cambridge: Cambridge University Press, 1995). Institutional charity in northern Italy and the way bequests by members of the elite were tied to struggles around prestige and gender. Reconceptualizes charitable giving.

Elaine Chalus, *Elite Women in English Political Life, c. 1754–1790* (Oxford: Clarendon, 2005). How electoral politics really worked in England before the Great Reform Bill. Despite the title there is also material on non-elite women in borough politics.

Nina Rattner Gelbart, *Feminine and Opposition Journalism in Old Regime France: Le Journal des Dames* (Berkeley: University of California Press, 1987). A classic study of the chequered history of the French women's journal, the *Journal des dames*, over three decades, with particular attention to the radical feminist journalist Mme de Beaumer.

Adele Lindenmeyr, *Poverty Is Not a Vice: Charity, Society and the State in Imperial Russia* (Princeton, NJ: Princeton University Press, 1996). Poverty, charity and welfare policy bottom to top, from blind singing beggars to local women renowned for their charity, to Peter I and Catherine II's efforts to control mendicity.

Rebecca Marie Messbarger, *The Century of Women: Representations of Women in Eighteenth-Century Italian Public Discourse* (Toronto, ON: University of Toronto Press, 2002). Extensive coverage of women in Italian intellectual life and institutions in the Age of Enlightenment, with a lot of attention to individual women intellectuals (feminists, scientists, journalists, etc.).

CHAPTER 9: AGE OF REVOLUTIONS

Primary sources

Lynn Avery Hunt, *The French Revolution and Human Rights: A Brief Documentary History* (Boston, MA: Bedford Books of St. Martin's Press, 1996). Excellent collection of primary sources dealing with racism, antisemitism, sexuality and gender in the French Revolution.

Darline Gay Levy, Harriet Branson Applewhite and Mary Durham Johnson, eds, *Women in Revolutionary Paris 1789–1795: Selected Documents* (Urbana: University of Illinois Press, 1979). Still the best collection in English of French Revolutionary documents pertaining to women.

Jeanne-Marie Phlipon Roland, *An Appeal to Impartial Posterity* (Oxford: Woodstock Books, 1990). One of the greatest of revolutionary memoirs, by a woman who died under the guillotine.

Secondary sources

Harriet B. Applewhite and Darline G. Levy, eds, *Women and Politics in the Age of the Democratic Revolution* (Ann Arbor: University of Michigan Press, 1990). Important collection of essays on women in the American, Dutch, Belgian and French Revolutions.

Suzanne Desan, *The Family on Trial in Revolutionary France*, Studies on the History of Society and Culture, 51 (Berkeley: University of California Press, 2004). Law reform and domestic relations during the 1790s.

Dominique Godineau, *The Women of Paris and Their French Revolution*, trans. Katherine Streip, Studies on the History of Society and Culture, 26 (Berkeley: University of California Press, 1998). The most detailed account of plebeian women's politics during the French Revolution.

Olwen Hufton, 'Women in Revolution 1789–1796', *Past & Present* 53 (1971):90–108. Classic article on poverty, food deprivation, motherhood, and female religiosity in the French Revolution.

Lynn Hunt, 'The Many Bodies of Marie Antoinette: Political Pornography and the Problem of the Feminine in the French Revolution', in Lynn Hunt, ed., *Eroticism and the Body Politic* (Baltimore, MD: Johns Hopkins University Press, 1991), 108–30. Classic article on the pornographic rhetoric of attacks on political women.

BIBLIOGRAPHY

———— ◆ ————

Aarne, Antti and Stith Thompson (1981) *The Types of the Folktale: A Classification and Bibliography*, Folk-Lore Fellows Communication, 184 (Helsinki: Academia Scientiarum Fennica).

Abreu-Ferreira, Darlene (2001) 'From Mere Survival to Near Success: Women's Economic Strategies in Early Modern Portugal', in *Journal of Women's History* 13 (2), pp. 58–79.

Adair, Richard (1996) *Courtship, Illegitimacy and Marriage in Early Modern England* (Manchester: Manchester University Press).

Adams, Christine (2007) 'In the Public Interest: Charitable Association, the State, and the Status of *Utilité Publique* in Nineteenth-Century France', in *Law and History Review* 25 (2), pp. 283–321.

Adler, Philip J. (1974) 'Habsburg School Reform among the Orthodox Minorities, 1770–1780', in *Slavic Review* 33 (1), pp. 23–45.

Agarwal, Bina (1997) '"Bargaining" And Gender Relations: Within and Beyond the Household', in *Feminist Economics* 3 (1), pp. 1–51.

Ågren, Maria (2003) 'A Partnership between Unequals: The Changing Meaning of Marriage in Eighteenth-Century Sweden', in *Eheschliessungen im Europa des 18. und 19. Jahrhunderts: Muster und Strategien*, ed. Christophe Duhamelle, Jürgen Schlumbohm and Pat Hudson (Göttingen: Vandenhoeck & Ruprecht), pp. 267–93.

Ågren, Maria (2009) *Domestic Secrets: Women and Property in Sweden circa 1600–1857* (Durham: University of North Carolina Press).

Ågren, Maria and Amy Louise Erickson, eds (2005) *The Marital Economy in Scandinavia and Britain, 1400–1900* (Aldershot: Ashgate).

Ahlgren, Gillian T.W. (1995) 'Negotiating Sanctity: Holy Women in Sixteenth-Century Spain', in *Church History* 64 (3), pp. 373–88.

Ahmed, Leila (1992) *Women and Gender in Islam: Historical Roots of a Modern Debate* (New Haven, CT: Yale University Press).

Ailes, Mary Elizabeth (2006) 'Wars, Widows and State Formation in 17th-Century Sweden', in *Scandinavian Journal of History* 31 (1), pp. 17–34.

Aïssé, Charlotte Élisabeth (1787) *Lettres de Mademoiselle Aïssé à Madame C[alendrini] qui contiennent plusieurs anecdotes de l'histoire du tems, depuis l'anée 1726 jusq'en 1733* (Paris: chez la Grange).

Aksan, Virginia H. and Daniel Goffman, eds (2007) *The Early Modern Ottomans: Remapping the Empire* (Cambridge: Cambridge University Press).

Alacoque, Marguerite-Marie (1961) *The Autobiography of Saint Margaret Mary*, trans. Vincent Kerns (London: Newman Press and Darton, Longman and Todd).

Alenius, Marianne (2004) 'Charlotta Dorothea Biehl (2 June 1731–17 May 1788)' in *Danish Writers from the Reformation to Decadence, 1550–1900*, ed. Marianne Stecher-Hansen (Detroit, MI: Gale), pp. 73–86.

Alexander, John T. (1989) *Catherine the Great: Life and Legend* (New York: Oxford University Press).

Algrant, Christine Pevitt (2002) *Madame de Pompadour: Mistress of France* (London: HarperCollins).

Allen, Robert C., Tommy Bengtsson and Martin Dribe, eds (2005) *Living Standards in the Past: New Perspectives on Well-Being in Asia and Europe* (Oxford: Oxford University).

Alter, George and Michel Oris (2000) 'Mortality and Economic Stress: Individual and Household Responses in a Nineteenth-Century Belgian Village', in *Population and Economy: From Hunger to*

Modern Economic Growth, ed. Tommy Bengtsson and Osamu Saito (Oxford: Oxford University Press), pp. 335–70.

Altinöz, Vuslat Devrim (2003) 'The Ottoman Women's Movement: The Women's Press, Journals, Magazines and Newspapers from 1875–1923' (Master's thesis, Department of History, Miami University, Oxford, Ohio).

Amussen, Susan Dwyer (2007) *Caribbean Exchanges: Slavery and the Transformation of English Society, 1640–1700* (Chapel Hill: University of North Carolina Press).

And, Metin (1963) *A History of Theatre and Popular Entertainment in Turkey* (Ankara: Forum Yayinlari).

Anderson, Bonnie S., and Judith P. Zinsser (2000) *A History of Their Own: Women in Europe from Prehistory to the Present*, rev. edn, 2 vols (New York: Oxford University Press).

Andor, Eszter and István György Tóth, eds (2001) *Frontiers of Faith: Religious Exchange and the Constitution of Religious Identities 1400–1750*, Cultural Exchange in Europe, 1400–1750, 1 (Budapest: Central European University, European Science Foundation).

Andorka, Rudolf (1971) 'La prévention des naissances en Hongrie dans la région Ormansag depuis la fin du XVIIIe siècle', in *Population* (French edn) 26 (1), pp. 63–78.

Andrea, Bernadette Diane (2007) *Women and Islam in Early Modern English Literature* (Cambridge: Cambridge University Press).

Andress, David (2006) *The Terror: The Merciless War for Freedom in Revolutionary France* (New York: Farrar, Straus and Giroux).

Andrew, Donna T. (1989) *Philanthropy and Police: London Charity in the Eighteenth Century* (Princeton, NJ: Princeton University Press).

Andrew, Donna T. (1994a) 'Reading the Demi-Rep: The Town and Country Magazine 1769–1795' Paper read at the North American Conference on British Studies, October (Vancouver, BC).

Andrew, Donna T., ed. (1994b) *London Debating Societies 1776–1799*, London Record Society Publications, 30 (London: London Record Society).

Andrew, Donna T. (1995) 'Noblesse Oblige: The Charity Letters of Margaret, Lady Spencer', in *Early Modern Conceptions of Property*, ed. John Brewer and Susan Staves (London: Routledge), pp. 275–300.

Andrew, Jean (1993) 'Diffusion of Mesoamerican Food Complex to Southeastern Europe', in *Geographical Review* 83 (2), pp. 194–204.

Ankarloo, Bengt and Stuart Clark, eds (1999) *Witchcraft and Magic in Europe: The Eighteenth and Nineteenth Centuries* (Philadelphia: University of Pennsylvania Press).

Ankarloo, Bengt and Gustav Henningsen, eds (1990) *Early Modern Witchcraft: Centres and Peripheries* (Oxford: Clarendon Press).

The Appearance of the Kaluzhsk Icon of the Mother of God (2007) trans. S. Janos (Baltimore, MD: Holy Trinity Russian Orthodox Church Web Site, http://holytrinityorthodox.com/calendar/los/ Epiphanyp+63.htm, accessed 26 June 2007).

Applewhite, Harriet B. and Darline G. Levy, eds (1990) *Women and Politics in the Age of the Democratic Revolution* (Ann Arbor: University of Michigan Press).

Arat, Zehra F., ed. (1998) *Deconstructing Images of 'the Turkish Woman'* (New York: St. Martin's Press).

Aravamudan, Srinivas (1995) 'Lady Mary Wortley Montagu in the Hammam: Masquerade, Womanliness, and Levantinization', in *ELH* 62 (1), pp. 68–104.

Arenal, Electa and Stacey Schlau, eds (1989) *Untold Sisters: Hispanic Nuns in Their Own Works* (Albuquerque: University of New Mexico Press).

Arnold, Elsie and Jane L. Berdes (2002) *Maddalena Lombardini Sirmen: Eighteenth-Century Composer, Violinist, and Businesswoman* (Lanham, MD: Scarecrow Press).

Arnold, Marina (2003) 'Mourning Widows: Portraits of Widows and Widowhood in Funeral Sermons from Brunswick-Wolfenbuettel', in *Widowhood and Visual Culture in Early Modern Europe*, ed. Allison M. Levy (Aldershot: Ashgate), pp. 55–74.

Arru, Angiolina (1990) 'The Distinguishing Features of Domestic Service in Italy', in *Journal of Family History* 15 (1), pp. 547–66.

Ashbridge, Elizabeth (1820) *Some Account of the Early Part of the Life of Elizabeth Ashbridge, Who Departed This Life in Truth's Service, in Ireland, the 16th of the 5th Month, 1755. Written by Herself. To Which Is Added, a Testimony Concerning Her, from the National Meeting of Ireland* (Dublin: Christopher Bentham).

Astell, Mary (1700) *Some Reflections Upon Marriage Occasion'd by the Duke & Dutchess of Mazarine's Case, Which Is Also Considered* (London: John Nutt).

Astell, Mary (1701) *A Serious Proposal to the Ladies for the Advancement of Their True and Greatest Interest*, Part 2 (London: R. Wilkin).

Azevedo, Celia M. (2003) 'Rocha's "the Ethiopian Redeemed" and the Circulation of Anti-Slavery Ideas', in *Slavery and Abolition* 24 (1), pp. 101–26.

Bächtold-Stäubli, Hanns (1930) 'Haar' in *Handwörterbuch des deutsches Aberglaubens*, ed. E. Hoffman-Krayer and Hanns Bächtold-Stäubli (Berlin/Leipzig: De Gruyter), vol. III, pp. 1239–88.

Baer, Marc David (2004a) 'The Great Fire of 1660 and the Islamization of Christian and Jewish Space in Istanbul', in *International Journal of Middle East Studies* 36 (2), pp. 159–81.

Baer, Marc David (2004b) 'Islamic Conversion Narratives of Women: Social Change and Gendered Religious Hierarchy in Early Modern Ottoman Istanbul', in *Gender & History* 16 (2), pp. 425–58.

Bailey, Joanne (2003) *Unquiet Lives: Marriage and Marriage Breakdown in England, 1660–1800* (Cambridge: Cambridge University Press).

Balikci, Asen (1965) 'Quarrels in a Balkan Village', in *American Anthropologist*, New Series 67 (1), pp. 1456–69.

Ballard, George (1752) *Memoirs of Several Ladies of Great Britain, Who Have Been Celebrated for Their Writings or Skill in the Learned Languages, Arts and Sciences* (Oxford: Printed by W. Jackson, for the author).

Barker, Adele Marie and Jehanne M. Gheith, eds (2002) *A History of Women's Writing in Russia* (Cambridge: Cambridge University Press).

Barnai, Jacob (2002) 'The Development of Community Organizational Structures: The Case of Izmir', in *Jews, Turks, Ottomans: A Shared History, Fifteenth through the Twentieth Century*, ed. Avigdor Levy (Syracuse, NY: Syracuse University Press), pp. 35–51.

Barta, Peter I., ed. (2001) *Gender and Sexuality in Russian Civilization*, Studies in Russian and European Literature, 5 (London: Routledge).

Başgöz, Ilhan (1971) *Turkish Folklore Reader* (Bloomington: Indiana University).

Başgöz, Ilhan and Andreas Tietze, eds (1973) *Bilmece: A Corpus of Turkish Riddles*, Folklore Studies, 22 (Berkeley: University of California Press).

Batalden, Stephen K., ed. (1993) *Seeking God: The Recovery of Religious Identity in Orthodox Russia, Ukraine, and Georgia* (DeKalb: Northern Illinois University Press).

Baxter, Richard (1681) *A Breviate of the Life of Margaret, the Daughter of Francis Charlton . . . and Wife of Richard Baxter* (London: B. Simmons).

Beales, Derek (1987) *Joseph II*, 2 vols (Cambridge: Cambridge University Press).

Beasley, Faith Evelyn (2006) *Salons, History, and the Creation of Seventeenth-Century France: Mastering Memory* (Aldershot: Ashgate).

Behar, Ruth (2001) 'Sexual Witchcraft, Colonialism, and Women's Powers: Views from the Mexican Inquisition', in *Gender and Witchcraft*, New Perspectives on Witchcraft, Magic and Demonology, 4, ed. Brian P. Levack (New York: Routledge), pp. 218–46.

Behn, Aphra (1987) *Love-Letters between a Nobleman and His Sister*, Virago Modern Classic, 240 (London: Virago).

Beik, William (1997) *Urban Protest in Seventeenth-Century France: The Culture of Retribution* (Cambridge: Cambridge University Press).

Bellini, Ligia (2005) 'Spirituality and Women's Monastic Life in Seventeenth and Eighteenth-Century Portugal', in *Portuguese Studies* 21 (1), pp. 126–41.

Benhabib, Seyla (1992) 'Models of Public Space: Hannah Arendt, the Liberal Tradition and Jürgen Habermas' in *Habermas and the Public Sphere*, ed. Craig J. Calhoun (Cambridge, MA: MIT Press), pp. 73–98.

Bennett, Judith M. (1988) 'History That Stands Still: Women's Work in the European Past', in *Feminist Studies* 14 (2), pp. 269–83.

Bennett, Judith M. (1993) 'Women's History: A Study in Continuity and Change', in *Women's History Review* 2 (2), pp. 173–84.

Bennett, Judith M. and Amy M. Froide, eds (1999) *Singlewomen in the European Past, 1250–1800* (Philadelphia: University of Pennsylvania Press).

Bérenguier, Nadine (1995) 'Victorious Victims: Women and Publicity in Mémoires Judiciaires', in *Going Public: Women and Publishing in Early Modern France*, ed. Elizabeth C. Goldsmith and Dena Goodman (Ithaca, NY: Cornell University Press), pp. 62–78.

Berg, Maxine (1988) 'Women's Work, Mechanization and the Early Phases of Industrialization in England', in *On Work*, ed. R.E. Pahl (Oxford: Basil Blackwell), pp. 61–94.

Berg, Maxine (1993) 'What Difference Did Women's Work Make to the Industrial Revolution?', in *History Workshop Journal* 35, pp. 22–44.

Berg, Maxine (1994) *The Age of Manufactures 1700–1820: Industry, Innovation and Work in Britain*, 2nd edn (London: Routledge).

Berg, Maxine (2005) *Luxury and Pleasure in Eighteenth-Century Britain* (Oxford: Oxford University Press).

Berlanstein, Lenard R. (1994) 'Women and Power in Eighteenth-Century France: Actresses at the Comédie-Française', in *Feminist Studies* 20 (3), pp. 475–506.

Bielecki, Robert (2001) 'Żubrowa, Joanna', in *Encyklopedia Wojen Napoleońskich*, ed. Robert Bielecki (Warsaw: TRIO), p. 618.

Bithell, Caroline (2003) 'A Man's Game? Engendered Song and the Changing Dynamics of Musical Activity in Corsica', in *Music and Gender: Perspectives from the Mediterranean*, ed. Tullia Magrini (Chicago: University of Chicago Press), pp. 33–66.

Black, Jeremy, ed. (2005) *Warfare in Europe 1650–1792* (Burlington, VT: Ashgate).

Blackburn, Robin (1988) *The Overthrow of Colonial Slavery 1776–1848* (London: Verso).

Blackstone, William (1770) *Commentaries on the Laws of England*, 4th edn, 4 vols (Oxford: Oxford University Press).

Blackwell, Jeannine and Susanne Zantop, eds (1990) *Bitter Healing: German Women Writers from 1700 to 1830: An Anthology* (Lincoln: University of Nebraska Press).

Blayo, Y. (1975) 'La proportion des naissances illégitimes en France de 1740 à 1829', in *Population* (French Edition) 30, pp. 65–70.

Blum, Alain and Irina Troitskaya (1997) 'Mortality in Russia During the 18th and 19th Centuries: Local Assessments Based on the *Revizii*', in *Population: An English Selection* 9, pp. 123–46.

Blum, Jerome (1961) *Lord and Peasant in Russia from the Ninth to the Nineteenth Century* (Princeton, NJ: Princeton University Press).

Boehm, Christopher (1984) *Blood Revenge: The Anthropology of Feuding in Montenegro and Other Tribal Societies* (Lawrence: University Press of Kansas).

Boéskov, Vanéco, Mark Alan Epstein and Stefan Andreev, eds (1990) *Ottoman Documents on Balkan Jews, XVI–XVII Centuries*, Balcanica 2, Inventaires et catalogues, 11 (Sofia, Bulgaria: Centre international d'information sur les sources de l'histoire balkanique et mediterranéenne).

Boggs, Ralph Steele (1930) *Index of Spanish Folktales* (Helsinki: Suomalainen Tiedeakatemia/ Academia Scientiarum Fennica).

Bogucka, Maria (1989) 'Women and Economic Life in the Polish Cities During the 16th–17th Centuries', in *La donna nell'economia secc. XIII–XVIII*, ed. Simonetta Cavaciocchi (Prato: Istituto internazionale di storia economica 'F.Datini'), pp. 185–94.

Bogucka, Maria (1999) 'Women and Culture in Poland in Early Modern Times', in *Acta Poloniae Historica* 80, pp. 61–97.

Bogucka, Maria (2001) 'Polish Women in Politics. The Case of Poland in the 16th–18th Centuries', in *Acta Poloniae Historica* 83, pp. 79–93.

Bogucka, Maria (2004) *Women in Early Modern Polish Society, Against the European Background* (Aldershot: Ashgate).

Bohlman, Philip V. (2003) '"And She Sang a New Song": Gender and Music on the Sacred Landscapes of the Mediterranean', in *Music and Gender: Perspectives from the Mediterranean*, ed. Tullia Magrini (Chicago: University of Chicago Press), pp. 329–49.

Bohstedt, John (1990) 'The Myth of the Feminine Food Riot: Women as Proto-Citizens in English Community Politics, 1790–1810', in *Women and Politics in the Age of the Democratic Revolution*, ed. Harriet B. Applewhite and Darline G. Levy (Ann Arbor: University of Michigan), pp. 21–59.

Bonner, Michael David, Mine Ener and Amy Singer, eds (2003) *Poverty and Charity in Middle Eastern Contexts* (Albany: State University of New York Press).

Boon, L.J. (1989) 'Those Damned Sodomites: Public Images of Sodomy in the Eighteenth-Century Netherlands', in *The Pursuit of Sodomy: Male Homosexuality in Renaissance and Enlightenment Europe*, ed. Kent Gerard and Gert Hekma (New York: Harrington Park Press), pp. 237–48.

Bordereau, Renée (1814) *Mémoires de Renée Bordereau dites Langevin, touchant sa vie militaire dans la Vendée* (Paris: chez L.G. Michaud, Imprimeur du Roi).

Boserup, Ester (1970) *Woman's Role in Economic Development* (New York: St. Martin's Press).

Boswell, James and Isabelle de Charrière (1952) *Boswell in Holland, 1763–1764, Including His Correspondence with Belle de Zuylen (Zélide)*, ed. F.A. Pottle (New York: McGraw-Hill).

Boulton, Jeremy (2000) '"It Is Extreme Necessity That Makes Me Do This": Some "Survival Strategies" of Pauper Households in London's West End During the Early Eighteenth Century', in *International Review of Social History* 45 (Supplement 8, Household Strategies for Survival 1600–2000: Fission, Faction and Cooperation), pp. 47–70.

Bourgoanne, Jean François (1790) *Travels in Spain: Containing a New, Accurate, and Comprehensive View of the Present State of that Country*, trans. from the French, 2 vols (Dublin: P. Byrne and W. Jones).

Bouton, Cynthia A. (1993) *The Flour War: Gender, Class, and Community in Late Ancien Regime French Society* (University Park: Pennsylvania State University Press).

Bowerbank, Sylvia (2004) 'Lead [née Ward], Jane (1624–1704), Mystic and Author', in *Oxford Dictionary of National Biography*, ed. H.C.G. Matthew and Brian Harrison (Oxford: Oxford University Press), online edn, ed. Lawrence Goldman, January 2008, http://www.oxforddnb.com, accessed 13 June 2008.

Bowers, Jane (1986) 'The Emergence of Women Composers in Italy, 1566–1700', in *Women Making Music: The Western Art Tradition, 1150–1950*, ed. Jane Bowers and Judith Tick (Urbana: University of Illinois Press), pp. 116–67.

Boxer, Marilyn J. and Jean H. Quataert, eds (1987) *Connecting Spheres: European Women in a Globalizing World, 1500 to the Present* (New York: Oxford University Press).

Boyd, Kenneth M. (1980) *Scottish Church Attitudes to Sex, Marriage and the Family, 1850–1914* (Edinburgh: Donald).

Bradshaw, Penelope (1749) *Bradshaw's Valuable Family Jewel . . . Containing All That Relates to Cookery, Pastry, Pickling, Preserving, Wine Making, Brewing, Bread Making, Oat Cakes, &c. . . . The 12th Edition* (London: Printed for P. Bradshaw).

Brake, Wayne P. te, Rudolf M. Dekker and Lotte C. Van de Pol (1990) 'Women and Political Culture in the Dutch Revolutions', in *Women and Politics in the Age of Democratic Revolution*, ed. Harriet B. Applewhite and Darline G. Levy (Ann Arbor: University of Michigan Press), pp. 109–46.

Bräker, Ulrich (1970) *The Life Story and Real Adventures of the Poor Man of Toggenburg*, trans. Derek Bowman (Edinburgh: Edinburgh University Press).

Brandes, Ute (1991) 'Baroque Women Writers and the Public Sphere', in *Women in German Yearbook: Feminist Studies in German Literature & Culture* 7, pp. 43–63.

Branson, Susan (2001) *These Fiery Frenchified Dames: Women and Political Culture in Early National Philadelphia* (Philadelphia: University of Pennsylvania Press).

Bray, Francesca (1997) *Technology and Gender: Fabrics of Power in Late Imperial China* (Berkeley: University of California Press).

Brewer, John and Susan Staves, eds (1995) *Early Modern Conceptions of Property* (London: Routledge).

Bringa, Tone (1995) *Being Muslim the Bosnian Way: Identity and Community in a Central Bosnian Village* (Princeton, NJ: Princeton University Press).

Brown, Canter, Jr. (1995) 'Race Relations in Territorial Florida, 1821–1845', in *Florida Historical Quarterly* 73 (3), pp. 287–307.

Brown, Laura (1993) *Ends of Empire: Women and Ideology in Early Eighteenth-Century English Literature* (Ithaca, NY: Cornell University Press).

Brown, P. (2000) 'Rational Fairies and the Pursuit of Virtue: Didactic Strategies in Early French Children's Literature', in *Studies on Voltaire and the Eighteenth Century* 5, pp. 341–53.

Brown, Stewart J. (2006) 'Movements of Christian Awakening in Revolutionary Europe, 1790–1815', in *Enlightenment, Reawakening, and Revolution, 1660–1815*, ed. Stewart J. Brown and Timothy Tackett (Cambridge: Cambridge University Press), pp. 575–95.

Browne, Alice (1987) *The Eighteenth-Century Feminist Mind* (Brighton: Harvester).

Bruneau, Marie-Florine (1998) *Women Mystics Confront the Modern World: Marie de l'Incarnation (1599–1672) and Madame Guyon (1648–1717)* (Albany: State University of New York Press).

Burckhardt, John Lewis (1968) *Travels in Arabia, Comprehending an Account of those Territories in Hedjaz which the Mohammedans Regard as Sacred* (London: Frank Cass & Co.).

Burić, Olivera (1976) 'The Zadruga and the Contemporary Family in Yugoslavia', in *Communal Families in the Balkans: The Zadruga; Essays by Philip E. Mosely and Essays in His Honor*, ed. Robert Byrnes (Notre Dame, IN: University of Notre Dame Press), pp. 117–38.

Burke, Janet M. and Margaret C. Jacob (1996) 'French Freemasonry, Women, and Feminist Scholarship', in *Journal of Modern History* 68 (3), pp. 513–49.

Burnette, Joyce and Joel Mokyr (1995) 'The Standard of Living through the Ages', in *The State of Humanity*, ed. Julian L. Simon (Oxford: Blackwell), pp. 135–48.

Burton, Antoinette (1994) *Burdens of History: British Feminists, Indian Women, and Imperial Culture, 1865–1915* (Chapel Hill: University of North Carolina Press).

Bush, Michael L. (1983–1988) *The European Nobility*, 2 vols (New York: Holmes & Meier Publishers).

Butler, Judith and Joan Wallach Scott, eds (1992) *Feminists Theorize the Political* (New York: Routledge).

Buttafuoco, Annarita (1977) 'Eleonora Fonseca Pimentel: una donna nella rivoluzione', in *Nuova dwf Donnawomanfemme* (3), pp. 51–92.

Butterwick, Richard (2005) 'Political Discourses of the Polish Revolution, 1788–92', in *English Historical Review* 120 (487), pp. 695–731.

Buttimer, Neil (2006) 'Literature in Irish, 1690–1800: From the Williamite Wars to the Act of Union' in *The Cambridge History of Irish Literature*, ed. Margaret Kelleher and Philip O'Leary, 2 vols (Cambridge: Cambridge University Press), vol. I, pp. 320–71.

Buturović, Amila and Irvin Cemil Schick, eds (2007) *Women in the Ottoman Balkans: Gender, Culture and History*, Library of Ottoman Studies, 15 (New York: I.B. Tauris).

Caffiero, Marina (1999) 'From the Late Baroque Mystical Explosion to the Social Apostolate, 1650–1850', in *Women and Faith: Catholic Religious Life in Italy from Late Antiquity to the Present*, ed. Lucetta Scaraffia and Gabriella Zarri (Cambridge, MA: Harvard University Press), pp. 176–204.

Calhoun, Craig J. (1992) *Habermas and the Public Sphere* (Cambridge, MA: MIT Press).

Calvi, Giulia (1989) *Histories of a Plague Year: The Social and the Imaginary in Baroque Florence*, ed. Bryant T. Ragan, Jr., trans. Dario Biocca (Berkeley: University of California Press).

Campbell, Gwyn, Suzanne Miers and Joseph Calder Miller, eds (2007) *Women and Slavery*, 2 vols (Athens: Ohio University Press).

Cannadine, David (1999) *The Decline and Fall of the British Aristocracy* (New York: Vintage Books).

Carbonell-Esteller, Montserrat (2000) 'Using Microcredit and Restructuring Households: Two Complementary Survival Strategies in Late Eighteenth-Century Barcelona', in *International Review of Social History* 45 (Supplement 8, Household Strategies for Survival 1600–2000: Fission, Faction and Cooperation), pp. 71–92.

Carlos, Anne M. and Larry Neal (2004) 'Women Investors in Early Capital Markets, 1720–1725', in *Financial History Review* 11 (2), pp. 197–224.

Carlson, Marybeth (1994) 'A Trojan Horse of Worldliness? Maidservants in the Burgher Household in Rotterdam at the End of the Seventeenth Century', in *Women of the Golden Age: An International Debate on Women in Seventeenth-Century Holland, England and Italy*, ed. Els Kloek, Nicole Teeuwen and Marijke Huisman (Hilversum: Verloren), pp. 87–96.

Carpenter, Kirsty (1999) *Refugees of the French Revolution: Émigrés in London, 1789–1802* (Houndmills: Macmillan).

Carpenter, Kirsty and Philip Mansel, eds (1999) *The French Émigrés in Europe and the Struggle Against Revolution, 1789–1814* (Houndmills: Macmillan Press).

Carrier, Hubert (2003) 'Women's Political and Military Action During the Fronde', in *Political and Historical Encyclopedia of Women*, ed. Christine Fauré (New York: Routledge), pp. 23–36.

Cassar, Carmel (2001) 'Malta: Language, Literacy and Identity in a Mediterranean Island Society', in *National Identities* 3 (3), pp. 257–75.

Catherine II (2006) *The Memoirs of Catherine the Great*, ed. Hilde Hoogenboom, trans. Mark Cruse (New York: Modern Library).

Cavaciocchi, Simonetta, ed. (1989) *La donna nell'economia secc. XIII–XVIII* (Prato: Istituto Internazionale de Storia Economica 'F. Datini'/Le Monnier).

Cavallo, Sandra (1995) *Charity and Power in Early Modern Italy: Benefactors and Their Motives in Turin, 1541–1789* (Cambridge: Cambridge University Press).

Cavallo, Sandra and Simona Cerutti (1990) 'Female Honor and the Social Control of Reproduction in Piedmont between 1600 and 1800', in *Sex and Gender in Historical Perspective*, ed. Edward Muir and Guido Ruggiero (Baltimore, MD: Johns Hopkins University Press), pp. 73–109.

Cavarnos, Constantine (1971) *St. Cosmas Aitolos: Great Missionary, Illuminator, and Martyr of Greece: An Account of His Life, Character, and Message, Together with Selections from His Teachings*, Modern Orthodox Saints, 1 (Belmont, MA: Institute for Byzantine and Modern Greek Studies).

Cavazza, Silvano (1994) 'Double Death: Resurrection and Baptism in a Seventeenth-Century Rite', in *History from Crime*, ed. Edward Muir and Guido Ruggiero (Baltimore, MD: Johns Hopkins University Press), pp. 1–31.

Cavendish, Margaret (1997) *Sociable Letters*, Garland Reference Library of the Humanities, 2009, ed. James Fitzmaurice (New York: Garland Publishing).

Chalus, Elaine (2003) 'The Rag Plot: The Politics of Influence in Oxford, 1754', in *Women and Urban Life in Eighteenth-Century England: 'On the Town'*, ed. Rosemary Sweet and Penelope Lane (Aldershot: Ashgate), pp. 43–63.

Chalus, Elaine (2005) *Elite Women in English Political Life, c. 1754–1790* (Oxford: Clarendon Press).

[Chapone, Sarah] (1735) *The Hardships of the English Laws in Relation to Wives. With an Explanation of the Original Curse of Subjection Passed Upon the Woman. In an Humble Address to the Legislature* (London: J. Roberts).

Chaudhuri, Nupur and Margaret Strobel, eds (1992) *Western Women and Imperialism: Complicity and Resistance* (Bloomington: Indiana University Press).

Chaves, Maria Eugenia (2000) 'Slave Women's Strategies for Freedom and the Late Spanish Colonial State', in *Hidden Histories of Gender and the State in Latin America*, ed. Elizabeth Dore and Maxine Molyneux (Durham, NC: Duke University Press), pp. 108–26.

Chaytor, Miranda (1995) 'Husband(ry): Narratives of Rape in the Seventeenth Century', in *Gender & History* 7 (3), pp. 378–407.

Cheek, Pamela (2003) *Sexual Antipodes: Enlightenment Globalization and the Placing of Sex* (Stanford, CA: Stanford University Press).

Cherry, Deborah (1993) *Painting Women: Victorian Women Artists* (London: Routledge).

Chesnais, Jean-Claude (1992) *The Demographic Transition: Stages, Patterns, and Economic Implications: A Longitudinal Study of Sixty-Seven Countries Covering the Period 1720–1984*, trans. Elizabeth Kreager and Philip Kreager (Oxford: Clarendon Press and Oxford University Press).

Chilcote, Paul Wesley (1991) *John Wesley and the Women Preachers of Early Methodism*, Atla Monograph Series, 25 (Metuchen, NJ: Scarecrow Press and American Theological Library Association).

Cholakian, Patricia Francis (2000) *Women and the Politics of Self-Representation in Seventeenth-Century France* (Newark: University of Delaware Press and Associated University Presses).

Choquette, Leslie (1992) ' "Ces Amazones du Grand Dieu": Women and Mission in Seventeenth-Century Canada', in *French Historical Studies* 17 (3), pp. 627–55.

Choudhury, Mita (2004) *Convents and Nuns in Eighteenth-Century French Politics and Culture* (Ithaca, NY: Cornell University Press).

Christian, William A. (1981) *Local Religion in Sixteenth-Century Spain* (Princeton, NJ: Princeton University Press).

Ciappara, Frans (2001) 'Perceptions of Marriage in Late-Eighteenth-Century Malta', in *Continuity and Change* 16 (3), pp. 379–98.

Ciappara, Frans (2005) ' "Una Messa in Perpetuum": Perpetual Mass Bequests in Traditional Malta, 1750–1797', in *Catholic Historical Review* 91 (2), pp. 278–99.

Cichocki, Nina (2005) 'Continuity and Change in Turkish Bathing Culture in Istanbul: The Life Story of the Çemberlitas Hamam', in *Turkish Studies* 6 (1), pp. 93–112.

Clancy-Smith, Julia (2005) 'Women, Gender and Migration Along a Mediterranean Frontier: Pre-Colonial Tunisia, c. 1815–1870', in *Gender & History* 17 (1), pp. 62–92.

Clark, Alice (1919) *Working Life of Women in the Seventeenth Century* (London: G. Routledge & Sons, E.P. Dutton & Co.).

Clark, Anna (1995) *The Struggle for the Breeches: Gender and the Making of the British Working Class*, Studies on the History of Society and Culture, 23 (Berkeley: University of California Press).

Clark, Christopher M. (1995) *The Politics of Conversion: Missionary Protestantism and the Jews in Prussia, 1728–1941* (Oxford: Clarendon Press and Oxford University Press).

Clark, Emily (1997) ' "By All the Conduct of Their Lives": A Laywomen's Confraternity in New Orleans, 1730–1744', in *William and Mary Quarterly* 3rd Series, 54 (4), pp. 769–94.

Clay, Lauren (2005) 'Provincial Actors, the Comédie-Française, and the Business of Performing in Eighteenth-Century France', in *Eighteenth-Century Studies* 38 (4), pp. 651–79.

Clinton, Katherine B. (1975) 'Femme et Philosophe: Enlightenment Origins of Feminism', in *Eighteenth-Century Studies* 8 (3), pp. 283–99.

Clodfelter, Michael (2002) *Warfare and Armed Conflicts: A Statistical Reference to Casualty and Other Figures, 1500–2000*, 2nd edn (Jefferson, NC: McFarland).

Clogg, Richard (1969) 'The "Dhidhaskalia Patriki" (1798): An Orthodox Reaction to French Revolutionary Propaganda', in *Middle Eastern Studies* 5 (2), pp. 87–115.

Coale, Ansley J. and Susan Cotts Watkins, eds (1986) *The Decline of Fertility in Europe: The Revised Proceedings of a Conference on the Princeton European Fertility Project* (Princeton, NJ: Princeton University Press).

Cody, Lisa Forman (2004) 'Living and Dying in Georgian London's Lying-in Hospitals', in *Bulletin of the History of Medicine* 78 (2), pp. 309–48.

Cohen, Elisabeth S. (1992) 'Honor and Gender in the Streets of Early Modern Rome', in *Journal of Interdisciplinary History* 22 (4), pp. 597–625.

Cohen, Sherrill (1992) *The Evolution of Women's Asylums since 1500: From Refuges for Ex-Prostitutes to Shelters for Battered Women* (New York: Oxford University Press).

Cole, John R. (1998) 'Debunking Roussel's "Report" on the Society of Revolutionary Republican Women', in *French Historical Studies* 21 (1), pp. 181–91.

Coleman, Deirdre (2003) 'Janet Schaw and the Complexions of Empire', in *Eighteenth-Century Studies* 36 (2), pp. 169–93.

Colley, Linda (2003) *Britons: Forging the Nation, 1707–1837*, 2nd edn (London: Pimlico).

Condorcet, Jean-Antoine-Nicolas de Caritat (1788) *Lettres d'un bourgeois de New-Haven à un citoyen de Virginie* (Paris: A Colle).

Conner, Susan P. (1989) 'Politics, Prostitution, and the Pox in Revolutionary Paris, 1789–1799', in *Journal of Social History* 22 (4), pp. 713–34.

Conrad, Robert Edgar (1973) 'Neither Slave nor Free: The Emancipados of Brazil, 1818–1868', in *Hispanic American Historical Review* 53 (1), pp. 50–70.

Conrad, Robert Edgar (1983) *Children of God's Fire: A Documentary History of Black Slavery in Brazil* (Princeton, NJ: Princeton University Press).

Constantinidis, Stratos E. (1998) 'Korai's Dream and Kairi's Drama: A Chorus of Greek Women', in *Journal of the Hellenic Diaspora* 24 (2), pp. 7–23.

Corley, T.A.B. (2004) 'Mapp [née Wallin], Sarah (bap. 1706, d. 1737), Bone-Setter', in *Oxford Dictionary of National Biography*, ed. H.C.G. Matthew and Brian Harrison (Oxford: Oxford University Press), online edn, ed. Lawrence Goldman, January 2008, http://www.oxforddnb.com, accessed 11 February 2008.

Cosson de la Cressonnière, Charlotte-Catherine and Riballier (1779) *De l'éducation physique et morale des femmes, avec une notice alphabétique de celles qui se sont distinguées dans les differentes carrières des sciences & des beaux-arts, ou par des talens & des actions mémorables* (Brussels: Estienne).

Cott, Nancy F. (1976) 'Divorce and the Changing Status of Women in Eighteenth-Century Massachusetts', in *William and Mary Quarterly* 33 (4), pp. 586–614.

Cowles, Mary Jane (2007) 'The Subjectivity of the Colonial Subject from Olympe de Gouges to Mme de Duras', in *L'esprit créateur* 47 (4), pp. 29–43.

Crankshaw, Edward (1983) *Maria Theresa* (London: Constable).

Crawford, Patricia (2004) *Blood, Bodies, and Families in Early Modern England* (Harlow: Pearson/Longman).

Cressy, David (1997) *Birth, Marriage, and Death: Ritual, Religion and Life-Cycle in Tudor and Stuart England* (Oxford: Oxford University Press).

Criep, F. (1627) *Vanden Keyser, Ghemaeckt Inden Jare Noopende't Contracteren Van Huwelicke Van Persoonen Zijnde Beneden Hare Jaren* (The Hague: de Weduwe [the widow]).

Crowston, Clare Haru (2001) *Fabricating Women: The Seamstresses of Old Regime France, 1675–1791* (Durham, NC: Duke University Press).

Cserey, Farkas (1800) *A' Magyar és Székely asszonyok' törvénye. Mellyet e' két nevezetü, de egy vérü. nemes nemzetnek törvényiből, törvényes szokásiból, végezésiből, birák itéletiből és más törvény-tudók irásiból egybe-szedett* (The Law of the Women of Hungary (Magyar) and that of the Hungarian Women of Eastern Transylvania (Szekely). Collected Works of Laws, Legitimate Customs, the Decrees, Verdicts of Judges, and Writings of Other Experts in Law of this Noble Nation, with Two Different Names, yet Sharing the Same Blood) (Kolozsváratt, Hungary: Márton Hochmeister).

Curtin, Nancy J. (1991) 'Women and Eighteenth-Century Irish Republicanism', in *Women in Early Modern Ireland*, ed. Margaret MacCurtain and Mary O'Dowd (Edinburgh: Edinburgh University Press), pp. 133–44.

Curtis, Maria (2001) 'Multiple Meanings of "Voice" in 'Ayoua: Gender, Improvisation, and Self in the Recording Studio', in *Text, Practice, Performance* 3, pp. 127–46.

Curzon, Robert (1955) *Visits to Monasteries in the Levant* (London: A. Barker).

Cynarski, Stanislaw (1968) 'The Shape of Sarmatian Ideology in Poland', in *Acta Poloniae Historica* 19, pp. 5–17.

Czap, Peter (1978) 'Marriage and the Peasant Joint Family in the Era of Serfdom' in *The Family in Imperial Russia: New Lines of Historical Research*, ed. David L. Ransel (Urbana: University of Illinois Press), pp. 103–23.

da Graça, Paula (1715) *Bondade das mulheres vendicada, e malicia dos homens manifesta* (Lisbon: Bernardo da Costa de Carvalho).

Da Molin, Giovanna (1990) 'Family Forms and Domestic Service in Southern Italy from the Seventeenth to the Nineteenth Centuries', in *Journal of Family History* 15 (1), pp. 503–27.

da Silva e Orta, Teresa Margarida (2002) *Aventuras de Diófanes*, ed. Maria de Santa-Cruz (Lisbon: Caminho).

Dabhoiwala, Faramerz (2008) 'Lust and Liberty', Conference on Civil and Religious Liberty: Ideas of Rights and Tolerance in England c. 1640–1800, 23–26 July (New Haven, Connecticut: Yale University).

Dabydeen, David (1987) *Hogarth's Blacks: Images of Blacks in Eighteenth-Century English Art* (Athens: University of Georgia Press).

d'Argenson, René (1891) *Rapports inédits du lieutenant de police René d'Argenson (1697–1715)*, ed. Paul Cottin (Paris: E. Plon, Nourrit et Cie).

Darnton, Robert (1968) *Mesmerism and the End of the Enlightenment in France* (Cambridge, MA: Harvard University Press).

Darrow, Margaret H. (1979) 'French Noblewomen and the New Domesticity, 1750–1850', in *Feminist Studies* 4 (1), pp. 41–65.

Darrow, Margaret H. (1989) *Revolution in the House: Family, Class and Inheritance in Southern France, 1775–1825* (Princeton, NJ: Princeton University Press).

Daumas, Maurice (1988) *L'affaire d'Esclans: Les conflits familiaux au XVIIIe siècle* (Paris: Editions du Seuil).

Davidoff, Leonore and Catherine Hall (1987) *Family Fortunes: Men and Women of the English Middle Class, 1750–1850* (Chicago: University of Chicago Press).

Davies, C. Stella (1960) *The Agricultural History of Cheshire 1750–1850* (Manchester: Chetham Society).

Davin, Anna (1978) 'Imperialism and Motherhood', in *History Workshop Journal* 5, pp. 9–63.

Davis, Fanny (1986) *The Ottoman Lady: A Social History from 1718 to 1918* (Westport, CT: Greenwood Press).

Davis, Natalie Zemon (1975) *Society and Culture in Early Modern France* (Stanford, CA: Stanford University Press).

Davis, Natalie Zemon (1978) 'Women on Top: Symbolic Sexual Inversion and Political Disorder in Early Modern Europe', in *The Reversible World: Symbolic Inversion in Art and Society*, ed. Barbara A. Babcock (Ithaca, NY: Cornell University Press), pp. 147–90.

Davis, Natalie Zemon (1987) *Fiction in the Archives: Pardon Tales and Their Tellers in Sixteenth-Century France* (Stanford, CA: Stanford University Press).

Davis, Natalie Zemon (1995) *Women on the Margins: Three Seventeenth-Century Lives* (Cambridge, MA: Harvard University Press).

Davis, Natalie Zemon and Arlette Farge (1993) 'Women as Historical Actors', in *History of Women in the West 3: Renaissance and Enlightenment Paradoxes*, ed. Natalie Zemon Davis and Arlette Farge (Cambridge, MA: Belknap Press of Harvard University Press), pp. 1–7.

Davis, Robert C. (1998) 'The Geography of Gender in the Renaissance', in *Gender and Society in Renaissance Italy*, ed. Judith C. Brown and Robert C. Davis (London: Longman), pp. 19–38.

Davis, Thomas J. (1985) *A Rumor of Revolt: The 'Great Negro Plot' In Colonial New York* (New York: Free Press).

Dayton, Cornelia Hughes (1995) *Women Before the Bar: Gender, Law, and Society in Connecticut, 1639–1789* (Chapel Hill: University of North Carolina Press).

de Charrière, Isabelle (1993) *Letters of Mistress Henley Published by Her Friend*, Texts and Translations. Translations, 1, trans. Joan Hinde Stewart and Philip Stewart (New York: Modern Language Association of America).

de Froes Perym, Damião (1736) *Theatro heroino, abecedario historico, e catalogo das mulheres illustres em armas, letras, acçoens heroicas, e artes liberaes*, 2 vols (Lisbon: Officina da Musica de Theotonio Antunes Lima).

de Gouges, Olympe (1994) 'L'esclavage des Noirs', in *Translating Slavery: Gender and Race in French Women's Writing, 1783–1823*, ed. Doris Y. Kadish and Françoise Massardier-Kenney (Kent, OH: Kent State University Press), pp. 87–119.

de Madariaga, Isabel (2002) *Catherine the Great: A Short History*, 2nd edn (New Haven, CT: Yale University Press).

Dean, Trevor (2004) 'Gender and Insult in an Italian City: Bologna in the Later Middle Ages', in *Social History of Medicine* 29 (2), pp. 217–31.

Decourdemanche, J. A. (1896) *Les ruses des femmes (Mikri-zenan). Et extraits du Plaisir après la peine (Férédj bad chiddeh)* (Paris: E. Leroux).

Dégh, Linda (1969) *Folktales and Society: Story-Telling in a Hungarian Peasant Community*, trans. Emily M. Schossberger (Bloomington: Indiana University Press).

DeJean, Joan E. (1991) *Tender Geographies: Women and the Origins of the Novel in France* (New York: Columbia University Press).

Dekker, Rudolf M. (1987) 'Women in Revolt: Collective Protest and Its Social Base in Holland', in *Theory and Society* 16 (3), pp. 337–63.

Dekker, Rudolf M. (2001) *Humour in Dutch Culture of the Golden Age* (Houndmills: Palgrave).

Dekker, Rudolf M. and Lotte van de Pol (1989) *The Tradition of Female Transvestism in Early Modern Europe* (New York: St. Martin's Press).

DeLong-Bas, Natana J. (2004) *Wahhabi Islam: From Revival and Reform to Global Jihad* (London: I.B. Tauris).

Derosas, Renzo and Michel Oris, eds (2002) *When Dad Died: Individuals and Families Coping with Family Stress in Past Societies* (Bern: P. Lang).

Desan, Suzanne (1992) '"Constitutional Amazons": Jacobin Women's Clubs in the French Revolution', in *Re-Creating Authority in Revolutionary France*, ed. Bryant T. Ragan and Elizabeth A. Williams (Rutgers, NJ: Rutgers University Press), pp. 11–35, 177–86.

Desan, Suzanne (1997) '"War between Brothers and Sisters": Inheritance Law and Gender Politics in Revolutionary France', in *French Historical Studies* 20 (4), pp. 597–634.

Desan, Suzanne (1999) 'Reconstituting the Social after the Terror: Family, Property and the Law in Popular Politics', in *Past & Present* 164, pp. 81–121.

Desan, Suzanne (2004) *The Family on Trial in Revolutionary France*, Studies on the History of Society and Culture, 51 (Berkeley: University of California Press).

d'Eszlary, Charles (1962) 'Le status de la femme dans le droit hongrois', in *Recueils de la société Jean Bodin* 12 (2), pp. 421–45.

Deutsch, Nathaniel (2003) *The Maiden of Ludmir: A Jewish Holy Woman and Her World* (Berkeley: University of California Press).

Di Simplicio, Oscar (1994) 'Perpetuas: The Women Who Kept Priests, Siena 1600–1800', in *History from Crime*, ed. Edward Muir and Guido Ruggiero (Baltimore, MD: Johns Hopkins University Press), pp. 32–64.

Dianina, Katia (2004) 'Art and Authority: The Hermitage of Catherine the Great', in *Russian Review* 63 (October 2004), pp. 630–54.

Dias, Maria Odila Leite da Silva (1995) *Power and Everyday Life: The Lives of Working Women in Nineteenth-Century Brazil* (Rutgers, NJ: Rutgers University Press).

DiCaprio, Lisa (2007) *The Origins of the Welfare State: Women, Work, and the French Revolution* (Urbana: University of Illinois Press).

Dickie, Simon (2003) 'Hilarity and Pitilessness in the Mid-Eighteenth Century: English Jestbook Humor', in *Eighteenth Century Studies* 37 (1), pp. 1–22.

Diefendorf, Barbara B. (1995) 'Women and Property in Ancien Régime France: Theory and Practice in Dauphiné and Paris', in *Early Modern Conceptions of Property*, ed. John Brewer and Susan Staves (London: Routledge), pp. 170–93.

Dijk, Suzanna van, Lia van Gemert and Sheila Ottway, eds (2001) *Writing the History of Women's Writing: Toward an International Approach: Proceedings of the Colloquium, Amsterdam, 9–11 September 1998* (Amsterdam: Royal Netherlands Academy of Arts and Sciences).

Dinc, Gulten and Yesim Isil Ulman (2007) 'The Introduction of Variolation "a La Turca" to the West by Lady Mary Montagu and Turkey's Contribution to This', in *Vaccine* 25 (21), pp. 4261–65.

Dirks, Robert (1993) 'Famine and Disease', in *The Cambridge World History of Human Disease*, ed. Kenneth F. Kiple (Cambridge: Cambridge University Press), pp. 157–63.

d'Ohsson, Ignatius Mouradgea and Constantin d'Ohsson (1787) *Tableau général de l'Empire Othoman, divisé en deux parties, dont l'une comprend la législation mahométane; l'autre, l'histoire de l'Empire Othoman,* 3 vols (Paris: Imp. de Monsieur [Firmin Didot]).

Donoghue, Emma (1995) *Passions between Women: British Lesbian Culture 1668–1801* (London: HarperCollins).

Dorwart, Reinholt August (1971) *The Prussian Welfare State Before 1740* (Cambridge, MA: Harvard University Press).

Douglas, A. and Mrs. M. Douglas (1797) *Notes of a Journey from Berne to England through France Made in the Year 1796* (London: W. Blackader).

Dresch, Catherine (1990) 'Maternal Nutrition and Infant Mortality Rates: An Evaluation of the Bourgeoisie of 18th-Century Montbéliard', in *Food and Foodways* 4 (1), pp. 1–38.

Drescher, Seymour (1994) 'The Long Goodbye: Dutch Capitalism and Antislavery in Comparative Perspective', in *American Historical Review* 98 (1), pp. 44–69.

Duben, Alan (1985) 'Nineteenth and Twentieth Century Ottoman-Turkish Family and Household Structure', in *Family in Turkish Society*, ed. Türköz Erder (Ankara: Turkish Social Science Association), pp. 105–26.

Dubert, Isidro (1999) 'Domestic Service and Social Modernization in Urban Galicia, 1752–1920', in *Continuity and Change* 14 (2), pp. 207–26.

Dubin, Lois C. (2007) 'Jewish Women, Marriage Law and Emancipation: A Civil Divorce in Late Eighteenth-Century Habsburg Trieste', in *Jewish Social Studies: History, Culture, Society* 13 (2), pp. 65–92.

Duchêne, Roger (1984) *Ninon de Lenclos, la courtisane du Grand Siècle* (Paris: Fayard).

Duden, Barbara (1991) *The Woman beneath the Skin: A Doctor's Patients in Eighteenth-Century Germany* (Cambridge, MA: Harvard University Press).

Dugaw, Dianne (1989) *Warrior Women and Popular Balladry 1650–1850* (Cambridge: Cambridge University Press).

Dülmen, Richard van (1991) *Frauen vor Gericht: Kindsmord in der frühen Neuzeit* (Frankfurt am Main: Fischer Taschenbuch Verlag).

D'Urfey, Thomas (1700) *The Famous History of the Rise and Fall of Massaniello. In Two Parts* (London: J. Nutt).

Durova, Nadezhda (1988) *The Cavalry Maid: The Memoirs of a Woman Soldier of 1812*, trans. John Mersereau and David Lapeza (Ann Arbor, MI: Ardis Publishers).

Dysa, Kateryna (2001) 'Attitudes Towards Witches in Germany and Ukraine', in *Frontiers of Faith: Religious Exchange and the Constitution of Religious Identities 1400–1750*, Cultural Exchange in Europe, 1400–1750, 1, ed. Eszter Andor and István György Tóth (Budapest: Central European University, European Science Foundation), pp. 285–90.

Earle, Peter (1989) 'The Female Labour Market in London in the Late Seventeenth and Early Eighteenth Centuries', in *Economic History Review* 2nd Series, 62 (3), pp. 328–53.

Edib, Mehemmed ibn Mehemmed (1825) *Itinéraire de Constantinople à la Mecque: extrait de l'ouvrage turc intitulé Kitab Menassik el-Hadj*, Extracted from Vol. 2 of *Recueil de voyages et de mémoires*, trans. Thomas Xavier Bianchi (Paris: Société du Géographie).

Egmond, Florike (2001) 'Incestuous Relations and Their Punishment in the Dutch Republic', in *Eighteenth-Century Life* 25 (3), pp. 20–42.

Ehrenreich, Barbara and Deirdre English (1973) *Witches, Midwives, and Nurses; a History of Women Healers* (Detroit, MI: Black & Red).

Eldem, Edhem (2007) 'Urban Voices from Beyond: Identity, Status and Social Strategies in Ottoman Muslim Funerary Epitaphs of Istanbul (1700–1850)', in *The Early Modern Ottomans: Remapping the Empire*, ed. Virginia H. Aksan and Daniel Goffman (Cambridge: Cambridge University Press), pp. 233–55.

Elias, Jamal (1988) 'Female and Feminine in Islamic Mysticism', in *Muslim World* 78 (3–4), pp. 209–24.

Ener, Mine (2005) 'Religious Prerogatives and Policing the Poor in Two Ottoman Contexts', in *Journal of Interdisciplinary History* 35 (3), pp. 501–11.

Engel, Barbara Alpern (1994) *Between the Fields and the City: Women, Work and Family in Russia, 1861–1914* (Cambridge: Cambridge University Press).

Englezakis, Benedict (1995) *Studies on the History of the Church of Cyprus, 4th–20th Centuries*, ed. Silouan Ioannou and Misael Ioannou, trans. Norman Russell (Aldershot: Variorum).

Erdem, Y. Hakan (1996) *Slavery in the Ottoman Empire and Its Demise, 1800–1909* (Houndmills: Macmillan and St. Martin's in association with St. Antony's College, Oxford).

Erder, Türköz, ed. (1985) *Family in Turkish Society* (Ankara: Turkish Social Science Association).

Erickson, Amy (1993) *Women and Property in Early Modern England* (London: Routledge).

Escrivá, José María (1944) *La abadesa de las Huelgas* (Madrid: Editorial Luz).

Etienne, Michel (1994) *Veuve Clicquot Ponsardin: Aux origines d'un grand vin de Champagne* (Paris: Economica).

Evans, Richard J., ed. (1988) *The German Underworld: Deviants and Outcasts in German History* (London: Routledge).

Evans, Richard J. (1998) *Tales from the German Underworld: Crime and Punishment in the Nineteenth Century* (New Haven, CT: Yale University Press).

Fábri, Anna (2001) 'Authoress or Romantic Heroine: The Problem of Plurality in the Hungarian Literary World around 1800', in *Writing the History of Women's Writing: Toward an International*

Approach, ed. Suzan van Dijk, Lia van Gemert and Sheila Ottway (Amsterdam: Royal Netherlands Academy of Arts and Sciences), pp. 47–56.

Faderman, Lillian (1981) *Surpassing the Love of Men: Romantic Friendship and Love between Women from the Renaissance to the Present* (London: Women's Press).

Fairchilds, Cissie C. (1978) 'Female Sexual Attitudes and the Rise of Illegitimacy: A Case Study', in *Journal of Interdisciplinary History* 8 (4), pp. 627–67.

Fairchilds, Cissie C. (1984) *Domestic Enemies: Servants and Their Masters in Old Regime France* (Baltimore, MD: Johns Hopkins University Press).

Fališevac, Dunja (2001) 'Women in Croatian Literary Culture, 16th to 18th Centuries', in *A History of Central European Women's Writing*, ed. Celia Hawkesworth (Houndmills: Palgrave, in association with School of Slavonic and East European Studies, University College, London), pp. 33–42.

Farge, Arlette and Jacques Revel (1991) *The Rules of Rebellion: Child Abductions in Paris in 1750*, trans. Claudia Miéville (Cambridge: Polity Press).

Farnsworth, Beatrice (1990) 'The Soldatka: Folk-Lore and Court Record', in *Slavic Review* 49 (1), pp. 58–73.

Faroqhi, Suraiya (2000) *Subjects of the Sultan: Culture and Daily Life in the Ottoman Empire* (London: I.B. Tauris).

Faroqhi, Suraiya (2001a) 'Quis Custodiet Custodes? Controlling Slave Identities and Slave Traders in Seventeenth- and Eighteenth-Century Istanbul', in *Frontiers of Faith: Religious Exchange and the Constitution of Religious Identities 1400–1750*, Cultural Exchange in Europe, 1400–1750, 1, ed. Eszter Andor and István György Tóth (Budapest: Central European University, European Science Foundation), pp. 121–36.

Faroqhi, Suraiya (2001b) 'Women's Work, Poverty and the Privileges of Guildsmen', in *Archiv orientalni* 69 (2), pp. 155–64.

Farrell, Diane Ecklund (1983) 'The Origins of Russian Popular Prints and Their Social Milieu in the Early Eighteenth Century', in *Journal of Popular Culture* 17 (1), pp. 9–47.

Farrow, Lee A. (2004) *Between Clan and Crown: The Struggle to Define Noble Property Rights in Imperial Russia* (Newark: University of Delaware Press).

Fauré, Christine, ed. (2003) *Political and Historical Encyclopedia of Women* (New York: Routledge).

Fauve-Chamoux, Antoinette (2000) 'Chestnuts', in *The Cambridge World History of Food*, ed. Kenneth F. Kiple and Kriemhild Coneé Ornelas, 2 vols (Cambridge: Cambridge University Press), vol. I, p. 361.

Fauve-Chamoux, Antoinette and Ludmilla Fialova, eds (1997) *Le phénomène de la domesticité en Europe, XVIe–XXe siècles* (Prague: Ceska Demografìcka Spolecnost).

Fay, Mary Ann (1997) 'Women and Waqf: Property, Power and the Domain of Gender in Eighteenth-Century Egypt', in *Women in the Ottoman Empire: Middle Eastern Women in the Modern Era*, ed. Madeline C. Zilfi (Leiden: Brill), pp. 28–47.

Fay, Mary Ann (1998) 'From Concubines to Capitalists: Women, Property, and Power in Eighteenth-Century Cairo', in *Journal of Women's History* 10 (3), pp. 118–40.

Felsenstein, Frank (1995) *Anti-Semitic Stereotypes: A Paradigm of Otherness in English Popular Culture, 1660–1830* (Baltimore, MD: Johns Hopkins University Press).

Ferguson, Moira (1992) *Subject to Others: British Women Writers and Colonial Slavery, 1670–1834* (New York: Routledge).

Ferguson, Moira (1993) *Colonialism and Gender Relations from Mary Wollstonecraft to Jamaica Kincaid: East Caribbean Connections* (New York: Columbia University Press).

Ferguson, Moira (1998) *Animal Advocacy and Englishwomen, 1780–1900: Patriots, Nation, and Empire* (Ann Arbor: University of Michigan Press).

Ferrer i Alòs, Llorenç (1993) 'Fratelli al celibate, sorelle al matrimonio. La parte dei cadetti nella riproduzione sociale dei gruppi agiati in Catalogna (secoli XVIII–XIX)', in *Quaderni storici* 83 (2), pp. 527–54.

Fieldhouse, R.T. (1972) 'Parliamentary Representation in the Borough of Richmond', in *Yorkshire Archaeological Journal* 44, pp. 207–16.

Filan, Kerima (2007) 'Women Founders of Pious Endowments in Ottoman Bosnia', in *Women in the Ottoman Balkans: Gender, Culture and History*, Library of Ottoman Studies, 15, ed. Amila Buturović and Irvin Cemil Schick (New York: I.B. Tauris), pp. 99–126.

Fildes, Valerie (1988) *Wet Nursing: A History from Antiquity to the Present* (Oxford: Basil Blackwell).

Filipović, Milenko S. (1954) 'The Bektashi in the District of Strumica (Macedonia)', in *Man* 54, pp. 10–13.

Filippini, Nadia Maria (1993) 'The Church, the State and Childbirth: The Midwife in Italy During the Eighteenth Century', in *The Art of Midwifery: Early Modern Midwives in Europe*, ed. Hilary Marland (London: Routledge), pp. 152–75.

Findley, Carter V. (1989) *Ottoman Civil Officialdom: A Social History* (Princeton, NJ: Princeton University Press).

Firth, C.H. and Robert S. Rait, eds (1911) *Acts and Ordinances of the Interregnum, 1642–1660*, 3 vols (London: H.M. Stationery Office, Printed by Wyman and Sons, Ltd).

Fisher, Alan W. (1968) 'Enlightened Despotism and Islam under Catherine II', in *Slavic Review* 27 (4), pp. 542–53.

Fogleman, Aaron Spencer (2007) *Jesus Is Female: Moravians and the Challenge of Radical Religion in Early America* (Philadelphia: University of Pennsylvania Press).

Fontaine, Laurence (1996) *History of Pedlars in Europe*, trans. Vicki Whittaker (Cambridge: Polity).

Fontaine, Laurence (2002) 'Women's Economic Spheres and Credit in Pre-Industrial Europe', in *Women and Credit: Researching the Past, Refiguring the Future*, ed. Beverly Lemire, Ruth Pearson and Gail Grace Campbell (Oxford: Berg), pp. 15–32.

Fontaine, Laurence (2003) 'The Circulation of Luxury Goods in Eighteenth-Century Paris: Social Redistribution and an Alternative Currency', in *Luxury in the Eighteenth Century: Debates, Desires and Delectable Goods*, ed. Maxine Berg and Elizabeth Eger (Basingstoke: Palgrave Macmillan), pp. 89–102.

Foucault, Michel (1973) *Madness and Civilization; a History of Insanity in the Age of Reason* (New York: Vintage Books).

Foyster, Elizabeth A. (2005) *Marital Violence: An English Family History, 1660–1875* (Cambridge: Cambridge University Press).

Francini, Giacomo (1997) 'Divorce and Separations in Eighteenth-Century France: An Outline for a Social History of Law', in *History of the Family: An International Quarterly* 2 (1), pp. 99–113.

Fraser, Antonia (2001) *Marie Antoinette: The Journey* (London: Phoenix).

Fraser, Nancy (1992) 'Rethinking the Public Sphere: A Contribution to the Critique of Actually Existing Democracy', in *Habermas and the Public Sphere*, ed. Craig J. Calhoun (Cambridge, MA: MIT Press), pp. 109–42.

Freke, Elizabeth (2001) *The Remembrances of Elizabeth Freke, 1671–1714*, Camden Fifth Series, 18, ed. Raymond A. Anselment (Cambridge: Cambridge University Press).

The Friendly Society for Widows: Being a Proposal for Supplying the Defect of Joyntures and Securing Women from Falling into Poverty and Distress at the Death of Their Husbands (1696) (London: Printed by F.C.).

Froide, Amy M. (2005) *Never Married: Singlewomen in Early Modern England* (Oxford: Oxford University Press).

Frost, Ginger (1994) 'Through the Medium of the Passions: Cohabitation Contracts in England, 1750–1850', in *Consortium on Revolutionary Europe, 1750–1850, Proceedings* 1993, pp. 181–93.

Fryer, Peter (1984) *Staying Power: The History of Black People in Britain* (London: Pluto Press).

Frykman, Jonas (1989) 'The Whore in Rural Society', in *Nordic Folklore: Recent Studies*, ed. Reimund Kvideland, Henning K. Sehmsdorf and Elizabeth Simpson (Bloomington: Indiana University Press), pp. 195–206.

Gaite, Carmen Martín (1991) *Love Customs in Eighteenth-Century Spain*, trans. Maria G. Tomsich (Berkeley: University of California Press).

Gallant, Thomas W. (1991) 'Agency, Structure, and Explanation in Social History: The Case of the Foundling Home on Kephallenia, Greece During the 1830s', in *Social Science History* 15 (4), pp. 479–508.

Gardiner, Judith Kegan (1989) 'The First English Novel: Aphra Behn's Love Letters, the Canon, and Women's Tastes', in *Tulsa Studies in Women's Literature* 8 (2), pp. 201–22.

Gárdonyi, Klára (1984) 'Brunsvik Teréz: Pestalozzi Követoje', in *Helikon világirodalmi figyelo* 30 (2–4), pp. 270–3.

Garrett, Clarke (1984) 'Swedenborg and the Mystical Enlightenment in Late Eighteenth-Century England', in *Journal of the History of Ideas* 45 (1), pp. 67–81.

Garrigus, John (2003) 'Race, Gender and Virtue in Haiti's Failed Foundational Fiction: La mulâtre comme il y a peu de blanches (1803)', in *The Color of Liberty: Histories of Race in France*, ed. Sue Peabody and Tyler Edward Stovall (Durham, NC: Duke University Press), pp. 73–94.

Gavigan, Shelley A.M. (1989) 'Petit Treason in Eighteenth Century England: Women's Inequality Before the Law', in *Canadian Journal of Women and the Law* 3 (2), pp. 335–74.

Gelbart, Nina (1993) 'Midwife to a Nation: Mme Du Coudray Serves France', in *The Art of Midwifery: Early Modern Midwives in Europe*, ed. Hilary Marland (London: Routledge), pp. 131–51.

Gelbart, Nina Rattner (1987) *Feminine and Opposition Journalism in Old Regime France: Le Journal Des Dames* (Berkeley: University of California Press).

Gemert, Lia van (1995) 'Hiding Behind Words? Lesbianism in 17th-Century Dutch Poetry', in *Thamyris* 2 (1), pp. 11–44.

Gendron, François (1993) *The Gilded Youth of Thermidor* (Montreal: McGill-Queen's University Press).

Gerber, Haim (1980) 'Social and Economic Position of Women in an Ottoman City, Bursa, 1600–1700', in *International Journal of Middle East Studies* 12 (3), pp. 231–44.

Gerhard, Ute, ed. (1997) *Frauen in der Geschichte des Rechts: von der frühen Neuzeit bis zur Gegenwart* (Munich: C.H. Beck).

Germani, Ian (1990) 'Les Bêtes Féroces: Thermidorian Images of Jacobinism', in *Proceedings of the Annual Meeting of the Western Society for French History* 17, pp. 205–19.

Gerolymatos, André (2002) *The Balkan Wars: Conquest, Revolution, and Retribution from the Ottoman Era to the Twentieth Century and Beyond* (New York: Basic Books).

Ghosh, Durba (2006) *Sex and the Family in Colonial India: The Making of Empire*, Cambridge Studies in Indian History and Society, 13 (Cambridge: Cambridge University Press).

Gibb, Elias John Wilkinson and Edward Granville Browne, eds (1963) *A History of Ottoman Poetry*, 6 vols (Cambridge: Printed for the Trustees of the 'E.J.W. Gibb Memorial' by Luzac & Co.).

Gibbons, B.J. (1996) *Gender in Mystical and Occult Thought: Behmenism and Its Development in England* (New York: Cambridge University Press).

Giladi, Avner (1990) 'Some Observations on Infanticide in Medieval Muslim Society', in *International Journal of Middle East Studies* 22 (2), pp. 185–200.

Ginio, Eyal (2001) '"Every Soul Shall Taste Death": Dealing with Death and the Afterlife in Eighteenth-Century Ottoman Salonica', in *Studia Islamica* 93, pp. 113–32.

Ginio, Eyal (2003) 'Living on the Margins of Charity: Coping with Poverty in an Ottoman Provincial City', in *Poverty and Charity in Middle Eastern Contexts*, ed. Michael David Bonner, Mine Ener and Amy Singer (Albany: State University of New York Press), pp. 165–84.

Ginio, Eyal (2006) 'The Shaping of a Sacred Space: The Tekke of Zühuri Seyh Ahmet Efendi in Eighteenth-Century Salonica', in *Medieval History Journal* 9 (2), pp. 271–96.

Ginsburg, C. and A. Swedlund (1986) 'Sex Specific Mortality and Economic Opportunity: Massachusetts, 1860–1899', in *Continuity and Change* 1 (3), pp. 415–45.

Giuli, Paola (1997) 'Querelle des Femmes: Eighteenth Century', in *The Feminist Encyclopedia of Italian Literature*, ed. Rinaldina Russell (Westport, CT: Greenwood Press), pp. 273–5.

Göçek, Fatma Müge (2003) 'Ottoman Empire: 15th to Mid-18th Century', in *Encyclopedia of Women & Islamic Cultures*, ed. Suad Joseph and Afsaneh Najmabadi, 6 vols (Leiden: Brill), vol. I, pp. 72–81.

Göçek, Fatma Müge and Marc David Baer (1997) 'Social Boundaries of Ottoman Women's Experience in Eighteenth-Century Galata Court Records', in *Women in the Ottoman Empire: Middle Eastern Women in the Early Modern Era*, ed. Madeline C. Zilfi (Leiden: Brill), pp. 48–65.

Godineau, Dominique (1998) *The Women of Paris and Their French Revolution*, Studies on the History of Society and Culture, 26, trans. Katherine Streip (Berkeley: University of California Press).

Godwin, William (1798) *Memoirs of the Author of a Vindication of the Rights of Woman [Mary Wollstonecraft]* (London: J. Johnson and G.G. and J. Robinson).

Goldberg, Halina (1999) 'Chopin in Warsaw's Salons', in *Polish Music Journal* 2 (1–2), online at: http://www.usc.edu/dept/polish_music/PMJ/issue/2.1.99/goldberg.html, accessed 1 May 2007.

Goldenberg, David M. (2003) *The Curse of Ham: Race and Slavery in Early Judaism, Christianity, and Islam* (Princeton, NJ: Princeton University Press).

Goldsmith, Elizabeth C. (1995) 'Publishing the Lives of Hortense and Marie Mancini', in *Going Public: Women and Publishing in Early Modern France*, ed. Elizabeth C. Goldsmith and Dena Goodman (Ithaca, NY: Cornell University Press), pp. 31–45.

Goldsmith, Elizabeth C. and Dena Goodman, eds (1995) *Going Public: Women and Publishing in Early Modern France* (Ithaca, NY: Cornell University Press).

Golos, George S. (1960) 'Some Slavic Predecessors of Chopin', in *Musical Quarterly* 46 (4), pp. 437–47.

Goncourt, Edmond de (1890) *Mademoiselle Clairon, d'après ses correspondances et les rapports de police du temps* (Paris: G. Charpentier et cie).

Goodman, Dena (1994) *The Republic of Letters: A Cultural History of the French Enlightenment* (Ithaca, NY: Cornell University Press).

Goodman, Katherine (1999) *Amazons and Apprentices: Women and the German Parnassus in the Early Enlightenment* (Columbia, SC: Camden House).

Görög-Karady, Veronika (1985) 'The Image of Gypsies in Hungarian Oral Literature', in *New York Folk-lore* 11 (1–4), pp. 149–59.

Gouk, Penelope (1999) *Music, Science, and Natural Magic in Seventeenth-Century England* (New Haven, CT: Yale University Press).

Gowing, Laura (1996) *Domestic Dangers: Women, Words and Sex in Early Modern London* (Oxford: Clarendon Press).

Gowing, Laura (2003) *Common Bodies: Women, Touch and Power in Seventeenth-Century England* (New Haven, CT: Yale University Press).

Grab, Alexander I. (1985) 'The Politics of Subsistence: The Liberalization of Grain Commerce in Austrian Lombardy under Enlightened Despotism', in *Journal of Modern History* 57 (2), pp. 186–210.

Graff, Harvey J. (1987) *The Legacies of Literacy: Continuities and Contradictions in Western Culture and Society* (Bloomington: Indiana University Press).

Gray, Richard (1987) 'The Papacy and the Atlantic Slave Trade: Lourenço Da Silva, the Capuchins and the Decisions of the Holy Office', in *Past & Present* (115), pp. 52–68.

Green, Llezlie L. (2002) 'Propaganda and Sexual Violence in the Rwandan Genocide: An Argument for Intersectionality in International Law', in *Columbia Human Rights Law Review* 33 (3), pp. 733–76.

Greenberg, David F. and Marcia H. Bystryn (1982) 'Christian Intolerance of Homosexuality', in *American Journal of Sociology* 88 (3), pp. 515–48.

Greene, Molly (2000) *A Shared World: Christians and Muslims in the Early Modern Mediterranean* (Princeton, NJ: Princeton University Press).

Greer, Donald (1935) *The Incidence of the Terror During the French Revolution: A Statistical Interpretation* (Cambridge, MA: Harvard University Press).

Grellman, Heinrich Moritz Gottlieb (1787) *Dissertation on the Gipsies, Being an Historical Enquiry, Concerning the Manner of Life, Economy, Customs and Conditions of These People in Europe, and Their Origin* (London: P. Elmsley, T. Cadell and J. Sewell).

Grenby, M.O. (2001) *The Anti-Jacobin Novel: British Conservatism and the French Revolution*, Cambridge Studies in Romanticism, 48 (Cambridge: Cambridge University Press).

Groppi, Angela (2002) 'A Matter of Fact Rather Than Principle: Women, Work and Property in Papal Rome (Eighteenth-Nineteenth Centuries)', in *Journal of Modern Italian Studies* 7 (1), pp. 37–55.

Guenzi, Alberto, Paola Massa and Fausto Piola Caselli, eds (1998) *Guilds, Markets, and Work Regulations in Italy, 16th–19th Centuries* (Aldershot: Ashgate).

Guest, Harriet (2000) *Small Change: Women, Learning, Patriotism, 1750–1810* (Chicago: University of Chicago Press).

Gullickson, Gay L. (2001) 'Protoindustrialization' in *Encyclopedia of European Social History from 1350 to 2000*, ed. Peter N. Stearns (New York: Charles Scribner), vol. III, pp. 39–47.

Gürtuna, Sevgi (2000) 'The Clothing of Ottoman Women', in *The Great Ottoman-Turkish Civilisation*, ed. Kemal Ciçek (Ankara: Yeni Tuerkiye), pp. 78–92.

Habermas, Jürgen (1989) *The Structural Transformation of the Public Sphere: An Inquiry into a Category of Bourgeois Society* (Cambridge, MA: MIT Press).

Hacker, Barton C. (1981) 'Women and Military Institutions in Early Modern Europe: A Reconnaissance', in *Signs: Journal of Women in Culture and Society* 6 (4), pp. 643–71.

Hadžijahic, Muhamed (1982) 'Badžijanije u Sarajevu i Bosni–prilog historiji duhovnosti u nas [Female Sufi Saints in Sarajevo and Bosnia: A Contribution to the History of Spirituality]', in *Anali gazi husrev-begove biblioteke* 7–8, pp. 109–33.

Hafter, Daryl M., ed. (1995a) *European Women and Preindustrial Craft* (Bloomington: Indiana University Press).

Hafter, Daryl M. (1995b) 'Women Who Wove in the Eighteenth-Century Silk Industry in Lyon', in *European Women and Preindustrial Craft*, ed. Daryl M. Hafter (Bloomington: Indiana University Press), pp. 42–64.

Hafter, Daryl M. (2001) 'Women in the Underground Business of Eighteenth-Century Lyon', in *Enterprise and Society* 2 (1), pp. 11–40.

Hagemann, Karen (2004) 'Female Patriots: Women, War and the Nation in the Period of the Prussian-German Anti-Napoleonic Wars', in *Gender & History* 16 (2), pp. 397–424.

Hall, Catherine (2002) *Civilising Subjects: Metropole and Colony in the English Imagination, 1830–1867* (Cambridge: Polity).

Hall, Catherine and Sonya O. Rose, eds (2006) *At Home with the Empire: Metropolitan Culture and the Imperial World* (Cambridge: Cambridge University Press).

Hamadeh, Shirine (2007) 'Public Spaces and the Garden Culture of Istanbul in the Eighteenth Century', in *The Early Modern Ottomans: Remapping the Empire*, ed. Virginia H. Aksan and Daniel Goffman (Cambridge: Cambridge University Press), pp. 277–312.

Hambly, Gavin, ed. (1998) *Women in the Medieval Islamic World: Power, Patronage, and Piety*, The New Middle Ages, 6 (New York: St. Martin's Press).

Hammel, E.A. and Aaron Gullickson (2004) 'Kinship Structures and Survival: Maternal Mortality on the Croatian-Bosnian Border 1750–1898', in *Population Studies* 58 (2), pp. 145–59.

Hammond, Cynthia Imogen (2006) '"Dearest City, I Am Thine": Selina Hastings' Architectural Vision', in *Women's Studies: An Interdisciplinary Journal* 35 (2), pp. 145–69.

Hanley, Sarah (2003) 'The Salic Law', in *Political and Historical Encyclopedia of Women*, ed. Christine Fauré (New York: Routledge), pp. 3–12.

Hanlon, Gregory (2003) 'L'infanticidio di coppie sposate in Toscana nella prima eta moderna', in *Quaderni storici* 38 (2), pp. 453–98.

Hanna, Nelly (1995) 'Marriage and the Family in the 17th Century Cairo [sic]', in *Histoire économique et sociale de l'Empire ottoman et de la Turquie (1326–1960): Actes du sixième congrés international tenu à Aix-en-Provence du 1er au 4 juillet 1992*, Collection Turcica, 8, ed. Daniel Panzac (Paris: Peeters), pp. 349–72.

Hardwick, Julie (2006) 'Early Modern Perspectives on the Long History of Domestic Violence: The Case of Seventeenth-Century France', in *Journal of Modern History* 78 (1), pp. 1–36.

Harries, Elizabeth Wanning (2001) *Twice Upon a Time: Women Writers and the History of the Fairy Tale* (Princeton, NJ: Princeton University Press).

Harrington, Joel F. (1999) 'Escape from the Great Confinement: The Genealogy of a German Workhouse', in *Journal of Modern History* 71 (2), pp. 308–45.

Harris, Ruth (1999) *Lourdes: Body and Spirit in the Secular Age* (Harmondsworth: Penguin).

Harten, Elke and Hans-Christian Harten (1989) *Frauen-Kultur-Revolution 1789–1799* (Pfaffenweiler: Centaurus-Verlaggesellschaft).

Harvey, A.D. (1978) 'Prosecutions for Sodomy in England at the Beginning of the Nineteenth Century', in *Historical Journal* 21 (4), pp. 939–48.

Hatem, Mervat F. (1997) 'The Professionalization of Health and the Control of Women's Bodies as Modern Governmentalities in Nineteenth-Century Egypt', in *Women in the Ottoman Empire: Middle Eastern Women in the Early Modern Era*, ed. Madeline C. Zilfi (Leiden: Brill), pp. 66–80.

Haug, Kate (1992) 'Myth and Matriarchy: An Analysis of the Mammy Stereotype', in *Dirt and Domesticity: Constructions of the Feminine*, ISP Papers, 2 (New York: Whitney Museum of American Art), pp. 38–57.

Hawkesworth, Celia (2000) *Voices in the Shadows: Women and Verbal Art in Serbia and Bosnia* (Budapest: Central European University Press).

Hawkesworth, Celia, ed. (2001) *A History of Central European Women's Writing* (Houndmills: Palgrave and School of Slavonic and East European Studies, University College, London).

Hay, Douglas (1980) 'Crime and Justice in Eighteenth- and Nineteenth-Century England', in *Crime & Justice* 2, pp. 45–84.

Haynes, Stephen R. (2002) *Noah's Curse: The Biblical Justification of American Slavery* (Oxford: Oxford University Press).

Heijden, Manon van der (2000) 'Women as Victims of Sexual and Domestic Violence in Seventeenth-Century Holland: Criminal Cases of Rape, Incest, and Maltreatment in Rotterdam and Delft', in *Journal of Social History* 33 (3), pp. 623–44.

Helie, Anissa, Farah Naqvi, Gabriela Mischkowski, Meera Vellayudan, Nira Yuval-Davis, Rhonda Copelon, Sunila Abeysekara, Uma Chakravarty and Vahida Nainar (2003) *Threatened Existence: A Feminist Analysis of the Genocide in Gujarat: Report by the International Initiative for Justice* (online at: http://www.coalitionagainstgenocide.org/reports.php, accessed 20 August 2008).

Hellie, Richard (1982) *Slavery in Russia 1450–1725* (Chicago: University of Chicago Press).

Helt, J.S.W. (2003) 'Memento Mori: Death, Widowhood and Remembering in Early Modern England', in *Widowhood and Visual Culture in Early Modern Europe*, ed. Allison M. Levy (Aldershot: Ashgate), pp. 39–54.

Henderson, John and Richard Wall, eds (1994) *Poor Women and Children in the European Past* (London: Routledge).

Henderson, Tony (1999) *Disorderly Women in Eighteenth-Century London: Prostitution and Control in the Metropolis, 1730–1830* (London: Longman).

Hertz, Deborah (1978) 'Salonières and Literary Women in Late Eighteenth-Century Berlin', in *New German Critique* 14, pp. 97–108.

Hesse, Carla (2001) *The Other Enlightenment: How French Women Became Modern* (Princeton, NJ: Princeton University Press).

Heuer, Jennifer Ngaire (2005) *The Family and the Nation: Gender and Citizenship in Revolutionary France, 1789–1830* (Ithaca, NY: Cornell University Press).

Heuvel, Danielle van den (2006) 'Sharing a Trade? The Cooperation of Spouses in Commerce in the Eighteenth-Century Dutch Republic', European Social Science History Conference, Panel on Partners in Business: Husbands and Wives Working Together, Part I: Married Couples Working Together in Commerce, 1500–1800, 25 March (Amsterdam, The Netherlands).

Heuvel, Danielle van den (2007) *Women and Entrepreneurship: Female Traders in the Northern Netherlands c. 1580–1815*, Women and Work in the Early Modern Period, 2 (Amsterdam: Uitgeverij Aksant).

Hickman, Trevor (2005) *The History of Stilton Cheese*, New edn (Stroud: Sutton).

Hilden, Patricia Penn (1993) *Women, Work, and Politics: Belgium, 1830–1914* (Oxford: Oxford Unversity Press).

Hill, Bridget (1987) 'A Refuge from Men: The Idea of a Protestant Nunnery', in *Past & Present* 117, pp. 107–30.

Hill, Bridget (1993) 'Women's History: A Study in Change, Continuity or Standing Still?', in *Women's History Review* 2 (1), pp. 5–22.

Hill, Bridget (1996) *Servants: English Domestics in the Eighteenth Century* (New York: Oxford University Press).

Hill, Bridget (2004) 'Macaulay, Catharine (1731–1791)', in *Oxford Dictionary of National Biography*, ed. H.C.G. Matthew and Brian Harrison (Oxford: Oxford University Press), online edn, ed. Lawrence Goldman, January 2008, http://www.oxforddnb.com, accessed 12 June 2008.

Hirst, Derek (1975) *The Representative of the People? Voters and Voting in England under the Early Stuarts* (Cambridge: Cambridge University Press).

Hitchcock, Tim (2004) 'Marsin, M. (Fl. 1696–1701)', in *Oxford Dictionary of National Biography*, ed. H.C.G. Matthew and Brian Harrison (Oxford: Oxford University Press), online edn, ed. Lawrence Goldman, January 2008, http://www.oxforddnb.com, accessed 13 June 2008.

Hitchcock, Tim (2005) 'Begging on the Streets of Eighteenth-Century London', in *Journal of British Studies* 44 (3), pp. 478–98.

Hobsbawm, E.J. and T.O. Ranger (1983) *The Invention of Tradition* (Cambridge: Cambridge University Press).

Hoch, Steven L. (1986) *Serfdom and Social Control in Russia: Petrovskoe, a Village in Tambov* (Chicago: University of Chicago Press).

Holst-Warhaft, Gail (1992) *Dangerous Voices: Women's Laments and Greek Literature* (London: Routledge).

Holthöfer, Ernst (1997) 'Die Geschleschtsvormundschaft. Ein Überblick von der Antike bis ins 19. Jahrhundert', in *Frauen in der Geschichte des Rechts: von der frühen Neuzeit bis zur Gegenwart*, ed. Ute Gerhard (Munich: C.H. Beck), pp. 390–451.

Hopkins, James K. (1982) *A Woman to Deliver Her People: Joanna Southcott and English Millenarianism in an Era of Revolution* (Austin: University of Texas Press).

Horrell, Sara and Jane Humphries (1992) 'Old Questions, New Data and Alternative Perspectives: Families' Living Standards in the Industrial Revolution', in *Journal of Economic History* 52 (4), pp. 849–80.

Horwitz, Henry (1998) *A Guide to Chancery Equity Records and Proceedings 1600–1800*, Public Record Office Handbook, 27, 2nd edn (Kew: Public Record Office).

Houston, R.A. (1988) *Literacy in Early Modern Europe: Culture and Education, 1500–1800* (London: Longman).

Hrdy, Sarah Blaffer (1992) 'Fitness Tradeoffs in the History and Evolution of Delegated Mothering with Special Reference to Wet-Nursing, Abandonment, and Infanticide', in *Ethology and Sociobiology* 13 (5–6), pp. 409–42.

Hrdy, Sarah Blaffer (2001) 'The Past, Present and Future of the Human Family', The Tanner Lectures on Human Values, 27–28 February (Salt Lake City: University of Utah, http://www.tannerlectures.utah.edu/lectures/Hrdy_02.pdf, accessed 23 June 2007).

Hsia, R. Po-chia (1988) *The Myth of Ritual Murder: Jews and Magic in Reformation Germany* (New Haven, CT: Yale University Press).

Hufton, Olwen (1971) 'Women in Revolution 1789–1796', in *Past & Present* 53, pp. 90–108.

Hufton, Olwen (1974) *The Poor of Eighteenth-Century France, 1750–1789* (Oxford: Clarendon Press).

Hufton, Olwen (1975) 'Women and the Family Economy in Eighteenth-Century France', in *French Historical Studies* 9 (1), pp. 1–22.

Hufton, Olwen (1995) *The Prospect Before Her: A History of Women in Western Europe* (London: HarperCollins).

Hufton, Olwen and Frank Tallett (1987) 'Communities of Women, the Religious Life, and Public Service in Eighteenth-Century France', in *Connecting Spheres: Women in the Western World, 1500 to the Present*, ed. Marilyn J. Boxer and Jean H. Quataert (New York: Oxford University Press), pp. 75–85.

Hughes, Lindsey (2001) 'From Caftans into Corsets: The Sartorial Transformation of Women During the Reign of Peter the Great', in *Gender and Sexuality in Russian Civilization*, ed. Peter I. Barta (London: Routledge), pp. 17–32.

Hughes, Lindsey (2004) 'Catherine I of Russia: Consort to Peter the Great', in *Queenship in Europe, 1660–1815: The Role of the Consort*, ed. Clarissa Campbell Orr (Cambridge: Cambridge University Press), pp. 131–54.

Hull, Isabel V. (1996) *Sexuality, State, and Civil Society in Germany, 1700–1815* (Ithaca, NY: Cornell University Press).

Humphreys, Jennett and Angela M. Leonard (2004) 'Candler [née More], Ann (1740–1814), Poet', in *Oxford Dictionary of National Biography*, ed. H.C.G. Matthew and Brian Harrison (Oxford: Oxford University Press), online edn, ed. Lawrence Goldman, January 2008, http://www.oxforddnb.com, accessed 23 May 2008.

Humphries, Jane (1990) 'Enclosures, Common Rights and Women: The Proletarianisation of Families in the Late Eighteenth and Early Nineteenth Centuries', in *Journal of Economic History* 50 (1), pp. 17–42.

Humphries, Jane (1991) '"Bread and a Pennyworth of Treacle": Excess Female Mortality in England in the 1840s', in *Cambridge Journal of Economics* 15 (4), pp. 451–73.

Hundert, Gershon David (2004) *Jews in Poland-Lithuania in the Eighteenth Century: A Genealogy of Modernity* (Berkeley: University of California Press).

Hunt, Lynn Avery (1991) 'The Many Bodies of Marie Antoinette: Political Pornography and the Problem of the Feminine in the French Revolution', in *Eroticism and the Body Politic*, ed. Lynn Hunt (Baltimore, MD: Johns Hopkins University Press), pp. 108–30.

Hunt, Lynn Avery (1992) *The Family Romance of the French Revolution* (Berkeley: University of California Press).

Hunt, Lynn Avery (1996) *The French Revolution and Human Rights: A Brief Documentary History* (Boston: Bedford Books of St. Martin's Press).

Hunt, Margaret R. (1984) 'Hawkers, Bawlers and Mercuries: Women and the London Press in the Early Enlightenment', in *Women and the Enlightenment*, ed. Margaret Hunt, Margaret Jacob, Phyllis Mack and Ruth Perry (New York: Institute for Research in History and the Haworth Press), pp. 41–68.

Hunt, Margaret R. (1995) '"The Great Danger She Had Reason to Believe She Was In": Wife-Beating in the Eighteenth Century', in *Women & History: Voices of Early Modern England*, ed. Valerie Frith (Toronto, ON: Coach House Press), pp. 81–102.

Hunt, Margaret R. (1996) *The Middling Sort: Commerce, Gender and the Family in England* (Berkeley: University of California Press).

Hunt, Margaret R. (1999) 'The Sapphic Strain: English Lesbians During the Long Eighteenth Century', in *Singlewomen in the European Past*, ed. Amy M. Froide and Judith Bennett (Philadelphia: University of Pennsylvania Press), pp. 270–96.

Hunt, Margaret R. (2000) 'Wives and Marital "Rights" In the Court of Exchequer in the Early Eighteenth Century', in *Londinopolis: Essays in the Cultural and Social History of Early Modern London*, ed. Mark S. R. Jenner and Paul Griffiths (Manchester: Manchester University Press), pp. 107–29.

Hunt, Margaret R. (2004a) 'Nutt, Elizabeth (b. in or before 1666, d. 1746), Printer and Bookseller', in *Oxford Dictionary of National Biography*, ed. H.C.G. Matthew and Brian Harrison (Oxford: Oxford University Press), online edn, ed. Lawrence Goldman, January 2008, http://www.oxforddnb.com, accessed 28 July 2008.

Hunt, Margaret R. (2004b) 'Women and the Fiscal-Imperial State in the Late Seventeenth and Early Eighteenth Centuries', in *A New Imperial History: Culture, Identity, and Modernity in Britain and the Empire, 1660–1840*, ed. Kathleen Wilson (Cambridge: Cambridge University Press), pp. 29–47.

Hurl-Eamon, Jennine (2005) *Gender and Petty Violence in London, 1680–1720* (Columbus: Ohio State University Press).

Hurwich, Judith J. (1993) 'Inheritance Practices in Early Modern Germany', in *Journal of Interdisciplinary History* 23 (4), pp. 699–718.

Huussen, Jr., Arend H. (1987) 'Sodomy in the Dutch Republic During the Eighteenth Century', in *'Tis Nature's Fault: Unauthorized Sexuality During the Enlightenment*, ed. Robert Purks Maccubbin (New York: Cambridge University Press), pp. 169–78.

Hyde, Melissa Lee and Jennifer Dawn Milam, eds (2003) *Women, Art, and the Politics of Identity in Eighteenth-Century Europe* (Burlington, VT: Ashgate).

Iggers, Wilma (1995) *Women of Prague: Ethnic Diversity and Social Change from the Eighteenth Century to the Present* (Providence, RI: Berghahn Books).

Imber, Colin (1997) 'Women, Marriage and Property: Mahr in the Behcetü'l-Fetava of Yeniserhirli Abdullah', in *Women in the Ottoman Empire: Middle Eastern Women in the Early Modern Era*, ed. Madeline C. Zilfi (Leiden: Brill), pp. 81–104.

Immel, Andrea and Michael Witmore, eds (2006) *Childhood and Children's Books in Early Modern Europe, 1550–1800* (London: Routledge).

Inalcik, Halil and Donald Quataert (1994) *An Economic and Social History of the Ottoman Empire, 1300–1914* (Cambridge: Cambridge University Press).

Ingrao, Charles (1982) '"Barbarous Strangers": Hessian State and Society During the American Revolution', in *American Historical Review* 87 (4), pp. 954–76.

Irwin, Joyce (1991) 'Anna Maria Van Schurman and Antoinette Bourignon: Contrasting Examples of Seventeenth-Century Pietism', in *Church History* 60 (3), pp. 301–15.

Ivanova, Svetlana (2007) 'Judicial Treatment of the Matrimonial Problems of Christian Women in Rumeli During the Seventeenth and Eighteenth Centuries', in *Women in the Ottoman Balkans: Gender, Culture and History*, Library of Ottoman Studies, 15, ed. Amila Buturović and Irvin Cemil Schick (New York: I.B. Tauris), pp. 153–200.

Jackson, Mark, ed. (2002) *Infanticide: Historical Perspectives on Child Murder and Concealment, 1550–2000* (Aldershot: Ashgate).

Jacob, Margaret C. and Dorothée Sturkenboom (2003) 'A Women's Scientific Society in the West: The Late Eighteenth-Century Assimilation of Science', in *Isis* 94 (2), pp. 217–52.

Jacob, Margaret C. (1984) 'Freemasons, Women and the Paradox of the Enlightenment', in *Women and the Enlightenment*, ed. Margaret Hunt, Margaret Jacob, Phyllis C. Mack and Ruth Perry (New York: The Institute for Research in History and the Haworth Press), pp. 69–93.

Jamgocyan, Onnik (1990) 'La révolution française vue et vécue de Constantinope (1789–1795)', in *Annales historiques de la révolution française* 282, pp. 462–69.

Jamieson, Ross W. (1995) 'Material Culture and Social Death: African-American Burial Practices', in *Historical Archaeology* 29 (4), pp. 39–58.

Jansson, Karin Hassan (2002) *Kvinnofrid: synen på våldtäkt och konstruktionen av kön i Sverige 1600–1800* (Conceptualizing rape: gendered notions of violence in Sweden 1600–1800), Studia Historica Upsaliensia, 205 (Uppsala: Acta Universitatis Upsaliensis).

Jennings, Ronald C. (1975) 'Women in Early 17th Century Ottoman Judicial Records – the Sharia Court of Anatolian Kayseri', in *Journal of the Economic and Social History of the Orient* 18 (1), pp. 53–114.

Jennings, Ronald C. (1993) *Christians and Muslims in Ottoman Cyprus and the Mediterranean World, 1571–1640*, New York University Studies in Near Eastern Civilization, 18 (New York: New York University Press).

Jespersen, Knud J.V. (1995) 'The Danish Nobility, 1600–1800', in *The European Nobilities in the Seventeenth and Eighteenth Centuries*, ed. H.M. Scott, 2 vols (London: Longman), vol. II (Northern, Central and Eastern Europe), pp. 41–70.

Jianu, Angela (2007) 'Women, Fashion and Europeanization: The Romanian Principalities, 1750–1830', in *Women in the Ottoman Balkans: Gender, Culture and History*, Library of Ottoman Studies, 15, ed. Amila Buturović and Irvin Cemil Schick (New York: I.B. Tauris), pp. 201–30.

Johansen, Hanne Marie (2005) 'Marriage Trouble: Separation and Divorce in Early Modern Norway', in *The Marital Economy in Scandinavia and Britain, 1400–1900*, ed. Maria Ågren and Amy Louise Erickson (Aldershot: Ashgate), pp. 175–89.

Johansson, Egil (1981) 'The History of Literacy in Sweden', in *Literacy and Social Development in the West: A Reader*, ed. Harvey J. Graff (Cambridge: Cambridge University Press), pp. 151–82.

Johnson, Joan Marie (2005) ' "Ye Gave Them a Stone": African American Women's Clubs, the Frederick Douglass Home, and the Black Mammy Monument', in *Journal of Women's History* 17 (1), pp. 62–86.

Johnson, Walter (1999) *Soul by Soul: Life inside the Antebellum Slave Market* (Cambridge, MA: Harvard University Press).

Johnson, Walter (2003) 'On Agency', in *Journal of Social History* 37 (1), pp. 113–24.

Jones, Colin (1978) 'Prostitution and the Ruling Class in Eighteenth-Century Montpellier', in *History Workshop Journal* 6, pp. 7–28.

Jones, Colin (1982) *Charity and Bienfaisance: The Treatment of the Poor in the Montpellier Region, 1740–1815* (Cambridge: Cambridge University Press).

Jones, Colin (1989) *The Charitable Imperative: Hospitals and Nursing in Ancien Regime and Revolutionary France* (New York: Routledge, Chapman and Hall).

Jones, David E. (2003) *Women Warriors: A History* (Washington, DC: Brassey's).

Jones, Jennifer Michelle (2004) *Sexing la Mode: Gender, Fashion and Commercial Culture in Old Regime France*, English edn (Oxford: Berg).

Jones, Peter (1983) 'Common Rights and Agrarian Individualism in the Southern Massif Central 1750–1880', in *Beyond the Terror: Essays in French Regional and Social History, 1794–1815*, ed. Gwynne Lewis and Colin Lucas (Cambridge: Cambridge University Press), pp. 121–51.

Jones, Verina R. (2000) 'Journalism, 1750–1850', in *A History of Women's Writing in Italy*, ed. Letizia Panizza and Sharon Wood (Cambridge: Cambridge University Press), pp. 120–34.

Jonsson, Inger (1995) 'Women Flax Scutchers in the Linen Production of Hälsingland, Sweden', in *European Women and Preindustrial Craft*, ed. Daryl M. Hafter (Bloomington: Indiana University Press), pp. 16–30.

Jónsson, Már (1998) 'Incest in Iceland 1500–1900', Páll Guðmundsson Lecture, 29 March (Winnipeg: University of Manitoba, online at http://gateway.uvic.ca/beck/media/text/incest.html, accessed 23 May 2007).

Joseph, Suad and Afsaneh Najmabadi, eds (2003) *Encyclopedia of Women and Islamic Cultures*, 6 vols (Leiden: Brill).

Jung, Martin H. (1998) *Frauen des Pietismus: zehn Porträts von Johanna Regina Bengel bis Erdmuthe Dorothea von Zinzendorf* (Gütersloh: Gütersloher).

Juratic, Sabine (1987) 'Solitude féminine et travail des femmes à Paris à la fin du XVIIIe siècle', in *Mélanges de l'école françaises de Rome: moyen age, temps modernes* 99 (2), pp. 779–900.

Jütte, Robert (1994) *Poverty and Deviance in Early Modern Europe* (Cambridge: Cambridge University Press).

Kabbani, Muhammad Hisham and Laleh Bakhtiar (1998) *Encyclopedia of Muhammad's Women Companions and the Traditions They Related* (Chicago: ABC International Group/Kazi Publications).

Kadin bestekârlar (Ottoman Women Composers) (2001), Osmanli Mozaiği/Mosaic of Ottoman Series, produced by Ahmet Kadri Rizeli (Istanbul: Sony/Columbia).

Kahan, Arcadius and Richard Hellie (1985) *The Plow, the Hammer, and the Knout: An Economic History of Eighteenth-Century Russia* (Chicago: University of Chicago Press).

Kaiser, Daniel H. (1992) 'Urban Household Composition in Early Modern Russia', in *Journal of Interdisciplinary History* 23 (1), pp. 39–71.

Kamler, Marcin (1988) 'Infanticide in the Towns of the Kingdom of Poland in the Second Half of the 16th and the First Half of the 17th Century', in *Acta Poloniae Historica* 58, pp. 33–49.

Kandiyoti, Deniz (1988) 'Bargaining with Patriarchy', in *Gender and Society* 2 (3), pp. 274–90.

Kant, Immanuel (1960) *Observations on the Feeling of the Beautiful and Sublime*, trans. John T. Goldthwait (Berkeley: University of California Press).

Kany, Charles (1932) *Life and Manners in Madrid, 1750–1800* (Berkeley: University of California Press).

Kaplan, Benjamin J. (2007) *Divided by Faith: Religious Conflict and the Practice of Toleration in Early Modern Europe* (Cambridge, MA: Belknap Press of Harvard University Press).

Kaplan, Steven Laurence (1982) 'The Famine Plot Persuasion in Eighteenth-Century France', in *Transactions of the American Philosophical Society*, New Series, 72 (3), pp. 1–79.

Kaplan, Temma (1982) 'Female Consciousness and Collective Action: The Barcelona Case, 1910–1918', in *Signs: Journal of Women in Culture and Society* 7 (3), pp. 545–66.

Karadžic, Vuk Stefanovic, ed. (1992) *Red Knight: Serbian Women's Songs* (London: Menard Press).

Karpinski, Andrzej (1989a) 'La prostitution dans les grandes villes polonaises aux XVIe et XVIIe siècles', in *Acta Poloniae Historica* 59, pp. 5–40.

Karpinski, Andrzej (1989b) 'The Woman on the Market Place. The Scale of Feminization of Retail Trade in Polish towns in the Second Half of the 16e and in the 17e Century [sic]' in *La donna nell'economia secc. XIII–XVIII*, ed. Simonetta Cavaciocchi (Prato: Istituto internazionale di storia economica 'F.Datini'), pp. 283–92.

Karpinski, Andrzej (1996) 'Female Servants in Polish Towns in the Late 16th and 17th Centuries', in *Acta Poloniae Historica* 74, pp. 21–44.

Karsch, Anna Luisa (1990) 'Autobiographical Letter to Professor Sulzer', in *Bitter Healing: German Women Writers from 1700 to 1830: An Anthology*, ed. Jeannine Blackwell and Susanne Zantop (Lincoln: University of Nebraska Press), pp. 131–9.

Kasdagli, Aglaia E. (1999) *Land and Marriage Settlements in the Aegean: A Case Study of Seventeenth-Century Naxos*, Oriens Graecolatinus, 6 (Venice: Hellenic Institute of Byzantine and Post-Byzantine Studies/Vikelea Municipal Library of Iraklion).

Kates, Gary (1990) '"The Powers of Husband and Wife Must Be Equal and Separate": The Cercle Social and the Rights of Women, 1790–1791', in *Women and Politics in the Age of the Democratic Revolution*, ed. Harriet B. Applewhite and Darline G. Levy (Ann Arbor: University of Michigan Press), pp. 163–80.

Kay, Devra, ed. (2004) *Seyder Tkhines: The Forgotten Book of Common Prayer for Jewish Women* (Philadelphia: Jewish Publication Society).

Keddie, Nikki R. and Beth Baron, eds (1991) *Women in Middle Eastern History: Shifting Boundaries in Sex and Gender* (New Haven, CT: Yale University Press).

Kefadar, Cemal (1992) 'The New Visibility of Sufism in Turkish Studies and Cultural Life', in *The Dervish Lodge: Architecture, Art, and Sufism in Ottoman Turkey*, ed. Raymond Lifchez (Berkeley: University of California Press), pp. 307–22.

Kefeli, Agnès (2001) 'The Role of Tatar and Kriashen Women in the Transmission of Islamic Knowledge, 1800–1870', in *Of Religion and Empire: Missions, Conversion, and Tolerance in Tsarist Russia*, ed. Robert P. Geraci and Michael Khodarkovsky (Ithaca, NY: Cornell University Press), pp. 250–73.

Kelly, Catriona (2001) 'Sappho, Corina, and Niobe: Genres and Personae in Russian Women's Writing, 1760–1820', in *History of Women's Writing in Russia*, ed. Adele Marie Barker (Port Chester, NY: Cambridge University Press), pp. 37–61.

Kelly, Gary, ed. (1999) *Bluestocking Feminism: Writings of the Bluestocking Circle, 1738–1785*, 6 vols (London: Pickering and Chatto).

Kelly, J. (1992) 'Infanticide in Eighteenth-Century Ireland', in *Irish Economic and Social History* 19, pp. 5–26.

Kenna, Margaret E. (1985) 'Icons in Theory and Practice: An Orthodox Christian Example', in *History of Religions* 24 (4), pp. 345–68.

Kertzer, David I. (1993) *Sacrificed for Honor: Italian Infant Abandonment and the Politics of Reproductive Control* (Boston: Beacon Press).

Kertzer, David I. (1999) 'Syphilis, Foundlings, and Wetnurses in Nineteenth-Century Italy', in *Journal of Social History* 32 (3), pp. 589–602.

Kertzer, David I. (2000) 'The Lives of Foundlings in Nineteenth-Century Italy', in *Abandoned Children*, ed. Catherine Panter-Brick and Malcolm T. Smith (Cambridge: Cambridge University Press), pp. 41–56.

Kettering, Sharon (1989) 'The Patronage Power of Early Modern French Noblewomen', in *Historical Journal* 32 (4), pp. 817–41.

Keymer, Thomas (2004) 'Chapone, Sarah (1699–1764)', in *Oxford Dictionary of National Biography*, ed. H.C.G. Matthew and Brian Harrison (Oxford: Oxford University Press), online edn, ed. Lawrence Goldman, January 2008, http://www.oxforddnb.com, accessed 11 March 2008.

Khoury, Dina Rizk (1996) 'Drawing Boundaries and Defining Spaces: Women and Space in Ottoman Iraq', in *Women, the Family, and Divorce Laws in Islamic History*, ed. Amira El-Azhary Sonbol (Syracuse, NY: Syracuse University Press), pp. 173–87.

Khoury, Dina Rizk (1997a) 'Slippers at the Entrance or Behind Closed Doors: Domestic and Public Spaces for Mosuli Women', in *Women in the Ottoman Empire: Middle Eastern Women in the Early Modern Era*, ed. Madeline C. Zilfi (Leiden: Brill), pp. 105–27.

Khoury, Dina Rizk (1997b) *State and Provincial Society in the Ottoman Empire: Mosul, 1540–1834* (Cambridge: Cambridge University Press).

Kingdon, Robert McCune (1995) *Adultery and Divorce in Calvin's Geneva* (Cambridge, MA: Harvard University Press).

Kiple, Kenneth F. (1993) *The Cambridge World History of Human Disease*: Cambridge University Press).

Kiple, Kenneth F. and Kriemhild Coneé Ornelas, eds (2000) *The Cambridge World History of Food*, 2 vols (Cambridge: Cambridge University Press).

Király, Béla K. (1969) *Hungary in the Late Eighteenth Century; the Decline of Enlightened Despotism* (New York: Columbia University Press).

Klaniczay, Gábor (1990) 'Hungary: The Accusations and the Universe of Popular Magic', in *Early Modern Witchcraft: Centres and Peripheries*, ed. Bengt Ankarloo and Gustav Henningsen (Oxford: Clarendon Press), pp. 219–55.

Klaniczay, Gábor (1992) 'The Decline of Witches and the Rise of Vampires under the Eighteenth-Century Habsburg Monarchy', in *Witch-Hunting in Early Modern Europe: Local and Regional Studies*, ed. Brian P. Levack (New York: Garland Publishing), pp. 262–86.

Klasen, Stephan (1998) 'Marriage, Bargaining and Intrahousehold Resource Allocation: Excess Female Mortality among Adults During Early German Development, 1740–1860', in *Journal of Economic History* 58 (2), pp. 432–67.

Kloek, Els, Nicole Teeuwen and Marijke Huisman, eds (1994) *Women of the Golden Age: An International Debate on Women in Seventeenth-Century Holland, England and Italy* (Hilversum: Verloren).

Knapp, Vincent J. (1998) 'Major Medical Explanations for High Infant Mortality in Nineteenth-Century Europe', in *Canadian Bulletin of Medical History / Bulletin canadien d'histoire de la médecine* 15 (2), pp. 317–36.

Knodel, John (1970) 'Two and a Half Centuries of Demographic History in a Bavarian Village', in *Population Studies* 24 (3), pp. 353–76.

Ko, Dorothy (1994) *Teachers of the Inner Chambers: Women and Culture in Seventeenth-Century China* (Stanford, CA: Stanford University Press).

Kohbach, M. (1986) 'Ein Fall von Steinigung wegen Ehebruch in Istanbul im Jahre 1680', in *Wiener Zeitschrift für die Kunde des Morgenlandes* 76, pp. 187–92.

Kollmann, Nancy Shields (1983) 'The Seclusion of Elite Muscovite Women', in *Russian History* 10 (2), pp. 170–87.

Komlos, John (1989) *Nutrition and Economic Development in the Eighteenth Century Habsburg Monarchy: An Anthropometric History* (Princeton, NJ: Princeton University Press).

Konczacki, J.M. and K. Aterman (2002) 'Regina Salomea Pilsztynowa, Ophthalmologist in 18th-Century Poland', in *Survey of Ophthalmology* 47 (2), pp. 189–95.

Kopczynski, Michal (1998) 'Old Age Gives no Joy? Old People in the Kujawy Countryside at the End of the 18th Century', in *Acta Poloniae Historica* 78, pp. 81–101.

Kord, Susanne (2003) *Women Peasant Poets in Eighteenth-Century England, Scotland, and Germany* (Rochester, NY: Camden House).

Kostroun, Daniella (2003) 'A Formula for Disobedience: Jansenism, Gender, and the Feminist Paradox', in *Journal of Modern History* 75 (3), pp. 483–522.

Krody, Sumru Belger (2000) *Flowers of Silk and Gold: Four Centuries of Ottoman Embroidery* (Washington, DC: Merrell in association with The Textile Museum).

Kuklo, Cezary (1997) 'La domesticité en Pologne à la fin du XVIIIe siècle, premiers resultats des recherches', in *Le phénomène de la domesticité en Europe, XVIe–XXe siècles*, ed. Antoinette Fauve-Chamoux and Ludmilla Fialova (Prague: Ceska Demograficka Spolecnost), pp. 51–56.

Kuklo, Cezary (1998) *Kobieta samotna w społeczeństwie miejskim u schyłku Rzeczypospolitej szlacheckiej: Studium demograficzno-społeczne* (Białystock, Poland: Wydawnictwo Uniwersytetu w Białymstoku).

Kushner, Nina (2001) 'Procuring Mothers, Sacrificed Daughters and "Helpful" Policemen: The Elite Prostitute as Family Breadwinner in Eighteenth-Century Paris', in *Proceedings of the Annual Meeting of the Western Society for French History* 29, pp. 11–20.

Kussmaul, Ann (1981) *Servants in Husbandry in Early Modern England* (Cambridge: Cambridge University Press).

Laine, Merit (1998) 'An Eighteenth-Century Minerva: Lovisa Ulrika and Her Collections at Drottningholm Palace 1744–1777', in *Eighteenth-Century Studies* 31 (4), pp. 493–503.

Laiou, Sophia (2007) 'Christian Women in an Ottoman World: Interpersonal and Family Cases Brought Before the Shari'a Courts During the Seventeenth and Eighteenth Centuries', in *Women in the Ottoman Balkans: Gender, Culture and History*, Library of Ottoman Studies, 15, ed. Amila Buturović and Irvin Cemil Schick (New York: I.B. Tauris), pp. 243–72.

Lampe, John R. and Marvin R. Jackson (1982) *Balkan Economic History, 1550–1950: From Imperial Borderlands to Developing Nations* (Bloomington: Indiana University Press).

Landers, Jane (1999) *Black Society in Spanish Florida* (Urbana: University of Illinois Press).

Landes, Joan B. (1988) *Women and the Public Sphere in the Age of the French Revolution* (Ithaca, NY: Cornell University Press).

Lanser, Susan S. (1998) 'Befriending the Body: Female Intimacies as Class Acts', in *Eighteenth-Century Studies* 32 (2), pp. 179–98.

Laqueur, Hans-Peter (1992) 'Dervish Gravestones', in *The Dervish Lodge: Architecture, Art, and Sufism in Ottoman Turkey*, ed. Raymond Lifchez (Berkeley: University of California Press), pp. 284–96.

Laqueur, Thomas Walter (1990) *Making Sex: Body and Gender from the Greeks to Freud* (Cambridge, MA: Harvard University Press).

Lavrin, Asunción (1999) 'Indian Brides of Christ: Creating New Spaces for Indigenous Women in New Spain', in *Mexican Studies / Estudios mexicanos* 15 (2), pp. 225–60.

Laytner, Anson (1990) *Arguing with God: A Jewish Tradition* (Northvale, NJ: J. Aronson).

Le Strange, Nicholas (1974) *Merry Passages and Jeasts: A Manuscript Jestbook*, Salzburg Studies in English Literature, Elizabethan and Renaissance Studies, 29, ed. Henry Frederick Lippincott (Salzburg: Institut für englische Sprache und Literatur, Universität Salzburg).

Leask, Nigel (1992) 'Shelley's "Magnetic Ladies": Romantic Mesmerism and the Politics of the Body', in *Beyond Romanticism: New Approaches to Texts and Contexts, 1780–1832*, ed. John C. Whale and Stephen Copley (London: Routledge), pp. 53–78.

Lee, W.R. (1977) 'Bastardy and the Socioeconomic Structure of South Germany', in *Journal of Interdisciplinary History* 7 (3), pp. 403–25.

LeGates, Marlene (1976) 'The Cult of Womanhood in Eighteenth-Century Thought', in *Eighteenth-Century Studies* 10 (1), pp. 21–39.

LeGates, Marlene (2001) *In Their Time: A History of Feminism in Western Society* (New York: Routledge).

Leib, Glickl bas Judah (1962) *The Life of Glückel of Hameln, 1646–1724 Written by Herself*, trans. Beth-Zion Abrahams (London: East and West Library).

Lemire, Beverly (1988) 'Consumerism in Pre-Industrial and Early Industrial England: The Trade in Second Hand Clothes', in *Journal of British Studies* 27 (1), pp. 1–24.

Lemire, Beverly (1998) 'Petty Pawns and Informal Lending: Gender and the Transformation of Small-Scale Credit in England, circa 1600–1800', in *From Family Firms to Corporate Capitalism: Essays in Business and Industrial History in Honour of Peter Mathias*, ed. Kristine Bruland and Patrick O'Brien (Oxford: Clarendon Press), pp. 112–38.

Lemire, Beverly (2005) *The Business of Everyday Life: Gender, Practice and Social Politics in England, c. 1600–1900* (Manchester: Manchester University Press).

Lemire, Beverly, Ruth Pearson and Gail Grace Campbell, eds (2002) *Women and Credit: Researching the Past, Refiguring the Future* (Oxford: Berg).

Leneman, Leah (1998) *Alienated Affections: The Scottish Experience of Divorce and Separation, 1684–1830* (Edinburgh: Edinburgh University Press).

Leneman, Leah and Rosalind Mitchison (1988) 'Girls in Trouble: The Social and Geographical Setting of Illegitimacy in Early Modern Scotland', in *Journal of Social History* 21 (3), pp. 483–97.

Leporin, Dorothea Christiana (1742) *Gründliche Untersuchung der Ursachen, die das weibliche Geschlecht vom Studiren abhalten. Darin deren Unerheblichkeit gezeiget, und wie möglich, nöthig und nützlich es sey dass dieses Geschlecht der Gelahrheit sich befleisse, umständlich dargeleget wird . . . Nebst einer Vorrede* (Berlin: Johann Andreas Rüdiger).

Letzter, Jacqueline and Robert Adelson (2001) *Women Writing Opera: Creativity and Controversy in the Age of the French Revolution*, Studies on the History of Society and Culture, 43 (Berkeley: University of California Press).

Levack, Brian P. (1995) *The Witch-Hunt in Early Modern Europe*, 2nd edn (London: Longman).

Levene, Alysa (2005) 'The Estimation of Mortality at the London Foundling Hospital, 1741–99', in *Population Studies* 59 (1), pp. 87–97.

Levin, Eve (1993) 'Dvoeverie and Popular Religion', in *Seeking God: The Recovery of Religious Identity in Orthodox Russia, Ukraine, and Georgia*, ed. Stephen K. Batalden (DeKalb: Northern Illinois University Press), pp. 31–52.

Levine, Baruch A. (1968) 'Mulugu/Melûg: The Origins of a Talmudic Legal Institution', in *Journal of the American Oriental Society* 88 (2), pp. 271–85.

Levy, Allison M., ed. (2003) *Widowhood and Visual Culture in Early Modern Europe* (Aldershot: Ashgate).

Levy, Avigdor, ed. (2002) *Jews, Turks, Ottomans: A Shared History, Fifteenth through the Twentieth Century* (Syracuse, NY: Syracuse University Press).

Levy, Darline Gay, Harriet Branson Applewhite and Mary Durham Johnson, eds (1979) *Women in Revolutionary Paris 1789–1795: Selected Documents* (Urbana: University of Illinois Press).

Lewin, Linda (1992) 'Natural and Spurious Children in Brazilian Inheritance Law from Colony to Empire: A Methodological Essay', in *The Americas* 48 (3), pp. 351–96.

Lewis, Bernard (1990) *Race and Slavery in the Middle East: An Historical Inquiry* (New York: Oxford University Press).

Lewis, Elizabeth Franklin (2004) *Women Writers in the Spanish Enlightenment: The Pursuit of Happiness* (Aldershot: Ashgate).

Lewis, Reina (2004) *Rethinking Orientalism: Women, Travel, and the Ottoman Harem* (Rutgers, NJ: Rutgers University Press).

Lifchez, Raymond, ed. (1992a) *The Dervish Lodge: Architecture, Art, and Sufism in Ottoman Turkey*, Comparative Studies on Muslim Societies, 10 (Berkeley: University of California Press).

Lifchez, Raymond (1992b) 'The Lodges of Istanbul', in *The Dervish Lodge: Architecture, Art, and Sufism in Ottoman Turkey*, ed. Raymond Lifchez (Berkeley: University of California Press), pp. 73–129.

Lin, Patricia Y.C.E. (2000) 'Citizenship, Military Families, and the Creation of a New Definition of "Deserving Poor" in Britain, 1793–1815', in *Social Politics: International Studies in Gender, State and Society* 7 (1), pp. 5–46.

Lindberg, Anna Lena (1998) 'Through the Needle's Eye: Embroidered Pictures on the Threshold of Modernity', in *Eighteenth-Century Studies* 31 (4), pp. 503–10.

Lindegren, Jan (2001) 'Men, Money and Means', in *War and Competition between States*, ed. Philippe Contamine (New York: Oxford University Press), pp. 129–62.

Lindemann, Mary (1996) *Health and Healing in Eighteenth-Century Germany* (Baltimore, MD: Johns Hopkins University Press).

Lindenmeyr, Adele (1996) *Poverty Is Not a Vice: Charity, Society and the State in Imperial Russia* (Princeton, NJ: Princeton University Press).

Lindkvist, Julia and Barbro Werkmäster (1998) *Kvinnor i naturalhistorien: från 1600-talets samlare och illustratörer till modern vetenskap: utställning på Observatoriemuseet, Stockholm* (Women in Natural History: from seventeenth-century collectors and illustrators to modern science: exhibition at the Observatory Museum) Bidrag till Kungl. Vetenskapsakademiens historia, 27 (Stockholm: Kungl. Vetenskapsakademien).

The Linwood Gallery: Pictures in Needle-Work with a Biographical Sketch of the Painter (early 19th century) (London).

Lister, Anne (1989) *I Know My Own Heart: The Diaries of Anne Lister*, ed. Helena Whitbread (New York: New York University Press).

Lister, Anne (1992) *No Priest but Love: Excerpts from the Diaries of Anne Lister, 1824–1826*, ed. Helena Whitbread (Otley: Smith Settle).

Livi-Bacci, Massimo (1968) 'Fertility and Nuptiality Changes in Spain from the Late 18th to the Early 20th Century: Part 2', in *Population Studies* 22 (2), pp. 211–34.

Livi-Bacci, Massimo (1986) 'Social-Group Forerunners of Fertility Control in Europe', in *The Decline of Fertility in Europe: The Revised Proceedings of a Conference on the Princeton European Fertility Project*, ed. Ansley J. Coale and Susan Cotts Watkins (Princeton, NJ: Princeton University Press), pp. 182–200.

Livi-Bacci, Massimo (2007) *A Concise History of World Population*, 4th edn (Malden, MA: Blackwell).

Lloyd, Sarah (2002) 'Pleasing Spectacles and Elegant Dinners: Conviviality, Benevolence, and Charity Anniversaries in Eighteenth-Century London', in *Journal of British Studies* 41 (1), pp. 23–57.

Lokken, Paul (2001) 'Marriage as Slave Emancipation in Seventeenth-Century Rural Guatemala', in *The Americas* 58 (2), pp. 175–200.

Lonsdale, Roger (1989) *Eighteenth-Century Women Poets: An Oxford Anthology* (Oxford: Oxford University Press).

Lopes, Maria Antónia (1989) *Mulheres, espaço e sociabilidade: A transformação dos papéis femininos em Portugal à luz de fontes literárias (segunda metade do século XVIII)* (Lisbon: Livros Horizonte).

Lopez, Pilar Ramos (2000) 'Walpurgis, Maria Antonia. Baroque Women VIII', in *Goldberg Magazine* 10, online at: http://www.goldberg-magazine.com/en/magazine/composers/2000/03/248.php, accessed 1 April 2006.

Lorence-Kot, Bogna (1985) *Childrearing and Reform. A Study of the Nobility in Eighteenth-Century Poland* (Westport, CT: Greenwood Press).

Loudon, Irvine (1992) *Death in Childbirth: An International Study of Maternal Care and Maternal Mortality 1800–1950* (Oxford: Clarendon Press).

Lövkrona, Inger (2002) 'Gender, Power and Honour: Child Murder in Premodern Sweden', in *Ethnologia europaea* 32 (1), pp. 5–14.

Lowe, Roger (1938) *The Diary of Roger Lowe, of Ashton-in-Makerfield, Lancashire, 1663–74*, ed. William L. Sachse (New Haven, CT: Yale University Press).

Lowry, Heath (2003) *Ottoman Bursa in Travel Accounts* (Bloomington: Indiana University).

Lozanova, Galina (2001) 'Local Saints (Evliya) among Bulgarian Pomaks in the Rhodopes: Idea and Fable', in *Ethnology of Sufi Orders: Theory and Practice*, ed. Antonina Zhelyazkova and Jorgen Nielsen (Sofia, Bulgaria: IMIR), pp. 470–89.

Luria, Keith P. (2001) 'Belief and Popular Religion', in *Encyclopedia of European Social History from 1350 to 2000*, ed. Peter N. Stearns, 6 vols (New York: Charles Scribner), vol. V, pp. 249–61.

Lynch, Katherine A. (2000) 'Infant Mortality, Child Neglect, and Child Abandonment in European History: A Comparative Analysis', in *Population and Economy: From Hunger to Modern Economic Growth*, ed. Tommy Bengtsson and Osamu Saito (Oxford: Oxford University Press), pp. 133–64.

MacDonald, Michael (1981) *Mystical Bedlam: Madness, Anxiety and Healing in Seventeenth-Century England* (Cambridge: Cambridge University Press).

Macintyre, Kate (2002) 'Famine and the Female Mortality Advantage', in *Famine Demography: Perspectives from the Past and Present*, ed. Tim Dyson and Cormac Ó Gráda (Oxford: Oxford University Press), pp. 240–59.

Mack, Phyllis (1992) *Visionary Women: Ecstatic Prophecy in Seventeenth-Century England* (Los Angeles: University of California Press).

MacKay, Lynn (1999) 'Why They Stole: Women in the Old Bailey, 1779–1789', in *Journal of Social History* 32 (3), pp. 623–39.

Macknight, Elizabeth C. (2007) 'Why Weren't They Feminists? Parisian Noble Women and the Campaigns for Women's Rights in France, 1880–1914', in *European Journal of Women's Studies* 14 (2), pp. 127–40.

Maclean, Ian (1977) *Woman Triumphant: Feminism in French Literature, 1610–1652* (Oxford: Clarendon Press).

Magrini, Tullia, ed. (2003) *Music and Gender: Perspectives from the Mediterranean* (Chicago: University of Chicago Press).

Mahmood, Saba (2005) *Politics of Piety: The Islamic Revival and the Feminist Subject* (Princeton, NJ: Princeton University Press).

Maksudyan, Nazan (2008) 'Foster Child or Servant, Charity or Abuse: *Beslemes* in the Late Ottoman Empire', in *Journal of Historical Sociology* 21 (4), pp. 488–512.

Maloney, Clarence, ed. (1976) *The Evil Eye* (New York: Columbia University Press).

Marcus, Abraham (1989) *The Middle East on the Eve of Modernity: Aleppo in the Eighteenth Century* (New York: Columbia University Press).

Marcus, Abraham (1990) 'Poverty and Poor Relief in Eighteenth-Century Aleppo', in *Revue du monde musulman et de la Méditeranée* 55/56, pp. 171–9.

Marienberg, Evyatar (2003) 'A Mystery on the Tombstones: "Women's Commandments" in Early-Modern Ashkenazi Culture', in *Women in Judaism: A Multidisciplinary Journal* 3 (2), pp. 1–18, online at: http://www.utoronto.ca/wjudaism/journal/vol3n2/Rosenwiller.pdf, accessed 23 June 2007.

Markau, Kornelia Steffi Gabriele (2006) 'Dorothea Christiana Erxleben (1715–1762): Die erste promovierte Ärztin Deutschlands. Eine Analyse ihrer lateinischen Promotionsschrift sowie der ersten deutschen Übersetzung' (Dr. Med. thesis, Department of Faculty of Medicine, Martin Luther University, Halle-Wittenberg).

Marker, Gary (2000) 'The Enlightenment of Anna Labzina: Gender, Faith, and Public Life in Catherinian and Alexandrian Russia', in *Slavic Review* 59 (2), pp. 369–90.

Marland, Hilary and Anne Marie Rafferty, eds (1997) *Midwives, Society, and Childbirth: Debates and Controversies in the Modern Period* (London: Routledge).

Marland, Hilary, ed. (1993) *The Art of Midwifery: Early Modern Midwives in Europe* (London: Routledge).

Marrese, Michelle Lamarche (2002) *A Woman's Kingdom: Noblewomen and the Control of Property in Russia, 1700–1861* (Ithaca, NY: Cornell University Press).

Marx, Karl (2005) *The Eighteenth Brumaire of Louis Bonaparte* (New York: Mondial).

Mathias, Peter, Kristine Bruland and Patrick Karl O'Brien (1998) *From Family Firms to Corporate Capitalism: Essays in Business and Industrial History in Honour of Peter Mathias* (Oxford: Clarendon Press and Oxford University Press).

Mattson, Ingrid (2008) *The Story of the Qur'an: Its History and Place in Muslim Life* (Malden, MA: Blackwell).

Maza, Sarah (1989) 'Domestic Melodrama as Political Ideology: The Case of the Comte de Sanois', in *American Historical Review* 94 (5), pp. 1249–64.

Mazarin, Hortense Mancini and Maria Mancini (2008) *Memoirs: Hortense Mancini and Marie Mancini*, trans. Sarah Nelson (Chicago: University of Chicago Press).

Mazzotti, Massimo (2001) 'Maria Gaetana Agnesi: Mathematics and the Making of the Catholic Enlightenment', in *Isis* 92 (4), pp. 657–83.

McAlister, Lyle N. (1984) *Spain and Portugal in the New World, 1492–1700*, Europe and the World in the Age of Expansion, 3 (Minneapolis: University of Minnesota Press).

McCants, Anne E.C. (1997) *Civic Charity in a Golden Age: Orphan Care in Early Modern Amsterdam* (Urbana: University of Illinois Press).

McCarthy, Justin (1979) 'Age, Family and Migration in Nineteenth Century Black Sea Provinces of the Ottoman Empire', in *International Journal of Middle East Studies* 10 (3), pp. 309–23.

McLeod, Norma and Marcia Herndon (1975) 'The *Bormliza*: Maltese Folksong Style and Women', in *Journal of American Folk-lore* 88 (347), pp. 81–100.

McNeill, John Robert (1992) *The Mountains of the Mediterranean World: An Environmental History* (Cambridge: Cambridge University Press).

Meehan, Brenda (1998) *Holy Women in Russia: The Lives of Five Orthodox Women Offer Spiritual Guidance for Today* (San Francisco: Harper).

Meehan-Waters, Brenda (1975) 'Catherine the Great and the Problem of Female Rule', in *Russian Review* 34 (3), pp. 293–307.

Meer, Jan van der (1989) 'The Persecutions of Sodomites in Eighteenth-Century Amsterdam: Changing Perceptions of Sodomy', in *The Pursuit of Sodomy: Male Homosexuality in Renaissance and Enlightenment Europe*, ed. Kent Gerard and Gert Hekma (New York: Harrington Park Press), pp. 263–310.

Meer, Jan Ij. van der (2002) *Literary Activities and Attitudes in the Stanislavian Age in Poland (1764–1795)*, Studies in Slavic Literature and Poetics, 36 (Amsterdam: Rodopi).

Meldrum, Tim (2000) *Domestic Service and Gender, 1660–1750: Life and Work in the London Household* (London: Longman).

Merians, Linda Evi (1996) *The Secret Malady: Venereal Disease in Eighteenth-Century Britain and France* (Lexington: University Press of Kentucky).

Meriwether, Margaret L. (1996) 'The Rights of Children and the Responsibilities of Women: Women as *Wasis* in Ottoman Aleppo, 1770–1840', in *Women, the Family, and Divorce Laws in Islamic History*, ed. Amira El-Azhary Sonbol (Syracuse, NY: Syracuse University Press), pp. 219–35.

Meriwether, Margaret L. (1997) 'Women and the *Waqf* revisited: The case of Aleppo, 1770–1840', in *Women in the Ottoman Empire: Middle Eastern Women in the Modern Era*, ed. Madeline C. Zilfi (Leiden: Brill), pp. 128–52.

Mernissi, Fatima (1991) *The Veil and the Male Elite: A Feminist Interpretation of Women's Rights in Islam* (Reading, MA: Addison-Wesley).

Merrick, Jeffrey (1999) 'Sodomitical Scandals and Subcultures in the 1720s', in *Men and Masculinities* 1 (1), pp. 373–92.

Messbarger, Rebecca Marie (2002) *The Century of Women: Representations of Women in Eighteenth-Century Italian Public Discourse* (Toronto, ON: University of Toronto Press).

Mezger, Fritz (1948) 'The Origin of a Specific Rule on Adultery in the Germanic Laws', in *Journal of the American Oriental Society* 68 (3), pp. 145–8.

Michel, Sonya and Seth Koven (1990) 'Womanly Duties: Maternalist Politics and the Origins of Welfare States in France, Germany, Great Britain, and the United States, 1880–1920', in *American Historical Review* 95 (4), pp. 1076–108.

Michels, Georg (1995) 'Muscovite Elite Women and Old Belief', in *Harvard Ukrainian Studies* 19 (2), pp. 428–50.

Midgley, Clare (1992) *Women Against Slavery: The British Campaigns, 1780–1870* (London: Routledge).

Midgley, Clare (2007) *Feminism and Empire: Women Activists in Imperial Britain, 1790–1865* (New York: Routledge).

Millennium Project Task Force 4 on Child Health and Maternal Health (2004) *Interim Report*, ed. Mushtaque Chowdhury and Allan Rosenfield (New York: Millennium Project of the UN Secretary General and Supported by the UN Development Group).

Minkov, Anton (2004) *Conversion to Islam in the Balkans: Kisve Bahası Petitions and Ottoman Social Life, 1670–1730* (Leiden: Brill).

Mintz, Sidney Wilfred (1986) *Sweetness and Power: The Place of Sugar in Modern History* (New York: Penguin Books).

Moch, Leslie Page (2001) 'Migration', in *Encyclopedia of European Social History from 1350 to 2000*, ed. Peter N. Stearns (New York: Charles Scribner), vol. II, pp. 133–44.

Momsen, Janet Henshall, ed. (1999) *Gender, Migration, and Domestic Service* (London: Routledge).

Monahan, W. Gregory (1990) 'Popular Violence and the Problem of Public Order in the Old Regime: The Case of Lyon in 1709', in *Consortium on Revolutionary Europe 1750–1850: Proceedings* 20, pp. 653–60.

Montagu, Mary Wortley (1965) *The Complete Letters of Lady Mary Wortley Montagu*, ed. Robert Halsband, 3 vols (Oxford: Clarendon Press).

Monter, E. William (1980) 'Women in Calvinist Geneva (1550–1800)', in *Signs: Journal of Women in Culture and Society* 6 (2), pp. 189–209.

Moring, Beatrice (1998) 'Motherhood, Milk, and Money. Infant Mortality in Pre-Industrial Finland', in *Social History of Medicine* 11 (2), pp. 177–96.

Morrow, Diane Batts (2002) *Persons of Color and Religious at the Same Time: The Oblate Sisters of Providence, 1828–1860* (Chapel Hill: University of North Carolina Press).

Mortimer, Margaret (1702) *The Case of Margaret Mortimer, Widow, and Seventeen More Sufferers by a Dreadful Fire, Which Happened in Derby Court, Westminster, the 16th of April, 1697 Humbly Submitted to the Honourable the House of Commons* (London).

Mosely, Philip E., Robert Francis Byrnes and Leonard Bertram Schapiro, eds (1976) *Communal Families in the Balkans: The Zadruga: Essays by Philip E. Mosely and Essays in His Honor* (Notre Dame, IN: University of Notre Dame Press).

Moses, Claire G. (1982) 'Saint-Simonian Men/Saint-Simonian Women: The Transformation of Feminist Thought in 1830s France', in *Journal of Modern History* 54 (2, Special Issue on Sex, Science, and Society in Modern France), pp. 240–67.

Mott, Maria Lucia de Barros (1989) 'Ser mãe: A escrava em face do aborto de do infanticido', in *Revista de historia [Brazil]* 120, pp. 85–96.

Mowry, Melissa M. (2004) *The Bawdy Politic in Stuart England, 1660–1714: Political Pornography and Prostitution* (Aldershot: Ashgate).

Mücke, Dorothea von (2000) 'Experience, Impartiality, and Authenticity in Confessional Discourse', in *New German Critique* 79 (Special Issue on Eighteenth-Century Literature and Thought), pp. 5–35.

Mui, Hoh-cheung and Lorna H. Mui (1989) *Shops and Shopkeeping in Eighteenth Century England* (Kingston, ON: McGill-Queen's University Press; Routledge).

Muldrew, Craig (1998) *The Economy of Obligation: The Culture of Credit and Social Relations in Early Modern England* (Basingstoke: Macmillan).

Murray, Judith Sargent (1995) *Selected Writings of Judith Sargent Murray*, ed. Sharon M. Harris (New York: Oxford University Press).

Murray, Stephen O. (1997) 'Woman-Woman Love in Islamic Societies', in *Islamic Homosexualities: Culture, History, and Literature, with Additional Contributions by Eric Allyn . . . [et al.]*, ed. Stephen O. Murray and Will Roscoe (New York: New York University Press), pp. 97–104.

Myrone, Martin (2004) 'Linwood, Mary (1755–1845)', in *Oxford Dictionary of National Biography*, ed. H.C.G. Matthew and Brian Harrison (Oxford: Oxford University Press), online edn, ed. Lawrence Goldman, January 2008, http://www.oxforddnb.com, accessed 20 March 2008.

Nadelhaft, Jerome (1966) 'The Somersett Case and Slavery: Myth, Reality, and Repercussions', in *Journal of Negro History* 51 (3), pp. 193–208.

Naess, Hans Eyvind (1990) 'Norway: The Criminological Context', in *Early Modern Witchcraft: Centres and Peripheries*, ed. Bengt Ankarloo and Gustav Henningsen (Oxford: Clarendon Press), pp. 367–82.

Nicholas, Stephen and Deborah Oxley (1993) 'The Living Standards of Women During the Industrial Revolution, 1795–1820', in *Economic History Review* 46 (4), pp. 723–49.

Nielsen, Marita Akhoj (2004) 'Leonora Christina Ulfeldt (8 July 1621–16 March 1698)', in *Danish Writers from the Reformation to Decadence, 1550–1900*, ed. Marianne Stecher-Hansen (Detroit, MI: Gale), pp. 460–70.

Noble, Anthony (2004) 'Gambarini, Elizabeth (1730–1765)', in *Oxford Dictionary of National Biography*, ed. H.C.G. Matthew and Brian Harrison (Oxford: Oxford University Press), online edn, ed. Lawrence Goldman, January 2008, http://www.oxforddnb.com, accessed 13 February 2008.

Noé, Gunther (1986) '"Amazonen" in der österreichischen Geschichte', in *Österreich in Geschichte und Literatur* 30 (6), pp. 350–61.

Noether, Emiliana P. and Frank J. Coppa (1989) 'Eleonora de Fonseca Pimentel and the Neapolitan Revolution of 1799', in *Consortium on Revolutionary Europe 1750–1850: Proceedings* 19 (1), pp. 76–88.

Nordenflycht, Hedvig Charlotta (1924–1938) *Samlade Skrifter*, Svenska författare, 11, ed. Hilma Johanna Ulrika Borelius and Anders Theodor Hjelmqvist, 3 vols (Stockholm: Albert Bonniers Förlag).

Norton, Mary Beth (1996) *Liberty's Daughters: The Revolutionary Experience of American Women, 1750–1800* (Ithaca, NY: Cornell University Press).

Ó Gráda, Cormac (1989) *The Great Irish Famine* (Dublin: Gill and Macmillan).

Ó Gráda, Cormac (2004) *Ireland's Great Famine: An Overview*, Working Paper Series, Wp04/25 (Dublin: University College Dublin, Centre for Economic Research).

O'Dowd, Mary and Margaret MacCurtain, eds (1991) *Women in Early Modern Ireland* (Edinburgh: Edinburgh University Press).

Offen, Karen M. (2000) *European Feminisms, 1700–1950: A Political History* (Stanford, CA: Stanford University Press).

Ogilvie, Sheilagh C. (2001) 'The Economic World of the Bohemian Serf: Economic Concepts, Preferences, and Constraints on the Estate of Friedland, 1583–1692', in *Economic History Review* 54 (3), pp. 430–53.

Ogilvie, Sheilagh C. (2003) *A Bitter Living: Women, Markets, and Social Capital in Early Modern Germany* (Oxford: Oxford University Press).

Ogilvie, Sheilagh C. (2004) 'How Does Social Capital Affect Women? Guilds and Communities in Early Modern Germany', in *American Historical Review* 109 (2), pp. 325–59.

Ogilvie, Sheilagh C. and Jeremy Edwards (2000) 'Women and the "Second Serfdom": Evidence from Early Modern Bohemia', in *Journal of Economic History* 60 (4), pp. 961–94.

Ogilvie, Sheilagh C. and Markus Cerman, eds (1996) *European Proto-Industrialization* (Cambridge: Cambridge University Press).

Old Bailey Proceedings Online (2008) (http://www.oldbaileyonline.org, accessed 1 July 2008).

Orr, Clarissa Campbell, ed. (2004) *Queenship in Europe, 1660–1815: The Role of the Consort* (Cambridge: Cambridge University Press).

Ortiz, Teresa (1993) 'From Hegemony to Subordination: Midwives in Early Modern Spain', in *The Art of Midwifery: Early Modern Midwives in Europe*, ed. Hilary Marland (London: Routledge), pp. 95–114.

Os, Nicole A.N.M. van (1999) 'Taking Care of Soldiers' Families: The Ottoman State and the *Muinsiz Aile Maaşı*', in *Arming the State: Military Conscription in the Middle East and Central Asia, 1775–1925*, ed. Erik J. Zürcher (London: I.B. Tauris), pp. 95–100.

Outhwaite, R.B. (1999) '"Objects of Charity": Petitions to the London Foundling Hospital, 1768–72', in *Eighteenth-Century Studies* 32 (4), pp. 497–510.

Özgüven, Burcu (2001) 'A Market Place in the Ottoman Empire: Avrat Pazari and Its Surroundings', in *Kadin/Woman 2000* 2 (2), pp. 67–86.

Öztürkman, Arzu (2002) 'From Constantinople to Istanbul: Two Source on the Historical Folklore of a City', in *Asian Folklore Studies* 61 (2), pp. 271–94.

Paert, Irina (2003) *Old Believers: Religious Dissent and Gender in Russia, 1760–1850* (Manchester: Manchester University Press).

Paert, Irina (2004) 'Regulating Old Believer Marriage: Ritual, Legality, and Conversion in Nicholas I's Russia', in *Slavic Review* 63 (3), pp. 555–76.

Palairet, Michael (1997) *The Balkan Economies c. 1800–1914: Evolution without Development*, Cambridge Studies in Modern Economic History, 6 (Cambridge: Cambridge University Press).

Palazzi, Maura (1990) 'Female Solitude and Patrilineage: Unmarried Women and Widows During the Eighteenth and Nineteenth Centuries', in *Journal of Family History* 15 (1), pp. 443–59.

Palazzi, Maura (1997) *Donne sole: storie dell'altra faccia dell'Italia tra antico regime e società contemporanea* (Milan: B. Mondadori).

Panizza, Letizia and Sharon Wood, eds (2000) *A History of Women's Writing in Italy* (Cambridge: Cambridge University Press).

Panter-Brick, Catherine and Malcolm T. Smith, eds (2000) *Abandoned Children* (Cambridge: Cambridge University Press).

Panzac, Daniel, ed. (1995) *Histoire économique et sociale de l'Empire Ottoman et de la Turquie (1326–1960): Actes du sixième congrés international tenu à Aix-en-Provence du 1er au 4 juillet 1992*, Collection turcica, 8 (Paris: Peeters).

Pardoe, Julia S. (1838) *The City of the Sultan; and Domestic Manners of the Turks in 1836*, 3 vols (London: Henry Colburn).

Parkes, Peter (2004) 'Milk Kinship in Southeast Europe. Alternative Social Structures and Foster Relations in the Caucasus and the Balkans', in *Social Anthropology* 12 (3), pp. 341–58.

Parush, Iris and Ann Brene (1995) 'The Politics of Literacy: Women and Foreign Languages in Jewish Society of 19th-Century Eastern Europe', in *Modern Judaism* 15 (2), pp. 183–206.

Paton, Diana (2001) 'Punishment, Crime, and the Bodies of Slaves in Eighteenth-Century Jamaica', in *Journal of Social History* 34 (4), pp. 923–54.

Patterson, Orlando (1982) *Slavery and Social Death: A Comparative Study* (Cambridge, MA: Harvard University Press).

Peabody, Sue (1994) 'Colonialism's Challenge to French and English Marriage and Citizenship Law: The Case of Mary Anne Raworth', in *Eighteenth-Century Life* 18, pp. 64–91.

Peabody, Sue (1996) *There Are No Slaves in France: The Political Culture of Race and Slavery in the Ancien Régime* (New York: Oxford University Press).

Peabody, Sue (2005) 'Négresse, Mulâtresse, Citoyenne: Gender and Emancipation in the French Caribbean, 1650/1848', in *Gender and Slave Emancipation in the Atlantic World*, ed. Pamela Scully and Diana Paton (Durham, NC: Duke University Press), pp. 56–78.

Peirce, Leslie Penn (1993) *The Imperial Harem: Women and Sovereignty in the Ottoman Empire* (New York: Oxford University Press).

Peirce, Leslie Penn (2003) *Morality Tales: Law and Gender in the Ottoman Court of Aintab* (Berkeley: University of California Press).

Peirce, Leslie Penn (2007) 'The Material World: Ideologies and Ordinary Things', in *The Early Modern Ottomans: Remapping the Empire*, ed. Virginia H. Aksan and Daniel Goffman (Cambridge: Cambridge University Press), pp. 213–32.

Penny, N.B. (1975) 'English Church Monuments to Women Who Died in Childbed between 1780 and 1835', in *Journal of the Warburg and Courtauld Institutes* 38, pp. 314–32.

Pérez, Janet and Maureen Ihrie, eds (2002) *The Feminist Encyclopedia of Spanish Literature* (Westport, CT: Greenwood Press).

Peri, Oded (1992) '*Waqf* and Ottoman Welfare Policy. The Poor Kitchen of Hasseki Sultan in Eighteenth-Century Jerusalem', in *Journal of the Economic and Social History of the Orient* 35 (2), pp. 167–86.

Peter, Fabienne (2005) 'Gender and the Foundations of Social Choice: the Role of Situated Agency', in *Amartya Sen's Work and Ideas: A Gender Perspective*, Bina Agarwal, Jane Humphries and Ingrid Robeyns, eds (New York: Routledge).

Peters, Rudolph (2005) *Crime and Punishment in Islamic Law: Theory and Practice from the Sixteenth to the Twenty-First Century* (Cambridge: Cambridge University Press).

Petersen, Johanna Eleonora (2005) *The Life of Lady Johanna Eleonora Petersen Written by Herself: Pietism and Women's Autobiography in Seventeenth-Century Germany*, ed. Barbara Becker-Cantarino (Chicago: University of Chicago Press).

Petrović, Ankica (1990) 'Women in the Music Creation Project in the Dinaric Cultural Zone of Yugoslavia', in *Music, Gender and Culture*, ed. Marcia Herdon and Susan Ziegler (Wilhelmshaven, Germany: Florian Noetzel Verlag), pp. 71–84.

Petschauer, Peter (1989) *The Education of Women in Eighteenth-Century Germany: New Directions from the German Female Perspective, Bending the Ivy*, Studies in German Thought and History, 9 (Lewiston, NY: Edwin Mellen Press).

Pettan, Svanibor (2003) 'Male, Female, and Beyond in the Culture and Music of Roma in Kosovo', in *Music and Gender: Perspectives from the Mediterranean*, ed. Tullia Magrini (Chicago: University of Chicago Press), pp. 287–305.

Phillips, Roderick (1980) *Family Breakdown in Late Eighteenth-Century France: Divorces in Rouen 1792–1803* (Oxford: Clarendon).

Phillips, Roderick (1988) *Putting Asunder: A History of Divorce in Western Society* (Cambridge: Cambridge University Press).

Pinchbeck, Ivy (1977) *Women Workers and the Industrial Revolution* (London: Frank Cass).

Pipelet de Leury, Constance Marie afterwards Princess Salm-Reifferscheid-Dyck (1800) *Rapport sur un ouvrage du c[itoy]e[n] Theremin, intitulé: De la condition des femmes dans une république . . . lu par l'auteur . . . 24 pluviose An 8, etc.* (Paris: Gille).

Plakans, Andrejs (1975) 'Seigneurial Authority and Peasant Family Life: The Baltic Area in the Eighteenth Century', in *Journal of Interdisciplinary History* 5 (4), pp. 629–54.

Pocket World in Figures, 2008 Edition (2007) (London: The Economist in association with Profile Books).

Pol, Lotte C. van de (1994) 'The Lure of the Big City. Female Migration to Amsterdam', in *Women of the Golden Age: An International Debate on Women in Seventeenth-Century Holland, England and Italy*, ed. Els Kloek, Nicole Teeuwen and Marijke Huisman (Hilversum: Verloren), pp. 73–81.

Pol, Lotte C. van de (1996) *Het Amsterdams hoerdom: prostitutie in de zeventiende en achttiende eeuw* (Amsterdam: Wereldbibliotheek).

Polasky, Janet L. (1986) 'Women in Revolutionary Belgium: From Stone Throwers to Hearth Tenders', in *History Workshop Journal* 21, pp. 87–104.

Polasky, Janet L. (1990) 'Women in Revolutionary Brussels: "The Source of Our Greatest Strength"', in *Women and Politics in the Age of the Democratic Revolution*, ed. Harriet B. Applewhite and Darline G. Levy (Ann Arbor: University of Michigan), pp. 147–62.

Pomeranz, Kenneth (2000) *The Great Divergence: China, Europe, and the Making of the Modern World Economy* (Princeton, NJ: Princeton University Press).

Poska, Allyson M. (1998) *Regulating the People: The Catholic Reformation in Seventeenth-Century Spain* (Leiden: Brill).

Poska, Allyson M. (2005) *Women and Authority in Early Modern Spain: The Peasants of Galicia* (Oxford: Oxford University Press).

Postma, Johannes (1990) *The Dutch in the Atlantic Slave Trade, 1600–1815* (Cambridge: Cambridge University Press).

Powitz, Dagmar (1995) 'Lebenswelten von Falschgeldhändlern und -händlerinnen in der ersten Hälfte des 18. Jahrhunderts: Eine Fallstudie' (M. Ed. Thesis, Department of University of Göttingen, Göttingen).

Prince, Mary (1997) *The History of Mary Prince: A West Indian Slave*, ed. Moira Ferguson, rev. edn (Ann Arbor: University of Michigan Press).

Prior, Mary (1990) 'Wives and Wills 1558–1700', in *English Rural Society, 1500–1800: Essays in Honour of Joan Thirsk*, ed. John Chartres, David Hey and Joan Thirsk (Cambridge: Cambridge University Press), pp. 201–25.

Pushkareva, Natalia (1997) *Women in Russian History from the Tenth to the Twentieth Century* (Armonk, NY: M.E. Sharpe).

Quataert, Donald (1991) 'Ottoman Women, Households and Textile Manufacturing, 1800–1914', in *Women in Middle Eastern History. Shifting Boundaries in Sex and Gender*, ed. Nikki Keddie and Beth Baron (New Haven, CT: Yale University Press), pp. 161–76.

Quataert, Jean (1985) 'The Shaping of Women's Work in Manufacturing, Guilds, Households and the State in Central Europe, 1648–1870', in *American Historical Review* 90 (5), pp. 1122–48.

Rabuzzi, Daniel A. (1995) 'Women as Merchants in Eighteenth-Century Northern Germany: The Case of Stralsund, 1750–1830', in *Central European History* 28 (4), pp. 435–56.

Radcliffe, Ann (1795) *A Journey Made in the Summer of 1794 through Holland and the Western Frontier of Germany with a Return Down the Rhine* (London: G.G. and J. Robinson).

Rafeq, Abdul-Karim (1990) 'Public Morality in 18th-century Ottoman Damascus', in *Revue du monde musulman et de la Méditeranée* 55/56 (Villes au Levant: Hommage à André Raymond), pp. 180–96.

Ragan, Bryant T. and Elizabeth A. Williams, eds (1992) *Re-Creating Authority in Revolutionary France* (New Brunswick, NJ: Rutgers University Press).

Ramos-González, Alicia (2005) 'Daughters of Tradition: Women in Yiddish Culture in the 16th–18th Centuries', in *European Journal of Women's Studies* 12 (2), pp. 213–26.

Ramsey, Matthew (1988) *Professional and Popular Medicine in France, 1770–1830: The Social World of Medical Practice* (Cambridge: Cambridge University Press).

Ransel, David L. (1988) *Mothers of Misery: Child Abandonment in Russia* (Princeton, NJ: Princeton University Press).

Ransel, David L. (1990) *Mothering, Medicine, and Infant Mortality in Russia*, Kennan Institute Occasional Papers, 236 (Washington, DC: Kennan Institute).

Rashid, Salim (1980) 'The Policy of Laissez-Faire During Scarcities', in *Economic Journal* 90 (359), pp. 493–503.

Raughter, Rosemary (2004) 'Nagle, Honora (1718–1784)', in *Oxford Dictionary of National Biography*, ed. H.C.G. Matthew and Brian Harrison (Oxford: Oxford University Press), online edn, ed. Lawrence Goldman, January 2008, http://www.oxforddnb.com, accessed 23 May 2008.

Razzell, Peter (2003) *The Conquest of Smallpox: The Impact of Inoculation on Smallpox Mortality in Eighteenth-Century Britain* (London: Caliban Books).

Reader, Nicola (2004) 'The Distribution of Female Friendly Societies across England in the Early Nineteenth Century', Economic History Society Annual Conference, 2–4 April (Royal Holloway: University of London).

Rebérioux, Madeleine and Paule-Marie Duhet, eds (1981) *1789 cahiers de doléances des femmes et autres textes* (Paris: Des Femmes/Antoinette Fouque).

Reher, David S. (1997) *Perspective on the Family in Spain, Past and Present* (Oxford: Clarendon Press).

Rey, Michael (1987) 'Parisian Homosexuals Create a Lifestyle, 1700–1750: The Police Archives', in *'Tis Nature's Fault: Unauthorized Sexuality During the Enlightenment*, ed. Robert Purks Maccubbin (New York: Cambridge University Press), pp. 179–91.

Reynolds, Glynis (1979) 'Infant Mortality and Sex Ratios at Baptism as Shown by Reconstruction of Willingham, a Parish at the End of the Fens in Cambridgeshire', in *Local Population Studies* 22, pp. 31–7.

Rice, John A. (2003) *Empress Marie Therese and Music at the Viennese Court, 1792–1807* (Cambridge: Cambridge University Press).

Richardson, Alan (2002) '"The Sorrows of Yamba," by Eaglesfield Smith and Hannah More: Authorship, Ideology, and the Fractures of Antislavery Discourse', in *Romanticism on the Net* 28, online at: http://www.erudit.org/revue/ron/2002/v/n28/007209ar.html, accessed 15 July 2007.

Richter, Jeffrey S. (1998) 'Infanticide, Child Abandonment, and Abortion in Imperial Germany', in *Journal of Interdisciplinary History* 28 (4), pp. 511–51.

Ritratti e vite di donne illustri che fiorirono dal secolo XI. sino al XVIII. (1775) (Venice: Coleti).

Rizzo, Betty (1994) *Companions without Vows: Relationships among Eighteenth-Century British Women* (Athens: University of Georgia Press).

Rizzo, Tracey (2004) 'Between Dishonor and Death: Infanticide in the Causes Célèbres of Eighteenth-Century France', in *Women's History Review* 13 (1), pp. 5–21.

Robbins, Horace H. and Francis Deak (1930) 'The Familial Property Rights of Illegitimate Children: A Comparative Study', in *Columbia Law Review* 30, pp. 308–29.

Robert, André (1933) *L'idée nationale autrichienne et les guerres de Napoléon: L'apostolat du Baron de Hromayr et le salon de Caroline Pichler* (Paris: Félix Alcan).

Robertson, John (1999) 'Enlightenment and Revolution: Naples 1799', in *Transactions of the Royal Historical Society* 6th Series, 10, pp. 17–44.

Robins, Joseph (1980) *The Lost Children: A Study of Charity Children in Ireland, 1700–1900* (Dublin: Institute of Public Administration).

Robinson, Mary (1994) *Perdita: The Memoirs of Mary Robinson*, ed. M.J. Levy (London: Peter Owen).

Robinson, Mary (2003 [orig. 1799]) *A Letter to the Women of England and the Natural Daughter*, ed. Sharon M. Setzer (Peterborough, ON: Broadview Press).

Rockstroh, K.C. (1932) *Norges forsvar 1717–1718*, Bidrag till det store nordiske krigs historie, 9 (Copenhagen: General Staff).

Rodríguez, Laura (1973) 'The Spanish Riots of 1766', in *Past & Present* (59), pp. 117–46.

Roessler, Shirley Elson (1998) *Out of the Shadows: Women and Politics in the French Revolution 1789–1795*, Studies in Modern European History, 14 (New York: Peter Lang).

Rogers, Katharine M. (1982) *Feminism in Eighteenth-Century England* (Urbana: University of Illinois Press).

Rogers, Nicholas (1991) 'Policing the Poor in Eighteenth-Century London: The Vagrancy Laws and their Administration', in *Histoire sociale/Social History* 24 (47), pp. 127–47.

Roggero, Marina (2001) 'L'alphabétisation en Italie: une conquête féminine?', in *Annales: histoire, sciences sociales* 56 (4–5), pp. 903–25.

Roland, Jeanne-Marie Phlipon (1990) *An Appeal to Impartial Posterity* (Oxford: Woodstock Books).

Romlid, Christina (1997) 'Swedish Midwives and Their Instruments in the Eighteenth and Nineteenth Centuries', in *Midwives, Society, and Childbirth: Debates and Controversies in the Modern Period*, ed. Hilary Marland and Anne Marie Rafferty (London: Routledge), pp. 38–60.

Roodenburg, Herman W. (1985) 'The Autobiography of Isabella de Moerloose: Sex, Child-rearing and Popular Belief in Seventeenth-Century Holland', in *Journal of Social History* 18 (4), pp. 517–40.

Roodenburg, Herman W. (1988) 'The Maternal Imagination. The Fears of Pregnant Women in Seventeenth-Century Holland', in *Journal of Social History* 21 (4), pp. 701–16.

Roosevelt, Priscilla R. (1995) *Life on the Russian Country Estate: A Social and Cultural History* (New Haven, CT: Yale University Press).

Roper, Lyndal (1994) *Oedipus and the Devil: Witchcraft, Sexuality, and Religion in Early Modern Europe* (London: Routledge).

Roper, Lyndal (2004) *Witch Craze: Terror and Fantasy in Baroque Germany* (New Haven, CT: Yale University Press).

Rosa, Maria de Lurdes (1995) *O morgadio em Portugal, sécs. XIV–XV: modelos e práticas comportamento linhagístico*, Histórias de Portugal, 16 (Lisbon: Editorial Estampa).

Roscoe, S. (1973) *John Newbery and His Successors, 1740–1814* (Wormley: Five Owls Press).

Rosman, Moshe (2002) 'A Prolegomenon to the Study of Jewish Cultural History', in *Jewish Studies: An Internet Journal* 1, pp. 109–27, online at: http://www.biu.ac.il/JS/JSIJ/, accessed 14 March 2007.

Rosman, Moshe (2005) 'The History of Jewish Women in Early Modern Poland', in *Polin: Studies in Polish Jewry* 18, pp. 25–56.

Rosslyn, Wendy and Alessandra Tosi, eds (2007) *Women in Russian Culture and Society, 1700–1825* (Basingstoke: Palgrave Macmillan).

Rothenberg, Gunther Erich, Béla K. Király and Peter F. Sugar, eds (1982) *East Central European Society and War in the Prerevolutionary Eighteenth Century*, East European Monographs, 122 (Boulder, CO: Social Science Monographs; distributed by Columbia University Press).

Rousseau, Jean-Jacques (2000) *Confessions*, ed. Patrick Coleman, trans. Angela Scholar (Oxford: Oxford University Press).

Roworth, Wendy Wassyng (2003) 'Ancient Matrons and Modern Patrons: Angelica Kauffman as a Classical History Painter', in *Women, Art and the Politics of Identity in Eighteenth-Century Europe*, ed. Melissa Lee Hyde and Jennifer Dawn Milam (Aldershot: Ashgate), pp. 188–210.

Rozman, Gilbert (1973) *Urban Networks in Ch'ing China and Tokugawa Japan* (Princeton, NJ: Princeton University Press).

Ruane, Christine (1995) 'Clothes Shopping in Imperial Russia: The Development of a Consumer Culture', in *Journal of Social History* 28 (4), pp. 765–82.

Rublack, Ulinka (1996) 'Pregnancy, Childbirth and the Female Body in Early Modern Germany', in *Past & Present* 150, pp. 84–110.

Rublack, Ulinka (1999) *The Crimes of Women in Early Modern Germany* (Oxford: Clarendon Press).

Ruggles, D. Fairchild, ed. (2000) *Women, Patronage and Self-Representation in Islamic Societies* (Albany: State University of New York Press).

Rusiecka, Regina Salomea (forthcoming) *The Conduct of My Life's Travels and Adventures*, trans. Wladyslaw Roczniak (Chicago: University of Chicago Press).

Russell, Alexander (1794) *The Natural History of Aleppo Containing a Description of the City, and the Principal Natural Productions in Its Neighbourhood*, ed. Pat Russell, 2 vols (London: G.G. and J. Robinson).

Russell, Rinaldina, ed. (1997) *The Feminist Encyclopedia of Italian Literature* (Westport, CT: Greenwood Press).

Russell-Wood, J.R. (2000) '"Acts of Grace": Portuguese Monarchs and Their Subjects of African Descent in Eighteenth-Century Brazil', in *Journal of Latin American Studies* 32 (2), pp. 307–32.

Sá, Isabel dos Guimarães (2000) 'Circulation of Children in Eighteenth-Century Portugal' in *Abandoned Children*, ed. Catherine Panter-Brick and Malcolm T. Smith (Cambridge: Cambridge University Press), pp. 27–40.

Sabean, David W. (1990) *Property, Production, and Family in Neckarhausen, 1700–1870*, Cambridge Studies in Social and Cultural Anthropology, 73 (Cambridge: Cambridge University Press).

Sadat, Deena R. (1972) 'Rumeli Ayanlari: The Eighteenth Century', in *Journal of Modern History* 44 (3), pp. 346–63.

Saint Cassia, Paul (1986) 'Religion, Politics and Ethnicity in Cyprus During the Turkocratia (1571–1878)', in *Archives européennes de sociologie* 27 (1), pp. 3–28.

Saito, Osamu (1979) 'Who Worked When: Life-Time Profiles of Labour Force Participation in Cardington and Corfe Castle in the Late Eighteenth and Mid-Nineteenth Centuries', in *Local Population Studies* 22, pp. 14–29.

Salve, Kristi (1997) 'Oh, My Pretty Hair: Belief, Tradition and Image', in *Folklore: Electronic Journal of Folklore* 3, pp. 36–59, online at: http://haldjas.folklore.ee/folklore/vol3/kris.htm, accessed 15 December 2005.

Sapurma, Kita and Pandora Petrovska (1997) *Children of the Bird Goddess: A Macedonian Autobiography* (Five Dock, NSW (Australia): Pollitecon Publications).

Sarasúa, Carmen (2001) 'Male and Female Temporary Migrants in Eighteenth- and Nineteenth-Century Spain', in *Women, Gender, and Labour Migration: Historical and Global Perspectives*, ed. Pamela Sharpe (London: Routledge), pp. 29–59.

Sarkar, Tanika and Urvashi Butalia, eds (1995) *Women and Right-Wing Movements: Indian Experiences* (London: Zed).

Sarti, Rafaella (1997) 'Notes on the Feminization of domestic service: Bologna as a case study, XVIIIth-XXth centuries', in *Le phénomène de la domesticité en Europe, XVIe–XXe siècles*, ed. Antoinette Fauve-Chamoux and Ludmilla Fialova (Prague: Ceska Demograficka Spolecnost), pp. 125–63.

Schaw, Janet (1921) *Journal of a Lady of Quality; Being the Narrative of a Journey from Scotland to the West Indies, North Carolina, and Portugal, in the Years 1774 to 1776*, ed. Evangeline Walker Andrews and Charles McLeon Andrews (New Haven, CT: Yale University Press and Oxford University Press).

Scheper-Hughes, Nancy (1992) *Death without Weeping: The Violence of Everyday Life in Brazil* (Berkeley: University of California Press).

Schick, Irvin Cemil (1998) 'The Women of Turkey as Sexual Personae: Images from Western Literature', in *Deconstructing Images of 'the Turkish Woman'*, ed. Zehra F. Arat (New York: St. Martin's Press), pp. 83–100.

Schick, Irvin Cemil (2007) 'Christian Maidens, Turkish Ravishers: The Sexualization of National Conflict in the Late Ottoman Period', in *Women in the Ottoman Balkans: Gender, Culture and History*, Library of Ottoman Studies, 15, ed. Amila Buturović and Irvin Cemil Schick (New York: I.B. Tauris), pp. 273–305.

Schiebinger, Londa (1986) 'Skeletons in the Closet: The First Illustrations of the Female Skeleton in Eighteenth-Century Anatomy', in *Representations* 14, pp. 42–82.

Schiebinger, Londa (1989) *The Mind Has No Sex? Women in the Origins of Modern Science* (Cambridge, MA: Harvard University Press).

Schiebinger, Londa (1993) *Nature's Body: Gender in the Making of Modern Science* (Boston: Beacon Press).

Schiebinger, Londa (2004) *Plants and Empire: Colonial Bioprospecting in the Atlantic World* (Cambridge, MA: Harvard University Press).

Schneider, Zoë A. (2000) 'Women Before the Bench: Female Litigants in Early Modern Normandy', in *French Historical Studies* 23 (1), pp. 2–32.

Schønau, Friederich Christian (1753) *Samling af danske lærde fruentimer, som ved deres lærdom, og udgivne eller efterladte skrifter have giort deres navne i den lærde verden bekiendte, med adskilllige mest historiske anmerkninger forøget*, 2 vols (Copenhagen: J.W. Bopp).

Schrader, Catharina (1987) *Mother and Child Were Saved: The Memoirs (1693–1740) of the Frisian Midwife Catharina Schrader*, Nieuwe nederlandse bijdragen tot de geschiedenis der geneeskunde en der natuurwetenschappen, 22, ed. Hilary Marland, M.J. van Lieburg and G.J. Kloosterman, trans. Hilary Marland (Amsterdam: Rodopi).

Schroder, Anne L. (1999) 'Going Public Against the Academy in 1784: Mme de Genlis Speaks out on Gender Bias', in *Eighteenth-Century Studies* 32 (3), pp. 376–82.

Schulte, Regina (1984) 'Infanticide in Rural Bavaria in the Nineteenth Century', in *Interest and Emotion: Essays on the Study of Family and Kinship*, ed. Hans Medick and David Warren Sabean (Cambridge: Cambridge University Press), pp. 77–102.

Schulte, Regina, ed. (2005) *The Body of the Queen: Gender and Rule in the Courtly World, 1500–2000* (New York: Berghahn Books).

Schumacher, John N (2002) 'Ignacia del Espiritu Santo: The Historical Reliability of her Principal Contemporary Biography', in *Philippine Studies* 50 (3), pp. 416–37.

Scott, H.M., ed. (1995) *The European Nobilities in the Seventeenth and Eighteenth Centuries*, 2 vols (London: Longman).

Scott, Joan Wallach (1988) *Gender and the Politics of History* (New York).

Scribner, Robert W. (1996) 'Elements of Popular Belief', in *Handbook of European History, 1400–1600: Late Middle Ages, Renaissance, and Reformation*, ed. Thomas A. Brady, Heiko Augustinus Oberman and James D. Tracy, 2 vols (Grand Rapids, MI: W.B. Eerdmans), vol. I, pp. 231–62.

Scully, Pamela and Diana Paton, eds (2005) *Gender and Slave Emancipation in the Atlantic World* (Durham, NC: Duke University Press).

Seifert, Lewis Carl (1996) *Fairy Tales, Sexuality, and Gender in France, 1690–1715: Nostalgic Utopias*, Cambridge Studies in French, 55 (Cambridge: Cambridge University Press).

Semerdjian, Elyse (2003) 'Sinful Professions: Illegal Occupations of Women in Ottoman Aleppo, Syria', in *Hawwa* 1 (1), pp. 60–85.

Sen, Amartya Kumar (1981) *Poverty and Famines: An Essay on Entitlement and Deprivation* (Oxford: Clarendon, 1982).

Seng, Yvonne (1998) 'Invisible Women: Residents of Early Sixteenth-Century Istanbul', in *Women in the Medieval Islamic World: Power, Patronage and Piety*, ed. Gavin R.G. Hambly (New York: St. Martin's Press), pp. 241–68.

Senior, Nancy (1983) 'Aspects of Infant Feeding in Eighteenth-Century France', in *Eighteenth-Century Studies* 16 (4), pp. 367–88.

Sharpe, Pamela (1990) 'Marital Separation in the Eighteenth and Early Nineteenth Centuries', in *Local Population Studies* 45, pp. 66–70.

Sharpe, Pamela (1991) 'Literally Spinsters: A New Interpretation of Local Economy and Demography in Colyton in the Seventeenth and Eighteenth Centuries', in *Economic History Review* 44 (1), pp. 46–65.

Sharpe, Pamela (1996) *Adapting to Capitalism: Working Women in the English Economy, 1700–1850* (New York: St. Martin's Press).

Sharpe, Pamela, ed. (2001) *Women, Gender, and Labour Migration: Historical and Global Perspectives*, Routledge Research in Gender and History, 5 (London: Routledge).

Shaw, Margaret Fay (1977) *Folksongs and Folk-Lore of South Uist* (London: Oxford University Press).

Shaw, Stanford J. (1991) *The Jews of the Ottoman Empire and the Turkish Republic* (New York: New York University Press).

Shea, Daniel B. (1990) 'Elizabeth Ashbridge and the Voice Within' (Introduction to 'Some Account of the Fore Part of the Life of Elizabeth Ashbridge'), in *Journeys in New Worlds: Early American Women's Narratives*, ed. William L. Andrews (Madison: University of Wisconsin Press), pp. 117–80.

Shefrin, Jill (2004) 'Newbery, Elizabeth (1745/6–1821, Bookseller and Publisher', in *Oxford Dictionary of National Biography*, ed. H.C.G. Matthew and Brian Harrison (Oxford: Oxford University Press), online edn, ed. Lawrence Goldman, January 2008, http://www.oxforddnb.com, accessed 9 July 2008.

Shefrin, Jill (2006) ' "Governesses to their Children": Royal and Aristocratic Mothers Educating Daughters in the Reign of George III', in *Childhood and Children's Books in Early Modern Europe, 1550–1800*, ed. Andrea Immel and Michael Witmore (London: Routledge), pp. 181–211.

Sheller, Mimi (1997) 'Sword-Bearing Citizens: Militarism and Manhood in Nineteenth-Century Haiti', in *Plantation Society in the Americas* 4 (2–3), pp. 233–78.

Shepard, Alexandra (2003) *Meanings of Manhood in Early Modern England* (Oxford: Oxford University Press).

Shevzov, Vera (1999) 'Miracle-Working Icons, Laity, and Authority in the Russian Orthodox Church', in *Russian Review* 58 (1), pp. 26–48.

Shoemaker, Robert Brink (2004) *The London Mob: Violence and Disorder in Eighteenth-Century England* (London: Hambledon and London).

Shteir, Ann B. (2004) 'Wakefield, Priscilla (1750–1832)', in *Oxford Dictionary of National Biography*, ed. H.C.G. Matthew and Brian Harrison (Oxford: Oxford University Press), online edn, ed. Lawrence Goldman, January 2008, http://www.oxforddnb.com, accessed 11 July 2008.

Sibbald, Robert (1709) *Provision for the Poor in Time of Dearth and Scarcity: Where There Is an Account of Such Food as May Be Easily Gotten When Corns Are Scarce, or Unfit for Use: And of Such Meats as May Be Used When the Ordinary Provisions Fail, or Are Very Dear* (Edinburgh: James Watson).

Siena, Kevin P. (2004) *Venereal Disease Hospitals and the Urban Poor: London's 'Foul Wards', 1600–1800* (Rochester, NY: University of Rochester Press).

Silverman, Carol (2003) 'The Gender of the Profession: Music, Dance, and Reputation among Balkan Muslim Rom Women', in *Music and Gender: Perspectives from the Mediterranean*, ed. Tullia Magrini (Chicago: University of Chicago Press), pp. 119–46.

Simonton, Deborah (1998) *A History of European Women's Work, 1700 to the Present* (London: Routledge).

Simonton, Deborah (2006) *The Routledge History of Women in Europe since 1700* (London: Routledge).

Simpson, Antony E. (1996) ' "The Mouth of Strange Women Is a Deep Pit": Male Guilt and Legal Attitudes toward Prostitution in Georgian London', in *Journal of Criminal Justice and Popular Culture* 4 (3), pp. 50–85, online at: http://www.scj.albany.edu:90/jcjpc, accessed 23 July 2007.

Sjögren, Åsa Karlsson and Peter Lindström (2004) 'Widows, Ownership and Political Culture: Sweden 1650–1800', in *Scandinavian Journal of History* 29 (3–4), pp. 241–62.

Skedd, Susan (1997) 'Women Teachers and the Expansion of Girls' Schooling in England c. 1760–1820', in *Gender in Eighteenth-Century England: Roles, Representations and Responsibilities*, ed. Hannah Barker and Elaine Chalus (London: Longman), pp. 101–25.

Skedd, Susan (2004) 'More, Hannah (1745–1833)', in *Oxford Dictionary of National Biography*, ed. H.C.G. Matthew and Brian Harrison (Oxford: Oxford University Press), online edn, ed. Lawrence Goldman, January 2008, http://www.oxforddnb.com, accessed 25 May 2008.

Skendi, Stavro (1976) 'Mosely on the Zadruga', in *Communal Families in the Balkans: The Zadruga; Essays by Philip E. Mosely and Essays in His Honor*, ed. Robert Byrnes (Notre Dame, IN: University of Notre Dame Press), pp. 14–17.

Slonik, Benjamin Aaron ben Abraham, Jacob ben Elhanan Heilbronn, Isaac ben Jacob 'The Levite' [sic] and Iseppo Venturin (1652) *Precetti da esser imparati dalle donne hebree = Mitsvot Nashim Melamdah, Hilkhot Nidah, Halah, Hadlakat Ha-Ner, Ve-Derekh Erets*, trans. Iacob B.M. Alpron (Venice: Gio. Imberti).

Smilianskaia, E.B. (2003) *Volshebniki, bogokhul'niki, eretiki: narodnai religioznost' i 'dukhovnye pre-stupleniia' v Rossii XVIII v.* (Magicians, Blasphemers, and Heretics: Popular Religiosity and 'Religious Crimes' in 18th-century Russia) (Moscow: Indrik).

Smith, Adam (1937) *An Inquiry into the Nature and Causes of the Wealth of Nations*, ed. Edwin Cannan and Max Lerner (New York: Modern Library).

Smith, Daniel Scott (1973) 'Family Limitation, Sexual Control, and Domestic Feminism in Victorian America', in *Feminist Studies* 1 (3–4), pp. 50–7.

Smith, Eaglesfield and Hannah More (1795) *The Sorrows of Yamba; or, a Negro Woman's Lamentation* (London: Cheap Repository Tracts).

Smith, Hilda L. (1982) *Reason's Disciples: Seventeenth-Century English Feminists* (Urbana: University of Illinois Press).

Smith, Hilda L., Mihoko Suzuki and Susan Wiseman, eds (2007) *Women's Political Writings, 1610–1725* (London: Pickering & Chatto Ltd).

Smith, R.E.F. and David Christian (1984) *Bread and Salt: A Social and Economic History of Food and Drink in Russia* (Cambridge: Cambridge University Press).

Smith, Raymond (1987) 'Hierarchy and the Dual Marriage System in West Indian Society', in *Gender and Kinship: Essays toward a Unified Analysis*, ed. Jane Collier and Sylvia Yanagisako (Stanford, CA: Stanford University Press), pp. 163–96.

Smith, Richard Michael, ed. (1984) *Land, Kinship, and Life-Cycle*, Cambridge Studies in Population, Economy, and Society in Past Time, 1 (Cambridge: Cambridge University Press).

Smith, Theresa Ann (2003) 'Writing out of the Margins: Women, Translation, and the Spanish Enlightenment', in *Journal of Women's History* 15 (1), pp. 116–43.

Smith, Timothy B. (2001) 'Marginal People', in *Encyclopedia of European Social History from 1350 to 2000*, ed. Peter N. Stearns (New York: Charles Scribner), vol. III, pp. 175–86.

Smith-Rosenberg, Carroll (1975) 'The Female World of Love and Ritual: Relations between Women in Nineteenth-Century America', in *Signs: Journal of Women in Culture and Society* 1 (1), pp. 1–29.

Snell, K.D.M. (1985) *Annals of the Labouring Poor: Social Change and Agrarian England, 1660–1900* (Cambridge: Cambridge University Press).

Soares, Mariza de Carvalho (2007) 'Can Women Guide and Govern Men? Gendering Politics among African Catholics in Colonial Brazil', in *Women and Slavery*, ed. Gwyn Campbell, Suzanne Miers and Joseph Calder Miller (Athens: Ohio University Press), vol. 2, The Modern Atlantic, pp. 79–99.

Sogner, Solvi (1997) 'Domestic Service in Norway: The Long View', in *Le phénomène de la domesticité en Europe, XVIe–XXe siècles*, ed. Antoinette Fauve-Chamoux and Ludmilla Fialova (Prague: Ceska Demograficka Spolecnost), pp. 95–103.

Sokoll, Thomas (2000) 'Negotiating a Living: Essex Pauper Letters from London, 1800–1834', in *International Review of Social History* 45 (Supplement 8, Household Strategies for Survival 1600–2000: Fission, Faction and Cooperation), pp. 19–46.

Sol, Antoinette (2002) 'The Second Time Around: Marriage and Remarriage in Riccoboni and La Guesnerie', in *Eighteenth-Century Life* 26 (2), pp. 53–68.

Šolic, Mirna (2007) 'Women in Ottoman Bosnia as Seen through the Eyes of Luka Botic, a Christian Poet', in *Women in the Ottoman Balkans: Gender, Culture and History*, Library of Ottoman Studies, 15, ed. Amila Buturović and Irvin Cemil Schick (New York: I.B. Tauris), pp. 307–34.

Somel, Selçuk Akşın (2001) *The Modernization of Public Education in the Ottoman Empire, 1839–1908: Islamization, Autocracy, and Discipline*, The Ottoman Empire and Its Heritage, 22 (Leiden: Brill).

Somerville, Diane Miller (1997) 'Rape, Race, and Castration in Slave Law in the Colonial and Early South', in *The Devil's Lane: Sex and Race in the Early South*, ed. Catherine Clinton and Michele Gillespie (New York: Oxford University Press), pp. 74–89.

Sonbol, Amira El-Azhary, ed. (1996) *Women, the Family, and Divorce Laws in Islamic History* (Syracuse, NY: Syracuse University Press).

Sonnino, Eugenio (1994) 'Between the Home and the Hospice: The Plight and Fate of Girl Orphans in Seventeenth- and Eighteenth-Century Rome', in *Poor Women and Children in the European Past*, ed. John Henderson and Richard Wall (London: Routledge), pp. 94–116.

Soulodre-La France, Renée (2001) 'Socially Not So Dead! Slave Identities in Bourbon Nueva Granada', in *Colonial Latin American Review* 10 (1), pp. 87–103.

Spavens, William (1998) *The Narrative of William Spavens, a Chatham Pensioner . . . A Unique Lower Deck View of the Navy of the Seven Years War*, ed. N.A.M. Rodger (London: Chatham Publishing).

Sperling, Jutta Gisela (2004) 'Marriage at the Time of the Council of Trent (1560–70): Clandestine Marriages, Kinship Prohibitions, and Dowry Exchange in European Comparison', in *Journal of Early Modern History* 8 (1–2), pp. 67–108.

Sperling, Jutta Gisela and Shona Kelly Wray, eds (2009) *Across the Religious Divide: Women's Property Rights in the Wider Mediterranean (ca. 1300–1800)* (New York: Routledge).

St John Williams, Noel T. (1988) *Judy O'Grady and the Colonel's Lady: The Army Wife and Camp Follower since 1660* (London: Brassey's Defence Publishers).

Staudacher, Anna (2002) *Jüdische Konvertiten in Wien, 1782–1868*, 2 vols (Frankfurt am Main: Peter Lang).

Staves, Susan (1990) *Married Women's Separate Property in England, 1660–1833* (Cambridge, MA: Harvard University Press).

Stearns, Peter N., ed. (2001) *Encyclopedia of European Social History from 1350 to 2000*, 6 vols (New York: Charles Scribner).

Steckel, Richard H. and Roderick Floud, eds (1997) *Health and Welfare During Industrialization* (Chicago: University of Chicago Press).

Steingrímsson, Jón (1998) *Fires of the Earth: The Laki Eruption, 1783–1784*, trans. Keneva Kunz (Reykjavík: Nordic Volcanological Institute and University of Iceland Press).

Stephens, W.B. (1990) 'Literacy in England, Scotland, and Wales, 1500–1900', in *History of Education Quarterly* 30 (4), pp. 545–71.

Stiglmayer, Alexandra (1994) *Mass Rape: The War Against Women in Bosnia-Herzegovina* (Lincoln: University of Nebraska Press).

Stiker, Henri-Jacques (1999) *A History of Disability*, trans. William Sayers (Ann Arbor: University of Michigan Press).

Stites, Richard (2007) 'Female Serfs in the Performing World', in *Women in Russian Culture and Society, 1700–1825*, ed. Wendy Rosslyn and Alessandra Tosi (Basingstoke: Palgrave Macmillan), pp. 24–38.

Stoddard, Eve W. (1995) 'A Serious Proposal for Slavery Reform: Sarah Scott's Sir George Ellison', in *Eighteenth-Century Studies* 28 (4), pp. 379–96.

Stolberg, Michael (2003) 'A Woman Down to Her Bones: The Anatomy of Sexual Difference in the Sixteenth and Early Seventeenth Centuries', in *Isis* 94 (2), pp. 274–99.

Stoler, Ann Laura (2002) *Carnal Knowledge and Imperial Power: Race and the Intimate in Colonial Rule* (Berkeley: University of California Press).

Stoppa, Giovanni Battista (1655) *A Collection of the Several Papers Sent to His Highness the Lord Protector . . . Concerning the Bloudy and Barbarous Massacres, Murthers, and Other Cruelties, Committed on Many Thousands of Reformed or Protestants Dwelling in the Valleys of Piedmont, by the Duke of Savoy's Forces* (London).

Storer, Mary Elizabeth (1947) 'Madame de Villedieu and the Academy of the Ricovrati', in *Modern Language Notes* 62 (6), pp. 418–20.

Stowasser, Barbara Freyer (1994) *Women in the Qur'an, Traditions, and Interpretation* (New York: Oxford University Press).

Stowasser, Barbara Freyer (1996) 'Women and Citizenship in the Qur'an', in *Women, the Family, and Divorce Laws in Islamic History*, ed. Amira El-Azhary Sonbol (Syracuse, NY: Syracuse University Press), pp. 23–38.

Strasser, Ulrike (2003) *State of Virginity: Gender, Religion, and Politics in an Early Modern Catholic State* (Ann Arbor: University of Michigan Press).

Strobel, Heidi A. (2005) 'Royal "Matronage" of Women Artists in the Late-18th Century', in *Woman's Art Journal* 26 (2), pp. 3–9.

Stuurman, Siep (1998) '"L'égalité des sexes qui ne se conteste plus en France": Feminism in the Seventeenth Century', in *Perspectives on Feminist Thought in European History: From the Middle Ages to the Present*, ed. Tjitske Akkerman and Siep Stuurman (London: Routledge), pp. 67–84.

Stuurman, Siep (2004) *François Poulain de la Barre and the Invention of Modern Equality* (Cambridge, MA: Harvard University Press).

Styles, John (2003) 'Custom or Consumption? Plebeian Fashion in Eighteenth-Century England', in *Luxury in the Eighteenth Century: Debates, Desires and Delectable Goods*, ed. Maxine Berg and Elizabeth Eger (Basingstoke: Palgrave Macmillan), pp. 103–18.

Suceska, Avdo (1982) 'The Eighteenth-Century Austro-Ottoman Wars' Economic Impact on the Population of Bosnia', in *East Central European Society and War in the Prerevolutionary Eighteenth Century*, East European Monographs, 122, ed. Gunther Erich Rothenberg, Béla K. Király and Peter F. Sugar (Boulder, CO: Columbia University Press), pp. 339–47.

Sullivan, Constance A. (1990) 'Spanish Literary History and the Politics of Gender', in *Journal of the Midwest Modern Language Association* 23 (2), pp. 26–41.

Sullivan, Constance A. (2001) 'Constructing Her Own Tradition: Ideological Selectivity in Josefa Amar y Borbón's Representation of Female Models', in *Recovering Spain's Feminist Tradition*, ed. Lisa Vollendorf (New York: Modern Language Association of America), pp. 142–59.

Sussman, Charlotte (2000) *Consuming Anxieties: Consumer Protest, Gender, and British Slavery, 1713–1833* (Stanford, CA: Stanford University Press).

Sussman, George D. (1982) *Selling Mothers Milk: The Wet-Nursing Business in France 1715–1914* (Urbana: University of Illinois Press).

Sweet, Rosemary and Penelope Lane, eds (2003) *Women and Urban Life in Eighteenth-Century England: 'On the Town'* (Aldershot: Ashgate).

Sweets, John F. (1995) 'The Lacemakers of Le Puy in the Nineteenth Century', in *European Women and Preindustrial Craft*, ed. Daryl M. Hafter (Bloomington: Indiana University Press), pp. 67–86.

Swett, Katharine Warner (1996) 'Widowhood, Custom and Property in Early Modern North Wales', in *Welsh History Review/Cylchgrawn Hanes Cymru* 18 (2), pp. 189–227.

Symanski, Richard (1981) *The Immoral Landscape: Female Prostitution in Western Societies* (Toronto, ON: Butterworths).

Taitz, Emily, Sondra Henry and Cheryl Tallan (2003) *The JPS Guide to Jewish Women: 600 B.C.E. To 1900 C.E* (Philadelphia: Jewish Publication Society).

Tapper, Nancy and Richard Tapper (1987) 'The Birth of the Prophet: Ritual and Gender in Turkish Islam', in *Man*, New Series, 22 (1), pp. 69–92.

Tari, Lujza (1999) 'Women, Musical Instruments and Instrumental Music', in *Studia Musicologica Academiae Scientiarum Hungaricae* 40 (1–3), pp. 95–143.

Taylor, Barbara (1983) *Eve and the New Jerusalem: Socialism and Feminism in the Nineteenth Century* (London: Virago Press Ltd).

Taylor, Peter Keir (1994) *Indentured to Liberty: Peasant Life and the Hessian Military State, 1688–1815* (Ithaca, NY: Cornell University Press).

Taylor, Peter Keir and Hermann Rebel (1981) 'Hessian Peasant Women, Their Families and the Draft: A Social-Historical Interpretation of Four Tales from the Grimm Collection', in *Journal of Family History* 6 (4), pp. 347–78.

Terpstra, Nicholas, ed. (1995) *Lay Confraternities and Civic Religion in Renaissance Bologna* (Cambridge: Cambridge University Press).

Teter, Magdalena (2003) 'Jewish Conversions to Catholicism in the Polish-Lithuanian Commonwealth of the Seventeenth and Eighteenth Centuries', in *Jewish History* 17 (3), pp. 257–83.

Thale, Mary (1989) 'London Debating Societies in the 1790s', in *Historical Journal* 32 (1), pp. 57–86.

Theiss, Janet M. (2004) *Disgraceful Matters: The Politics of Chastity in Eighteenth-Century China* (Berkeley: University of California Press).

Théré, Christine (1999) 'Women and Birth Control in Eighteenth-Century France', in *Eighteenth-Century Studies* 32 (4), pp. 552–64.

Theremin, Charles Guillaum (1799) *De la condition des femmes dans les républiques* (Paris: chez Laran).

Thirsk, Joan (2007) *Food in Early Modern England: Phases, Fads, Fashions 1500–1760* (London: Hambledon Continuum).

Thomas, Claudia (1992) 'Samuel Johnson and Elizabeth Carter: Pudding, Epictetus, and the Accomplished Woman', in *South Central Review* 9 (4, Special issue: Johnson and Gender), pp. 18–30.

Thompson, Elizabeth (2003) 'Public and Private in Middle Eastern Women's History', in *Journal of Women's History* 15 (1, Special issue: Women's History in the New Millennium: Rethinking Public and Private), pp. 52–69.

Thompson, Jack George (1996) *Women in Celtic Law and Culture*, Women's Studies, 12 (Lewiston, NY: Edwin Mellen Press).

Thomson, J.K.J. (1992) *A Distinctive Industrialization: Cotton in Barcelona, 1728–1832* (Cambridge: Cambridge University Press).

Thornton, John K. (1991) 'Legitimacy and Political Power: Queen Njinga, 1624–1663', in *The Journal of African History* 32 (1), pp. 25–40.

Thwaites, Wendy (1984) 'Women in the Marketplace: Oxfordshire c. 1690–1800', in *Midland History* 9, pp. 23–42.

Thys-Senocak, Lucienne (2006) *Ottoman Women Builders: The Architectural Patronage of Hadice Turhan Sultan* (Burlington, VT: Ashgate).

Tikoff, Valentina K. (2008) 'Gender and Juvenile Charity, Tradition and Reform: Assistance for Young People in Eighteenth-Century Seville', in *Eighteenth-Century Studies* 41 (3), pp. 307–35.

Tilly, Louise A. (1983) 'Food Entitlement, Famine, and Conflict', in *Journal of Interdisciplinary History* 14 (2), pp. 333–49.

Tilly, Louise A. and Joan Scott (1978) *Women, Work and the Family* (New York: Holt Rinehart and Winston).

Tinkova, Daniela (2003) 'Predchazet ci trestat? Problem infanticidia v osvicenske spolecnosti', in *Cesky casopis historicky* 101, pp. 27–76.

Tinkova, Daniela (2005) 'Protéger ou punir? Les voies de la décriminalisation de l'infanticide en France et dans le domaine des Habsbourg (XVIIIe–XIXe siècles)', in *Crime, histoire & sociétés* 9 (2), pp. 43–72.

Todd, Barbara J. (1999) 'Small Sums to Risk: Women's Investments in the Age of the Financial Revolution', North American Conference of British Studies, November 19 (Boston, Massachusetts).

Todorova, Maria (1983) 'Population Structure, Marriage Patterns, Family and Household (According to Ottoman Documentary Material from North-Eastern Bulgaria in the 60s of the 19th Century)', in *Études balkaniques* 19 (1), pp. 59–72.

Toepfer, Karl (1990) 'Orgy Salon: Aristocracy and Pornographic Theatre in Pre-Revolutionary Paris', in *Performing Arts Journal* 12 (2–3), pp. 110–36.

Toledano, Ehud R. (1997) *Slavery and Abolition in the Ottoman Middle East* (Seattle: Washington University Press).

Toledano, Ehud R. (2006) 'Shemsigul: A Circassian Slave in Mid-Nineteenth-Century Cairo', in *Struggle and Survival in the Modern Middle East*, ed. Edmund Burke III and David N. Yaghoubian (Berkeley: University of California Press), pp. 59–74.

Toledano, Ehud R. (2007) *As if Silent and Absent: Bonds of Enslavement in the Islamic Middle East* (New Haven, CT: Yale University Press).

Tolmacheva, Marina (1998) 'Female Piety and Patronage in the Medieval "Hajj"', in *Women in the Medieval Islamic World: Power, Patronage and Piety*, ed. Gavin R.G. Hambly (New York: St. Martin's Press), pp. 161–79.

Tomasson, Richard F. (1977) 'A Millennium of Misery; the Demography of the Icelanders', in *Population Studies* 31, pp. 405–27.

Tóth, István György (1991) 'Peasant Sexuality in Eighteenth-Century Hungary', in *Continuity and Change* 6 (1), pp. 43–59.

Tóth, István György (2000) *Literacy and Written Culture in Early Modern Central Europe*, ed. Miklós Bodóczky, trans. Tunde Vajda (Budapest: Central European University Press).

Tóth, István György (2001) 'The Missionary and the Devil: Ways of Conversion in Catholic Missions in Hungary', in *Frontiers of Faith: Religious Exchange and the Constitution of Religious Identities 1400–1750*, Cultural Exchange in Europe, 1400–1750, 1, ed. Eszter Andor and István György Tóth (Budapest: Central European University and European Science Foundation), pp. 79–88.

Townsend, Camilla (1998) '"Half My Body Free, the Other Half Enslaved": The Politics of the Slaves of Guayaquil at the End of the Colonial Era', in *Colonial Latin American Review* 7 (1), pp. 105–28.

Townsend, Camilla (2000) *Tales of Two Cities: Race and Economic Culture in Early Republican North and South America: Guayaquil, Ecuador, and Baltimore, Maryland* (Austin: University of Texas Press).

Traer, James F. (1980) *Marriage and the Family in Eighteenth-Century France* (Ithaca, NY: Cornell University Press).

Traub, Valerie (2001) 'The Renaissance of Lesbianism in Early Modern England', in *GLQ: A Journal of Lesbian and Gay Studies* 7 (2), pp. 245–63.

A Treatise of Feme Coverts, or, the Lady's Law: Containing All the Laws and Statutes Relating to Women (1732) (London: E. and R. Nutt, and R. Gosling).

Truant, Cynthia Maria (1995) 'Parisian Guildswomen and the (Sexual) Politics of Privilege: Defending Their Patrimonies in Print', in *Going Public: Women and Publishing in Early Modern France*, ed. Elizabeth C. Goldsmith and Dena Goodman (Ithaca, NY: Cornell University Press), pp. 46–61.

Tucker, Holly (2003) *Pregnant Fictions: Childbirth and the Fairy Tale in Early-Modern France* (Detroit, MI: Wayne State University Press).

Tucker, Judith E. (1998) *In the House of the Law: Gender and Islamic Law in Ottoman Syria and Palestine* (Berkeley: University of California Press).

Tugay, Emine Foat (1963) *Three Centuries; Family Chronicles of Turkey and Egypt* (London: Oxford University Press).

Turin, Yvonne (1989) *Femmes et religieuses au XIXe siècle: Le féminisme 'en religion'* (Paris: Nouvelle Cité).

Turniansky, Chava (1988) 'Yiddish Song as Historical Source Material: Plague in the Judenstadt of Prague in 1713', in *Jewish History: Essays in Honour of Chimen Abramsky*, ed. Chimen Abramsky, Ada Rapoport-Albert and Steven J. Zipperstein (London: P. Halban), pp. 189–98.

Ty, Eleanor Rose (1993) *Unsex'd Revolutionaries: Five Women Novelists of the 1790s* (Toronto, ON: University of Toronto Press).

Tyson, John R. (1995) 'Lady Huntingdon's Reformation', in *Church History* 64 (4), pp. 580–93.

Ulbrich, Otto (1988) 'Infanticide in Eighteenth-Century Germany', in *The German Underworld: Deviants and Outcasts in German History*, ed. Richard J. Evans (London: Routledge), pp. 108–40.

Ullmann, Sabine (2000) 'Poor Jewish Families in Early Modern Rural Swabia', in *International Review of Social History* 45 (Supplement 8, Household Strategies for Survival 1600–2000: Fission, Faction and Cooperation), pp. 93–114.

Ullrich, Hermann (1946) 'Maria Theresia Paradis and Mozart', in *Music and Letters* 27 (4), pp. 224–33.

Ulman, Yesim Isil (2006) 'The Imperial School of Medicine of Galatasaray as an Example of Medical Modernisation in Turkey (1839–1848)', 40th International Congress on the History of Medicine, 29 August (Budapest, Hungary: http://www.ishm2006.hu/scientific/abstract.php?ID=153, accessed 25 November 2008).

Valenze, Deborah (1995) *The First Industrial Woman* (New York: Oxford University Press).

Vanpée, Janie (1999) 'Performing Justice: The Trials of Olympe de Gouges', in *Theatre Journal* 51 (1), pp. 47–65.

Vanzan, A. (1996) 'In Search of Another Identity: Female Muslim-Christian Conversions in the Mediterranean World', in *Islam and Christian-Muslim Relations* 7 (3), pp. 327–33.

Viazzo, Pier Paolo, Maria Bortolotto and Andrea Zanotto (2000) 'Five Centuries of Foundling History in Florence: Changing Patterns of Abandonment, Care and Mortality', in *Abandoned Children*, ed. Catherine Panter-Brick and Malcolm T. Smith (Cambridge: Cambridge University Press), pp. 70–91.

Vicente, Marta V. (2000) 'Artisans and Work in a Barcelona Cotton Factory (1770–1816)', in *International Review of Social History* 45 (1), pp. 1–23.

Vicente, Marta V. (2003) 'Textual Uncertainties: The Written Legacy of Women Entrepreneurs in Eighteenth-Century Barcelona', in *Women, Texts and Authority in the Early Modern Spanish World*, ed. Marta V. Vicente and Luis R. Corteguera (Aldershot: Ashgate), pp. 183–95.

Vickery, Amanda (1993) 'Golden Age to Separate Spheres? A Review of the Categories and Chronology of English Women's History', in *Historical Journal* 36 (2), pp. 383–414.

Vickery, Amanda (1994) 'Women and the World of Goods: A Lancashire Consumer and Her Possessions, 1751–81', in *Consumption and the World of Goods*, ed. John Brewer and Roy Porter (London: Routledge), pp. 274–301.

Vigée-Lebrun, Louise-Elisabeth (1989) *The Memoirs of Elisabeth Vigée-Le Brun*, trans. Sian Evans (Bloomington: Indiana University Press).

Voekel, Pamela (2002) *Alone Before God: The Religious Origins of Mexican Modernity* (Durham, NC: Duke University Press).

Vollendorf, Lisa (2005) *The Lives of Women: A New History of Inquisitional Spain* (Nashville, TN: Vanderbilt University Press).

Vollendorf, Lisa, ed. (2001) *Recovering Spain's Feminist Tradition* (New York: Modern Language Association of America).

Voltaire (2002) *Micromégas and Other Short Fictions*, ed. Haydn Trevor Mason, trans. Theo Cuffe (London: Penguin).

Vowles, Judith (1994) 'The "Feminization" of Russian Literature: Women, Language, and Literature in Eighteenth-Century Russia', in *Women Writers in Russian Literature*, ed. Toby W. Clyman and Diana Greene (Westport, CT: Greenwood Press), pp. 35–60.

Vukanović, T.P. (1989) 'Witchcraft in the Central Balkans I: Characteristics of Witches', in *Folklore* 100 (1), pp. 9–24.

Vukanović, T.P. (1989) 'Witchcraft in the Central Balkans II: Protection Against Witches', in *Folklore* 100 (2), pp. 221–36.

Wagner, William G. (2007) 'Female Orthodox Monasticism in Eighteenth-Century Imperial Russia: The Experience of Nizhnii Novgorod', in *Women in Russian Culture and Society, 1700–1825*, ed. Wendy Rosslyn and Alessandra Tosi (Basingstoke: Palgrave Macmillan), pp. 191–218.

Waigand, J. (1970) 'Totenklage über Panna Czinka', in *Studia Musicologica Academiae Scientiarum Hungaricae* 12 (1/4), pp. 299–310.

Waldron, Mary (1996) *Lactilla, Milkwoman of Clifton: The Life and Writings of Ann Yearsley, 1753–1806* (Athens: University of Georgia Press).

Wales, Tim (1984) 'Poverty, Poor Relief and the Life Cycle: Some Evidence from Seventeenth-Century Norfolk', in *Land, Kinship and Life-Cycle*, ed. Richard M. Smith (Cambridge: Cambridge University Press), pp. 351–88.

Walker, Barbara K. (1990) *The Art of the Turkish Tale*, trans. Helen Siegl, 2 vols (Lubbock, TX: Texas Tech University Press).

Walker, Garthine (1998) 'Rereading Rape and Sexual Violence in Early Modern England', in *Gender & History* 10 (1), pp. 1–25.

Walkowitz, Judith (1980) *Prostitution and Victorian Society: Women, Class and the State* (Cambridge: Cambridge University Press).

Walle, Francine van de (1986) 'Infant Mortality and the European Demographic Transition', in *The Decline of Fertility in Europe: The Revised Proceedings of a Conference on the Princeton European Fertility Project*, ed. Ansley J. Coale and Susan Cotts Watkins (Princeton, NJ: Princeton University Press), pp. 201–33.

Walton, John and David Seddon (1994) *Free Markets & Food Riots: The Politics of Global Adjustment* (Oxford: Blackwell).

Wangermann, Ernst (1977) 'Maria Theresa: A Reforming Monarchy', in *The Courts of Europe: Politics, Patronage and Royalty, 1400–1800*, ed. A.G. Dickens (London: Thames and Hudson), pp. 283–303.

Watanabe-O'Kelly, Helen (2000) 'Women's Writing in the Early Modern Period', in *A History of Women's Writing in Germany, Austria, and Switzerland*, ed. Jo Catling (Cambridge: Cambridge University Press), pp. 27–44.

Watanabe-O'Kelly, Helen (2004) 'Religion and the Consort: Two Electresses of Saxony and Queens of Poland (1697–1757)', in *Queenship in Europe, 1660–1815: The Role of the Consort*, ed. Clarissa Campbell Orr (Cambridge: Cambridge University Press), pp. 252–75.

Watkins, Susan Cotts and Jane Menken (1985) 'Famines in Historical Perspective', in *Population and Development Review* 11 (4), pp. 647–75.

Weaver, Elissa (2002) *Convent Theatre in Early Modern Italy: Spiritual Fun and Learning for Women* (Cambridge: Cambridge University Press).

Weaver, F. Ellen (2002a) *La contre-réforme et les constitutions de Port-Royal* (Paris: Éditions du Cerf).

Weaver, F. Ellen (2002b) *Mademoiselle de Joncoux: polémique janséniste à la veille de la bulle Unigenitus* (Paris: Éditions du Cerf).

Weisbrod, Bernd (2005) 'Theatrical Monarchy: The Making of Victoria, the Modern Family Queen', in *The Body of the Queen: Gender and Rule in the Courtly World, 1500–2000*, ed. Regina Schulte (New York: Berghahn Books), pp. 238–53.

Weissler, Chava (1998) *Voices of the Matriarchs: Listening to the Prayers of Early Modern Jewish Women* (Boston: Beacon Press).

Welter, Barbara (1966) 'The Cult of True Womanhood: 1820–1860', in *American Quarterly* 18 (2, Part 1), pp. 151–74.

Wetherell, Charles, Andrejs Plakans and Barry Wellman (1994) 'Social Networks, Kinship, and Community in Eastern Europe', in *Journal of Interdisciplinary History* 24 (4), pp. 639–63.

Wheelwright, Julie (1989) *Amazons and Military Maids: Women Who Dressed as Men in the Pursuit of Life, Liberty and Happiness* (London: Pandora).

Whelan, Kevin (2004) 'The Green Atlantic: Radical Reciprocities between Ireland and America in the Long Eighteenth Century', in *A New Imperial History: Culture, Identity, and Modernity in Britain and the Empire, 1660–1840*, ed. Kathleen Wilson (Cambridge: Cambridge University Press), pp. 216–38.

Wichmann, Christian August (1772) *Geschichte berühmter Frauenzimmer nach alphabetischer Ordnung aus alten und neuen in- und ausländischen Geschicht- Sammlungen und Wörterbüchern zusammen getragen*, 3 vols (Leipzig: A.F. Böhmen).

Wiersma, Geertje (1998) *Johanna Borski: Financier van Nederland, 1764–1846* (Amsterdam: Prometheus).

Wiesner, Merry E. (1986) *Working Women in Renaissance Germany* (Rutgers, NJ: Rutgers University Press).

Wiesner, Merry E. (1997a) 'Guilds, Male Bonding and Women's Work in Early Modern Germany', in *Gender, Church, and State in Early Modern Germany: Essays* (London: Longman), pp. 163–77.

Wiesner, Merry E. (1997b) 'The Reformation of the Women' in *Gender, Church, and State in Early Modern Germany: Essays* (London: Longman), pp. 63–78.

Wiesner, Merry E. (2008) *Women and Gender in Early Modern Europe*, 3rd edn (Cambridge: Cambridge University Press).

Wiesner-Hanks, Merry E. (2006) *Early Modern Europe, 1450–1789* (Cambridge: Cambridge University Press).

Wijngaarden, Hilde van (1998) 'Credit as a Way to Make Ends Meet: The Use of Credit by Poor Women in Zwolle, 1650–1700', Twelfth International Economic History Congress, 24–28 August (Madrid, Spain).

Williams, David (1980) 'The Fate of French Feminism: Boudier de Villemert's *Ami des Femmes*', in *Eighteenth-Century Studies* 14 (1), pp. 37–55.

Wilson, Duncan (1970) *The Life and Times of Vuk Stefanović Karadžić, 1787–1864: Literacy, Literature, and National Independence in Serbia* (Oxford: Clarendon Press).

Wilson, Kathleen (1995) *The Sense of the People: Politics, Culture and Imperialism in England, 1715–1785* (Cambridge: Cambridge University Press).

Wilson, Kathleen (2003) *The Island Race: Englishness, Empire, and Gender in the Eighteenth Century* (London: Routledge).

Wilson, Kathleen (2004) 'Thinking Back: Gender Misrecognition and Polynesian Subversions Aboard the Cook Voyages', in *A New Imperial History: Culture, Identity, and Modernity in Britain and the Empire, 1660–1840*, ed. Kathleen Wilson (Cambridge: Cambridge University Press), pp. 345–62.

Wilson, Peter H. (1995) *War, State and Society in Württemberg, 1677–1793* (Cambridge: Cambridge University Press).

Wilson, Peter H. (2005) 'German Women and War, 1500–1800', in *Warfare in Europe 1650–1792*, ed. Jeremy Black (Aldershot: Ashgate), pp. 45–78.

Wilson, Stephen (1988) 'Infanticide, Child Abandonment, and Female Honour in Nineteenth-Century Corsica', in *Comparative Studies in Society and History*, 30 (4), pp. 762–83.

Wolff, Larry (2003) 'The Innocence and Natural Liberty of Morlacchia: European Identity, Enlightened Anthropology and the Ambivalent Significance of Gender Among Noble Savages', in *Dialectical Anthropology* 27 (2), pp. 93–104.

Wollstonecraft, Mary (1988) *A Vindication of the Rights of Woman: An Authoritative Text, Backgrounds, the Wollstonecraft Debate, Criticism*, ed. Carol H. Poston, 2nd edn (New York: Norton).

Woloch, Isser (1976) 'War-Widows' Pensions: Social Policy in Revolutionary and Napoleonic France', in *Societas* 6 (4), pp. 235–54.

Wong, David C. (1996) 'A Theory of Petty Trading: The Jamaican Higgler', in *Economic Journal* 106 (435), pp. 507–18.

Worobec, Christine D. (2006) 'Lived Orthodoxy in Imperial Russia', in *Kritika: Explorations in Russian and Eurasian History* 7 (2), pp. 329–50.

Wrigley, E.A. (1985) 'Urban Growth and Agricultural Change: England and the Continent in the Early Modern Period', in *Journal of Interdisciplinary History* 15 (4), pp. 683–728.

Wunder, Heide (1998) *He Is the Sun, She Is the Moon: Women in Early Modern Germany*, trans. Thomas Dunlap (Cambridge, MA: Harvard University Press).

Yi, Eunjeong (2004) *Guild Dynamics in Seventeenth-Century Istanbul: Fluidity and Leverage*, The Ottoman Empire and Its Heritage, 27 (Leiden: Brill).

Yıldırım, Onur (2000) 'Craft Guilds in the Ottoman Empire (c. 1650–1826): A Survey', in *METU Studies in Development* 27 (3–4), pp. 349–70.

Young, Alfred F. (1990) 'The Women of Boston: "Persons of Consequence" in the Making of the American Revolution, 1765–76', in *Women and Politics in the Age of the Democratic Revolution*, ed. Harriet B. Applewhite and Darline G. Levy (Ann Arbor: University of Michigan), pp. 181–226.

Young, Antonia (2000) *Women Who Become Men: Albanian Sworn Virgins* (Oxford: Berg).

Zarinebaf-Shahr, Fariba (1997) 'Ottoman Women and the Tradition of Seeking Justice in the Eighteenth Century', in *Women in the Ottoman Empire: Middle Eastern Women in the Early Modern Era*, ed. Madeline C. Zilfi (Leiden: Brill), pp. 253–63.

Zarinebaf-Shahr, Fariba (1998) 'Women and the Public Eye in Eighteenth-Century Istanbul', in *Women in the Medieval Islamic World: Power, Patronage and Piety*, ed. Gavin R.G. Hambly (New York: St. Martin's Press), pp. 301–24.

Zečević, Selma (2007) 'Missing Husbands, Waiting Wives, Bosnian Muftis: Fatwa Texts and the Interpretation of Gendered Presences and Absences in Late Ottoman Bosnia', in *Women in the Ottoman Balkans: Gender, Culture and History*, Library of Ottoman Studies, 15, ed. Amila Buturović and Irvin Cemil Schick (New York: I.B. Tauris), pp. 335–60.

Ze'evi, Dror (1995) 'Women in 17th-Century Jerusalem: Western and Indigenous Perspectives', in *International Journal of Middle East Studies* 27 (2), pp. 157–73.

Ze'evi, Dror (2001) 'Changes in Legal-Sexual Discourses: Sex Crimes in the Ottoman Empire', in *Continuity and Change* 16 (4), pp. 219–42.

Zentai, Tünde (1979) 'The Sign-Language of Hungarian Graveyards', in *Folklore* 90 (2), pp. 131–40.

Zhelyazkova, Antonina and Jorgen Nielsen, eds (2001) *Ethnology of Sufi Orders: Theory and Practice*, The Fate of Muslim Communities in the Balkans, 8 (Sofia, Bulgaria: IMIR).

Zilfi, Madeline C. (1995) 'Ibrahim Pasha and the Women', in *Histoire économique et sociale de l'Empire Ottoman et de la Turquie (1326–1960): Actes du sixième congrès international tenu à Aix-en-Provence du 1er au 4 Juillet 1992*, Collection Turcica, 8, ed. Daniel Panzac (Aix-en-Provence: Peeters), pp. 555–9.

Zilfi, Madeline C. (1997a) ' "We Don't Get Along": Women and Hul Divorce in the Eighteenth Century', in *Women in the Ottoman Empire: Middle Eastern Women in the Early Modern Era*, ed. Madeline C. Zilfi (Leiden: Brill), pp. 264–96.

Zilfi, Madeline C., ed. (1997b) *Women in the Ottoman Empire: Middle Eastern Women in the Early Modern Era*, The Ottoman Empire and Its Heritage, 10 (Leiden: Brill).

Zilfi, Madeline C. (2004) 'Servants, Slaves, and the Domestic Order in the Ottoman Middle East', in *Hawwa* 2 (1), pp. 1–33.

INDEX